DAFX: Digital Audio Effects

Second Edition

DAFX: Digital Audio Effects

Second Edition

Edited by

Udo Zölzer

Helmut Schmidt University – University of the Federal Armed Forces, Hamburg, Germany

A John Wiley and Sons, Ltd., Publication

Library of Congress Cataloguing-in-Publication Data

Zölzer, Udo.
  DAFX : digital audio effects / Udo Zölzer. – 2nd ed.
    p. cm.
  Includes bibliographical references and index.
  ISBN 978-0-470-66599-2 (hardback)
  1. Computer sound processing. 2. Sound–Recording and reproducing–Digital techniques.
3. Signal processing–Digital techniques. I. Title.
  TK5105.8863.Z65 2011
  006.5 – dc22

                                                                    2010051411

A catalogue record for this book is available from the British Library.

Print ISBN: 978-0-470-66599-2 [HB]
e-PDF ISBN: 978-1-119-99130-4
o-Book ISBN: 978-1-119-99129-8
e-Pub ISBN: 978-0-470-97967-9

Typeset in 9/11pt Times by Laserwords Private Limited, Chennai, India

Contents

Preface

DAFX is a synonym for digital audio effects. It is also the name for a European research project for co-operation and scientific transfer, namely EU-COST-G6 "Digital Audio Effects" (1997–2001). It was initiated by Daniel Arfib (CNRS, Marseille). In the past couple of years we have had four EU-sponsored international workshops/conferences on DAFX, namely, in Barcelona (DAFX-98), Trondheim (DAFX-99), Verona (DAFX-00) and Limerick (DAFX-01). A variety of DAFX topics have been presented by international participants at these conferences. The papers can be found on the corresponding web sites.

This book not only reflects these conferences and workshops, it is intended as a profound collection and presentation of the main fields of digital audio effects. The contents and structure of the book were prepared by a special book work group and discussed in several workshops over the past years sponsored by the EU-COST-G6 project. However, the single chapters are the individual work of the respective authors.

Chapter 1 gives an introduction to digital signal processing and shows software implementations with the MATLAB® programming tool. Chapter 2 discusses digital filters for shaping the audio spectrum and focuses on the main building blocks for this application. Chapter 3 introduces basic structures for delays and delay-based audio effects. In Chapter 4 modulators and demodulators are introduced and their applications to digital audio effects are demonstrated. The topic of nonlinear processing is the focus of Chapter 5. First, we discuss fundamentals of dynamics processing such as limiters, compressors/expanders and noise gates, and then we introduce the basics of nonlinear processors for valve simulation, distortion, harmonic generators and exciters. Chapter 6 covers the wide field of spatial effects starting with basic effects, 3D for headphones and loudspeakers, reverberation and spatial enhancements. Chapter 7 deals with time-segment processing and introduces techniques for variable speed replay, time stretching, pitch shifting, shuffling and granulation. In Chapter 8 we extend the time-domain processing of Chapters 2–7. We introduce the fundamental techniques for time-frequency processing, demonstrate several implementation schemes and illustrate the variety of effects possible in the 2D time-frequency domain. Chapter 9 covers the field of source-filter processing, where the audio signal is modeled as a source signal and a filter. We introduce three techniques for source-filter separation and show source-filter transformations leading to audio effects such as cross-synthesis, formant changing, spectral interpolation and pitch shifting with formant preservation. The end of this chapter covers feature extraction techniques. Chapter 10 deals with spectral processing, where the audio signal is represented by spectral models such as sinusoids plus a residual signal. Techniques for analysis, higher-level feature analysis and synthesis are introduced, and a variety of new audio effects based on these spectral models are discussed. Effect applications range from pitch transposition, vibrato, spectral shape shift and gender change to harmonizer and morphing effects. Chapter 11 deals with fundamental principles of time and frequency warping techniques for deforming the time and/or the frequency axis. Applications of these techniques are presented for pitch-shifting inharmonic sounds, the inharmonizer, extraction of excitation signals, morphing and classical effects. Chapter 12 deals with the control of effect processors ranging from general control techniques to control based on sound features and gestural interfaces. Finally, Chapter 13 illustrates new challenges of bitstream signal representations, shows the fundamental basics and introduces filtering concepts for bitstream signal processing. MATLAB implementations in several chapters of the book illustrate software implementations of DAFX algorithms. The MATLAB files can be found on the web site http://www.dafx.de.

I hope the reader will enjoy the presentation of the basic principles of DAFX in this book and will be motivated to explore DAFX with the help of our software implementations. The creativity of a DAFX designer can only grow or emerge if intuition and experimentation are combined with profound knowledge of physical and musical fundamentals. The implementation of DAFX in software needs some knowledge of digital signal processing and this is where this book may serve as a source of ideas and implementation details.

I would like to thank the authors for their contributions to the chapters and also the EU-Cost-G6 delegates from all over Europe for their contributions during several meetings, especially Nicola Bernadini, Javier Casajús, Markus Erne, Mikael Fernström, Eric Feremans, Emmanuel Favreau, Alois Melka, Jøran Rudi and Jan Tro. The book cover is based on a mapping of a time-frequency representation of a musical piece onto the globe by Jøran Rudi. Thanks to Catja Schümann for her assistance in preparing drawings and LaTeX formatting, Christopher Duxbury for proof-reading and Vincent Verfaille for comments and cleaning up the code lines of Chapters 8 to 10. I also express my gratitude to my staff members Udo Ahlvers, Manfred Chrobak, Florian Keiler, Harald Schorr and Jörg Zeller for providing assistance during the course of writing this book. Finally, I would like to thank Birgit Gruber, Ann-Marie Halligan, Laura Kempster, Susan Dunsmore and Zoë Pinnock from John Wiley & Sons, Ltd for their patience and assistance.

My special thanks are directed to my wife Elke and our daughter Franziska.

Hamburg, March 2002   Udo Zölzer

Preface 2nd Edition

This second edition is the result of an ongoing DAFX conference series over the past years. Each chapter has new contributing co-authors who have gained experience in the related fields over the years. New emerging research fields are introduced by four new Chapters on Adaptive-DAFX, Virtual Analog Effects, Automatic Mixing and Sound Source Separation. The main focus of the book is still the audio effects side of audio research. The book offers a variety of proven effects and shows directions for new audio effects. The MATLAB files can be found on the web site http://www.dafx.de.

I would like to thank the co-authors for their contributions and effort, Derry FitzGerald and Nuno Fonseca for their contributions to the book and finally, thanks go to Nicky Skinner, Alex King, and Georgia Pinteau from John Wiley & Sons, Ltd for their assistance.

Hamburg, September 2010   Udo Zölzer

List of Contributors

Jonathan S. Abel is a Consulting Professor at the Center for Computer Research in Music and Acoustics (CCRMA) in the Music Department at Stanford University, where his research interests include audio and music applications of signal and array processing, parameter estimation and acoustics. From 1999 to 2007, Abel was a co-founder and chief technology officer of the Grammy Award-winning Universal Audio, Inc. He was a researcher at NASA/Ames Research Center, exploring topics in room acoustics and spatial hearing on a grant through the San Jose State University Foundation. Abel was also chief scientist of Crystal River Engineering, Inc., where he developed their positional audio technology, and a lecturer in the Department of Electrical Engineering at Yale University. As an industry consultant, Abel has worked with Apple, FDNY, LSI Logic, NRL, SAIC and Sennheiser, on projects in professional audio, GPS, medical imaging, passive sonar and fire department resource allocation. He holds PhD and MS degrees from Stanford University, and an SB from MIT, all in electrical engineering. Abel is a Fellow of the Audio Engineering Society.

Xavier Amatriain is Researcher in Telefonica R&D Barcelona which he joined in June 2007. His current focus of research is on recommender systems and other web science-related topics. He is also associate Professor at Universitat Pompeu Fabra, where he teaches software engineering and information retrieval. He has authored more than 50 publications, including several book chapters and patents. Previous to this, Dr. Amatriain worked at the University of California Santa Barbara as Research Director, supervising research on areas that included multimedia and immersive systems, virtual reality and 3D audio and video. Among others, he was Technical Director of the Allosphere project and he lectured in the media arts and technology program. During his PhD at the UPF (Barcelona), he was a researcher in the Music Technology Group and he worked on music signal processing and systems. At that time he initiated and co-ordinated the award-winning CLAM open source project for audio and music processing.

Daniel Arfib (1949–) received his diploma as "ingénieur ECP" from the Ecole Centrale of Paris in 1971 and is a "docteur-ingénieur" (1977) and "docteur es sciences" (1983) from the Université of Marseille II. After a few years in education or industry jobs, he has devoted his work to research, joining the CNRS (National Center for Scientific Research) in 1978 at the Laboratory of Mechanics and Acoustics (LMA) in Marseille (France). His main concern is to provide a combination of scientific and musical points of view on synthesis, transformation and interpretation of sounds using the computer as a tool, both as a researcher and a composer. As the chairman of the COST-G6 action named "Digital Audio Effects" he has been in the middle of a galaxy of researchers working on this subject. He also has a strong interest in the gesture and sound relationship, especially concerning creativity in musical systems. Since 2008, he is working in the field of sonic interaction design at the Laboratory of Informatics (LIG) in Grenoble, France.

David Berners is a Consulting Professor at the Center for Computer Research in Music and Acoustics (CCRMA) at Stanford University, where he has taught courses in signal processing and audio effects since 2004. He is also Chief Scientist at Universal Audio, Inc., a hardware and software manufacturer for the professional audio market. At UA, Dr Berners leads research and development efforts in audio effects processing, including dynamic range compression, equalization, distortion and delay effects, and specializing in modeling of vintage analog equipment. Dr Berners has previously held positions at the Lawrence Berkeley Laboratory, NASA Jet Propulsion Laboratory and Allied Signal. He received his PhD from Stanford University, MS from the California Institute of Technology, and his SB from Massachusetts Institute of Technology, all in electrical engineering.

Stefan Bilbao received his BA in Physics at Harvard University (1992), then spent two years at the Institut de Recherche et Coordination Acoustique Musicale (IRCAM) under a fellowship awarded by Harvard and the Ecole Normale Superieure. He then completed the MSc and PhD degrees in Electrical Engineering at Stanford University (1996 and 2001, respectively), while working at the Center for Computer Research in Music and Acoustics (CCRMA). He was subsequently a post-doctoral researcher at the Stanford Space Telecommunications and Radioscience Laboratory, and a lecturer at the Sonic Arts Research Centre at the Queen's University Belfast. He is currently a senior lecturer in music at the University of Edinburgh.

Jordi Bonada (1973–) received an MSc degree in electrical engineering from the Universitat Politècnica de Catalunya (Barcelona, Spain) in 1997, and a PhD degree in computer science and digital communications from the Universitat Pompeu Fabra (Barcelona, Spain) in 2009. Since 1996 he has been a researcher at the Music Technology Group of the same university, while leading several collaboration projects with Yamaha Corp. He is mostly interested in the field of spectral-domain audio signal processing, with focus on time scaling and singing-voice modeling and synthesis.

Giovanni De Poli is an Associate Professor of computer science at the Department of Electronics and Informatics of the University of Padua, where he teaches "Data Structures and Algorithms" and "Processing Systems for Music". He is the Director of the Centro di Sonologia Computazionale (CSC) of the University of Padua. He is a member of the Executive Committee (ExCom) of the IEEE Computer Society Technical Committee on Computer Generated Music, a member of the board of directors of AIMI (Associazione Italiana di Informatica Musicale), a member of the board of directors of CIARM (Centro Interuniversitario di Acustica e Ricerca Musicale), a member of the Scientific Committee of ACROE (Institut National Politechnique Grenoble), and Associate Editor of the *International Journal of New Music Research*. His main research interests are in algorithms for sound synthesis and analysis, models for expressiveness in music, multimedia systems and human–computer interaction, and the preservation and restoration of audio documents. He is the author of several scientific international publications, and has served in the Scientific Committees of international conferences. He is co-editor of the books *Representations of Music Signals*, MIT Press 1991, and *Musical Signal Processing*, Swets & Zeitlinger, 1996. Systems and research developed in his lab have been exploited in collaboration with digital musical instruments industry (GeneralMusic). He is the owner of patents on digital music instruments.

Kristjan Dempwolf was born in Osterode am Harz, Germany, in 1978. After finishing an apprenticeship as an electronic technician in 2002 he studied electrical engineering at the Technical University Hamburg-Harburg (TUHH). He spent one semester at the Norwegian University of Science and Technology (NTNU) in 2006 and obtained his Diplom-Ingenieur degree in 2008. He is currently working on a doctoral degree at the Helmut Schmidt University – University of the Federal Armed Forces, Hamburg, Germany. His main research interests are real-time modeling and nonlinear audio systems.

Sascha Disch received his Diplom-Ingenieur degree in electrical engineering from the Technische Universität Hamburg-Harburg (TUHH), Germany in 1999. From 1999 to 2007 he was with the Fraunhofer Institut für Integrierte Schaltungen (FhG-IIS), Erlangen, Germany. At Fraunhofer, he worked in research and development in the field of perceptual audio coding and audio processing, including the MPEG standardization of parametric coding of multi-channel sound (MPEG Surround). From 2007 to 2010 he was a researcher at the Laboratorium für Informationstechnologie, Leibniz Universität Hannover (LUH), Germany and is also a PhD candidate. Currently, he is again with Fraunhofer and is involved with research and development in perceptual audio coding. His research interests include audio signal processing/coding and digital audio effects, primarily pitch shifting and time stretching.

Pierre Dutilleux graduated in thermal engineering from the Ecole Nationale Supérieure des Techniques Industrielles et des Mines de Douai (ENSTIMD) in 1983 and in information processing from the Ecole Nationale Supérieure d'Electronique et de Radioélectricité de Grenoble (ENSERG) in 1985. From 1985 to 1991, he developed audio and musical applications for the Syter real-time audio processing system designed at INA-GRM by J.-F.Allouis. After developing a set of audio-processing algorithms as well as implementing the first wavelet analyser on a digital signal processor, he got a PhD in acoustics and computer music from the university of Aix-Marseille II in 1991 under the direction of J.-C.Risset. From 1991 through to 2000 he worked as a research and development engineer at the ZKM (Center for Art and Media Technology) in Karlsruhe where he planned computer and digital audio networks for a large digital-audio studio complex, and he introduced live electronics and physical modeling as tools for musical production. He contributed to multimedia works with composers such as K. Furukawa and M. Maiguashca. He designed and realised the AML (Architecture and Music Laboratory) as an interactive museum installation. He has been a German delegate of the Digital Audio Effects (DAFX) project. In 2000 he changed his professional focus from music and signal processing to wind energy. He applies his highly differentiated listening skills to the characterisation of the noise from wind turbines. He has been Head of Acoustics at DEWI, the German Wind-Energy Institute. By performing diligent reviews of the acoustic issues of wind farm projects before construction, he can identify at an early stage the acoustic risks which might impair the acceptance of the future wind farm projects by neighbours.

Gianpaolo Evangelista is Professor in Sound Technology at the Linköping University, Sweden, where he has headed the Sound and Video Technology research group since 2005. He received the Laurea in physics (summa cum laude) from "Federico II" University of Naples, Italy, and the M.Sc. and Ph.D. degrees in electrical engineering from the University of California, Irvine. He has previously held positions at the Centre d'Etudes de Mathématique et Acoustique Musicale (CEMAMu/CNET), Paris, France; the Microgravity Advanced Research and Support (MARS) Center, Naples, Italy; the University of Naples Federico II and the Laboratory for Audiovisual Communications, Swiss Federal Institute of Technology (EPFL), Lausanne, Switzerland. He is the author or co-author of about 100 journal or conference papers and book chapters. He is a senior member of the IEEE and an active member of the DAFX (Digital Audio Effects) Scientific Committee. His interests are centered in audio signal representations, sound synthesis by physical models, digital audio effects, spatial audio, audio coding, wavelets and multirate signal processing.

Martin Holters was born in Hamburg, Germany, in 1979. He received the Master of Science degree from Chalmers Tekniska Högskola, Göteborg, Sweden, in 2003 and the Diplom-Ingenieur degree in computer engineering from the Technical University Hamburg-Harburg, Germany, in 2004. He then joined the Helmut-Schmidt-University – University of the Federal Armed Forces,

Hamburg, Germany where he received the Dr-Ingenieur degree in 2009. The topic of his dissertation was delay-free audio coding based on adaptive differential pulse code modulation (ADPCM) with adaptive pre- and post-filtering. Since 2009 he has been chief scientist in the department of signal processing and communications. He is active in various fields of audio signal processing research with his main focus still on audio coding and transmission.

Florian Keiler was born in Hamburg, Germany, in 1972. He received the Diplom-Ingenieur degree in electrical engineering from the Technical University Hamburg-Harburg (TUHH) in 1999 and the Dr.-Ingenieur degree from the Helmut-Schmidt-University – University of the Federal Armed Forces, Hamburg, Germany in 2006. The topic of his dissertation was low-delay audio coding based on linear predictive coding (LPC) in subbands. Since 2005 he has been working in the audio and acoustics research laboratory of Technicolor (formerly Thomson) located in Hanover, Germany. He is currently working in the field of spatial audio.

Tapio Lokki was born in Helsinki, Finland, in 1971. He has studied acoustics, audio signal processing, and computer science at the Helsinki University of Technology (TKK) and received an MSc degree in electrical engineering in 1997 and a DSc (Tech.) degree in computer science and engineering in 2002. At present Dr. Lokki is an Academy Research Fellow with the Department of Media Technology at Aalto University. In addition, he is an adjunct professor at the Department of Signal Processing and Acoustics at Aalto. Dr. Lokki leads his virtual acoustics team which aims to create novel objective and subjective ways to evaluate concert hall acoustics. In addition, the team develops physically based room acoustics modeling methods to obtain authentic auralization. Furthermore, the team studies augmented reality audio and eyes-free user interfaces. The team is funded by the Academy of Finland and by Dr Lokki's starting grant from the European Research Council (ERC). Dr. Lokki is a member of the editorial board of Acta Acustica united with Acustica. Dr. Lokki is a member of the Audio Engineering Society, the IEEE Computer Society, and Siggraph. In addition, he is the president of the Acoustical Society of Finland.

Alex Loscos received BS and MS degrees in signal processing engineering in 1997. In 1998 he joined the Music Technology Group of the Universitat Pompeu Fabra of Barcelona. After a few years as a researcher, lecturer, developer and project manager he co-founded Barcelona Music & Audio Technologies in 2006, a spin-off company of the research lab. In 2007 he gained a PhD in computer science and immediately started as Chief Strategy Officer at BMAT. A year and a half later he took over the position of Chief Executive Officer which he currently holds. Alex is also passionate about music, an accomplished composer and a member of international distribution bands.

Sylvain Marchand has been an associate professor in the image and sound research team of the LaBRI (Computer Science Laboratory), University of Bordeaux 1, since 2001. He is also a member of the "Studio de Création et de Recherche en Informatique et Musique Électroacoustique" (SCRIME). Regarding the international DAFX (Digital Audio Effects) conference, he has been a member of the Scientific Committee since 2006, Chair of the 2007 conference held in Bordeaux and has attended all DAFX conferences since the first one in 1998–where he gave his first presentation, as a Ph.D. student. Now, he is involved in several international conferences on musical audio, and he is also associate editor of the *IEEE Transactions on Audio, Speech, and Language Processing*. Dr Marchand is particularly involved in musical sound analysis, transformation, and synthesis. He focuses on spectral representations, taking perception into account. Among his main research topics are sinusoidal models, analysis/synthesis of deterministic and stochastic sounds, sound localization/spatialization ("3D sound"), separation of sound entities (sources) present in polyphonic music, or "active listening" (enabling the user to interact with the musical sound while it is played).

Jyri Pakarinen (1979–) received MSc and DSc (Tech.) degrees in acoustics and audio signal processing from the Helsinki University of Technology, Espoo, Finland, in 2004 and 2008, respectively. He is currently working as a post-doctoral researcher and a lecturer in the Department of Signal Processing and Acoustics, Aalto University School of Science and Technology. His main research interests are digital emulation of electric audio circuits, sound synthesis through physical modeling, and vibro- and electroacoustic measurements. As a semiprofessional guitar player, he is also interested and involved in music activities.

Enrique Perez Gonzalez was born in 1978 in Mexico City. He studied engineering communications and electronics at the ITESM University in Mexico City, where he graduated in 2002. During his engineering studies he did a one-year internship at RMIT in Melbourne, Australia where he specialized in Audio. From 1999 to 2005 he worked at the audio rental company SAIM, one of the biggest audio companies in Mexico, where he worked as a technology manager and audio system engineer for many international concerts. He graduated with distinction with an MSc in music technology at the University of York in 2006, where he worked on delta sigma modulation systems. He completed his PhD in 2010 on Advanced Tools for Automatic Mixing at the Centre for Digital Music in Queen Mary, University of London.

Mark Plumbley has investigated audio and music signal analysis, including beat tracking, music transcription, source separation and object coding, using techniques such as neural networks, independent component analysis, sparse representations and Bayesian modeling. Professor Plumbley joined Queen Mary, University of London (QMUL) in 2002, he holds an EPSRC Leadership Fellowship on Machine Listening using Sparse Representations, and in September 2010 became Director of the Centre for Digital Music at QMUL. He is chair of the International Independent Component Analysis (ICA) Steering Committee, a member of the IEEE Machine Learning in Signal Processing Technical Committee, and an Associate Editor for *IEEE Transactions on Neural Networks*.

Ville Pulkki received his MSc and DSc (Tech.) degrees from Helsinki University of Technology in 1994 and 2001, respectively. He majored in acoustics, audio signal processing and information sciences. Between 1994 and 1997 he was a full time student at the Department of Musical Education at the Sibelius Academy. In his doctoral dissertation he developed vector base amplitude panning (VBAP), which is a method for positioning virtual sources to any loudspeaker configuration. In addition, he studied the performance of VBAP with psychoacoustic listening tests and with modeling of auditory localization mechanisms. The VBAP method is now widely used in multi-channel virtual auditory environments and in computer music installations. Later, he developed with his group, a method for spatial sound reproduction and coding, directional audio coding (DirAC). DirAC takes coincident first-order microphone signals as input, and processes output to arbitrary loudspeaker layouts or to headphones. The method is currently being commercialized. Currently, he is also developing a computational functional model of the brain organs devoted to binaural hearing, based on knowledge from neurophysiology, neuroanatomy, and from psychoacoustics. He is leading a research group in Aalto University (earlier: Helsinki University of Technology, TKK or HUT), which consists of 10 researchers. The group also conducts research on new methods to measure head-related transfer functions, and conducts psychoacoustical experiments to better understand the spatial sound perception by humans. Dr. Pulkki enjoys being with his family (wife and two children), playing various musical instruments, and building his summer place. He is the Northern Region Vice President of AES and the co-chair of the AES Technical Committee on Spatial Audio.

Josh Reiss is a senior lecturer with the Centre for Digital Music at Queen Mary, University of London. He received his PhD in physics from Georgia Tech. He made the transition to audio and musical signal processing through his work on sigma delta modulators, which led to patents and a nomination for a best paper award from the IEEE. He has investigated music retrieval systems, time scaling and pitch-shifting techniques, polyphonic music transcription, loudspeaker design, automatic mixing for live sound and digital audio effects. Dr. Reiss has published over 80 scientific papers and serves on several steering and technical committees. As coordinator of the EASAIER project, he led an international consortium of seven partners working to improve access to sound archives in museums, libraries and cultural heritage institutions. His primary focus of research, which ties together many of the above topics, is on state-of-the-art signal processing techniques for professional sound engineering.

Davide Rocchesso received the PhD degree from the University of Padua, Italy, in 1996. Between 1998 and 2006 he was with the Computer Science Department at the University of Verona, Italy, as an Assistant and Associate Professor. Since 2006 he has been with the Department of Art and Industrial Design of the IUAV University of Venice, as Associate Professor. He has been the coordinator of EU project SOb (the Sounding Object) and local coordinator of the EU project CLOSED (Closing the Loop Of Sound Evaluation and Design) and of the Coordination Action S2S^2 (Sound-to-Sense; Sense-to-Sound). He has been chairing the COST Action IC-0601 SID (Sonic Interaction Design). Davide Rocchesso authored or co-authored over one hundred publications in scientific journals, books, and conferences. His main research interests are sound modelling for interaction design, sound synthesis by physical modelling, and design and evaluation of interactions.

Xavier Serra is Associate Professor of the Department of Information and Communication Technologies and Director of the Music Technology Group at the Universitat Pompeu Fabra in Barcelona. After a multidisciplinary academic education he obtained a PhD in computer music from Stanford University in 1989 with a dissertation on the spectral processing of musical sounds that is considered a key reference in the field. His research interests cover the understanding, modeling and generation of musical signals by computational means, with a balance between basic and applied research and approaches from both scientific/technological and humanistic/artistic disciplines.

Julius O. Smith teaches a music signal-processing course sequence and supervises related research at the Center for Computer Research in Music and Acoustics (CCRMA). He is formally a Professor of music and Associate Professor (by courtesy) of electrical engineering at Stanford University. In 1975, he received his BS/EE degree from Rice University, where he got a solid start in the field of digital signal processing and modeling for control. In 1983, he received the PhD/EE degree from Stanford University, specializing in techniques for digital filter design and system identification, with application to violin modeling. His work history includes the Signal Processing Department at Electromagnetic Systems Laboratories, Inc., working on systems for digital communications; the Adaptive Systems Department at Systems Control Technology, Inc., working on research problems in adaptive filtering and spectral estimation, and NeXT Computer, Inc., where he was responsible for sound, music, and signal processing software for the NeXT computer workstation. Professor Smith is a Fellow of the Audio Engineering Society and the Acoustical Society of America. He is the author of four online books and numerous research publications in his field.

Vesa Välimäki (1968–) is Professor of Audio Signal Processing at the Aalto University, Department of Signal Processing and Acoustics, Espoo, Finland. He received the Doctor of Science in technology degree from Helsinki University of Technology (TKK), Espoo, Finland, in 1995. He has published more than 200 papers in international journals and conferences. He has organized several special issues in scientific journals on topics related to musical signal processing. He was the chairman of the 11th International Conference on Digital Audio Effects (DAFX-08), which was held in Espoo in 2008. During the academic year 2008–2009 he was on sabbatical leave under a grant from the Academy of Finland and spent part of the year as a Visiting Scholar at the

Center for Computer Research in Music and Acoustics (CCRMA), Stanford University, CA. He currently serves as an Associate Editor of the *IEEE Transactions on Audio, Speech and Language Processing*. His research interests are sound synthesis, audio effects processing, digital filters, and musical instrument acoustics.

Vincent Verfaille (1974–) studied applied mathematics at INSA (Toulouse, France) to become an engineer in 1997. He then adapted to a carrier change, where he studied music technology (DEA-ATIAM, Université Paris VI, France, 2000; PhD in music technology at CNRS-LMA and Université Aix-Marseille II, France, 2003) and adaptive audio effects. He then spent a few years (2003–2009) as a post-doctoral researcher and then as a research associate in both the Sound Processing and Control Lab (SPCL) and the Input Device for Musical Interaction Lab (IDMIL) at the Schulich School of Music (McGill University, CIRMMT), where he worked on sound synthesis and control. He also taught digital audio effects and sound transformation at ENSEIRB and Université Bordeaux I (Bordeaux, France, 2002–2006), signal processing at McGill University (Montreal, Canada, 2006) and musical acoustics at University of Montréal (Montréal, Canada, 2008). He is now doing another carrier change, far away from computers and music.

Emmanuel Vincent received the BSc degree in mathematics from École Normale Supérieure in 2001 and the PhD degree in acoustics, signal processing and computer science applied to music from Université Pierre et Marie Curie, Paris, France, in 2004. After working as a research assistant with the Center for Digital Music at Queen Mary College, London, UK, he joined the French National Research Institute for Computer Science and Control (INRIA) in 2006 as a research scientist. His research focuses on probabilistic modeling of audio signals applied to source separation, information retrieval and coding. He is the founding chair of the annual Signal Separation Evaluation Campaign (SiSEC) and a co-author of the toolboxes BSS Eval and BSS Oracle for the evaluation of source separation systems.

Adrian von dem Knesebeck (1982–) received his Diplom-Ingenieur degree in electrical engineering from the Technical University Hamburg-Harburg (TUHH), Germany in 2008. Since 2009 he has been working as a research assistant in the Department of Signal Processing and Communications at the Helmut Schmidt University – University of the Federal Armed Forces in Hamburg, Germany. He was involved in several audio research projects and collaboration projects with external companies so far and is currently working on his PhD thesis.

Udo Zölzer (1958–) received the Diplom-Ingenieur degree in electrical engineering from the University of Paderborn in 1985, the Dr.-Ingenieur degree from the Technical University Hamburg-Harburg (TUHH) in 1989 and completed a Habilitation in communications engineering at the TUHH in 1997. Since 1999 he has been a Professor and Head of the Department of Signal Processing and Communications at the Helmut Schmidt University – University of the Federal Armed Forces in Hamburg, Germany. His research interests are audio and video signal processing and communication. He is a member of the AES and the IEEE.

1

Introduction

V. Verfaille, M. Holters and U. Zölzer

1.1 Digital audio effects DAFX with MATLAB®

Audio effects are used by all individuals involved in the generation of musical signals and start with special playing techniques by musicians, merge to the use of special microphone techniques and migrate to effect processors for synthesizing, recording, production and broadcasting of musical signals. This book will cover several categories of sound or audio effects and their impact on sound modifications. Digital audio effects – as an acronym we use DAFX – are boxes or software tools with input audio signals or sounds which are modified according to some sound control parameters and deliver output signals or sounds (see Figure 1.1). The input and output signals are monitored by loudspeakers or headphones and some kind of visual representation of the signal, such as the time signal, the signal level and its spectrum. According to acoustical criteria the sound engineer or musician sets his control parameters for the sound effect he would like to achieve. Both input and output signals are in digital format and represent analog audio signals. Modification of the sound characteristic of the input signal is the main goal of digital audio effects. The settings of the control parameters are often done by sound engineers, musicians (performers, composers, or digital instrument makers) or simply the music listener, but can also be part of one specific level in the signal processing chain of the digital audio effect.

The aim of this book is the description of digital audio effects with regard to:

- *Physical and acoustical effect:* we take a short look at the physical background and explanation. We describe analog means or devices which generate the sound effect.

- *Digital signal processing:* we give a formal description of the underlying algorithm and show some implementation examples.

- *Musical applications:* we point out some applications and give references to sound examples available on CD or on the web.

DAFX: Digital Audio Effects, Second Edition. Edited by Udo Zölzer.
© 2011 John Wiley & Sons, Ltd. Published 2011 by John Wiley & Sons, Ltd.

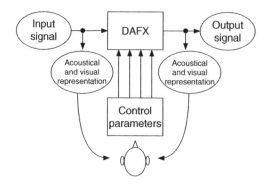

Figure 1.1   Digital audio effect and its control [Arf99].

The physical and acoustical phenomena of digital audio effects will be presented at the beginning of each effect description, followed by an explanation of the signal processing techniques to achieve the effect, some musical applications and the control of effect parameters.

In this introductory chapter we next introduce some vocabulary clarifications, and then present an overview of classifications of digital audio effects. We then explain some simple basics of digital signal processing and show how to write simulation software for audio effects processing with the **MATLAB**[1] simulation tool or freeware simulation tools[2]. **MATLAB** implementations of digital audio effects are a long way from running in real time on a personal computer or allowing real-time control of its parameters. Nevertheless the programming of signal processing algorithms and in particular sound-effect algorithms with **MATLAB** is very easy and can be learned very quickly.

Sound effect, audio effect and sound transformation

As soon as the word "effect" is used, the viewpoint that stands behind is the one of the subject who is observing a phenomenon. Indeed, "effect" denotes an impression produced in the mind of a person, a change in perception resulting from a cause. Two uses of this word denote related, but slightly different aspects: "sound effects" and "audio effects." Note that in this book, we discuss the latter exclusively. The expression – "sound effects" – is often used to depict sorts of earcones (icons for the ear), special sounds which in production mode have a strong signature and which therefore are very easily identifiable. Databases of sound effects provide natural (recorded) and processed sounds (resulting from sound synthesis and from audio effects) that produce specific effects on perception used to simulate actions, interaction or emotions in various contexts. They are, for instance, used for movie soundtracks, for cartoons and for music pieces. On the other hand, the expression "audio effects" corresponds to the tool that is used to apply transformations to sounds in order to modify how they affect us. We can understand those two meanings as a shift of the meaning of "effect": from the perception of a change itself to the signal processing technique that is used to achieve this change of perception. This shift reflects a semantic confusion between the object (what is perceived) and the tool to make the object (the signal processing technique). "Sound effect" really deals with the subjective viewpoint, whereas "audio effect" uses a subject-related term (effect) to talk about an objective reality: the tool to produce the sound transformation.

Historically, it can arguably be said that audio effects appeared first, and sound transformations later, when this expression was tagged on refined sound models. Indeed, techniques that made use of an analysis/transformation/synthesis scheme embedded a transformation step performed on a refined model of the sound. This is the technical aspect that clearly distinguishes "audio effects"

---

[1] http://www.mathworks.com
[2] http://www.octave.org

and "sound transformations," the former using a simple representation of the sound (samples) to perform signal processing, whereas the latter uses complex techniques to perform enhanced signal processing. Audio effects originally denoted simple processing systems based on simple operations, e.g. chorus by random control of delay line modulation; echo by a delay line; distortion by non-linear processing. It was assumed that audio effects process sound at its *surface*, since sound is represented by the wave form samples (which is not a high-level sound model) and simply processed by delay lines, filters, gains, etc. By surface we do not mean how strongly the sound is modified (it in fact can be deeply modified; just think of distortion), but we mean how far we go in unfolding the sound representations to be accurate and refined in the data and model parameters we manipulate. Sound transformations, on the other hand, denoted complex processing systems based on analysis/transformation/synthesis models. We, for instance, think of the phase vocoder with fundamental frequency tracking, the source-filter model, or the sinusoidal plus residual additive model. They were considered to offer deeper modifications, such as high-quality pitch-shifting with formant preservation, timbre morphing, and time-scaling with attack, pitch and panning preservation. Such deep manipulation of control parameters allows in turn the sound modifications to be heard as very subtle.

Over time, however, practice blurred the boundaries between audio effects and sound transformations. Indeed, several analysis/transformation/synthesis schemes can simply perform various processing that we consider to be audio effects. On the other hand, usual audio effects such as filters have undergone tremendous development in terms of design, in order to achieve the ability to control the frequency range and the amplitude gain, while taking care to limit the phase modulation. Also, some usual audio effects considered as simple processing actually require complex processing. For instance, reverberation systems are usually considered as simple audio effects because they were originally developed using simple operations with delay lines, even though they apply complex sound transformations. For all those reasons, one may consider that the terms "audio effects," "sound transformations" and "musical sound processing" are all refering to the same idea, which is to apply signal processing techniques to sounds in order to modify how they will be perceived, or in other words, to transform a sound into another sound with a perceptually different quality. While the different terms are often used interchangeably, we use "audio effects" throughout the book for the sake of consistency.

1.2 Classifications of DAFX

Digital audio effects are mainly used by composers, performers and sound engineers, but they are generally described from the standpoint of the DSP engineers who designed them. Therefore, their classification and documentation, both in software documentation and textbooks, rely on the underlying techniques and technologies. If we observe what happens in different communities, there exist other classification schemes that are commonly used. These include signal processing classification [Orf96, PPPR96, Roa96, Moo90, Zöl02], control type classification [VWD06], perceptual classification [ABL+03], and sound and music computing classification [CPR95], among others. Taking a closer look in order to compare these classifications, we observe strong differences. The reason is that each classification has been introduced in order to best meet the needs of a specific audience; it then relies on a series of features. Logically, such features are relevant for a given community, but may be meaningless or obscure for a different community. For instance, signal-processing techniques are rarely presented according to the perceptual features that are modified, but rather according to acoustical dimensions. Conversely, composers usually rely on perceptual or cognitive features rather than acoustical dimensions, and even less on signal-processing aspects.

An interdisciplinary approach to audio effect classification [VGT06] aims at facilitating the communication between researchers and creators that are working on or with audio effects.[3] Various

---

[3] e.g. DSP programmers, sound engineers, sound designers, electroacoustic music composers, performers using augmented or extended acoustic instruments or digital instruments, musicologists.

disciplines are then concerned: from acoustics and electrical engineering to psychoacoustics, music cognition and psycholinguistics. The next subsections present the various standpoints on digital audio effects through a description of the communication chain in music. From this viewpoint, three discipline-specific classifications are described: based on underlying techniques, control signals and perceptual attributes, then allowing the introduction of interdisciplinary classifications linking the different layers of domain-specific descriptors. It should be pointed out that the presented classifications are not classifications *stricto sensu*, since they are neither exhaustive nor mutually exclusive: one effect can be belong to more than one class, depending on other parameters such as the control type, the artefacts produced, the techniques used, etc.

Communication chain in music

Despite the variety of needs and standpoints, the technological terminology is predominantly employed by the actual users of audio effects: composers and performers. This technological classification might be the most rigorous and systematic one, but it unfortunately only refers to the techniques used, while ignoring our perception of the resulting audio effects, which seems more relevant in a musical context.

We consider the communication chain in music that essentially produces musical sounds [Rab, HMM04]. Such an application of the communication-chain concept to music has been adapted from linguistics and semiology [Nat75], based on Molino's work [Mol75]. This adaptation in a tripartite semiological scheme distinguishes three levels of musical communication between a composer (producer) and a listener (receiver) through a physical, neutral trace such as a sound. As depicted in Figure 1.2, we apply this scheme to a complete chain in order to investigate all possible standpoints on audio effects. In doing so, we include all actors intervening in the various processes of the conception, creation and perception of music, who are instrument-makers, composers, performers and listeners. The *poietic level* concerns the conception and creation of a *musical message* to which instrument-makers, composers and performers participate in different ways and at different stages. The *neutral level* is that of the physical "trace" (instruments, sounds or scores). The *aesthetic level* corresponds to the perception and reception of the *musical message* by a listener. In the case of audio effects, the instrument-maker is the signal-processing engineer who designs the effect and the performer is the user of the effect (musician, sound engineer). In the context of home studios and specific musical genres (such as mixed music creation), composers, performers and instrument-makers (music technologists) are usually distinct individuals who need to efficiently communicate with one another. But all actors in the chain are also listeners who can share descriptions of what they hear and how they interpret it. Therefore we will consider the perceptual and cognitive standpoints as the entrance point to the proposed interdisciplinary network of the various domain-specific classifications. We also consider the specific case of the home studio where a performer may also be his very own sound engineer, designs or sets his processing chain, and performs the mastering. Similarly, electroacoustic music composers often combine such tasks with additional programming and performance skills. They conceive their own processing system, control and perform on their instruments. Although all production tasks are performed by a single multidisciplinary artist in these two cases, a transverse classification is still helpful to achieve a

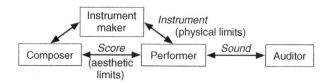

Figure 1.2 Communication chain in music: the composer, performer and instrument maker are also listeners, but in a different context than the auditor.

better awareness of the relations, between the different description levels of an audio effect, from technical to perceptual standpoints.

1.2.1 Classification based on underlying techniques

Using the standpoint of the "instrument-maker" (DSP engineer or software engineer), this first classification focuses on the underlying techniques that are used in order to implement the audio effects. Many digital implementations of audio effects are in fact emulations of their analog ancestors. Similarly, some analog audio effects implemented with one technique were emulating audio effects that already existed with another analog technique. Of course, at some point analog and/or digital techniques were also creatively used so as to provide new effects. We can distinguish the following analog technologies, in chronological order:

- Mechanics/acoustics (e.g., musical instruments and effects due to room acoustics)

- Electromechanics (e.g., using vinyls)

- Electromagnetics (e.g., flanging and time-scaling with magnetic tapes)

- Electronics (e.g., filters, vocoder, ring modulators).

With mechanical means, such as designing or choosing a specific room for its acoustical properties, music was modified and shaped to the wills of composers and performers. With electromechanical means, vinyls could be used to time-scale and pitch-shift a sound by changing disk rotation speed.[4] With electromagnetic means, flanging was originally obtained when pressing the thumb on the flange of a magnetophone wheel[5] and is now emulated with digital comb filters with varying delays. Another example of electromagnetic means is the time-scaling effect without pitch-shifting (i.e., with "not-too-bad" timbre preservation) performed by the composer and engineer Pierre Schaeffer back in the early 1950s. Electronic means include ring modulation, which refers to the multiplication of two signals and borrows its name from the analog ring-shaped circuit of diodes originally used to implement this effect.

Digital effects emulating acoustical or perceptual properties of electromechanic, electric or electronic effects include filtering, the wah-wah effect,[6] the vocoder effect, reverberation, echo and the Leslie effect. More recently, electronic and digital sound processing and synthesis allowed for the creation of new unprecedented effects, such as robotization, spectral panoramization, prosody change by adaptive time-scaling and pitch-shifting, and so on. Of course, the boundaries between imitation and creative use of technology is not clear cut. The vocoding effect, for example, was first developed to encode voice by controlling the spectral envelope with a filter bank, but was later used for musical purposes, specifically to add a vocalic aspect to a musical sound. A digital synthesis counterpart results from a creative use (LPC, phase vocoder) of a system allowing for the imitation of acoustical properties. Digital audio effects can be organized on the basis of implementation techniques, as it is proposed in this book:

- Filters and delays (resampling)

- Modulators and demodulators

---

[4] Such practice was usual in the first cinemas with sound, where the person in charge of the projection was synchronizing the sound to the image, as explained with a lot of humor by the awarded filmmaker Peter Brook in his autobiography: Threads of Time: Recollections, 1998.

[5] It is considered that flanging was first performed by George Martin and the Beatles, when John Lennon was asking for a technical way to replace dubbing.

[6] It seems that the term wah-wah was first coined by Miles Davis in the 1950s to describe how he manipulated sound with his trumpet's mute.

- Non-linear processing

- Spatial effects

- Time-segment processing

- Time-frequency processing

- Source-filter processing

- Adaptive effects processing

- Spectral processing

- Time and frequency warping

- Virtual analog effects

- Automatic mixing

- Source separation.

Another classification of digital audio effects is based on the domain where the signal processing is applied (namely time, frequency and time-frequency), together with the indication whether the processing is performed sample-by-sample or block-by-block:

- Time domain:

  - block processing using overlap-add (OLA) techniques (e.g., basic OLA, synchronized OLA, pitch synchronized OLA)

  - sample processing (filters, using delay lines, gain, non-linear processing, resampling and interpolation)

- Frequency domain (with block processing):

  - frequency-domain synthesis with inverse Fourier transform (e.g., phase vocoder with or without phase unwrapping)

  - time-domain synthesis (using oscillator bank)

- Time and frequency domain (e.g., phase vocoder plus LPC).

The advantage of such kinds of classification based on the underlying techniques is that the software developer can easily see the technical and implementation similarities of various effects, thus simplifying both the understanding and the implementation of multi-effect systems, which is depicted in the diagram in Figure 1.3. It also provides a good overview of technical domains and signal-processing techniques involved in effects. However, several audio effects appear in two places in the diagram (illustrating once again how these diagrams are not real classifications), belonging to more than a single class, because they can be performed with techniques from various domains. For instance, time-scaling can be performed with time-segment processing as well as with time-frequency processing. One step further, adaptive time-scaling with time-synchronization [VZA06] can be performed with SOLA using either block-by-block or time-domain processing, but also with the phase vocoder using a block-by-block frequency-domain analysis with IFFT synthesis.

Depending on the user expertise (DSP programmer, electroacoustic composer), this classification may not be the easiest to understand, even more since this type of classification does not explicitly handle perceptual features, which are the common vocabulary of all listeners. Another reason for introducing the perceptual attributes of sound in a classification is that when users can choose between various implementations of an effect, they also make their choice depending on

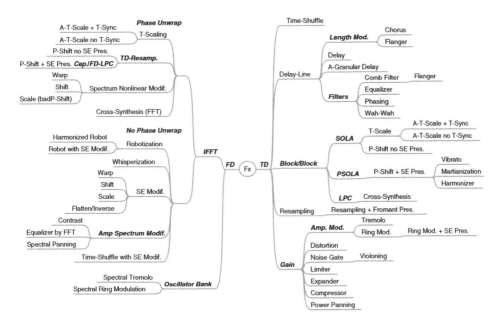

Figure 1.3   A technical classification of audio effects that could be used to design multi-effect systems. "TD" stands for "time-domain," "FD" for "frequency domain," "t-scale" for "time-scaling," "p-shift" for "pitch-shifting," "+" for "with," "A-" for adaptive control," "SE" for "spectral envelope," "osc" for "oscillator," "mod." for "modulation" and "modif." for "modification." Bold italic font words denote technical aspects, whereas regular font words denote audio effects.

the audible artifacts of each effect. For instance, with time-scaling, resampling does not preserve pitch nor formants; OLA with circular buffer adds the window modulation and sounds rougher and filtered; a phase vocoder sounds a bit reverberant, the "sinusoidal + noise" additive model sounds good except for attacks, the "sinusoidal + transients + noise" additive model preserves attacks, but not the spatial image of multi-channel sounds, etc. Therefore, in order to choose a technique, the user must be aware of the audible artifact of each technique. The need to link implementation techniques to perceptual features thus becomes clear and will be discussed next.

1.2.2   Classification based on perceptual attributes

Using the perceptual categorization, audio effects can be classified according to the perceptual attribute that is mainly altered by the digital processing (examples of "musical gestures" are also provided):

- Loudness: related to dynamics, nuances and phrasing (*legato*, and *pizzicato*), accents, *tremolo*

- Time: related to duration, tempo, and rhythmic modifications (*accelerando*, *deccelerando*)

- Pitch: composed of height and chroma, related to and organized into melody, intonation and harmony; sometimes shaped with *glissandi*

- Spatial hearing: related to source localization (distance, azimuth, elevation), motion (Doppler) and directivity, as well as to the room effect (reverberation, echo)

- Timbre: composed of short-term time features (such as transients and attacks) and long-term time features that are formants (color) and ray spectrum properties (texture, harmonicity), both coding aspects such as brightness (or spectral height), sound quality, timbral metamorphosis; related musical gestures contain various playing modes, ornamentation and special effects such as *vibrato*, trill, flutter tonguing, *legato, pizzicato*, harmonic notes, multiphonics, etc.

We consider this classification to be among the most natural to musicians and audio listeners, since such perceptual attributes are usually clearly identified in music scores. It has already been used to classify content-based transformations [ABL+03] as well as adaptive audio effects [VZA06]. Therefore, we now discuss a more detailed overview of those perceptual attributes by highlighting some basics of psychoacoustics for each perceptual attribute. We also name commonly used digital audio effects, with a specific emphasis on timbre, as this more complex perceptive attribute offers the widest range of sound possibilities. We also highlight the relationships between perceptual attributes (or high-level features) and their physical counterparts (signal or low-level features), which are usually simpler to compute.

Loudness: Loudness is the perceived intensity of the sound through time. Its computational models perform time and frequency integration of the energy in critical bands [ZS65, Zwi77]. The sound intensity level computed by RMS (root mean square) is its physical counterpart. Using an additive analysis and a transient detection, we extract the sound intensity levels of the harmonic content, the transient and the residual. We generally use a logarithmic scale named decibels: loudness is then $L_{dB} = 20 \log_{10} I$, with I the intensity. Adding 20 dB to the loudness is obtained by multiplying the sound intensity level by 10. The musical counterpart of loudness is called dynamics, and corresponds to a scale ranging from *pianissimo* (*pp*) to *fortissimo* (*ff*) with a 3 dB space between two successive dynamic levels. *Tremolo* describes a loudness modulation with a specific frequency and depth. Commonly used loudness effects modify the sound intensity level: the volume change, the tremolo, the compressor, the expander, the noise gate and the limiter. The tremolo is a sinusoidal amplitude modulation of the sound intensity level with a modulation frequency between 4 and 7 Hz (around the 5.5 Hz frequency modulation of the vibrato). The compressor and the expander modify the intensity level using a non-linear function; they are among the first adaptive effects that were created. The former compresses the intensity level, thus giving more percussive sounds, whereas the latter has the opposite effect and is used to extend the dynamic range of the sound. With specific non-linear functions, we obtain noise gate and limiter effects. The noise gate bypasses sounds with very low loudness, which is especially useful to avoid the background noise that circulate throughout an effect system involving delays. Limiting the intensity level protects the hardware. Other forms of loudness effects include automatic mixers and automatic volume/gain control, which are sometimes noise-sensor equipped.

Time and Rhythm: Time is perceived through two intimately intricate attributes: the duration of sound and gaps, and the rhythm, which is based on repetition and inference of patterns [DH92]. Beat can be extracted with autocorrelation techniques, and patterns with quantification techniques [Lar01]. Time-scaling is used to fit the signal duration to a given duration, thus affecting rhythm. Resampling can perform time-scaling, resulting in an unwanted pitch-shifting. The time-scaling ratio is usually constant, and greater than 1 for time-expanding (or time-stretching, time-dilatation: sound is slowed down) and lower than 1 for time-compressing (or time-contraction: sound is sped up). Three block-by-block techniques avoid this: the phase vocoder [Por76, Dol86, AKZ02a], SOLA [MC90, Lar98] and the additive model [MQ86, SS90, VLM97]. Time-scaling with the phase vocoder technique consists of using different analysis and synthesis step increments. The phase vocoder is performed using the short-time Fourier transform (STFT) [AR77]. In the analysis step, the STFT of windowed input blocks is performed with an R_A samples step increment. In the synthesis step, the inverse Fourier transform delivers output blocks which are windowed, overlapped and then added with an R_S samples step increment. The phase vocoder step increments have to be suitably chosen to provide a perfect reconstruction of the signal [All77, AR77]. Phase computation is needed for each frequency bin of the synthesis STFT. The phase vocoder technique can time-scale any type of sound, but adds phasiness if no care is taken: a peak phase-locking technique solves this problem [Puc95, LD97]. Time-scaling with the SOLA technique[7] is performed by duplication or suppression of temporal grains or blocks, with pitch synchronization of the overlapped grains in order to avoid low frequency modulation due to phase cancellation. Pitch-synchronization implies that the SOLA technique only correctly processes the monophonic sounds. Time-scaling with the additive model results in scaling the time axis of the partial frequencies and their amplitudes. The additive model can process harmonic as well as inharmonic sounds while having a good quality spectral line analysis.

Pitch: Harmonic sounds have their pitch given by the frequencies and amplitudes of the harmonics; the fundamental frequency is the physical counterpart. The attributes of pitch are height (high/low frequency) and chroma (or color) [She82]. A musical sound can be either perfectly harmonic (e.g., wind instruments), nearly harmonic (e.g., string instruments) or inharmonic (e.g., percussions, bells). Harmonicity is also related to timbre. Psychoacoustic models of the perceived pitch use both the spectral information (frequency) and the periodicity information (time) of the sound [dC04]. The pitch is perceived in the quasi-logarithmic *mel* scale, which is approximated by the log-Hertz scale. Tempered scale notes are transposed up by one octave when multiplying the fundamental frequency by 2 (same chroma, doubling the height). The pitch organization through time is called melody for monophonic sounds and harmony for polyphonic sounds. The pitch of harmonic sounds can be shifted, thus transposing the note. Pitch-shifting is the dual transformation of time-scaling, and consists of scaling the frequency axis of a time-frequency representation of the sound. A pitch-shifting ratio greater than 1 transposes up; lower than 1 it transposes down. It can be performed by a combination of time-scaling and resampling. In order to preserve the timbre and the spectral envelope [AKZ02b], the phase vocoder decomposes the signal into source and filter for each analysis block: the formants are pre-corrected (in the frequency domain [AD98]), the source signal is resampled (in the time domain) and phases are wrapped between two successive blocks (in the frequency domain). The PSOLA technique preserves the spectral envelope [BJ95, ML95], and performs pitch-shifting by using a synthesis step increment that differs from the analysis step increment. The additive model scales the spectrum by multiplying the frequency of each partial by the pitch-shifting ratio. Amplitudes are then linearly interpolated from the spectral envelope. Pitch-shifting of inharmonic sounds such as bells can also be performed by ring modulation. Using a pitch-shifting effect, one can derive harmonizer and auto tuning effects. Harmonizing consists of mixing a sound with several pitch-shifted versions of it, to obtain chords. When controlled by the input pitch and the melodic context, it is called smart harmony [AOPW99] or intelligent harmonization.[8] Auto tuning[9] consists of pitch-shifting a monophonic signal so that the pitch fits to the tempered scale [ABL+03].

Spatial Hearing: Spatial hearing has three attributes: the location, the directivity, and the room effect. The sound is localized by human beings with regards to distance, elevation and azimuth, through interaural intensity (IID) and inter-aural time (ITD) differences [Bla83], as well as through filtering via the head, the shoulders and the rest of the body (head-related transfer function, HRTF). When moving, sound is modified according to pitch, loudness and timbre, indicating the speed and direction of its motion (Doppler effect) [Cho71]. The directivity of a source is responsible for the differences in transfer functions according to the listener position relative to the source. The sound is transmitted through a medium as well as reflected, attenuated and filtered by obstacles (reverberation and echoes), thus providing cues for deducing the geometrical and material properties of the room. Spatial effects describe the spatialization of a sound with headphones or loudspeakers. The position in the space is simulated using intensity panning (e.g., constant power panoramization

---

[7] When talking about SOLA techniques, we refer to all the synchronized and overlap-add techniques: SOLA, TD-PSOLA, TF-PSOLA, WSOLA, etc.

[8] http://www.tc-helicon.tc/

[9] http://www.antarestech.com/

with two loudspeakers or headphones [Bla83], vector-based amplitude panning (VBAP) [Pul97] or Ambisonics [Ger85] with more loudspeakers), delay lines to simulate the precedence effect due to ITD, as well as filters in a transaural or binaural context [Bla83]. The Doppler effect is due to the behaviour of sound waves approaching or going away; the sound motion throughout the space is simulated using amplitude modulation, pitch-shifting and filtering [Cho71, SSAB02]. Echoes are created using delay lines that can eventually be fractional [LVKL96]. The room effect is simulated with artificial reverberation units that use either delay-line networks or all-pass filters [SL61, Moo79] or convolution with an impulse response. The simulation of instruments' directivity is performed with linear combination of simple directivity patterns of loudspeakers [WM01]. The rotating speaker used in the Leslie/Rotary is a directivity effect simulated as a Doppler [SSAB02].

Timbre: This attribute is difficult to define from a scientific point of view. It has been viewed for a long time as "that attribute of auditory sensation in terms of which a listener can judge that two sounds similarly presented and having the same loudness and pitch are dissimilar" [ANS60]. However, this does not take into account some basic facts, such as the ability to recognize and to name any instrument when hearing just one note or listening to it through a telephone [RW99]. The frequency composition of the sound is concerned, with the attack shape, the steady part and the decay of a sound, the variations of its spectral envelope through time (e.g., variations of formants of the voice), and the phase relationships between harmonics. These phase relationships are responsible for the whispered aspect of a voice, the roughness of low-frequency modulated signals, and also for the phasiness[10] introduced when harmonics are not phase aligned. We consider that timbre has several other attributes, including:

- The brightness or spectrum height, correlated to spectral centroid[11] [MWdSK95], and computed with various models [Cab99]

- The quality and noisiness, correlated to the signal-to-noise ratio (e.g., computed as the ratio between the harmonics and the residual intensity levels [ABL+03]) and to the voiciness (computed from the autocorrelation function [BP89] as the second-highest peak value of the normalized autocorrelation)

- The texture, related to jitter and shimmer of partials/harmonics [DT96] (resulting from a statistical analysis of the partials' frequencies and amplitudes), to the balance of odd/even harmonics (given as the peak of the normalized autocorrelation sequence situated half way between the first- and second-highest peak values [AKZ02b]) and to harmonicity

- The formants (especially vowels for the voice [Sun87]) extracted from the spectral envelope, the spectral envelope of the residual and the mel-frequency critical bands (MFCC), perceptual correlate of the spectral envelope.

Timbre can be verbalized in terms of roughness, harmonicity, as well as openness, acuteness and laxness for the voice [Sla85]. At a higher level of perception, it can also be defined by musical aspects such as *vibrato* [RDS+99], *trill* and *Flatterzunge*, and by note articulation such as *appoyando, tirando* and *pizzicato*.

Timbre effects is the widest category of audio effects and includes vibrato, chorus, flanging, phasing, equalization, spectral envelope modifications, spectral warping, whisperization, adaptive filtering and transient enhancement or attenuation.

- Vibrato is used for emphasis and timbral variety [MB90], and is defined as a complex timbre pulsation or modulation [Sea36] implying frequency modulation, amplitude modulation and

---

[10] Phasiness is usually involved in speakers reproduction, where phase inproperties make the sound poorly spatialized. In the phase vocoder technique, the phasiness refers to a reverberation artifact that appears when neighboring frequency bins representing the same sinusoid have different phase unwrapping.

[11] The spectral centroid is also correlated to other low-level features: the spectral slope, the zero-crossing rate, the high frequency content [MB96].

sometimes spectral-shape modulation [MB90, VGD05], with a nearly sinusoidal control. Its modulation frequency is around 5.5 Hz for the singing voice [Hon95]. Depending on the instruments, the vibrato is considered as a frequency modulation with a constant spectral shape (e.g., voice, [Sun87], stringed instruments [MK73, RW99]), an amplitude modulation (e.g., wind instruments), or a combination of both, on top of which may be added a complex spectral-shape modulation, with high-frequency harmonics enrichment due to non-linear properties of the resonant tube (voice [MB90], wind and brass instruments [RW99]).

- A chorus effect appears when several performers play together the same piece of music (same in melody, rhythm, dynamics) with the same kind of instrument. Slight pitch, dynamic, rhythm and timbre differences arise because the instruments are not physically identical, nor are perfectly tuned and synchronized. It is simulated by adding to the signal the output of a randomly modulated delay line [Orf96, Dat97]. A sinusoidal modulation of the delay line creates a flanging or sweeping comb filter effect [Bar70, Har78, Smi84, Dat97]. Chorus and flanging are specific cases of phase modifications known as phase shifting or phasing.

- Equalization is a well-known effect that exists in most of the sound systems. It consists in modifying the spectral envelope by filtering with the gains of a constant-Q filter bank. Shifting, scaling or warping of the spectral envelope is often used for voice sounds since it changes the formant places, yielding to the so-called Donald Duck effect [AKZ02b].

- Spectral warping consists of modifying the spectrum in a non-linear way [Fav01], and can be achieved using the additive model or the phase vocoder technique with peak phase-locking [Puc95, LD97]. Spectral warping allows for pitch-shifting (or spectrum scaling), spectrum shifting, and in-harmonizing.

- Whisperization transforms a spoken or sung voice into a whispered voice by randomizing either the magnitude spectrum or the phase spectrum of a short-time Fourier transform [AKZ02a]. Hoarseness is a quite similar effect that takes advantage of the additive model to modify the harmonic-to-residual ratio [ABL$^+$03].

- Adaptive filtering is used in telecommunications [Hay96] in order to avoid the feedback loop effect created when the output signal of the telephone loudspeaker goes into the microphone. Filters can be applied in the time domain (comb filters, vocal-like filters, equalizer) or in the frequency domain (spectral envelope modification, equalizer).

- Transient enhancement or attenuation is obtained by changing the prominence of the transient compared to the steady part of a sound, for example using an enhanced compressor combined with a transient detector.

Multi-Dimensional Effects: Many other effects modify several perceptual attributes of sounds simultaneously. For example, robotization consists of replacing a human voice with a metallic machine-like voice by adding roughness, changing the pitch and locally preserving the formants. This is done using the phase vocoder and zeroing the phase of the grain STFT with a step increment given as the inverse of the fundamental frequency. All the samples between two successive non overlapping grains are zeroed[12] [AKZ02a]. Resampling consists of interpolating the wave form, thus modifying duration, pitch and timbre (formants). Ring modulation is an amplitude modulation without the original signal. As a consequence, it duplicates and shifts the spectrum and modifies pitch and timbre, depending on the relationship between the modulation frequency and the signal fundamental frequency [Dut91]. Pitch-shifting without preserving the spectral envelope modifies

---

[12] The robotization processing preserves the spectral shape of a processed grain at the local level. However, the formants are slightly modified at the global level because of overlap-add of grains with non-phase-aligned grain (phase cancellation) or with zeros (flattening of the spectral envelope).

both pitch and timbre. The use of multi-tap monophonic or stereophonic echoes allow for rhythmic, melodic and harmonic constructions through superposition of delayed sounds.

Summary of Effects by Perceptual Attribute: For the main audio effects, Tables 1.1, 1.2, and 1.3 indicate the perceptual attributes modified, along with complementary information for programmers and users about real-time implementation and control type. When the user chooses an effect to modify one perceptual attribute, the implementation technique used may introduce artifacts, implying modifications of other attributes. For that reason, we differentiate the perceptual attributes that we primarily want to modify ("main" perceptual attributes, and the corresponding dominant modification perceived) and the "secondary" perceptual attributes that are slightly modified (on purpose or as a by-product of the signal processing).

Table 1.1 Digital audio effects according to modified perceptual attributes (L for loudness, D for duration and rhythm, P for pitch and harmony, T for timbre and quality, and S for spatial qualities). We also indicate if real-time implementation (RT) is not possible (using "—"), and the built-in control type (A for adaptive, cross-A for cross-adaptive, and LFO for low-frequency oscillator).

Effect name	Perceptual Attributes		RT	Control
	Main	Other		
Effects mainly on loudness (L)				
compressor, limiter, expander, noise gate	L	T		A
gain/amplification	L			
normalization	L		–	
tremolo	L			LFO
violoning (attack smoothing)	L	T		A
Effects mainly on duration (D)				
time inversion	D	P,L,T	–	
time-scaling	D			
time-scaling with formant preservation	D		–	
time-scaling with vibrato preservation	D		–	
time-scaling with attack preservation	D		–	A
rhythm/swing change	D	T	–	A
Effects mainly on pitch (P)				
pitch-shifting without formant preservation	P	T		
pitch-shifting with formant preservation	P			
pitch change	P			A
pitch discretization (auto-tune)	P	T		A
harmonizer/smart harmony	P			A
(in-)harmonizer	P			A
Effects mainly on spatial aspects (S)				
distance change	S	L,T		
directivity	S	P,T		
Doppler effect	S	L,P		
echo	S	L		
granular delay	S	L,D,P,T		A
reverberation	S	L,D,T		
panning (2D, 3D)	S			
spectral panning	S	L,T		
rotary/Leslie	S	P,T		LFO

Table 1.2 Digital audio effects that mainly modify timbre only.

Effect name	Perceptual Attributes		RT	Control
	Main	Other		
Effects mainly on timbre (T)				
Effects on spectral envelope:				
filter	T	L		
arbitrary resolution filter	T	L		
comb filter	T	L,P		
resonant filter	T	L,P		
equalizer	T	L		
wah-wah	T	L,P		
auto-wah (sensitive wah)	T	L,D,P		LFO
envelope shifting	T	L		
envelope scaling	T	L		
envelope warping	T	L		
spectral centroid change	T	L		
Effects on phase:				
chorus	T			random
flanger	T	P		LFO
phaser	T	P		LFO
Effects on spectral structure:				
spectrum shifting	T	P		
adaptive ring modulation	T	P		A
texture change	T			
Effects on spectrum & envelope:				
distortion	T	L,P		
fuzz	T	L,P		
overdrive	T	L,P		
spectral (in-)harmonizer	T			
mutation	T	L,P		cross-A
spectral interpolation:	T	L,P		cross-A
vocoding	T	L,P		cross-A
cross-synthesis	T	L,P		cross-A
voice morphing	T	L,P		cross-A
timbral metamorphosis	T	L,P		cross-A
timbral morphing	T	L,P		cross-A
whispering/hoarseness	T	L	–	
de-esser	T	L		A
declicking	T	L	–	
denoising	T	L		
exciter	T	L		
enhancer	T	L		

Table 1.3 Digital audio effects that modify several perceptual attributes (on purpose).

Effect name	Perceptual Attributes		RT	Control
	Main	Other		
Effects modifying several perceptual attributes				
spectral compressor	L,T			
gender change	P,T	L		A
intonation change	L,P			A
martianisation	P,T	L		A
prosody change	L,D,P			A
resampling	D,T	L,P	–	
ring modulation	P,T			
robotization	P,T	L		
spectral tremolo	L,T	D		LFO
spectral warping	T,P	L		
time shuffling	L,D,P,T		–	
vibrato	L,P	T,D		LFO

By making use of heuristic maps [BB96] we can represent the various links between an effect and perceptual attributes, as depicted in Figure 1.4, where audio effects are linked in the center to the main perceptual attribute modified. Some sub-attributes (not necessarily perceptual) are introduced. For the sake of simplicity, audio effects are attached to the center only for the main modified perceptual attributes. When other attributes are slightly modified, they are indicated on the opposite side, i.e., at the figure bounds. When other perceptual attributes are slightly modified by an audio effect, those links are not connected to the center, in order to avoid overloading the heuristic map, but rather to the outer direction. A perceptual classification has the advantage of presenting audio effects according to the way they are perceived, taking into account the audible artifacts of the implementation techniques. The diagram in Figure 1.4, however, only represents each audio effect in its expected use (e.g., a compressor set to compress the dynamic range, which in turn slightly modifies the attacks and possibly timbre; it does not indicate all the possible settings, such as the attack smoothing and resulting timbral change when the attack time is set to 2s for instance). Of course, none of the presented classifications is perfect, and the adequacy of each depends on the goal we have in mind when using it. However, for sharing and spreading knowledge about audio effects between DSP programmers, musicians and listeners, this classification offers a vocabulary dealing with our auditory perception of the sound produced by the audio effect, that we all share since we all are listeners in the communication chain.

1.2.3 Interdisciplinary classification

Before introducing an interdisciplinary classification of audio effects that links the different layers of domain-specific descriptors, we recall sound effect classifications, as they provide clues for such interdisciplinary classifications. Sound effects have been thoroughly investigated in electroacoustic music. For instance, Schaeffer [Sch66] classified sounds according to: (i) *matter*, which is constituted of mass (noisiness; related to spectral density), harmonic timbre (harmonicity) and grain (the micro-structure of sound); (ii) *form*, which is constituted of dynamic (intensity evolution), and allure (e.g., frequency and amplitude modulation); (iii) *variation*, which is constituted of melodic profile (e.g., pitch variations) and mass profile (e.g., mass variations). In the context

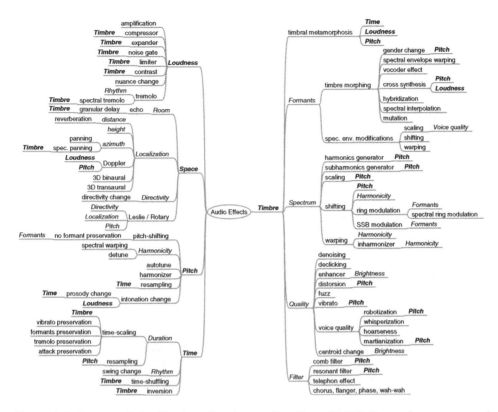

Figure 1.4 Perceptual classification of various audio effects. Bold-italic words are perceptual attributes (pitch, loudness, etc.). Italic words are perceptual sub-attributes (formants, harmonicity, etc.). Other words refer to the corresponding audio effects.

of ecological acoustics, Schafer [Sch77] introduced the idea that soundscapes reflect human activities. He proposed four main categories of environmental sounds: mechanical sounds (traffic and machines), human sounds (voices, footsteps), collective sounds (resulting from social activities) and sounds conveying information about the environment (warning signals or spatial effects). He considers four aspects of sounds: (i) emotional and affective qualities (aesthetics), (ii) function and meaning (semiotics and semantics), (iii) psychoacoustics (perception), (iv) acoustics (physical characteristics). That in turn can be used to develop classification categories [CKC+04]. Gaver [Gav93] also introduced the distinction between musical listening and everyday listening. Musical listening focuses on perceptual attributes of the sound itself (e.g., pitch, loudness), whereas everyday listening focuses on events to gather relevant information about our environment (e.g., car approaching), that is, not about the sound itself but rather about sound sources and actions producing sound. Recent research on soundscape perception validated this view by showing that people organize familiar sounds on the basis of source identification. But there is also evidence that the same sound can give rise to different cognitive representations which integrate semantic features (e.g., meaning attributed to the sound) into physical characteristics of the acoustic signal [GKP+05]. Therefore, semantic features must be taken into consideration when classifying sounds, but they cannot be matched with physical characteristics in a one-to-one relationship.

Similarly to sound effects, audio effects give rise to different semantic interpretations depending on how they are implemented or controlled. Semantic descriptors were investigated in the context of distortion [MM01] and different standpoints on reverberation were summarized in [Ble01]. An interdisciplinary classification links the various layers of discipline-specific classifications ranging from low-level to high-level features as follows:

- Digital implementation technique

- Processing domain

- Applied processing

- Control type

- Perceptual attributes

- Semantic descriptors.

It is an attempt to bridge the gaps between discipline-specific classifications by extending previous research on isolated audio effects.

Chorus Revisited. The first example in Figure 1.5 concerns the chorus effect. As previously said, a chorus effect appears when several performers play together the same piece of music (same in melody, rhythm, dynamics) with the same kind of instrument. Slight pitch, dynamic, rhythm and timbre differences arise because the instruments are not physically identical, nor are perfectly tuned and synchronized. This effect provides some warmth to a sound, and can be considered as an effect on timbre: even though it performs slight modifications of pitch and time unfolding, the resulting effect is mainly on timbre. While its usual implementation involves one or many delay lines, with modulated length and controlled by a white noise, an alternative and more realistic sounding implementation consists in using several slightly pitch-shifted and time-scaled versions of the same sound with refined models (SOLA, phase vocoder, spectral models) and mixing them together. In this case, the resulting audio effect sounds more like a chorus of people or instruments playing the same harmonic and rhythmic patterns together. Therefore, this effect's control is a random generator (white noise), that controls a processing either in the time domain (using SOLA

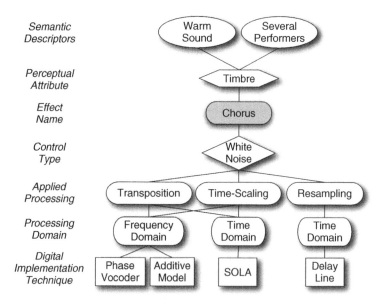

Figure 1.5 Transverse diagram for the chorus effect.

or a delay line), in the time-frequency domain (using the phase vocoder) or in the frequency domain (using spectral models).

Wah-Wah Revisited. The wah-wah is an effect that simulates vowel coarticulation. It can be implemented in the time domain using either a resonant filter or a series of resonant filters to simulate several formants of each vowels. In any case, these filters can be implemented in the time domain as well as in the time-frequency domain (phase vocoder) and in the frequency domain (with spectral models). From the usual wah-wah effect, variations can be derived by modifying its control. Figure 1.6 illustrates various control types for the wah-wah effect. With an LFO, the control is periodic and the wah-wah is called an "auto-wah." With gestural control, such as a foot pedal, it becomes the usual effect rock guitarists use since Jimmy Hendrix gave popularity to it. With an adaptive control based on the attack of each note, it becomes a "sensitive wah" that moves from "a" at the attack to "u" during the release. We now can better see the importance of specifying the control type as part of the effect definition.

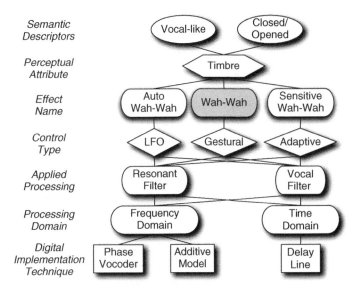

Figure 1.6   Transverse diagram for the wah-wah effect: the control type defines the effect's name, i.e., wah-wah, automatic wah-wah (with LFO) or sensitive wah-wah (adaptive control).

Comb Filter Revisited. Figure 1.7 depicts the interdisciplinary classification for the comb filter. This effect corresponds to filtering a signal using a comb-shaped frequency response. When the signal is rich and contains either a lot of partials, or a certain amount of noise, its filtering gives rise to a timbral pitch that can easily be heard. The sound is then similar to a sound heard through the resonances of a tube, or even vocal formants when the tube length is properly adjusted. As any filter, the effect can be implemented in both the time domain (using delay lines), the time-frequency domain (phase vocoder) and the frequency domain (spectral models). When controlled with a LFO, the comb filter changes its name to "phasing," which sounds similar to a plane landing, and has been used in songs during the late 1960s to simulate the effects of drugs onto perception.

Cross-synthesis revisited. The transverse diagram for cross-synthesis shown in Figure 1.8 consists in applying the time-varying spectral envelope of one sound onto the source of a second sound, after having separated their two source and filter components. Since this effect takes the whole spectral envelope of one sound, it also conveys some amplitude and time information, resulting in modifications of timbre, but also loudness, and time and rhythm. It may provide the

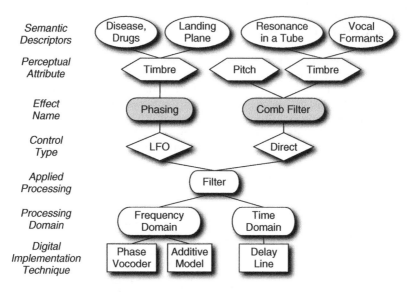

Figure 1.7 Transverse diagram for the comb-filter effect: a modification of the control by adding a LFO results in another effect called "phasing."

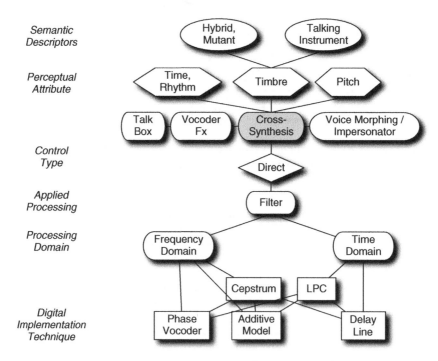

Figure 1.8 Transverse diagram for the cross-synthesis effect.

illusion of a talking instrument when the resonances of a human voice are applied onto the source of a musical instrument. It then provides a hybrid, mutant voice. After the source-filter separation, the filtering of the source of sound A with the filter from sound B can be applied in the time domain as well as in the frequency and the time-frequency domains. Other perceptually similar effects on voice are called voice morphing (as the processing used to produce the castrato's voice in the movie Farinelli's soundtrack), "voice impersonator" (the timbre of a voice from the database is mapped to your singing voice in real time), the "vocoder effect" (based on the classical vocoder), or the "talk box" (where the filter of a voice is applied to a guitar sound without removing its original resonances, then adding the voice's resonances to the guitar's resonances; as in Peter Frampton's famous "Do you feel like I do").

Distortion revisited. A fifth example is the distortion effect depicted in Figure 1.9. Distortion is produced from a soft or hard clipping of the signal, and results in a harmonic enrichment of a sound. It is widely used in popular music, especially through electric guitar that conveyed it from the beginning, due to amplification. Distortions can be implemented using amplitude warping (e.g., with Chebyshev polynomials or wave shaping), or with physical modeling of valve amplifiers. Depending on its settings, it may provide a warm sound, an aggressive sound, a bad quality sound, a metallic sound, and so on.

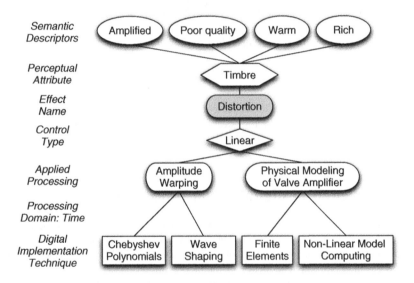

Figure 1.9 Transverse diagram for the distortion effect.

Equalizer revisited. A last example is the equalizer depicted in Figure 1.10. Its design consists of a series of shelving and peak filters that can be implemented in the time domain (filters), in the time-frequency domain (phase vocoder) or in the frequency domain (with spectral models). The user directly controls the gain, bandwidth and center frequency in order to apply modifications of the energy in each frequency band, in order to better suit aesthetic needs and also correct losses in the transducer chain.

We illustrated and summarized various classifications of audio effects elaborated in different disciplinary fields. An interdisciplinary classification links the different layers of domain-specific features and aims to facilitate knowledge exchange between the fields of musical acoustics, signal processing, psychoacoustics and cognition. Besides addressing the classification of audio effects, we further explained the relationships between structural and control parameters of signal processing algorithms and the perceptual attributes modified by audio effects. A generalization of this

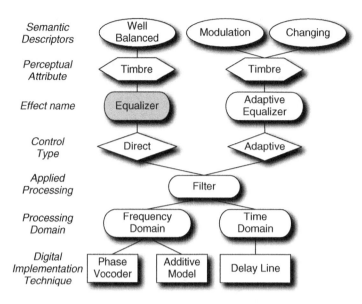

Figure 1.10   Transverse diagram for the equalizer effect.

classification to all audio effects would have a strong impact on pedagogy, knowledge sharing across disciplinary fields and musical practice. For example, DSP engineers conceive better tools when they know how it can be used in a musical context. Furthermore, linking perceptual features to signal processing techniques enables the development of more intuitive user interfaces providing control over high-level perceptual and cognitive attributes rather than low-level signal parameters.

1.3   Fundamentals of digital signal processing

The fundamentals of digital signal processing consist of the description of *digital signals* – in the context of this book we use digital audio signals – as a sequence of numbers with appropriate number representation and the description of *digital systems*, which are described by software algorithms to calculate an output sequence of numbers from an input sequence of numbers. The visual representation of digital systems is achieved by functional block diagram representations or signal flow graphs. We will focus on some simple basics as an introduction to the notation and refer the reader to the literature for an introduction to digital signal processing [ME93, Orf96, Zöl05, MSY98, Mit01].

1.3.1   Digital signals

The digital signal representation of an analog audio signal as a sequence of numbers is achieved by an analog-to-digital converter (ADC). The ADC performs *sampling* of the amplitudes of the analog signal $x(t)$ on an equidistant grid along the horizontal time axis and *quantization* of the amplitudes to fixed samples represented by numbers $x(n)$ along the vertical amplitude axis (see Fig. 1.11). The samples are shown as vertical lines with dots on the top. The analog signal $x(t)$ denotes the signal amplitude over continuous time t in micro seconds. Following the ADC, the digital (discrete time and quantized amplitude) signal is a sequence (stream) of samples $x(n)$ represented by numbers over the discrete time index n. The time distance between two consecutive samples is termed *sampling interval* T (sampling period) and the reciprocal is the *sampling frequency*

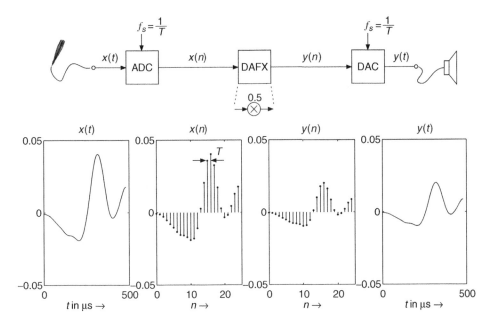

Figure 1.11 Sampling and quantizing by ADC, digital audio effects and reconstruction by DAC.

$f_S = 1/T$ (sampling rate). The sampling frequency reflects the number of samples per second in Hertz (Hz). According to the sampling theorem, it has to be chosen as twice the highest frequency f_{max} (signal bandwidth) contained in the analog signal, namely $f_S > 2 \cdot f_{max}$. If we are forced to use a fixed sampling frequency f_S, we have to make sure that our input signal to be sampled has a bandwidth according to $f_{max} = f_S/2$. If not, we have to reject higher frequencies by filtering with a lowpass filter which only passes all frequencies up to f_{max}. The digital signal is then passed to a DAFX box (digital system), which in this example performs a simple multiplication of each sample by 0.5 to deliver the output signal $y(n) = 0.5 \cdot x(n)$. This signal $y(n)$ is then forwarded to a digital-to-analog converter DAC, which reconstructs the analog signal $y(t)$. The output signal $y(t)$ has half the amplitude of the input signal $x(t)$.

Figure 1.12 shows some digital signals to demonstrate different graphical representations (see M-file 1.1). The upper part shows 8000 samples, the middle part the first 1000 samples and the lower part shows the first 100 samples out of a digital audio signal. Only if the number of samples inside a figure is sufficiently low, will the line with dot graphical representation be used for a digital signal.

M-file 1.1 (figure1_03.m)

```
% Author: U. Zölzer
[x,FS,NBITS]=wavread('ton2.wav');

figure(1)
subplot(3,1,1);
plot(0:7999,x(1:8000));ylabel('x(n)');
subplot(3,1,2);
plot(0:999,x(1:1000));ylabel('x(n)');
subplot(3,1,3);
stem(0:99,x(1:100),'.');ylabel('x(n)');
xlabel('n \rightarrow');
```

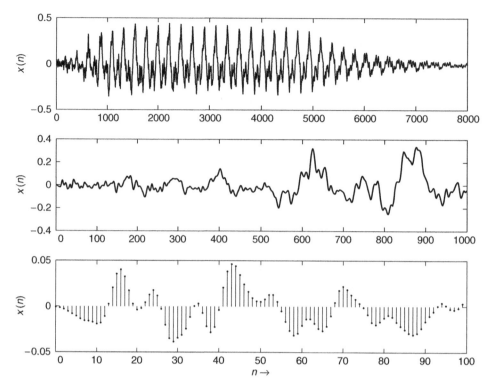

Figure 1.12 Different time representations for digital audio signals.

Two different vertical scale formats for digital audio signals are shown in Figure 1.13. The quantization of the amplitudes to fixed numbers in the range $-32768\ldots32767$ is based on a 16-bit representation of the sample amplitudes which allows 2^{16} quantized values in the range $-2^{15}\ldots2^{15}-1$. For a general w-bit representation the number range is $-2^{w-1}\ldots2^{w-1}-1$. This representation is called the integer number representation. If we divide all integer numbers by the maximum absolute value, for example 32768, we come to the normalized vertical scale in Figure 1.13, which is in the range $-1\ldots1-Q$, where Q is the quantization step size. It and can be calculated by $Q=2^{-(w-1)}$, which leads to $Q=3.0518\times10^{-5}$ for $w=16$. Figure 1.13 also displays the horizontal scale formats, namely the continuous-time axis, the discrete-time axis and the normalized discrete-time axis, which will be used normally. After this narrow description we can define a digital signal as a discrete-time and discrete-amplitude signal, which is formed by sampling an analog signal and by quantization of the amplitude onto a fixed number of amplitude values. The digital signal is represented by a sequence of numbers $x(n)$. Reconstruction of analog signals can be performed by DACs. Further details of ADCs and DACs and the related theory can be found in the literature. For our discussion of digital audio effects this short introduction to digital signals is sufficient.

Signal processing algorithms usually process signals by either *block processing* or *sample-by-sample processing*. Examples for digital audio effects are presented in [Arf98]. For block processing, samples are first collected in a memory buffer and then processed each time the buffer is completely filled with new data. Examples of such algorithms are *fast Fourier transforms (FFTs)* for spectra computations and *fast convolution*. In sample processing algorithms, each input sample is processed on a sample-by-sample basis.

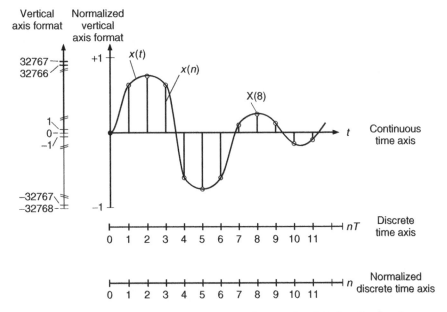

Figure 1.13   Vertical and horizontal scale formats for digital audio signals.

A basic algorithm for weighting of a sound $x(n)$ (see Figure 1.11) by a constant factor a demonstrates a sample-by-sample processing (see M-file 1.2). The input signal is represented by a vector of numbers `[x(1), x(2),..., x(length(x))]`.

M-file 1.2 (sbs_alg.m)

```
% Author: U. Zölzer
% Read input sound file into vector x(n) and sampling frequency FS
[x,FS]=wavread('input filename');
% Sample-by sample algorithm y(n)=a*x(n)
for n=1:length(x),
    y(n)=a * x(n);
end;
% Write y(n) into output sound file with number of
% bits Nbits and sampling frequency FS
wavwrite(y,FS,Nbits,'output filename');
```

1.3.2   Spectrum analysis of digital signals

The spectrum of a signal shows the distribution of energy over the frequency range. The upper part of Figure 1.14 shows the spectrum of a short time slot of an analog audio signal. The frequencies range up to 20 kHz. The sampling and quantization of the analog signal with sampling frequency of $f_S = 40$ kHz leads to a corresponding digital signal. The spectrum of the digital signal of the same time slot is shown in the lower part of Figure 1.14. The sampling operation leads to a replication of the baseband spectrum of the analog signal [Orf96]. The frequency contents from 0 Hz up to 20 kHz of the analog signal now also appear from 40 kHz up to 60 kHz and the folded version of it from 40 kHz down to 20 kHz. The replication of this first image of the baseband spectrum at 40 kHz will now also appear at integer multiples of the sampling frequency of $f_S = 40$ kHz. But notice that the spectrum of the digital signal from 0 up to 20 kHz shows exactly the same shape as the spectrum of the analog signal. The reconstruction of the analog signal out of the digital signal is achieved by simply lowpass filtering the digital signal, rejecting frequencies higher than $f_S/2 = 20$ kHz. If we consider the spectrum of the digital signal in the lower part of Fig. 1.14 and reject all frequencies higher than 20 kHz, we come back to the spectrum of the analog signal in the upper part of the figure.

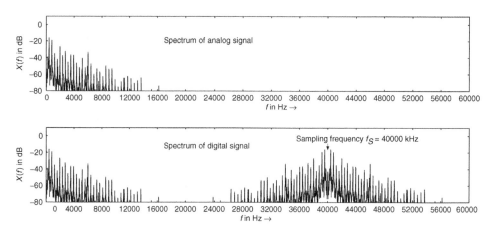

Figure 1.14 Spectra of analog and digital signals.

Discrete Fourier transform

The spectrum of a digital signal can be computed by the discrete Fourier transform (DFT) which is given by

$$X(k) = \text{DFT}[x(n)] = \sum_{n=0}^{N-1} x(n)e^{-j2\pi nk/N} \quad k = 0, 1, \ldots, N-1. \tag{1.1}$$

The fast version of the above formula is called the fast Fourier transform (FFT). The FFT takes N consecutive samples out of the signal $x(n)$ and performs a mathematical operation to yield N samples $X(k)$ of the spectrum of the signal. Figure 1.15 demonstrates the results of a 16-point FFT applied to 16 samples of a cosine signal. The result is normalized by N according to X=abs(fft(x,N))/N;.

The N samples $X(k) = X_R(k) + jX_I(k)$ are complex-valued with a real part $X_R(k)$ and an imaginary part $X_I(k)$ from which one can compute the absolute value

$$|X(k)| = \sqrt{X_R^2(k) + X_I^2(k)} \quad k = 0, 1, \ldots, N-1 \tag{1.2}$$

which is the magnitude spectrum, and the phase

$$\varphi(k) = \arctan \frac{X_I(k)}{X_R(k)} \quad k = 0, 1, \ldots, N-1 \tag{1.3}$$

which is the phase spectrum. Figure 1.15 also shows that the FFT algorithm leads to N equidistant frequency points which give N samples of the spectrum of the signal starting from 0 Hz in steps of $\frac{f_S}{N}$ up to $\frac{N-1}{N}f_S$. These frequency points are given by $k\frac{f_S}{N}$, where k is running from $0, 1, 2, \ldots,$ $N-1$. The magnitude spectrum $|X(f)|$ is often plotted over a logarithmic amplitude scale

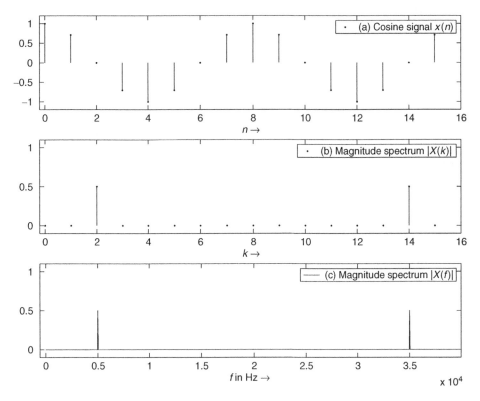

Figure 1.15 Spectrum analysis with FFT algorithm: (a) digital cosine with $N = 16$ samples, (b) magnitude spectrum $|X(k)|$ with $N = 16$ frequency samples and (c) magnitude spectrum $|X(f)|$ from 0 Hz up to the sampling frequency $f_S = 40\,000$ Hz.

according to $20 \log_{10}\left(\frac{X(f)}{0.5}\right)$ which gives 0 dB for a sinusoid of maximum amplitude ± 1. This normalization is equivalent to $20 \log_{10}\left(\frac{X(k)}{N/2}\right)$. Figure 1.16 shows this representation of the example from Fig. 1.15. Images of the baseband spectrum occur at the sampling frequency f_S and multiples of f_S. Therefore we see the original frequency at 5 kHz and in the first image spectrum the folded frequency $f_S - f_{cosine} = 40\,000$ Hz $- 5000$ Hz $= 35\,000$ Hz.

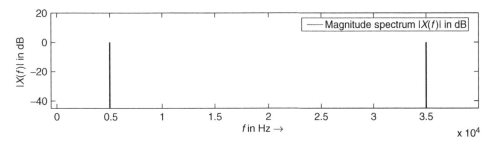

Figure 1.16 Magnitude spectrum $|X(f)|$ in dB from 0 Hz up to the sampling frequency $f_S = 40000$ Hz.

Inverse discrete Fourier transform (IDFT)

Whilst the DFT is used as the transform from the discrete-time domain to the discrete-frequency domain for spectrum analysis, the inverse discrete Fourier transform (IDFT) allows the transform from the discrete-frequency domain to the discrete-time domain. The IDFT algorithm is given by

$$x(n) = \text{IDFT}[X(k)] = \frac{1}{N} \sum_{k=0}^{N-1} X(k) e^{j2\pi nk/N} \quad n = 0, 1, \ldots, N-1. \tag{1.4}$$

The fast version of the IDFT is called the inverse Fast Fourier transform (IFFT). Taking N complex-valued numbers with the property $X(k) = X^*(N-k)$ in the frequency domain and then performing the IFFT gives N discrete-time samples $x(n)$, which are real-valued.

Frequency resolution: zero-padding and window functions

To increase the frequency resolution for spectrum analysis we simply take more samples for the FFT algorithm. Typical numbers for the FFT resolution are $N = 256, 512, 1024, 2048, 4096$ and 8192. If we are only interested in computing the spectrum of 64 samples and would like to increase the frequency resolution from $f_S/64$ to $f_S/1024$, we have to extend the sequence of 64 audio samples by adding zero samples up to the length 1024 and then perform an 1024-point FFT. This technique is called zero-padding and is illustrated in Figure 1.17 and by M-file 1.3. The upper left

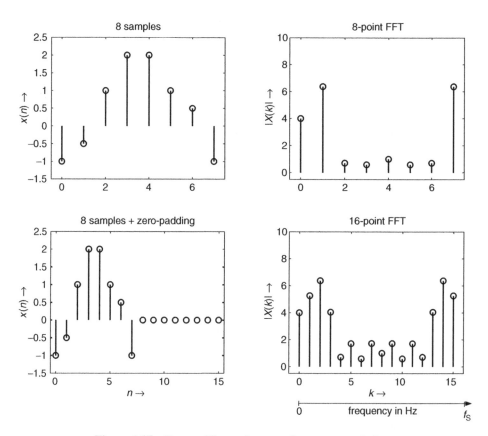

Figure 1.17   Zero-padding to increase frequency resolution.

part shows the original sequence of eight samples and the upper right part shows the corresponding eight-point FFT result. The lower left part illustrates the adding of eight zero samples to the original eight-sample sequence up to the length $N = 16$. The lower right part illustrates the magnitude spectrum $|X(k)|$ resulting from the 16-point FFT of the zero-padded sequence of length $N = 16$. Notice the increase in frequency resolution between the eight-point and 16-point FFT. Between each frequency bin of the upper spectrum a new frequency bin in the lower spectrum is calculated. Bins $k = 0, 2, 4, 6, 8, 10, 12, 14$ of the 16-point FFT correspond to bins $k = 0, 1, 2, 3, 4, 5, 6, 7$ of the eight-point FFT. These N frequency bins cover the frequency range from 0 Hz up to $\frac{N-1}{N} fs$.

M-file 1.3 (figure1_17.m)

```
%Author: U. Zölzer
x1=[-1 -0.5 1 2 2 1 0.5 -1];
x2(16)=0;
x2(1:8)=x1;

subplot(221);
stem(0:1:7,x1);axis([-0.5 7.5 -1.5 2.5]);
ylabel('x(n) \rightarrow');title('8 samples');
subplot(222);
stem(0:1:7,abs(fft(x1)));axis([-0.5 7.5 -0.5 10]);
ylabel('|X(k)| \rightarrow');title('8-point FFT');

subplot(223);
stem(0:1:15,x2);axis([-0.5 15.5 -1.5 2.5]);
xlabel('n \rightarrow');ylabel('x(n) \rightarrow');
title('8 samples+zero-padding');

subplot(224);
stem(0:1:15,abs(fft(x2)));axis([-1 16 -0.5 10]);
xlabel('k \rightarrow');ylabel('|X(k)| \rightarrow');
title('16-point FFT');
```

The leakage effect occurs due to cutting out N samples from the signal. This effect is shown in the upper part of Figure 1.18 and demonstrated by the corresponding M-file 1.4. The cosine spectrum is smeared around the frequency. We can reduce the leakage effect by selecting a window function like Blackman window and Hamming window

$$w_B(n) = 0.42 - 0.5\cos(2\pi n/N) + 0.08\cos(4\pi n/N), \tag{1.5}$$

$$w_H(n) = 0.54 - 0.46\cos(2\pi n/N) \tag{1.6}$$

$$n = 0, 1, \ldots N - 1.$$

and weighting the N audio samples by the window function. This weighting is performed according to $x_w = w(n) \cdot x(n) / \left(\sum_k w(k)\right)$ with $0 \leq n \leq N - 1$ and then an FFT of the weighted signal is performed. The cosine weighted by a window and the corresponding spectrum is shown in the middle part of Figure 1.18. The lower part of Figure 1.18 shows a segment of an audio signal weighted by the Blackman window and the corresponding spectrum via a FFT. Figure 1.19 shows further simple examples for the reduction of the leakage effect and can be generated by the M-file 1.5.

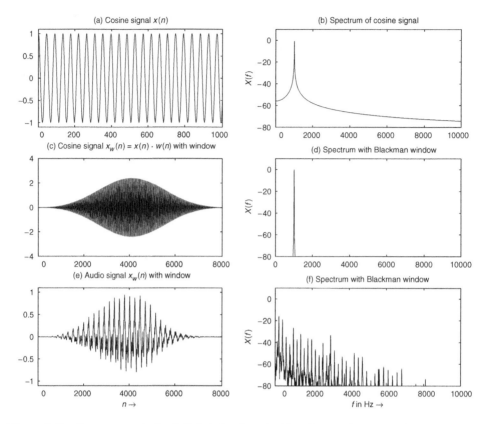

Figure 1.18 Spectrum analysis of digital signals: take N audio samples and perform an N point discrete Fourier transform to yield N samples of the spectrum of the signal starting from 0 Hz over $k\frac{f_S}{N}$ where k is running from $0, 1, 2, \ldots, N-1$. For (a)–(d), $x(n) = \cos(2 \cdot \pi \cdot \frac{1\,kHz}{44.1\,kHz} \cdot n)$.

M-file 1.4 (figure1_18.m)

```
%Author: U. Zölzer
x=cos(2*pi*1000*(0:1:N-1)/44100)';
figure(2)
W=blackman(N);
W=N*W/sum(W); % scaling of window
f=((0:N/2-1)/N)*FS;

xw=x.*W;
subplot(3,2,1);plot(0:N-1,x);
axis([0 1000 -1.1 1.1]);
title('a) Cosine signal x(n)')

subplot(3,2,3);plot(0:N-1,xw);axis([0 8000 -4 4]);
title('c) Cosine signal x_w(n)=x(n) \cdot w(n) with window')

X=20*log10(abs(fft(x,N))/(N/2));
subplot(3,2,2);plot(f,X(1:N/2));
axis([0 10000 -80 10]);
```

```
ylabel('X(f)');
title('b) Spectrum of cosine signal')

Xw=20*log10(abs(fft(xw,N))/(N/2));
subplot(3,2,4);plot(f,Xw(1:N/2));
axis([0 10000 -80 10]);
ylabel('X(f)');
title('d) Spectrum with Blackman window')

s=u1(1:N).*W;
subplot(3,2,5);plot(0:N-1,s);axis([0 8000 -1.1 1.1]);
xlabel('n \rightarrow');
title('e) Audio signal x_w(n) with window')

Sw=20*log10(abs(fft(s,N))/(N/2));
subplot(3,2,6);plot(f,Sw(1:N/2));
axis([0 10000 -80 10]);
ylabel('X(f)');
title('f) Spectrum with Blackman window')
xlabel('f in Hz \rightarrow');
```

M-file 1.5 (figure1_19.m)

```
%Author: U. Zölzer
x=[-1 -0.5 1 2 2 1 0.5 -1];
w=blackman(8);
w=w*8/sum(w);
x1=x.*w';
x2(16)=0;
x2(1:8)=x1;

subplot(421);
stem(0:1:7,x);axis([-0.5 7.5 -1.5 2.5]);
ylabel('x(n) \rightarrow');
title('a) 8 samples');
subplot(423);
stem(0:1:7,w);axis([-0.5 7.5 -1.5 3]);
ylabel('w(n) \rightarrow');
title('b) 8 samples Blackman window');

subplot(425);
stem(0:1:7,x1);axis([-0.5 7.5 -1.5 6]);
ylabel('x_w(n) \rightarrow');
title('c) x(n)\cdot w(n)');

subplot(427);
stem(0:1:15,x2);axis([-0.5 15.5 -1.5 6]);
xlabel('n \rightarrow');ylabel('x_w(n) \rightarrow');
title('d) x(n)\cdot w(n) + zero-padding');

subplot(222);
stem(0:1:7,abs(fft(x1)));axis([-0.5 7.5 -0.5 15]);
ylabel('|X(k)| \rightarrow');
title('8-point FFT of c)');
```

```
subplot(224);
stem(0:1:15,abs(fft(x2)));axis([-1 16 -0.5 15]);
xlabel('k \rightarrow');ylabel('|X(k)| \rightarrow');
title('16-point FFT of d)');
```

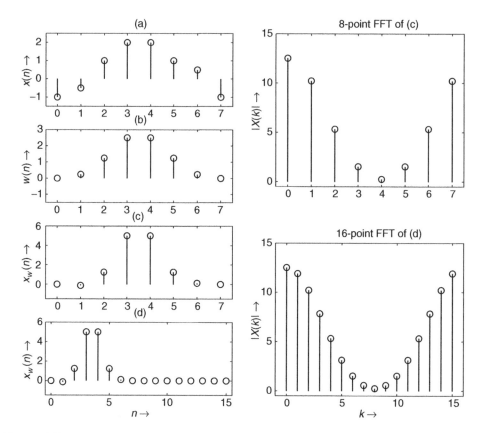

Figure 1.19 Reduction of the leakage effect by window functions: (a) the original signal, (b) the Blackman window function of length $N = 8$, (c) product $x(n) \cdot w_B(n)$ with $0 \le n \le N - 1$, (d) zero-padding applied to $x(n) \cdot w_B(n)$ up to length $N = 16$ and the corresponding spectra are shown on the right side.

Spectrogram: time-frequency representation

A special time-frequency representation is the spectrogram which gives an estimate of the short-time, time-localized frequency content of the signal. To obtain the spectrogram the signal is split into segments of length N, which are multiplied by a window and an FFT is performed (see Figure 1.20). To increase the time-localization of the short-time spectra an overlap of the weighted segments can be used. A special visual representation of the short-time spectra is the spectrogram in Figure 1.21. Time increases linearly across the horizontal axis and frequency increases across the vertical axis. So each vertical line represents the absolute value $|X(f)|$ over frequency by a

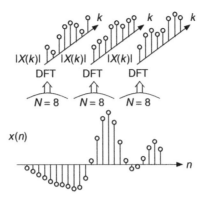

Figure 1.20   Short-time spectrum analysis by FFT.

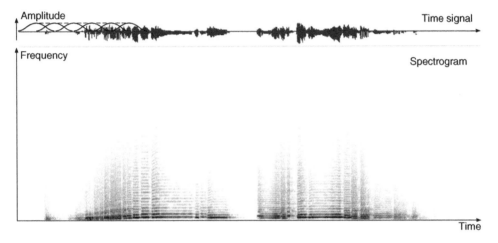

Figure 1.21   Spectrogram via FFT of weighted segments.

grey-scale value (see Figure 1.21). Only frequencies up to half the sampling frequency are shown. The calculation of the spectrogram from a signal can be performed by the **MATLAB** function `B = specgram(x,nFFT,Fs,window,nOverlap)`.

Another time-frequency representation of the short-time Fourier transforms of a signal $x(n)$ is the waterfall representation in Figure 1.22, which can be produced by M-file 1.6 that calls the waterfall computation algorithm given by M-file 1.7.

M-file 1.6 (figure1_22.m)

```
%Author: U. Zölzer
[signal,FS,NBITS]=wavread('ton2');
subplot(211);plot(signal);
subplot(212);
waterfspec(signal,256,256,512,FS,20,-100);
```

M-file 1.7 (waterfspec.m)

```
function yy=waterfspec(signal,start,steps,N,fS,clippingpoint,baseplane)
% Authors: J. Schattschneider, U. Zölzer
% waterfspec( signal, start, steps, N, fS, clippingpoint, baseplane)
%
% shows short-time spectra of signal, starting
% at k=start, with increments of STEP with N-point FFT
% dynamic range from -baseplane in dB up to 20*log(clippingpoint)
% in dB versus time axis
echo off;
if nargin<7, baseplane=-100; end
if nargin<6, clippingpoint=0; end
if nargin<5, fS=48000; end
if nargin<4, N=1024; end          % default FFT
if nargin<3, steps=round(length(signal)/25); end
if nargin<2, start=0; end

windoo=blackman(N);                % window - default
windoo=windoo*N/sum(windoo);       % scaling
% Calculation of number of spectra nos
  n=length(signal);
  rest=n-start-N;
  nos=round(rest/steps);
  if nos>rest/steps, nos=nos-1; end
% vectors for 3D representation
  x=linspace(0, fS/1000 ,N+1);
  z=x-x;
  cup=z+clippingpoint;
  cdown=z+baseplane;

  signal=signal+0.0000001;
% Computation of spectra and visual representation
  for i=1:1:nos,
    spek1=20.*log10(abs(fft(windoo.*signal(1+start+....
    ....i*steps:start+N+i*steps)))./(N)/0.5);
    spek=[-200 ; spek1(1:N)];
    spek=(spek>cup').*cup'+(spek<=cup').*spek;
    spek=(spek<cdown').*cdown'+(spek>=cdown').*spek;
    spek(1)=baseplane-10;
    spek(N/2)=baseplane-10;
    y=x-x+(i-1);
    if i==1,
      p=plot3(x(1:N/2),y(1:N/2),spek(1:N/2),'k');
      set(p,'Linewidth',0.1);
    end
      pp=patch(x(1:N/2),y(1:N/2),spek(1:N/2),'w','Visible','on');
      set(pp,'Linewidth',0.1);
  end;
set(gca,'DrawMode','fast');
axis([-0.3 fS/2000+0.3 0 nos baseplane-10 0]);
set(gca,'Ydir','reverse');
view(12,40);
```

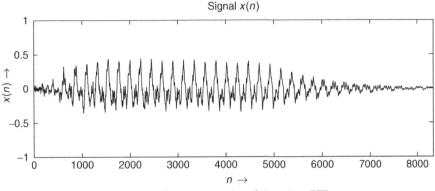

Signal $x(n)$

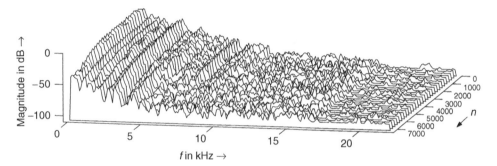

Waterfall representation of short-time FFTs

Figure 1.22   Waterfall representation via FFT of weighted segments.

1.3.3   Digital systems

A digital system is represented by an algorithm which uses the input signal $x(n)$ as a sequence (stream) of numbers and performs mathematical operations upon the input signal such as additions, multiplications and delay operations. The result of the algorithm is a sequence of numbers or the output signal $y(n)$. Systems which do not change their behavior over time and fulfill the superposition property [Orf96] are called linear time-invariant (LTI) systems. The input/output relations for a LTI digital system describe time-domain relations which are based on the following terms and definitions:

- Unit impulse, impulse response and discrete convolution;
- Algorithms and signal flow graphs.

For each of these definitions an equivalent description in the frequency domain exists, which will be introduced later.

Unit impulse, Impulse response and Discrete convolution

- Test signal: a very useful test signal for digital systems is the unit impulse

$$\delta(n) = \begin{cases} 1 & \text{for} \quad n = 0 \\ 0 & \text{for} \quad n \neq 0, \end{cases} \tag{1.7}$$

which is equal to one for $n = 0$ and zero elsewhere (see Figure 1.23).

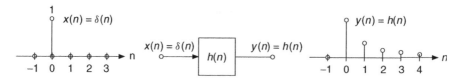

Figure 1.23   Impulse response $h(n)$ as a time-domain description of a digital system.

- Impulse response: if we apply a unit-impulse function to a digital LTI system, the digital system will lead to an output signal $y(n) = h(n)$, which is called the impulse response $h(n)$ of the digital system. The digital LTI system is completely described by the impulse response, which is pointed out by the label $h(n)$ inside the box, as shown in Figure 1.23.

- Discrete convolution: if we know the impulse response $h(n)$ of a digital system, we can calculate the output signal $y(n)$ from a freely chosen input signal $x(n)$ by the discrete convolution formula given by

$$y(n) = \sum_{k=-\infty}^{\infty} x(k) \cdot h(n-k) = x(n) * h(n), \tag{1.8}$$

which is often abbreviated by the second term $y(n) = x(n) * h(n)$. This discrete sum formula (1.8) represents an input–output relation for a digital system in the time domain. The computation of the convolution sum formula (1.8) can be achieved by the **MATLAB** function `y=conv(x,h)`.

Algorithms and signal flow graphs

The above given discrete convolution formula shows the mathematical operations which have to be performed to obtain the output signal $y(n)$ for a given input signal $x(n)$. In the following we will introduce a visual representation called a signal flow graph which represents the mathematical input/output relations in a graphical block diagram. We discuss some example algorithms to show that we only need three graphical representations for the multiplication of signals by coefficients, delay and summation of signals.

- A delay of the input signal by two sampling intervals is given by the algorithm

$$y(n) = x(n-2) \tag{1.9}$$

and is represented by the block diagram in Figure 1.24.

- A weighting of the input signal by a coefficient a is given by the algorithm

$$y(n) = a \cdot x(n) \tag{1.10}$$

and represented by a block diagram in Figure 1.25.

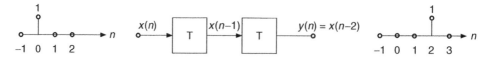

Figure 1.24   Delay of the input signal.

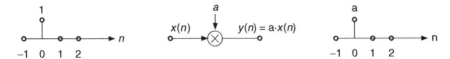

Figure 1.25 Weighting of the input signal.

- The addition of two input signals is given by the algorithm

$$y(n) = a_1 \cdot x_1(n) + a_2 \cdot x_2(n) \qquad (1.11)$$

and represented by a block diagram in Figure 1.26.

- The combination of the above algorithms leads to the weighted sum over several input samples, which is given by the algorithm

$$y(n) = \frac{1}{3}x(n) + \frac{1}{3}x(n-1) + \frac{1}{3}x(n-2) \qquad (1.12)$$

and represented by a block diagram in Fig. 1.27.

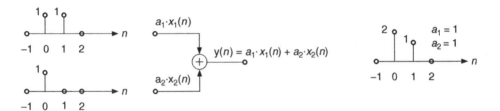

Figure 1.26 Addition of two signals $x_1(n)$ and $x_2(n)$.

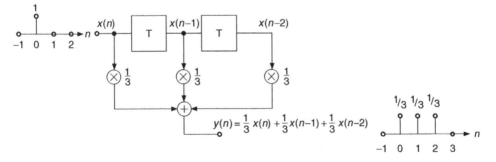

Figure 1.27 Simple digital system.

Transfer function and frequency response

So far our description of digital systems has been based on the time-domain relationship between the input and output signals. We noticed that the input and output signals and the impulse response of the digital system are given in the discrete time domain. In a similar way to the frequency-domain description of digital signals by their spectra given in the previous subsection we can have a frequency-domain description of the digital system which is represented by the impulse response $h(n)$. The frequency-domain behavior of a digital system reflects its ability to pass, reject and enhance certain frequencies included in the input signal spectrum. The common terms for the frequency-domain behavior are the transfer function $H(z)$ and the frequency response $H(f)$ of the digital system. Both can be obtained by two mathematical transforms applied to the impulse response $h(n)$.

The first transform is the *Z-Transform*

$$X(z) = \sum_{n=-\infty}^{\infty} x(n) \cdot z^{-n} \tag{1.13}$$

applied to the signal $x(n)$ and the second transform is the *discrete-time Fourier transform*

$$X(e^{j\omega}) = \sum_{n=-\infty}^{\infty} x(n) \cdot e^{-j\omega n}, \tag{1.14}$$

$$\text{with} \quad \omega = 2\pi f / f_S \tag{1.15}$$

applied to the signal $x(n)$. Both are related by the substitution $z \leftrightarrow e^{j\omega}$. If we apply the Z-transform to the impulse response $h(n)$ of a digital system according to

$$H(z) = \sum_{n=-\infty}^{\infty} h(n) \cdot z^{-n} \tag{1.16}$$

we denote $H(z)$ as the *transfer function*. The transfer function is of special interest as it relates the Z-transforms of input signal and output signal of the described system by

$$Y(z) = H(z) \cdot X(z). \tag{1.17}$$

If we apply the discrete-time Fourier transform to the impulse response $h(n)$ we get

$$H(e^{j\omega}) = \sum_{n=-\infty}^{\infty} h(n) \cdot e^{-j\omega n}. \tag{1.18}$$

Substituting (1.15) we define the *frequency response* of the digital system by

$$H(f) = \sum_{n=-\infty}^{\infty} h(n) \cdot e^{-j2\pi f / f_S n}. \tag{1.19}$$

Causal and stable systems

A realizable digital system has to fulfill the following two conditions:

- Causality: a discrete-time system is *causal*, if the output signal $y(n) = 0$ for $n < 0$ for a given input signal $x(n) = 0$ for $n < 0$. This means that the system cannot react to an input before the input is applied to the system.

- Stability: a digital system is stable if

$$\sum_{n=-\infty}^{\infty} |h(n)| < M_2 < \infty \tag{1.20}$$

holds. The sum over the absolute values of $h(n)$ has to be less than a fixed number $M_2 < \infty$.

The stability implies that the transfer function (Z-transform of impulse response) and the frequency response (discrete-time Fourier transform of impulse response) of a digital system are related by the substitution $z \leftrightarrow e^{j\omega}$. Realizable digital systems have to be *causal* and *stable* systems. Some Z-transforms and their discrete-time Fourier transforms of a signal $x(n)$ are given in Table 1.4.

Table 1.4   Z-transforms and discrete-time Fourier transforms of $x(n)$.

Signal	Z-transform	Discrete-time Fourier transform
$x(n)$	$X(z)$	$X(e^{j\omega})$
$x(n - M)$	$z^{-M} \cdot X(z)$	$e^{-j\omega M} \cdot X(e^{j\omega})$
$\delta(n)$	1	1
$\delta(n - M)$	z^{-M}	$e^{-j\omega M}$
$x(n) \cdot e^{j\omega_0 n}$	$X(e^{-j\omega_0} \cdot z)$	$X(e^{j(\omega-\omega_0)})$

IIR and FIR systems

IIR systems: A system with an infinite impulse response $h(n)$ is called an IIR system. From the block diagram in Figure 1.28 we can read the difference equation

$$y(n) = x(n) - a_1 y(n - 1) - a_2 y(n - 2). \tag{1.21}$$

The output signal $y(n)$ is fed back through delay elements and a weighted sum of these delayed outputs is summed up to the input signal $x(n)$. Such a feedback system is also called a recursive system. The Z-transform of (1.21) yields

$$Y(z) = X(z) - a_1 z^{-1} Y(z) - a_2 z^{-2} Y(z) \tag{1.22}$$

$$X(z) = Y(z)(1 + a_1 z^{-1} + a_2 z^{-2}) \tag{1.23}$$

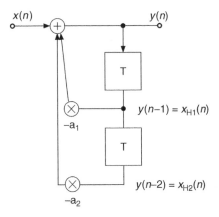

Figure 1.28   Simple IIR system with input signal $x(n)$ and output signal $y(n)$.

and solving for $Y(z)/X(z)$ gives transfer function

$$H(z) = \frac{Y(z)}{X(z)} = \frac{1}{1 + a_1 z^{-1} + a_2 z^{-2}}.$$ (1.24)

Figure 1.29 shows a special signal flow graph representation, where adders, multipliers and delay operators are replaced by weighted graphs.

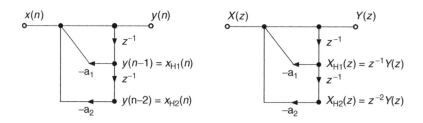

Figure 1.29   Signal flow graph of digital system in Figure 1.28 with time-domain description in the left block diagram and corresponding frequency-domain description with Z-transform.

If the input delay line is extended up to $N - 1$ delay elements and the output delay line up to M delay elements according to Figure 1.30, we can write for the difference equation

$$y(n) = -\sum_{k=1}^{M} a_k\, y(n - k) + \sum_{k=0}^{N-1} b_k\, x(n - k),$$ (1.25)

the Z-transform of the difference equation

$$Y(z) = -\sum_{k=1}^{M} a_k\, z^{-k} Y(z) + \sum_{k=0}^{N-1} b_k\, z^{-k} X(z),$$ (1.26)

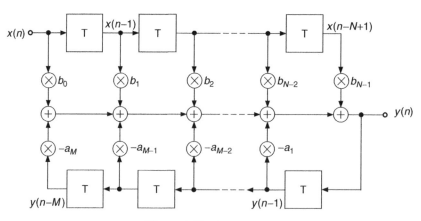

Figure 1.30   IIR system.

and the resulting transfer function

$$H(z) = \frac{\sum\limits_{k=0}^{N-1} b_k z^{-k}}{1 + \sum\limits_{k=1}^{M} a_k z^{-k}}. \tag{1.27}$$

The block processing approach for the IIR filter algorithm can be performed with the **MATLAB**/Octave function y = filter(b, a, x), where b and a are vectors with the filter coefficients as above and x contains the input signal.

A sample-by-sample processing approach for a second-order IIR filter algorithm is demonstrated by M-file 1.8.

M-file 1.8 (DirectForm01.m)

```
% Author: U. Zölzer
% Impulse response of 2nd order IIR filter
% Sample-by-sample algorithm
clear

% Coefficients for a high-pass
a=[1, -1.28, 0.47];
b=[0.69, -1.38, 0.69];

% Initialization of state variables
xh1=0;xh2=0;
yh1=0;yh2=0;

% Input signal: unit impulse
N=20;   % length of input signal
x(N)=0;x(1)=1;

% Sample-by-sample algorithm
for n=1:N
y(n)=b(1)*x(n)+b(2)*xh1+b(3)*xh2 - a(2)*yh1 - a(3)*yh2;
xh2=xh1;xh1=x(n);
yh2=yh1;yh1=y(n);
end;

% Plot results
subplot(2,1,1)
stem(0:1:length(x)-1,x,'.');axis([-0.6 length(x)-1 -1.2 1.2]);
xlabel('n \rightarrow');ylabel('x(n) \rightarrow');
subplot(2,1,2)
stem(0:1:length(x)-1,y,'.');axis([-0.6 length(x)-1 -1.2 1.2]);
xlabel('n \rightarrow');ylabel('y(n) \rightarrow');
```

Computation of the frequency response based on the coefficients of the transfer function $H(z) = \frac{B(z)}{A(z)}$ can be made with the **MATLAB**/Octave function freqz(b, a), while the poles and zeros can be determined with zplane(b, a).

FIR systems: A system with a finite impulse response $h(n)$ is called an FIR system. From the block diagram in Figure 1.31 we can read the difference equation

$$y(n) = b_0 x(n) + b_1 x(n-1) + b_2 x(n-2). \tag{1.28}$$

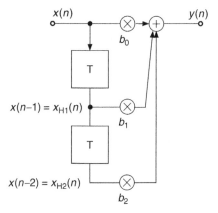

Figure 1.31   Simple FIR system with input signal $x(n)$ and output signal $y(n)$.

The input signal $x(n)$ is fed forward through delay elements and a weighted sum of these delayed inputs is summed up to the input signal $y(n)$. Such a feed-forward system is also called a non-recursive system. The Z-transform of (1.28) yields

$$Y(z) = b_0 X(z) + b_1 z^{-1} X(z) + b_2 z^{-2} X(z) \tag{1.29}$$

$$= X(z)(b_0 + b_1 z^{-1} + b_2 z^{-2}) \tag{1.30}$$

and solving for $Y(z)/X(z)$ gives transfer function

$$H(z) = \frac{Y(z)}{X(z)} = b_0 + b_1 z^{-1} + b_2 z^{-2}. \tag{1.31}$$

A general FIR system in Figure 1.32 consists of a feed-forward delay line with $N-1$ delay elements and has the difference equation

$$y(n) = \sum_{k=0}^{N-1} b_k \, x(n-k). \tag{1.32}$$

The finite impulse response is given by

$$h(n) = \sum_{k=0}^{N-1} b_k \, \delta(n-k), \tag{1.33}$$

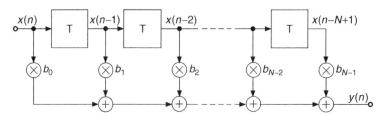

Figure 1.32   FIR system.

which shows that each impulse of $h(n)$ is represented by a weighted and shifted unit impulse. The Z-transform of the impulse response leads to the transfer function

$$H(z) = \sum_{k=0}^{N-1} b_k z^{-k}. \tag{1.34}$$

The time-domain algorithms for FIR systems are the same as those for IIR systems with the exception that the recursive part is missing. The previously introduced M-files for IIR systems can be used with the appropriate coefficients for FIR block processing or sample-by-sample processing.

The computation of the frequency response $H(f) = |H(f)| \cdot e^{j\angle H(f)}$ ($|H(f)|$ magnitude response, $\varphi = \angle H(f)$ phase response) from the Z-transform of an FIR impulse response according to (1.34) is shown in Figure 1.33 and is calculated by the following M-file 1.9.

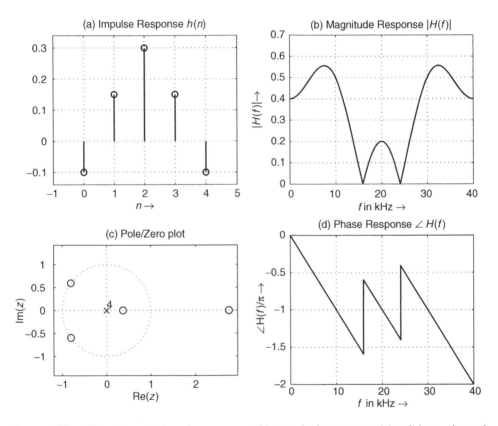

Figure 1.33 FIR system: (a) impulse response, (b) magnitude response, (c) pole/zero plot and (d) phase response (sampling frequency $f_S = 40$ kHz).

M-file 1.9 (figure1_33.m)

```
function magphasresponse(h)
% Author: U. Zölzer
FS=40000;
fosi=10;
```

```
if nargin==0
  h=[-.1 .15 .3 .15 -.1];
end
hmax=max(h);
hmin=min(h);
dh=hmax-hmin;
hmax=hmax+.1*dh;
hmin=hmin-.1*dh;

N=length(h);
% denominator polynomial:
a=zeros(1,N);
a(1)=1;

subplot(221)
stem(0:N-1,h)
axis([-1 N, hmin hmax])
title('a) Impulse Response h(n)','Fontsize',fosi);
xlabel('n \rightarrow','Fontsize',fosi)
grid on;

subplot(223)
zplane(h,a)
title('c) Pole/Zero plot','Fontsize',fosi);
xlabel('Re(z)','Fontsize',fosi)
ylabel('Im(z)','Fontsize',fosi)

subplot(222)
[H,F]=freqz(h,a,1024,'whole',FS);
plot(F/1000,abs(H))
xlabel('f in kHz  \rightarrow','Fontsize',fosi);
ylabel('|H(f)| \rightarrow','Fontsize',fosi);
title('b) Magnitude response |H(f)|','Fontsize',fosi);
grid on;

subplot(224)
plot(F/1000,unwrap(angle(H))/pi)
xlabel('f  in kHz \rightarrow','Fontsize',fosi)
ylabel('\angle H(f)/\pi \rightarrow','Fontsize',fosi)
title('d) Phase Response \angle H(f)','Fontsize',fosi);
grid on;
```

1.4 Conclusion

In this first chapter we introduced definitions and classifications of audio effects, to provide an overview of the territory to be explored. Then, some basic concepts of digital signals, their spectra and digital systems have been introduced. The description is intended for persons with little or no knowledge of digital signal processing. The inclusion of **MATLAB** M-files for all stages of processing may serve as a basis for further programming in the following chapters. As well as showing simple tools for graphical representations of digital audio signals we have calculated the spectrum of a signal $x(n)$ by the use of the FFT M-file

- ```
  Xmagnitude=abs(fft(x))
  Xphase=angle(fft(x)).
  ```
  ```

Time-domain processing for DAFX can be performed by block-based input–output computations which are based on the convolution formula (if the impulse response of a system is known) or difference equations (if the coefficients a and b are known). The computations can be done by the following M-files:

- ```
  y=conv(h,x)      %length of output signal l_y = l_h +l_x -1
  y=filter(b,a,x) %l_y = l_x
  ```

These M-files deliver an output vector containing the output signal $y(n)$ in a vector of corresponding length. Of course, these block processing algorithms perform their inner computations on a sample-by-sample basis. Therefore, we have also shown an example for the sample-by-sample programming technique, which can be modified according to different applications:

- ```
  y=dafxalgorithm(parameters,x)
  % Sample-by sample algorithm y(n)=function(parameters,x(n))
        for n=1:length(x),
        y(n)=....do something algorithm with x(n) and parameters;
        end;
  ```

That is all we need for DAFX exploration and programming, good luck!

References

[ABL+03]   X. Amatriain, J. Bonada, A. Loscos, J. L. Arcos and V. Verfaille. Content-based transformations. *J. New Music Research*, 32(1): 95–114, 2003.

[AD98]   D. Arfib and N. Delprat. Selective transformations of sound using time-frequency representations: An application to the vibrato modification. In *104th Conv. Audio Eng. Soc., Amsterdam*, 1998.

[AKZ02a]   D. Arfib, F. Keiler and U. Zölzer. *DAFX–Digital Audio Effects*, First edition, Time-Frequency Processing, pp. 237–97. U. Zölzer ed., J. Wiley & Sons, Ltd, 2002.

[AKZ02b]   D. Arfib, F. Keiler and U. Zölzer. *DAFX - Digital Audio Effects*, First edition, Source-filter processing, pp. 299–372. U. Zölzer ed., J. Wiley & Sons, Ltd, 2002.

[All77]   J. B. Allen. Short term spectral analysis, synthesis and modification by discrete fourier transform. *IEEE Trans. on Acoustics, Speech, and Signal Processing*, 25(3): 235–8, 1977.

[ANS60]   ANSI. *USA Standard Acoustic Terminology*. American National Standards Institute, 1960.

[AOPW99]   S. Abrams, D. V. Oppenheim, D. Pazel and J. Wright. Higher-level composition control in lusic sketcher: Modifiers and smart harmony. In *Proc. Int. Computer Music Conf. (ICMC'99), Beijing*, pp. 13–6, 1999.

[AR77]   J. B. Allen and L. R. Rabiner. A unified approach to short-time fourier analysis and synthesis. *Proc. IEEE*, 65(11): 1558–64, 1977.

[Arf98]   D. Arfib. Different ways to write digital audio effects programs. In *Proc. DAFX-98 Digital Audio Effects Workshop*, pp. 188–191, Barcelona, November 1998.

[Arf99]   D. Arfib. Visual representations for digital audio effects and their control. In *Proc. DAFX-99 Digital Audio Effects Workshop*, pp. 63–68, Trondheim, December 1999.

[Bar70]   B. Bartlett. A scientific explanation of phasing (flanging). *J. Audio Eng. Soc.*, 18(6): 674–5, 1970.

[BB96]   T. Buzan and B. Buzan. *Mind Map Book*. Plume, 1996.

[BJ95]   R. Bristow-Johnson. A detailed analysis of time-domain formant-corrected pitch-shifting algorithm. *J. Audio Eng. Soc.*, 43(5): 340–52, 1995.

[Bla83]   J. Blauert. *Spatial Hearing: the Psychophysics of Human Sound Localization*. MIT Press, 1983.

[Ble01]   B. Blesser. An interdisciplinary synthesis of reverberation viewpoints. *J. Audio Eng. Soc.*, 49(10): 867–903, 2001.

[BP89]   J. C. Brown and M S. Puckette. Calculation of a narrowed autocorrelation function. *J. Ac. Soc. of America*, 85: 1595–601, 1989.

[Cab99]   D. Cabrera. PsySound: a computer program for psychoacoustical analysis. In *Proc. Australian Ac. Soc. Conf., Melbourne*, pp. 47–53, November 1999.

[Cho71]   J. Chowning. The simulation of moving sound sources. *J. Audio Eng. Soc.*, 19(1): 1–6, 1971.

[CKC+04]   P. Cano, M. Koppenberger, O. Celma, P. Herrera and V. Tarasov. Sound effects taxonomy management in production environments. In *Int. Conf. Audio Eng. Soc.*, London UK, 2004.

[CPR95]   A. Camurri, G. De Poli and D. Rocchesso. A taxonomy for sound and music computing. *Computer Music J.*, 19(2): 4–5, 1995.

[Dat97]   J. Dattoro. Effect design, part 2: Delay-line modulation and chorus. *J. Audio Eng. Soc.*, pp. 764–88, 1997.

[dC04]   A. de Cheveigné. *Pitch*, Pitch perception models. C. Plack and A. Oxenham eds, Springer-Verlag, Berlin, 2004.

[DH92]   P. Desain and H. Honing. *Music, Mind and Machine: Studies in Computer Music, Music Cognition, and Artificial Intelligence*. Thesis Publishers, 1992.

[Dol86]   M. Dolson. The phase vocoder: a tutorial. *Computer Music J.*, 10(4): 14–27, 1986.

[DT96]   S. Dubnov and N. Tishby. Testing for gaussianity and non linearity in the sustained portion of musical sounds. In *Proc. Journées Informatique Musicale (JIM'96)*, 1996.

[Dut91]   P. Dutilleux. *Vers la machine à sculpter le son, modification en temps-réel des caractéristiques fréquentielles et temporelles des sons*. PhD thesis, University of Aix-Marseille II, 1991.

[Fav01]   E. Favreau. Phase vocoder applications in GRM tools environment. In *Proc. of the COST-G6 Workshop on Digital Audio Effects (DAFx-01), Limerick*, pp. 134–7, 2001.

[Gav93]   W. W. Gaver. What in the world do we hear? An ecological approach to auditory event perception. *Ecological Psychology*, 5(1): 1–29, 1993.

[Ger85]   M. A. Gerzon. Ambisonics in multichannel broadcasting and video. *J. Audio Eng. Soc.*, 33(11), 1985.

[GKP+05]   C. Guastavino, B. F. Katz, J.-D. Polack, D. J. Levitin and D. Dubois. Ecological validity of soundscape reproduction. *Acta Acust. United Ac.*, 91(2): 333–341, 2005.

[Har78]   W. M. Hartmann. Flanging and phasers. *J. Audio Eng. Soc.*, 26: 439–43, 1978.

[Hay96]   S. Haykin. *Adaptive Filter Theory*, Third edition Prentice Hall, 1996.

[HMM04]   D. Hargreaves, D. Miell and R. MacDonald. What do we mean by musical communication, and why it is important?, introduction of "*Musical communication (part 1)*" session, ICMPC CD-ROM. In *Proc. Int. Conf. Music Perc. and Cog.*, 391–394, 2004.

[Hon95]   H. Honing. The vibrato problem, comparing two solutions. *Computer Music J.*, 19(3): 32–49, 1995.

[Lar98]   J. Laroche. Time and pitch scale modification of audio signals. In M. Kahrs and K. Brandenburg, eds, *Applications of Digital Signal Processing to Audio & Acoustics*, pp. 279–309. Kluwer Academic Publishers, 1998.

[Lar01]   J. Laroche. Estimating tempo, swing and beat locations in audio recordings. In *Proc. IEEE Workshop on Applications of Digital Signal Processing to Audio and Acoustics*, pp. 135–8, 2001.

[LD97]   J. Laroche and M. Dolson. About this phasiness business. In *Proc. Int. Computer Music Conf. (ICMC'97), Thessaloniki*, pp. 55–8, 1997.

[LVKL96]   T. I. Laakso, V. Välimäki, M. Karjalainen and U. K. Laine. Splitting the unit delay. In *IEEE Signal Proc. Mag.*, pp. 30–60, 1996.

[MB90]   R. C. Maher and J. Beauchamp. An investigation of vocal vibrato for synthesis. *Appl. Acoust.*, 30: 219–45, 1990.

[MB96]   P. Masri and A. Bateman. Improved modelling of attack transients in music analysis-resynthesis. In *Proc. Int. Computer Music Conf. (ICMC'96), Hong Kong*, pp. 100–3, 1996.

[MC90]   E. Moulines and F. Charpentier. Pitch synchronous waveform processing techniques for text-to-speech synthesis using diphones. *Speech Com.*, 9(5/6): 453–67, 1990.

[ME93]   C. Marvin and G. Ewers. *A Simple Approach to Digital Signal Processing*. Texas Instruments, 1993.

[Mit01]   S.K Mitra. *Digital Signal Processing–A Computer-Based Approach*, Second edition. McGraw-Hill, 2001.

[MK73]   M. Mathews and J. Kohut. Electronic simulation of violin resonances. *J. Ac. Soc. of America*, 53(6): 1620–6, 1973.

[ML95]   E. Moulines and J. Laroche. Non-parametric technique for pitch-scale and time-scale modification. *Speech Com.*, 16: 175–205, 1995.

[MM01]   A. Marui and W. L. Martens. Perceptual and semantic scaling for user-centered control over distortion-based guitar effects. In *110th Conv. Audio Eng. Soc., Paris, France*, 2001. Preprint 5387.

[Mol75]   J. Molino. Fait musical et sémiologie de la musique. *Musique en Jeu*, 17: 37–62, 1975.

[Moo79]   J. A. Moorer. About this reverberation business. *Computer Music J.*, 3(2): 13–8, 1979.

[Moo90]   F. R. Moore. *Elements of Computer Music*. University of California, San Diego, Prentice Hall Inc., 1990.

[MQ86]   R. J. McAulay and T. F. Quatieri. Speech analysis/synthesis based on a sinusoidal representation. *IEEE Trans. Acoust., Speech Signal Proc.*, 34(4): 744–54, 1986.

[MSY98]   J. McClellan, R. Schafer and M. Yoher. *DSP FIRST: A Multimedia Approach*. Prentice-Hall, 1998.

[MWdSK95]   S. McAdams, S. Winsberg, G. de Soete and J. Krimphoff. Perceptual scaling of synthesized musical timbres: common dimensions, specificities, and latent subject classes. *Psychol. Res.*, 58: 177–92, 1995.

[Nat75]   J.-J. Nattiez. *Fondements d'une Sémiologie de la Musique*. U. G. E., Coll. 10/18, Paris, 1975.

[Orf96]   S.J. Orfanidis. *Introduction to Signal Processing*. Prentice-Hall, 1996.

[Por76]   M. Portnoff. Implementation of the digital phase vocoder using the fast Fourier transform. *IEEE Trans. Acoust. Speech Signal Proc.*, 24(3): 243–8, 1976.

[PPPR96]   G. De Poli, A. Picialli, S. T. Pope, and C. Roads (eds). *Musical Signal Processing*. Swets & Zeitlinger, 1996.

[Puc95]   M. S. Puckette. Phase-locked vocoder. In *Proc. IEEE ASSP Conf. on Appl. of Signal Proc. Audio Acoust. (Mohonk, NY)*, 1995.

[Pul97]   V. Pulkki. Virtual sound source positioning using vector base amplitude panning. *J. Audio Eng. Soc.*, 45(6): 456–66, 1997.

[Rab]   C. A. Rabassó. L'improvisation: du langage musical au langage littéraire. *Intemporel: Bulletin de la Société Nationale de Musique*, 15.

[RDS+99]   S. Rossignol, P. Depalle, J. Soumagne, X. Rodet and J.-L. Collette. Vibrato: Detection, estimation, extraction, modification. In *Proc. COST-G6 Workshop on Digital Audio Effects (DAFx-99), Trondheim*, 1999.

[Roa96]   C. Roads. *The Computer Music Tutorial*. MIT Press, 1996.

[RW99]   J.-C. Risset and D. L. Wessel. *Exploration of Timbre by Analysis and Synthesis*, pp. 113–69. D. Deutsch, Academic Press, 1999.

[Sch66]   P. Schaeffer. *Traité des Objets Musicaux*. Seuil, 1966.

[Sch77]   R. M. Schafer. *The Tuning of the World*. Knopf: New York, 1977.

[Sea36]   C. E. Seashore. Psychology of the vibrato in voice and speech. *Studies Psychol. Music*, 3, 1936.

[She82]   R. Shepard. Geometrical approximations to the structure of musical pitch. *Psychol. Rev.*, 89(4): 305–33, 1982.

[SL61]   M. R. Schrœder and B. Logan. "Colorless" artificial reverberation. *J. Audio Eng. Soc.*, 9: 192–7, 1961.

[Sla85]   W. Slawson. *Sound Color*. University of California Press, 1985.

[Smi84]   J. O. Smith. An allpass approach to digital phasing and flanging. In *Proc. Int. Computer Music Conf. (ICMC'84), Paris*, pp. 103–8, 1984.

[SS90]   X. Serra and J. O. Smith. A sound decomposition system based on a deterministic plus residual model. *J. Ac. Soc. of America, Sup. 1*, 89(1): 425–34, 1990.

[SSAB02]   J. O. Smith, S. Serafin, J. Abel and D. Berners. Doppler simulation and the Leslie. In *Proc. Int. Conf. on Digital Audio Effects (DAFx-02), Hamburg*, pp. 13–20, 2002.

[Sun87]   J. Sundberg. *The Science of the Singing Voice*. Northern Illinois University Press, 1987.

[VGD05]   V. Verfaille, C. Guastavino and P. Depalle. Perceptual evaluation of vibrato models. In *Colloq. Interdisc. Musicol., Montréal (CIM'05)*, 2005.

[VGT06]   Vincent Verfaille, Catherine Guastavino and Caroline Traube. An interdisciplinary approach to audio effect classification. In *Proc. 9th Int. Conf. Digital Audio Effects (DAFx-06), Montreal, Canada*, pp. 107–13, 2006.

[VLM97]   T. Verma, S. Levine and T. Meng. Transient modeling synthesis: a flexible analysis/synthesis tool for transient signals. In *Proc. Int. Computer Music Conf. (ICMC'97), Thessaloniki*, 164–167, 1997.

[VWD06]   V. Verfaille, M. M. Wanderley and Ph. Depalle. Mapping strategies for gestural control of adaptive digital audio effects. *J. New Music Res.*, 35(1): 71–93, 2006.

[VZA06]   Vincent Verfaille, U. Zölzer and Daniel Arfib. Adaptive digital audio effects (A-DAFx): A new class of sound transformations. *IEEE Trans. Audio, Speech and Lang. Proc.*, 14(5): 1817–1831, 2006.

[WM01]   O. Warusfel and N. Misdariis. Directivity synthesis with a 3D array of loudspeakers - Application for stage performance. In *Proc. of the COST-G6 Workshop on Digital Audio Effects (DAFx-01), Limerick*, pp. 232–6, 2001.

[Zöl02]   U. Zölzer (ed). *DAFX–Digital Audio Effects*, First edition. J. Wiley & Sons, Ltd, 2002.

[Zöl05]   U. Zölzer. *Digital Audio Signal Processing*, Second edition. John Wiley & Sons, Ltd, 2005.

[ZS65]   E. Zwicker and B. Scharf. A model of loudness summation. *Psychol. Rev.*, 72: 3–26, 1965.

[Zwi77]   E. Zwicker. Procedure for calculating loudness of temporally variable sounds. *J. Ac. Soc. of America*, 62(3): 675–82, 1977.

2

Filters and delays

P. Dutilleux, M. Holters, S. Disch and U. Zölzer

2.1 Introduction

The term filter can have a large number of different meanings. In general it can be seen as a way to select certain elements with desired properties from a larger set. Let us focus on the particular field of digital audio effects and consider a signal in the frequency domain. The signal can be seen as a set of partials having different frequencies and amplitudes. The filter will perform a selection of the partials according to the frequencies that we want to reject, retain or emphasize. In other words: the filter will modify the amplitude of the partials according to their frequency. Once implemented, it will turn out that this filter is a linear transformation. As an extension, linear transformations can be said to be filters. According to this new definition of a filter, any linear operation could be said to be a filter, but this would go far beyond the scope of digital audio effects. It is possible to demonstrate what a filter is by using one's voice and vocal tract. Utter a vowel, *a*, for example, at a fixed pitch and then utter other vowels at the same pitch. By doing that we do not modify our vocal cords, but we modify the volume and the interconnection pattern of our vocal tract. The vocal cords produce a signal with a fixed harmonic spectrum, whereas the cavities act as acoustic filters to enhance some portions of the spectrum. We have described filters in the frequency domain here because it is the usual way to consider them, but they also have an effect in the time domain. After introducing a filter classification for basic filter types in the frequency domain, we will review typical implementation methods.

Beyond their effects in the frequency domain, filters can also be considered in the time domain leading to a family of delay-based audio effects such as those which can be experienced in acoustical spaces. A sound wave reflected by a wall will be superimposed on the sound wave at the source. If the wall is far away, such as a cliff, we will hear an echo. If the wall is close to us, we will notice the reflections through a modification of the sound color. Repeated reflections can appear between parallel boundaries. In a room, such reflections will be called *flatter echo*. The distance between the boundaries determines the delay that is imposed on each reflected sound wave. In a cylinder, successive reflections will develop at both ends. If the cylinder is long, we will hear

---

an iterative pattern, whereas if the cylinder is short, we will hear a pitched tone. Equivalents of these acoustical phenomena have been implemented as signal processing units. In the case of a time-varying delay the direct physical correspondence can be a relative movement between sound source and listener imposing a frequency shift on the perceived signal, which is commonly referred to as the "Doppler effect."

2.2 Basic filters

2.2.1 Filter classification in the frequency domain

The various types of filters can be defined according to the following classification (see Figure 2.1):

- **Lowpass (LP)** filters select low frequencies up to the cut-off frequency f_c and attenuate frequencies higher than f_c. Additionally, a resonance may amplify frequencies around f_c.

- **Highpass (HP)** filters select frequencies higher than f_c and attenuate frequencies below f_c, possibly with a resonance around f_c.

- **Bandpass (BP)** filters select frequencies between a lower cut-off frequency f_{cl} and a higher cut-off frequency f_{ch}. Frequencies below f_{cl} and frequencies higher than f_{ch} are attenuated.

- **Bandreject (BR)** filters attenuate frequencies between a lower cut-off frequency f_{cl} and a higher cut-off frequency f_{ch}. Frequencies below f_{cl} and frequencies higher than f_{ch} are passed.

- **Allpass** filters pass all frequencies, but modify the phase of the input signal.

The lowpass with resonance is very often used in computer music to simulate an acoustical resonating structure; the highpass filter can remove undesired very low frequencies; the bandpass can produce effects such as the imitation of a telephone line or of a mute on an acoustical instrument; the bandreject can divide the audible spectrum into two bands that seem to be uncorrelated.

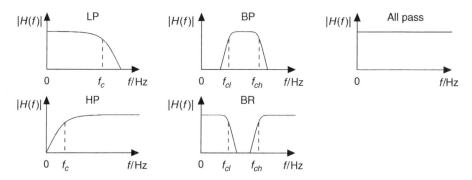

Figure 2.1   Filter classification.

2.2.2 Canonical filters

There are various ways to implement a filter, the simplest being the canonical filter, as shown in Figure 2.2 for a second-order filter, which can be implemented by the difference equations

$$x_h(n) = x(n) - a_1 x_h(n-1) - a_2 x_h(n-2) \tag{2.1}$$

$$y(n) = b_0 x_h(n) + b_1 x_h(n-1) + b_2 x_h(n-2) \tag{2.2}$$

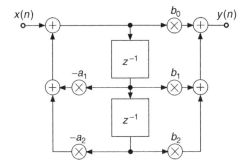

Figure 2.2   Canonical second-order digital filter.

Table 2.1   Coefficients for first-order filters.

	b_0	b_1	a_1
Lowpass	$K/(K+1)$	$K/(K+1)$	$(K-1)/(K+1)$
Highpass	$1/(K+1)$	$-1/(K+1)$	$(K-1)/(K+1)$
Allpass	$(K-1)/(K+1)$	1	$(K-1)/(K+1)$

and leads to the transfer function

$$H(z) = \frac{b_0 + b_1 z^{-1} + b_2 z^{-2}}{1 + a_1 z^{-1} + a_2 z^{-2}}. \tag{2.3}$$

By setting $a_2 = b_2 = 0$, this reduces to a first-order filter which, can be used to implement an allpass, lowpass or highpass with the coefficients of Table 2.1 where K depends on the cut-off frequency f_c by

$$K = \tan(\pi f_c / f_S). \tag{2.4}$$

For the allpass filter, the coefficient K likewise controls the frequency f_c when $-90°$ phase shift is reached.

For the second-order filters with coefficients shown in Table 2.2, in addition to the cut-off frequency (for lowpass and highpass) or the center frequency (for bandpass, bandreject and allpass) we additionally need the Q factor with slightly different meanings for the different filter types:

- For the lowpass and highpass filters, it controls the height of the resonance. For $Q = \frac{1}{\sqrt{2}}$, the filter is maximally flat up to the cut-off frequency; for lower Q, it has higher pass-band attenuation, while for higher Q, amplification around f_c occurs.

- For the bandpass and bandreject filters, it is related to the bandwidth f_b by $Q = \frac{f_c}{f_b}$, i.e., it is the inverse of the relative bandwidth $\frac{f_b}{f_c}$.

- For the allpass filter, it likewise controls the bandwidth, which here depends on the points where $\pm 90°$ phase shift relative to the $-180°$ phase shift at f_c are reached.

While the canonical filters are relatively simple, the calculation of their coefficients from parameters like cut-off frequency and bandwidth is not. In the following, we will therefore study filter structures that are slightly more complicated, but allow for easier parameterization.

Table 2.2 Coefficients for second-order filters.

	b_0	b_1	b_2	a_1	a_2
Lowpass	$\dfrac{K^2Q}{K^2Q+K+Q}$	$\dfrac{2K^2Q}{K^2Q+K+Q}$	$\dfrac{K^2Q}{K^2Q+K+Q}$	$\dfrac{2Q\cdot(K^2-1)}{K^2Q+K+Q}$	$\dfrac{K^2Q-K+Q}{K^2Q+K+Q}$
Highpass	$\dfrac{Q}{K^2Q+K+Q}$	$-\dfrac{2Q}{K^2Q+K+Q}$	$\dfrac{Q}{K^2Q+K+Q}$	$\dfrac{2Q\cdot(K^2-1)}{K^2Q+K+Q}$	$\dfrac{K^2Q-K+Q}{K^2Q+K+Q}$
Bandpass	$\dfrac{K}{K^2Q+K+Q}$	0	$-\dfrac{K}{K^2Q+K+Q}$	$\dfrac{2Q\cdot(K^2-1)}{K^2Q+K+Q}$	$\dfrac{K^2Q-K+Q}{K^2Q+K+Q}$
Bandreject	$\dfrac{Q\cdot(1+K^2)}{K^2Q+K+Q}$	$\dfrac{2Q\cdot(K^2-1)}{K^2Q+K+Q}$	$\dfrac{Q\cdot(1+K^2)}{K^2Q+K+Q}$	$\dfrac{2Q\cdot(K^2-1)}{K^2Q+K+Q}$	$\dfrac{K^2Q-K+Q}{K^2Q+K+Q}$
Allpass	$\dfrac{K^2Q-K+Q}{K^2Q+K+Q}$	$\dfrac{2Q\cdot(K^2-1)}{K^2Q+K+Q}$	1	$\dfrac{2Q\cdot(K^2-1)}{K^2Q+K+Q}$	$\dfrac{K^2Q-K+Q}{K^2Q+K+Q}$

2.2.3   State variable filter

A nice alternative to the canonical filter structure is the state variable filter shown in Figure 2.3 [Cha80], which combines second-order lowpass, bandpass and highpass for the same f_c and Q. Its difference equation is given by

$$y_l(n) = F_1 y_b(n) + y_l(n-1) \tag{2.5}$$

$$y_b(n) = F_1 y_h(n) + y_b(n-1) \tag{2.6}$$

$$y_h(n) = x(n) - y_l(n-1) - Q_1 y_b(n-1), \tag{2.7}$$

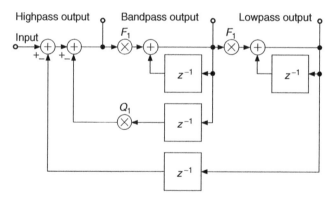

Figure 2.3   Digital state variable filter.

where $y_l(n)$, $y_b(n)$ and $y_h(n)$ are the outputs of lowpass, bandpass, and highpass, respectively. The tuning coefficients F_1 and Q_1 are related to the tuning parameters f_c and Q by

$$F_1 = 2\sin(\pi f_c/f_S) \qquad Q_1 = 1/Q. \tag{2.8}$$

It can be shown that the transfer function of lowpass, bandpass, and highpass, respectively, are

$$H_l(z) = \frac{r^2}{1 + (r^2 - q - 1)z^{-1} + qz^{-2}} \tag{2.9}$$

$$H_b(z) = \frac{r\cdot(1 - z^{-1})}{1 + (r^2 - q - 1)z^{-1} + qz^{-2}} \tag{2.10}$$

$$H_h(z) = \frac{(1 - z^{-1})^2}{1 + (r^2 - q - 1)z^{-1} + qz^{-2}}, \tag{2.11}$$

with $r = F_1$ and $q = 1 - F_1 Q_1$.

This structure is particularly effective not only as far as the filtering process is concerned, but above all because of the simple relations between control parameters and tuning coefficients. One should consider the stability of this filter, because at higher cut-off frequencies and smaller Q factors it becomes unstable. A "usability limit" given by $F_1 < 2 - Q_1$ assures the stable operation of the state variable implementation [Dut91, Die00]. In most musical applications, however, it is not a problem because the tuning frequencies are usually small compared to the sampling frequency and the Q factor is usually set to sufficiently high values [Dut89a, Dat97a]. This filter has proven its suitability for a large number of applications. The nice properties of this filter have been exploited to produce endless glissandi out of natural sounds and to allow smooth transitions between extreme settings [Dut89b, m-Vas93]. It is also used for synthesizer applications [Die00].

2.2.4 Normalization

Filters are usually designed in the frequency domain and as a consequence, they are expected to primarily affect the frequency content of the signal. However, the side effect of loudness modification must not be forgotten because of its importance for the practical use of the filter. The filter might produce the right effect, but the result might be useless because the sound has become too weak or too strong. The method of compensating for these amplitude variations is called normalization. Normalization is performed by scaling the filter such that the norm

$$L_p = \left(\frac{1}{2\pi} \int_{-\pi}^{\pi} |H(e^{j\omega})|^p d\omega \right)^{\frac{1}{p}} = 1, \tag{2.12}$$

where typically L_2 or $L_\infty = \max \left(|H(e^{j\omega})| \right)$ are used [Zöl05]. To normalize the loudness of the signal, the L_2 norm is employed. It is accurate for broadband signals and fits many practical musical applications. L_∞ normalizes the maximum of the frequency response and avoids overloading the filter. With a suitable normalization scheme the filter can prove to be very easy to handle whereas with the wrong normalization, the filter might be rejected by musicians because they cannot operate it.

The normalization of the state variable filter has been studied in [Dut91], where several effective implementation schemes are proposed. In practice, a first-order lowpass filter that processes the input signal will perform the normalization in f_c and an amplitude correction in $\sqrt{\zeta}$ will normalize in ζ (see Figure 2.4). This normalization scheme allows us to operate the filter with damping factors down to 10^{-4} where the filter gain reaches about 74 dB at f_c.

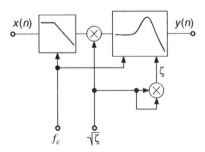

Figure 2.4 L_2-normalization in f_c and ζ for the state variable filter.

2.2.5 Allpass-based filters

In this subsection we introduce a special class of parametric filter structures for lowpass, highpass, bandpass and bandreject filter functions. Parametric filter structures denote special signal flow graphs where a coefficient inside the signal flow graph directly controls the cut-off frequency and bandwidth of the corresponding filter. These filter structures are easily tunable by changing only one or two coefficients. They play an important role for real-time control with minimum computational complexity.

The basis for parametric first- and second-order IIR filters is the first- and second-order allpass filter. We will first discuss the first-order allpass and show simple lowpass and highpass filters, which consist of a tunable allpass filter together with a direct path.

First-order allpass

A first-order allpass filter is given by the transfer function (see 2.2.2)

$$A(z) = \frac{z^{-1} + c}{1 + cz^{-1}} \tag{2.13}$$

$$c = \frac{\tan(\pi f_c/f_S) - 1}{\tan(\pi f_c/f_S) + 1}. \tag{2.14}$$

and the corresponding difference equation

$$x_h(n) = x(n) - cx_h(n - 1) \tag{2.15}$$

$$y(n) = cx_h(n) + x_h(n - 1), \tag{2.16}$$

which can be realized by the block diagram shown in Figure 2.5.

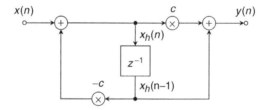

Figure 2.5   Block diagram for a first-order allpass filter.

The magnitude/phase response and the group delay of a first-order allpass are shown in Figure 2.6. The magnitude response is equal to one and the phase response is approaching $-180°$ for high frequencies. The group delay shows the delay of the input signal in samples versus frequency. The coefficient c in (2.13) controls the frequency where the phase response passes $-90°$ (see Figure 2.6).

For simple implementations a table with a number of coefficients for different cut-off frequencies is sufficient, but even for real-time applications this structure offers very few computations. In the following we use this first-order allpass filter to perform low/highpass filtering.

First-order low/highpass

A first-order lowpass/highpass filter can be achieved by adding or subtracting (+/−) the output signal from the input signal of a first-order allpass filter. As the output signal of the first-order allpass filter has a phase shift of $-180°$ for high frequencies, this operation leads to low/highpass

Magnitude response, Phase response, Group delay

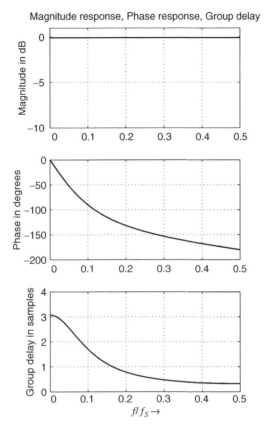

Figure 2.6 First-order allpass filter with $f_c = 0.1 \cdot f_S$.

filtering. The transfer function of a lowpass/highpass filter is then given by

$$H(z) = \frac{1}{2}(1 \pm A(z)) \quad (\text{LP/HP} + /-) \tag{2.17}$$

$$A(z) = \frac{z^{-1} + c}{1 + cz^{-1}} \tag{2.18}$$

$$c = \frac{\tan(\pi f_c / f_S) - 1}{\tan(\pi f_c / f_S) + 1}, \tag{2.19}$$

where a tunable first-order allpass $A(z)$ with tuning parameter c is used. The plus sign (+) denotes the lowpass operation and the minus sign (−) the highpass operation. The block diagram in Figure. 2.7 represents the operations involved in performing the low/highpass filtering. The allpass

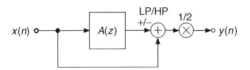

Figure 2.7 Block diagram of a first-order low/highpass filter.

filter can be implemented by the difference equation (2.16), as shown in Figure 2.5 to obtain the lowpass implementation of M-file 2.1.

M-file 2.1 (aplowpass.m)

```
function y = aplowpass (x, Wc)
% y = aplowpass (x, Wc)
% Author: M. Holters
% Applies a lowpass filter to the input signal x.
% Wc is the normalized cut-off frequency 0<Wc<1, i.e. 2*fc/fS.
c = (tan(pi*Wc/2)-1) / (tan(pi*Wc/2)+1);
xh = 0;
for n = 1:length(x)
  xh_new = x(n) - c*xh;
  ap_y = c * xh_new + xh;
  xh = xh_new;
  y(n) = 0.5 * (x(n) + ap_y);   % change to minus for highpass
end;
```

The magnitude/phase response and group delay are illustrated for low- and highpass filtering in Figure 2.8. The -3 dB point of the magnitude response for lowpass and highpass is passed at the cut-off frequency. With the help of the allpass subsystem in Figure 2.7, tunable first-order low- and highpass systems are achieved.

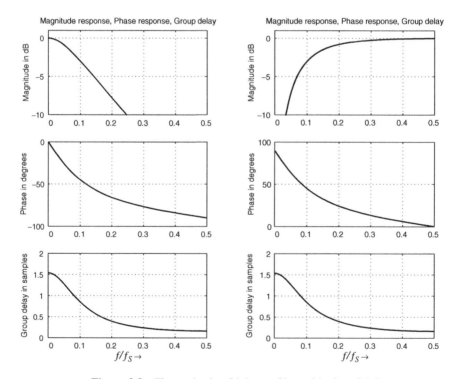

Figure 2.8 First-order low/highpass filter with $f_c = 0.1 f_S$.

Second-order allpass

The implementation of tunable bandpass and bandreject filters can be achieved with a second-order allpass filter. The transfer function of a second-order allpass filter is given by

$$A(z) = \frac{-c + d(1-c)z^{-1} + z^{-2}}{1 + d(1-c)z^{-1} - cz^{-2}} \tag{2.20}$$

$$c = \frac{\tan(\pi f_b/f_S) - 1}{\tan(\pi f_b/f_S) + 1} \tag{2.21}$$

$$d = -\cos(2\pi f_c/f_S), \tag{2.22}$$

with the corresponding difference equations (compare Section 2.2.2)

$$x_h(n) = x(n) - d(1-c)x_h(n-1) + cx_h(n-2) \tag{2.23}$$

$$y(n) = -cx_h(n) + d(1-c)x_h(n-1) + x_h(n-2). \tag{2.24}$$

The parameter d adjusts the center frequency and the parameter c the bandwidth. The magnitude/phase response and the group delay of a second-order allpass are shown in Figure 2.9. The magnitude response is again equal to one and the phase response approaches $-360°$ for high frequencies. The cut-off frequency f_c determines the point on the phase curve where the phase response passes $-180°$. The width or slope of the phase transition around the cut-off frequency is controlled by the bandwidth parameter f_b.

Second-order bandpass/bandreject

Second-order bandpass and bandreject filters can be described by the following transfer function

$$H(z) = \frac{1}{2}[1 \mp A(z)] \quad (\text{BP/BR} - /+) \tag{2.25}$$

$$A(z) = \frac{-c + d(1-c)z^{-1} + z^{-2}}{1 + d(1-c)z^{-1} - cz^{-2}} \tag{2.26}$$

$$c = \frac{\tan(\pi f_b/f_S) - 1}{\tan(\pi f_b/f_S) + 1} \tag{2.27}$$

$$d = -\cos(2\pi f_c/f_S), \tag{2.28}$$

where a tunable second-order allpass $A(z)$ with tuning parameters c and d is used. The minus sign $(-)$ denotes the bandpass operation and the plus sign $(+)$ the bandreject operation. The block diagram in Figure 2.10 shows the bandpass and bandreject filter implementation based on a second-order allpass subsystem, M-file 2.2 shows the corresponding MATLAB® code. The magnitude/phase response and group delay are illustrated in Figure 2.11 for both filter types.

M-file 2.2 (apbandpass.m)

```
function y = apbandpass (x, Wc, Wb)
% y = apbandpass (x, Wc, Wb)
% Author: M. Holters
% Applies a bandpass filter to the input signal x.
% Wc is the normalized center frequency 0<Wc<1, i.e. 2*fc/fS.
% Wb is the normalized bandwidth 0<Wb<1, i.e. 2*fb/fS.
c = (tan(pi*Wb/2)-1) / (tan(pi*Wb/2)+1);
d = -cos(pi*Wc);
```

```
xh = [0, 0];
for n = 1:length(x)
  xh_new = x(n) - d*(1-c)*xh(1) + c*xh(2);
  ap_y = -c * xh_new + d*(1-c)*xh(1) + xh(2);
  xh = [xh_new, xh(1)];
  y(n) = 0.5 * (x(n) - ap_y);   % change to plus for bandreject
end;
```

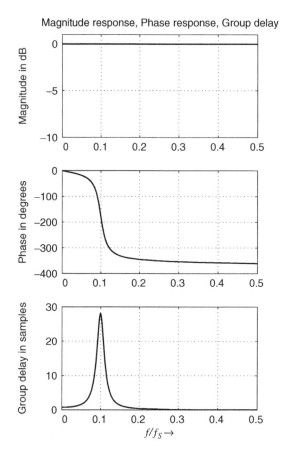

Figure 2.9   Second-order allpass filter with $f_c = 0.1 f_S$ and $f_b = 0.022 f_S$.

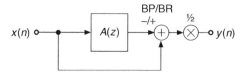

Figure 2.10   Second-order bandpass and bandreject filter.

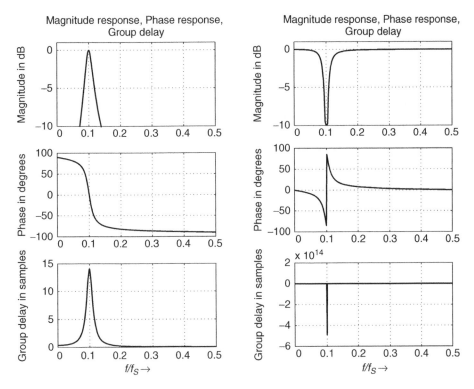

Figure 2.11   Second-order bandpass/bandreject filter with $f_c = 0.1 f_S$ and $f_b = 0.022 f_S$.

2.2.6   FIR filters

Introduction

The digital filters that we have seen before are said to have an infinite impulse response. Because of the feedback loops within the structure, an input sample will excite an output signal whose duration is dependent on the tuning parameters and can extend over a fairly long period of time. There are other filter structures without feedback loops (Figure 2.12). These are called finite impulse response filters (FIR), because the response of the filter to a unit impulse lasts only for a fixed period of time. These filters allow the building of sophisticated filter types where strong attenuation of unwanted frequencies or decomposition of the signal into several frequency bands is necessary.

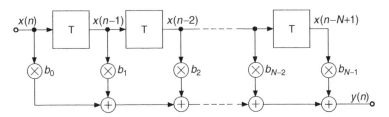

Figure 2.12   Finite impulse response filter.

They typically require higher filter orders and hence more computing power than IIR structures to achieve similar results, but when they are implemented in the form known as fast convolution they become competitive, thanks to the FFT algorithm. It is rather unwieldy to tune these filters interactively. As an example, let us briefly consider the vocoder application. If the frequency bands are fixed, then the FIR implementation can be most effective but if the frequency bands have to be subtly tuned by a performer, then the IIR structures will certainly prove superior [Mai97]. However, the filter structure in Figure 2.12 finds widespread applications for head-related transfer functions and the approximation of first room reflections, as will be shown in Chapter 5. For applications where the impulse response of a real system has been measured, the FIR filter structure can be used directly to simulate the measured impulse response.

Signal processing

The output/input relation of the filter structure in Figure 2.12 is described by the difference equation

$$y(n) = \sum_{i=0}^{N-1} b_i \cdot x(n-i) \tag{2.29}$$

$$= b_0 x(n) + b_1 x(n-1) + \cdots + b_{N-1} x(n-N+1), \tag{2.30}$$

which is a weighted sum of delayed input samples. If the input signal is a unit impulse $\delta(n)$, which is one for $n = 0$ and zero for $n \neq 0$, we get the impulse response of the system according to

$$h(n) = \sum_{i=0}^{N-1} b_i \cdot \delta(n-i) = b_n. \tag{2.31}$$

A graphical illustration of the impulse response of a five-tap FIR filter is shown in Figure 2.13. The Z-transform of the impulse response gives the transfer function

$$H(z) = \sum_{i=0}^{N-1} b_i \cdot z^{-i} \tag{2.32}$$

and with $z = e^{j\omega}$ the frequency response

$$H(e^{j\omega}) = b_0 + b_1 e^{-j\omega} + b_2 e^{-j2\omega} + \cdots + b_{N-1} \cdot e^{-j(N-1)\omega} \tag{2.33}$$

with $\quad \omega = 2\pi f/f_s$.

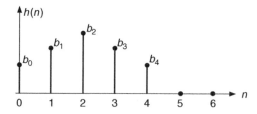

Figure 2.13   Impulse response of an FIR filter.

Filter design

The filters already described such as LP, HP, BP and BR are also possible with FIR filter structures (see Figure 2.14). The N coefficients $b_0, \ldots, b_{N-1}$ of a nonrecursive filter have to be computed by special design programs, which are discussed in all DSP text books. The N coefficients of the impulse response can be designed to yield a linear phase response, when the coefficients fulfill certain symmetry conditions. The simplest design is based on the inverse discrete-time Fourier transform of the ideal lowpass filter, which leads to the impulse response

$$h(n) = \frac{2f_c}{f_S} \cdot \frac{\sin\left[2\pi f_c/f_S\left(n - \frac{N-1}{2}\right)\right]}{2\pi f_c/f_S\left(n - \frac{N-1}{2}\right)}, \quad n = 0, \ldots, N-1. \tag{2.34}$$

To improve the frequency response this impulse response can be weighted by an appropriate window function like Hamming or Blackman according to

$$h_B(n) = h(n) \cdot w_B(n) \tag{2.35}$$

$$h_H(n) = h(n) \cdot w_H(n) \tag{2.36}$$

$$n = 0, 1, \ldots, N-1.$$

If a lowpass filter is designed and an impulse response $h_{LP}(n)$ is derived, a *frequency transformation* of this lowpass filter leads to highpass, bandpass and bandreject filters (see Fig. 2.14).

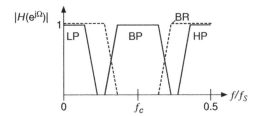

Figure 2.14   Frequency transformations: LP and frequency transformations to BP and HP.

Frequency transformations are performed in the time domain by taking the lowpass impulse response $h_{LP}(n)$ and computing the following equations:

- LP-HP

$$h_{HP}(n) = h_{LP}(n) \cdot \cos\left[\pi\left(n - \frac{N-1}{2}\right)\right] \qquad n = 0, \ldots, N-1 \tag{2.37}$$

- LP-BP

$$h_{BP}(n) = 2h_{LP}(n) \cdot \cos\left[2\pi\frac{f_c}{f_S}\left(n - \frac{N-1}{2}\right)\right] \qquad n = 0, \ldots, N-1 \tag{2.38}$$

- LP-BR

$$h_{BR}(n) = \delta\left(n - \frac{N-1}{2}\right) - h_{BP}(n) \qquad n = 0, \ldots, N-1. \tag{2.39}$$

Another simple FIR filter design is based on the FFT algorithm and is called *frequency sampling*. Its main idea is to specify the desired frequency response at discrete frequencies uniformly distributed over the frequency axis and calculate the corresponding impulse response. Design examples for audio processing with this design technique can be found in [Zöl05].

Musical applications

If linear phase processing is required, FIR filter offer magnitude equalization without phase distortions. They allow real-time equalization by making use of the frequency sampling design procedure [Zöl05] and are attractive equalizer counterparts to IIR filters, as shown in [McG93]. A discussion of more advanced FIR filters for audio processing can be found in [Zöl05].

2.2.7   Convolution

Introduction

Convolution is a generic signal processing operation like addition or multiplication. In the realm of computer music, however, it has the particular meaning of imposing a spectral or temporal structure onto a sound. These structures are usually not defined by a set of a few parameters, such as the shape or the time response of a filter, but are given by a signal which lasts typically a few seconds or more. Although convolution has been known and used for a very long time in the signal-processing community, its significance for computer music and audio processing has grown with the availability of fast computers that allow long convolutions to be performed in a reasonable period of time.

Signal processing

We could say in general that the convolution of two signals means filtering one with the other. There are several ways of performing this operation. The straightforward method is a direct implementation in a FIR filter structure, but it is computationally very inefficient when the impulse response is several thousand samples long. Another method, called fast convolution, makes use of the FFT algorithm to dramatically speed up the computation. The drawback of fast convolution is that it has a processing delay equal to the length of two FFT blocks, which is objectionable for real-time applications, whereas the FIR method has the advantage of providing a result immediately after the first sample has been computed. In order to take advantage of the FFT algorithm while keeping the processing delay to a minimum, low-latency convolution schemes have been developed which are suitable for real-time applications [Gar95, MT99].

The result of convolution can be interpreted in both the frequency and time domains. If $a(n)$ and $b(n)$ are the two convolved signals, the output spectrum will be given by the product of the two spectra $S(f) = A(f) \cdot B(f)$. The time interpretation derives from the fact that if $b(n)$ is a pulse at time k, we will obtain a copy of $a(n)$ shifted at time k_0, i.e., $s(n) = a(n - k)$. If $b(n)$ is a sequence of pulses, we will obtain a copy of $a(n)$ in correspondence to every pulse, i.e., a rhythmic, pitched or reverberated structure, depending on the pulse distance. If $b(n)$ is pulse-like, we obtain the same pattern with a filtering effect. In this case $b(n)$ should be interpreted as an impulse response. Thus convolution will result in subtractive synthesis, where the frequency shape of the filter is determined by a real sound. For example convolution with a bell sound will be heard as filtered by the resonances of the bell. In fact the bell sound is generated by a strike on the bell and can be considered as the impulse response of the bell. In this way we can simulate the effect of a sound hitting a bell, without measuring the resonances and designing the filter. If both sounds $a(n)$ and $b(n)$ are complex in time and frequency, the resulting sound will be blurred and will tend to lack the original sound's character. If both sounds are of long duration and each has a strong pitch and smooth attack, the result will contain both pitches and the intersection of their spectra.

Musical applications

When a sound is convolved with the impulse responses of a room, it is projected in the corresponding virtual auditory space [DMT99]. A diffuse reverberation can be produced by convolving with broad-band noise having a sharp attack and exponentially decreasing amplitude. Another example is obtained by convolving a tuba glissando with a series of snare-drum strokes. The tuba is transformed into something like a Tibetan trumpet playing in the mountains. Each stroke of the snare drum produces a copy of the tuba sound. Since each stroke is noisy and broadband, it acts like a reverberator. The series of strokes acts like several diffusing boundaries and produces the type of echo that can be found in natural landscapes [DMT99].

The convolution can be used to map a rhythm pattern onto a sampled sound. The rhythm pattern can be defined by positioning a unit impulse at each desired time within a signal block. The convolution of the input sound with the time pattern will produce copies of the input signal at each of the unit impulses. If the unit impulse is replaced by a more complex sound, each copy will be modified in its timbre and in its time structure. If a snare drum stroke is used, the attacks will be smeared and some diffusion will be added. The convolution has an effect both in the frequency and in the time domain. Take a speech sound with sharp frequency resonances and a rhythm pattern defined by a series of snare-drum strokes. Each word will appear with the rhythm pattern and the rhythm pattern will be heard in each word with the frequency resonances of the initial speech sound.

Convolution as a tool for musical composition has been investigated by composers such as Horacio Vaggione [m-Vag96, Vag98] and Curtis Roads [Roa97]. Because convolution has a combined effect in the time and frequency domains, some expertise is necessary to foresee the result of the combination of two sounds.

2.3 Equalizers

Introduction and musical applications

In contrast to low/highpass and bandpass/reject filters, which attenuate the audio spectrum above or below a cut-off frequency, equalizers shape the audio spectrum by enhancing certain frequency bands while others remain unaffected. They are typically built by a series connection of first- and second-order shelving and peak filters, which are controlled independently (see Figure 2.15). Shelving filters boost or cut the low- or high-frequency bands with the parameters cut-off frequency f_c and gain G. Peak filters boost or cut mid-frequency bands with parameters center frequency f_c, bandwidth f_b and gain G. One often-used filter type is the constant Q peak filter. The Q factor is defined by the ratio of the bandwidth to center frequency $Q = \frac{f_b}{f_c}$. The center frequency of peak filters is then tuned while keeping the Q factor constant. This means that the bandwidth is increased when the center frequency is increased and vice versa. Several proposed digital filter structures for shelving and peak filters can be found in the literature [Whi86, RM87, Dut89a, HB93, Bri94, Orf96, Orf97, Zöl05].

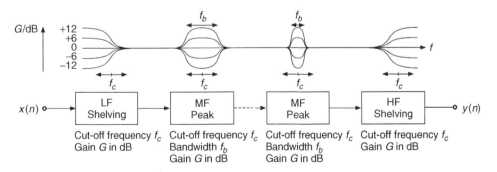

Figure 2.15   Series connection of shelving and peak filters.

Applications of these parametric filters can be found in parametric equalizers, octave equalizers ($f_c = 31.25, 62.5, 125, 250, 500, 1000, 2000, 4000, 8000, 16\,000$ Hz) and all kinds of equalization devices in mixing consoles, outboard equipment and foot-pedal controlled stomp boxes.

2.3.1 Shelving filters

First-order design

Similar to the first-order lowpass/highpass filters described in Section 2.2.5, first-order low/high frequency shelving filters can be constructed based on a first-order allpass [Zöl05], yielding the transfer function

$$H(z) = 1 + \frac{H_0}{2}[1 + \pm A(z)] \quad \text{(LF/HF} + /-) \tag{2.40}$$

with the first-order allpass

$$A(z) = \frac{z^{-1} + c_{B/C}}{1 + c_{B/C}z^{-1}}. \tag{2.41}$$

The block diagram in Figure 2.16 shows a first-order low/high-frequency shelving filter, which leads to the difference equations

$$x_h(n) = x(n) - c_{B/C}x_h(n-1) \tag{2.42}$$

$$y_1(n) = c_{B/C}x_h(n) + x_h(n-1) \tag{2.43}$$

$$y(n) = \frac{H_0}{2}\left[x(n) \pm y_1(n)\right] + x(n). \tag{2.44}$$

The gain G in dB for low/high frequencies can be adjusted by the parameter

$$H_0 = V_0 - 1 \quad \text{with} \quad V_0 = 10^{G/20}. \tag{2.45}$$

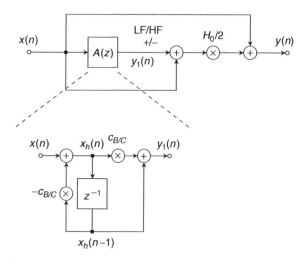

Figure 2.16   First-order low/high-frequency shelving filter.

The cut-off frequency parameters, c_B for boost and c_C for cut, for a first-order low-frequency shelving filter can be calculated [Zöl05] as

$$c_B = \frac{\tan(\pi f_c/f_S) - 1}{\tan(\pi f_c/f_S) + 1},$$ (2.46)

$$c_C = \frac{\tan(\pi f_c/f_S) - V_0}{\tan(\pi f_c/f_S) + V_0}$$ (2.47)

and for a high-frequency shelving filter as

$$c_B = \frac{\tan(\pi f_c/f_S) - 1}{\tan(\pi f_c/f_S) + 1}$$

$$c_C = \frac{V_0 \tan(\pi f_c/f_S) - 1}{V_0 \tan(\pi f_c/f_S) + 1}.$$

An implementation of this approach is given in M-file 2.3

M-file 2.3 (lowshelving.m)

```
function y = lowshelving (x, Wc, G)
% y = lowshelving (x, Wc, G)
% Author: M. Holters
% Applies a low-frequency shelving filter to the input signal x.
% Wc is the normalized cut-off frequency 0<Wc<1, i.e. 2*fc/fS
% G is the gain in dB
V0 = 10^(G/20); H0 = V0 - 1;
if G > = 0
  c = (tan(pi*Wc/2)-1) / (tan(pi*Wc/2)+1);      % boost
else
  c = (tan(pi*Wc/2)-V0) / (tan(pi*Wc/2)+V0);    % cut
end;
xh = 0;
for n = 1:length(x)
  xh_new = x(n) - c*xh;
  ap_y = c * xh_new + xh;
  xh = xh_new;
  y(n) = 0.5 * H0 * (x(n) + ap_y) + x(n);  % change to minus for HS
end;
```

Magnitude responses for a low-frequency shelving filter are illustrated in the left part of Figure 2.17 for several cut-off frequencies and gain factors. The slope of the frequency curves for these first-order filters are 6 dB per octave.

Higher-order designs

For several applications, especially in advanced equalizer designs, the slope of the shelving filter is further increased by second-order or even higher-order transfer functions. There are several approaches for designing higher-order shelving filters with relatively simple computation of the coefficients at the cost of slightly more complicated filter structures [KZ04, Orf05, HZ06].

Design formulas for canonical second-order shelving filters are given in Table 2.3 from [Zöl05]. Their magnitude responses are illustrated in the right part of Figure 2.17 for two cut-off frequencies and several gain factors.

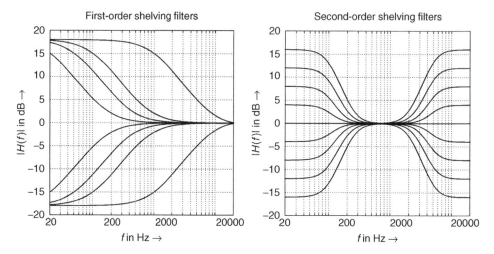

Figure 2.17   Frequency responses for first-order and second-order shelving filters.

Table 2.3   Second-order shelving filter design with $K = \tan(\pi f_c / f_S)$ and $V_0 = 10^{G/20}$ [Zöl05].

	b_0	b_1	b_2	a_1	a_2
LF boost	$\dfrac{1+\sqrt{2V_0}K+V_0K^2}{1+\sqrt{2}K+K^2}$	$\dfrac{2(V_0K^2-1)}{1+\sqrt{2}K+K^2}$	$\dfrac{1-\sqrt{2V_0}K+V_0K^2}{1+\sqrt{2}K+K^2}$	$\dfrac{2(K^2-1)}{1+\sqrt{2}K+K^2}$	$\dfrac{1-\sqrt{2}K+K^2}{1+\sqrt{2}K+K^2}$
LF cut	$\dfrac{V_0(1+\sqrt{2}K+K^2)}{V_0+\sqrt{2V_0}K+K^2}$	$\dfrac{2V_0(K^2-1)}{V_0+\sqrt{2V_0}K+K^2}$	$\dfrac{V_0(1-\sqrt{2}K+K^2)}{V_0+\sqrt{2V_0}K+K^2}$	$\dfrac{2(K^2-V_0)}{V_0+\sqrt{2V_0}K+K^2}$	$\dfrac{V_0-\sqrt{2V_0}K+K^2}{V_0+\sqrt{2V_0}K+K^2}$
HF boost	$\dfrac{V_0+\sqrt{2V_0}K+K^2}{1+\sqrt{2}K+K^2}$	$\dfrac{2(K^2-V_0)}{1+\sqrt{2}K+K^2}$	$\dfrac{V_0-\sqrt{2V_0}K+K^2}{1+\sqrt{2}K+K^2}$	$\dfrac{2(K^2-1)}{1+\sqrt{2}K+K^2}$	$\dfrac{1-\sqrt{2}K+K^2}{1+\sqrt{2}K+K^2}$
HF cut	$\dfrac{V_0(1+\sqrt{2}K+K^2)}{1+\sqrt{2V_0}K+V_0K^2}$	$\dfrac{2V_0(K^2-1)}{1+\sqrt{2V_0}K+V_0K^2}$	$\dfrac{V_0(1-\sqrt{2}K+K^2)}{1+\sqrt{2V_0}K+V_0K^2}$	$\dfrac{2(V_0K^2-1)}{1+\sqrt{2V_0}K+V_0K^2}$	$\dfrac{1-\sqrt{2V_0}K+V_0K^2}{1+\sqrt{2V_0}K+V_0K^2}$

2.3.2   Peak filters

Similarly, a second-order peak filter [Zöl05] is given by the transfer function

$$H(z) = 1 + \frac{H_0}{2}\left[1 - A_2(z)\right], \tag{2.48}$$

where

$$A_2(z) = \frac{-c_{B/C} + d(1 - c_{B/C})z^{-1} + z^{-2}}{1 + d(1 - c_{B/C})z^{-1} - c_{B/C}z^{-2}} \tag{2.49}$$

is a second-order allpass filter. The block diagram in Figure 2.18 shows the second-order peak filter, which leads to the difference equations

$$x_h(n) = x(n) - d(1 - c_{B/C})x_h(n-1) + c_{B/C}x_h(n-2) \tag{2.50}$$

$$y_1(n) = -c_{B/C}x_h(n) + d(1 - c_{B/C})x_h(n-1) + x_h(n-2) \tag{2.51}$$

$$y(n) = \frac{H_0}{2}\left[x(n) - y_1(n)\right] + x(n). \tag{2.52}$$

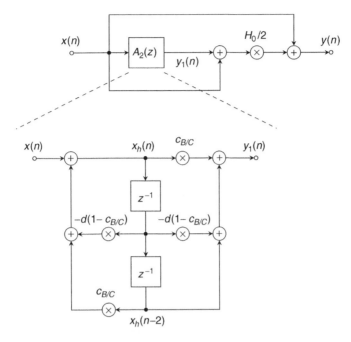

Figure 2.18   Second-order peak filter.

The center frequency parameter d and the coefficient H_0 are given by

$$d = -\cos(2\pi f_c/f_S) \tag{2.53}$$

$$V_0 = H(e^{j2\pi f_c/f_S}) = 10^{G/20} \tag{2.54}$$

$$H_0 = V_0 - 1. \tag{2.55}$$

The bandwidth f_b is adjusted through the parameters c_B and c_C for boost and cut given by

$$c_B = \frac{\tan(\pi f_b/f_S) - 1}{\tan(\pi f_b/f_S) + 1} \tag{2.56}$$

$$c_C = \frac{\tan(\pi f_b/f_S) - V_0}{\tan(\pi f_b/f_S) + V_0}. \tag{2.57}$$

A possible peak filter implementation using this approach is given in M-file 2.4.

M-file 2.4 (peakfilt.m)

```
function y = peakfilt (x, Wc, Wb, G)
% y = peakfilt (x, Wc, Wb, G)
% Author: M. Holters
% Applies a peak filter to the input signal x.
% Wc is the normalized center frequency 0<Wc<1, i.e. 2*fc/fS.
% Wb is the normalized bandwidth 0<Wb<1, i.e. 2*fb/fS.
% G is the gain in dB.
V0 = 10^(G/20); H0 = V0 - 1;
if G >= 0
   c = (tan(pi*Wb/2)-1) / (tan(pi*Wb/2)+1);     % boost
```

```
else
  c = (tan(pi*Wb/2)-V0) / (tan(pi*Wb/2)+V0);    % cut
end;
d = -cos(pi*Wc);
xh = [0, 0];
for n = 1:length(x)
  xh_new = x(n) - d*(1-c)*xh(1) + c*xh(2);
  ap_y = -c * xh_new + d*(1-c)*xh(1) + xh(2);
  xh = [xh_new, xh(1)];
  y(n) = 0.5 * H0 * (x(n) - ap_y) + x(n);
end;
```

This peak filter offers almost independent control of all three musical parameters center frequency, bandwidth and gain. Another design approach from [Zöl05] shown in Table 2.4 allows direct computation of the five coefficients for a second-order transfer function as given in the difference equation (2.2).

Table 2.4 Peak filter design with $K = \tan(\pi f_c/f_s)$ and $V_0 = 10^{G/20}$ [Zöl05].

	b_0	b_1	b_2	a_1	a_2
Boost	$\dfrac{1+\frac{V_0}{Q}K+K^2}{1+\frac{1}{Q}K+K^2}$	$\dfrac{2(K^2-1)}{1+\frac{1}{Q}K+K^2}$	$\dfrac{1-\frac{V_0}{Q}K+K^2}{1+\frac{1}{Q}K+K^2}$	$\dfrac{2(K^2-1)}{1+\frac{1}{Q}K+K^2}$	$\dfrac{1-\frac{1}{Q}K+K^2}{1+\frac{1}{Q}K+K^2}$
Cut	$\dfrac{1+\frac{1}{Q}K+K^2}{1+\frac{1}{V_0 Q}K+K^2}$	$\dfrac{2(K^2-1)}{1+\frac{1}{V_0 Q}K+K^2}$	$\dfrac{1-\frac{1}{Q}K+K^2}{1+\frac{1}{V_0 Q}K+K^2}$	$\dfrac{2(K^2-1)}{1+\frac{1}{V_0 Q}K+K^2}$	$\dfrac{1-\frac{1}{V_0 Q}K+K^2}{1+\frac{1}{V_0 Q}K+K^2}$

Frequency responses for several settings of a peak filter are shown in Figure 2.19. The left part shows a variation of the gain with a fixed center frequency and bandwidth. The right part shows for fixed gain and center frequency a variation of the bandwidth or Q factor.

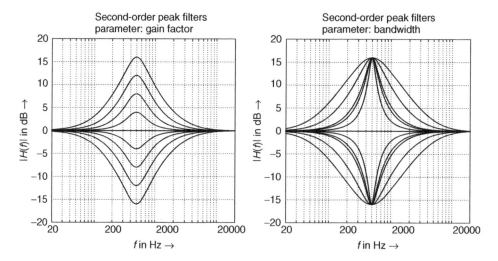

Figure 2.19 Frequency responses second-order peak filters.

2.4 Time-varying filters

The parametric filters discussed in the previous sections allow the time-varying control of the filter parameters gain, cut-off frequency, and bandwidth or Q factor. Special applications of time-varying audio filters will be shown in the following.

2.4.1 Wah-wah filter

The wah-wah effect is produced mostly by foot-controlled signal processors containing a bandpass filter with variable center frequency and a small bandwidth. Moving the pedal back and forth changes the bandpass center frequency. The "wah-wah" effect is then mixed with the direct signal, as shown in Figure 2.20. This effect leads to a spectrum shaping similar to speech and produces a speech-like "wah-wah" sound. Instead of manually changing the center frequency, it is also possible to let a low-frequency oscillator control the center frequency, which in turn is controlled based on parameters derived from the input signal, e.g., the signal envelope (see Section 3.3). Such an effect is called an auto-wah filter. If the effect is combined with a low-frequency amplitude variation, which produces a tremolo, the effect is denoted a tremolo-wah filter. Replacing the unit delay in the bandpass filter by an M tap delay leads to the M-fold wah-wah filter [Dis99], which is shown in Figure 2.21. M bandpass filters are spread over the entire spectrum and simultaneously change their center frequency. When a white noise input signal is applied to an M-fold wah-wah filter, a spectrogram of the output signal shown in Figure 2.22 illustrates the periodic enhancement of the output spectrum. Table 2.5 contains several parameter settings for different effects.

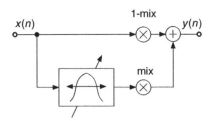

Figure 2.20 Wah-wah: time-varying bandpass filter.

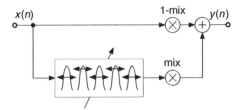

Figure 2.21 M-fold wah-wah filter.

Table 2.5 Effects with M-fold wah-wah filter [Dis99].

	M	Q^{-1}/f_m	Δf
Wah-Wah	1	$-/3$ kHz	200 Hz
M-fold Wah-Wah	5–20	0.5/-	200–500 Hz
Bell effect	100	0.5/-	100Hz

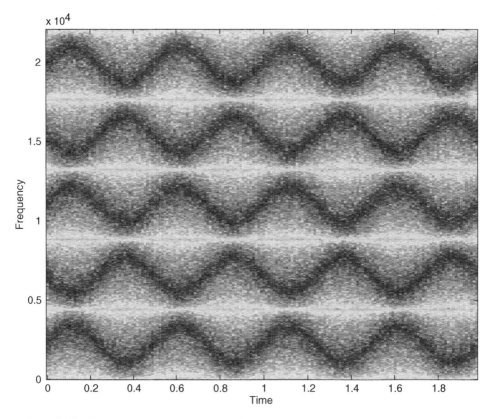

Figure 2.22   Spectrogram of output signal of a time-varying M-fold wah-wah filter [Dis99].

2.4.2   Phaser

The previous effect relies on varying the center frequency of a bandpass filter. Another effect uses notch filters: *phasing*. A set of notch filters, that can be realized as a cascade of second-order IIR sections, is used to process the input signal. The output of the notch filters is then combined with the direct sound. The frequencies of the notches are slowly varied using a low-frequency oscillator (Figure 2.23) [Smi84]. "The strong phase shifts that exist around the notch frequencies combine with the phases of the direct signal and cause phase cancellations or enhancements that sweep up and down the frequency axis" [Orf96]. Although this effect does not rely on a delay line, it is often considered to go along with delay-line-based effects because the sound effect is similar

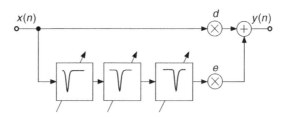

Figure 2.23   Phasing.

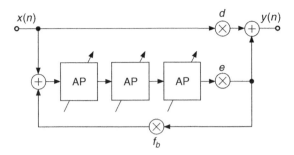

Figure 2.24 Phasing with time-varying allpass filters.

to that of *flanging*. An extensive discussion on this topic is found in [Str83]. A different phasing approach is shown in Figure 2.24. The notch filters have been replaced by second-order allpass filters with time-varying center frequencies. The cascade of allpass filters produces time-varying phase shifts which lead to cancellations and amplifications of different frequency bands when used in the feedforward and feedback configuration.

2.4.3 Time-varying equalizers

There is a wide range of effects that are based on time-varying equalizers, some of which are briefly described in the following:

- Time-varying octave bandpass filters, as shown in Figure 2.25, offer the possibility of achieving wah-wah-like effects. The spectrogram of the output signal in Figure 2.26 demonstrates the octave spaced enhancement of this approach.

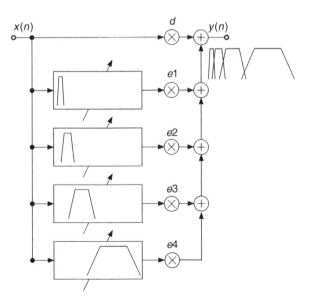

Figure 2.25 Time-varying octave filters.

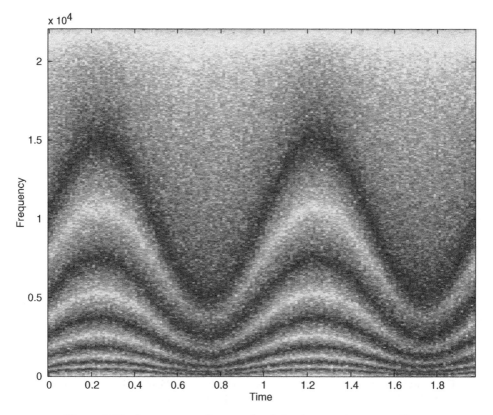

Figure 2.26   Spectrogram of output signal for time-varying octave filters.

- Time-varying shelving and peak filters: the special allpass realization of shelving and peak filters has shown that a combination of lowpass, bandpass and allpass filters gives access to several frequency bands inside such a filter structure. Integrating level measurement or envelope followers (see Chapter 4) into these frequency bands can be used for adaptively changing the filter parameters gain, cut-off/center frequency and bandwidth or Q factor. The combination of dynamics processing, which will be discussed in Chapter 4, and parametric filter structures allows the creation of signal dependent filtering effects with a variety of applications.

- Feedback cancellers, which are based on time-varying notch filters, play an important role in sound reinforcement systems. The spectrum is continuously monitored for spectral peaks and a very narrow-band notch filter is applied to the signal path.

2.5   Basic delay structures

2.5.1   FIR comb filter

The A network that simulates a single delay is called a FIR comb filter. The input signal is delayed by a given time duration. The effect will be audible only when the processed signal is combined (added) to the input signal, which acts here as a reference. This effect has two tuning parameters:

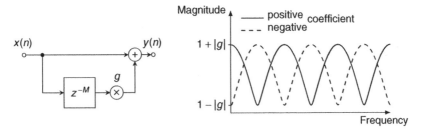

Figure 2.27   FIR comb filter and magnitude response.

the amount of time delay τ and the relative amplitude of the delayed signal to that of the reference signal. The difference equation and the transfer function are given by

$$y(n) = x(n) + gx(n - M) \tag{2.58}$$

$$\text{with} \quad M = \tau/f_s \tag{2.59}$$

$$H(z) = 1 + gz^{-M}. \tag{2.60}$$

The time response of this filter is made up of the direct signal and the delayed version. This simple time-domain behavior comes along with interesting frequency-domain patterns. For positive values of g, the filter amplifies all frequencies that are multiples of $1/\tau$ and attenuates all frequencies that lie in-between. The transfer function of such a filter shows a series of spikes and it looks like a comb (Figure 2.27), hence the name. For negative values of g, the filter attenuates frequencies that are multiples of $1/\tau$ and amplifies those that lie in-between. The gain varies between $1 + g$ and $1 - g$ [Orf96]. The following M-file 2.5 demonstrates a sample-by-sample based FIR comb filter. For plotting the output signal use the command stem(0:length(y)-1,y) and for the evaluation of the magnitude and phase response use the command freqz(y,1).

M-file 2.5 (fircomb.m)

```
% Authors: P. Dutilleux, U Zölzer
x=zeros(100,1);x(1)=1; % unit impulse signal of length 100
g=0.5;
Delayline=zeros(10,1);% memory allocation for length 10
for n=1:length(x);
      y(n)=x(n)+g*Delayline(10);
      Delayline=[x(n);Delayline(1:10-1)];
end;
```

Just as with acoustical delays, the FIR comb filter has an effect both in the time and frequency domains. Our ear is more sensitive to the one aspect or to the other depending on the range in which the time delay is set. For larger values of τ, we can hear an echo that is distinct from the direct signal. The frequencies that are amplified by the comb are so close to each other that we barely identify the spectral effect. For smaller values of τ, our ear can no longer segregate the time events, but can notice the spectral effect of the comb.

2.5.2 IIR comb filter

Similar to the endless reflections at both ends of a cylinder, the IIR comb filter produces an endless series of responses $y(n)$ to an input $x(n)$. The input signal circulates in a delay line that is fed back

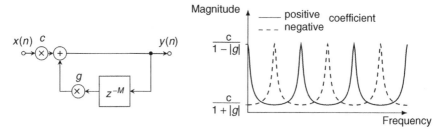

Figure 2.28   IIR comb filter and magnitude response.

to the input. Each time the signal goes through the delay line it is attenuated by g. It is sometimes necessary to scale the input signal by c in order to compensate for the high amplification produced by the structure. It is implemented by the structure shown in Figure 2.28, with the difference equation and transfer function given by

$$y(n) = cx(n) + gy(n - M), \text{ with } M = \tau/f_s \tag{2.61}$$

$$H(z) = c/(1 - gz^{-M}). \tag{2.62}$$

Due to the feedback loop, the time response of the filter is infinite. After each time delay τ a copy of the input signal will come out with an amplitude g^p, where p is the number of cycles that the signal has gone through the delay line. It can readily be seen, that $|g| \leq 1$ is a stability condition. Otherwise the signal would grow endlessly. The frequencies that are affected by the IIR comb filter are similar to those affected by the FIR comb filter. The gain varies between $1/(1 - g)$ and $1/(1 + g)$. The main differences between the IIR comb and the FIR comb is that the gain grows very high and that the frequency peaks get narrower as $|g|$ comes closer to 1 (see Figure 2.28). The following M-file 2.6 shows the implementation of a sample-by-sample based IIR comb filter.

M-file 2.6 (iircomb.m)

```
% Authors: P. Dutilleux, U Zölzer
x=zeros(100,1);x(1)=1; % unit impulse signal of length 100
g=0.5;
Delayline=zeros(10,1); % memory allocation for length 10
for n=1:length(x);
        y(n)=x(n)+g*Delayline(10);
        Delayline=[y(n);Delayline(1:10-1)];
end;
```

2.5.3   Universal comb filter

The combination of FIR and IIR comb filters leads to the universal comb filter. This filter structure, shown in Figure 2.29, reverts to an allpass structure in the special case of $-BL = FB, FF = 1$ (see Figure 2.5), where the one sample delay operator z^{-1} is replaced by the M sample delay operator z^{-M}. The special cases for differences in feedback parameter FB, feedforward parameter FF and blend parameter BL are given in Table 2.6. M-file 2.7 shows the implementation of a sample-by-sample universal comb filter.

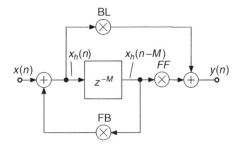

Figure 2.29   Universal comb filter.

Table 2.6   Parameters for universal comb filter.

	BL	FB	FF
FIR comb filter	1	0	g
IIR comb filter	c	g	0
Allpass	a	$-a$	1
Delay	0	0	1

M-file 2.7 (unicomb.m)

```
% Authors: P. Dutilleux, U Zölzer
x=zeros(100,1);x(1)=1; % unit impulse signal of length 100
BL=0.5;
FB=-0.5;
FF=1;
M=10;
Delayline=zeros(M,1); % memory allocation for length 10
for n=1:length(x);
    xh=x(n)+FB*Delayline(M);
    y(n)=FF*Delayline(M)+BL*xh;
    Delayline=[xh;Delayline(1:M-1)];
end;
```

The extension of the above universal comb filter to a parallel connection of N comb filters is shown in Figure 2.30. The feedback, feedforward and blend coefficients are now $N \times N$ matrices to mix the input and output signals of the delay network. The use of different parameter sets leads to the applications shown in Table 2.7.

2.5.4   Fractional delay lines

Variable-length delays of the input signal are used to simulate several acoustical effects. Therefore, delays of the input signal with noninteger values of the sampling interval are necessary. A delay of the input signal by M samples plus a fraction of the normalized sampling interval with $0 \leq \text{frac} \leq 1$ is given by

$$y(n) = x(n - [M + \text{frac}]) \tag{2.63}$$

and can be implemented by a fractional delay shown in Figure 2.31.

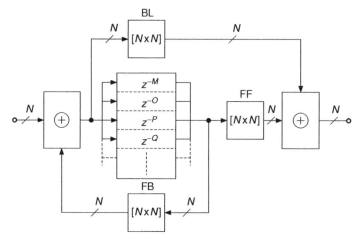

Figure 2.30   Generalized structure of parallel allpass comb filters.

Table 2.7   Effects with generalized comb filter.

	Delay	BL	FB	FF
Slapback	50 ms	1	0	X
Echo	>50 ms	1	$0 < X < 1$	0
Reverb		Matrix	Matrix	Matrix

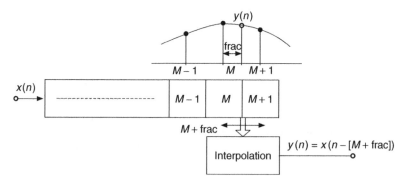

Figure 2.31   Fractional delay line with interpolation.

Design tools for fractional delay filters can be found in [LVKL96]. An interpolation algorithm has to compute the output sample $y(n)$, which lies in-between the two samples at time instants M and $M + 1$. Several interpolation algorithms have been proposed for audio applications:

• Linear interpolation [Dat97b]

$$y(n) = x(n - [M + 1])\text{frac} + x(n - M)(1 - \text{frac}) \tag{2.64}$$

- Allpass interpolation [Dat97b]

$$y(n) = x(n - [M + 1])\text{frac} + x(n - M)(1 - \text{frac}) - y(n - 1)(1 - \text{frac}) \qquad (2.65)$$

- Sinc interpolation [FC98]

- Fractionally addressed delay lines [Roc98, Roc00]

- Spline interpolation [Dis99], e.g., of third order

$$
\begin{aligned}
y(n) = {} & x(n - [M + 1]) \cdot \frac{\text{frac}^3}{6} \\
& + x(n - M) \cdot \frac{(1 + \text{frac})^3 - 4 \cdot \text{frac}^3}{6} \\
& + x(n - [M - 1]) \cdot \frac{(2 - \text{frac})^3 - 4(1 - \text{frac})^3}{6} \\
& + x(n - [M - 2]) \cdot \frac{(1 - \text{frac})^3}{6}.
\end{aligned}
\qquad (2.66)
$$

They all perform interpolation of a fractional delayed output signal with different computational complexity and different performance properties, which are discussed in [Roc00]. The choice of the algorithm depends on the specific application.

2.6 Delay-based audio effects

2.6.1 Vibrato

When a car is passing by, we hear a pitch deviation due to the Doppler effect [Dut91]. This effect will be explained in another chapter, but we can keep in mind that the pitch variation is due to the fact that the distance between the source and our ears is being varied. Varying the distance is, for our application, equivalent to varying the time delay. If we keep on varying periodically the time delay we will produce a periodical pitch variation. This is precisely a vibrato effect. For that purpose we need a delay line and a low-frequency oscillator to drive the delay time parameter. We should only listen to the delayed signal. Typical values of the parameters are 5 to 10 ms as the average delaytime and 5 to 14 Hz rate for the low-frequency oscillator (see Figure 2.32) [And95, Whi93]. M-file 2.8 shows the implementation for vibrato [Dis99].

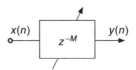

Figure 2.32 Vibrato.

M-file 2.8 (vibrato.m)

```
function y=vibrato(y,SAMPLERATE,Modfreq,Width)
% Author: S. Disch
ya_alt=0;
Delay=Width; % basic delay of input sample in sec
```

```
DELAY=round(Delay*SAMPLERATE); % basic delay in # samples
WIDTH=round(Width*SAMPLERATE); % modulation width in # samples
if WIDTH>DELAY
   error('delay greater than basic delay !!!');
   return;
end
MODFREQ=Modfreq/SAMPLERATE; % modulation frequency in # samples
LEN=length(x);          % # of samples in WAV-file
L=2+DELAY+WIDTH*2;      % length of the entire delay
Delayline=zeros(L,1);  % memory allocation for delay
y=zeros(size(x));      % memory allocation for output vector
for n=1:(LEN-1)
   M=MODFREQ;
   MOD=sin(M*2*pi*n);
   TAP=1+DELAY+WIDTH*MOD;
   i=floor(TAP);
   frac=TAP-i;
   Delayline=[x(n);Delayline(1:L-1)];
   %---Linear Interpolation---------------------------
   y(n,1)=Delayline(i+1)*frac+Delayline(i)*(1-frac);
   %---Allpass Interpolation--------------------------
   %y(n,1)=(Delayline(i+1)+(1-frac)*Delayline(i)-(1-frac)*ya_alt);
   %ya_alt=ya(n,1);
   %---Spline Interpolation---------------------------
   %y(n,1)=Delayline(i+1)*frac^3/6
   %....+Delayline(i)*((1+frac)^3-4*frac^3)/6
   %....+Delayline(i-1)*((2-frac)^3-4*(1-frac)^3)/6
   %....+Delayline(i-2)*(1-frac)^3/6;
   %3rd-order Spline Interpolation
end
```

2.6.2   Flanger, chorus, slapback, echo

A few popular effects can be realized using the comb filter. They have special names because of the peculiar sound effects that they produce. Consider the FIR comb filter. If the delay is in the range 10 to 25 ms, we will hear a quick repetition named *slapback* or *doubling*. If the delay is greater than 50 ms we will hear an *echo*. If the time delay is short (less than 15 ms) and if this delay time is continuously varied with a low frequency such as 1 Hz, we will hear the *flanging* effect. "The flanging effect can be commonly observed outdoors, when a jet flies overhead, and the direct sound is summed in the ear of the observer with the sound reflected from the ground, resulting in the cancellation of certain frequencies and producing the comb filter effect, commonly referred to as 'jet sound'" [Bod84]. The name "flanging" derives from alternatively braking two turntables or tape machines playing the same recording by slightly pressing a finger on their respective flange. The audio effect becomes audible by summation of the outputs of both playback devices. If several copies of the input signal are delayed in the range 10 to 25 ms with small and random variations in the delay times, we will hear the *chorus* effect, which is a combination of the vibrato effect with the direct signal (see Table 2.8 and Figure 2.33) [Orf96, And95, Dat97b]. The chorus effect can be interpreted as a simulation of several musicians playing the same tones, but affected by slight time and pitch variations. These effects can also be implemented as IIR comb filters. The feedback will then enhance the effect and produce repeated slapbacks or echoes.

Normalization. To avoid clipping of the output signal, it is important to compensate for the intrinsic gain of the filter structure. Whereas in practice the FIR comb filter does not amplify the signal by more than 6 dB, the IIR comb filter can yield a very large amplification when $|g|$ comes

Table 2.8 Typical delay-based effects.

Delay range (ms) (Typ.)	Modulation (Typ.)	Effect name
0 ... 20	–	Resonator
0 ... 15	Sinusoidal	Flanging
10 ... 25	Random	Chorus
25 ... 50	–	Slapback
> 50	–	Echo

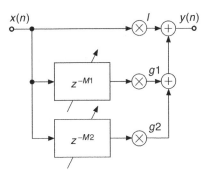

Figure 2.33 Chorus.

close to 1. The L_2 and L_∞ norms are given by

$$L_2 = 1/\sqrt{1 - g^2} \quad L_\infty = 1/(1 - |g|). \tag{2.67}$$

The normalization coefficient $c = 1/L_\infty$, when applied, ensures that no overload will occur with, for example, periodical input signals. $c = 1/L_2$ ensures that the loudness will remain approximatively constant for broadband signals.

A standard effect structure was proposed by Dattorro [Dat97b] and is shown in Figure 2.34. It is based on the allpass filter modification towards a general allpass comb, where the fixed delay line is replaced by a variable-length delay line. Dattorro [Dat97b] proposed keeping the feedback tap of the delay line fixed, that means the input signal to the delay line $x_h(n)$ is delayed by a fixed integer delay K and with this $x_h(n - K)$ is weighted and fed back. The delay K is the center tab delay of the variable-length delay line for the feed forward path. The control signal MOD(n) for changing the length of the delay line can either be a sinusoid or lowpass noise. Typical settings of the parameters are given in Table 2.9.

Table 2.9 Industry standard audio effects. [Dis99]

	BL	FF	FB	DELAY	DEPTH	MOD
Vibrato	0	1	0	0 ms	0–3 ms	0.1–5 Hz sine
Flanger	0.7	0.7	0.7	0 ms	0–2 ms	0.1–1 Hz sine
(White) Chorus	0.7	1	(−0.7)	1–30 ms	1–30 ms	Lowpass noise
Doubling	0.7	0.7	0	10–100 ms	1–100 ms	Lowpass noise

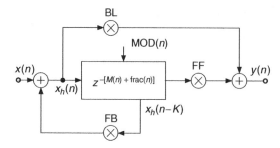

Figure 2.34   Standard effects with variable-length delay line.

2.6.3   Multiband effects

New interesting sounds can be achieved after splitting the signal into several frequency bands, for example, lowpass, bandpass and highpass signals, as shown in Figure 2.35.

Variable-length delays are applied to these signals with individual parameter settings and the output signals are weighted and summed to the broadband signal [FC98, Dis99]. Efficient frequency-splitting schemes are available from loudspeaker crossover designs and can be applied for this purpose directly. One of these techniques uses complementary filtering [Fli94, Orf96], which consists of lowpass filtering and subtracting the lowpass signal from the broadband signal to derive the highpass signal, as shown in Figure 2.36. The lowpass signal is then further processed by a following stage of the same complementary technique to deliver the bandpass and lowpass signals.

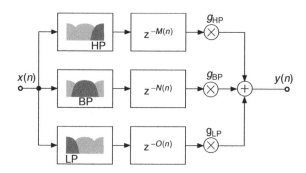

Figure 2.35   Multiband effects.

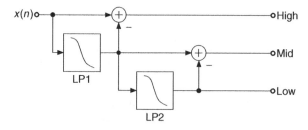

Figure 2.36   Filter bank for multiband effects.

2.6.4   Natural sounding comb filter

We have made the comparison between acoustical cylinders and IIR comb filters. This comparison might seem inappropriate because the comb filters sound *metallic*. They tend to amplify greatly the high-frequency components and they appear to resonate much too long compared to the acoustical cylinder. To find an explanation, let us consider the boundaries of the cylinder. They reflect the acoustic waves with an amplitude that decreases with frequency. If the comb filter should sound like an acoustical cylinder, then it should also have a frequency-dependent feedback coefficient $g(f)$. This frequency dependence can be realized by using a first-order lowpass filter in the feedback loop (see Figure 2.37) [Moo85].

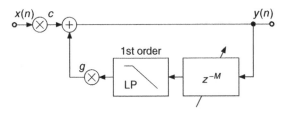

Figure 2.37   Lowpass IIR comb filter.

These filters sound more *natural* than the plain IIR comb filters. They find application in room simulators. Further refinements such as fractional delays and compensation of the frequency-dependent group delay within the lowpass filter make them suitable for the imitation of acoustical resonators. They have been used, for example, to impose a definite pitch onto broadband signals such as sea waves or to detune fixed-pitched instruments such as a Celtic harp [m-Ris92]. M-file 2.9 shows the implementation for a sample-by-sample based lowpass IIR comb filter.

M-file 2.9 (lpiircomb.m)

```
% Authors: P.Dutilleux, U. Zölzer
x=zeros(100,1);x(1)=1; % unit impulse signal of length 100
g=0.5;
b_0=0.5;
b_1=0.5;
a_1=0.7;
xhold=0;yhold=0;
Delayline=zeros(10,1); % memory allocation for length 10
for n=1:length(x);
    yh(n)=b_0*Delayline(10)+b_1*xhold-a_1*yhold;
    % 1st-order difference equation
    yhold=yh(n);
    xhhold=Delayline(10);
    y(n)=x(n)+g*yh(n);
    Delayline=[y(n);Delayline(1:10-1)];
end;
```

2.7   Conclusion

Filtering is still one of the most commonly used effect tools for sound recording and production. Nevertheless, its successful application is heavily dependent on the specialized skills of the operator. In this chapter we have described basic filter algorithms for time-domain audio processing.

These algorithms perform the filtering operations by the computation of difference equations. The coefficients for the difference equations are given for several filter functions such as lowpass, highpass, bandpass, shelving and peak filters. Simple design formulas for various equalizers lead to efficient implementations for time-varying filter applications.

Delays are used in audio processing to solve several practical problems, for example delay compensation for sound reinforcement systems, and as basic building blocks for delay-based audio effects, artificial reverberation and physical models for instrument simulation. The variety of applications of delays to *spatial effects* will be presented in Chapter 5.

This brief introduction has described some of the basic delay structures, which should enable the reader to implement and experiment with delay algorithms on their own. We have further pointed out that a comb-filter effect emerges if a delayed copy of the signal is mixed with the nondelayed signal. Thus we established an intuitive link between delays and filters, which is especially helpful in understanding their time-varying application. We have focused on a small set of important delay-based effects such as echo, vibrato, flanger and chorus and introduced the principle of multiband effects. These basic building blocks may serve as a source of ideas for designing new digital audio effects.

Sound and music

[m-Vag96] H. Vaggione: MYR-S, *Composition for cello, electroacoustic set-up and tape*. Festival Synthèse, Bourges 1996.
[m-Vas93] P. Vasseur: Purple Frame, in *Le sens caché 100 mystères*, CD. Free Way Musique, No. 869193, 1993.
[m-Ris92] J.-C. Risset: *Lurai, pour harpe celtique et bande*. Radio France, 21.3. 1992.

References

[And95] C. Anderton. *Multieffects for Musicians*. Amsco Publications, 1995.
[Bod84] H. Bode. History of electronic sound modification. *J. Audio Eng. Soc.*, 32(10): 730–739, October 1984.
[Bri94] R. Bristow. The equivalence of various methods of computing biquad coefficients for audio parametric equalizers. In *Proc. 97th AES Convention*, Preprint 3906, San Francisico, 1994.
[Cha80] H. Chamberlin. *Musical Applications of Microprocessors*. Hayden Book Company, 1980.
[Dat97a] J. Dattoro. Effect design, part 1: Reverberator and other filters. *J. Audio Eng. Soc.*, 45(9): 660–684, September 1997.
[Dat97b] J. Dattoro. Effect design, part 2: Delay-line modulation and chorus. *J. Audio Eng. Soc.*, 45(10): 764–788, October 1997.
[Die00] S. Diedrichsen. Personal communication. emagic GmbH, 2000.
[Dis99] S. Disch. *Digital audio effects – modulation and delay lines*. Master's thesis, Technical University Hamburg-Harburg, 1999.
[DMT99] P. Dutilleux and C. Müller-Tomfelde. AML|Architecture and Music Laboratory, a museum installation. In *Proc. of the 16th AES Int. Conf. on Spatial Sound Reprod. Rovaniemi, Finland. Audio Engineering Society*, pp. 191–206, April 10–12 1999.
[Dut89a] P. Dutilleux. Simple to operate digital time-varying filters. In *Proc. 86th AES Convention*, Preprint 2757, Hamburg, March 1989.
[Dut89b] P. Dutilleux. Spinning the sounds in real-time. In *Proc. Int. Comp. Music Conf.*, pp. 94–97, Columbus November, 1989.
[Dut91] P. Dutilleux. *Vers la machine à sculpter le son, modification en temps réel des caractéristiques fréquentielles et temporelles des sons*. PhD thesis, University of Aix-Marseille II, 1991.
[FC98] P. Fernández-Cid and F.J. Casajús-Quirós. Enhanced quality and variety of chorus/flange units. In *Proc. DAFX-98 Digital Audio Effects Workshop*, pp. 35–39, Barcelona, November 1998.
[Fli94] N.J. Fliege. *Multirate Digital Signal Processing*. John Wiley & Sons, Ltd, 1994.
[Gar95] W.G. Gardner. Efficient convolution without input-output delay. *J. Audio Eng. Soc.*, 43(3): 127–136, March 1995.

[HB93]   F. Harris and E. Brooking. A versatile parametric filter using an imbeded all-pass sub-filter to independently adjust bandwidth, center frequency, and boost or cut. In *95th AES Conv.*, Preprint 3757, New York, 1993.

[HZ06]   M. Holters and U. Zölzer. Parametric higher-order shelving filters. In *Proc. of 14th Eur. Signal Proces. Conf. (EUSIPCO)*, Florence, Italy, September 2006.

[KZ04]   F. Keiler and U. Zölzer. Parametric second- and fourth-order shelving filters for audio applications. In *Proc. of IEEE 6th Workshop on Multimedia Signal Proces.*, pp. 231–234, Siena, Italy, September 2004.

[LVKL96] T.I. Laakso, V. Välimäki, M. Karjalainen and U.K. Laine. Splitting the unit delay. *IEEE Signal Proces. Mag.*, 13: 30–60, 1996.

[Mai97]   M. Maiguashca. *Reading Castañeda. Booklet*. Wergo2053-2, zkm 3rd edition, 1997.

[McG93]   D.S. McGrath. An efficient 30-band graphic equalizer implementation for a low cost dsp processor. In *Proc. 95th AES Conv.*, Preprint 3756, New York, 1993.

[Moo85]   J.A. Moorer. About this reverberation business. In *Foundations of Computer Music*, pp. 605–639. MIT Press, 1985.

[MT99]   C. Müller-Tomfelde. Low-latency convolution for real-time applications. In *Proc. of the 16th AES Int. Conf. on Spatial Sound Reprod., Rovaniemi, Finland*, pp. 454–460. Audio Engineering Society, April 10–12 1999.

[Orf96]   S.J. Orfanidis. *Introduction to Signal Processing*. Prentice-Hall, 1996.

[Orf97]   S.J. Orfanidis. Digital parametric equalizer design with prescribed nyquist-frequency gain. *J. Audio Eng. Soc.*, 45(6): 444–455, June 1997.

[Orf05]   S.J. Orfanidis. Higher-order digital parametric equalizer design. *J. Audio Eng. Soc.*, 53(11): 1026–1046, November 2005.

[RM87]   P.A. Regalia and S.K. Mitra. Tunable digital frequency response equalization filters. *IEEE Trans. Acoustics, Speech and Signal Proces.*, 35(1): 118–120, January 1987.

[Roa97]   C. Roads. Sound transformation by convolution. In C. Roads, St. Pope, A. Piccialli, and G. De Poli (eds), *Musical Signal Processing*, pp. 411–438. Swets & Zeitlinger Publishers, 1997.

[Roc98]   D. Rochesso. Fractionally-adressed delay lines. In *Proc. DAFX-98 Digital Audio Effects Workshop*, pp. 40–43, Barcelona, November 1998.

[Roc00]   D. Rochesso. Fractionally addressed delay lines. *IEEE Trans. on Speech and Audio Process.*, 8(6): 717–727, November 2000.

[Smi84]   J.O. Smith. An all-pass approach to digital phasing and flanging. In *Proc. International Computer Music Conference*, pp. 103–109, 1984.

[Str83]   A. Strange. *Electronic Music, Systems, Techniques and Controls*. W. C. Brown, 1983.

[Vag98]   H. Vaggione. Transformations morphologiques: quelques exemples. In *Proc. of JIM98, CNRS-LMA*, pp. G1.1–G1.10, Marseille 1998.

[Whi86]   S.A. White. Design of a digital biquadratic peaking or notch filter for digital audio equalization. *J. Audio Eng. Soc.*, 34(6): 479–482, June 1986.

[Whi93]   P. White. *L'enregistrement créatif, Effets et processeurs, Tomes 1 et 2*. Les cahiers de l'ACME, 1993.

[Zöl05]   U. Zölzer. *Digital Audio Signal Processing*. John Wiley & Sons, Ltd, 2nd edition, 2005.

3

Modulators and demodulators

P. Dutilleux, M. Holters, S. Disch and U. Zölzer

3.1 Introduction

The word *modulate* means to impress a modulator signal on a carrier signal. This can be accomplished by modifying the amplitude and/or the phase of the carrier signal by means of the modulator. The typical application domain of modulators are communication systems, where a low-frequency information-bearing signal modulates a radio-frequency carrier to obtain a signal with a frequency range suitable for transmission.

Numerous techniques have been designed to achieve this goal, some of which have found applications in digital audio effects. An interesting historical review of such audio effects can be found in [Bod84]. In the field of audio processing, these modulation techniques are mainly used with modulators having variations of very low frequency (up to 20 Hz), so that these variations are perceived as temporal fluctuations rather than a continuous sound, while the carrier is situated in the audible frequency region.

To gain a deeper understanding of the possibilities of modulation techniques, we will first introduce simple schemes for amplitude modulation, single-side-band modulation and phase modulation and point out their use for audio effects. We will then describe several demodulators, which extract parameters of the incoming signal for further effects processing. The combination of these techniques will lead to more advanced digital audio effects, which will be demonstrated by several examples.

3.2 Modulators

3.2.1 Ring modulator

In the *ring modulation* (RM), the audio signal $x(n)$ is multiplied by a sinusoid $m(n)$ with carrier frequency f_c, as in Figure 3.1. While difficult in the analog domain, the multiplication is straightforward to realize in the digital domain [Ste87]. The input signal is called the modulator $x(n)$ and

DAFX: Digital Audio Effects, Second Edition. Edited by Udo Zölzer.
© 2011 John Wiley & Sons, Ltd. Published 2011 by John Wiley & Sons, Ltd.

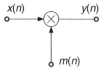

Figure 3.1   Ring modulation of a signal $x(n)$ by a sinusoidal carrier signal $m(n)$.

the second operand is called the carrier $m(n)$, giving the output signal

$$y(n) = x(n) \cdot m(n). \tag{3.1}$$

If $m(n)$ is a sine wave of frequency f_c, the spectrum of the output $y(n)$ is made up of two copies of the input spectrum: the lower side band (LSB) and the upper side band (USB). The LSB is reversed in frequency and both side band are centered around f_c (see Figure 3.2). Depending on the width of the spectrum of $x(n)$ and on the carrier frequency, the side bands can be partly mirrored around the origin of the frequency axis. If the carrier signal comprises several spectral components, the same effect happens with each component. Although the audible result of a ring modulation is fairly easy to comprehend for elementary signals, it gets very complicated with signals having numerous partials. The carrier itself is not audible in this kind of modulation. When carrier and modulator are sine waves of frequencies f_c and f_x, one hears the sum and the difference frequencies $f_c + f_x$ and $f_c - f_x$ [Hal95].

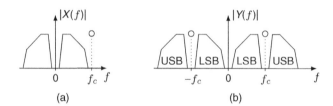

Figure 3.2   Ring modulation of a signal $x(n)$ by a sinusoidal carrier signal $m(n)$. The spectrum of the modulator $x(n)$ (a) is shifted to the carrier frequency (b).

When the input signal is periodic with fundamental frequency f_0, a sinusoidal carrier of frequency f_c produces a spectrum with amplitude lines at the frequencies $|kf_0 \pm f_c|$ [DP00]. A musical application of this effect is applied in the piece "Ofanim" by Luciano Berio. The first section is dominated by a duet between a child voice and a clarinet. The transformation of the child voice into a clarinet is desired. For this purpose a pitch detector computes the instantaneous frequency $f_0(n)$ of the voice. Then the child voice passes through a ring modulator, where the frequency of the carrier f_c is set to $f_0(n)/2$. This emphasizes odd harmonics, which is similar to the sound of a clarinet in the low register [Vid91].

3.2.2   Amplitude modulator

The *amplitude modulation* (AM) was easier to realize with analog electronic means than the ring modulation and has therefore been in use for a much longer time. It can be implemented by

$$y(n) = [1 + \alpha m(n)] \cdot x(n) \tag{3.2}$$

where it is assumed that the peak amplitude of $m(n)$ is 1. The coefficient α determines the modulation depth. The modulation effect is maximum when $\alpha = 1$ and the effect is disengaged

Carrier
(audio)

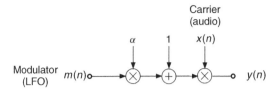

Figure 3.3 Typical application of AM.

when $\alpha = 0$. A typical application is with an audio signal as carrier $x(n)$ and a *low-frequency oscillator* (LFO) as modulator $m(n)$ (see Figure 3.3). The amplitude of the audio signal varies according to the instantaneous amplitude value of the LFO.

When the modulator is an audible signal and the carrier a sine wave of frequency f_c, the spectrum of the output $y(t)$ is similar to that of the ring modulator except that the carrier frequency can be also heard. When carrier and modulator are sine waves of frequencies f_c and f_x, one hears three components: carrier, difference and sum frequencies $(f_c - f_x, f_c, f_c + f_x)$. The effect is perceived in a different manner depending on the frequency range of the signals. A modulation with frequencies below 20 Hz will be heard in the time domain (variation of the amplitude, *tremolo* in Figure 3.4), whereas modulations by medium frequencies (20–70 Hz) introduce auditory roughness into the signal. Modulations by high frequencies will be heard as distinct spectral components (LSB, carrier, USB).

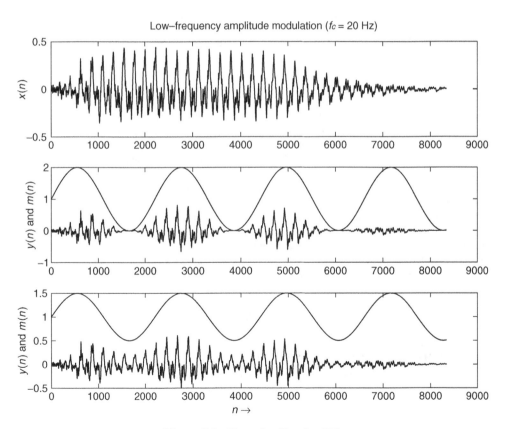

Figure 3.4 Tremolo effect by AM.

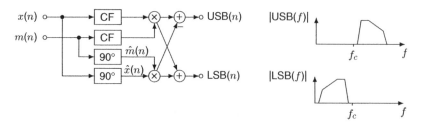

Figure 3.5   Single-side-band modulator with compensation filter CF and Hilbert filter (90° block).

3.2.3   Single-side-band modulator

The upper and lower side bands of RM and AM carry the same information, although organized differently. In order to save bandwidth and transmitter power, radio-communication engineers have designed the single-side band (SSB) modulation scheme (Figure 3.5). Either the LSB or the USB is transmitted. Phase shifted versions by 90° of the modulating audio signal $x(n)$ are denoted by $\hat{x}(n)$ and of the carrier signal $m(n)$ by $\hat{m}(n)$, and are produced by Hilbert transform filters [Orf96]. The upper and lower side-band signals can be computed as follows:

$$USB(n) = x(n)m(n) - \hat{x}(n)\hat{m}(n) \tag{3.3}$$

$$LSB(n) = x(n)m(n) + \hat{x}(n)\hat{m}(n). \tag{3.4}$$

A discrete-time Hilbert transform can be approximated by a FIR filter with the impulse response

$$a(n) = \frac{1 - \cos(\pi n)}{\pi n} = \begin{cases} 2/(\pi n) & \text{for } n \text{ odd} \\ 0 & \text{for } n \text{ even.} \end{cases} \tag{3.5}$$

After truncation to the desired length N, these coefficients are multiplied with a suitable window function, for example a Hamming window, and shifted right by $\frac{N-1}{2}$ to make the filter causal. Note that the use of the FIR Hilbert filter requires a delay in the direct path for the audio and the carrier signal. Figure 3.6 shows an example with the compensation delay of 30 samples and a FIR Hilbert filter of length $N = 61$. This effect is typically used with a sine wave as carrier of frequency f_c. The use of a complex oscillator for $m(n)$ simplifies the implementation. By using positive or negative frequencies it is then possible to select the USB or the LSB. The spectrum of $x(n)$ is frequency-shifted up or down according to f_c. The results are detune effects and non-harmonic sounds: a piano tone may sound like a bell after processing or a plucked-string sound is heard like a drum sound. The modification in perceived pitch is much less than expected, probably because our ear recovers pitch height and salience information also from cues other than the absolute frequency of the lowest partial ("fundamental") present in the actual tone [Dut91], the most prominent of which being the frequency difference between the different partials ("overtones"). These effects are explained and modeled by, for example, the theory of "virtual pitch" [TSS82a, TSS82b]. A review of legacy frequency-shifters can be found in [Bod84].

3.2.4   Frequency and phase modulator

The *frequency modulation* (FM) is widely used for broadcasting and has found interesting applications for sound synthesis [Roa96]. The continuous-time description of an angle-modulated carrier signal is given by

$$x_{PM/FM}(t) = A_c \cos[2\pi f_c t + \phi(t)], \tag{3.6}$$

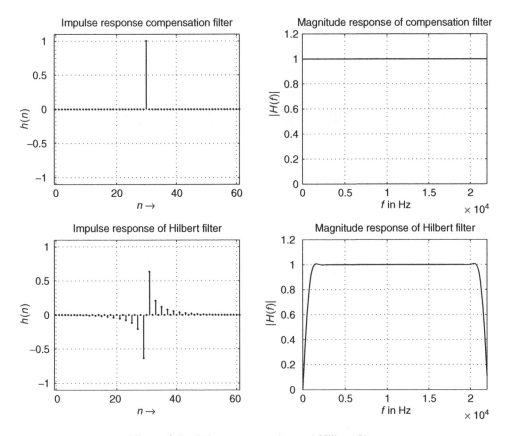

Figure 3.6   Delay compensation and Hilbert filter.

where A_c is the amplitude of the signal and the argument of the cosine is given by the carrier frequency f_c and the modulating signal $m(t)$ according to

$$\phi_{PM}(t) = k_{PM} \cdot m(t) \tag{3.7}$$

$$\phi_{FM}(t) = 2\pi \cdot k_{FM} \cdot \int_{-\infty}^{t} m(\tau)\mathrm{d}\tau. \tag{3.8}$$

For phase modulation (PM) the phase $\phi(t)$ is directly proportional to the modulating signal $m(t)$, while for frequency modulation the phase $\phi(t)$ is the integral of the modulating signal $m(t)$. Some examples of frequency and phase modulation are shown in Figure 3.7. In the first example the modulating signal is a sinusoid which shows that the resulting FM and PM signals are the same except for a time shift in the modulation characteristic. The second example in (c) and (d) depicts the difference between FM and PM, where the modulating signal is now a bipolar pulse signal. The last example in (e) and (f) depicts the result of a ramp type signal. The main idea behind using these techniques is the control of the carrier frequency by a modulating signal $m(n)$.

Applying phase modulation to audio signals for audio effects is different from the previous discussion, where a modulating signal $m(n)$ is used to modify the phase $\phi(t)$ of a cosine of fixed carrier frequency f_c. By contrast, for audio effects the phase of the audio signal $x(n)$ is modified by a control parameter or modulating signal $m(n)$. The phase modulator system can be described by a time-variant impulse response $h(n)$ and leads to a phase modulated output signal $x_{PM}(n)$

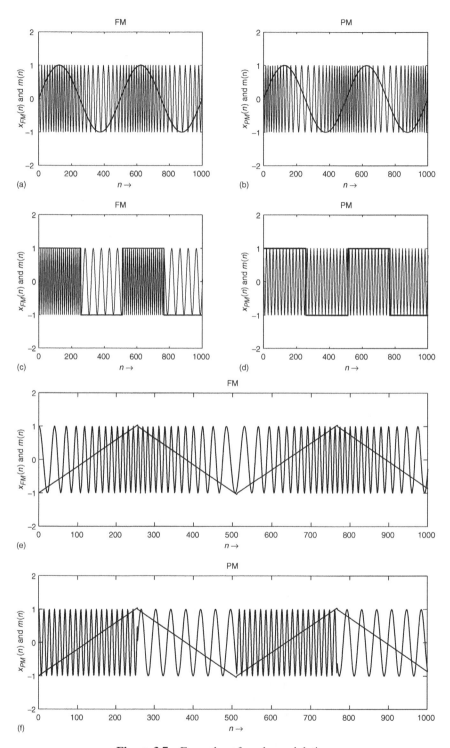

Figure 3.7   Examples of angle modulation.

according to

$$h(n) = \delta[n - m(n)] \tag{3.9}$$

$$y(n) = x_{PM}(n) = x(n) * h(n) = x(n) * \delta[n - m(n)]. \tag{3.10}$$

The result for phase modulation (PM) of the signal $x(n)$ can then be written as

$$y(n) = x_{PM}(n) = x(n - m(n)) \tag{3.11}$$

where $m(n)$ is a continuous variable, which changes every discrete time instant n. Therefore $m(n)$ is decomposed into an integer and a fractional part [Dat97]. The integer part is implemented by a series of M unit delays, the fractional part is approximated by interpolation filters, e.g., linear, Lagrange, allpass [Dat97, LVKL96, Zöl05] or spline filters [Dis99] (see Figure 3.8 and Section 2.5.4). The discrete-time Fourier transform of (3.11) yields

$$Y(e^{j\Omega}) = X_{PM}(e^{j\Omega}) = X(e^{j\Omega})e^{-j\Omega m(n)}, \tag{3.12}$$

which expresses the phase modulation of the input signal by a time-variant delay $m(n)$.

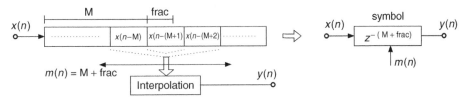

Figure 3.8 Phase modulation by delay-line modulation.

For sine-type modulation, useful for vibrato effects, the modulation signal can be written as

$$m(n) = M + \text{DEPTH} \cdot \sin(\omega_M n T). \tag{3.13}$$

For a sinusoidal input signal the so-called resampling factor for sine-type modulation can be derived as

$$\alpha(n) = \frac{f_I}{f} = 1 - \text{DEPTH} \cdot \omega_M T \cos(\omega_M n T). \tag{3.14}$$

The instantaneous frequency is denoted by f_I and the frequency of the input sinusoid is denoted by f. The resampling factor is regarded as the pitch-change ratio in [Dat97]. For sine-type modulation the mean value of the resampling factor $\alpha(n)$ is one. The consequence is an output signal which has the same length as the input signal, but exhibits a pitch variation centered around the original pitch, implementing a *vibrato* effect.

For ramp-type modulation according to

$$m(n) = M \pm \text{SLOPE} \cdot n, \tag{3.15}$$

the resampling factor $\alpha(n)$ for the sinusoidal input signal is given by

$$\alpha(n) = \frac{f_I}{f} = 1 \mp \text{SLOPE}. \tag{3.16}$$

The output signal is pitch transposed by a factor α and the length of the output data is altered by the factor $1/\alpha$. This behavior is useful for pitch-transposing applications, as will be detailed in Section 6.4.3.

3.3   Demodulators

Each modulation has a suitable demodulation scheme and we will focus on the ring and amplitude modulations in this section. The demodulator for the ring modulator uses exactly the same scheme as the modulator, so no new effect is to be expected there. The demodulator for the amplitude modulator is called an amplitude follower in the realm of digital audio effects. Several implementation schemes are available, some are inspired from analog designs, some are much easier to realize using digital techniques. These demodulators comprise three parts: a detector, an averager and a scaler.

3.3.1   Detectors

The detector can be a half-wave rectifier $d_h(t)$, a full-wave rectifier $d_f(t)$, a squarer $d_r(t)$ or an instantaneous envelope detector $d_i^2(t)$. The first two detectors are directly inspired by analog designs. They are still useful to achieve effects having typical analog behavior. The third and fourth types are much easier to realize in the digital domain (Figure 3.9). The four detectors are computed by

$$d_h(n) = \max[0, x(n)] \qquad d_f(n) = |x(n)|$$
$$d_r(n) = x^2(n) \qquad d_i^2(n) = x^2(n) + \hat{x}^2(n), \qquad (3.17)$$

respectively, where $x(n)$ denotes the input signal and $\hat{x}(n)$ its Hilbert transform.

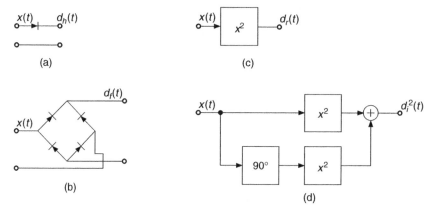

Figure 3.9   Detectors: (a) half-wave, (b) full-wave, (c) squarer, (d) instantaneous envelope.

3.3.2   Averagers

In the analog domain, the averager is realized with a resistor-capacitor (RC) network and in the digital domain using a first-order lowpass filter. Both structures are characterized by a time constant τ. The filter is implemented as:

$$y(n) = (1 - g)d(n) + gy(n - 1) \quad \text{with } g = \exp[-1/(f_s \tau)], \qquad (3.18)$$

where $d(n)$ denotes the detector output. The time constant τ must be chosen in accordance with the application. A short time constant is suitable when fast variations of the input signal must be followed. A larger time constant is better to measure the long-term amplitude of the input signal.

For many applications, however, this averager is not suitable. It is often necessary to follow short attacks of the input signal. This calls for a very small time constant, 5 ms typically. The output of the averager will then react very fast to any amplitude variation, even to the intrinsic variations within a period of a low-frequency signal. We understand that we need an averager with two time constants: an attack time constant τ_a and a release time constant τ_r. To distinguish it from the basic averager, we will call this one the *AR-averager*. McNally has proposed an implementation having two fixed coefficients [McN84, Zöl05] and Jean-Marc Jot has an alternative where a single coefficient is varied according to the relationship between the input and the output of the averager (Figure 3.10):

$$g_a = \exp[-1/(f_s\tau_a)]$$

$$g_r = \exp[-1/(f_s\tau_r)]$$

$$g = \begin{cases} g_a & \text{if } y_{ar}(n-1) < d(n) \\ g_r & \text{else} \end{cases}$$

$$y_{ar}(n) = (1-g)d(n) + gy_{ar}(n-1), \tag{3.19}$$

where $d(n)$ again denotes the detector output.

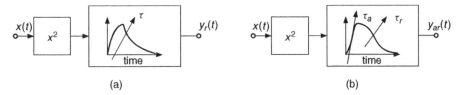

(a)   (b)

Figure 3.10   RMS (root mean square) detectors. (a) single time constant; (b) attack and release time constants.

3.3.3   Amplitude scalers

The systems described above lead to slightly different outputs. In order to get measures that are comparable with each other, it would be necessary to scale the outputs. Although scaling schemes are typically defined for sine waves, each type of signal would require a different scaling scheme. To build a RMS detector or an instantaneous envelope detector, furthermore a root extractor would be necessary, a computationally intensive operation. Fortunately, it is often possible to avoid the root extraction by modifying the circuit that makes use of the averager output, so that it works fine with squared measures. For these practical reasons the scaling is taken into account most of the time within the device that follows the averager output.

3.3.4   Typical applications

Well-known devices or typical applications relate to the previous schemes as follows:

- The AM-detector comprises the half-wave rectifier and the basic averager.

- The volume meter (VU-meter) is an AM-detector. It measures the average amplitude of the audio signal.

- The peak-program-meter (PPM) is, according to DIN45406, a full-wave rectifier followed by an AR-averager with 10 ms attack time and 1500 ms release time.

- The RMS detector, as found in electronic voltmeters, uses the squarer and the basic averager.

- A sound-level-meter uses a RMS detector along with an AR-averager to measure impulsive signals.

- The RMS detector associated with an AR-averager is the best choice for amplitude follower applications in vocoders, computer music and live electronics [Dut98b, m-Fur93].

- Dynamics processors (see Section 4.2) use various types of the above-mentioned schemes in relation to the effect and to the quality that has to be achieved.

- The instantaneous envelope detector, without averager, is useful to follow the amplitude of a signal with the finest resolution. The output contains typically audio band signals. A particular application of the $d_i^2(t)$ detector is the amplification of difference tones [Dut96, m-MBa95].

- Otherwise static audio effects can be made more natural and lively by controlling certain parameters by characteristics of the input signal. One of these characteristics is the temporal envelope, which is, for example, used in the auto-wah or touch-wah effects, where the center frequency of a peak filter is controlled by the envelope of the input signal, see Section 2.4.1.

3.4   Applications

Several applications of modulation techniques for audio effects are presented in the literature [Dut98a, War98, Dis99]. We will now summarize some of these effects.

3.4.1   Vibrato

The cyclic variation of the pitch of the input signal is the basic application of the phase modulator described in the previous section. A detailed description can be found in Section 2.6.1.

3.4.2   Stereo phaser

The application of a SSB modulator for a stereo phaser is described in [War98]. Figure 3.11 shows a SSB modulator performed by a recursive allpass implementation of a Hilbert filter. The phase difference of $90°$ is achieved through specially designed allpass filters.

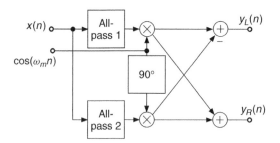

Figure 3.11   Stereo phaser based on SSB modulation [War98].

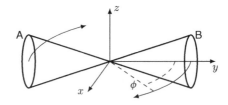

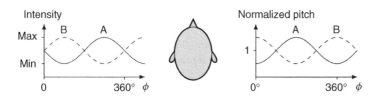

Figure 3.12   Rotary loudspeaker [DZ99].

3.4.3   Rotary loudspeaker effect

Introduction

The rotary loudspeaker effect was first used for the electronic reproduction of organ instruments. Figure 3.12 shows the configuration of a rotating bi-directional loudspeaker horn in front of a listener. The sound in the listener's ears is altered by the Doppler effect, the directional characteristic of the speakers and phase effects due to air turbulence. The Doppler effect raises and lowers the pitch according to the rotation speed. The directional characteristic of the opposite horn arrangement performs an intensity variation in the listener's ears. Both the pitch modification and the intensity variation are performed by speaker A and in the opposite direction by speaker B.

Signal processing

A combination of modulation and delay line modulation can be used for a rotary loudspeaker effect simulation [DZ99], as shown in Figure 3.13. The simulation makes use of a modulated delay line

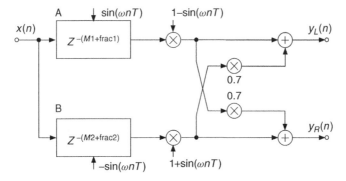

Figure 3.13   Rotary loudspeaker simulation [DZ99].

for pitch modifications and amplitude modulation for intensity modifications. The simulation of the Doppler effect of two opposite horns is done by the use of two delay lines modulated with 180° phase shifted signals in vibrato configuration (see Figure 3.13). A directional sound characteristic similar to rotating speakers can be achieved by amplitude modulating the output signal of the delay lines. The modulation is synchronous to the delay modulation in a manner that the back-moving horn has lower pitch and decreasing amplitude. At the return point the pitch is unaltered and the amplitude is minimum. The movement in direction to the listener causes a raised pitch and increasing amplitude. A stereo rotary speaker effect is perceived due to unequal mixing of the two delay lines to the left and right channel output.

Musical applications

By imprinting amplitude and pitch modulations as well as some spatialization, this effect makes the sounds more lively. At lower rotation speeds it is reminiscent of the echoes in a cathedral, whereas at higher rotation speeds it gets a ring-modulation flavor. This effect is known as "Leslie" from the name of Donald E. Leslie, who invented it in the early forties. It was licensed to electronic organ manufacturers such as Baldwin, Hammond or Wurlitzer, but it has also found applications for other musical instruments such as the guitar or even the voice ("Blue Jay Way" on the Beatles LP "Magical Mystery Tour" [Sch94].) A demonstration of a Leslie simulator can be heard on [m-Pie99]. This effect can also be interpreted as a rotating microphone between two loudspeakers. You may also imagine that you are sitting on a merry-go-round and you pass by two loudspeakers.

3.4.4   SSB effects

Single-side-band modulation can be used for detuning of percussion instruments or voices. The harmonic frequency relations are modified by using this technique. Another application is time-variant filtering: first use SSB modulation to shift the input spectrum, apply filtering or phase modulation and then perform the demodulation of the signal, as shown in Figure 3.14 [Dis99, DZ99]. The frequency shift of the input signal is achieved by a low-frequency sinusoid. Arbitrary filters can be used in-between modulation and demodulation.

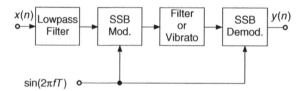

Figure 3.14   SSB modulation-filtering-demodulation: if a vibrato is performed instead of the filter a mechanical vibrato bar simulation is achieved.

The simulation of the mechanical vibrato bar of an electric guitar can be achieved by applying a vibrato instead of a filter [DZ99]. Such a vibrato bar alters the pitch of the lower strings of the guitar in larger amounts than the higher strings and thus a non-harmonic vibrato results. The SSB approach can also be used for the construction of modified flangers. Further applications of SSB modulation techniques for audio effects are presented in [Dut98a, War98].

3.4.5   Simple morphing: amplitude following

In the context of audio effects, "morphing" means to impose a feature of one sound onto another. The amplitude envelope and the spectrum, as well as the time structure are features that can be morphed. Morphing the amplitude envelope can be achieved by the amplitude follower, whereas morphing a spectrum or a time structure can be achieved by the use of convolution (see Section 2.2.7).

Introduction

Envelope following is one of various methods developed to breathe more life into synthetic sounds. The amplitude envelope of a control signal, usually coming from a real acoustical source, is measured and used to control the amplitude of the synthetic sounds. For example, the amplitude envelope of speech can be used to control the amplitude of broadband noise. Through this process the noise seems to have been articulated like voice. A refinement of this method has led to the development of the vocoder, where the same process is applied in each of the frequency bands into which the voice as well as the noise are divided.

Signal processing

The input signal is multiplied with the output of the envelope generator for the controlling signal. When an accurate measurement is desired, a RMS detector should be used. However, signals from acoustic instruments usually have fairly limited amplitude variations and their loudness variations are more dependent on spectrum modifications than on amplitude modifications. If the loudness of the output signal has to be similar to that of the controlling signal, then an expansion of the dynamic of the controlling signal should be performed. An effective way to expand the dynamic by a factor of 2 is to eliminate the root extraction from the scaler and use a much simpler MS (mean square) detector.

Musical applications and control

In "Swim, swan," Kiyoshi Furukawa has extended the sound of a clarinet by additional synthetic sounds. In order to link these sounds intimately to the clarinet, their amplitude is controlled by that of the clarinet. In this case, the input sound is the synthetic sound and the controlling sound is the clarinet. The mixing of the synthetic sounds with the clarinet is done in the acoustic domain of the performance space [m-Fur93].

The amplitude variations of the controlling signal applied to the input signal produce an effect that is perceived in the time domain or in the frequency domain, according to the frequency content of the modulating signal. For sub-audio rates (below 20 Hz) the effect will appear in the time domain and we will call it "amplitude following," whereas for audio modulation rates (above 20 Hz), the effect will be perceived in the frequency domain and will be recognized as an amplitude modulation.

If the control signal has a large bandwidth, the spectrum of the amplitude will have to be reduced by the averager. Typical settings for the decay time constant of the averager are in the range of 30 to 100 ms. Such values will smooth out the amplitude signal so that it remains in the sub-audio range. However, it is often desired that the attacks that are present in the control signal, are morphed onto the input signal as attacks and are not smoothed out by the averager. This is why it is recommended to use a shorter attack time constant than the decay time constant. Typical values are in the range of 1 to 30 ms.

The amplitude variations of the input signal could be opposite to those of the controlling signal, hence reducing the impact of the effect, or be similar and provoke an expansion of the dynamic. In order to get amplitude variations at the output that are similar to those of the controlling signal, it is recommended to process the input signal through a compressor-limiter beforehand [Hal95, p. 40], leading to the system in Figure 3.15.

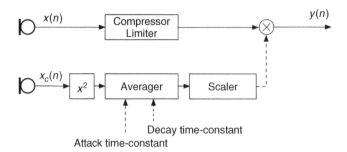

Figure 3.15   The amplitude of an input signal $x(n)$ is controlled by that of another signal $x_c(n)$. The amplitude of the input signal is leveled in a pre-processing step before modulation by the amplitude of the controlling signal is performed.

In his work "Diario polacco," Luigi Nono specifies how the singer should move away from her microphone in order to produce amplitude modifications that are used to control the amplitude of other sounds [(Hal95, p. 67–68)].

Applying an amplitude envelope can produce interesting modifications of the input signal. Take, for example, the sustained sound of a flute and apply iteratively a triangular amplitude envelope. By varying the slopes of the envelope and the iteration rate, the original sound can be affected by a tremolo or a *Flatterzunge* and evoke percussive instruments [Dut88]. Such sound transformations are reminiscent of those (anamorphoses) that the early electroacoustic composers were fond of [m-Sch98].

3.4.6   Modulation vocoder

Novel modulation based effects can be realized within a so-called modulation vocoder (MODVOC). A multi-band modulation decomposition [DE09b] dissects the audio signal into a signal adaptive set of analytic bandpass signals, each of which is further divided into a sinusoidal carrier and its amplitude modulation (AM) and frequency modulation (FM). A set of bandpass filters is computed such that on the one hand the full-band spectrum is covered seamlessly and on the other hand the filters are aligned with local *centers of gravity* (COGs). The local COG corresponds to the mean frequency that is perceived by a listener due to the spectral contributions in that frequency region and can be modeled by a sinusoidal carrier. Both AM and FM are captured in the amplitude envelope and the phase of the bandpass signals heterodyned by their respective carriers.

A block diagram of the signal decomposition is depicted in Figure 3.16. In the diagram, the schematic signal flow for the extraction of one of the multi-band components is shown. All other components are obtained in a similar fashion. First, a broadband input signal x is fed into a front-end bandpass filter that has been designed signal adaptively, yielding an output signal $\tilde{x}$. Next, the analytic signal is derived by the Hilbert transform according to Equation 3.20

$$\widehat{x}(t) = \tilde{x}(t) + j\mathcal{H}(\tilde{x}(t)). \tag{3.20}$$

The AM is given by the amplitude envelope of $\widehat{x}$

$$AM(t) = |\widehat{x}(t)|, \tag{3.21}$$

while the FM is the *instantaneous frequency* (IF) obtained by the phase derivative of the analytic signal heterodyned by a stationary sinusoidal carrier with the angular frequency ω_c of the local

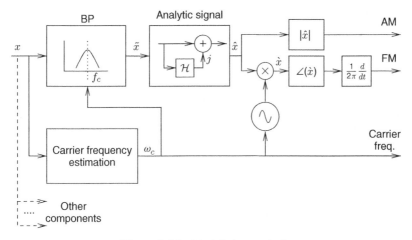

Figure 3.16 Modulation analysis.

COG. The FM can be interpreted as the IF variation of the carrier frequency f_c.

$$\grave{x}(t) = \widehat{x}(t) \cdot \exp(-j\omega_c t)$$

$$FM(t) = \frac{1}{2\pi} \cdot \frac{\mathrm{d}}{\mathrm{d}t} \angle (\grave{x}(t)) \tag{3.22}$$

The estimation of local COGs and the signal adaptive design of the front-end filterbank is one of the key parts of the modulation analysis [DE09a]. The MODVOC synthesis renders the output signal on an additive basis from all components. Each component is re-synthesized by modulating its carrier frequency by the associated AM and FM [DE09b].

A global *transposition* that alters the musical key of an audio signal can be obtained by a simple multiplication of all component carriers with a constant transposition factor. In contrast to other transposition techniques, the transposition of selected MODVOC components also becomes feasible due to the signal adaptive multi-band processing, enabling applications which alter the key mode (e.g., major to minor scale) [DE09b]. However, in the selective transposition there exists an inherent ambiguity with respect to the musical function of each component. Most instruments excite harmonic sounds consisting of a fundamental frequency and its overtones. Since musical intervals obey a logarithmic scale, each harmonic overtone resembles a different musical interval with respect to the fundamental. If the component originates from a fundamental it has to be transposed according to the desired scale mapping; if it is dominated by an overtone to be attributed to a certain fundamental it has to be transposed by the transposition factor of its fundamental in order to best preserve the original timbre. From this, the need emerges for an assignment of each component in order to select the most appropriate transposition factor [DE10].

Another audio effect that can be accomplished within the MODVOC environment, for example, relates to the manipulation of auditory roughness by filtering AM and FM data prior to synthesis [DE08].

3.5 Conclusion

In this chapter we presented the application of modulators and demodulators in digital audio effects. We transfered concepts that are well known in communication engineering and in the design of music synthesizers into the realm of audio effects and pointed out the importance of these techniques for digital discrete-time implementations of well-known effects like ring modulation, detune effects, chorus, vibrato, flanger and rotating speaker simulation. A strong focus was put on the interaction of modulators and demodulators with filters and delays since this combination is one of the fundamental processes for many audio effects.

Using the demodulation techniques presented in this chapter, the temporal envelope of a signal can be obtained, for example. Parameters of a given audio effect to be applied to this signal may be controlled by the temporal envelope of the same, in order to arrive at a more lively and expressive sound quality. As examples, we presented the auto-wah and, more advanced, an audio morphing scheme. These applications examples may serve as a basis for experiments and further research.

Sound and music

[m-MBa95] M. Bach: 55 *Sounds for Cello*. Composition for cello and live electronics. 1995.

[m-Fur93] K. Furukawa: *Swim, Swan. Composition for clarinet and live electronics*. ZKM, 1993.

[m-Hoe82] K. Hörmann and M. Kaiser: *Effekte in der Rock- und Popmusik: Funktion, Klang, Einsatz*. Bosse-Musik-Paperback; 21, 1982. Sound examples. Cassette BE 2240 MC.

[m-Pie99] F. Pieper: Leslie-Simulatoren. CD, Tr. 33. of *Das Effekte Praxisbuch*. Ch. 12. GC Carstensen, 1999.

[m-Sch98] P. Schaeffer and G. Reibel: *Solfège de L'objet Sonore*. Booklet + 3 CDs. First published 1967. INA-GRM, 1998.

References

[Bod84] H. Bode. History of electronic sound modification. *J. Audio Eng. Soc.*, 32(10): 730–739, 1984.

[Dat97] J. Dattoro. Effect design, part 2: Delay-line modulation and chorus. *J. Audio Eng. Soc.*, 45(10): 764–788, 1997.

[DE08] S. Disch and B. Edler. An amplitude- and frequency modulation vocoder for audio signal processing. In *Proc. DAFX-08 Digital Audio Effects Workshop*, pp. 257–263, Espoo, September 2008.

[DE09a] S. Disch and B. Edler. An iterative segmentation algorithm for audio signal spectra depending on estimated local centers of gravity. In *Proc. DAFX-09 Digital Audio Effects Workshop*, Como, September 2009.

[DE09b] S. Disch and B. Edler. Multiband perceptual modulation analysis, processing and synthesis of audio signals. In *Proc. ICASSP '09*, Taipei, April 2009.

[DE10] S. Disch and B. Edler. An enhanced modulation vocoder for selective transposition of pitch. *13th Int. Conf. Digital Audio Effects (DAFx-10)*, 2010.

[Dis99] S. Disch. *Digital audio effects – modulation and delay lines*. Master's thesis, Technical University Hamburg–Harburg, 1999.

[DP00] G. De Poli. Personal communication, 2000.

[Dut88] P. Dutilleux. *Mise en œ uvre de transformations sonores sur un système temps-réel*. Technical report, Rapport de stage de DEA, CNRS-LMA, June 1988.

[Dut91] P. Dutilleux. *Vers la machine à sculpter le son, modification en temps réel des caractéristiques fréquentielles et temporelles des sons*. PhD thesis, University of Aix-Marseille II, 1991.

[Dut96] P. Dutilleux. Verstärkung der Differenztöne (f2-f1). In *Bericht der 19. Tonmeistertagung Karlsruhe*, Verlag K.G. Saur, pp. 798–806, 1996.

[Dut98a] P. Dutilleux. Filters, delays, modulations and demodulations: A tutorial. In *Proc. DAFX-98 Digital Audio Effects Workshop*, pp. 4–11, Barcelona, November 1998.

[Dut98b] P. Dutilleux. Opéras multimédias, le rôle des ordinateurs dans trois créations du zkm. in musique et arts plastiques. In *GRAME et Musée d'Art contemporain, Lyon*, pp. 73–79, 1998.

[DZ99] S. Disch and U. Zölzer. Modulation and delay line based digital audio effects. In *Proc. DAFX-99 Digital Audio Effects Workshop*, pp. 5–8, Trondheim, December 1999.

[Hal95] H. P. Haller. Das Experimental Studio der Heinrich-Strobel-Stiftung des Südwest-funks Freiburg 1971–1989, Die Erforschung der Elektronischen Klangumformung und ihre Geschichte. Nomos, 1995.

[LVKL96] T. I. Laakso, V. Välimäki, M. Karjalainen and U. K. Laine. Splitting the unit delay. *IEEE Signal Process. Mag.*, 13: 30–60, 1996.

[McN84] G. W. McNally. Dynamic range control of digital audio signals. *J. Audio Eng. Soc.*, 32(5): 316–327, 1984.

[Orf96]   S. J. Orfanidis. *Introduction to Signal Processing*. Prentice-Hall, 1996.

[Roa96]   C. Roads. *The Computer Music Tutorial*. MIT Press, 1996.

[Sch94]   W. Schiffner. *Rock und Pop und ihre Sounds*. Elektor-Verlag, 1994.

[Ste87]   M. Stein. *Les modems pour transmission de données*. Masson CNET-ENST, 1987.

[TSS82a]   E. Terhardt, G. Stoll, and M. Seewann. Algorithm for extraction of pitch and pitch salience from complex tonal signals. *J. Acoust. Soc. Am.*, 71(3): 679–688, 1982.

[TSS82b]   E. Terhardt, G. Stoll, and M. Seewann. Pitch of complex signals according to virtual-pitch theory: Tests, examples, and predictions. *J. Acoust. Soc. Am.*, 71(3): 671–678, 1982.

[Vid91]   A. Vidolin. Musical interpretation and signal processing. In G. De Poli, A. Piccialli, and C. Roads (eds), *Representations of Musical Signals*, pp. 439–459. MIT Press, 1991.

[War98]   S. Wardle. A Hilbert-transformer frequency shifter for audio. In *Proc. DAFX-98 Digital Audio Effects Workshop*, pp. 25–29, Barcelona, November 1998.

[Zöl05]   U. Zölzer. *Digital Audio Signal Processing*. John Wiley & Sons, Ltd, 2nd edition, 2005.

4

Nonlinear processing

P. Dutilleux, K. Dempwolf, M. Holters and U. Zölzer

4.1 Introduction

Audio effect algorithms for dynamics processing, valve simulation, overdrive and distortion for guitar and recording applications, psychoacoustic enhancers and exciters fall into the category of nonlinear processing. They create intentional or unintentional harmonic or inharmonic frequency components which are not present in the input signal. Harmonic distortion is caused by nonlinearities within the effect device. For most of these signal processing devices, a lot of listening and recording experience is necessary to obtain sound results which are preferred by most listeners. The effect parameters have to be adjusted carefully by ear while monitoring the output signal by a level meter. The application of these signal processing devices is an art of its own and of course one of the main tools for recording engineers and musicians.

The terms nonlinear processing or nonlinear processors are used for all signal processing algorithms or signal processing devices in the analog or digital domains which do *not* satisfy the condition of linearity. A system with input $x(n)$ and output $y(n)$ is called linear if the property

$$x(n) = Ax_1(n) + Bx_2(n) \rightarrow y(n) = Ay_1(n) + By_2(n) \tag{4.1}$$

is fullfilled. In all other cases it is called nonlinear. A difference can be made between static or memoryless nonlinearities, that can be described by a static input-to-output mapping, and dynamic nonlinear systems.

If a sinusoid of known amplitude and frequency according to $x(n) = A \sin(2\pi f_1 T n)$ is fed to a linear system the output signal can be written as $y(n) = A_{\text{out}} \sin(2\pi f_1 T n + \varphi_{\text{out}})$ which again is a sinusoid where the amplitude is modified by the magnitude response $|H(f_1)|$ of the transfer function according to $A_{\text{out}} = |H(f_1)| \cdot A$ and the phase response $\varphi_{\text{out}} = \varphi_{\text{in}} + \angle H(f_1)$. In contrast, a

DAFX: Digital Audio Effects, Second Edition. Edited by Udo Zölzer.
© 2011 John Wiley & Sons, Ltd. Published 2011 by John Wiley & Sons, Ltd.

nonlinear system will deliver a sum of sinusoids $y(n) = A_0 + A_1 \sin(2\pi f_1 T n) + A_2 \sin(2 \cdot 2\pi f_1 T n) + \ldots + A_N \sin(N \cdot 2\pi f_1 T n)$. Block diagrams in Figure 4.1 showing both input and output signals of a linear and a nonlinear system illustrate the difference between both systems.

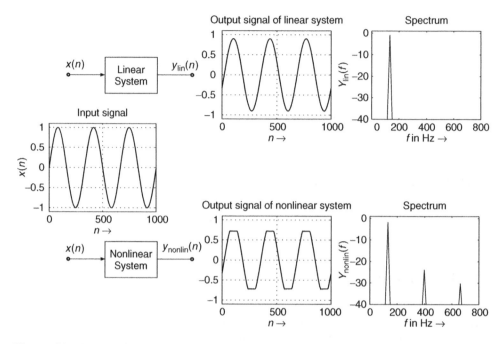

Figure 4.1 Input and output signals of a linear and nonlinear system. The output signal of the linear system is changed in amplitude and phase. The output signal of the nonlinear system is strongly shaped by the nonlinearity and consists of a sum of harmonics, as shown by the spectrum.

A measurement of the total harmonic distortion gives an indication of the nonlinearity of the system. Total harmonic distortion is defined by

$$\text{THD} = \sqrt{\frac{A_2^2 + A_3^2 + \cdots + A_N^2}{A_1^2 + A_2^2 + \cdots + A_N^2}}, \tag{4.2}$$

which is the square root of the ratio of the sum of powers of all harmonic frequencies above the fundamental frequency to the power of all harmonic frequencies, including the fundamental frequency.

The example of a sine wave has been used as an introduction to non linear distortion, but musical signals are usually comprised of several partials which induce many distortion products. If the input signal $x(n)$ is a sum of harmonics of a fundamental frequency f_0, the individual distortion products are also harmonics of f_0. The resulting signal $y(n)$ hence contains only harmonics, the relative amplitudes of which are non monotonously related to the amplitude of the input signal. If the input signal $x(n)$ is a sum of non harmonically related partials, the non linear system generates a series of harmonics for each input partial, as well as new partials at the frequencies of the sum and difference of the input partials and of their harmonics [CVAT01]. The non harmonic components produced by the non linear system are called intermodulation products because they can also be interpreted as the result of an amplitude modulation of one partial by another. In digital systems, foldover of the distortion products around $f_s/2$ are additional distortion products which have to be dealt with (refer to Section 4.1.1 and Figure 4.6).

In most usual musical applications, the intermodulation products are not welcome because they blur the input signal, impeding the identification of the individual musical sources or even introducing new musical parts which are out of tune. However, these effects can sometimes be used in a controlled and creative way, such as the amplification of the difference tones $f_2 - f_1$ [Dut96]. A general recommendation when applying non linear processing is to carefully control, before processing, the input signal $x(n)$ as to its harmonic content, amplitude and bandwidth, because filtering out the unpleasant or unwanted distortion products is usually challenging.

We will discuss nonlinear processing in three main musical categories. The first category consists of dynamic range controllers where the main purpose is the control of the signal envelope according to some control parameters. The amount of harmonic distortion introduced by these control algorithms should be kept as low as possible. Dynamics processing algorithms will be introduced in Section 4.2. The second class of nonlinear processing is designed for the creation of strong harmonic distortion such as guitar amplifiers, guitar effect processors, etc. and will be introduced in Section 4.3. The third category can be described by the same theoretical approach and is represented by signal-processing devices called exciters and enhancers. Their main field of application is the creation of additional harmonics for a subtle improvement of the main sound characteristic. The amount of harmonic distortion is usually kept small to avoid a pronounced effect. Exciters and enhancers are based on psycho-acoustic fundamentals and will be discussed in Section 4.4.

4.1.1   Basics of nonlinear modeling

Digital signal processing is mainly based on linear time-invariant systems. The assumption of linearity and time invariance is certainly valid for a variety of technical systems, especially for systems where input and output signals are bounded to a specified amplitude range. However, several analog audio processing devices have nonlinearities like valve amplifiers, analog effect devices, analog tape recorders, loudspeakers and at the end of the chain the human hearing mechanism. A compensation and the simulation of these nonlinearities need nonlinear signal processing and of course a theory of nonlinear systems. From several models for different nonlinear systems discussed in the literature, the Volterra series expansion is a suitable approach, because it is an extension of the linear systems theory. Not all technical and physical systems can be described by the Volterra series expansion, especially systems with extreme nonlinearities. If the inner structure of a nonlinear system is unknown, a typical measurement set-up, as shown in Figure 4.2, with a pseudo-random signal as the input signal and recording the output signal is used. Input and output signals allow the calculation of the linear impulse response $h_1(n)$ by cross-correlation and *kernels* (impulse responses) of higher order $h_2(n_1, n_2), h_3(n_1, n_2, n_3), \cdots, h_N(n_1, \cdots, n_N)$ by higher order cross-correlations. The linear impulse response $h_1(n)$ is a one-dimensional, $h_2(n_1, n_2)$ is a two-dimensional and $h_N(n_1, \cdots, n_N)$ is an N-dimensional kernel. An exhaustive treatment of these techniques can be found in [Sch80]. These N kernels can be used for an N-order Volterra system model given by

$$y(n) = \sum_{i=1}^{N} y_i(n) = \sum_{v_1=0}^{\infty} h_1(v_1)x(n - v_1) \tag{4.3}$$

$$+ \sum_{v_1=0}^{\infty} \sum_{v_2=0}^{\infty} h_2(v_1, v_2)x(n - v_1)x(n - v_2)$$

$$+ \sum_{v_1=0}^{\infty} \sum_{v_2=0}^{\infty} \sum_{v_3=0}^{\infty} h_3(v_1, v_2, v_3)x(n - v_1)x(n - v_2)x(n - v_3) + \cdots$$

$$+ \sum_{v_1=0}^{\infty} \cdots \sum_{v_N=0}^{\infty} h_N(v_1, \ldots, v_N)x(n - v_1) \cdots x(n - v_N). \tag{4.4}$$

Figure 4.2   Measurement of nonlinear systems.

Figure 4.3 shows the block diagram representing (4.4).

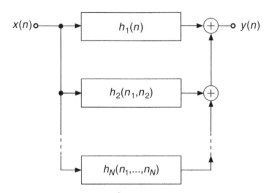

Figure 4.3   Simulation of nonlinear systems by an N-order Volterra system model.

A further simplification [Fra97] is possible if the kernels can be factored according to

$$h_i(n_1, n_2, \cdots, n_i) = h_i^f(n_1)h_i^f(n_2) \cdots h_i^f(n_i). \tag{4.5}$$

Then (4.4) can be written as

$$y(n) = \sum_{v=0}^{\infty} h_1^f(v)x(n-v) + \left(\sum_{v=0}^{\infty} h_2^f(v)x(n-v)\right)^2 + \cdots + \left(\sum_{v=0}^{\infty} h_N^f(v)x(n-v)\right)^N, \tag{4.6}$$

which is shown in block diagram representation in Figure 4.4. This representation shows several advantages, especially from the implementation point of view, because every subsystem can be realized by a one-dimensional impulse response. At the output of each subsystem we have to perform the $()^i$ operation on the corresponding output signals. The discussion so far can be applied to nonlinear systems with memory, which means that besides nonlinearities linear filtering operations are also included. Further material on nonlinear audio systems can be found in [Kai87, RH96, Kli98, FUB+98].

A simulation of a nonlinear system without memory, namely static nonlinear curves, can be done by a Taylor series expansion given by

$$y(n) = f[x(n)] = \sum_{i=0}^{N} b_i x^i(n). \tag{4.7}$$

Static nonlinear curves can be applied directly to the input signal, where each input amplitude is mapped to an output amplitude according to the nonlinear function $y = f[x(n)]$. If one applies

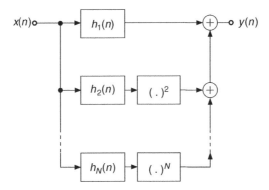

Figure 4.4 Simulation of nonlinear systems by an N-order Volterra system model with factored kernels.

a squarer operation to the input signal of a given bandwidth, the output signal $y(n) = x^2(n)$ will double its bandwidth. As soon as the highest frequency after passing a nonlinear operation exceeds half the sampling frequency $f_s/2$, aliasing will fold this frequency back to the base band. This means that for digital signals we first have to perform over-sampling of the input signal before applying any nonlinear operation to the input signal in order to avoid any aliasing distortions. This over-sampling is shown in Figure 4.5 where first up-sampling is performed and then an interpolation filter H_I is used to suppress images up to the new sampling frequency Lf_s. Then the nonlinear operation can be applied followed by a band-limiting filter to $f_s/2$ and down-sampling.

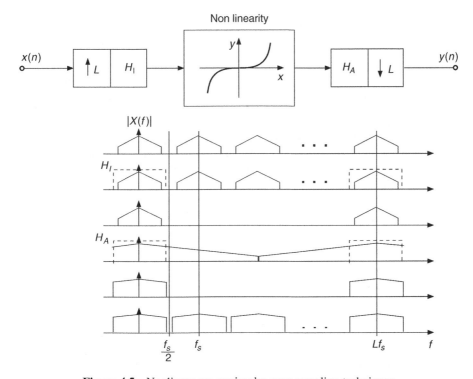

Figure 4.5 Nonlinear processing by over-sampling techniques.

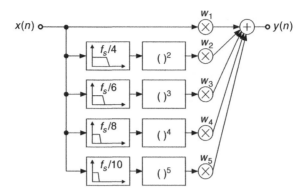

Figure 4.6   Nonlinear processing by band-limiting input range [SZ99].

As can be noticed, the output spectrum only contains frequencies up to $f_s/2$. Based on this fact the entire nonlinear processing can be performed without over-sampling and down-sampling by the system shown in Figure 4.6 [SZ99]. The input signal is split into several lowpass versions which are forwarded to an individual nonlinearity. The output signal is a weighted combination of the individual output signals after passing a nonlinearity. With this approach the problem of aliasing is avoided and an approximation to the over-sampling technique is achieved. A comparison with our previous discussion on factored Volterra kernels shows also a close connection. As a conclusion for a special static nonlinearity applied to an input signal, the input signal has to be filtered by a lowpass of cut-off frequency $f_s/(2 \cdot \text{order of the Taylor series})$, otherwise aliasing distortions will occur.

4.2   Dynamic range control

Dynamics processing is performed by amplifying devices where the gain is automatically controlled by the level of the input signal. We will discuss limiters, compressors, expanders and noise gates. A good introduction to the parameters of dynamics processing can be found in [Ear76, pp. 242–248].

Dynamics processing is based on an amplitude/level detection scheme sometimes called an envelope follower, a static curve to derive a gain factor from the result of the envelope follower, a smoothing filter to prevent too abrupt gain changes and a multiplier to weight the input signal (see Figure 4.7). Optionally, the input signal is delayed to compensate for any delay in the *side chain*, the lower path in Figure 4.7. Normally, the gain factor is derived from the input signal, but the side chain path can also be connected to another signal for controlling the gain factor of the input signal.

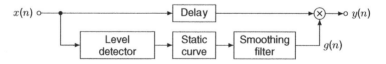

Figure 4.7   Block diagram of a dynamic range controller [Zöl05].

An example of a dynamic range controller's impact on a signal is shown in Figure 4.8. In this example, the dynamic range controller is a *compressor*: during periods of low signal level (first half of the shown input signal $x(n)$), the gain $g(n)$ is set to 1, while for higher input levels (second half), the gain is decreased to reduce the signal's amplitude. Thus the difference in signal levels along time is reduced, compressing the signal's dynamic range.

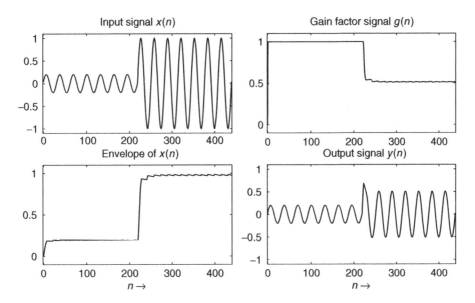

Figure 4.8 The input signal $x(n)$, the envelope of $x(n)$, the derived gain factor $g(n)$ and the output signal $y(n)$.

Signal processing

The level detector follows one of the approaches described in Section 4.3. Two commonly used choices are:

- A full-wave rectifier in combination with an AR-averager (see Figure 4.9) with very short attack time may be used to track the peak value of the signal.

- A squarer averaged with only a single time-constant (see Figure 4.10) provides the RMS value, measuring the signal's power.

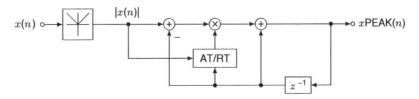

Figure 4.9 Peak measurement (envelope detector/follower) for a dynamic range controller.

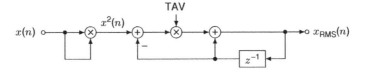

Figure 4.10 RMS measurement (envelope detector/follower) for a dynamic range controller [McN84, Zöl05].

Typical dynamic range controllers contain one of these level detectors, or even both, to be able to react to sudden level increases with the peak detector, while usually operating based on the RMS measurement.

The static curve decides which function (limiter, compressor, expander, ...) the dynamic range controller assumes. It is best described on a dB scale, so we introduce X, G and Y for the levels of the respective signals in dB, i.e., $X = 20 \cdot \log_{10}(x_{PEAK}(n))$ or $X = 10 \cdot \log_{10}(x_{RMS}(n))$. The multiplication at the dynamic range controller's output then becomes $Y = X + G$.

In this logarithmic domain, the gain is typically derived from the input level by a piecewise linear function. Figure 4.11 shows the characteristic curve of a typical compressor, mapping input to output level (on the left) and input level to gain (on the right). Up to a certain input level, the compressor threshold CT (-30 dB in this example), the gain is left at 0 dB. Above the threshold, the characteristic curve is defined by the ratio R, specifying the relation between input level change ΔX to output level change ΔY by $\Delta Y = \frac{1}{R} \cdot \Delta X$. Alternatively, the slope factor $S = 1 - \frac{1}{R}$ may be specified instead of the ratio R.

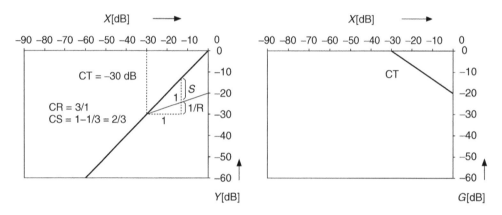

Figure 4.11 Static characteristic: definition of slope S and ratio R [Zöl05] exemplified for a compressor.

The *dynamic behavior* of a dynamic range controller is influenced by the level measurement approach (with attack AT and release time RT for peak measurement and averaging time TAV for RMS measurement) and further adjusted with a smoothing filter, as shown in Figure 4.12,

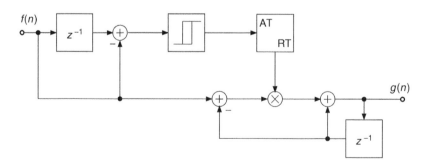

Figure 4.12 Dynamic filter: attack and release time adjustment for a dynamic range controller [McN84, Zöl05].

which also employs special attack/release times. The calculation of the attack time parameter is carried out by

$$AT = 1 - e^{-2.2T/t_{AT}},$$

where t_{AT} is the time parameter in seconds and T is the sampling period. The release time parameter RT and the averaging parameter TAV can be computed by the same formula by replacing t_{AT} by t_{RT} or t_{TAV}, respectively. Further details and derivations can be found in [McN84, Zöl05]. The output of the static function is used as the input signal to the dynamic filter with attack and release times in Figure 4.12. The output signal $g(n)$ is the gain factor for weighting the delayed input signal $x(n - D)$ as shown in Figure 4.7. In the following sections some special dynamic range controllers are discussed in detail.

4.2.1   Limiter

The purpose of a limiter is to provide control over the highest peaks in the signal, but to otherwise change the dynamics of the signal as little as possible. This is achieved by employing a characteristic curve with an infinite ratio $R = \infty$ above a limiter threshold LT, i.e.,

$$G = \begin{cases} 0 \text{ dB} & \text{if } X < LT \\ LT - X & \text{else.} \end{cases} \qquad (4.8)$$

Thus, the output level $Y = X + G$ should never exceed the threshold LT. By lowering the peaks, the overall signal can be boosted. Beside limiting single instrument signals, limiting is also often performed on the final mix of a multichannel application.

A limiter makes use of peak level measurement and should react very quickly when the input signal exceeds the limiter threshold. Typical parameters for a limiter are $t_{AT} = 0.02 \ldots 10$ ms and $t_{RT} = 1 \ldots 5000$ ms, for both the peak measurement and the smoothing filter.

An actual implementation, like the one in Figure 4.13, may perform the gain computation in linear values by

$$g(n) = \min\left(1, \frac{lt}{x_{\text{PEAK}}(n)}\right) \qquad (4.9)$$

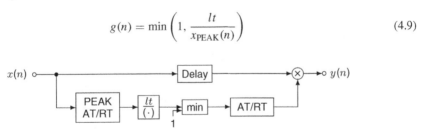

Figure 4.13   Block diagram of a limiter.

where $lt = 10^{\frac{LT}{20}}$ is the threshold on the linear scale. This approach is also used in M-file 4.1, a very simple limiter implementation with the same filter coefficients in the level detector and the smoothing filter. Figure 4.14 demonstrates the behavior of the time signals inside a limiter configuration of Figure 4.13.

M-file 4.1 (limiter.m)

```
function y = limiter(x, lt)
% function y = limiter(x, lt)
% Author: M. Holters
```

```
at = 0.3;
rt = 0.01;
delay = 5;

xpeak = 0;
g = 1;
buffer = zeros(1,delay);

for n = 1:length(x)
  a = abs(x(n));
  if a > xpeak
    coeff = at;
  else
    coeff = rt;
  end;
  xpeak = (1-coeff) * xpeak + coeff * a;
  f = min(1, lt/xpeak);
  if f < g
    coeff = at;
  else
    coeff = rt;
  end;
  g = (1-coeff) * g + coeff * f;
  y(n) = g * buffer(end);
  buffer = [x(n) buffer(1:end-1)];
end;
```

4.2.2   Compressor and expander

While a limiter completely eliminates any dynamics above a certain threshold by keeping the output level constant, a compressor only reduces the dynamics, compressing the dynamic range. The reduced dynamics can be exploited to increase the overall level, thereby boosting the loudness, without exceeding the allowed amplitude range. An expander does just the opposite of the compressor, increasing dynamics by mapping small level changes of the input to larger changes of the output level. Applying an expander to low-level signals gives a lively sound characteristic. The corresponding ratios and slopes of the characteristic curve are $CR > 1$ and $0 < CS < 1$ for the compressor and $0 < ER < 1$ and $ES < 0$ for the expander.

Compressors and expanders typically employ RMS level detectors with an averaging time in the range $t = 5 \ldots 130$ ms and a smoothing filter with $t_{AT} = 0.1 \ldots 2600$ ms and $t_{RT} = 1 \ldots 5000$ ms.

Combining a compressor for high signal levels with an expander for low signal levels leads to the gain computation

$$G = \begin{cases} CS \cdot (CT - X) & \text{if} \quad X > CT \\ 0 \text{ dB} & \text{if} \quad ET \leq X \leq CT \\ ES \cdot (ET - X) & \text{if} \quad X < ET \end{cases} \tag{4.10}$$

$$= \min\left(0, CS \cdot (CT - X), ES \cdot (ET - X)\right). \tag{4.11}$$

Here CT and ET denote the thresholds above which the compressor and below which the expander affect the signal, respectively. The resulting combined system is depicted in Figure 4.15. Again, the

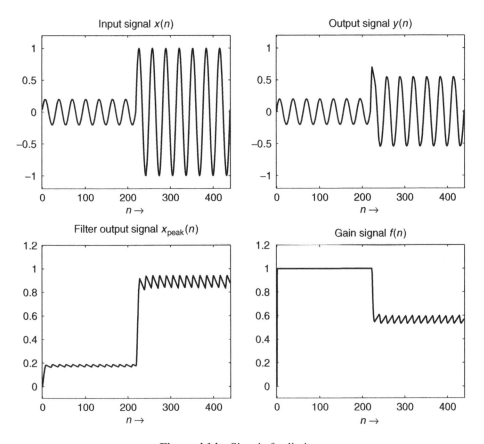

Figure 4.14   Signals for limiter.

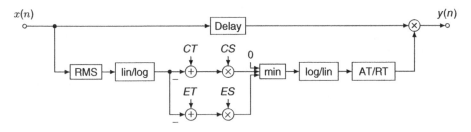

Figure 4.15   Block diagram of a compressor/expander [Zöl05].

gain can alternatively be calculated without using logarithmic values by

$$g(n) = \min\left(1, \left(\frac{x_{\mathrm{RMS}}(n)}{ct^2}\right)^{-CS/2}, \left(\frac{x_{\mathrm{RMS}}(n)}{et^2}\right)^{-ES/2}\right), \tag{4.12}$$

where the square root operation of the RMS measurement is moved to the exponents by halving the respective slopes. This approach makes conversion to and from the logarithmic domain unnecessary, but requires exponentiation. An implementation following the approach of Figure 4.15 is given in M-file 4.2.

M-file 4.2 (compexp.m)

```
function y = compexp(x, CT, CS, ET, ES)
% function y = compexp(x, CT, CS, ET, ES)
% Author: M. Holters

tav = 0.01;
at = 0.03;
rt = 0.003;
delay = 150;

xrms = 0;
g = 1;
buffer = zeros(1,delay);

for n = 1:length(x)
  xrms = (1-tav) * xrms + tav * x(n)^2;
  X = 10*log10(xrms);
  G = min([0, CS*(CT-X), ES*(ET-X)]);
  f = 10^(G/20);
  if f < g
    coeff = at;
  else
    coeff = rt;
  end;
  g = (1-coeff) * g + coeff * f;
  y(n) = g * buffer(end);
  buffer = [x(n) buffer(1:end-1)];
end;
```

Parallel compression

The usual application of compressors is the reduction of the amplitude variations above a specified threshold. In some circumstances however, e.g., for percussion instruments or an acoustic guitar, it is desired to leave unaffected the high-amplitude transients while enhancing the weaker parts of the signal. For such applications, parallel compression is recommended, where a heavily compressed version of the signal is added to the unaffected signal. The soft parts of the sound are heavily compressed using typically a low threshold, a high ratio and a short attack time. The compressed part is then amplified and mixed to the original signal. The resulting sound retains the transparency of the original sound because the transients are unaffected. This type of processing is sometimes referred to as New-York compression or side-chain compression [Bev77, Hul97, Kat07, Izh10].

Multiband compression

Depending on the spectral content of the sound to process, compression might be required only on a selected frequency band. Let us consider the musical example of a piece for tuba and live electronics where the fingering and the breathing noises had to be processed irrespective of the overwhelming low frequency tones of the instrument. The solution was the insertion of a high-pass filter in the main path as well as the side-chain of a compressor so that the device left the lower part of the spectrum unaffected by the compression.

For the general case where several frequency bands of the spectrum have to be processed individually, the multiband compressor has been developed. A filter bank splits the input signal in several bands (usually three to five) which are then individually processed. The side-chain signal of each compressor is also derived from a band-limited version of the input signal. The filter-bank for the side-chain is usually the same as the for the input signal, but it is sometimes implemented as an independent processing unit so that intricate relations can be set up where the content of the input signal in a limited frequency band drives the compression in another frequency band.

Multiband dynamics processors are often used during mastering. At this stage, no direct correction of the individual musical parts is possible since the mix is finished and the music is usually available as a stereo track. Under the assumption that each musical part or instrument mainly occupies a particular frequency band, minor corrections are still possible if they are band limited.

One advantage of multiband compression is that the unwanted side-effects of compression, such as alteration of the tonal balance or distortions, can be limited to a given frequency band. With the objective of dynamic range compression, the reduction of the ratio of peak to RMS amplitude can be more effectively implemented in individual frequency bands than at the full audio bandwidth. This allows the increase of the overall loudness of the track. Considering that the casual listener often gives preference to the louder of two musical works, a trend has developed towards always higher average levels. Moderation is, however, necessary because the "loudness war" can induce severe degradations of the audio and musical quality [Kat07, Lun07].

4.2.3   Noise gate

A noise gate can be considered as an extreme expander with a slope of $-\infty$. This results in the complete muting of signals below the chosen threshold NT. As the name implies, the noise gate is typically used to gate out noise by setting the threshold just above the level of the background noise, such that the gate only opens when a desired signal with a level above the threshold is present. A particular application is found when recording a drum set. Each element of the drum set has a different decay time. When they are not manually damped, their sounds mix together and the result is no longer distinguishable. When each element is processed by a noise gate, every sound can automatically be faded out after the attack part of the sound. This results in an overall cleaner sound.

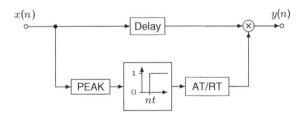

Figure 4.16   Block diagram of a noise gate [Zöl05].

The functional units of a noise gate are shown in Figure 4.16. The decision to activate the gate is typically based on a peak measurement which leads to a fade in/fade out of the gain factor $g(n)$ with appropriate attack and release times. Further possible refinements include the use of two thresholds to realize a hysteresis and a hold time to avoid unpleasant effects when the input level fluctuates around the threshold. These are demonstrated in the implementation given in M-file 4.3 [Ben97].

M-file 4.3 (noisegt.m)

```
function y=noisegt(x,holdtime,ltrhold,utrhold,release,attack,a,Fs)
% function y=noisegt(x,holdtime,ltrhold,utrhold,release,attack,a,Fs)
% Author: R. Bendiksen
```

```
% noise gate with hysteresis
% holdtime     - time in seconds the sound level has to be below the
%                  threshhold value before the gate is activated
% ltrhold      - threshold value for activating the gate
% utrhold      - threshold value for deactivating the gate > ltrhold
% release      - time in seconds before the sound level reaches zero
% attack       - time in seconds before the output sound level is the
%                  same as the input level after deactivating the gate
% a            - pole placement of the envelope detecting filter <1
% Fs           - sampling frequency
rel=round(release*Fs);  %number of samples for fade
att=round(attack*Fs);    %number of samples for fade
g=zeros(size(x));
lthcnt=0;
uthcnt=0;
ht=round(holdtime*Fs);
h=filter([(1-a)^2],[1.0000 -2*a a^2],abs(x));%envelope detection
h=h/max(h);
for i=1:length(h)
   if (h(i)<=ltrhold) | ((h(i)<utrhold) & (lthcnt>0))
% Value below the lower threshold?
      lthcnt=lthcnt+1;
      uthcnt=0;
      if lthcnt>ht
% Time below the lower threshold longer than the hold time?
         if lthcnt>(rel+ht)
            g(i)=0;
         else
            g(i)=1-(lthcnt-ht)/rel;    % fades the signal to zero
         end;
      elseif ((i<ht) & (lthcnt==i))
         g(i)=0;
      else
         g(i)=1;
      end;
   elseif (h(i)>=utrhold) | ((h(i)>ltrhold) & (uthcnt>0))
% Value above the upper threshold or is the signal being faded in?
      uthcnt=uthcnt+1;
      if (g(i-1)<1)
% Has the gate been activated or isn't the signal faded in yet?
         g(i)=max(uthcnt/att,g(i-1));
      else
         g(i)=1;
      end;
      lthcnt=0;
   else
      g(i)=g(i-1);
      lthcnt=0;
      uthcnt=0;
   end;
end;
y=x.*g;
y=y*max(abs(x))/max(abs(y));
```

Further implementations of limiters, compressors, expanders and noise gates can be found in [Orf96] and in [Zöl05], where special combined dynamic range controllers are also discussed.

4.2.4 De-esser

A de-esser is a signal processing device for processing speech and vocals. It consists of a bandpass filter tuned to the frequency range between 2 and 6 kHz to detect the level of the signal in this frequency band. If a certain threshold is exceeded, the gain factor of a peak or notch filter tuned to the same frequency band is controlled to realize a compressor for that band only, as shown in Figure 4.17. De-essers are mainly applied to speech or vocal signals to avoid high frequency sibilance.

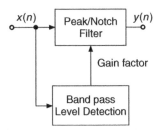

Figure 4.17   Block diagram of a de-esser.

As an alternative to the bandpass/notch filters, highpass and shelving filters are used with good results. In order to make the de-esser more robust against input level changes, the threshold should depend on the overall level of the signal – that is, a relative threshold [Nie00].

4.2.5 Infinite limiters

In order to catch overshoots from a compressor and limiter, a clipper or *infinite limiter* may be used [Nie00]. In contrast to the previously considered dynamic range controllers, the infinite limiter is a nonlinear operation working directly on the waveform by flattening the signal above a threshold. The simplest one is hard clipping, which generates lots of high-order harmonics. A gentler infinite limiter is the soft clipper, which rounds the signal shape before the absolute clipping threshold. Although infinite limiting should usually be avoided during mix down of multi channel recordings and recording sessions, several CDs make use of infinite limiting or saturation (see wave file in Figure 4.18 and listen to Carlos Santana/Smooth [m-San99]). A more detailed description of clipping effects and their artistic use is given in the following section.

4.3 Musical distortion and saturation effects

4.3.1 Valve simulation

Introduction

Valve or tube devices dominated electronic signal processing circuits during the first part of the last century and have experienced a revival in audio processing every decade since their introduction [Bar98, Ham73]. One of the most commonly used effects for electric guitars is the amplifier and especially the valve amplifier. The typical behavior of the amplifier and the connected loudspeaker

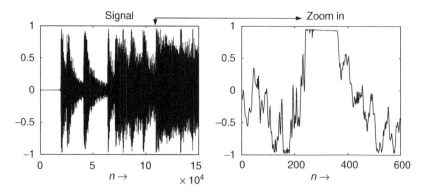

Figure 4.18   Infinite limiting (Santana – "Smooth").

cabinet have demonstrated their influence on the sound of rock music over the past decades. Besides the two most important guitars, namely the Fender Stratocaster and the Gibson Les Paul, several valve amplifiers have helped in creating exciting sounds from these classic guitars.

Valve microphones, preamplifiers and effect devices such as compressors, limiters and equalizers are also used for vocal recordings where the warm and subtle effect of valve compression is applied. A lot of vocalists prefer recording with valve condenser microphones because of their warm low end and smooth top end frequency response. Also the recording of acoustical instruments such as acoustic guitars, brass instruments and drums benefit from being processed with valve outboard devices. Valve processors also assist the mixing process for individual track enhancing and on the mix buses. The demand for valve outboard effects and classic mixing consoles used in combination with digital audio workstations has led back to entire valve technology mixing consoles. For the variety of digital audio workstations a lot of plug-in software modules for valve processing are available.

Vintage valve amplifiers

An introduction to valve amplifiers and their history can be found in [Fli93, Bar98], where several comments on sound characteristics are published. We will concentrate on the most important amplifier manufacturers over the years and point out some characteristic features.

- **Fender:** The Fender series of guitar amplifiers goes back to the year 1946 when the first devices were introduced. These were based on standard tube schematics supplied by the manufacturers of tubes. Over the years modifications of the standard design approach were integrated in response to musicians' needs and proposals. The range of Fender amplifiers is still expanding, but also reissues of the originals are very popular with musicians. The sound of Fender amplifiers is the "classic tube sound" and was made famous by blues musicians like Buddy Guy and Stevie Ray Vaughan. A detailed analysis of a Fender amplifier and a discussion on its similarity to other amplifier designs is presented in [Kue05].

- **Vox:** The manufacturer Vox is always associated with its most famous amplifier, the Vox AC30/4. Its sound is best characterized by guitar player Brian May in [PD93] where he states "the quality at low levels is broad and crisp and unmistakably *valve like*, and as the volume is turned up it slides into a pleasant, creamy compression and distortion." There is always a ringing treble quality through all level settings of the amp. The real "soul of the amp" comes out if you play it at full volume and control your sound with the volume knob of your guitar. The heart of the sound characteristic of the Vox AC30/4 is claimed to be the use of EL84 pentodes, negative feedback and cathode biasing in Class A configuration. The four small EL84s should sound more lively than the bigger EL34s. The sound of the Vox AC30 can be found on recordings by Brian May, Status Quo, Tom Petty and Bryan Adams.

- **Marshall:** The Fender Bassman 5F6 was the basis for the Marshall JTM 45. The differences between both are discussed in [Doy93] and [Kue05], and are claimed to be the output transformers, speakers, input valve and feedback circuit, although the main circuit diagrams are nearly identical. The sound of Marshall is characterized by an aggressive and "crunchy" tone with brilliant harmonics, as Eric Clapton says, "I was probably playing full volume to get that sound" [Doy93]. Typical representatives of the early Marshall sound are Jimi Hendrix, Eric Clapton, Jimmy Page and Ritchie Blackmore. The JCM800 series established the second generation of Marshall amplifiers featuring the typical hardrock and heavy metal sound as played by Zakk Wylde or Slash.

- **Mesa-Boogie:** The "creamy" tone and the high gain of Mesa-Boogie amplifiers has its seeds in a wrongly connected test arrangement of two preamp stages. Founder Randall Smith stated in an interview [Sal02]: "Then when we plugged it in right, Lee hit a big power chord and practically blew both our bodies right through the back wall! (. . .) It was just HUGE sounding. And it would sustain forever. That was the beginning of cascading high-gain pre-amp architecture". Through this assembly Mesa-Boogie amplifiers featured 50 to 80 times more gain compared to amplifier designs of that time, leading to a long sustaining tone. An ambassador for Mesa-Boogie amplifiers is Carlos Santana.

Signal processing

The sound of a valve amplifier is based on a combination of several important factors. First of all the main processing features of valves or tubes are important [Bar98, Ham73]. Then the amplifier circuit has its influence on the sound and, last but not least, the chassis and loudspeaker combination play an important role in sound shaping. We will discuss all three factors now.

Valve basics. Valves or vacuum tubes are active electronic components used for amplifying, rectifying, switching, modulating or generating electrical signals. Prior to the invention of transistors, valves were the main active components in electronic equipment. In today's electronics, valves are replaced completely by semiconductors, except for some special applications. In the following we will discuss the reasons why these components are still very popular in hi-fi and guitar amplifiers.

Triode valves [Rat95, RCA59] consist of three electrodes, namely anode (or plate), cathode (or filament) and grid. Applying a voltage between anode and cathode, electrons are emitted by the heated cathode and flow to the positively charged anode. The grid is placed between these electrodes and can be used to modulate the rate of electron flow. A negative charge on the grid electrode affects the electron flow: the larger the charge, the smaller the current from anode to cathode. Thus, the triode can be used as voltage-controlled amplifier. The corresponding transfer function relates the anode current I_A to the input grid voltage V_G, as depicted in Figure 4.19. This nonlinear curve has a quadratic shape. An input signal represented by the grid voltage V_G delivers an anode output current $I_A = f(V_G)$ representing the output signal. The corresponding output spectrum shows a second harmonic in addition to the input frequency. This second harmonic can be lowered in amplitude when the operating point of the nonlinear curve is shifted right and the input voltage is applied to the more linear region of the quadratic curve. As a consequence of this, triodes are considered to provide a warm and soft sound coloration when used in preamplifiers.

The dc component in the output signal can be suppressed by a subsequent highpass filter. Note also the asymmetrical soft clipping of the negative halves of the output sinusoid, which is the result of the quadratic curve of the triode. Input stages of valve amplifiers make use of these triode valves. A design parameter is the operating point which controls the amplitude of the second harmonic.

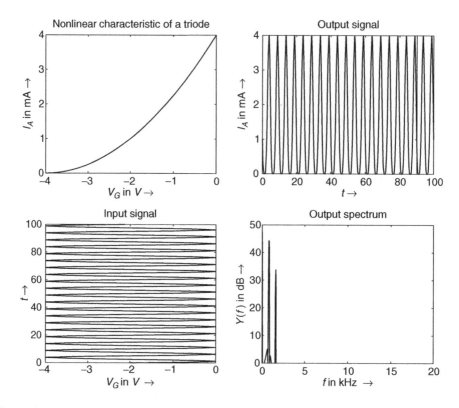

Figure 4.19   Triode: nonlinear characteristic curve $I_A = f(V_G)$ and nonlinear effect on input signal. The output spectrum consists of the fundamental input frequency and a second harmonic generated by the quadratic curve of the triode.

Pentode valves feature two additional electrodes, the screen and the suppressor grid. With this arrangement oscillations can be suppressed which can arise in triodes. When driving a load resistance the characteristic curve $I_A = f(V_G)$ is shaped like a S-curve, as shown in Figure 4.20. Through this, the output signal is compressed for higher-input amplitudes, leading to a symmetrical soft clipping. The corresponding output spectrum shows the creation of odd order harmonics. For lower input amplitudes the static characteristic curve operates in a nearly linear region, which again shows the control of the nonlinear behavior by properly selecting the operating point.

The technical parameters of valves have wide variation, which leads to a wide variation of sound features, although selected valves (so-called "matched pairs") with limited deviations of parameters are of course available. All surrounding environmental parameters like humidity and temperature have their influence as well.

Valve amplifier circuits. Valve amplifier circuits are based on the block diagram in Figure 4.21. Several measured signals from a Vox AC30 at different stages of the signal flow path are also displayed. This will give an indication of typical signal distortions in valve amplifiers. The corresponding spectra of the signals for the Vox AC30/4 measurements are shown in Figure 4.22. The distortion characteristic can be visualized by the waterfall representation of short-time FFTs for a chirp input signal in Figure 4.23. The main stages of a valve amplifier are given below:

- The *input stage* consists of a triode circuit providing the input matching and preamplification followed by a volume control for the next stages.

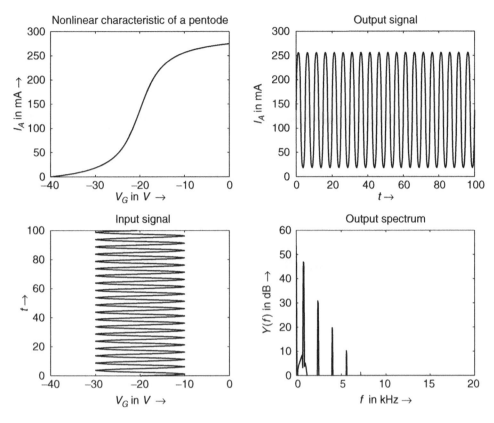

Figure 4.20   Pentode: nonlinear characteristic curve $I_A = f(V_G)$ and nonlinear effect on input signal.

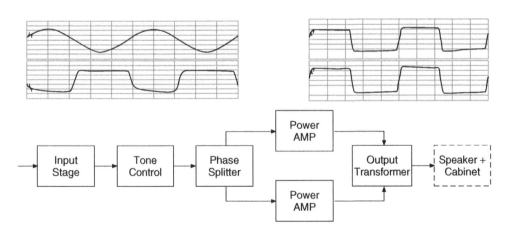

Figure 4.21   Main stages of a valve amplifier. Upper left plot shows signal after pre-amplifier, lower left plot shows signal after phase splitter, upper right plot shows signal after power amplifier and lower right plot shows signal after output transformer.

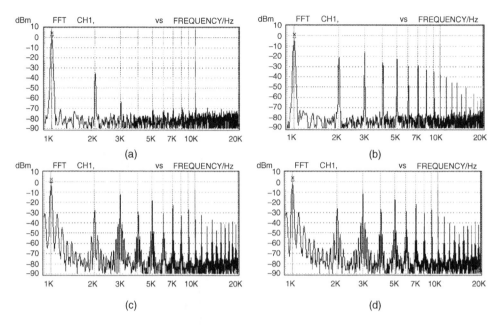

Figure 4.22 Vox AC30/4 spectra at different stages: (a) input stage, (b) output phase splitter, (c) output power amp and (d) output of transformer.

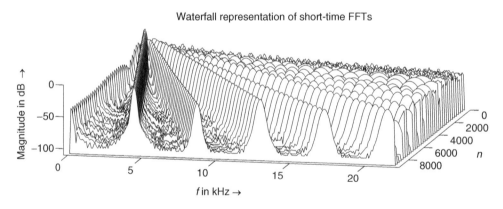

Figure 4.23 Short-time FFTs (waterfall representation) of Vox AC30 with a chirp input signal. The amplifier is operating with full volume setting.

- The *tone control* circuitry is based on passive filter networks, typically with three controls for bass, mid and treble.

- The *phase splitter* stage provides symmetrical power amp feeding. This phase splitter delivers the original input for the upper power amp and a phase inverted replica of the input for the lower power amp.

- The *power amp* stage in push-pull configuration performs individual amplification of the original and the phase inverted replica in a class A, class B or class AB configuration (see Figure 4.24). Class A is shown in the left plot, where the output signal is valid all the

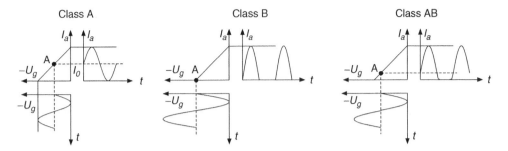

Figure 4.24   Power amplifier operation with idealized transfer characteristic (left class A, middle class B, right class AB operation).

time. Class B performs amplification only for one half wave, as depicted in the middle plot. The working point for class AB operation (right plot) lies in-between class A and class B, also amplifying a part of the negative half wave. Class A and class AB are the main configurations for guitar power amplifiers.

- The *output transformer* performs the subtraction of both waveforms delivered by the power amplifiers, which leads to a doubling of the output amplitude. Figure 4.25 shows the principle of push-pull amplification and the typical connection of the output transformer. The nonlinear behavior of transformers is beyond the scope of this discussion.

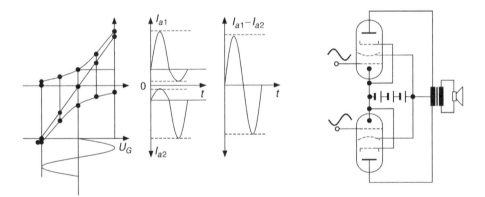

Figure 4.25   Power amplifier stage and output transformer. Left: principle and waveforms for class AB push-pull power amplifier. Right: simplified circuit with two pentodes, output transformer and loudspeaker.

Speaker and cabinet. Guitar amplifiers are built either as a *combo*, where amplifier chassis and one or more loudspeakers are combined in the same enclosure or as a *stack* with separated amplifier *head* and loudspeaker *cabinet*. The traditional guitar cabinet is closed-back and houses four 12″ speakers (4×12), but different combinations with loudspeakers in the range from 8″ to 15″ in closed or open enclosures are also available. The frequency responses of common guitar cabinets show an uneven bandpass characteristic with many resonances at mid frequencies. Simulations can be done by impulse response measurements of the loudspeaker and cabinet combination. The nonlinear behavior of a loudspeaker cabinet was analyzed and modeled in [YBK08].

As well as the discussed topics, the influence of the power supply with valve rectifier [zL97, pp. 51–54] is claimed to be of importance. A soft reduction of the power supply voltage occurs when in a high-power operation short transients need a high current. This power supply effect leads to a soft clipping of the audio signal.

A proposal for tube simulation by using asymmetrical clipping [Ben97] is given by

$$f(x) = \begin{cases} \frac{x-Q}{1-e^{-dist\cdot(x-Q)}} + \frac{Q}{1-e^{dist\cdot Q}}, & Q \neq 0, x \neq Q, \\ \frac{1}{dist} + \frac{Q}{1-e^{dist\cdot Q}}, & x = Q. \end{cases} \tag{4.13}$$

The underlying design parameters for the simulation of tube distortion are based on the mathematical model [Ben97] where no distortion should occur when the input level is low (the derivative of $f(x)$ has to be $f'(0) \approx 1$ and $f(0) = 0$). The static characteristic curve should perform clipping and limiting of large negative input values and be approximately linear for positive values. The result of Equation (4.13) is shown in Figure 4.26.

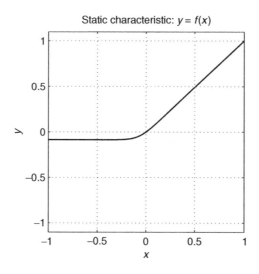

Figure 4.26 Static characteristic curve of asymmetric soft clipping for tube simulation $Q = -0.2$ and $dist = 8$.

The following M-file 4.4 performs Equation (4.13) from [Ben97]. To remove the dc component and to shape higher harmonics, additional lowpass and highpass filtering of the output signal is performed.

M-file 4.4 (tube.m)

```
function y=tube(x, gain, Q, dist, rh, rl, mix)
% function y=tube(x, gain, Q, dist, rh, rl, mix)
% Author: Bendiksen, Dutilleux, Zölzer

% y=tube(x, gain, Q, dist, rh, rl, mix)
% "Tube distortion" simulation, asymmetrical function
% x     - input
% gain - the amount of distortion, >0->
% Q     - work point. Controls the linearity of the transfer
%               function for low input levels, more negative=more linear
% dist - controls the distortion's character, a higher number gives
%               a harder distortion, >0
```

```
% rh    - abs(rh)<1, but close to 1. Placement of poles in the HP
%            filter which removes the DC component
% rl    - 0<rl<1. The pole placement in the LP filter used to
%            simulate capacitances in a tube amplifier
% mix   - mix of original and distorted sound, 1=only distorted
q=x*gain/max(abs(x));                       %Normalization
if Q==0
  z=q./(1-exp(-dist*q));
  for i=1:length(q)                         %Test because of the
    if q(i)==Q                              %transfer function's
      z(i)=1/dist;                          %0/0 value in Q
    end;
  end;
else
  z=(q-Q)./(1-exp(-dist*(q-Q)))+Q/(1-exp(dist*Q));
  for i=1:length(q)                         %Test because of the
    if q(i)==Q                              %transfer function's
      z(i)=1/dist+Q/(1-exp(dist*Q));        %0/0 value in Q
    end;
  end;
end;
y=mix*z*max(abs(x))/max(abs(z))+(1-mix)*x;
y=y*max(abs(x))/max(abs(y));
y=filter([1 -2 1],[1 -2*rh rh^2],y);        %HP filter
y=filter([1-rl],[1 -rl],y);                 %LP filter
```

Short-time FFTs (waterfall representation) of this algorithm applied to a 1 kHz sinusoid are shown in Figure 4.27. The waterfall representation shows strong even-order harmonics and also odd-order harmonics.

Digital amp modeling

New guitar amplifier designs with digital preamplifiers are based on digital modeling technology, featuring the simulation of classic valve amplifiers. Available are combos, amplifier heads or separated preamplifiers, mostly providing a wide variety of amplifier models in combination with additional effects. Besides these guitar amplifiers, software models are very popular which can be used as plug-ins together with a recording software. The principles of established modeling techniques will be introduced in Section 12.3.

Musical applications

Musical applications of valve amplifiers can be found on nearly every recording featuring guitar tracks. Ambassadors of innovative guitar players from the blues to the early rock period are B. B. King, Albert King and Chuck Berry, who mainly used valve amplifiers for their warm and soft sound. Representatives of the classic rock period are Jimi Hendrix [m-Hen67a, m-Hen67b, m-Hen68], Eric Clapton [m-Cla67], Jimmy Page [m-Pag69], Ritchie Blackmore [m-Bla70], Jeff Beck [m-Bec89] and Carlos Santana [m-San99]. All make extensive use of valve amplification and special guitar effect units. There are also players from the new classic period like Eddie van Halen, Steve Ray Vaughan and Steve Morse up to the new guitar heroes such as Steve Lukather, Joe Satriani, Gary Moore, Steve Vai and Paul Gilbert, who are using effect devices together with valve amplifiers.

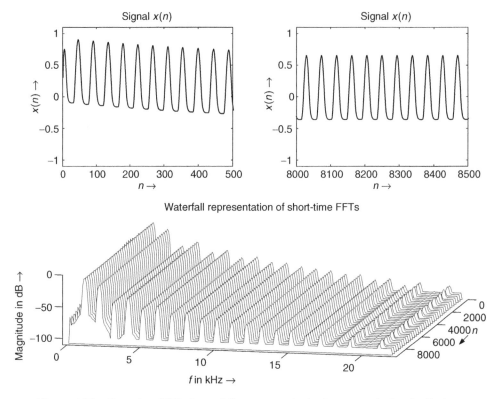

Figure 4.27   Short-time FFTs (waterfall representation) of asymmetrical soft clipping.

4.3.2   Overdrive, distortion and fuzz

Introduction

As pointed out in the section on valve simulation, the distorted electric guitar is a central part of rock music. In addition to the guitar amplifier as a major sound effect device, several stomp boxes (foot-operated pedals) have been used by guitar players for the creation of their typical guitar sound. Guitar heroes like Jimi Hendrix have made use of several small analog effect devices to achieve their unmistakable sound. Most of these effect devices have been used to create higher harmonics for the guitar sound in a faster way and at a much lower sound level compared to valve amplifiers. In this context terms like overdrive, distortion and fuzz are used. Several definitions of these terms for musical applications especially in the guitar player world are available [Kee00]. For our discussion we will define *overdrive* as a first state where a nearly linear audio effect device at low input levels is driven by higher input levels into the nonlinear region of its characteristic curve. The operating region is in the linear region as well as in the nonlinear region, with a smooth transition. The main sound characteristic is of course from the nonlinear part. Overdrive has a warm and smooth sound. The second state is termed *distortion*, where the effects device mainly operates in the nonlinear region of the characteristic curve and reaches the upper input level, where the output level is fixed to a maximum level. Distortion covers a wide tonal area starting beyond tube warmth to buzz saw effects. All metal and grunge sounds fall into this category. The operating status of *fuzz* is represented by a completely nonlinear behavior of the effect device with a sound characterized by the guitar player terms "harder" and "harsher" than distortion. The fuzz effect is generally used on single-note lead lines.

Signal processing

Overdrive. For overdrive simulations a soft clipping of the input values has to be performed. One possible approach for a soft saturation nonlinearity [Sch80] is given by

$$f(x) = \begin{cases} 2x & \text{for} \quad 0 \leq x \leq 1/3 \\ \frac{3-(2-3x)^2}{3} & \text{for} \quad 1/3 \leq x \leq 2/3 \\ 1 & \text{for} \quad 2/3 \leq x \leq 1. \end{cases} \qquad (4.14)$$

The static input to output relation is shown in Figure 4.28. Up to the threshold of $1/3$ the input is multiplied by two and the characteristic curve is in its linear region. Between input values of $1/3$ up to $2/3$, the characteristic curve produces a soft compression described by the middle term of Equation (4.14). Above input values of $2/3$ the output value is set to one. The corresponding M-file 4.5 for overdrive with symmetrical soft clipping is shown next.

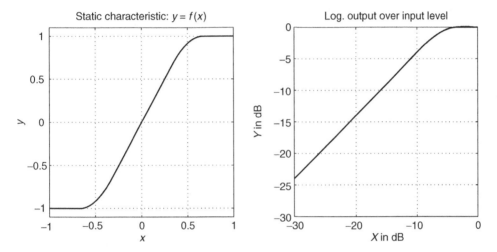

Figure 4.28   Static characteristic curve of symmetrical soft clipping (right part shows logarithmic output value versus input value).

M-file 4.5 (symclip.m)

```
function y=symclip(x)
% function y=symclip(x)
% Author: Dutilleux, Zölzer
% "Overdrive" simulation with symmetrical clipping
% x    - input
N=length(x);
th=1/3; % threshold for symmetrical soft clipping
        % by Schetzen Formula
for i=1:1:N,
    if abs(x(i))< th, y(i)=2*x(i);end;
    if abs(x(i))>=th,
        if x(i)> 0, y(i)=(3-(2-x(i)*3).^2)/3; end;
        if x(i)< 0, y(i)=-(3-(2-abs(x(i))*3).^2)/3; end;
    end;
    if abs(x(i))>2*th,
```

```
        if x(i)> 0, y(i)=1;end;
        if x(i)< 0, y(i)=-1;end;
    end;
end;
```

Figure 4.29 shows the waveforms of a simulation with the above-described characteristic curve and a decaying sinusoid of 1 kHz. In the upper left plot the first part of the output signal is shown with high signal levels, which corresponds to the saturated part of the characteristic curve. The tops and bottoms of the sinusoid run with a soft curve towards the saturated maximum values. The upper right plot shows the output signal where the maximum values are in the soft clipping region of the characteristic curve. Both the negative and the positive top of the sinusoid are rounded in their shape. The lower waterfall representation shows the entire decay of the sinusoid down to -12 dB. Notice the odd order harmonics produced by this nonlinear symmetrical characteristic curve, which appear in the nonlinear region of the characteristic curve and disappear as soon as the lower threshold of the soft compression is reached. The prominent harmonics are the third and the fifth harmonic. The slow increase or decrease of higher harmonics is the major property of symmetrical soft clipping. As soon as simple hard clipping without a soft compression is performed, higher harmonics appear with significantly higher levels (see Figure 4.30). The discussion of overdrive and distortion has so far only considered the creation of harmonics for a single sinusoid as the input signal. Since a single guitar tone itself consists of the fundamental frequency plus all odd- and even-order harmonics, it is always the sum of sinusoids that is processed by the nonlinearity. The nonlinearity also produces sum and difference frequencies.

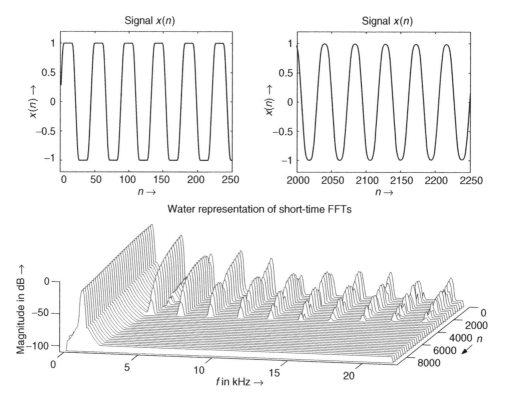

Figure 4.29 Short-time FFTs (waterfall representation) of symmetrical soft clipping for a decaying sinusoid of 1 kHz.

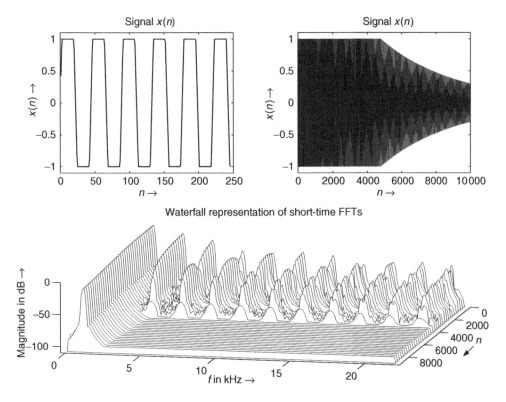

Figure 4.30   Short-time FFTs (waterfall representation) of symmetrical hard clipping for a decaying sinusoid of 1 kHz.

Distortion.   A nonlinearity suitable for the simulation of distortion [Ben97] is given by

$$f(x) = \mathrm{sgn}(x)\left(1 - e^{-|x|}\right). \tag{4.15}$$

The M-file 4.6 for performing Equation (4.15) is shown next.

M-file 4.6 (expdist.m)

```
function y=expdist(x, gain, mix)
% function y=expdist(x, gain, mix)
% Author: Bendiksen, Dutilleux, Zölzer, Dempwolf
% y=expdist(x, gain, mix)
% Distortion based on an exponential function
% x    - input
% gain - amount of distortion, >0
% mix  - mix of original and distorted sound, 1=only distorted
q=x*gain;
z=sign(q).*(1-exp(-abs(q)));
y=mix*z+(1-mix)*x;
```

The static characteristic curve is illustrated in Figure 4.31 and short-time FFTs of a decaying 1 kHz sinusoid are shown in Figure 4.32.

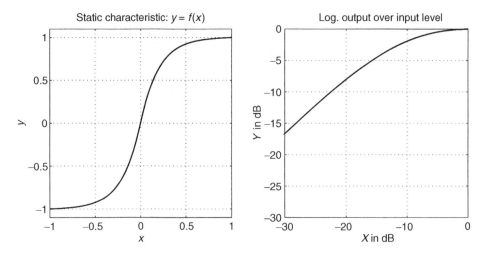

Figure 4.31   Static characteristic curve of exponential distortion.

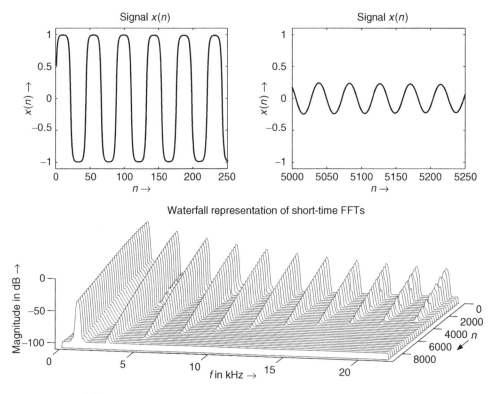

Figure 4.32   Short-time FFTs (waterfall representation) of exponential distortion.

Fuzz.   We have already discussed the behavior of triode valves in the previous section which produce an asymmetrical overdrive. One famous representative of asymmetrical clipping is the *Fuzz Face* [Kee98a], which was used by Jimi Hendrix. The basic analog circuit is shown in Figure 4.33 and consists only of a few components with two transistors in a feedback arrangement.

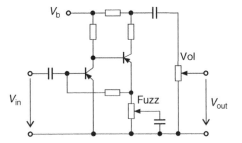

Figure 4.33   Analog circuit of Fuzz Face.

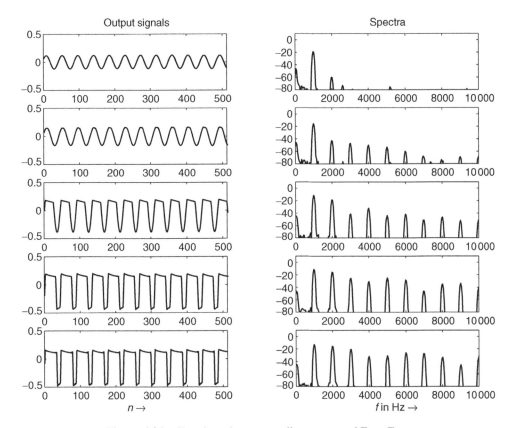

Figure 4.34   Signals and corresponding spectra of Fuzz Face.

The output signals for various input levels are presented in Figure 4.34 in conjunction with the corresponding spectra for a 1 kHz sinusoid. The upper plots down to the lower plots show an increasing input level. For low-level input signals the typical second harmonic of a triode valve can be noticed, although the time signal shows no distortion components. With increasing input level the second harmonic and all even-order harmonics as well as odd-order harmonics appear. The asymmetrical clipping produces enhanced even-order harmonics, as shown in the third row of Figure 4.34. Notice that only the top of the positive maximum values are clipped. As soon as the input level further increases, the negative part of the waveform is clipped. The negative clipping level is lower than the positive clipping value and so asymmetrical clipping is performed.

Short-time Fourier transforms (in waterfall representation) for an increasing 1 kHz sinusoid, together with two waveforms are shown in Figure 4.35.

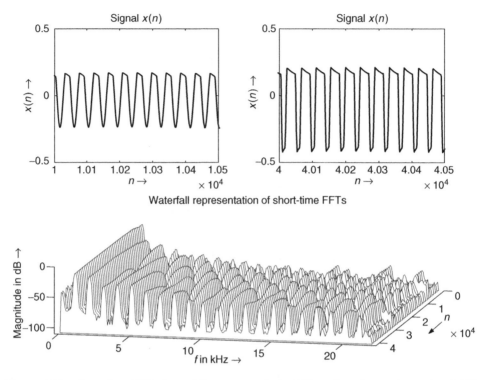

Figure 4.35 Short-time FFTs (waterfall representation) of Fuzz Face for an increasing 1 kHz sinusoid. The upper plots show segments of samples from the complete analyzed signal.

Musical applications

There are a lot of commercial stomp effects for guitarists on the market. Some of the most interesting distortion devices for guitars are the *Fuzz Face* which performs asymmetrical clipping towards symmetrical soft clipping and the *Tube Screamer* [Kee98b], which performs symmetrical soft clipping. The *Fuzz Face* was used by Jimi Hendrix and the *Tube Screamer* by Stevie Ray Vaughan. They both offer classical distortion and are well known because of their famous users. It is difficult to explain the sound of a distortion unit without listening personally to it. The technical specifications for the sound of distortion are missing, so the only way to choose a distortion effect is by a comparative listening test. Investigations about the sound coloration caused by typical distortion or overdrive effects can be found in [MM05, DHMZ09].

4.3.3 Harmonic and subharmonic generation

Introduction

Harmonic and subharmonic generation are performed by simple analog or digital effect devices, which should produce an octave above and/or an octave below a single note. Advanced techniques to achieve pitch shifting of instrument sounds will be introduced in Chapter 6. Here, we will focus on simple techniques, which lead to the generation of harmonics and subharmonics.

Signal processing

The signal-processing algorithms for harmonic and subharmonic generation are based on simple mathematical operations like absolute value computation and counting of zero crossings, as shown in Figure 4.36 when an input sinusoid has to be processed (first row shows time signal and corresponding spectrum).

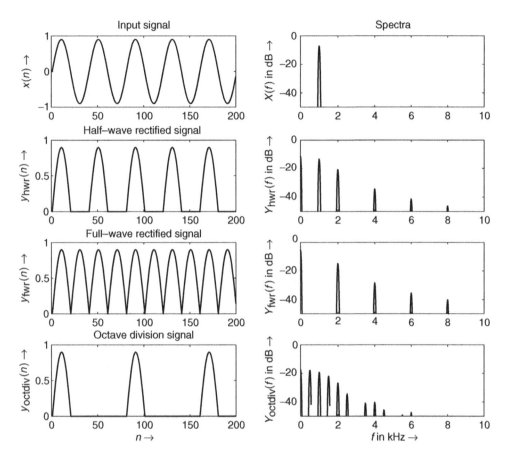

Figure 4.36 Signals and corresponding spectra of half-wave rectification, full-wave rectification and octave division.

The second row of Figure 4.36 demonstrates half-wave rectification, where positive values are kept and negative values are set to zero. This operation leads to the generation of even-order harmonics. Full-wave rectification, where the absolute value is taken from the input sequence, leads to even-order harmonics, as shown in the third row of Figure 4.36. Notice the absence of the fundamental frequency. If a zero crossing counter is applied to the half-wave or the full-wave rectified signal, a predefined number of positive wave parts can be set to zero to achieve the signal in the last row of Figure 4.36. This signal has a fundamental frequency which is one octave lower than the input frequency in the first row of the figure, but also shows harmonics of this new fundamental frequency. If appropriate lowpass filtering is applied to such a signal, only the fundamental frequency can be obtained, which is then added to the original input signal.

Musical applications

Harmonic and subharmonic generation is mostly used on single-note lead lines, where an additional harmonic or subharmonic frequency helps to enhance the octave effect. Harmonic generators can be found in stomp boxes for guitar or bass guitar and appear under the name *octaver*. Subharmonic generation is often used for solo and bass instruments to give them an extra bass boost or simply a fuzz bass character.

4.3.4   Tape saturation

Introduction and musical application

The special sound characteristic of analog tape recordings has been acknowledged by a variety of producers and musicians in the field of rock music. They prefer doing multi track recordings with analog tape-based machines and use the special physics of magnetic tape recording as an analog effects processor for sound design. One reason for their preference for analog recording is the fact that magnetic tape goes into distortion gradually [Ear76, pp. 216-218] and produces those kinds of harmonics which help special sound effects on drums, guitars and vocals.

Signal processing

Tape saturation can be simulated by the already introduced techniques for valve simulation. An input-level-derived weighting curve is used for generating a gain factor, which is used to compress the input signal. A variety of measurements of tape recordings can help in the design of such processing devices. An example of the input/output behavior is shown in Figure 4.37 and a short-time FFT of a sinusoid input signal in Figure 4.38 illustrates a tape saturation algorithm. For low-level inputs the transfer characteristic is linear without any distortions. A smooth soft compression simulates the gradually increasing distortion of magnetic tape.

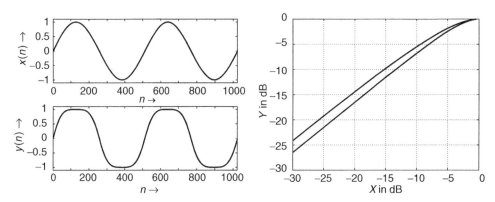

Figure 4.37   Tape saturation: input and output signal (left) and characteristic curve.

4.4   Exciters and enhancers

4.4.1   Exciters

Introduction

An exciter is a signal processor that emphasizes or de-emphasizes certain frequencies in order to change a signal's timbre. An exciter increases brightness without necessarily adding equalization.

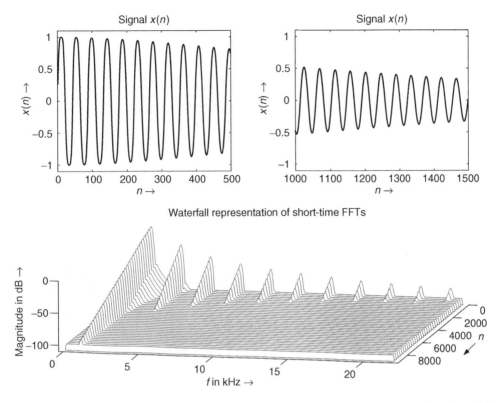

Figure 4.38 Tape saturation: short-time FFTs (waterfall representation) for decaying sinusoid of 1 kHz.

The result is a brighter, "airier" sound without the stridency that can sometimes occur by simply boosting the treble. This is often accomplished with subtle amounts of high-frequency distortion, and sometimes by phase shifting. Usually there will only be one or two parameters, such as exciter mix and exciter frequency. The former determines how much "excited" sound gets added to the straight sound, and the latter determines the frequency at which the exciter effect starts [Whi93, And95, Dic87, WG94].

This effect was discovered by the Aphex company and "Aural Exciter" is a trademark of this company. The medium and treble parts of the original signal are processed by a nonlinear circuit that generates higher overtones. These components are then mixed to some extent to the original signal. A compressor at the output of the nonlinear element makes the effect dependent on the input signal. The initial part of percussive sounds will be more enriched than the following part, when the compressor limits the effect depth. The enhanced imaging or spaciousness is probably the result of the phase rotation within the filter [Alt90].

Signal processing

Measurement results of the APHEX Aural Exciter are shown in Figures 4.39 and 4.40, where the generation of a second harmonic is clearly visible. The input signal is a chirp signal with an increasing frequency up to 5 kHz. Signal-processing techniques to achieve the effect have already been discussed in the previous sections. The effect is created in the side-chain path and is mixed with the input signal.

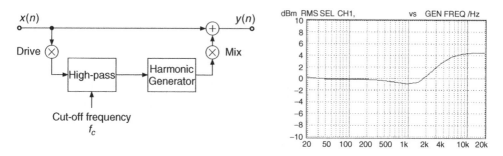

Figure 4.39   Block diagram of the psycho-acoustic equalizer APHEX Aural Exciter and frequency response.

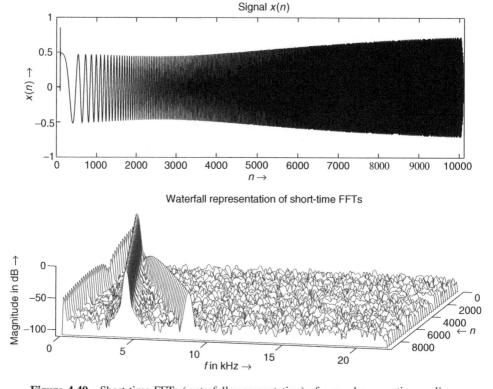

Figure 4.40   Short-time FFTs (waterfall representation) of a psycho-acoustic equalizer.

Musical applications

The applications of this effect are widespread and range from single-instrument enhancement to enhancement of mix buses and stereo signals. The effect increases the presence and clarity of a single instrument inside a mix and helps to add natural brightness to stereo signals. Applied to vocals and speech the effect increases intelligibility. Compared to equalizers the sound level is only increased slightly. The application of this effect only makes sense if the input signal lacks high-frequency content.

4.4.2 Enhancers

Introduction

Enhancers are signal processors which combine equalization together with nonlinear processing. They perform equalization according to the fundamentals of psychoacoustics [ZF90] and introduce a small amount of distortion in a just noticeable manner. An introduction to the ear's own nonlinear distortions, sharpness, sensory pleasantness and roughness can be also be found in [ZF90].

Signal processing

As an example of this class of devices the block diagram and the frequency response of the SPL vitalizer are shown in Figure 4.41. This effect processor has also a side-chain path which performs equalization with a strong bass enhancement, a mid-frequency cut and a high-frequency boost. The short-time FFT of the output signal when a chirp input signal is applied is shown in Figure 4.42. The resulting waterfall representation clearly shows higher harmonics generated by this effect processor.

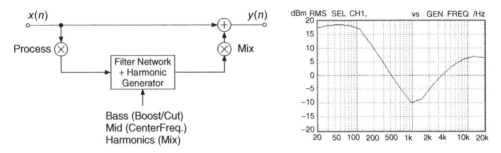

Figure 4.41 Block diagram of the psycho-acoustic equalizer SPL Vitalizer and frequency response.

Further refinements of enhancers can be achieved through multiband enhancers which split the input signal into several frequency bands. Inside each frequency band nonlinear processing plus filtering is performed. The output signals of each frequency band are weighted and summed up to form the output signal (see Figure 4.43).

Musical applications

The main applications of such effects are single-track processing as a substitute for the equalizers inside the input channels of mixing consoles and processing of final mixes. The side-chain processing allows the subtle mix of the effects signal together with the input signal. Further applications are stereo enhancement for broadcast stations and sound reinforcement.

4.5 Conclusion

The most challenging tools for musicians and sound engineers are nonlinear processors such as dynamics processors, valve simulators and exciters. The successful application of these audio processors depends on the appropriate control of these devices. A variety of interactive control parameters influences the resulting sound quality.

The primary purpose of this chapter is to enable the reader to attain a fundamental understanding of different types of nonlinear processors and the special properties of nonlinear operations applied

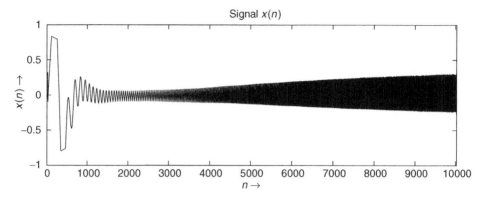

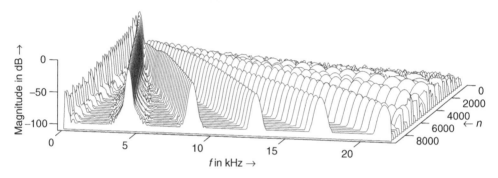

Figure 4.42 Short-time FFTs (waterfall representation) of psycho-acoustic equalizer SPL Vitalizer.

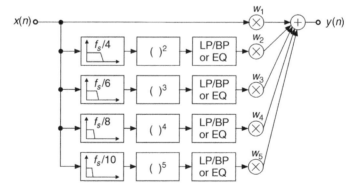

Figure 4.43 Multiband enhancer with nonlinear processing in frequency bands.

to the audio signal. Dynamics processors need a careful consideration of the interaction of thresholds and time constants to achieve sonic purity and avoid harmonic distortion. On the other hand, nonlinear processors are used for the simulation of valve amplifiers or nonlinear audio systems, where a special kind of nonlinearity provides a sound distortion with an accepted sound characteristic. We have presented the basics of nonlinear modeling and focused on the combination of filters and nonlinearities. Several applications demonstrate the importance of nonlinear processors. The basic building blocks of the previous chapters such as filters, delays and modulators/demodulators are particularly useful for exploring new, improved nonlinear processors.

Sound and music

[m-Bec89]   Jeff Beck: *Guitar Shop*. 1989.

[m-Bla70]   Deep Purple: *Deep Purple in Rock*. 1970.

[m-Cla67]   Cream: *Disraeli Gears*. 1967.

[m-Hen67a] Jimi Hendrix: *Are You Experienced?* 1967.

[m-Hen67b] Jimi Hendrix: *Axis: Bold as Love*. 1967.

[m-Hen68]   Jimi Hendrix: *Electric Ladyland*. 1968.

[m-Pag69]   Led Zeppelin: *I/II/III/IV*. 1969-1971.

[m-San99]   Santana: *Supernatural*. 1999.

References

[Alt90]   S. R. Alten. *Audio in Media*. Wadsworth, 1990.

[And95]   C. Anderton. *Multieffects for Musicians*. Amsco Publications, 1995.

[Bar98]   E. Barbour. The cool sound of tubes. *IEEE Spectrum*, pp. 24–32, 1998.

[Ben97]   R. Bendiksen. Digitale Lydeffekter. *Master's thesis*, Norwegian University of Science and Technology, 1997.

[Bev77]   M. Bevelle. Compressors and limiters. *Studio Sound*, p. 32, 1977.

[CVAT01]   E. Czerwinski, A. Voishvillo, S. Alexandrov and A. Terekhov. Multitone testing of sound system components - some results and conclusions. Part 1: History and theory. *J. Audio Eng. Soc.*, 49(11), 2001. 1011–1048

[DHMZ09]   K. Dempwolf, M. Holters, S. Möller and U. Zölzer. The influence of small variations in a simplified guitar amplifier model. In *Proc. of the 12th Int. Conf. on Digital Audio Effects (DAFx-09)*, Como, Italy, Sept. 1–4 2009.

[Dic87]   M. Dickreiter. *Handbuch der Tonstudiotechnik, Band I und II*. K.G. Saur, 1987.

[Doy93]   M. Doyle. *The History of Marshall*. Hal Leonhard Publishing Corporation, 1993.

[Dut96]   P. Dutilleux. Verstärkung der Differenztöne (f2-f1). In *Bericht der 19. Tonmeistertagung Karlsruhe*, Verlag K.G. Saur, pp. 798–806, 1996.

[Ear76]   J. Eargle. *Sound Recording*. Van Nostrand, 1976.

[Fli93]   R. Fliegler. *AMPS! The Other Half of Rock"n'Roll*. Hal Leonhard Publishing Corporation, 1993.

[Fra97]   W. Frank. *Aufwandsarme Modellierung und Kompensation nichtlinearer Systeme auf Basis von Volterra-Reihen*. PhD thesis, University of the Federal Armed Forces Munich, Germany, 1997.

[FUB+98]   A. Farina, E. Ugolotti, A. Bellini, G. Cibelli and C. Morandi. Inverse numerical filters for linearisation of loudspeaker's responses. In *Proc. DAFX-98 Digital Audio Effects Workshop*, pp. 12–16, Barcelona, November 1998.

[Ham73]   R. O. Hamm. Tubes versus transistors – is there an audible difference ? *J. Audio Eng. Soc.*, 21(4): 267–273, May 1973.

[Hul97]   R. Hulse. A different way of looking at compression. *Studio Sound*, 1997.

[Izh10]   R. Izhaki. *Mixing Audio: Concepts, Practices and Tools*. Focal Press, 2010.

[Kai87]   A. J. M. Kaizer. Modeling of the nonlinear response of an electrodynamic loudspeaker by a volterra series expansion. *J. Audio Eng. Soc.*, 35(6): 421–433, 1987.

[Kat07]   B. Katz. *Mastering Audio*. Focal Press, 2007.

[Kee98a]   R. G. Keen. The technology of the fuzz face. [online] www.geofex.com, 1998.

[Kee98b]   R. G. Keen. The technology of the tube screamer. [online] www.geofex.com, 1998.

[Kee00]   R. G. Keen. A musical distortion primer. [online] www.geofex.com, 1993–2000.

[Kli98]   W. Klippel. Direct feedback linearization of nonlinear loudspeaker systems. *J. Audio Eng. Soc.*, 46(6): 499–507, 1998.

[Kue05]   R. Kuehnel. *Circuit Analysis of a Legendary Tube Amplifier: The Fender Bassman 5F6-A*, 2nd edition. Pentode Press, 2005.

[Lun07]   T. Lund. Level and distortion in digital broadcasting. *EBU Technical Review*, April 2007.

[McN84]   G. W. McNally. Dynamic range control of digital audio signals. *J. Audio Eng. Soc.*, 32(5): 316–327, May 1984.

[MM05]   A. Marui and W. L. Martens. Timbre of nonlinear distortion effects: Perceptual attributes beyond sharpness. In *Proc. of Conf. Interdisc. Musicol. (CIM05)*, Montréal, Canada, March 2005.

[Nie00]   S. Nielsen. Personal communication. TC Electronic A/S, 2000.

[Orf96]   S. J. Orfanidis. *Introduction to Signal Processing*. Prentice-Hall, 1996.

[PD93]   D. Peterson and D. Denney. *The VOX Story*. The Bold Strummer Ltd., 1993.

[Rat95]   L. Ratheiser. *Das Große Röhrenhandbuch*. Reprint. Franzis-Verlag, 1995.

[RCA59]   RCA. *Receiving Tube Manual. Technical Series RC-19*. Radio Corporation of America, 1959.

[RH96]   M. J. Reed and M. O. Hawksford. Practical modeling of nonlinear audio systems using the volterra series. In *Proc. 100th AES Convention*, Preprint 4264, 1996.

[Sal02]   T. Salter. *Talking Shop with Randall Smith of Mesa Boogie, Interview*. Musicians Hotline, May/June 2002.

[Sch80]   M. Schetzen. *The Volterra and Wiener Theories of Nonlinear Systems*. Robert Krieger Publishing, 1980.

[SZ99]   J. Schattschneider and U. Zölzer. Discrete-time models for nonlinear audio systems. In *Proc. DAFX-99 Digital Audio Effects Workshop*, pp. 45–48, Trondheim, December 1999.

[WG94]   M. Warstat and T. Görne. *Studiotechnik – Hintergrund und Praxiswissen*. Elektor-Verlag, 1994.

[Whi93]   P. White. *L'enregistrement Créatif, Effets et Processeurs, Tomes 1 et 2*. Les Cahiers de l'ACME, 1993.

[YBK08]   D. Yeh, B. Bank and M. Karjalainen. Nonlinear modeling of a guitar amplifier cabinet. In *Proc. DAFX-08 Conf. Digital Audio Effects*, pp. 89–96, Espoo, Finland, Sept 1–4 2008.

[ZF90]   E. Zwicker and H. Fastl. *Psychoacoustics*. Springer-Verlag, 1990.

[zL97]   R. zur Linde. *Röhrenverstärker*. Elektor-Verlag, 1997.

[Zöl05]   U. Zölzer. *Digital Audio Signal Processing*, 2nd edition. John Wiley & Sons, Ltd, 2005.

5

Spatial effects

V. Pulkki, T. Lokki and D. Rocchesso

5.1 Introduction

A listener is capable of sensing his surroundings in some degree using only hearing, for example directions, distances, and spatial extents of sound sources, and also some characteristics of the rooms. This information is obtained by comparing the sound signals in ear canals to a set of spatial cues, used by the brain. Understanding the cues used by the hearing system helps the audio engineer to introduce some artificial features in the sound material in order to project the sound events in space. In the first half of this chapter, the most important techniques for sound projection are described, both for individual listeners using headphones and for an audience listening through a set of loudspeakers.

In natural listening conditions, sounds propagate from a source to the listener and during this trip they are widely modified by the environment. Therefore, there are some spatial effects imposed by the physical and geometric characteristics of the environment on the sound signals arriving to the listener's ears. Generally speaking, we call reverberation the kind of processing operated by the environment. The second half of this chapter illustrates this kind of effect and describes audio-processing techniques that have been devised to imitate and extend the reverberation that occurs in nature.

The importance of space has been largely emphasized in electroacoustic compositions, with the result that sophisticated spatial orchestrations often result in poor musical messages to the listener. Indeed, space cannot be treated as a composition parameter in the same way as pitch or timbre are orchestrated, just because space for sounds is not an "indispensable attribute" [KV01] as it is for images. This relative weakness is well explained if we think of two loudspeakers playing the same identical sound track: the listener will perceive one apparent source. The phenomenon is analogous to two colored spotlights that fuse to give one new, apparent, colored spot. In fact, color is considered a non-indispensable attribute for visual perception. However, just as color is a very important component in visual arts, the correct use of space can play a fundamental role

DAFX: Digital Audio Effects, Second Edition. Edited by Udo Zölzer.
© 2011 John Wiley & Sons, Ltd. Published 2011 by John Wiley & Sons, Ltd.

in music composition, especially for improving the effectiveness of other musical parameters of sound, such as pitch, timbre, and intensity.

5.2   Concepts of spatial hearing

As already mentioned, using only hearing, humans can localize sound sources, and they are also able to perceive some properties of the space they are in. This section considers both physical and perceptual issues which are related to such perception of spatial sound.

5.2.1   Head-related transfer functions

As a sound signal travels from a sound source to the ear canals of the listener, the signals in both ear canals will be different from the original sound signal and from each other. The transfer functions from a sound source to the ear canals are called the head-related transfer functions (HRTF) [Bla97]. They are dependent on the direction of a sound source related to the listener, and they yield temporal and spectral differences between left and right ear canals. Due to the fact that the ears are located on different sides of the skull, the arrival times of a sound signal vary with direction. Also, the skull casts an acoustic shadow that causes the contralateral ear signal to be attenuated. The shadowing is most prominent at frequencies above about 2 kHz, and does not exist when the frequency is below about 800 Hz. The pinna and other parts of the body may also change the sound signal. In some cases, it is advantageous to think about these filtering effects in the time domain, thus considering them *head-related impulse responses* (HRIR). Several authors have measured HRTFs by means of manikins or human subjects. A popular collection of measurements was taken by Gardner and Martin using a KEMAR dummy head, and made freely available [GM94, Gar97a]. A large set of HRTFs measured from humans have also been made available [ADDA01]. The HRTFs are also dependent on distance [BR99] with sources close to the listener. If the distance is more than about 1 m the dependence can be omitted. It will always be assumed in this chapter that the sources are in far field.

5.2.2   Perception of direction

Humans decode the differences of sound between the ear channels and use them to localize sound sources. These differences are called binaural directional cues. Temporal difference is called the interaural time difference (ITD) and spectral difference is called the interaural level difference (ILD) [Bla97]. Humans are sensitive to ILD at all frequencies, and to ITD mainly at frequencies lower than about 1.5 kHz. At higher frequencies, humans are also slightly sensitive to ITDs between signal envelopes, and not at all to ITD between the carriers of the signals. In typical HRTFs there exists a region near 2 kHz, where ILD is not monotonic with azimuth angle, and listeners easily localize the sources erroneously if the ITD between signal envelopes does not provide information of sound source direction [MHR10].

ITD and ILD provide information on where a sound source is in the left–right dimension. The angle between the sound source direction and the median plane can thus be decoded by the listener. The median plane is the vertical plane which divides the space related to a listener into left and right parts. The angle between the median plane and the sound source defines the cone of confusion, which is a set of points that all satisfy the following condition: the difference in distance from both ears to any point on the cone is constant, as shown in Figure 5.1. The angular coordinate system used in this chapter is also shown in the figure, which utilizes clockwise azimuth angle θ, being zero in front of the listener, and elevation angle ϕ, which defines the angle between the horizontal plane and the sound source direction, where positive is above the horizontal plane.

The information of the cone of confusion provided by the ITD and ILD is only an intermediate phase in the localization process. It is known that there are two mechanisms, which refine the

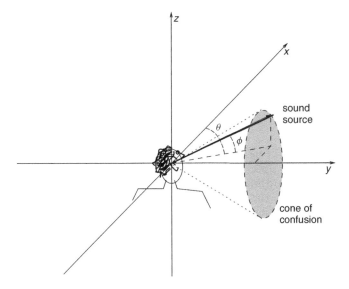

Figure 5.1 The azimuth-elevation coordinate system and cone of confusion.

perceived direction. One is related to monaural spectral cues, and the other is the monitoring of the effect of head rotation to binaural cues.

The monaural spectral cues are caused by the pinna of the listener, which filters the sound depending on the direction of arrival. For example, the concha, which is the cavity just around the ear canal opening, is known to have a direction-dependent resonance around 5–6 kHz [Bla97]. This effect with other direction-dependent filtering by the pinna and torso of the listener introduces spectral changes into the sound signal entering the ear canal at frequencies above 1–2 kHz. This provides information on the direction within the cone of confusion obtained from the ITD and ILD cues. Note that this mechanism is thus dependent on the spectrum of the signal, and a sufficiently broad and locally smooth spectrum is needed to decode the direction from the monaural spectrum. If the signal has too narrow a bandwidth, monaural spectral cues cannot be decoded. For example, some birds have a narrow bandwidth in their calls, and their localization using only hearing is relatively hard.

The effect of head movements on binaural cues, and how humans use this information in sound source localization [Bla97, GA97] are now discussed. For example, when a source is in front of the listener, and the listener rotates his head to the right, the left ear becomes closer the source, and the ITD and ILD cues change favoring the left ear. If the source is in the back of the listener, the cues would change favoring the right ear. This dynamic cue gives information on the source direction. Humans seem to use the information in a relatively coarse manner, such as if the source is in front, back or above of the listener. However, it is a very strong cue. A simple and very effective spatial effect can be composed by switching the ear canal signals of the listener in dynamic conditions either with tubes or microphones and loudspeakers. In this device, the sound signal captured on one side of the head of the listener is delivered to the ear on the other side. When wearing such a device, a striking directional effect is obtained, where the perceived direction of the voice of the visible speaker in front is perceived at the back of the listener.

5.2.3   Perception of the spatial extent of the sound source

It is also possible to perceive the extent of a sound source in some cases. For example, the sea shore and grand piano can be perceived to have a substantial width only using audition. Unfortunately, the knowledge of the corresponding perceptual phenomena and mechanisms is relatively sparse.

A basic result is, that point-like broadband sound sources are perceived to be point-like, and when incoherent broadband sound arrives from multiple directions evenly it is perceived to surround the listener [Bla97]. In these cases, the perception corresponds well to the physical situation. When the frequency content is narrower, or the duration of the stimulus is short, the perceived widths of the sources are perceived to be narrower than in reality [PB82, CT03, Hir07, HP08]. When the frequency bands of a broad sound signal are presented using loudspeakers in different directions, the listener perceives the source to be wide, though not as wide as the loudspeaker ensemble is [Hir07].

5.2.4   Room effect

So far we have discussed only the direct sound coming from the source to the listener. In real rooms and in many outdoor spaces there exist reflections and reverberation, which do not carry information on the direction of the sound. A mechanism has evolved which helps to localize sources in such environments. The precedence effect [Bla97, Zur87, LCYG99] is a suppression of early delayed versions of the direct sound in source direction perception. This has been researched a lot in classical studies, where a direct sound and a delayed sound are presented to a listener in anechoic conditions with two loudspeakers. When the delay is about 0–3 ms, no echo is perceived, and the perceived direction depends on the amplitude relationship and on the delay between the loudspeakers. The perceived direction may also be dependent on the frequency content of the sound. When the delay is about 5–30 ms, the presence of the lagging sound may be perceived, but it is not localized correctly. With larger delays, the delayed loudspeaker starts to be localizable. The effect is dependent on the signal, in principle: the more transient-like the nature of the signal, the more the precedence effect is salient. The precedence effect manifests itself in the Franssen effect, where the rapid onset of a sinusoid with a slow fadeout in one loudspeaker is interleaved with a slow fade in of the same sinusoid in another loudspeaker. The listener does not perceive that the second loudspeaker is emitting sound, but he erroneously perceives that the first loudspeaker is still active [Bla97].

Humans can also perceive the effect of the room in some manner. Indeed, in real life, a free-field condition very seldom occurs and sound always contains some reverberation, composed of reflections from surfaces. Humans can estimate the size of a room and even surface materials by listening to sounds. The perception relies on the density of the reflections and the length of the reverberation. Consider a concert hall and a bathroom, which both can have a reverberation time of 2 to 3 seconds, i.e., the sound is audible 2 to 3 seconds after the source has stopped emitting sound. The density of reflections, as well as their frequency characteristics modify the sound color, based on which humans can tell the size of space, even though the reverberation time in both cases is the same. The shape of the space can be also perceived to some extent, at least if it is a long narrow corridor, or a big concert hall.

5.2.5   Perception of distance

Humans also perceive the distance of sound sources to some extent [Bla97]. There are some main cues used for this. The perceived loudness created by a sound source has been proven to affect the perceived distance: the softer the auditory event, that farther away it is perceived. However, the signal has to be somewhat known by the listener, and is effective only with sources in about 1 m–10 m distances.

Listeners use the acoustical room effect caused by the source in perception of distance: the more the room effect is present in the ear canals of the listener, the farther away is the source perceived. This is quantified with the direct-to-reverberant ratio (DRR) of sound energies expressed in decibels. Besides the DRR, the room also has another well-known effect on perceived distance. If the impulse response of the room contains no strong early reflections, the source is perceived to be relatively near. This is utilized in studio reverberators with a predelay parameter, which controls the delay between the direct sound and the reverb tail. If the value of the predelay is long enough, the source is perceived at the distance of the loudspeakers, and if it is very short, then the source is perceived to be farther away.

When the source is very near to the listener, there are also some binaural effects which are used in distance perception [DM98]. With close sources the magnitude of ILD is higher and appears at lower frequencies than a far source with the same direction, which creates the perception of a nearby source.

5.3 Basic spatial effects for stereophonic loudspeaker and headphone playback

The most common loudspeaker layout is the two-channel setup, called the standard stereophonic setup. It was widely taken into use after the development of single-groove 45°/45° two-channel records in the late 1950s. Two loudspeakers are positioned in front of the listener, separated by 60° from the listener's viewpoint, as presented in Figure 5.2. The setup of two loudspeakers is very common, though quite often the setup is not as shown in the figure. In domestic use, or in car audio typically the listener is not situated in the centre, but the loudspeakers are located in different directions and distances from him than in Figure 5.2. However, even then two-channel reproduction is preferred from monophonic presentation in most cases. On the other hand, in some cases the listener can be assumed to be in the best listening position, as in computer audio.

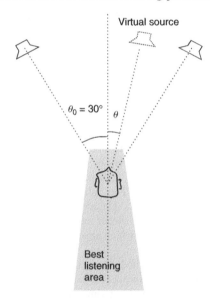

Figure 5.2 Standard stereophonic listening configuration.

This section deals with the spatial effects obtainable with such two-channel reproduction and simple processing. Two types of effects are presented, the creation of point-like sources, and the creation of spatially spread sources. More advanced methods for loudspeaker reproduction with HRTF processing are discussed in Section 5.4.5, which provide some more degrees of freedom, but unfortunately also introduce some limitations in listening position and listening room acoustics.

5.3.1 Amplitude panning in loudspeakers

Amplitude panning is the most frequently used virtual-source-positioning technique. In it a sound signal is applied to loudspeakers with different amplitudes, which can be formulated as

$$x_i(t) = g_i x(t), \quad i = 1, \ldots, N, \tag{5.1}$$

where $x_i(t)$ is the signal to be applied to loudspeaker i, g_i is the gain factor of the corresponding channel, N is the number of loudspeakers, and t is the time. The listener perceives a virtual source, the direction of which is dependent on the gain factors.

If the listener is located equally distant from the loudspeakers, the panning law estimates the perceived direction θ from the gain factors of loudspeakers. The estimated direction is called the panning direction or panning angle. In [Pul01] it has been found that amplitude panning provides consistent ITD cues up to 1.1 kHz, and roughly consistent ILD cues above 2 kHz for a listener in the best listening position. The *level* differences between the loudspeakers are changed a bit surprisingly to *phase* differences between the ears, which is due to the fact that the sound arrives from both loudspeakers to both ears, which is called cross-talk. This effect is valid at low frequencies. At high frequencies, the level differences of the loudspeakers turn into level differences due to lack of the cross-talk caused by the shadowing of the head.

There exist many published methods to estimate the perceived direction. In practice, all the proposed methods are equally good for audio effects, and the tangent law by Bennett *et al.* [BBE85] is formulated as

$$\frac{\tan \theta}{\tan \theta_0} = \frac{g_1 - g_2}{g_1 + g_2}, \qquad (5.2)$$

which has been found to estimate perceived direction best in listening tests in anechoic listening [Pul01]. There are also other panning laws, reviewed in [Pul01].

The panning laws set only the ratio between the gain factors. To prevent undesired changes in loudness of the virtual source depending on panning direction, the sum-of-squares of the gain factors should be normalized:

$$\sqrt{\sum_{n=1}^{N} g_n^2} = 1. \qquad (5.3)$$

This normalization equation is used in real rooms with some reverberation. Depending on listening room acoustics, different normalization rules may be used [Moo90].

The presented analysis is valid only if the loudspeakers are equidistant from the listener, and if the base angle is not larger than about 60°. This defines the best listening area where the virtual sources are localized between the loudspeakers. The area is located around the axis of symmetry of the setup, as shown in Figure 5.2. When the listener moves away from the area, the virtual source is localized towards the nearest loudspeaker which emanates a considerable amount of sound, due to the precedence effect.

In principle, the amplitude-panning method creates a comb-filter effect in the sound spectrum, as the same sound arrives from both loudspeakers to each ear. However, this effect is relatively mild, and when heard in a normal room, the room reverberation smooths the coloring effect prominently. The sound color is also very similar when heard in different positions in the room. The lack of prominent coloring and the relatively robust directional effect provided by it are very probably the reasons why amplitude panning is included in all mixing consoles as "panpot" control, which makes it the most widely used technique to position virtual sources.

M-file 5.1 (stereopan.m)

```
% stereopan.m
% Author: V. Pulkki

% Stereophonic panning example with tangent law
Fs=44100;
theta=-20; % Panning direction
% Half of opening angle of loudspeaker pair
lsbase=30;
```

```
% Moving to radians
theta=theta/180*pi;
lsbase=lsbase/180*pi;
% Computing gain factors with tangent law
g(2)=1; % initial value has to be one
g(1)=- (tan(theta)-tan(lsbase)) / (tan(theta)+tan(lsbase)+eps);
% Normalizing the sum-of-squares
g=g/sqrt(sum(g.^2));
% Signal to be panned
signal=mod([1:20000]',200)/200;
% Actual panning
loudsp_sig=[signal*g(1) signal*g(2)];
% Play audio out with two loudspeakers
soundsc(loudsp_sig,Fs);
```

5.3.2 Time and phase delays in loudspeaker playback

When a constant delay is applied to one loudspeaker in stereophonic listening, virtual sources with transient signals are perceived to migrate towards the loudspeaker that radiates the earlier sound signal [Bla97]. Maximal effect is achieved asymptotically when the delay is approximately 1.0 ms or more. However, the effect depends on the signal used. With continuous signals containing low frequencies, the effect is much less prominent than with modulated signals containing high frequencies.

In such processing the *phase* or *time* delays between the loudspeakers are turned at low frequencies into *level* differences between the ears, and at high frequencies to *time* differences between the ears. This all makes the virtual source direction depend on frequency [Coo87, Lip86]. The produced binaural cues vary with frequency, and different cues suggest different directions for virtual sources [PKH99]. It may thus generate a "spread" perception of direction of sound, which is desirable in some cases. The effect is dependent on listening position. For example, if the sound signal is delayed by 1 ms in one loudspeaker, the listener can compensate the delay by moving 30 cm towards the delayed loudspeaker.

M-file 5.2 (delaypan.m)

```
% delaypan.m
% Author: V. Pulkki
% Creating spatially spread virtual source by delaying one channel
Fs=44100;
% Delay parameter for channel 1 in seconds
delay=0.005;
% Corresponding number of delayed samples
delaysamp=round(delay*Fs)
% Signal to be used
signal=mod([1:20000]',400)/400;
signal(1:2000)=signal(1:2000).*[1:2000]'/2000; % Fade in
% Delaying first channel
loudsp_sig=[[zeros(delaysamp,1); signal(1:end-delaysamp)] signal];
% Play audio with loudspeakers
soundsc(loudsp_sig,Fs);
```

A special case of a phase difference in stereophonic reproduction is the use of antiphasic signals in the loudspeakers. In such a technique, the same signal is applied to both loudspeakers, however, the polarity of the other loudspeaker signal is inverted, which produces a constant 180°

phase difference between the signals at all frequencies. This changes the perceived sound color, and also spreads the virtual sources. Depending on the listening position, the low frequencies may be cancelled out. At higher frequencies this effect is milder. This effect is also milder in rooms with longer reverberation. The directional perception of the antiphasic virtual source depends on the listening position. In the sweet spot, the high frequencies are perceived to be at the center, and low frequencies in random directions. Outside the sweet spot, the direction is either random, or towards the closest loudspeaker. In the language of professional audio engineers this effect is called "phasy", or "there is phase error in here".

M-file 5.3 (phaseinvert.m)

```
% phaseinvert.m
% Author: V. Pulkki
% Create a spread virtual source by inverting phase in one loudspeaker
Fs=44100;
signal=mod([1:20000]',400)/400; %signal to be used
% Inverting one loudspeaker signal
loudsp_sig=[-signal signal];
% Play audio out with two loudspeakers
soundsc(loudsp_sig,Fs);
```

A further method to spread the virtual source between the loudspeakers is to change the phase spectrum of the sound differently at different frequencies. A basic method is to convolve the signal for the loudspeakers with two different short bursts of white noise. Another method is to apply a different delay to different frequencies. This effectively spreads out the virtual source between the loudspeakers, and the effect is audible over a large listening area. Unfortunately, the processing changes the temporal response slightly, which may be audible as temporal smearing of transients of the signal.

Below is a example creating spread virtual sources for stereophonic listening by convolving the sound with short noise bursts:

M-file 5.4 (spreadnoise.m)

```
% spreadnoise.m
% Author: V. Pulkki
% Example how to spread a virtual source over N loudspeakers
Fs=44100;
signal=mod([1:20000]',400)/400; % Signal to be used
NChan=2; % Number of channels
% Generate noise bursts for all channels
nois=rand(round(0.05*Fs),NChan)-0.5;
% Convolve signal with bursts
loudsp_sig=conv(signal,nois(:,1));
for i=2:NChan
    loudsp_sig=[loudsp_sig conv(signal,nois(:,i))];
end
if NChan == 2
    % Play audio out with  loudspeakers
    soundsc(loudsp_sig,Fs);
else
    % Write file to disk
    loudsp_sig=loudsp_sig/max(max(loudsp_sig))*0.9;
    wavwrite([loudsp_sig],Fs,16,'burstex.wav');
end
```

5.3.3 Listening to two-channel stereophonic material with headphones

The headphone listening is significantly different to loudspeaker listening. In headphones the cross-talk present in loudspeaker listening is missing, meaning that the sound from the left headphone enters only to the left ear canal, and similarly with the right side. Typically, the audio engineers create the stereophonic audio content in studios with two-channel loudspeaker listening. It is then relevant to ask how the spatial perception of the content changes, when listened to over headphones.

With amplitude-panned virtual sources the level difference between headphone channels is turned directly into ILD, and ITD remains zero. This is very different from loudspeaker listening, where the direction of amplitude-panned sources relies on ITD cues, and ILD remains zero at low frequencies. Although this seems a potential source for large differences in spatial perception of resulting virtual sources, the resulting spatial image is similar. The virtual sources are ordered from the left to right in about the same order as in loudspeaker listening, however in headphone listening the sources are perceived inside the listener's head. This internalization is due to two facts: the dynamic cues propose internalized sources since the ITD and ILD do not change with listener movements, and also the monaural spectral cues do not suggest external sources, since the spectral cues are very different from the cues produced with distant sources.

If the stereophonic material includes virtual sources which have been spatialized by applying time delays, as in Section 5.3.2, this may result in a vastly different spatial perception in headphone listening, e.g., a 5 ms delay in the left loudspeaker may produce a spread perception of the sound in loudspeaker listening, but in headphone listening the sound can be perceived to originate only from the right headphone.

In Section 5.3.2 the technique to spread out virtual sources by convolution with noise burst was also described. This effect provides a similar effect in both headphone and loudspeaker listening. The frequency-dependent alteration of signal phase and magnitude creates ITD and ILD cues which change as a function of frequency in both loudspeaker and headphone listening. Of course, the effect is not the same, as in headphone listening the sound is perceived inside the head, and in loudspeaker listening it is perceived between the loudspeakers.

5.4 Binaural techniques in spatial audio

Binaural techniques are loosely defined to be methods which aim to control directly the sound in the ear canals to match a recorded real case or with a simulated virtual case. This is done by careful binaural recordings, or by utilizing measured or modeled head-related transfer functions (HRTFs) and acoustical modeling of the listening space.

5.4.1 Listening to binaural recordings with headphones

The basic technique is to reproduce a recorded binaural sound-track with headphones. The recording is made by inserting miniature microphones in to the ear canals of a real human listener, or by using a manikin with microphones in the ears [Bla97]. This recording is reproduced by playing the recorded signals in the ears of the listener. This is a very simple technique in principle, and can provide effective results. A simple implementation is to replace the transducers of in-ear headphones with insert miniature microphones, to use a portable audio recorder to record the sounds of the surroundings, and to play back the sound with headphones. Already without any equalization, a nice spatial effect is achieved, as the left–right directions of the sound sources and reverberant sound field are reproduced naturally. Especially, if the person who did the recording is listening, the effect can be striking.

Unfortunately, there are also problems with the technique. The sound may appear colored, the perceived directions move from front to back, and everything may be localized inside head. To partially avoid these problems, the recording and the reproduction should be equalized carefully to get a flat frequency response from the ear drum of the person in the recording position to the ear drum of the listener. Such equalization requires very careful measurements, and is not discussed further here.

A further problem in listening to binaural recordings is the fact that listeners use also dynamic cues to localize sound. When a binaural recording is listened with headphones, the movements of the listener do not naturally change the binaural recording at all. This is also a reason why binaural recordings easily tend to be localized inside head of the listener.

Another issue is the problem of individuality. Each listener has different pinna, and head size, and the sound in similar conditions appears different in different individuals' ears. When a binaural recording made by another individual is listened to, similar problems occur as with non-optimal equalization.

5.4.2 Modeling HRTF filters

Modeling the structural properties of the system pinna–head–torso gives us the possibility to research spatial hearing. Much of the physical/geometric properties can be understood by careful analysis of the HRIRs, plotted as surfaces, functions of the variables time and azimuth, or time and elevation. This is the approach taken by Brown and Duda [BD98] who came up with a model which can be structurally divided into three parts: (1) head shadow and ITD, (2) shoulder echo, and (3) pinna reflections.

Starting from the approximation of the head as a rigid sphere that diffracts a plane wave, the shadowing effect can be effectively approximated by a first-order continuous-time system, i.e., a pole-zero couple in the Laplace complex plane:

$$s_z = \frac{-2\omega_0}{\alpha(\theta)} \tag{5.4}$$

$$s_p = -2\omega_0 , \tag{5.5}$$

where ω_0 is related to the effective radius a of the head and the speed of sound c by

$$\omega_0 = \frac{c}{a} . \tag{5.6}$$

The position of the zero varies with the azimuth θ according to the function

$$\alpha(\theta) = 1.05 + 0.95 \cos\left(\frac{\theta + \frac{\pi}{2}}{150°} 180°\right) . \tag{5.7}$$

The pole-zero couple can be directly translated into a stable IIR digital filter by bilinear transformation [Mit98], and the resulting filter (with proper scaling) is

$$H_{hs} = \frac{(\omega_0 + \alpha F_s) + (\omega_0 - \alpha F_s)z^{-1}}{(\omega_0 + F_s) + (\omega_0 - F_s)z^{-1}} . \tag{5.8}$$

The ITD can be obtained by simple delay in seconds as is the following function of the azimuth angle θ:

$$\tau_h(\theta) = \begin{cases} -\frac{a}{c} \cos\left(\theta + \frac{\pi}{2}\right) & \text{if } 0 \leq |\theta + \frac{\pi}{2}| < \frac{\pi}{2} \\ \frac{a}{c}\left(|\theta + \frac{\pi}{2}| - \frac{\pi}{2}\right) & \text{if } \frac{\pi}{2} \leq |\theta + \frac{\pi}{2}| < \pi \end{cases} . \tag{5.9}$$

The overall magnitude responses of the block responsible for head shadowing is reported in Figure 5.3.

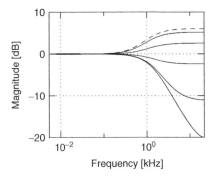

Figure 5.3 Magnitude responses of the simplified HRTFs for the ear in negative azimuth side. Azimuth ranging from $-\frac{\pi}{2}$ (dashed line) to $\frac{\pi}{2}$ at steps of $\pi/6$.

The M-file implementing the head-shadowing filter as a time-domain HRIR is:

M-file 5.5 (simpleHRIR.m)

```
function [output] = simpleHRIR(theta, Fs)
% [output] = simpleHRIR(theta, Fs)
% Author: F. Fontana and D. Rocchesso, V.Pulkki
%
% computes simplified HRTFs with only simple ITD-ILD approximations
% theta is the azimuth angle in degrees
% Fs is the sample rate
theta = theta + 90;
theta0 = 150 ;
alfa_min = 0.05 ;
c = 334; % speed of sound
a = 0.08; % radius of head
w0 = c/a;
input=zeros(round(0.003*Fs),1); input(1)=1;
alfa = 1+ alfa_min/2 + (1- alfa_min/2)* cos(theta/ theta0* pi) ;
B = [(alfa+w0/Fs)/(1+w0/Fs), (-alfa+w0/Fs)/(1+w0/Fs)] ;
    % numerator of Transfer Function
A = [1, -(1-w0/Fs)/(1+w0/Fs)] ;
    % denominator of Transfer Function
if (abs(theta) < 90)
 gdelay = round(- Fs/w0*(cos(theta*pi/180) - 1))  ;
else
 gdelay = round(Fs/w0*((abs(theta) - 90)*pi/180 + 1) );
end;
out_magn = filter(B, A, input);
output = [zeros(gdelay,1); out_magn(1:end-gdelay);  ];
```

The function simpleHRIR gives a rough approximation of HRIR of one ear with one direction. To obtain a HRIR for the left and right ears the same function has to be used with opposite values of argument theta. An example is presented in Section 5.4.3.

5.4.3   HRTF processing for headphone listening

A monophonic sound signal can be positioned virtually in any direction in headphone listening, if HRTFs for both ears are available for the desired virtual source direction [MSHJ95, Beg94]. The result of the measurements is a set of HRIRs that can be directly used as coefficients of a pair of FIR filters. Since the decay time of the HRIR is always less than a few milliseconds, 256 to 512 taps are sufficient at a sampling rate of 44.1 kHz. A sound signal is filtered with a digital filter modeling the measured HRTFs. The method simulates the ear-canal signals that would have been produced if a sound source existed in a desired direction.

A point-like virtual source is created with this example:

M-file 5.6 (simplehrtfconv.m)

```
function [binauralsig] = simplehrtfconv(theta)
% [binauralsig] = simplehrirconv(theta)
% Author: V. Pulkki
% Convolve a signal with HRIR pair corresponding to direction theta
% Theta is azimuth angle of virtual source
Fs =44100; % Sample rate
HRTFpair=[simpleHRIR(theta,Fs) simpleHRIR(-theta,Fs)];
signal=rand(Fs*5,1);
% Convolution
binauralsig=[conv(HRTFpair(:,1),signal) conv(HRTFpair(:,2),signal)];
%soundsc(binauralsig,Fs);% Uncomment to play sound for headphones
```

The demonstration above produces very probably the perception of inside-head virtual source, which may also sound colored. If a head tracker is available, much more realistic perception of external sound sources can be obtained with headphones. In head tracking, the direction of the listener's head is monitored about 10–100 times a second, and the HRTF filter is changed dynamically to keep the perceived direction of sound constant with the space where the listener is. In practice, the updating of the HRTF filter has to be done carefully in order not to produce audible artifacts.

The technique discussed above simulates anechoic listening of a distant sound source. It is also possible to simulate with the same technique the binaural listening of a sound source in a real room. In this approach, the binaural room impulse responses (BRIRs) are measured from the ear canals of a subject in a room with a relatively distant loudspeaker. The main difference to HRTFs is that typically the lengths of HRTFs are of the order of a few milliseconds and include only the acoustical response of the subject, whereas the BRIRs include the room responses, and they can be even few seconds long. The same MATLAB® example can also be used to process sound with BRIRs, although the required processing is much heavier in that case, since the convolution with such long responses is computationally a complex process.

HRTFs can also be used for cross-talk-canceled loudspeaker listening. In that case, the binaural signals are computed as shown in this section, and then played back with a stereo dipole, as shown in Section 5.4.5.

5.4.4   Virtual surround listening with headphones

An interesting application for HRTF technologies with headphones is listening to existing multichannel audio material. In such cases, each loudspeaker in the multichannel loudspeaker layout is simulated using an HRTF pair. For example, a signal meant to be applied to the loudspeaker in a $30°$ direction is convolved with the HRTF pair measured from the same direction, and the convolved signals are applied to the headphones. The usage of HRTFs measured in anechoic conditions is often suboptimal in this case, and the use of BRIRs is beneficial, which have similar responses to the room in which the subject is located. This can be done using measured room impulse responses, or by simulating the effect or room with a reverberator, see Section 5.6.

An example of virtual loudspeaker listening with headphones:

M-file 5.7 (virtualloudspeaker.m)

```
% virtualloudspeaker.m
% Author: V. Pulkki
% Virtual playback of 5.0 surround signal over headphones using HRIRs
Fs=44100;
% generate example 5.0 surround signal
cnt=[0:20000]';
signal=[(mod(cnt,200)/200) (mod(cnt,150)/150) (mod(cnt,120)/120)...
    (mod(cnt,90)/90) (mod(cnt,77)/77)];
i=1;
% go through the input channels
outsigL=0; outsigR=0;
for theta=[30 -30 -110 110 0]
  HRIRl=simpleHRIR(theta,Fs);
  HRIRr=simpleHRIR(-theta,Fs);
  outsigL=outsigL+conv(HRIRl,signal(:,i));
  outsigR=outsigR+conv(HRIRr,signal(:,i));
  i=i+1;
end
% sound output to headphones
soundsc([outsigL outsigR],Fs)
```

5.4.5   Binaural techniques with cross-talk canceled loudspeakers

Binaural recordings are meant to be played back in such a way that the sound which originates from the left ear is played back only to the left ear, and correspondingly with the right ear. If such a recording is played back with stereophonic setup of loudspeakers, the sound from the left loudspeaker also travels to the right ear, and vice versa, called *cross-talk*, which ruins the spatial audio quality.

In order to be able to listen to binaural recordings over two loudspeakers, some methods have been proposed [CB89, KNH98]. In these methods, the loudspeakers are driven in such a way that in practice the cross-talk is canceled as much as possible.

A system can be formed as presented in Figure 5.4 to deliver binaurally recorded signals to the listener's ears using two closely spaced loudspeakers with cross-talk cancellation. The binaural signals are represented as a 2x1 vector in $\mathbf{x}(n)$, and the produced ear canal signals also as 2x1 vector $\mathbf{d}(n)$. The system can be formulated in the z-domain

$$\mathbf{d}(z) = \mathbf{C}(z)\mathbf{H}(z)\mathbf{x}(z), \tag{5.10}$$

where $\mathbf{C}(z) = \begin{bmatrix} C_{11}(z) & C_{12}(z) \\ C_{21}(z) & C_{22}(z) \end{bmatrix}$ contains the electro-acoustical responses of the loudspeakers measured in the ear canals, as shown in the figure, and $\mathbf{H}(z) = \begin{bmatrix} H_{11}(z) & H_{12}(z) \\ H_{21}(z) & H_{22}(z) \end{bmatrix}$ contains the responses for performing inverse filtering to minimize the cross-talk.

Ideally, $\mathbf{x}(z) = \mathbf{d}(z)$, which can be obtained if $\mathbf{H}(z) = \mathbf{C}(z)^{-1}$. Unfortunately, the direct inversion is not feasible due to unidealities of the loudspeakers and the listening conditions. A regularized method to find an optimal $\mathbf{H}_{opt}(z)$ has been proposed in [KNH98],

$$\mathbf{H}_{opt}(z) = \left[\mathbf{C}^T(z^{-1})\mathbf{C}(z) + \beta\mathbf{I}\right]^{-1}\mathbf{C}^T(z^{-1})z^{-m}, \tag{5.11}$$

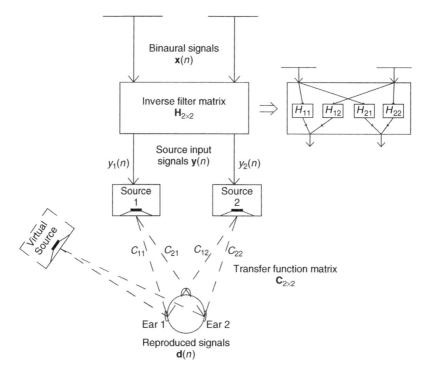

Figure 5.4   Presentation of binaurally recorded signals with loudspeakers with cross-talk canceling [Pol07].

where β is a positive scalar regularization factor, and z^{-m} models the time delay due to the sound reproduction system. If β is selected very low, there will be sharp peaks in the resulting time-domain inverse filters, which may exceed the dynamic range of the loudspeakers. If β is selected to be higher, the inverse filter will have longer duration in time, which is less demanding on the loudspeakers, but unfortunately the inversion is also less accurate [KNH98].

A **MATLAB** example is provided in the following to compute inverse filters for a cross-talk canceling system:

- The responses in $\mathbf{C}$ are moved into the frequency domain with discrete Fourier transform (DFT) with the desired length of time window.

- The filter responses are computed by $\mathbf{H}_{opt}(k) = \left[\mathbf{C}^{H}(k)\mathbf{C}(k) + \beta\mathbf{I}\right]^{-1}\mathbf{C}^{H}(k)$, where k presents the frequency bin indexes and H Hermitian transposition.

- The inverse DFT is taken of $\mathbf{H}$, resulting in the inverse filters for cross-talk cancellation.

- A circular shift of half of the applied time-window length is implemented on the inverse filters.

M-file 5.8 (`crosstalkcanceler.m`)

```
% crosstalkcanceler.m
% Author: A. Politis, V. Pulkki
% Simplified cross-talk canceler
theta=10;  % spacing of stereo loudspeakers in azimuth
Fs=44100; % sample rate
```

```
b=10^-5;    % regularization factor
% loudspeaker HRIRs for both ears (ear_num,loudspeaker_num)
% If more realistic HRIRs are available, pls use them
HRIRs(1,1,:)=simpleHRIR(theta/2,Fs);
HRIRs(1,2,:)=simpleHRIR(-theta/2,Fs);
HRIRs(2,1,:)=HRIRs(1,2,:);
HRIRs(2,2,:)=HRIRs(1,1,:);
Nh=length(HRIRs(1,1,:));
%transfer to frequency domain
for i=1:2;for j=1:2
        C_f(i,j,:)=fft(HRIRs(i,j,:),Nh)
    end;end
% Regularized inversion of matrix C
H_f=zeros(2,2,Nh);
for k=1:Nh
    H_f(:,:,k)=inv((C_f(:,:,k)'*C_f(:,:,k)+eye(2)*b))*C_f(:,:,k)';
end
% Moving back to time domain
for k=1:2; for m=1:2
        H_n(k,m,:)=real(ifft(H_f(k,m,:)));
        H_n(k,m,:)=fftshift(H_n(k,m,:));
    end; end
% Generate binaural signals.  Any binaural recording shoud also be ok
binauralsignal=simplehrtfconv(70);
%binauralsignal=wavread('road_binaural.wav');
% Convolve the loudspeaker signals
loudspsig=[conv(reshape(H_n(1,1,:),Nh,1),binauralsignal(:,1)) + ...
    conv(reshape(H_n(1,2,:),Nh,1),binauralsignal(:,2)) ...
    conv(reshape(H_n(2,1,:),Nh,1),binauralsignal(:,1)) + ...
    conv(reshape(H_n(2,2,:),Nh,1),binauralsignal(:,2))];
soundsc(loudspsig,Fs)        % play sound for loudspeakers
```

In practice, this method works best with loudspeakers close to each other, as a larger loudspeaker base angle would lead to coloration at lower frequencies. The listening area in which the effect is audible is very small, as if the listener departs from the mid line between the loudspeakers by about 1–2 cm, the effect is lost.

A nice feature of this technique is that the sound is typically externalized. This may be due to the fact that head movements of the listener produce somewhat relevant cues, and since the sound is reproduced using far-field loudspeakers generating plausible monaural spectral cues. However, although the sound is externalized, a surrounding spatial effect is hard to obtain with this technique. With a stereo dipole in the front, the reproduced sound scene is typically perceived only at the front.

The technique also is affected by the reflections and reverberation of the listening room. It works best only in spaces without prominent reflections. To get the best results, the HRTFs of the listener should be known, however already very plausible results can be obtained with generic responses.

5.5 Spatial audio effects for multichannel loudspeaker layouts

5.5.1 Loudspeaker layouts

In the history of multichannel audio [Ste96, Dav03, Tor98] multiple different loudspeaker layouts with more than two loudspeakers have been specified. The most frequently used layouts are presented in this chapter. In the 1970s, the quadraphonic setup was proposed, in which four loudspeakers are placed evenly around the listener at azimuth angles $\pm 45°$ and $\pm 135°$. This layout was never successful because of problems related to reproduction techniques of that time, and because the layout itself had too few loudspeakers to provide good spatial quality in all directions around the listener [Rum01].

For cinema sound, a system was evolved in which the frontal image stability of the standard stereophonic setup was enhanced by one extra center channel, and two surround channels were used to create atmospheric effects and room perception. This kind of setup was first used in Dolby's surround sound system for cinemas from 1976 [Dav03]. Later, the layout was investigated [The91], and ITU gave a recommendation about the layout in 1992 [BS.94]. In the late 1990s, this layout also became common in domestic use. It is widely referred to as the 5.1 system, where 5 stands for the number of loudspeakers, and .1 stands for the low-frequency channel. In the recommendation, three frontal loudspeakers are at directions $0°$ and $\pm 30°$, and two surround channels at $\pm (110 \pm 10)°$, as shown in Figure 5.5. The system has been criticized for not delivering good directional quality anywhere but in front [Rum01]. To achieve better quality, it can be extended by adding loudspeakers. Layouts with 6–12 loudspeakers have been proposed, and are presented in [Rum01].

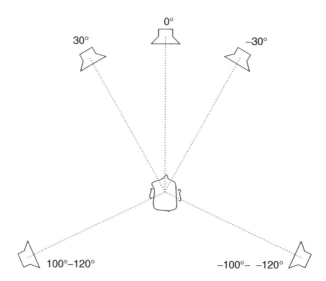

Figure 5.5 Five channel surround loudspeaker layout based on ITU recommendation BS775.1.

In computer music, media installations and in academic projects, loudspeaker setups, in which the loudspeakers have equal spacing, have been used. In horizontal arrays the number of loudspeakers can be, for example, six (hexagonal array) or eight (octagonal array). In wave-field synthesis, see Section 5.5.6, the number of loudspeakers is typically between 20 and 200. In theaters and in virtual environment systems there exist systems in which loudspeakers are also placed above and/or below the listener.

5.5.2 2-D loudspeaker setups

In 2-D loudspeaker setups all loudspeakers are on the horizontal plane. Pair-wise amplitude panning [Cho71] is the best method to position virtual sources with such setups, when the number of loudspeakers is less than about 20. In pair-wise panning the sound signal is applied only to two adjacent loudspeakers of the loudspeaker setup at one time. The pair between which the panning direction lies is selected. Different formulations for pair-wise panning are Chowning's law [Cho71], which is not based on any psychoacoustic criteria, or 2-D vector-base amplitude panning (VBAP) [Pul97], which is a generalization of the tangent law (Equation (5.2)) for stereophonic panning.

In VBAP a loudspeaker pair is specified with two vectors. The unit-length vectors $\mathbf{l}_m$ and $\mathbf{l}_n$ point from the listening position to the loudspeakers. The intended direction of the virtual source (panning direction) is presented with a unit-length vector $\mathbf{p}$. Vector $\mathbf{p}$ is expressed as a linear weighted sum of the loudspeaker vectors

$$\mathbf{p} = g_m\mathbf{l}_m + g_n\mathbf{l}_n. \tag{5.12}$$

Here g_m and g_n are the gain factors of the respective loudspeakers. The gain factors can be solved as

$$\mathbf{g} = \mathbf{p}^T\mathbf{L}_{mn}^{-1}, \tag{5.13}$$

where $\mathbf{g} = [g_m\ g_n]^T$ and $\mathbf{L}_{mn} = [\mathbf{l}_m\ \mathbf{l}_n]$. The calculated factors are used in amplitude panning as gain factors of the signals applied to respective loudspeakers after suitable normalization, e.g., $\|\mathbf{g}\| = 1$.

The directional quality achieved with pair-wise panning was studied in [Pul01]. When the loudspeakers are symmetrically placed on the left and right of the listener, VBAP estimates the perceived angle accurately. When the loudspeaker pair is not symmetrical with the median plane, the perceived direction is biased towards the median plane [Pul01], which can be more or less compensated [Pul02].

When there is a loudspeaker in the panning direction, the virtual source is sharp, but when panned between loudspeakers, the binaural cues are unnatural to some degree. This means that the directional perception of the virtual source varies with panning direction, which can be compensated by always applying sound to more than one loudspeaker [Pul99, SK04]. As in pair-wise panning, outside the best listening position the perceived direction collapses to the nearest loudspeaker producing a specific sound. This implies that the maximal directional error is of the same order of magnitude with the angular separation of loudspeakers from the listener's viewpoint in pair-wise panning. In practice, when the number of loudspeakers exceeds about eight, the virtual sources are perceived to be in the similar directions in a large listening area.

A basic implementation of 2-D VBAP is included here as a **MATLAB** function.

M-file 5.9 (VBAP2.m)

```
function [gains] = VBAP2(pan_dir)
% function [gains] = VBAP2(pan_dir)
% Author: V. Pulkki
% Computes 2D VBAP gains for horizontal loudspeaker setup.
% Loudspeaker directions in clockwise or counterclockwise order.
% Change these numbers to match with your system.
ls_dirs=[30 -30 -90 -150 150 90];
ls_num=length(ls_dirs);
ls_dirs=[ls_dirs ls_dirs(1)]/180*pi;
% Panning direction in cartesian coordinates.
panvec=[cos(pan_dir/180*pi) sin(pan_dir/180*pi)];
for i=1:ls_num
    % Compute inverse of loudspeaker base matrix.
    lsmat=inv([[cos(ls_dirs(i)) sin(ls_dirs(i))];...
        [cos(ls_dirs(i+1)) sin(ls_dirs(i+1))]]);
    % Compute unnormalized gains
    tempg=panvec*lsmat;
```

```
    % If gains nonnegative, normalize the gains and stop
    if min(tempg) > -0.001
        g=zeros(1,ls_num);
        g([i mod(i,ls_num)+1])=tempg;
        gains=g/sqrt(sum(g.^2));
        return
    end
end
```

5.5.3   3-D loudspeaker setups

A 3-D loudspeaker setup denotes here a setup in which all loudspeakers are not in the same plane as the listener. Typically this means that there are some elevated and/or lowered loudspeakers added to a horizontal loudspeaker setup. Triplet-wise panning can be used in such setups [Pul97]. In it, a sound signal is applied to a maximum of three loudspeakers at one time that form a triangle from the listener's viewpoint. If more than three loudspeakers are available, the setup is divided into triangles, one of which is used in the panning of a single virtual source at one time, as shown in Figure 5.6. 3-D vector-base amplitude panning (3-D VBAP) is a method to formulate such setups [Pul97]. It is formulated in an equivalent way to pair-wise panning in the previous section. However, the number of gain factors and loudspeakers is naturally three in the equations. The angle between the median plane and virtual source is estimated correctly with VBAP in most cases, as in pair-wise panning. However, the perceived elevation of a sound source is individual to each subject [Pul01].

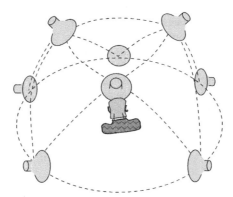

Figure 5.6   A 3-D triangulated loudspeaker system for triplet-wise panning.

A basic implementation of 3-D VBAP for the loudspeaker setup in Figure 5.6 is shown here as a **MATLAB** function.

M-file 5.10 (VBAP3.m)

```
function [gains] = VBAP3(pan_dir)
% function [gains] = VBAP3(pan_dir)
% Author: V. Pulkki
% Computes 3D VBAP gains for loudspeaker setup shown in Fig.6.4
% Change the lousdpeaker directions to match with your system,
% the directions are defined as azimuth elevation; pairs
loudspeakers=[0 0; 50 0; 130 0; -130 0; -50 0;  40 45; 180 45;-40 45];
ls_num=size(loudspeakers,1);
```

```
% Define the triangles from the loudspeakers here
ls_triangles=[1 2 6; 2 3 6; 3 4 7; 4 5 8; 5 1 8; 1 6 8;
    3 6 7; 4 7 8; 6 7 8];
% Go through all triangles
for tripl=1:size(ls_triangles,1)
    ls_tripl=loudspeakers(ls_triangles(tripl,:),:);
    % Panning direction in cartesian coordinates
    cosE=cos(pan_dir(2)/180*pi);
    panvec(1:2)=[cos(pan_dir(1)/180*pi)*cosE sin(pan_dir(1)/180*pi)*cosE];
    panvec(3)=sin(pan_dir(2)/180*pi);
    % Loudspeaker base matrix for current triangle.
    for i=1:3
        cosE=cos(ls_tripl(i,2)/180*pi);
        lsmat(i,1:2)=[cos(ls_tripl(i,1)/180*pi)*cosE...
            sin(ls_tripl(i,1)/180*pi)*cosE];
        lsmat(i,3)=sin(ls_tripl(i,2)/180*pi);
    end
    tempg=panvec*inv(lsmat); % Gain factors for current triangle.
    % If gains nonnegative, normalize g and stop computation
    if min(tempg) > -0.01
        tempg=tempg/sqrt(sum(tempg.^2));
        gains=zeros(1,ls_num);
        gains(1,ls_triangles(tripl,:))=tempg;
        return
    end
end
```

5.5.4 Coincident microphone techniques and Ambisonics

In coincident microphone technologies first- or higher-order microphones positioned ideally in the same position are used to capture sound for multichannel playback. The ambisonics technique [Ger73, ED08] is a form of this. The most common microphone for these applications is the first-order four-capsule B-format microphone, producing a signal $w(t)$ with omnidirectional characteristics, which has been scaled down by $\sqrt{2}$. The B-format microphone also outputs three signals $x(t)$, $y(t)$, and $z(t)$ with figure-of-eight characteristics pointing to corresponding Cartesian directions. The microphones are ideally in the same position. Higher-order microphones have also been proposed and are commercially available, which have much more capsules than the first-order microphones.

In most cases, the microphones are of first order. When the loudspeaker signals are created from the recorded signal, the channels are simply added together with different gains. Thus each loudspeaker signal can be considered as a virtual microphone signal having first-order directional characteristics. This is expressed as

$$s(t) = \frac{2-\kappa}{2}w(t) + \frac{\kappa}{2\sqrt{2}}[\cos(\theta)\cos(\phi)x(t) + \sin(\theta)\cos(\phi)y(t) + \sin(\phi)z(t)], \quad (5.14)$$

where $s(t)$ is the produced virtual microphone signal having an orientation of azimuth θ and elevation ϕ. The parameter $\kappa \in [0, 2]$ defines the directional characteristics of the virtual microphone from omnidirectional to cardioid and dipole, as shown in Figure 5.7.

In multichannel reproduction of such first-order B-format recordings, a virtual microphone signal is computed for each loudspeaker. In practice such methods provide good quality only in certain loudspeaker configurations [Sol08] and at frequencies well below 1 kHz. At higher frequencies the high coherence between the loudspeaker signals, which is caused by the broad

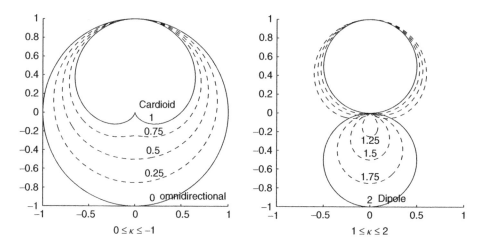

Figure 5.7 The directional pattern of virtual microphones which can be generated from first-order B-format recordings. Figure reprinted with permission from [Vil08].

directional patterns of the microphones, leads to undesired effects such as coloration and loss of spaciousness. Using higher-order microphones these problems are less severe, though some problems with microphone self-noise may appear.

The decoding of first-order B-format microphone signals to a horizontal loudspeaker layout with directional characteristics controllable by κ is shown in the following example:

M-file 5.11 (kappa.m)

```
% kappa.m
% Author: V. Pulkki
% Simple example of cardioid decoding of B-format signals
Fs=44100;
% mono signal
signal=(mod([0:Fs*2],220)/220);
% Simulated horizontal-only B-format recording of single
% sound source in direction of theta azimuth.
% This can be replaced with a real B-format recording.
theta=0;
w=signal/sqrt(2);
x=signal*cos(theta/180*pi);
y=signal*sin(theta/180*pi);
% Virtual microphone directions
% (In many cases the values equal to the directions of loudspeakers)
ls_dir=[30 90 150 -150 -90 -30]/180*pi;
ls_num=length(ls_dir);
% Compute virtual cardioids (kappa = 1) out of the B-format signal
kappa=1;
for i=1:ls_num
    LSsignal(:,i)=(2-kappa)/2*w...
        +kappa/(2*sqrt(2))*(cos(ls_dir(i))*x+sin(ls_dir(i))*y);
end
% File output
wavwrite(LSsignal,Fs,16,'firstorderB-formatexample.wav')
```

The previous example was of reproducing a recorded sound scenario. Such coincident recording can also be simulated to perform synthesis of spatial audio [MM95] for 2-D or 3-D loudspeaker setups. In this case it is an amplitude-panning method in which a sound signal is applied to all loudspeakers placed evenly around the listener with gain factors

$$g_i = \frac{1}{N} \sum_{m=1}^{M} \{1 + 2p_m \cos{(m\alpha_i)}\}, \tag{5.15}$$

where g_i is the gain of ith speaker, N is the number of loudspeakers, α is the angle between loudspeaker and panning direction, $\cos{(m\alpha_i)}$ represents a single spherical harmonic with order m, M is the order of Ambisonics, and p_m are the gains for each spherical harmonic [DNM03, Mon00]. When the order is low, the sound signal emanates from all the loudspeakers, which causes some spatial artifacts due to unnatural behavior of binaural cues [PH05]. In such cases, when listening outside the best listening position, the sound is also perceived at the nearest loudspeaker which produces the sound. This effect is more prominent with first-order ambisonics than with pair- or triplet-wise panning, since in ambisonics virtually all loudspeakers produce the same sound signal. The sound is also colored, for the same reason, i.e., multiple propagation paths of the same signal to ears produce comb-filter effects. Conventional microphones can be used to realize first-order ambisonics.

When the order is increased, the cross-talk between loudspeakers can be minimized by optimizing gains of spherical harmonics for each loudspeaker in a listening setup [Cra03]. Using higher-order spatial harmonics increases both directional and timbral virtual source quality, since the loudspeaker signals are less coherent. The physical wave field reconstruction is then more accurate, and different curvatures of wavefronts, as well as planar wavefronts can be produced [DNM03], if a large enough number of loudspeakers is in use. The selection of the coefficients for different spherical harmonics has to be done carefully for each loudspeaker layout.

A simple implementation of computing second-order ambisonic gains for a hexagonal loudspeaker layout is shown here:

M-file 5.12 (ambisonics.m)

```
% ambisonics.m
% Author: V. Pulkki
% Second-order harmonics to compute gains for loudspeakers
% to position virtual source to a loudspeaker setup
theta=30;% Direction of virtual source
loudsp_dir=[30 -30 -90 -150 150 90]/180*pi; % loudspeaker setup
ls_num=length(loudsp_dir);
harmC=[1 2/3 1/6]; % Coeffs for harmonics "smooth solution", [Mon00]
theta=theta/180*pi;
for i=1:ls_num
    g(i)= (harmC(1) + 2*cos(theta-loudsp_dir(i))*harmC(2) +...
        2*cos(2*(theta-loudsp_dir(i)))*harmC(3));
end
% use gains in g for amplitude panning
```

5.5.5 Synthesizing the width of virtual sources

A loudspeaker layout having loudspeakers around the listener can also be used to control the width of the sound source, or even to produce an enveloping perception of the sound source. A simple demonstration can be made by playing back pink noise with all loudspeakers, where the noises are independent of each other [Bla97]. The sound source is then perceived to surround the listener totally.

The precise control of the width of the virtual source is a complicated topic. However, simple and effective spatial effects can be performed by using some of the loudspeakers to generate a wide virtual source. The example of decorrelating a monophonic input signal for stereophonic listening shown in Section 5.3.2 can be also used with multichannel loudspeaker setups. In such cases, the number of columns in the noise matrix corresponds to the number of loudspeakers to which the decorrelated sound is applied, and the convolution has to be computed for each loudspeaker channel. The virtual source will be more or less perceived to originate evenly from the loudspeakers and from the space between them. Unfortunately, the drawback of time-smearing of transients is also present in this case.

Note that this is a different effect than the effect generated with reverberators, which are discussed in Section 5.6, although the processing is very similar. The reverberators simulate the room effect, and try to create the perception of a surrounding reverberant tail, and in contrast the effect discussed in this section generates the perception of a surrounding non-reverberant sound. However, such effects cannot be achieved with all types of signals, due to human perceptual capabilities, as discussed briefly in Section 5.2.3.

5.5.6   Time delay-based systems

There are a number of methods proposed, which instead of using amplitude differences use time-delays in positioning the virtual sources. The most complete one, the wave field synthesis is presented first, after which Moore's room-inside-room approach is discussed.

Wave-field synthesis is a technique that requires a large number of carefully equalized loud-speakers [BVV93, VB99]. It aims to reconstruct the whole sound field in a listening room. When a virtual source is reproduced, the sound for each loudspeaker is delayed and amplified in a manner that a desired circular or planar sound wave occurs as a superposition of sounds from each loudspeaker. The virtual source can be positioned far behind the loudspeakers, or in some cases even in the space inside the loudspeaker array, as shown in Figure 5.8. The loudspeaker signals have to be equalized depending on virtual source position [ARB04].

Theoretically the wave-field synthesis is superior as a technique, as the perceived position of the sound source is correct within a very large listening area. Unfortunately, to create a desired wave field in the total area inside the array, it demands that the loudspeakers are at a distance of maximally a half wavelength from each other. The area in which a perfect sound field synthesis is achieved

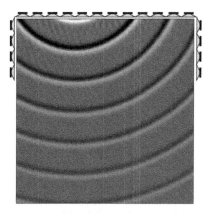 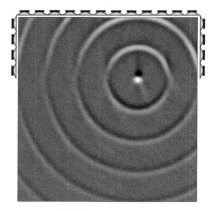

Figure 5.8   Wave-field synthesis concept. A desired 2-D sound field can be constructed using a large loudspeaker array. Figure reprinted with IEEE permission from [VB99].

shrinks with increasing frequency [DNM03]. In practice, due to the perception mechanisms of humans, more error can be allowed above approximately 1.5 kHz. Arrays for wave-field synthesis have been built for room acoustics control and enhancement to be used in theaters and multipurpose auditoria [VB99].

Time delays also can be used when creating spatial effects with loudspeaker setups with fewer loudspeakers than used in wave-field synthesis. The use of time delays for positioning virtual sources was considered for a two-channel stereophonic layout in Section 5.3.2. It was noted that short delays of a few milliseconds make the virtual sources perceived as spatially spread. This effect of course also applies with multi-loudspeaker setups. With longer delays, the precedence effect makes the sound direction perceived to be form the loudspeaker where the sound arrived first. This technique has also been used for multichannel loudspeaker layouts, as in Moore's approach, where the relative time delay between the loudspeaker feeds is controlled. A model supporting this approach was introduced by Moore [Moo83], and can be described as a physical and geometric model. The metaphor underlying the Moore model is that of a room-within-a-room, where the inner room has holes in the walls, corresponding to the positions of the loudspeakers, and the outer room is the virtual room where the sound events take place. When a single virtual source is applied in the virtual world, all the loudspeakers emanate the same sound with different amplitudes and delays. This is a similar idea to wave-field synthesis, though the mathematical basis is less profound, and the number of loudspeakers utilized is typically smaller. The recreated sound field will be limited to low frequencies, and at higher frequencies comb-filter effects and unstable directions for virtual sources will appear. However, if the delays are large enough, the virtual source will be perceived at all listening positions to the loudspeaker which emanates the sound first. The effects introduced by the Moore model are directly related with the artifacts one would get when listening to the outside world through windows.

5.5.7 Time-frequency processing of spatial audio

The directional resolution of spatial hearing is limited within auditory frequency bands [Bla97]. In principle, all sound within one critical band can be only perceived as a single source with broader or narrower extent. In some special cases a binaural narrow-band sound stimulus can be perceived as two distinct auditory objects, but the perception of three or more concurrent sources is generally not possible. This is different from visual perception, where already one eye can detect the directions of a large number of visual objects sharing the same color.

The limitations of spatial auditory perception imply that the spatial realism needed in visual reproduction is not needed in audio. In other words, the spatial accuracy in reproduction of acoustical wave field can be compromised without decrease in perceptual quality. There are some recent technologies which exploit this assumption. Methods to compress multichannel audio files to 1–2 audio signals with metadata have been proposed [BF08, GJ06], where the level and time differences between the channels are analyzed in the time-frequency domain, and are coded as metadata to the signal. A related technology for spatial audio, directional audio coding (DirAC) [Pul07], is a signal-processing method for spatial sound, which can be applied to spatial sound reproduction for any multichannel loudspeaker layout, or for headphones. The other applications suggested for it include teleconferencing and perceptual audio coding.

In DirAC, it is assumed that at one time instant and at one critical band the spatial resolution of auditory system is limited to decoding one cue for direction and another for inter-aural coherence. It is further assumed that if the direction and diffuseness of sound field is measured and reproduced correctly, a human listener will perceive the directional and coherence cues correctly.

The concept of DirAC is illustrated in Figure 5.9. In the analysis phase, the direction and diffuseness of the sound field is estimated in auditory frequency bands depending on time, forming the metadata transmitted together with a few audio channels. In the "low-bitrate" approach shown in the figure, only one channel of audio is transmitted. The audio channel may also be further compressed to obtain a lower transmission data rate. The version with more channels is shown

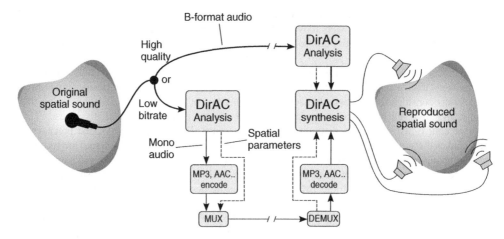

Figure 5.9 Two typical approaches of DirAC: High quality (top) and low bitrate (bottom). Figure reprinted with AES permission from [Vil08].

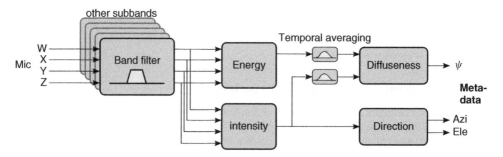

Figure 5.10 DirAC analysis. Figure reprinted with AES permission from [Vil08].

as a "high-quality version," where the number of transmitted channels is three for horizontal reproduction, and four for 3-D reproduction. In the high-quality version the analysis may be conducted at the receiving end. It has been proven that the high-quality version of DirAC produces better perceptual quality in loudspeaker listening than other available techniques using the same microphone input [VLP09].

The processing in DirAC and in other time-frequency-domain processing for spatial audio is typically organized as an analysis-transmission-synthesis chain. To give an idea of the analysis process, the analysis part of DirAC is now discussed in detail, followed by a code example.

The aim of directional analysis, which is shown in Figure 5.10, is to estimate at each frequency band the direction of arrival of sound, together with an estimate of if the sound is arriving from one or multiple directions at the same time. In principle this can be performed with a number of techniques, however, an energetic analysis of the sound field has been found to be suitable, which is shown in Figure 5.10. The energetic analysis can be performed when the pressure signal and velocity signals in one, two or three dimensions are captured from a single position.

The first-order B-format signals described in Section 5.5.4 can be used for directional analysis. The sound pressure can be estimated using the omnidirectional signal $w(t)$ as $P = \sqrt{2}W$, expressed in the STFT domain. The figure-of-eight signals $x(t)$, $y(t)$, and $z(t)$ are grouped in the STFT domain into a vector $\mathbf{U} = [X, Y, Z]$, which estimates the 3-D sound field velocity vector. The energy E of sound field can be computed as

$$E = \frac{\rho_0}{4}||\mathbf{U}||^2 + \frac{1}{4\rho_0 c^2}|P|^2, \tag{5.16}$$

where ρ_0 is the mean density of air, and c is the speed of sound. The capturing of B-format signals can be obtained with either coincident positioning of directional microphones, or with closely spaced set of omnidirectional microphones. In some applications, the microphone signals may be formed in the computational domain, i.e., simulated. The analysis is repeated as frequently as is needed for the application, typically with an update frequency of 100–1000 Hz.

The intensity vector $\mathbf{I}$ expresses the net flow of sound energy as a 3-D vector, and can be computed as

$$\mathbf{I} = \overline{P}\mathbf{U}, \tag{5.17}$$

where $\overline{(\cdot)}$ denotes complex conjugation. The direction of sound is defined as the opposite direction to the intensity vector at each frequency band. The direction is denoted as the corresponding angular azimuth and elevation values in the transmitted metadata. The diffuseness of the sound field is computed as

$$\psi = 1 - \frac{||\mathrm{E}\{\mathbf{I}\}||}{c\mathrm{E}\{E\}}, \tag{5.18}$$

where E is the expectation operator. Typically the expectation operator is implemented with temporal integration, as in the example below. This process is also called "smoothing." The outcome of this equation is a real-valued number between zero and one, characterizing whether the sound energy is arriving from a single direction, or from all directions.

An example of directional analysis of B-format signals is presented in the following. The synthesis of sound is not shown here, however the reader is encouraged to use the analysis results to build different spatial effects of his own.

M-file 5.13 (diranalysis.m)

```
% diranalysis.m
% Author: V. Pulkki
% Example of directional analysis of simulated B-format recording
Fs=44100; % Generate signals
sig1=2*(mod([1:Fs]',40)/80-0.5) .* min(1,max(0,(mod([1:Fs]',Fs/5)-Fs/10)));
sig2=2*(mod([1:Fs]',32)/72-0.5) .* min(1,max(0,(mod([[1:Fs]+Fs/6]',...
Fs/3)-Fs/6)));
% Simulate two sources in directions of -45 and 30 degrees
w=(sig1+sig2)/sqrt(2);
x=sig1*cos(50/180*pi)+sig2*cos(-170/180*pi);
y=sig1*sin(50/180*pi)+sig2*sin(-170/180*pi);
% Add fading in diffuse noise with  36 sources evenly in the horizontal plane
for dir=0:10:350
    noise=(rand(Fs,1)-0.5).*(10.^((([1:Fs]'/Fs)-1)*2));
    w=w+noise/sqrt(2);
    x=x+noise*cos(dir/180*pi);
    y=y+noise*sin(dir/180*pi);
end
hopsize=256; % Do directional analysis with STFT
winsize=512; i=2; alpha=1./(0.02*Fs/winsize);
Intens=zeros(hopsize,2)+eps; Energy=zeros(hopsize,2)+eps;
for time=1:hopsize:(length(x)-winsize)
```

```
% moving to frequency domain
W=fft(w(time:(time+winsize-1)).*hanning(winsize));
X=fft(x(time:(time+winsize-1)).*hanning(winsize));
Y=fft(y(time:(time+winsize-1)).*hanning(winsize));
W=W(1:hopsize);X=X(1:hopsize);Y=Y(1:hopsize);
%Intensity computation
tempInt = real(conj(W) * [1 1 ] .* [X Y])/sqrt(2);%Instantaneous
Intens = tempInt * alpha + Intens * (1 - alpha); %Smoothed
% Compute direction from intensity vector
Azimuth(:,i) = round(atan2(Intens(:,2), Intens(:,1))*(180/pi));
%Energy computation
tempEn=0.5 * (sum(abs([X Y]).^2, 2) * 0.5 + abs(W).^2 + eps);%Inst
Energy(:,i) = tempEn*alpha + Energy(:,(i-1)) * (1-alpha); %Smoothed
%Diffuseness computation
Diffuseness(:,i) = 1 - sqrt(sum(Intens.^2,2)) ./ (Energy(:,i));
i=i+1;
end
% Plot variables
figure(1); imagesc(log(Energy)); title('Energy');set(gca,'YDir','normal')
xlabel('Time frame'); ylabel('Freq bin');
figure(2); imagesc(Azimuth);colorbar; set(gca,'YDir','normal')
title('Azimuth'); xlabel('Time frame'); ylabel('Freq bin');
figure(3); imagesc(Diffuseness);colorbar; set(gca,'YDir','normal')
title('Diffuseness'); xlabel('Time frame'); ylabel('Freq bin');
```

5.6   Reverberation

5.6.1   Basics of room acoustics

Most of the techniques presented in previous sections have concentrated on reproducing one sound source in a free field from a certain direction. However, in a real space reverberation is always present. Reverberation is composed of reflections which are delayed and attenuated copies of the direct sound. The frequency content of each reflection is also modified due to the directivity of the sound source and due to the material absorption of reflecting surfaces.

The most important concept in room acoustics is an impulse response which describes the acoustics of a room from a static sound source to a listening position. Engineers often divide the impulse response into three parts, the direct sound, early reflections and late reverberation. This division is illustrated with a simulated impulse response in Figure 5.11. The direct sound is the sound reaching the listener first. The early reflections are the first reflections that are not perceived separately as human hearing integrates them with the direct sound. Although their individual directions are not perceived due to the precedence effect, they contribute to the perception of the sound color and the size of the sound source, as well as the size of the room. Late reverberation is considered after a time moment, which is sometimes called the mixing time, when the reflection density is so high that individual reflections cannot be seen in the response. Late reverberation gives cues of the size of the room as well as the distance of the sound source.

The room impulse response can be measured [MM01] or modeled with room acoustics modeling techniques [SK02, Sil10]. Section 5.7 presents various ways to create the impulse response, but before that the basic method to add the room effect to a sound signal is presented.

5.6.2   Convolution with room impulse responses

If the impulse response of a target room is readily available, the most faithful reverberation method would be to convolve the input signal with such a response. Direct convolution can be done by

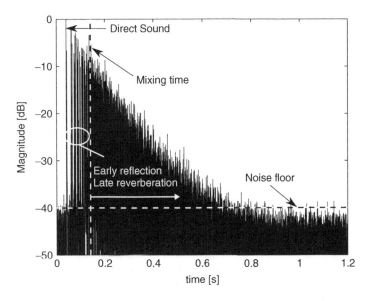

Figure 5.11 Simulated room energy response illustrating the direct sound, early reflections and late reverberation.

storing each sample of the impulse response as a coefficient of an FIR filter whose input is the dry signal. Direct convolution becomes easily impractical if the length of the target response exceeds small fractions of a second, as it would translate into several hundreds of taps in the filter structure. A solution is to perform the convolution block by block in the frequency domaing given the Fourier transform of the impulse response, and the Fourier transform of a block of input signal, the two can be multiplied point by point and the result transformed back to the time domain. As this kind of processing is performed on successive blocks of the input signal, the output signal is obtained by overlapping and adding the partial results [OS89]. Thanks to the FFT computation of the discrete Fourier transform, such a technique can be significantly faster. A drawback is that, in order to be operated in real time, a block of N samples must be read and then processed while a second block is being read. Therefore, the input–output latency in samples is twice the size of a block, and this is not tolerable in practical real-time environments.

The complexity–latency tradeoff is illustrated in Figure 5.12, where the direct-form and the block-processing solutions can be located, together with a third efficient yet low-latency solution [Gar95, MT99]. This third realization of convolution is based on a decomposition of the

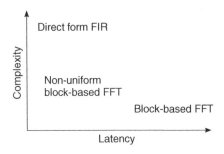

Figure 5.12 Complexity vs. latency tradeoff in convolution.

impulse response into increasingly large chunks. The size of each chunk is twice the size of its predecessor, so that the latency of prior computation can be occupied by the computations related to the following impulse response chunk. Details and discussion on convolution were presented in Section 2.2.7.

When the reproduction is monaural the convolution is a trivial task, but when spatial sound reproduction is applied the process is more complicated. In real life the reflections reach the listening position (or a microphone) from all directions and the reflections can be considered to be virtual sources (discussed in previous sections). Thus, each reflection should be reproduced from the correct direction, which means that the impulse response has to contain such information. Currently, the most common technique is to measure or model the first or higher-order B-format response that is convolved with source signals. Then the reproduction with multi loudspeaker setups is performed with spatial-sound rendering techniques (see Sections 5.5.4 and 5.5.7).

5.7   Modeling of room acoustics

The room effect, i.e., the room impulse response, can be created by modeling how sound propagates and reflects from surfaces if the geometry of a room is available. Such a process is called room acoustics modeling and several techniques are discussed in Section 5.7.4. In many cases the geometry of a room is not needed since an artificial room impulse response can be created from a perceptual point of view. In fact, the human hearing is not very sensitive to details in the reverberant tail and any decaying response can be used as an effect.

Even if we have enough computer power to compute convolutions by long impulse responses in real time, there are still reasons to prefer reverberation algorithms based on feedback delay networks in many practical contexts. The reasons are similar to those that make a CAD description of a scene preferable to a still picture whenever several views have to be extracted or the environment has to be modified interactively. In fact, it is not easy to modify a room impulse response to reflect some of the room attributes, e.g., its high-frequency absorption. If the impulse response is coming from a room acoustics modeling algorithm, these manipulations can be operated at the level of room description, and the coefficients of the room impulse response are transmitted to the real-time convolver. In low-latency block-based implementations, we can even have faster update rates for the smaller early chunks of the impulse response, and slower update rates for the reverberant tail. Still, continuous variations of the room impulse response are easier to render using a model of reverberation operating on a sample-by-sample basis. For this purpose dozens of reverberation algorithms have been developed and in the following some of them are introduced in more detail.

5.7.1   Classic reverb tools

In the second half of the twentieth century, several engineers and acousticians tried to invent electronic devices capable of simulating the long-term effects of sound propagation in enclosures. The most important pioneering work in the field of *artificial reverberation* has been that of Manfred Schroeder at the Bell Laboratories in the early sixties [Sch61, Sch62, Sch70, Sch73, SL61]. Schroeder introduced the recursive *comb filters* and the delay-based *allpass filters* as computational structures suitable for the inexpensive simulation of complex patterns of echoes. In particular, the allpass filter based on the recursive delay line has the form

$$y(n) = -g \cdot x(n) + x(n - m) + g \cdot y(n - m) \,, \tag{5.19}$$

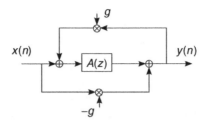

Figure 5.13   The allpass filter structure.

where m is the length of the delay in samples. The filter structure is depicted in Figure 5.13, where $A(z)$ is usually replaced by a delay line. This filter allows one to obtain a dense impulse response and a flat frequency response. Such a structure became rapidly a standard component used in almost all the artificial reverberators designed up to now [Moo79]. It is usually assumed that the allpass filters do not introduce coloration in the input sound. However, this assumption is valid from a perceptual viewpoint only if the delay line is much shorter than the integration time of the ear, i.e., about 50 ms [ZF90]. If this is not the case, the time-domain effects become much more relevant and the timbre of the incoming signal is significantly affected.

In the seventies, Michael Gerzon generalized the single-input single-output allpass filter to a multi-input multi-output structure, where the delay line of m samples has been replaced by an order-N unitary network [Ger76]. Examples of trivial unitary networks are orthogonal matrices, and parallel connections of delay lines or allpass filters. The idea behind this generalization is that of increasing the complexity of the impulse response without introducing appreciable coloration in frequency. According to Gerzon's generalization, allpass filters can be nested within allpass structures, in a telescopic fashion. Such embedding is shown to be equivalent to lattice allpass structures [Gar97b], and it is realizable as long as there is at least one delay element in the block $A(z)$ of Figure 5.13. An example **MATLAB** code with a delay of 40 samples is:

M-file 5.14 (comballpass.m)

```
% Author: T. Lokki
% Create an impulse
x = zeros(1,2500); x(1) = 1;
% Delay line and read position
A = zeros(1,100);
Adelay=40;
% Output vector
ir = zeros(1,2500);
% Feedback gain
g=0.7;
% Comb-allpass filtering
for n = 1:length(ir)
    tmp = A(Adelay) + x(n)*(-g);
    A = [(tmp*g + x(n))' A(1:length(A)-1)];
    ir(n) = tmp;
end
% Plot the filtering result
plot(ir)
```

Extensive experimentation on structures for artificial reverberation was conducted by Moorer in the late seventies [Moo79]. He extended the work done by Schroeder [Sch70] in relating some basic computational structures (e.g., tapped delay lines, comb and allpass filters) with the physical behavior of actual rooms. In particular, it was noticed that the early reflections have great importance in the perception of the acoustic space, and that a direct-form FIR filter can reproduce these early reflections explicitly and accurately. Usually this FIR filter is implemented as a tapped delay line, i.e., a delay line with multiple reading points that are weighted and summed together to provide a single output. This output signal feeds, in Moorer's architecture, a series of allpass filters and parallel comb filters. Another improvement introduced by Moorer was the replacement of the simple gain of feedback delay lines in comb filters with lowpass filters resembling the effects of air absorption and lossy reflections.

An original approach to reverberation was taken by Julius Smith in 1985, when he proposed *digital waveguide networks* (*DWNs*) as a viable starting point for the design of numerical reverberators [Smi85]. The idea of *waveguide reverberators* is that of building a network of waveguide branches (i.e., bidirectional delay lines simulating wave propagation in a duct or a string) capable of producing the desired early reflections and a diffuse, sufficiently dense reverb. If the network is augmented with lowpass filters it is possible to shape the decay time with frequency. In other words, waveguide reverberators are built in two steps: the first step is the construction of a prototype lossless network, the second step is the introduction of the desired amount of losses. This procedure ensures good numerical properties and good control over stability [Smi86, Vai93]. In ideal terms, the quality of a prototype lossless reverberator is evaluated with respect to the whiteness and smoothness of the noise that is generated in response to an impulse. The fine control of decay time at different frequencies is decoupled from the structural aspects of the reverberator.

Among the classic reverberation tools we should also mention the structures proposed by Stautner and Puckette [SP82], and by Jot [Jot92]. These structures form the basis of feedback delay networks, which are discussed in detail in Section 5.7.2.

Clusters of comb/allpass filters

The construction of high-quality reverberators is half an art and half a science. Several structures and many parameterizations have been proposed in the past, especially in non-disclosed form within commercial reverb units [Dat97]. In most cases, the various structures are combinations of comb and allpass elementary blocks, as suggested by Schroeder in the early work. As an example, we briefly describe Moorer's preferred structure [Moo79], depicted in Figure 5.14. The block (a) of Moorer's reverb takes care of the early reflections by means of a tapped delay line. The resulting signal is forwarded to the block (b), which is the parallel of a direct path on one branch, and a delayed, attenuated diffuse reverberator on the other branch. The output of the reverberator is delayed in such a way that the last of the early echoes coming out of block (a) reaches the output before the first of the non-null samples coming out of the diffuse reverberator. In Moorer's preferred implementation, the reverberator of block (b) is best implemented as a parallel of six comb filters, each with a first-order lowpass filter in the loop, and a single allpass filter. In [Moo79], it is suggested to set the allpass delay length to 6 ms and the allpass coefficient to 0.7. Despite the fact that any allpass filter does not add coloration in the magnitude frequency response, its time response can give a metallic character to the sound, or add some unwanted roughness and granularity. The feedback attenuation coefficients and the lowpass filters of the comb filters can be tuned to resemble a realistic and smooth decay. In particular, the attenuation coefficients g_i determine the overall decay time of the series of echoes generated by each comb filter. If the desired decay time (usually defined for an attenuation level of 60 dB) is T_d, the gain of each comb filter has to be set to

$$g_i = 10^{-3 \frac{T_d F_s}{m_i}} \, , \qquad (5.20)$$

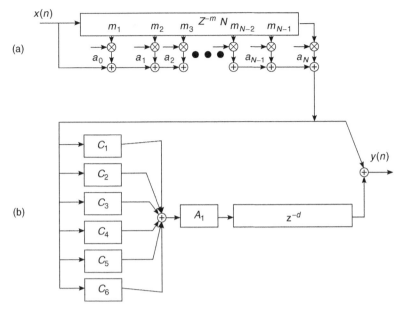

Figure 5.14 Moorer's reverberator.

where F_s is the sample rate and m_i is the delay length in the samples. Further attenuation at high frequencies is provided by the feedback lowpass filters, whose coefficient can also be related to decay time at a specific frequency or fine tuned by direct experimentation. In [Moo79], an example set of feedback attenuation and allpass coefficients is provided, together with some suggested values of the delay lengths of the comb filters. As a general rule, they should be distributed over a ratio 1:1.5 between 50 and 80 ms. Schroeder suggested a number-theoretic criterion for a more precise choice of the delay lengths [Sch73]: the lengths in samples should be mutually coprime (or incommensurate) to reduce the superimposition of echoes in the impulse response, thus reducing the so-called flutter echoes. This same criterion might be applied to the distances between each echo and the direct sound in early reflections. However, as was noticed by Moorer [Moo79], the results are usually better if the taps are positioned according to the reflections computed by means of some geometric modeling technique, such as the image method. As is explained next, even the lengths of the recirculating delays can be computed from the geometric analysis of the normal modes of actual room shapes.

5.7.2 Feedback delay networks

In 1982, J. Stautner and M. Puckette [SP82] introduced a structure for artificial reverberation based on delay lines interconnected in a feedback loop by means of a matrix (see Figure 5.15). Later, structures such as this have been called *feedback delay networks* (*FDN*s). The Stautner–Puckette FDN was obtained as a vector generalization of the recursive comb filter

$$y(n) = x(n - m) + g \cdot y(n - m) , \tag{5.21}$$

where the m-sample delay line was replaced by a bunch of delay lines of different lengths, and the feedback gain g was replaced by a feedback matrix $\mathbf{G}$. Stautner and Puckette proposed the

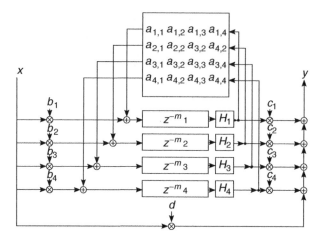

Figure 5.15 Fourth-order feedback delay network.

following feedback matrix:

$$
\mathbf{G} = g \begin{bmatrix} 0 & 1 & 1 & 0 \\ -1 & 0 & 0 & -1 \\ 1 & 0 & 0 & -1 \\ 0 & 1 & -1 & 0 \end{bmatrix} / \sqrt{2}.
\tag{5.22}
$$

Due to its sparse special structure, $\mathbf{G}$ requires only one multiple per output channel.
An example of FDN without lowpass filters H_n is:

M-file 5.15 (delaynetwork.m)

```
% delaynetwork.m
% Author: T. Lokki
fs=44100;
gain=0.97;
% Create an impulse
x = zeros(1,1*fs); x(1) = 1;
y = zeros(1,fs);
b = [1 1 1 1];
c = [0.8 0.8 0.8 0.8];
% Feedback matrix
a(1,:)=[0 1 1 0];
a(2,:)=[-1 0 0 -1];
a(3,:)=[1 0 0 -1];
a(4,:)=[0 1 -1 0];
a2=a*(1/sqrt(2)) * gain;
% Delay lines, use prime numbers
m=[149 211 263 293]';
z1=zeros(1,max(max(m)));
z2=zeros(1,max(max(m)));
z3=zeros(1,max(max(m)));
z4=zeros(1,max(max(m)));
```

```
for n = 1:length(y)
    tmp = [z1(m(1)) z2(m(2)) z3(m(3)) z4(m(4))];
    y(n) = x(n) + c(1)*z1(m(1)) + c(2)*z2(m(2)) ...
           + c(3)*z3(m(3)) + c(4)*z4(m(4));
    z1 = [(x(n)*b(1) + tmp*a2(1,:)') z1(1:length(z1)-1)];
    z2 = [(x(n)*b(2) + tmp*a2(2,:)') z2(1:length(z2)-1)];
    z3 = [(x(n)*b(3) + tmp*a2(3,:)') z3(1:length(z3)-1)];
    z4 = [(x(n)*b(4) + tmp*a2(4,:)') z4(1:length(z4)-1)];
end
plot(y)
```

More recently, Jean-Marc Jot has investigated the possibilities of FDNs very thoroughly. He proposed to use some classes of unitary matrices allowing efficient implementation. Moreover, he showed how to control the positions of the poles of the structure in order to impose a desired decay time at various frequencies [Jot92]. His considerations were driven by perceptual criteria and the general goal was to obtain an ideal diffuse reverb. In this context, Jot introduced the important design criterion that all the modes of a frequency neighborhood should decay at the same rate, in order to avoid the persistence of isolated, ringing resonances in the tail of the reverb [JC91]. This is not what happens in real rooms though, where different modes of close resonance frequencies can be differently affected by wall absorption [Mor91]. However, it is generally believed that the slow variation of decay rates with frequency produces smooth and pleasant impulse responses.

General structure

Referring to Figure 5.15, an *FDN* is built starting from N delay lines, each being $\tau_i = m_i T_s$ seconds long, where $T_s = 1/F_s$ is the sampling interval. The FDN is completely described by the following equations:

$$y(n) = \sum_{i=1}^{N} c_i s_i(n) + dx(n)$$

$$s_i(n + m_i) = \sum_{j=1}^{N} a_{i,j} s_j(n) + b_i x(n), \qquad (5.23)$$

where $s_i(n)$, $1 \leq i \leq N$, are the delay outputs at the nth time sample. If $m_i = 1$ for every i, we obtain the well-known *state space description* of a discrete-time linear system [Kai80]. In the case of FDNs, m_i are typically numbers on the orders of hundreds or thousands, and the variables $s_i(n)$ are only a small subset of the system state at time n, being the whole state represented by the content of all the delay lines.

From the state-variable description of the FDN it is possible to find the system transfer function [Roc96, RS97] as

$$H(z) = \frac{Y(z)}{X(z)} = \mathbf{c}^T [\mathbf{D}z^{-1} - \mathbf{A}]^{-1} \mathbf{b} + d. \qquad (5.24)$$

The diagonal matrix $\mathbf{D}(z) = \text{diag}\left(z^{-m_1}, z^{-m_2}, \ldots z^{-m_N}\right)$ is called the *delay matrix*, and $\mathbf{A} = [a_{i,j}]_{N \times N}$ is called the *feedback matrix*.

The stability properties of a FDN are all ascribed to the feedback matrix. The fact that $\|A\|^n$ decays exponentially with n ensures that the whole structure is stable [Roc96, RS97].

The poles of the FDN are found as the solutions of

$$\det[\mathbf{A} - \mathbf{D}z^{-1}] = 0 .\tag{5.25}$$

In order to have all the poles on the unit circle it is sufficient to choose a unitary matrix. This choice leads to the construction of a *lossless prototype*, but this is not the only choice allowed.

The zeros of the transfer function can also be found [Roc96, RS97] as the solutions of

$$\det\left[\mathbf{A} - \mathbf{b}\frac{1}{d}\mathbf{c}^T - \mathbf{D}z^{-1}\right] = 0 .\tag{5.26}$$

In practice, once we have constructed a lossless FDN prototype, we must insert attenuation coefficients and filters in the feedback loop. For instance, following the indications of Jot [JC91], we can cascade every delay line with a gain

$$g_i = \alpha^{m_i} .\tag{5.27}$$

This corresponds to replacing $D(z)$ with $D(z/\alpha)$ in (5.24). With this choice of the attenuation coefficients, all the poles are contracted by the same factor α. As a consequence, all the modes decay with the same rate, and the reverberation time (defined for a level attenuation of 60 dB) is given by

$$T_d = \frac{-3T_s}{\log \alpha} .\tag{5.28}$$

In order to have a faster decay at higher frequencies, as happens in real enclosures, we must cascade the delay lines with lowpass filters. If the attenuation coefficients g_i are replaced by lowpass filters, we can still get a local smoothness of decay times at various frequencies by satisfying the condition (5.27), where g_i and α have been made frequency dependent:

$$G_i(z) = A^{m_i}(z),\tag{5.29}$$

where $A(z)$ can be interpreted as per-sample filtering [JSer, JC91, Smi92].

It is important to notice that a uniform decay of neighbouring modes, even though commonly desired in artificial reverberation, is not found in real enclosures. The *normal modes* of a room are associated with stationary waves, whose absorption depends on the spatial directions taken by these waves. For instance, in a rectangular enclosure, axial waves are absorbed less than oblique waves [Mor91]. Therefore, neighboring modes associated with different directions can have different reverberation times. Actually, for commonly found rooms having irregularities in the geometry and in the materials, the response is close to that of a room having diffusive walls, where the energy rapidly spreads among the different modes. In these cases, we can find that the decay time is quite uniform among the modes [Kut95].

Parameterization

The main questions arising after we established a computational structure called FDN are: What are the numbers that can be put in place of the many coefficients of the structure? How should these numbers be chosen?

The most delicate part of the structure is the feedback matrix. In fact, it governs the stability of the whole structure. In particular, it is desirable to start with a lossless prototype, i.e., a reference structure providing an endless, flat decay. The reader interested in general matrix classes that might work as prototypes is referred to the literature [Jot92, RS97, Roc97, Gar97b]. Here we only mention the class of *circulant matrices*, having the general form

$$\mathbf{A} = \begin{bmatrix} a(0) & a(1) & \ldots & a(N-1) \\ a(N-1) & a(0) & \ldots & a(N-2) \\ \ldots & & & \\ a(1) & & \ldots & a(N-1) & a(0) \end{bmatrix}. \tag{5.30}$$

The stability of an FDN is related to the magnitude of its eigenvalues, which can be computed by the discrete Fourier transform of the first row, in the case of a circulant matrix. By keeping these eigenvalues on the unit circle (i.e., magnitude one) we ensure that the whole structure is stable and lossless. The control over the angle of the eigenvalues can be translated into a direct control over the degree of diffusion of the enclosure that is being simulated by the FDN. The limiting cases are the diagonal matrix, corresponding to perfectly reflecting walls, and the matrix whose rows are sequences of equal-magnitude numbers and (pseudo-)randomly distributed signs [Roc97].

Another critical set of parameters is given by the lengths of the delay lines. Several authors suggested to use lengths in samples that are mutually coprime numbers in order to minimize the collision of echoes in the impulse response. However, if the FDN is linked to a physical and geometrical interpretation, as it is done in the ball-within-a-box model [Roc95], the delay lengths are derived from the geometry of the room being simulated and the resulting digital reverb quality is related to the quality of the actual room. A delay line is associated with a harmonic series of normal modes, all obtainable from a plane-wave loop that bounces back and forth within the enclosure. The delay length for the particular series of normal modes is given by the time interval between two consecutive collisions of the plane wavefront along the main diagonal, i.e., twice the time taken to travel the distance

$$l = \frac{c}{2 f_0}, \tag{5.31}$$

being f_0 the fundamental frequency of the harmonic modal series.

5.7.3 Time-variant reverberation

Reverberation algorithms are usually time invariant, meaning that the response does not change as a function of time. This is reasonable, since reverberation algorithms model an LTI system, an impulse response. However, in live performances and installations, it is sometimes beneficial to have a time-variant reverberation to prevent and reduce the coloration and instability due to the feedback caused by the proximity of microphones and loudspeakers. The frequency response of such a system is not ideally flat, which easily leads to acoustical feedback at the frequency with the highest loop gain. Several algorithms exist [NS99] to modify the frequency response of the system so that resonance frequencies vary over time.

One efficient implementation of time-variance to an FDN type reverberator has been proposed [LH01]. The FDN is modified to contain a comb-allpass filter at each delay line. The time variance is implemented by modulating the feedback coefficient of this comb-allpass filter with a few Hertz modulation frequency. Such modulations change the group delay of each delay line, resulting in the frequency shift of resonant frequencies. However, this shift is not constant at all frequencies and if all delay lines in the FDN have different modulation frequencies no audible pitch shift is perceived. Such an algorithm has been successfully applied in the creation of a physically small, but sonically large rehearsal space for a symphony orchestra [LPPS09].

5.7.4 Modeling reverberation with a room geometry

In some applications, it is beneficial to have a room effect based on the defined room geometry. Then, the impulse response is created with computational room acoustics modeling methods.

The methods can be divided into ray-based and wave-based methods, based on the underlying assumptions of the sound propagation [Sil10].

Wave-based methods

Wave-based acoustic modeling aims to numerically solve the wave equation. Traditional techniques are the finite element (FEM) and the boundary element (BEM) methods [SK02]. However, these techniques are computationally too heavy for the whole audible frequency range, although at low frequencies they could be applied in combination with other techniques more suitable at higher frequencies. The digital waveguide mesh method is a newer wave-based technique, being computationally less expensive and thus more suitable for room impulse response creation or even for real-time auralization [MKMS07, Sav10]. A novel, very interesting wave-based method is the adaptive rectangular decomposition method [RNL09].

Ray-based methods

In ray-based acoustic modeling sound is assumed to behave similarly to light. This approximation is valid at high frequencies, and makes it possible to utilize plenty of algorithms developed in computer graphics in the field of global illumination. All the ray-based methods are covered by the room acoustic rendering equation [SLKS07], and all methods can be seen as a special solution for this equation. The detailed presentation of the room acoustic rendering equation is outside the scope of this book, but the most common ray-based modeling methods are briefly introduced here.

The *image-source method* and *beam-tracing methods* are the most common techniques to find specular reflection paths. The image-source method [AB79, Bor84] is based on recursive reflection of sound sources against all the surfaces in the room. This results in a combinatory explosion, and in practice only low-order, i.e., early reflections can be found. Figure 5.16 illustrates the process by showing image sources up to fourth order in a very simple 2-D geometry. Beam-tracing methods, such as [FCE+98, LSLS09], are optimized versions for the same purpose capable of dealing with more complicated geometries and higher reflection orders. A related approach to beam tracing is frustum tracing [LCM07], which scales even better to very large models. For image-source computation with **MATLAB** see [CPB05][1] and [LJ08].[2]

Ray tracing [KSS68] is the most popular offline algorithm for modeling sound propagation since it enables more advanced reflection modeling than the image-source method. A common approach is to shoot rays from the sound source in every direction, according to the directivity pattern of the source, and trace each ray until its energy level has decayed below a given threshold and at the same time keep track of instants when the ray hits a receiver, see Figures 5.17a and 5.17b.

The *acoustic radiance transfer* is a recently presented acoustic modeling technique based on progressive radiosity and arbitrary reflection models [SLKS07]. The acoustic energy is shot from the sound source to the surfaces of the model, which have been divided into patches, as illustrated in Figure 5.17c. Then, the propagation of the energy is followed from patch to patch and the intermediate results are stored on the patches. Finally, when the desired accuracy is achieved, the energy is collected from the patches to the listener.

These three methods have different properties for room-effect simulation. The image source method can only model specular reflections, but it is very efficient in finding perceptually relevant early reflections. As a reverberation effect the image source method is suitable for real-time processing, since the image sources, i.e., early reflections, can be spatially rendered and the late reverberation can be added with, for example, an FDN reverberator [SHLV99, LSH+02]. The ray-tracing method is not suitable for real-time reverberation processing. However, it is good at off line creation of the whole impulse response, which can be applied later with a real-time convolver.

---

[1] http://media.paisley.ac.uk/~campbell/Roomsim/
[2] http://www.eric-lehmann.com/ism_code.html

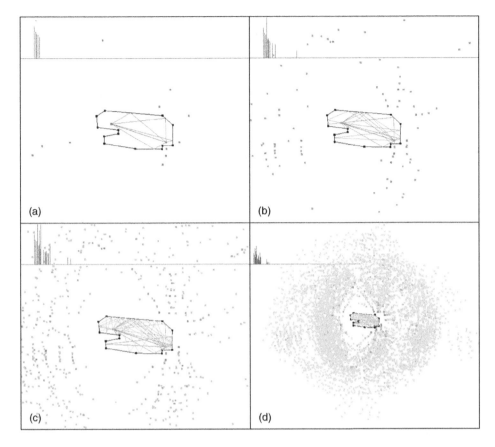

Figure 5.16 Visualization of the image source method. The dots outside of the concert hall silhouette are the image sources. The response above is the energy response at the receiver position, which is on the balcony. Figures (a)–(d) contain first–fourth-order image sources, respectively.

The acoustic radiance transfer method is the most advanced ray-based room acoustics modeling method, since it can handle both specular and diffuse reflections. Although the method is computationally extensive, the usage of the GPUs makes it possible to run the final gathering and sound rendering in real time, thus enabling interactive reverberation effects of environments with arbitrary reflection properties [SLS09].

5.8 Other spatial effects

5.8.1 Digital versions of classic reverbs

In the past, before the era of digital signal processing, many systems were used to create a reverberation effect. In studios the common way was to replay the recorded signals in a reverberant room or a corridor and record it again in that particular space. In addition, plates and springs were applied to create a decaying tail to the sound. Recently, researchers have modeled the physical principles of old-school reverberators and they have proposed digital implementations of them. For example, plate reverbs have been implemented with finite difference schemes [BAC06, Bil07]. An extension to digital plate reverbs to handle objects of any shape has been made with modal

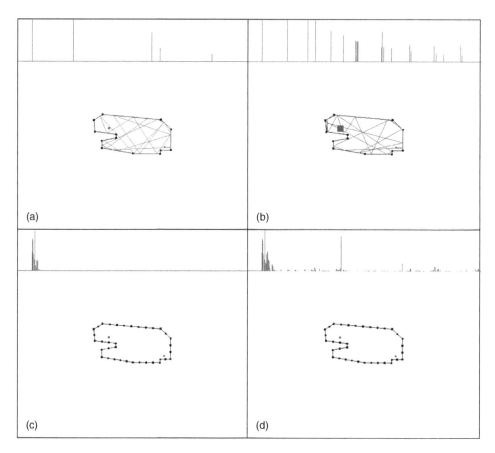

Figure 5.17   The ray-tracing method produces (a) a sparse response. (b) If the receiver area is larger more reflections are modeled. (c) The acoustics radiance transfer method when the initial energy is distributed to the surface patches. (d) The whole response after 100 energy distributions.

synthesis methods. Thus, simulations of the vibration of many different shapes and materials can be performed in real time [Max07]. Spring reverbs have also been modeled and it seems that efficient implementation can be achieved with parallel waveguides, which include dispersive all pass filters [ABCS06].

5.8.2   Distance effects

In digital audio effects, the control of apparent distance can be effectively introduced even in mono-phonic audio systems. In fact, the impression of distance of a sound source is largely controllable by insertion of artificial wall reflections or reverberant room responses.

There are not reliable cues for distance in anechoic or open spaces. Familiarity with the sound source can provide distance cues related with air absorption of high frequency. For instance, familiarity with a musical instrument tells us what is the average intensity of its sound when coming from a certain distance. The fact that timbral qualities of the instrument will change when playing loud or soft is also a cue that does help the identification of distance. These cues seem to vanish when using unfamiliar sources or synthetic stimuli that do not resemble any physical-sounding

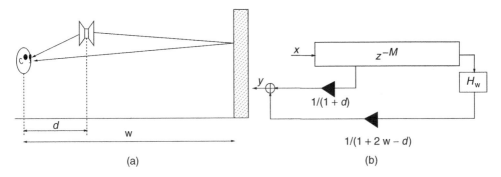

Figure 5.18 Distance rendering via single wall reflection: (a) physical situation, (b) signal-processing scheme

object. Conversely, in an enclosure the ratio of reverberant to direct acoustic energy has proven to be a robust distance cue [Bla97]. It is often assumed that in a small space the amplitude of the reverberant signal changes little with distance, and that in a large space it is roughly proportional to $1/\sqrt{\text{distance}}$ [Cho71]. The direct sound attenuates as $1/\text{distance}$ if spherical waves are propagated.

A single reflection from a wall can be enough to provide some distance cues in many cases. The physical situation is illustrated in Figure 5.18a, together with the signal-processing circuit that reproduces it. A single delay line with two taps is enough to reproduce this basic effect. Moreover, if the virtual source is close enough to the listening point, the first tap can be taken directly from the source, thus reducing the signal-processing circuitry to a simple non-recursive comb filter. To be physically consistent, the direct sound and its reflection should be attenuated as much as the distance they travel, and the wall reflection should also introduce some additional attenuation and filtering in the reflected sound, represented by the filter H_w in Figure 5.18b. The distance attenuation coefficients of Figure 5.18b have been set in such a way that they become one when the distance goes to zero, just to avoid the divergence to infinity that would come from the physical laws of a point source.

From this simple situation it is easy to see how the direct sound attenuates faster than the reflected sound, as long as the source approaches the wall.[3] This idea can be generalized to closed environments adding a full reverberant tail to the direct sound. An artificial yet realistic reverberant tail can be obtained just by taking an exponentially decayed gaussian noise and convolving it with the direct sound. The reverberant tail should be added to the direct sound after some delay (proportional to the size of the room) and should be attenuated with distance to a lesser extent than the direct sound. Figure 5.19 shows the signal-processing scheme for distance rendering via room reverberation.

The following M-file allows one to experiment with the situations depicted in Figures 5.18 and 5.19, with different listener positions, provided that x is initialized with the input sound, and y, z, and w are long-enough vectors initialized to zero.

M-file 5.16 (distfx.m)

```
% distfx.m
% Author: T. Lokki
h = filter([0.5,0.5],1, ...
    random('norm',0,1,1,lenh).*exp(-[1:lenh]*0.01/distwall)/100);
    % reverb impulse response
```

[3] Indeed, in this single-reflection situation, the intensity of the reflected sound increases as the source approaches the wall.

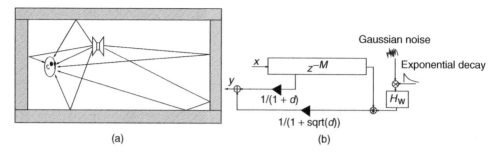

Figure 5.19 Distance rendering via room reverberation: (a) physical situation, (b) signal-processing scheme

```
offset = 100;
st = Fs/2;

for i = 1:1:distwall-1 % several distances listener-source
  del1 = floor(i/c*Fs);
  del2 = floor((distwall*2 - i)/c*Fs);
  y(i*st+1:i*st+del1) = zeros(1,del1);
  y(i*st+del1+1:i*st+del1+length(x)) = x./(1+i); % direct signal
  w(i*st+del2+1:i*st+del2+length(x)) = ...
        y(i*st+del2+1:i*st+del2+length(x)) + ...
        x./(1+(2*distwall-i));    % direct signal + echo
  z(i*st+del2+1:i*st+del2+length(x)+lenh-1+offset) = ...
        y(i*st+del2+1:i*st+del2+length(x)+lenh-1+offset) + ...
        [zeros(1,offset),conv(x,h)]./sqrt(1+i);
                    % direct signal + delayed reverb
end
```

5.8.3 Doppler effect

Movements of the sound sources are detected as changes in direction and distance cues. The Doppler effect is a further (strong) cue that intervenes whenever there is a radial component of motion between the sound source and the listener. In a closed environment, radial components of motion are likely to show up via reflections from the walls. Namely, even if a sound source is moving at constant distance from the listener, the paths taken by the sound waves via wall reflections are likely to change in length. If the source motion is sufficiently fast, in all of these cases we will have transpositions in frequency of the source sound.

The principle of the Doppler effect is illustrated in Figure 5.20, where the listener is moving toward the sound source with speed c_s. If the listener meets f_s wave crests per second at rest, it ends up meeting crests at the higher rate

$$f_d = f_s \left(1 + \frac{c_s}{c}\right) \tag{5.32}$$

when the source is moving. Here c is the speed of sound in air. We usually appreciate the pitch shift due to Doppler effect in non-musical situations, such as when an ambulance or a train is passing by. The perceived cue is so strong that it can evocate the relative motion between source and listener even when other cues indicate a constant relative distance between the two. In fact, ambulance or insect sounds having a strong Doppler effect are often used to demonstrate how good a spatialization system is, thus deceiving the listener who doesn't think that much of the spatial

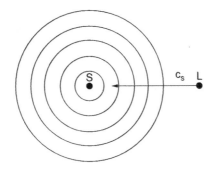

Figure 5.20   Illustration of the Doppler effect.

Figure 5.21   Control signal for simulating the Doppler effect with a delay-based pitch shifter

effect is already in the monophonic recording. Research into psychoacoustics has also shown how the perception of pitch can be strongly affected by dynamic changes in intensity, as they are found in situations where the Doppler effect occurs [Neu98]. Namely, a sound source approaching the listener at constant speed produces a rapid increase in intensity when it traverses the neighborhood of the listener. On the other hand, while the frequency shift is constant and positive before passing the listener, and constant and negative after it has passed, most listeners perceive an increase in pitch shift as the source is approaching. Such apparent pitch increase is due to the simultaneous increase in loudness.

The Doppler effect can be faithfully reproduced by a pitch shifter (see Chapter 6) controlled by the relative velocity between source and listener. In particular, the circuit in Figure 6.13 can be used with sawtooth control signals whose slope increases with the relative speed. Figure 5.21 shows the signal used to control one of the delays in Figure 6.13 for a sound source that approaches the listening point and passes it. Before the source reaches the listener, the sound is raised in pitch, and it is lowered right after.

Any sound-processing model based on the simulation of wave propagation, implements an implicit simulation of the Doppler effect. In fact, these models are based on delay lines that change their length according to the relative position of source and listener, thus providing positive or negative pitch transpositions.

In general, the accuracy and naturalness of a Doppler shift reproduced by digital means depends on the accuracy of interpolation in variable-length delays. If this is not good enough, modulation products affect the transposed signal, producing remarkable artifacts.

5.9   Conclusion

Playing with the spatial attributes of sound has been an intriguing and challenging task for many musicians and sound designers. The multiplicity of techniques developed so far has been roughly overviewed in the previous pages. Despite the length of this chapter, we have certainly missed many important contributions to the field. However, we have tried to communicate which are the main structural, perceptual, or technological limitations and possibilities of spatial audio. We hope that the sound designer, after reading this chapter, will be able to model some spatial features of sound or, at least, to be conscious of those features that will be part of the aesthetics of the design process rather than part of the sonic outcome.

Acknowledgements

The Academy of Finland, project [218238], have supported this work. The research leading to these results has received funding from the European Research Council under the European Community's Seventh Framework Programme (FP7/2007-2013) / ERC grant agreements no. [240453] and no. [203636].

References

[AB79]   J. B. Allen and D. A. Berkley. Image method for efficiently simulating small-room acoustics. *J. Acoust. Soc. Am.*, 65(4): 943–950, 1979.

[ABCS06]   J. S. Abel, D. P. Berners, S. Costello, and J. O. Smith. Spring reverb emulation using dispersive allpass filters in a waveguide structure. In *the 121st Audio Eng. Soc. (AES) Conv.*, 2006. Paper # 6954.

[ADDA01]   V. R. Algazi, R. O Duda, Thompson D. M., and C. Avendano. Parameters for auditory display of height and size. In *Proc. 2001 IEEE Workshop Appl. Signal Proces. Audio Electroacoust.*, Mohonk Mountain House, New Paltz, NY, 2001.

[ARB04]   A. Apel, T. Röder, and S. Brix. Equalization of wave field synthesis systems. In *Proc. 116th AES Convention, 2004 Paper # 6121.*

[BAC06]   S. Bilbao, K. Arcas, and A. Chaigne. A physical model for plate reverberation. In *Proc. Int. Conf. Acoust., Speech, Signal Proces. (ICASSP 2006)*, volume V, pp. 165–168, 2006.

[BBE85]   J. C. Bennett, K. Barker, and F. O. Edeko. A new approach to the assessment of stereophonic sound system performance. *J. Audio Eng. Soc.*, 33(5): 314–321, 1985.

[BD98]   C. P. Brown and R. O. Duda. A structural model for binaural sound synthesis. *IEEE Trans. Speech and Audio Process.*, 6(5): 476–488, 1998.

[Beg94]   D. R. Begault. *3-D Sound For Virtual Reality and Multimedia*. AP Professional, 1994.

[BF08]   J. Breebaart and C. Faller. *Spatial Audio Processing: MPEG Surround and Other Applications*. Wiley-Interscience, 2008.

[Bil07]   S. Bilbao. A digital plate reverberation algorithm. *J. Audio Eng. Soc.*, 55(3): 135–144, 2007.

[Bla97]   J. Blauert. *Spatial Hearing. The Psychophysics of Human Sound Localization*, 2nd edition MIT Press, 1997.

[Bor84]   J. Borish. Extension of the image model to arbitrary polyhedra. *J. Acoust. Soc. Am.*, 75(6): 1827–1836, 1984.

[BR99]   D. S. Brungart and W. M. Rabinowitz. Auditory localization of nearby sources. head-related transfer functions. *J. Acoust. Soc. Am.*, 106(3): 1465–1479, 1999.

[BS.94]   ITU-R Recommendation BS.775-1. Multichannel stereophonic sound system with and without accompanying picture. Technical report, International Telecommunication Union, Geneva, Switzerland, 1992-1994.

[BVV93]   A. J. Berkhout, D. de Vries, and P. Vogel. Acoustics control by wave field synthesis. *J. Acoust. Soc. Am.*, 93(5): 2764–2778, May 1993.

[CB89]   D. H. Cooper and J. L. Bauck. Prospects for transaural recording. *J. Audio Eng. Soc.*, 37(1/2): 3–39, 1989.

[Cho71]   J. Chowning. The simulation of moving sound sources. *J. Audio Eng. Soc.*, 19(1): 2–6, 1971.

[Coo87]   D. H. Cooper. Problems with shadowless stereo theory: Asymptotic spectral status. *J. Audio Eng. Soc.*, 35(9): 629–642, 1987.

[CPB05]   D. R. Campbell, K. J. Palomäki, and G. Brown. A matlab simulation of "shoebox" room acoustics for use in research and teaching. *Comp. Inform. Syst. J.*, 9(3), 2005.

[Cra03]   P. G. Craven. Continuous surround panning for 5-speaker reproduction. In *AES 24th Int. Conf. Multichannel Audio*, 2003.

[CT03]   D. Cabrera and S. Tilley. Parameters for auditory display of height and size. In *Proc. ICAD*, 2003.

[Dat97]   J. Dattorro. Effects design, part 1: Reverberator and other filters. *J. Audio Eng. Soc.*, 45(9): 660–683, 1997.

[Dav03]   M. F. Davis. History of spatial coding. *J. Audio Eng. Soc.*, 51(6): 554–569, 2003.

[DM98]   R. Duda and W. Martens. Range-dependence of the HRTF of a spherical head. *Appl. Signal Process. Audio Acoust*. 104(5): 3048–3058, November 1998.

[DNM03]   J. Daniel, R. Nicol, and S. Moreau. Further investigations of high order ambisonics and wavefield synthesis for holophonic sound imaging. In *Proc. 114th AES Conv.*, 2003. Paper # 5788.

[ED08]   N. Epain and J. Daniel. Improving Spherical Microphone Arrays. In *Proc. 124th AES Convention*, 2008. Paper #7479.

[FCE+98]   T. Funkhouser, I. Carlbom, G. Elko, G. Pingali, M. Sondhi, and J. West. A beam tracing approach to acoustics modeling for interactive virtual environments. In *Proc. 25th Ann. Conf. Comp. Graphics Interactive techniques (SIGGRAPH'98)*, pp. 21–32, 1998.

[GA97]   R. H. Gilkey and T. R. Anderson (eds). *Binaural and Spatial Hearing in Real and Virtual Environments*. Lawrence Erlbaum Assoc., 1997.

[Gar95]   W. G. Gardner. Efficient convolution without input-output delay. *J. Audio Eng. Soc.*, 43(3): 127–136, 1995.

[Gar97a]   W. G. Gardner. *3-D Audio Using Loudspeakers*. PhD thesis, MIT Media Lab, 1997.

[Gar97b]   W. G. Gardner. Reverberation algorithms. In M. Kahrs and K. Brandenburg (eds), *Applications of Digital Signal Processing to Audio and Acoustics*, pp. 85–131. Kluwer Academic Publishers, 1997.

[Ger73]   M. J. Gerzon. Periphony: With height sound reproduction. *J. Audio Eng. Soc.*, 21(1): 2–10, 1973.

[Ger76]   M. A. Gerzon. Unitary (energy preserving) multichannel networks with feedback. *Electron. Lett. V*, 12(11): 278–279, 1976.

[GJ06]   M. M. Goodwin and J.-M. Jot. A frequency-domain framework for spatial audio coding based on universal spatial cues. In *Proc. 120th AES Convention*, 2006. Paper # 6751.

[GM94]   W. G. Gardner and K. Martin. HRTF measurements of a KEMAR dummy-head microphone. Technical Report 280, MIT Media Lab Perceptual Computing, 1994.

[Hir07]   T. Hirvonen. *Perceptual and Modeling Studies on Spatial Sound*. PhD thesis, Helsinki University of Technology, 2007. http://lib.tkk.fi/Diss/2007/isbn9789512290512/.

[HP08]   T. Hirvonen and V. Pulkki. Perceived Spatial Distribution and Width of Horizontal Ensemble of Independent Noise Signals as Function of Waveform and Sample Length signals as Function of Waveform and Sample length. In *Proc. 124th AES Convention*, 2008. Paper # 7408.

[JC91]   J.-M. Jot and A. Chaigne. Digital delay networks for designing artificial reverberators. In *Proc. AES Convention*, 1991. Preprint no. 3030.

[Jot92]   J.-M. Jot. *Etude et réalisation d'un spatialisateur de sons par modèles physique et perceptifs*. PhD thesis, l'Ecole Nationale Superieure des Telecommunications, Télécom Paris 92 E 019, 1992.

[JSer]   D. Jaffe and J. O. Smith. Extensions of the Karplus-Strong plucked string algorithm. *Comp. Music J.*, 7(2): 56–69, 1983 Summer. Reprinted in C. Roads (ed.), *The Music Machine*. (MIT Press, 1989, pp. 481–49.

[Kai80]   T. Kailath. *Linear Systems*. Prentice-Hall, 1980.

[KNH98]   O. Kirkeby, P. A. Nelson, and H. Hamada. Local sound field reproduction using two closely spaced loudspeakers. *J. Acoust. Soc. Am.*, 104: 1973–1981, 1998.

[KSS68]   A. Krokstad, S. Strom, and S. Sorsdal. Calculating the acoustical room response by the use of a ray tracing technique. *J. Sound Vibr.*, 8: 118–125, 1968.

[Kut95]   H. Kuttruff. A simple iteration scheme for the computation of decay constants in enclosures with diffusely reflecting boundaries. *J. Acous. Soc. Am.*, 98(1): 288–293, 1995.

[KV01]   M. Kubovy and D. Van Valkenburg. Auditory and visual objects. *Cognition*, 80(1–2): 97–126, 2001.

[LCM07]   C. Lauterbach, A. Chandak, and D. Manocha. Interactive sound rendering in complex and dynamic scenes using frustum tracing. *IEEE Trans. Visualization Comp. Graphics*, 13(6): 1672–1679, 2007.

[LCYG99]   R. Y. Litovsky, H. S. Colburn, W. A. Yost, and S. J. Guzman. The precedence effect. *J. Acoust. Soc. Am.*, 106: 1633, 1999.

[LH01]   T. Lokki and J. Hiipakka. A time-variant reverberation algorithm for reverberation enhancement systems. In *Proc. Digital Audio Effects Conf. (DAFx-01)*, 2001, pp. 28–32.

[Lip86]   S. P. Lipshitz. Stereophonic microphone techniques ... are the purists wrong? *J. Audio Eng. Soc.*, 34(9): 716–744, 1986.

[LJ08]   E. A. Lehmann and A. M. Johansson. Prediction of energy decay in room impulse responses simulated with an image-source model. *J. Acoust. Soc. Am.*, 124(1): 269–277, 2008.

[LPPS09]   T. Lokki, J. Pätynen, T. Peltonen, and O. Salmensaari. A rehearsal hall with virtual acoustics for symphony orchestras. In *Proc. 126th AES Conv.*, 2009. paper no. 7695.

[LSH+02]   T. Lokki, L. Savioja, J. Huopaniemi, R. Väänänen, and T. Takala. Creating interactive virtual auditory environments. *IEEE Comp. Graphics Appl.*, 22(4): 49–57, 2002.

[LSLS09]   S. Laine, S. Siltanen, T. Lokki, and L. Savioja. Accelerated beam tracing algorithm. *Appl. Acoust.*, 70(1): 172–181, 2009.

[Max07]   C. B. Maxwell. Real-time reverb simulation for arbitrary object shapes. In *Proc. 10th Int. Conf. Digital Audio Effects (DAFX-07)*, 15–20, 2007.

[MHR10]   E. J. Macaulay, W. M. Hartmann, and B. Rakerd. The acoustical bright spot and mislocalization of tones by human listeners. *J. Acoust. Soc. Am.*, 127: 1440, 2010.

[Mit98]   S. K. Mitra. *Digital Signal Processing: A Computer-Based Approach*. McGraw-Hill, 1998.

[MKMS07]   D. Murphy, A. Kelloniemi, J. Mullen, and S. Shelley. Acoustic modeling using the digital waveguide mesh. *IEEE Signal Proces. Mag.*, 24(2): 55–66, 2007.

[MM95]   D. G. Malham and A. Myatt. 3-D sound spatialization using ambisonic techniques. *Comp. Music J.*, 19(4): 58–70, 1995.

[MM01]   S. Müller and P. Massarani. Transfer function measurement with sweeps. *J. Audio Eng. Soc.*, 49(6): 443–471, 2001.

[Mon00]   G. Monro. In-phase corrections for ambisonics. In *Proc. Int. Comp. Music Conf.*, 2000, pp. 292–295.

[Moo79]   J. A. Moorer. About this reverberation business. *Comp. Music J.*, 3(2): 13–28, 1979.

[Moo83]   F. R. Moore. A general model for spatial processing of sounds. *Comp. Music J.*, 7(3): 6–15, 1983.

[Moo90]   F. R. Moore. *Elements of Computer Music*. Prentice Hall, 1990.

[Mor91]   P. M. Morse. *Vibration and Sound*. American Institute of Physics for the Acoustical Society of America, 1991.

[MSHJ95]   H. Møller, M. F. Sørensen, D. Hammershøi, and C. B. Jensen. Head-related transfer functions of human subjects. *J. of Audio Eng. Soc.*, 43(5): 300–321, May 1995.

[MT99]   C. Müller-Tomfelde. Low-latency convolution for real-time applications. In *Proc. 16th AES Int. Conf*, 1999 pp. 454–459.

[Neu98]   J. G. Neuhoff. A perceptual bias for rising tones. *Nature*, 395(6698): 123–124, 1998.

[NS99]   J. L. Nielsen and U. P. Svensson. Performance of some linear time-varying systems in control of acoustic feedback. *J. Acoust. Soc. Am.*, 106(1): 240–254, 1999.

[OS89]   A. V. Oppenheim and R. W. Schafer. *Discrete-Time Signal Processing*. Prentice-Hall, Inc., 1989.

[PB82]   D. R. Perrott and T. N. Buell. Judgments of sound volume: Effects of signal duration, level, and interaural characteristics on the perceived extensity of broadband noise. *J. Acoust. Soc. Am.*, 72: 1413, 1982.

[PH05]   V. Pulkki and T. Hirvonen. Localization of virtual sources in multi-channel audio reproduction. *IEEE Trans. Speech Audio Proc.*, 2005.

[PKH99]   V. Pulkki, M. Karjalainen, and J. Huopaniemi. Analyzing virtual sound source attributes using a binaural auditory model. *J. Audio Eng. Soc.*, 47(4): 203–217, April 1999.

[Pol07]   A. Politis. *Subjective evaluation of the performance of virtual acoustic imaging systems under suboptimal conditions of implementation*, MSc thesis. University of Southampton, 2007.

[Pul97]   V. Pulkki. Virtual source positioning using vector base amplitude panning. *J. Audio Eng. Soc.*, 45(6): 456–466, 1997.

[Pul99]   V. Pulkki. Uniform spreading of amplitude panned virtual sources. In *1999 IEEE Workshop Appl. Signal Proces. Acoust.*, 1999.

[Pul01]   V. Pulkki. *Spatial Sound Generation and Perception by Amplitude Panning Techniques*. PhD thesis, Helsinki University of Technology, Laboratory of Acoustics and Audio Signal Processing, 2001.

[Pul02]   V. Pulkki. Compensating displacement of amplitude-panned virtual sources. In *22nd AES Int. Conf. on Virtual, Synth. Enter. Audio*, 2002 pp. 186–195.

[Pul07]   V. Pulkki. Spatial sound reproduction with directional audio coding. *J. Audio Eng. Soc.*, 55(6): 503–516, June 2007.

[RNL09]   N. Raghuvanshi, R. Narain, and M. Lin. Efficient and accurate sound propagation using adaptive rectangular decomposition. *IEEE Trans. Visual. Comp. Graphics*, 15(5): 789–801, 2009.

[Roc95]   D. Rocchesso. The ball within the box: a sound-processing metaphor. *Comp Music J.*, 19(4): 47–57, 1995.

[Roc96]   D. Rocchesso. *Strutture ed Algoritmi per l'Elaborazione del Suono basati su Reti di Linee di Ritardo Interconnesse. Tesi sottoposta per il conseguimento del titolo di dottore di ricerca in ingegneria informatica ed elettronica industriali*. PhD thesis, Universita di Padova, Dipartimento di Elettronica e Informatica, 1996.

[Roc97]   D. Rocchesso. Maximally diffusive yet efficient feedback delay networks for artificial reverberation. *IEEE Signal Process. Lett*., 4(9): 252–255, Sep. 1997.

[RS97]   D. Rocchesso and J. O. Smith. Circulant and elliptic feedback delay networks for artificial reverberation. *IEEE Trans. Speech Audio Process*., 5(1): 51–63, 1997.

[Rum01]   F. Rumsey. *Spatial Audio*. Focal Press, 2001.

[Sav10]   L. Savioja. Real-time 3D finite-difference time-domain simulation of low- and mid-frequency room acoustics. In *13th Int. Conf. Digital Audio Effects*, 2010.

[Sch61]   M. R. Schroeder. Improved quasi-stereophony and "colorless" artificial reverberation. *J. Acoust. Soc. Am*., 33(8): 1061–1064, 1961.

[Sch62]   M. R. Schroeder. Natural-sounding artificial reverberation. *J. Audio Eng. Soc*., 10(3): 219–223, 1962.

[Sch70]   M. R. Schroeder. Digital simulation of sound transmission in reverberant spaces. *J. Acoust. Soc. Am*., 47(2 (Part 1)): 424–431, 1970.

[Sch73]   M. R. Schroeder. Computer models for concert hall acoustics. *Am. J. Physics*, 41: 461–471, 1973.

[SHLV99] L. Savioja, J. Huopaniemi, T. Lokki, and R. Väänänen. Creating interactive virtual acoustic environments. *J. Audio Eng. Soc*., 47(9): 675–705, 1999.

[Sil10]   S. Siltanen. *Efficient physics-based room-acoustics modeling and auralization*. PhD thesis, Aalto University School of Science and Technology, 2010. Available at http://lib.tkk.fi/Diss/2010/isbn9789522482645/.

[SK02]   U. P. Svensson and U. R. Kristiansen. Computational modeling and simulation of acoustic spaces. In *Proc. 22nd AES Int. Conf. on Virtual, Synth. Entert. Audio*, 2002 pp. 11–30.

[SK04]   R. Sadek and C. Kyriakakis. A novel multichannel panning method for standard and arbitrary loudspeaker configurations. In Proc. *117th AES Conv.,* 2004 Paper #6263.

[SL61]   M. R. Schroeder and B. Logan. "Colorless" artificial reverberation. *J. Audio Eng. Soc*., 9: 192–197, 1961.

[SLKS07] S. Siltanen, T. Lokki, S. Kiminki, and L. Savioja. The room acoustic rendering equation. *J. Acoust. Soc. Am*., 122(3): 1624–1635, 2007.

[SLS09]   S. Siltanen, T. Lokki, and L. Savioja. Frequency domain acoustic radiance transfer for real-time auralization. *Acta Acust. United AC*, 95(1): 106–117, 2009.

[Smi85]   J. O. Smith. A new approach to digital reverberation using closed waveguide networks. In *Proc. Int. Comp. Music Conf. (ICMC'85)*, 1985 pp. 47–53.

[Smi86]   J. O. Smith. Elimination of limit cycles and overflow oscillations in time-varying lattice and ladder digital filters. In *Proc. IEEE Conf. Circuits Syst*., 197–299, 1986.

[Smi92]   J. O. Smith. Physical modeling using digital waveguides. *Comp. Music J*., 16(4): 74–87, 1992.

[Sol08]   A. Solvang. Spectral impairment of two-dimensional higher order ambisonics. *J. Audio Eng. Soc*., 56(4): 267–279, 2008.

[SP82]   J. Stautner and M. Puckette. Designing multi-channel reverberators. *Comp. Music J*., 6(1): 569–579, 1982.

[Ste96]   G. Steinke. Surround sound–the new phase. an overview. In *Proc. 100th AES Conv*, 1996. Preprint #4286.

[The91]   G. Theile. HDTV sound systems: How many channnels ? In *Proc. 9th AES Int. Conf. "Television Sound Today and Tomorrow"*, 1991. pp. 217–232.

[Tor98]   E. Torick. Highlights in the history of multichannel sound. *J. Audio Eng. Soc*., 46(1/2): 27–31, 1998.

[Vai93]   P. P. Vaidyanathan. *Multirate Systems and Filter Banks*. Prentice Hall, 1993.

[VB99]   D. Vries and M. Boone. Wave field synthesis and analysis using array technology. In *Proc. 1999 IEEE Workshop Appl. Signal Proces. Audio Acoust*., 1999. pp. 15–18.

[Vil08]   J. Vilkamo. *Spatial sound reproduction with frequency band processing of b-format audio signals*, MSc thesis. Helsinki University Technology, 2008.

[VLP09]   J. Vilkamo, T. Lokki, and V. Pulkki. Directional audio coding: virtual microphone-based synthesis and subjective evaluation. *J. Audio Eng. Society*, 57(9): 709–724, 2009.

[ZF90]   E. Zwicker and H. Fastl. *Psychoacoustics: Facts and Models*. Springer-Verlag, 1990.

[Zur87]   P. M. Zurek. The precedence effect. In W. A. Yost and G. Gourewitch (eds), *Directional Hearing*, pp. 3–25. Springer-Verlag, 1987.

6

Time-segment processing

P. Dutilleux, G. De Poli, A. von dem Knesebeck and U. Zölzer

6.1 Introduction

In this chapter we discuss several time-domain algorithms which are a combination of smaller processing blocks like amplitude/phase modulators, filters and delay lines. These effects mainly influence the pitch and the time duration of the audio signal. We will first introduce some basic effects like variable speed replay and pitch-controlled resampling. They are all based on delay-line modulation and amplitude modulation. Then we will discuss two approaches for time stretching (time scaling) of audio signals. They are based on an analysis stage, where the input signal is divided into segments (blocks) of fixed or variable length, and a synthesis stage where the blocks of the analysis stage are recombined by an overlap and add procedure. These time-stretching techniques perform time scaling without modifying the pitch of the signal. The fourth section focuses on pitch shifting, and introduces three techniques: block processing based on time stretching and resampling, delay line modulation and pitch-synchronous block processing. Block processing based on delay line modulation performs pitch shifting by scaling the spectral envelope of each block. Pitch-synchronous block processing performs pitch shifting by resampling the spectral envelope of each block and thus preserving the spectral envelope. The last section on time shuffling and granulation presents a more creative use of time-segment processing. Short segments of the input signal are freely assembled and placed along time in the output signal. In this case the input sound can be much less recognizable in the output. The wide choice of strategies for segment organization implies a sound composition attitude from the user.

6.2   Variable speed replay

Introduction

Analog audio tape recorders allow replay with a wide range of tape speeds. Particularly in fast forward/backward transfer mode, a monitoring of the audio signal is possible which can be used to locate a sound. During faster playback the pitch of the sound is raised and during slower playback the pitch is lowered. With this technique the duration of the sound is lengthened if the tape is slowed down, and shortened if the tape speed is increased. Figure 6.1 illustrates a sound segment which is lengthened and shortened, and the corresponding spectra.

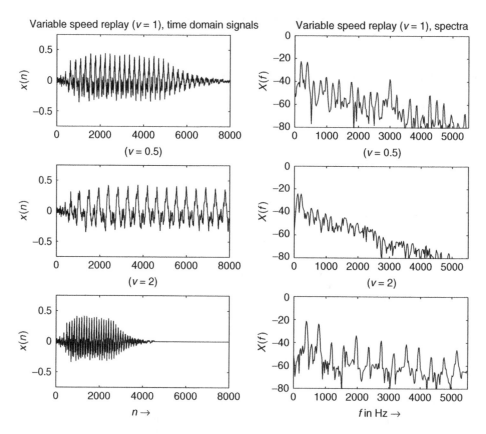

Figure 6.1   Pitch shifting: Variable speed replay leads to time compression/expansion and compression and expansion of the spectral envelope.

Signal processing

The phrase "variable speed replay" denotes that what has happened initially during the time period $nT_{s,in}$ is now happening during

$$nT_{s,replay} = nT_{s,in}/v \tag{6.1}$$

at the relative speed v, where $T_{s,in}$ and $T_{s,replay}$ are the initial and replay sampling periods. Time expansion corresponds to $v < 1$. A straightforward method of implementing the variable speed replay is hence to modify the sampling frequency while playing back the sound according to

$$f_{s,replay} = f_{s,in} \cdot v \qquad (6.2)$$

where $f_{s,in}$ and $f_{s,replay}$ are the initial and replay sampling frequencies. One should distinguish whether the output should be digital or may be analog. If the output is analog, then a very effective method is to modify the sampling frequency of the output DAC. The spectrum of the signal is scaled by v and the analog reconstruction filter should be tuned in order to remove the spectral images after the conversion [Gas87, Mas98].

If a digital output is required, then a sampling frequency conversion has to be performed between the desired replay frequency $f_{s,replay}$ and the output sampling frequency $f_{s,out}$, which is usually equal to $f_{s,in}$.

If $v < 1$ (time expansion) then $f_{s,in} > f_{s,replay} < f_{s,out}$ and more output samples are needed than available from the input signal. The output signal is an interpolated (over-sampled) version by a factor $1/v$ of the input signal. If $v > 1$ (time compression) then $f_{s,in} < f_{s,replay} > f_{s,out}$ and less output samples than available in the input signal are necessary. The input signal is decimated by a factor v. Before decimation, the bandwidth of the input signal has to be reduced to $f_{s,replay}/2$ by a digital lowpass filter [McN84]. The quality of the sampling rate conversion depends very much on the interpolation filter used. A very popular method is the linear interpolation between two adjacent samples. A review of interpolation methods can be found in [Mas98, CR83].

A discrete-time implementation can be achieved by increasing/decreasing the transfer rate of a recorded digital audio signal to the DA converter, thus changing the output sampling frequency compared to the recording sampling frequency. If the output signal has to be in digital format again, we have to resample the varispeed analog signal with the corresponding sampling frequency. A discrete-time implementation without a DA conversion and new AD conversion was proposed in [McN84] and is shown in Figure 6.2. It makes use of multirate signal-processing techniques and performs an approximation of the DA/AD conversion approach. A further signal-processing algorithm to achieve the acoustical result of a variable speed replay is delay line modulation with a constant pitch change, which will be discussed in Section 6.4.3.

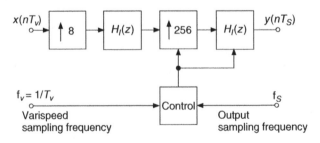

Figure 6.2 Variable speed replay scheme.

Musical applications and control

As well as for analog tape-based audio editing, variable-speed replay is very popular in digital audio editing systems. See [m-Wis94c, ID 2.9 and 2.10] for a straightforward demonstration of the effect on a voice signal.

The effect of tape-speed transposition has been used by Les Paul in the piece called "Whispering" in 1951 [Lee72]. This method is very often used in electro-acoustic music when the pitch of concrete sounds cannot be controlled at the time of recording. P. Schaeffer designed the *Phonogène chromatique* to transpose a sound to any one of the 12 degrees of the equal tempered scale. The device was based on a tape recorder with 12 capstans and pinch rollers. The operation of the pinch rollers could be controlled by a piano-like keyboard. An additional gear extended the range of operation to two octaves [Mol60, p. 71]; [Roa96, p. 119]; [Ges00]. Jacques Poullin developed another version, the *Phonogène à coulisse*, which allowed continuous speed modifications. A pair of cones, with a friction wheel in between, constitutes a variable-ratio mechanical link between the motor and the capstan of the tape player. The position of the friction wheel, and hence the replay speed, is controlled by a mechanical lever. Stockhausen, in "Hymnen," transposed orchestral sounds to give them an overwhelming and apocalyptic character [Chi82, p. 53].

In computer music too, variable-speed replay provides an effective transposition scheme. J.-C. Risset says: by "mixing a sound with transpositions of itself with a minute frequency difference (say, a twentieth of a Hertz), one can turn steady periodic tones into a pattern where the harmonics of the tone wax and wave at different rates, proportional to the rank of the harmonic" [Ris98, p. 255]; [m-INA3, Sud]. In "The Gates of H.," Ludger Brümmer exploits the fact that variable speed replay modifies both the pitch and the duration of a sample [m-Bru93, 14'40''–17'25'']. Seven copies of the same phrase, played simultaneously at speeds 7.56, 4.49, 2.24, 1.41, 0.94, 0.67, 0.42, 0.31 are overlapped. The resulting sound begins with a complex structure and an extended spectrum. As the piece continues, the faster copies vanish and the slower versions emerge one after the other. The sound structure simplifies and it evolves towards the very low registers.

The character of the transposed sounds is modified because all the features of the spectrum are simultaneously scaled. The formants are scaled up, leading to a "Mickey Mouse effect," or down, as if the sounds were produced by oversized objects. The time structure is modified as well. The transients are spread or contracted. A vibrato in the initial sound will lose its character and will appear as a slower or faster modulation. The sounds can also be played at negative speeds. A speed −1 yields a sound with the same average spectrum, although sounding very different. Think about speech or percussive sounds played backwards. Other transposition schemes that are free from these drawbacks are achieved by more sophisticated methods described in further sections of this book.

A particular application was desired by the composer Kiyoshi Furukawa. He wanted a sampler for which the speed would be controlled by the amplitude of an acoustical instrument. A sound is stored in a sampler and is played as a loop. In the meantime, the RMS amplitude of an incoming controlling signal is computed and time averaged with independent attack and decay time constants. This amplitude is converted to decibels and scaled before driving the speed of the sampler. The parameters have to be tuned in such a way that the speed remains within a valid range and the speed variations are intimately related to the loudness and the dynamics of the instrument (see Figure 6.3).

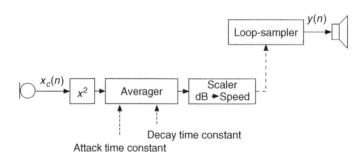

Figure 6.3 A loop-sampler controlled by an acoustical signal.

This effect is controlled by a clarinet in "Swim, swan" and by a viola in "Den Ungeborenen Göttern" [m-Fur93, m-Fur97]. The pitch of the acoustical instrument selects words out of a predefined set, whereas the loudness controls the replay speed of these words.

6.3 Time stretching

Introduction

In order to understand the issue of time stretching, let us take the example of a signal whose duration does not fit the time slot that is allocated to its application. Think about a speaker that has already recorded 33 seconds of speech, but whose contribution to a commercial may not be longer than 30 seconds. If he does not want to record his text again, the sound engineer may artificially contract his speech by 10%. With the term "time stretching" we mean the contraction or expansion of the duration of an audio signal. We have studied in 6.2 a method that alters the duration of a sound, the variable speed replay, but it has the drawback of simultaneously transposing the sound. The *Harmonizer* could be used to transpose the sound in the opposite direction and the combination of both methods leads to a time-stretching algorithm.

The main task of time-stretching algorithms is to shorten or lengthen a sound file of M samples to a new particular length $M' = \alpha \cdot M$, where α is the scaling factor. For performing time stretching algorithms the sound file has to be available in a stored form on a storage medium like a sampler, DAT or a hard disc. Time stretching of a sequence of audio samples is demonstrated in Figure 6.4.

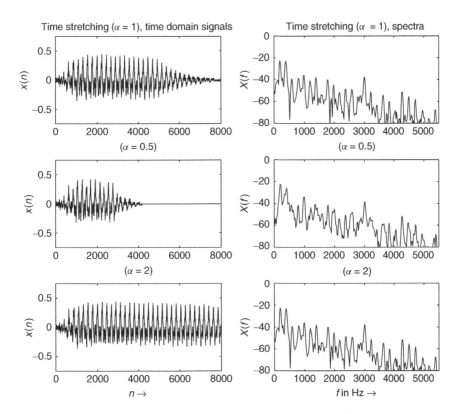

Figure 6.4 Time stretching with scaling factor $\alpha = 0.5, 2$.

The original signal is shown in the upper plot. The middle plot shows a sequence which is shortened by a scaling factor $\alpha = 0.5$ and the lower plot shows stretching by a scaling factor $\alpha = 2$.

Signal processing

The intended time scaling does not correspond to the mathematical time scaling as realized by vary-ispeed. We rather require a scaling of the perceived timing attributes, such as speaking rate, without affecting the perceived frequency attributes, such as pitch. We could say that we want the time-scaled version of an acoustic signal to be perceived as the same sequence of acoustic events as the original signal being reproduced according to a scaled time pattern. The time-stretching algorithms should not affect the pitch or the frequency contents of the processed signals. This is demonstrated by the corresponding spectra (first 2000 samples) of the discrete-time signals in Figure 6.4. For comparison, the traditional technique for time stretching based on variable speed replay introduces a pitch shift (see Section 6.2 and Figure 6.1). The basic idea of time stretching by time-segment processing is to divide the input sound into segments. Then if the sound is to be lengthened, some segments are repeated, while if the sound is to be shortened, some segments are discarded. A possible problem is amplitude and phase discontinuity at the boundaries of the segments. Amplitude discontinuities are avoided by partially overlapping the blocks, while phase discontinuities are avoided by a proper time alignment of the blocks. Two different strategies will be presented in Sections 6.3.2 and 6.3.3.

Applications

Special machines such as the *Phonogène universel* of Pierre Schaeffer or the Tempophon used by Herbert Eimerts allowed alteration of the time duration as well as the pitch of sounds. The *Phonogène* found many applications in *musique concrète* as a "time regulator." In his composition "Epitaph für Aikichi Kuboyama," Herbert Eimerts uses the Tempophon in order to iterate spoken word fragments. The device allowed the scanning of syllables, vowels and plosives and could make them shorter, longer or iterate them at will [Hal95, p. 13]; [m-Eim62].

As mentioned in the Introduction, the stretching of signals can be used to match their duration to an assigned time slot. In Techno music, different pieces of music are played one after the other as a continuous stream. This stream is supposed to have only very smooth tempo or *bpm* (beat per minute) transitions, although the musical excerpts usually do not have the same tempo. In order to adjust the tempi to each other, the disc jockey modifies the replay speeds at the transition from one excerpt to the other. This method leads to temporary pitch modifications which could be objectionable. The use of time-stretching methods could eliminate this problem.

After a brief presentation of the technology of the Phonogène, the following sections discuss two signal-processing techniques which perform time stretching without pitch modifications.

6.3.1   Historical methods – Phonogène

Fairbanks, Everitt and Jaeger report in 1954 on a modified tape recorder for time or frequency compression-expansion of speech [Lee72, Lar98]. Springer develops a similar machine [Spr55, Spr59] and Pierre Schaeffer praises a machine called *Phonogène universel* that was designed as a combination of the aforementioned *Phonogène chromatique* and *Phonogène à coulisse*, with the rotating head drum of Springer [Mol60, p. 71–76]; [Sch73, p. 47–48]; [m-Sch98, CD2, ID. 50–52]; [Pou54, PS57, Ges00].

The modified tape recorder has several playback heads mounted on a rotating head drum. The absolute speed of the tape at the capstan determines the duration of the sound, whereas the relative speed of the heads to that of the tape determines the amount of transposition. By electrical summation of the outputs of the different heads, a continous sound is delivered (Figure 6.5). Moles

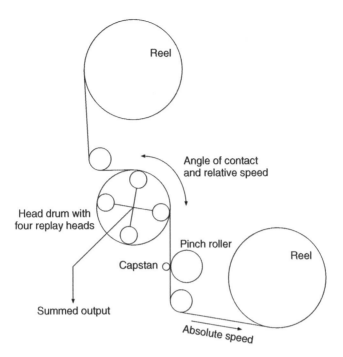

Figure 6.5 Tape-based time compression – expansion system, according to [Mol60].

reports a typical operating range of $+10\%$ to -40% [Mol60, p. 76]. The Springer machine was also known as *Laufzeitregler* or *Zeitdehner* [Car92, p. 479–480]; [End97].

6.3.2 Synchronous overlap and add (SOLA)

A simple algorithm for time stretching based on correlation techniques is proposed in [RW85, MEJ86]. Figure 6.6 illustrates the algorithm. The input signal $x(n)$ is divided into overlapping blocks of a fixed length N (see Figure 6.6a). S_a is the analysis step size, which determines the progression of the successive blocks along the input signal. In a second step these overlapping blocks are shifted according to the time-scaling factor α leading to the synthesis step size $S_s = \alpha \cdot S_a$ (see Figure 6.6b). Then the similarities in an interval of length L within the area of the overlap are searched for a discrete-time lag k_m of maximum similarity. The shift of two succeeding blocks is corrected by this time lag to synchronize the blocks and reduce artifacts (see Figure 6.6c). Finally at this point of maximum similarity the overlapping blocks are weighted by a fade-in and fade-out function and summed sample by sample (see Figure 6.6d).

Algorithm description:

(1) Segmentation of the input signal into overlapping blocks of length N with time shift of S_a samples.

(2) Repositioning of blocks with time shift $S_s = \alpha \cdot S_a$ using scaling factor α.

(3) Computation of the cross-correlation

$$r_{x_{L1}x_{L2}}(k) = \begin{cases} \frac{1}{L} \sum_{n=0}^{L-k-1} x_{L1}(n) \cdot x_{L2}(n+k) & , \quad 0 \leq k \leq L-1 \\ r_{x_{L2}x_{L1}}(-k) & , \quad -L+1 \leq k < 0 \end{cases} \qquad (6.3)$$

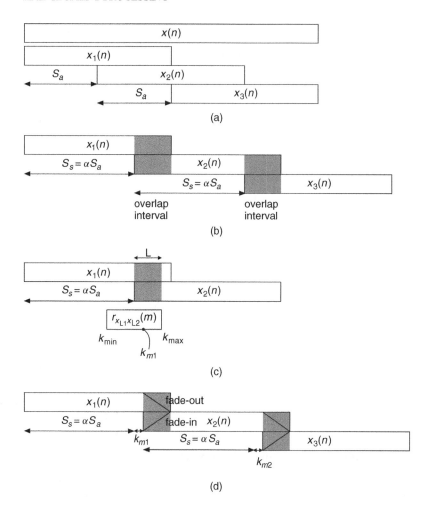

Figure 6.6   (a) Segmentation of the input signal, (b) repositioning of the blocks, (c) computation of the cross-correlation and synchronization of the blocks, (d) fading and overlap-add.

between $x_{L1}(n)$ and $x_{L2}(n)$, which are the segments of $x_1(n)$ and $x_2(n)$ in the overlap interval of length L.

(4) Extracting the discrete-time lag k_m where the cross-correlation $r_{x_{L1}x_{L2}}(k_m) = r_{max}$ has its maximum value.

(5) Using this discrete-time lag k_m, adjust the time shift to synchronize blocks $x_1(n)$ and $x_2(n)$ for maximum similarity.

(6) *Fade-out* $x_1(n)$ and *fade-in* $x_2(n)$. Overlap-add of $x_1(n)$ and $x_2(n)$ for new output signal.

The SOLA implementation leads to time scaling with little complexity, where the parameters S_a, N, L are independent of the pitch period of the input signal.

There are a number of similar approaches derived from the SOLA algorithm. The SOLAFS, as proposed in [HM91], realizes the time-scale modification with a fixed synthesis step size, while the analysis step size is varied to achieve maximum similarity between the output and the new window in the overlap region. A similar approach is proposed in [VR93] in the form of a waveform similarity overlap-add algorithm (WSOLA).

The following M-file 6.1 demonstrates the implementation of the SOLA time-scaling algorithm:

M-file 6.1 (TimeScaleSOLA.m)

```
% TimeScaleSOLA.m
% Authors: U. Zölzer, G. De Poli, P. Dutilleux
% Time Scaling with Synchronized Overlap and Add
%
% Parameters:
%
% analysis hop size    Sa = 256 (default parameter)
% block length         N  = 2048 (default parameter)
% time scaling factor  0.25 <= alpha <= 2
% overlap interval     L  = 256*alpha/2

clear all,close all

[DAFx_in,Fs]   =         wavread('x1.wav');
DAFx_in        =         signal';

% Parameters:
Sa       =      256;    % Sa must be less than N
N     = 2048;
alpha = 1;       % 0.25 <= alpha <= 2
Ss       = round(Sa*alpha);
L          = 128;    % L must be chosen to be less than N-Ss

% Segmentation into blocks of length N every Sa samples
% leads to M segments
M      =      ceil(length(DAFx_in)/Sa);

DAFx_in(M*Sa+N)=0;
Overlap  =  DAFx_in(1:N);

% **** Main TimeScaleSOLA loop ****
for ni=1:M-1
  grain=DAFx_in(ni*Sa+1:N+ni*Sa);
  XCORRsegment=xcorr(grain(1:L),Overlap(1,ni*Ss:ni*Ss+(L-1)));
  [xmax(ni),km(ni)]=max(XCORRsegment);

  fadeout=1:(-1/(length(Overlap)-(ni*Ss-(L-1)+km(ni)-1))):0;
  fadein=0:(1/(length(Overlap)-(ni*Ss-(L-1)+km(ni)-1))):1;
  Tail=Overlap(1,(ni*Ss-(L-1))+ ...
          km(ni)-1:length(Overlap)).*fadeout;
  Begin=grain(1:length(fadein)).*fadein;
  Add=Tail+Begin;
  Overlap=[Overlap(1,1:ni*Ss-L+km(ni)-1) ...
          Add grain(length(fadein)+1:N)];
end;
% **** end TimeScaleSOLA loop ****
% Output in WAV file
sound(Overlap,44100);
wavwrite(Overlap,Fs,'x1_time_stretch');
```

6.3.3 Pitch-synchronous overlap and add (PSOLA)

A variation of the SOLA algorithm for time stretching is the pitch synchronous overlap and add (PSOLA) algorithm proposed by Moulines *et al.* [HMC89, MC90] especially for voice processing. It is based on the hypothesis that the input sound is characterized by a pitch, as, for example, the human voice and monophonic musical instruments.

In this case PSOLA can exploit knowledge of the pitch to correctly synchronize the time segments, avoiding pitch discontinuities. When we perform time stretching of an input sound, the time variation of the pitch period $P(t)$ should be stretched accordingly. If $\tilde{t} = \alpha t$ describes the time-scaling function or time-warping function that maps the time t of the input signal into the time $\tilde{t}$ of the output signal, the local pitch period of the output signal $\tilde{P}(\tilde{t})$ will be defined by $\tilde{P}(\tilde{t}) = \tilde{P}(\alpha t) = P(t)$. More generally, when the scaling factor α is not constant, a nonlinear time-scaling function can be defined as $\tilde{t} = T(t) = \int_0^t \alpha(\tau)d\tau$ and used instead of $\tilde{t} = \alpha t$.

The algorithm is composed of two phases: the first phase analyses and segments the input sound (see Figure 6.7), and the second phase synthesizes a time-stretched version by overlapping and adding time segments extracted by the analysis algorithm.

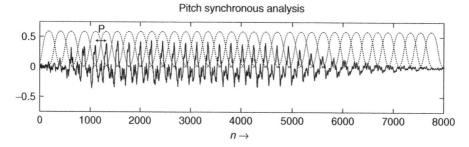

Figure 6.7 caption area:

Pitch synchronous analysis

Figure 6.7   PSOLA: Pitch analysis and block windows.

Analysis algorithm (see Figure 6.8):

(1) Determination of the pitch period $P(t)$ of the input signal and of time instants (pitch marks) t_i. These pitch marks are in correspondence with the maximum amplitude or glottal pulses at a pitch-synchronous rate during the periodic part of the sound and at a constant rate during the unvoiced portions. In practice $P(t)$ is considered constant $P(t) = P(t_i) = t_{i+1} - t_i$ on the time interval (t_i, t_{i+1}).

(2) Extraction of a segment centered at every pitch mark t_i by using a Hanning window with length $L_i = 2P(t_i)$ (two pitch periods) to ensure fade-in and fade-out.

Synthesis algorithm (see Figure 6.9): for every synthesis pitch mark $\tilde{t}_k$

(1) Choice of the corresponding analysis segment i (identified by the time mark t_i) minimizing the time distance $|\alpha t_i - \tilde{t}_k|$.

(2) Overlap and add the selected segment. Notice that some input segments will be repeated for $\alpha > 1$ (time expansion) or discarded when $\alpha < 1$ (time compression).

(3) Determination of the time instant $\tilde{t}_{k+1}$ where the next synthesis segment will be centered, in order to preserve the local pitch, by the relation

$$\tilde{t}_{k+1} = \tilde{t}_k + \tilde{P}(\tilde{t}_k) = \tilde{t}_k + P(t_i).$$

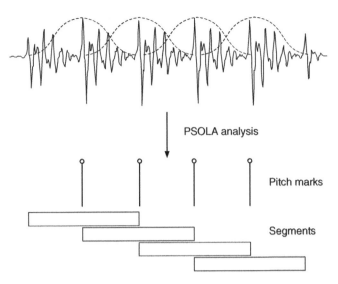

Figure 6.8   PSOLA pitch analysis.

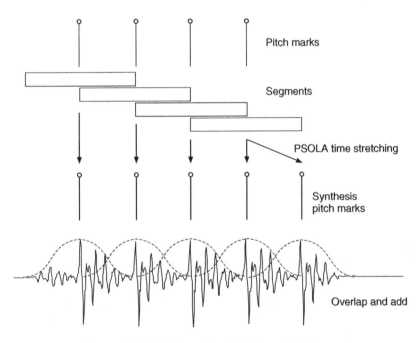

Figure 6.9   PSOLA synthesis for time stretching.

The basic PSOLA synthesis algorithm can be implemented in MATLAB® by the following M-file 6.2:

M-file 6.2 (psola.m)

```
function out=psola(in,m,alpha,beta)
% Authors: G. De Poli, U. Zölzer, P. Dutilleux
%      in    input signal
%      m     pitch marks
%      alpha time stretching factor
%      beta  pitch shifting factor

P = diff(m);   %compute pitch periods

if m(1)<=P(1), %remove first pitch mark
    m=m(2:length(m));
    P=P(2:length(P));
end

if m(length(m))+P(length(P))>length(in) %remove last pitch mark
    m=m(1:length(m)-1);
    else
    P=[P P(length(P))];
end

Lout=ceil(length(in)*alpha);
out=zeros(1,Lout); %output signal

tk = P(1)+1;         %output pitch mark

while round(tk)<Lout
    [minimum i] = min( abs(alpha*m - tk) ); %find analysis segment
    pit=P(i);
    gr = in(m(i)-pit:m(i)+pit) .* hanning(2*pit+1);
    iniGr=round(tk)-pit;
    endGr=round(tk)+pit;
    if endGr>Lout, break; end
    out(iniGr:endGr) = out(iniGr:endGr)+gr; %overlap new segment
    tk=tk+pit/beta;
end %while
```

Stretching factors typically range from $\alpha = 0.25$ to 2 for speech. Audible buzziness appears in unvoiced sound when larger values are applied, due to the regular repetition of identical input segments. In order to prevent the algorithm from introducing such an artificial short-term correlation in the synthesis signal, it is advisable to reverse the time axis of every repeated version of an unvoiced segment. With such an artifice, speech can be slowed down by a factor of four, even though some tonal effect is encountered in voiced fricatives, which combine voiced and unvoiced frequency regions and thus cannot be reversed in time.

It is possible to further exploit the analysis phase. In fact, uniformly applied time stretching can produce some artifacts on the non periodic parts of the sound. For example a plosive consonant may be repeated if the synthesis algorithm selects twice the time segment which contains the consonant. The analysis can then be extended in order to detect the presence of fast transitions

[PR99, KZZ10]. During synthesis, the time scale will not be modified at these points, thus the segments will not be repeated. This approach can be generalized for non-speech sounds where a large time-scale change during transitions (e.g., attacks) would dramatically change the timbre identity. Also in this case it is possible to limit time stretching during transitions and apply it mainly to the steady-state portion of the input sound. This technique is usually applied to digital musical instruments based on wavetable synthesis. On the other hand, the deformation of transient parts can be considered an interesting timbre transformation and can be appreciated as a musically creative audio effect.

Pitch marks

It should be noted that the determination of the pitch and of the position of pitch marks is not a trivial problem and could be difficult to implement robustly. The pitch periods can be determined with one of the pitch extraction algorithms presented in Chapter 9.2. Once the pitch periods are known, the position of the pitch marks can be determined. The sound quality of the modification results of the PSOLA algorithm essentially depends on the positioning of the pitch marks, since the pitch marks provide the centers of the segmentation windows of the PSOLA.

Obviously the pitch marks can only be positioned corresponding to the pitch period for voiced signal parts. As mentioned before, one way to handle unvoiced parts is to keep the "pitch period" at a constant value until the next voiced part. A method which determines the pitch marks of a complete voiced frame is proposed in [LJ04, MVV06]. The global maximum peak of the waveform is searched and the first pitch mark t_i is located at this position. Then the pitch marks to the right of t_i are positioned using the pitch period as a first estimate of the pitch mark locations, followed by a refinement of the location by searching the maximum within a certain region. The new pitch mark is determined as $t_{i+1} = max\,([t_i + \delta P_0, t_i + (2 - \delta)\, P_0])$, where P_0 is the pitch period and δ is a factor in the range of 0.5 to 0.9. This procedure is repeated until the right end of the frame is reached. Then the pitch marks to the left of t_i are positioned respectively by proceeding with the maximum search in the region $t_{i-1} = max\,([t_i - \delta P_0, t_i - (2 - \delta)\, P_0])$, until the left end of the frame is reached. This method is basically a peak-search approach.

A similar function to position the pitch marks can be implemented in a frame-based manner with overlapping frames of fixed length. With knowledge of the pitch period of the current frame and the position of the last pitch mark in the previous frame, the new pitch mark position can be first estimated and then refined. This enables the real-time usage of the peak-picking approach.

For steady-state periodic signals this approach yields good results. But in cases where the signal has rich harmonic content, the maximum peak may jump from one period to another. This leads to an erroneous positioning of the pitch mark, meaning the pitch mark distance of two succeeding pitch marks does not correspond to the true pitch period. The result are artifacts in the resynthesized signal. Therefore the pitch marks should be carefully positioned and rapid pitch mark jumps should be avoided. Since it is desireable to place the window in such a way that it contains a high amount of signal energy, using a center of energy approach [KZZ10] instead of peak picking yields a more robust pitch mark placement. In cases where the fundamental pitch period changes within a frame, the center of energy approach allows the pitch marks to follow the period change in a continuous manner, rather than jumping to the next maximum peak. There are methods to determine the pitch mark positions using spectral information. A method based on a weighted sum of frequency component group delays, which also ensures that the markers are positioned close to the local energy maximum, is described in [PR99].

A basic pitch mark placement algorithm is implemented in **MATLAB** by the following M-file 6.3. The pitch marks are placed in a frame-based manner at a constant rate corresponding to the fundamental pitch period of the current frame. In case of unvoiced frames the pitch period of the preceding voiced frame is used.

M-file 6.3 (findpitchmarks.m)

```
function [m] = findPitchMarks(x,Fs,F0,hop,frameLen)
% Author: A. von dem Knesebeck
% x         input signal
% Fs        sampling frequency
% F0        fundamental frequencies
% hop       hop size of F0 detection
% frameLen  length of frame

% Initialization
m          = 0;    % vector of pitch mark positions
P0         = zeros (1,length(F0));
index      = 1;
local_m    = [];   % local pitch marker position

% processing frames i
for i = 1:length(F0);
% set pitch periods of unvoiced frames
    if (i==1 && F0(i)==0); F0(i) = 120;    % 120Hz in case no preceding pitch
    elseif (F0(i)==0);     F0(i) = F0(i-1);
    end
    P0(i) = round(Fs/F0(i));                   % fundamental period of frame i
    frameRange = (1:frameLen) + (i-1)*hop; % hopping frame
    last_m = index;                        % last found pitch mark

% beginning periods of 1st frame
    j = 1;  %period number
    if i==1
        % define limits of searchFrame
        searchUpLim = 1 * P0(i);
        searchRange = (1 : searchUpLim);
        [pk,loc]  = max(x(searchRange));
        local_m(j) = round(loc);

% beginning periods of 2nd - end frame
    else
        searchUpLim = searchUpLim + P0(i);
        local_m(j)  = last_m + P0(i);
    end % beginning periods of 1st - end frame

% remaining periods of 1st - end frame
    index = local_m(1);
    j = 2;  % grain/period number
    while( searchUpLim + P0(i) <= frameRange(end))
        % define range in which a marker is to be found
        searchUpLim = searchUpLim + P0(i);
        local_m(j)  = local_m(j-1) + P0(i);
        index = local_m(j);
        j = j+1;
    end %while frame end not reached
    m = [m local_m];
end % processing frames i

% finishing calculated pitch marks
m = sort(m);
m = unique(m);
m = m(2:end);
```

6.4   Pitch shifting

Introduction

Transposition is one of the basic tools of musicians. When we think about providing this effect by signal-processing means, we need to think about the various aspects of it. For a musician, transposing means repeating a melody after pitch shifting it by a fixed interval. Each time the performer transposes the melody, he makes use of a different register of his instrument. By doing so, not only is the pitch of the sound modified, but also the timbre is affected.

In the realm of DAFX, it is a matter of choice to transpose without taking into account the timbre modification or whether the characteristic timbre of the instrument has to be maintained in each of its registers. The first method could be called "variable timbre transposition," whereas the second approach would be called "constant timbre transposition." To get an insight into the problem we have to consider the physical origins of the audio signal.

The timbre of a sound heavily depends on the organization of its spectrum. A model can be derived from the study of the singing voice. The pitch of a singing voice is determined by the vocal chords and it can be correlated with the set of frequencies available in the spectrum. The timbre of the voice is mainly determined by the vocal cavities. Their effect is to emphasize some parts of the spectrum, which are called formants. A signal model can be derived where an excitation part is modified by a resonance part. In the case of the voice, the excitation is provided by the vocal chords, hence it is related to the frequencies of the spectrum, whereas the resonances correspond to the formants. When a singer transposes a tune, he has, to some extent, the possibility of modifying the pitch and the formants independently. In a careful signal-processing implementation of this effect, each of these two aspects should be considered.

If only the spectrum of the excitation is stretched or contracted, a pitch transposition up or down, with a constant timbre, is achieved. If only the resonances are stretched or contracted, then the pitch remains the same, but the timbre is varied. Harmonic singing relies on this effect. If both excitation and resonance are deliberately and independently altered, then we enter the domain of effects that can be perceived as unnatural, but that might have a vast musical potential.

The separation of a sound into its excitation and resonance part is a complex process that will be addressed in Chapter 8. We will present here methods which simultaneously alter both aspects, such as the harmonizer or pitch shifting by delay-line modulation in Section 6.4.3. A more refined method based on PSOLA, which allows pitch shifting with formant preservation, will be discussed in Section 6.4.4. For more advanced pitch-shifting methods we refer the reader to Chapters 7–11.

Musical applications

Typical applications of pitch shifting in pop music are the correction of the intonation of instruments or singers, as well as the production of an effect similar to a chorus. When the voice of a singer is mixed with copies of itself that are slightly transposed, a subtle effect appears that gives the impression that one is listening to a choir instead of a single singer.

The harmonizer can also produce surprising effects, such as a man speaking with a tiny high-pitched voice or a female with a gritty low-pitched one. Extreme sounds can be produced such as the deep snare drum sound on David Bowie's "Let's Dance" record [Whi99]. It has also been used for scrambling and unscrambling speech [GRH73]. In combination with a delay line and with feedback of the transposed sound to the input, a kind of spiral can be produced where the sound is always transposed higher or lower at each iteration.

A subtle effect, similar to phasing, can be achieved with a set of harmonizers [Dut88] coupled in parallel and mixed to the input sound, as shown in Figure 6.10. The transposition ratio of the nth harmonizer should be set to $1 + nr$ where r is of the order of 1/3000. If f_0 is the pitch of the sound, the outputs of the nth harmonizer will provide a pitch of $f_0 + n\Delta f$, where $\Delta f = r f_0$. If Δf is small enough (a few 1/100 Hz) the interferences between the various outputs of the harmonizers

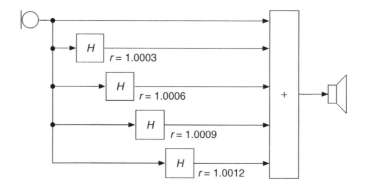

Figure 6.10 A set of harmonizers that produce a phasing-like effect. It is particularly effective for low-pitched (typically 100 Hz) signals of long duration.

will be clearly audible. When applied, for example, to a low-pitched tuba sound, one harmonic after the other will be emphasized. Flanging and chorus effects can also be achieved by setting the pitch control for a very slight amount of transposition (say, 1/10 to 1/5 of a semitone) and adding regeneration [And95, p. 53]. It appears here that tuning an audio effect is very dependent on the sound being processed. It frequently happens that the tuning has to be adjusted for each new sound or each new pitch.

Hans Peter Haller describes in [Hal95, pp. 51–55] some applications of the harmonizer for the production of musical works from Luigi Nono and André Richard.

6.4.1   Historical methods – Harmonizer

The tape-based machines described in 6.3.1 were also able to modify the pitch of sounds while keeping their initial duration. The *Phonogène universel* was bulky and could not find a broad diffusion, but in the middle of the 1970s, a digital device appeared that was called a *Harmonizer*. It implemented in the digital domain a process similar to that of the *Phonogène universel*. From there on the effect became very popular. Since *Harmonizer* is a trade mark of the Eventide company, other companies offer similar devices under names such as *pitch transposer* or *pitch shifter*.

The main limitation of the use of the harmonizer is the characteristic quality that it gives to the processed sounds. Moles states that the operating range of the *Phonogène universel*, used as a pitch regulator, was at least −4 to +3 semitones [Mol60, p. 74]. Geslin estimates that the machines available in the late 60s also found application in *musique concrète* at much larger transposition ratios [Ges00].

The digital implementations in the form of the harmonizer might allow for a better quality, but there are still severe limitations. For transpositions of the order of a semitone, almost no objectionable alteration of the sounds can be heard. As the transposition ratio grows larger, in the practical range of plus or minus two octaves, the timbre of the output sound obtains a character that is specific to the harmonizer.

This modification can be heard both in the frequency domain and in the time domain and is due to the modulation of the signal by the chopping window. The spectrum of the input signal is indeed convolved with that of the window. The time-domain modulation can be characterized by its rate and by the spectrum of the window, which is dependent on its shape and its size. The longer the window, the lower the rate and hence the narrower the spectrum of the window and the less disturbing the modulation. The effect of a trapezoidal window will be stronger than that of a smoother one, such as the raised cosine window.

On the other hand, a larger window tends to deliver, through the overlap-add process, audible iterated copies of the input signals. For the transposition of percussive sounds, it is necessary to reduce the size of the window. Furthermore, to accurately replay transients and not smooth them out, the window should have sharp transitions. We see that a trade-off between audible spectral modulation and iterated transients has to be found for each type of sound. Musicians using the computer as a musical instrument might exploit these peculiarities in the algorithm to give their sound a unique flavor.

6.4.2   Pitch shifting by time stretching and resampling

The variable speed replay discussed in Section 6.2 leads to a compression or expansion of the duration of a sound and to a pitch shift. This is accomplished by resampling in the time domain. Figure 6.1 illustrates the discrete-time signals and the corresponding spectra. The spectrum of the sound is compressed or expanded over the frequency axis. The harmonic relations

$$f_i = i \cdot f_{\text{fundamental}} \tag{6.4}$$

of the sound are not altered, but are scaled according to

$$f_i^{\text{new}} = \alpha \cdot f_i^{\text{old}}. \tag{6.5}$$

The amplitudes of the harmonics remain the same $a_i^{\text{new}} = a_i^{\text{old}}$. In order to rescale the pitch-shifted sound towards the original length, a further time-stretching algorithm can be applied to the sound. The result of pitch shifting followed by a time-stretching algorithm is illustrated in Figure 6.11.

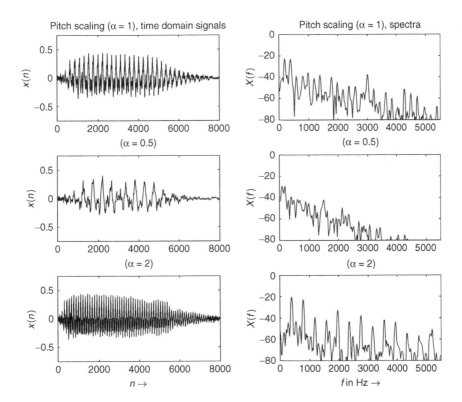

Figure 6.11   Pitch shifting followed by time correction.

The order of pitch shifting and time scaling can be changed, as shown in Figure 6.12. First, a time-scaling algorithm expands the input signal from length N_1 to length N_2. Then a resampling operation with the inverse ratio N_1/N_2 performs pitch shifting and a reduction of length N_2 back to length N_1. The following M-file 6.4 demonstrates the implementation of the SOLA time-scaling and pitch-scaling algorithm:

M-file 6.4 (PitchScaleSOLA.m)

```
% PitchScaleSOLA.m
% Authors: G. De Poli, U. Zölzer, P. Dutilleux
% Parameters:
%     analysis hop size      Sa = 256 (default parmater)
%     block length           N  = 2048 (default parameter)
%     pitch scaling factor   0.25 <= alpha <= 2
%     overlap interval       L  = 256*alpha/2
clear all,close all
[signal,Fs]       =       wavread('x1.wav');
DAFx_in           =       signal';

Sa=256;N=2048;              % time scaling parameters
M=ceil(length(DAFx_in)/Sa);

n1=512;n2=256;              % pitch scaling n1/n2
Ss=round(Sa*n1/n2);
L=256*(n1/n2)/2;

DAFx_in(M*Sa+N)=0;
Overlap=DAFx_in(1:N);

% ****** Time Stretching with alpha=n2/n1******
....... % include main loop TimeScaleSOLA.m
% ****** End Time Stretching ******

% ****** Pitch shifting with alpha=n1/n2 ******
lfen=2048;lfen2=lfen/2;
w1=hanningz(lfen);w2=w1;

% for linear interpolation of a grain of length lx to length lfen
lx=floor(lfen*n1/n2);
x=1+(0:lfen-1)'*lx/lfen;
ix=floor(x);ix1=ix+1;
dx=x-ix;dx1=1-dx;
%
lmax=max(lfen,lx);
Overlap=Overlap';
DAFx_out=zeros(length(DAFx_in),1);

pin=0;pout=0;
pend=length(Overlap)-lmax;
% Pitch shifting by resampling a grain of length lx to length lfen
while pin<pend
  grain2=(Overlap(pin+ix).*dx1+Overlap(pin+ix1).*dx).* w1;
  DAFx_out(pout+1:pout+lfen)=DAFx_out(pout+1:pout+lfen)+grain2;
  pin=pin+n1;pout=pout+n2;
end;
```

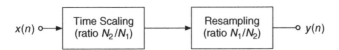

Figure 6.12   Pitch shifting by time scaling and resampling.

6.4.3   Pitch shifting by delay-line modulation

Pitch shifting or pitch transposing based on block processing is described in several publications. In [BB89] a pitch shifter based on an overlap-add scheme with two time-varying delay lines is proposed (see Figure 6.13). A cross-fade block combines the outputs of the two delay lines according to a cross-fade function. The signal is divided in small chunks. The chunks are read faster to produce higher pitches or slower to produce lower pitches. In order to produce a continuous signal output, two chunks are read simultaneously with a time delay equal to one half of the block length. A cross-fade is made from one chunk to the other at each end of a chunk [WG94, pp. 257–259].

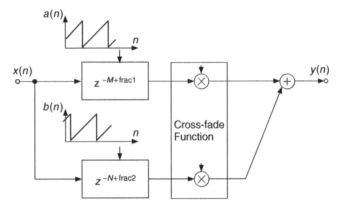

Figure 6.13   Pitch shifting.

The length of the delay lines is modulated by a sawtooth-type function. A similar approach is proposed in [Dat87], where the same configuration is used for time compression and expansion. A periodicity detection algorithm is used for calculating the cross-fade function in order to avoid cancellations during the cross-fades.

An enhanced method for transposing audio signals is presented in [DZ99]. The method is based on an overlap-add scheme and does not need any fundamental frequency estimation. The difference from other applications is the way the blocks are modulated and combined to the output signal. The enhanced transposing system is based on an overlap-add scheme with three parallel time-varying delay lines (see Figure 6.15).

Figure 6.14 illustrates how the input signal is divided into blocks, which are resampled (phase modulation with a ramp-type signal), amplitude modulated and summed yielding an output signal of the same length as the input signal. Adjacent blocks overlap with 2/3 of the block length.

The modulation signals form a system of three 120°-phase shifted raised cosine functions. The sum of these functions is constant for all arguments. Figure 6.15 also shows the topology of the pitch transposer. Since a complete cosine is used for modulation, the perceived sound quality of the processed signal is much better than in simple twofold overlap-add applications using several windows. The amplitude modulation only produces sum and difference frequencies with the base

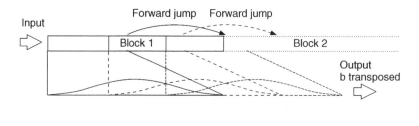

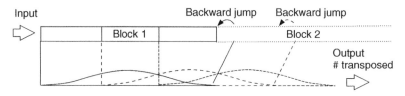

Figure 6.14   Enhanced pitch transposer: block processing, time shifting and overlap-add.

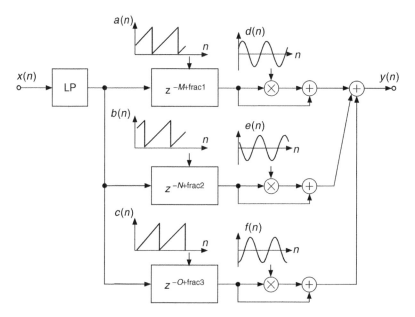

Figure 6.15   Enhanced pitch transposer: block diagram.

frequency of the modulation signal, which can be very low (6–10 Hz). Harmonics are not present in the modulation signal and hence cannot form sum or difference frequencies of higher order. The perceived artifacts are phasing-like effects and are less annoying than local discontinuities of other applications based on twofold overlap-add methods.

   If we want to change the pitch of a signal controlled by another signal or signal envelope, we can also make use of delay-line modulation. The effect can be achieved by performing a phase modulation of the recorded signal according to $y(n) = x(n - D(n))$. The modulating factor $D(n) = M + \text{DEPTH} \cdot x_{\text{mod}}(n)$ is now dependent on a modulating signal $x_{\text{mod}}(n)$. With this approach the pitch of the input signal $x(n)$ is changed according to the envelope of the modulating signal (see Figure 6.16).

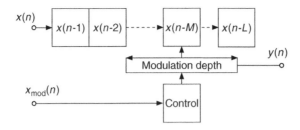

Figure 6.16 Pitch controlled by envelope of signal $x_{\mathrm{mod}}(n)$.

6.4.4 Pitch shifting by PSOLA and formant preservation

This technique is the dual operation to resampling in the time domain, but in this case a resampling of the short-time spectral envelope is performed. The short-term spectral envelope describes a frequency curve going through all amplitudes of the harmonics. This is demonstrated in Figure 6.17, where the spectral envelope is shown. The harmonics are again scaled according to $f_i^{\mathrm{new}} = \beta \cdot f_i^{\mathrm{old}}$, but the amplitudes of the harmonics $a_i^{\mathrm{new}} = \mathrm{env}(f_i^{\mathrm{new}}) \neq a_i^{\mathrm{old}}$ are now determined by sampling the spectral envelope. Some deviations of the amplitudes from the precise envelope can be noticed. This depends on the chosen pitch-shifting algorithm.

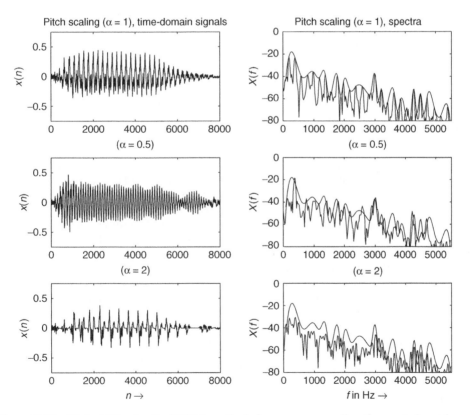

Figure 6.17 Pitch shifting by the PSOLA method: frequency resampling the spectral envelope.

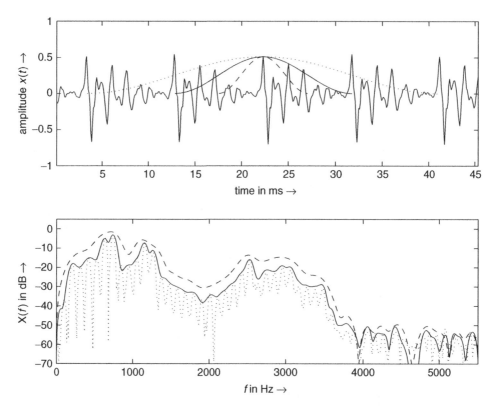

Figure 6.18 Spectrum of segments extracted from a vowel /a/ by using a Hanning window 4 (dotted line), 2 (solid line) and 1 (dashed line) pitch periods long, respectively. It can be noticed that the solid line approximates the local spectral envelope.

The PSOLA algorithm can be conveniently used for pitch shifting a voice sound maintaining the formant position, and thus the vowel identity [ML95, BJ95]. The basic idea consists of time stretching the position of pitch marks, while the segment waveform is not changed. The underlining signal model of speech production is a pulse train filtered by a time-varying filter corresponding to the vocal tract. The input segment corresponds to the filter impulse response and determines the formant position. Thus, it should not be modified. Conversely, the pitch mark distance determines the speech period, and thus should be modified accordingly. The aim of PSOLA analysis is to extract the local filter impulse response. As can be seen in Figure 6.18, the spectrum of a segment extracted using a Hanning window with a length of two periods approximates the local spectral envelope. Longer windows tend to resolve the fine line structure of the spectrum, while shorter windows tend to blur the formant structure of the spectrum. Thus if we do not stretch the segment, the formant position is maintained. The operation of overlapping the segments at the new pitch mark position will resample the spectral envelope at the desired pitch frequency. When we desire a pitch shift by a factor β, defined as the ratio of the local synthesis pitch frequency to the original one $\beta = \tilde{f}_0(\tilde{t})/f_0(t)$, the new pitch period will be given by $\tilde{P}(\tilde{t}) = P(t)/\beta$, where in this case $\tilde{t} = t$ because time is not stretched.

The analysis algorithm is the same as that previously seen for PSOLA time stretching in Section 6.3.3 (see Figure 6.8). The synthesis algorithm is modified (see Figure 6.19) according to the following steps:

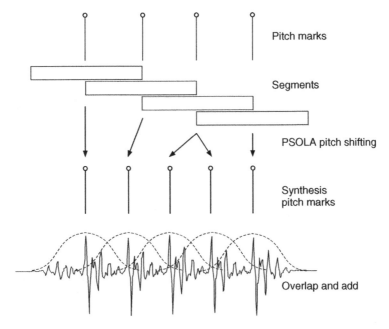

Figure 6.19 PSOLA: synthesis algorithm for pitch shifting.

- For every synthesis pitch mark $\tilde{t}_k$:

  (1) Choice of the corresponding analysis segment i (identified by the time mark t_i) minimizing the time distance $|t_i - \tilde{t}_k|$.

  (2) Overlap and add the selected segment. Notice that some input segments will be repeated for $\beta > 1$ (higher pitch) or discarded when $\beta < 1$ (lower pitch).

  (3) Determination of the time instant $\tilde{t}_{k+1}$ where the next synthesis segment will be centered, in order to preserve the local pitch, by the relation

$$\tilde{t}_{k+1} = \tilde{t}_k + \tilde{P}(\tilde{t}_k) = \tilde{t}_k + P(t_i)/\beta.$$

- For large pitch shifts, it is advisable to compensate the amplitude variation, introduced by the greater or lesser overlapping of segments, by multiplying the output signal by $1/\beta$.

It is possible to combine time stretching by a factor α with pitch shifting. In this case, for every synthesis pitch mark $\tilde{t}_k$ the first step of the synthesis algorithm above presented will be modified by the choice of the corresponding analysis segment i (identified by the time mark t_i), minimizing the time distance $|\alpha t_i - \tilde{t}_k|$.

The PSOLA algorithm is very effective for speech processing and is computationally very efficient, once the sound has been analyzed, so it is widely used for speech synthesis from a database of diphones, for prosody modification, for automatic answering machines etc. For wide variation of the pitch it presents some artifacts. On the other hand, the necessity of a preliminary analysis stage for obtaining a pitch contour makes the real-time implementation of an input-signal modification difficult. Also the estimation of glottal pulses can be difficult. A solution is to place the pitch marks at a pitch synchronous rate, regardless of the true position of the glottal pulses. The resulting synthesis quality will be only slightly decreased (see, for example, Figure 6.20).

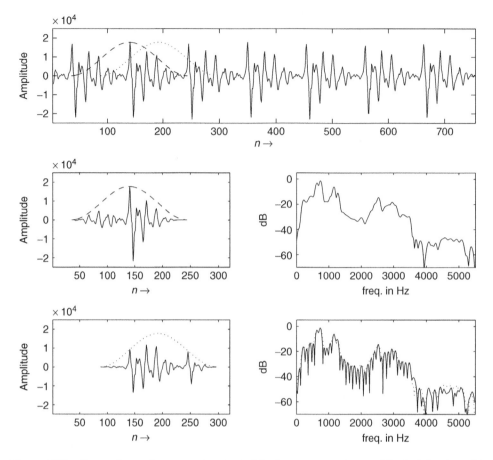

Figure 6.20 Comparison of a segment extracted in the correspondence with glottal pulse with one extracted between pitch pulses.

A further effect that can be obtained by a variation of PSOLA is linear scaling of formant frequencies (see Figure 6.21). In fact, we saw that the time scale of a signal corresponds to an inverse frequency scale. Thus when we perform time scaling of the impulse response of a filter, we inversely scale the frequency of formants. In PSOLA terms, this corresponds to time scaling the selected input segments before overlap and adding the synthesis step, without any change in the pitch marks calculation. To increase the frequencies of formants by a factor γ, every segment should be shortened by a factor $1/\gamma$ by resampling. For example, the average formant frequencies of female adults are about 16% higher than those of male adults, and children's formants are about 20% higher than female formants. Notice that care should be taken when the frequencies increase in order to avoid foldover. Ideally band-limited resampling should be used.

The PSOLA pitch shifter can be used to synthesize multiple voices from one real singer to create a *virtual choir* effect [SPLR02].

The following M-file 6.5 shows the implementation of the basic PSOLA synthesis algorithm. It is based on the PSOLA time-stretching algorithm shown in Section 6.3.3.

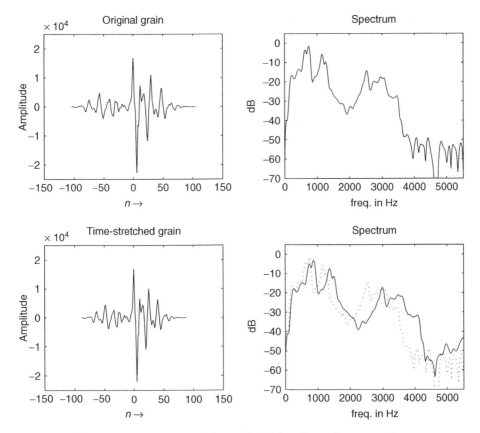

Figure 6.21   PSOLA: variation of PSOLA as linear formant scaling.

M-file 6.5 (psolaf.m)

```
function out=psolaF(in,m,alpha,beta,gamma)
% Authors: G. De Poli, U. Zölzer, P. Dutilleux
%      . . .
%      gamma newFormantFreq/oldFormantFreq
%      . . .
%      the internal loop as
tk = P(1)+1;                      %output pitch mark
while round(tk)<Lout
 [minimum i]=min(abs(alpha*m-tk) );    % find analysis segment
 pit=P(i);pitStr=floor(pit/gamma);
 gr=in(m(i)-pit:m(i)+pit).*hanning(2*pit+1);
 gr=interp1(-pit:1:pit,gr,-pitStr*gamma:gamma:pit);% stretch segm.
 iniGr=round(tk)-pitStr;endGr=round(tk)+pitStr;
 if endGr>Lout, break; end
 out(iniGr:endGr)=out(iniGr:endGr)+gr; % overlap new segment
 tk=tk+pit/beta;
end % end of while
```

6.5   Time shuffling and granulation

6.5.1   Time shuffling

Introduction

Musique concrète has made intensive use of splicing of tiny elements of magnetic tape. When mastered well, this assembly of hundreds of fragments of several tens of milliseconds allows an amalgamation of heterogeneous sound materials, at the limit of the time discrimination threshold. This manual operation, called micro-splicing, is very time-consuming. Bernard Parmegiani suggested in 1980 at the Groupe de Recherches Musicales (GRM) that this could be done by computers. An initial version of the software was produced in the early 80s. After being rewritten, improved and ported several times, it was eventually made available on personal computers in the form of a program called *brassage* in French that will be translated here as *time shuffling* [Ges98, Ges00].

Signal processing

Let us describe here an elementary algorithm for time shuffling that is based on the superposition of two time segments that are picked randomly from the input signal (see Figure 6.22):

(1) Let $x(n)$ and $y(n)$ be the input and output signals.

(2) Specify the duration d of the fragments and the duration $D \geq d$ of the time period $[n - D, n]$ from which the time segments will be selected.

(3) Store the incoming signal $x(n)$ in a delay line of length D.

(4) Choose at random the delay time τ_1 with $d \leq \tau_1 \leq D$.

(5) Select the signal segment x_{1d} of duration d beginning at $x(n - \tau_1)$.

(6) Follow the same procedure (steps 4 and 5) for a second time segment x_{2d}.

(7) Read x_{1d} and x_{2d} and apply an amplitude envelope W to each of them in order to smooth out the discontinuities at the borders.

(8) When the reading of x_{1d} or x_{2d} is finished, iterate the procedure for each of them.

(9) Compute the output as the overlap add of the sequence of x_{1d} and x_{2d} with a time shift of $d/2$.

Musical applications and control

The version described above introduces local disturbances into the signal's actual timing, while preserving the overall continuity of its time sequence. Many further refinements of this algorithm are possible. A random amplitude coefficient could be applied to each of the input segments in order to modify the density of the sound material. The shape of the envelope could be modified in order to retain more of the input time structure or, on the other hand, to smooth it out and blend different events with each other. The replay speed of the segments could be varied in order to produce transposition or glissandi.

At a time when computer tools were not yet available, Bernard Parmegiani magnificently illustrated the technique of tape-based micro-splicing in works such as "Violostries" (1964) or "Dedans-Dehors" (1977) [m-Par64, m-Par77]. The elementary algorithm presented above can be operated in real time, but other off-line versions have also been implemented which offer many more features. They have the ability to merge fragments of any size, sampled from a random field, and of any dimension; from a few samples to several minutes. Thus, apart from generating

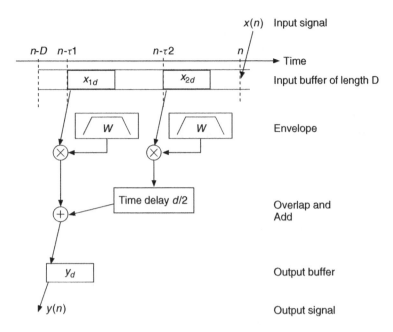

Figure 6.22 Time shuffling: two input segments, selected at random from the past input signal, are overlap-added to produce an output time segment. When one of the input segments is finished, a new one is selected.

fusion phenomena, for which the algorithm was conceived, the software was able to produce cross-fading of textured sound and other sustained chords, infinitely small variations in signal stability, interpolation of fragments with silence or sounds of other types [Ges98]. Jean-Claude Risset used this effect to perform sonic developments from short sounds, such as stones and metal chimes [m-INA3, Sud-I, 3'44'' to 4'38'']; [Ris98, Ges00] and to produce a "stuttering" piano, further processed by ring modulation [m-INA3, Sud-I, 4'30'', 5'45'']. Starting from "found objects" such as bird songs, he rearranged them in a compositional manner to obtain first a pointillistic rendering, then a stretto-like episode [m-INA3, Sud-I, 1'42'' to 2'49''].

6.5.2 Granulation

Introduction

In the previous sections about pitch shifting and time stretching we have proposed algorithms that have limitations as far as their initial purpose is concerned. Beyond a limited range of modification of pitch or of time duration, severe artifacts appear. The time-shuffling method considers these artifacts from an artistic point of view and takes them for granted. Out of the possibilities offered by the methods and by their limitations, it aims to create new sound structures. Whereas the time-shuffling effect exploits the possibilities of a given software arrangement, which could be considered here as a "musical instrument," the idea of building a complex sound out of a large set of elementary sounds could find a larger framework.

The physicist Dennis Gabor proposed in 1947 the idea of the quantum of sound, an indivisible unit of information from the psychoacoustical point of view. According to his theory, a granular representation could describe any sound. Granular synthesis was first suggested as a computer music technique for producing complex sounds by Iannis Xenakis (1971) and Curtis Roads (1978). This technique builds up acoustic events from thousands of sound grains. A sound grain lasts a brief moment (typically 1 to 100 ms), which approaches the minimum perceivable event time for duration, frequency and amplitude discrimination [Roa96, Roa98, Tru00a].

The granulation effect is an application of granular synthesis where the material out of which the grains are formed is an input signal. Barry Truax has developed this technique [Tru88, Tru94] by first real-time implementation and using it extensively in his compositional pieces.

Signal processing

Let $x(n)$ and $y(n)$ be the input and output signals. The grains $g_k(i)$ are extracted from the input signal with the help of a window function $w_k(i)$ of length L_k by

$$g_k(i) = x(i + i_k)w_k(i), \qquad (6.6)$$

with $i = 0, \ldots, L_{k-1}$. The time instant i_k indicates the point where the segment is extracted; the length L_k determines the amount of signal extracted; the window waveform $w_k(i)$ should ensure fade-in and fade-out at the border of the grain and affects the frequency content of the grain. Long grains tend to maintain the timbre identity of the portion of the input signal, while short ones acquire a pulse-like quality. When the grain is long, the window has a flat top and is used only to fade-in and fade-out the borders of the segment.

The following M-files 6.6 and 6.7 show the extraction of short and long grains:

M-file 6.6 (grainSh.m)

```
function y = grainSh(x,init,L)
% Authors: G. De Poli
% extract a short grain
% x     input signal
% init  first sample
% L     grain length (in samples)
y=x(init:init+L-1).*hanning(L)';
```

M-file 6.7 (grainLn.m)

```
function y = grainLn(x,iniz,L,Lw)
% Authors: G. De Poli
% extract a long grain
% x     input signal
% init  first sample
% L     grain length (in samples)
% Lw    length fade-in and fade-out (in samples)
if length(x) <= iniz+L , error('length(x) too short.'),    end
y = x(iniz:iniz+L-1);                        % extract segment
w = hanning(2*Lw+1)';
y(1:Lw)      = y(1:Lw).*w(1:Lw);             % fade-in
y(L-Lw+1:L) = y(L-Lw+1:L).*w(Lw+2:2*Lw+1);  % fade-out
```

The synthesis formula is given by

$$y(n) = \sum_k a_k g_k(n - n_k), \qquad (6.7)$$

where a_k is an eventual amplitude coefficient and n_k is the time instant where the grain is placed in the output signal. Notice that the grains can overlap. To overlap a grain g_k (grain) at instant $n_k = $ (iniOLA) with amplitude ak, the following **MATLAB** instructions can be used

```
endOLA = iniOLA+length(grain)-1;
y(iniOLA:endOLA) = y(iniOLA:endOLA) + ak * grain;
```

An example of granulation with random values of the parameters grain initial point and length, output point and amplitude is shown in Figure 6.23. The M-file 6.8 shows the implementation of the granulation algorithm.

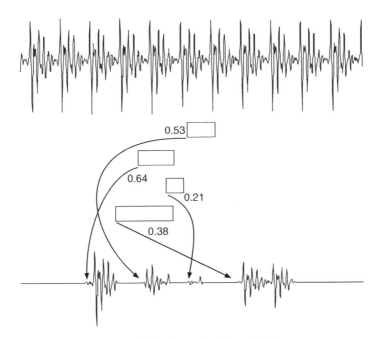

Figure 6.23   Example of granulation.

M-file 6.8 (granulation.m)

```
% granulation.m
% Authors: G. De Poli
f=fopen('a_male.m11');
x=fread(f,'int16')';
fclose(f);

Ly=length(x);  y=zeros(1,Ly);              %output signal
% Constants
nEv=4; maxL=200;  minL=50;  Lw=20;
% Initializations
L = round((maxL-minL)*rand(1,nEv))+minL;   %grain length
initIn = ceil((Ly-maxL)*rand(1,nEv));      %init grain
initOut= ceil((Ly-maxL)*rand(1,nEv));      %init out grain
a = rand(1,nEv);                           %ampl. grain
endOut=initOut+L-1;
% Synthesis
```

```
for k=1:nEv,
  grain=grainLn(x,initIn(k),L(k),Lw);
  y(initOut(k):endOut(k))=y(initOut(k):endOut(k))+a(k)*grain;
end
```

This technique is quite general and can be employed to obtain very different sound effects. The result is greatly influenced by the criterion used to choose the instants n_k. If these points are regularly spaced in time and the grain waveform does not change too much, the technique can be interpreted as a filtered pulse train, i.e., it produces a periodic sound whose spectral envelope is determined by the grain waveform interpreted as an impulse response. An example is the PSOLA algorithm shown in the previous Sections 6.3.3 and 6.4.4. When the distance between two subsequent grains is much greater than L_k, the sound will result in grains separated by interruptions or silences, with a specific character. When many short grains overlap (i.e., the distance is less than L_k), a sound texture effect is obtained.

The strategies for choosing the synthesis instants can be grouped into two rather simplified categories: synchronous, mostly based on deterministic functions, and asynchronous, based on stochastic functions. Grains can be organized in streams. There are two main control variables: the delay between grains for a single stream, and the degree of synchronicity among grains in different streams. Given that the local spectrum affects the global sound structure, it is possible to use input sounds that can be parsed in grains without altering the complex characteristics of the original sound, as water drops for stream-like sounds.

It is further possible to modify the grain waveform with a time transformation, such as modulation for frequency shifting or time stretching for frequency scaling [DP91]. The main parameters of granulation are: grain duration, selection order from input sound, amplitude of grains, temporal pattern in synthesis and grain density (i.e., grains per second). Density is a primary parameter, as it determines the overall texture, whether sparse or continuous. Notice that it is possible to extract grains from different sound files to create hybrid textures, e.g., evolving from one texture to another.

Musical applications

Examples of the effect can be found in [m-Wis94c]. Barry Truax has used the technique of granulation to process sampled sound as compositional material. In "The Wings of Nike" (1987) he has processed only short "phonemic" fragments, but longer sequences of environmental sound have been used in pieces such as "Pacific" (1990). In each of these works, the granulated material is time stretched by various amounts and thereby produces a number of perceptual changes that seem to originate from within the sound [Tru00b, m-Tru95].

In "Le Tombeau de Maurice," Ludger Brümmer uses the granulation technique in order to perform timbral, rhythmic as well as harmonic modifications [m-Bru97]. A transition from the original sound color of an orchestral sample towards noise pulses is achieved by reducing progressively the size of the grains. At an intermediate grain size, the pitch of the original sound is still recognizable, although the time structure has already disappeared [m-Bru97, 3'39''-4'12'']. A melody can be played by selecting grains of different pitches and by varying the tempo at which the grains are replayed [m-Bru97, 8'38''-9'10'']. New melodies can even appear out of a two-stage granulation scheme. A first series of grains is defined from the original sample, whereas the second is a granulation of the first one. Because of the stream segregation performed by the hearing system, the rhythmic as well as the harmonic grouping of the grains is constantly evolving [m-Bru97, 9'30''-10'33''].

6.6   Conclusion

The effects described in this chapter are based on the division of the input sound into short segments. These segments are processed by simple methods such as time scaling by resampling, or amplitude multiplication by an envelope. The segment waveform is not changed, thus maintaining the characteristic of the source signal.

Two categories of effects can be obtained, depending on the strategy used to place the segments in time during the synthesis. If the order and organization of extracted segments are carefully maintained, time stretching or pitch shifting can be performed. Basic methods, SOLA and PSOLA, are presented and their characteristics are discussed. These effects aim to produce sounds that are perceived as similar to the original, but are modified in duration or pitch. As often happens with digital audio effects, the artifacts produced by these methods can be used as a method for deformation of the input sound, whilst maintaining its main characteristics. The low computational complexity of time-segment processing allows efficient real-time applications. Nevertheless, these algorithms produce artifacts that limit their scope of application. More advanced methods for time stretching and pitch shifting will be introduced in Chapters 7–11.

The second category changes the organization and the order of the segments to a great extent, and thus leads to time shuffling and granulation. In this case, the input sound can be much less recognizable in the output. The central element becomes the grain with its amplitude envelope and time organization. These techniques can produce results from sparse grains to dense textures, with a very loose relationship with the original sound. It should be noticed that the wide choice of strategies for grain organization implies a sound composition attitude from the user. Thus granulation has became a sort of metaphor for music composition starting from the micro level.

Sound and music

[m-Bru93]   L. Brümmer: *The Gates of H*. Computer music. CCRMA 1993. In: CRI, *The Listening Room*, CD edel 0014522TLR, Hamburg, 1995.

[m-Bru97]   L. Brümmer: *Le Tombeau de Maurice, for computer-generated tape*. In: *Computer Music @ CCRMA*. CD CCRMAV02, 1997.

[m-Eim62]   H. Eimert: *Epitaph für Aikichi Kuboyama*. Electronic music composition, 1962. Studio-Reihe neuer Musik, Wergo, LP WER 60014. Reedition as a CD, Koch/Schwann, 1996.

[m-Fur93]   K. Furukawa: *Swim, Swan, composition for clarinet and live-electronics*. ZKM, 1993.

[m-Fur97]   K. Furukawa: *Den ungeborenen Göttern*. Multimedia-Opera, ZKM, 1997.

[m-INA3]   J.-C. Risset: *Sud, Dialogues, Inharmonique, Mutations*. CD INA C1003.

[m-Par64]   B. Parmegiani: *Violostries*, 1964. IDEAMA CD 051 Target Collection, ZKM and CCRMA, 1996.

[m-Par77]   B. Parmegiani: *Dedans-Dehors*, 1977. INA-GRM.

[m-Sch98]   P. Schaeffer and G. Reibel: *Solfège de L'objet Sonore*. Booklet + 3 CDs. First published 1967. INA-GRM, 1998.

[m-Tru95]   B. Truax: Granular time-shifting and transposition composition examples. In *Computer Music Journal*, Volume 19 Compact Disc, Index 6, 1995.

[m-Wis94c]   T. Wishart: *Audible Design*, Sound examples. CD. Orpheus the Pantomime, York, 1994.

References

[And95]   C. Anderton. *Multieffects for Musicians*. Amsco Publications, 1995.

[BB89]   K. Bogdanowicz and R. Blecher. Using multiple processors for real-time audio effects. In *Proc. AES 7th Int. Conf.*, pp. 337–342, 1989.

[BJ95]   R. Bristow-Johnson. A detailed analysis of a time-domain formant-corrected pitch shifting algorithm. *J. Audio Eng. Soc.*, 43(5): 340–352, 1995.

[Car92]   T. Cary. *Illustrated Compendium of Musical Technology*. Faber and Faber, 1992.

[Chi82]   M. Chion. *La Musique Électroacoustique*. QSJ No 1990, PUF, 1982.

[CR83]   R. E. Crochiere and L. R. Rabiner. *Multirate Digital Signal Processing*. Prentice-Hall, 1983.

[Dat87]   J. Dattoro. Using digital signal processor chips in a stereo audio time compressor/expander. In *Proc. 83rd AES Convention*, Preprint 2500, 1987.

[DP91]   G. De Poli and A. Piccialli. Pitch-synchronous granular synthesis. In G. De Poli, A. Piccialli, and C. Roads (eds), *Representations of Musical Signals*, pp. 187–219. MIT Press, 1991.

[Dut88]   P. Dutilleux. Mise en œuvre de transformations sonores sur un système temps-réel. Technical report, Rapport de stage de DEA, CNRS-LMA, June 1988.

[DZ99]   S. Disch and U. Zölzer. Modulation and delay line based digital audio effects. In *Proc. DAFX-99 Digital Audio Effects Workshop*, pp. 5–8, 1999.

[End97]   B. Enders. *Lexikon Musikelektronik*. Atlantis Schott, 1997.

[Gas87]   P. S. Gaskell. A hybrid approach to the variable speed replay of digital audio. *J. Audio Eng. Soc.*, 35: 230–238, April 1987.

[Ges98]   Y. Geslin. Sound and music transformation environments: A twenty-year experiment at the "Groupe de Recherches Musicales." In *Proc. DAFX-98 Digital Audio Effects Workshop*, pp. 241–248, 1998.

[Ges00]   Y. Geslin. About the various types of Phonogènes. GRM, Personal communication, 2000.

[GRH73]   T. A. Giordano, H. B. Rothman and H. Hollien. Helium speech unscramblers – a critical review of the state of the art. *IEEE Trans. Audio and Electroacoust.*, AU-21(5), 1973.

[Hal95]   H. P. Haller. *Das Experimental Studio der Heinrich-Strobel-Stiftung des Südwestfunks Freiburg 1971-1989, Die Erforschung der Elektronischen Klangumformung und ihre Geschichte*. Nomos, 1995.

[HM91]   Don Hejna and Bruce R. Musicus. The SOLAFS time-scale modification algorithm. Technical report, BBN, July 1991.

[HMC89]   C. Hamon, E. Moulines and F. Charpentier. A diphone synthesis system based on time-domain prosodic modifications of speech. In *Proc. ICASSP*, pp. 238–241, 1989.

[KZZ10]   A. von dem Knesebeck, P. Ziraksaz and U. Zölzer. High quality time-domain pitch shifting using PSOLA and transient preservation. In *Proc. of the 129th AES Convention*, 2010.

[Lar98]   J. Laroche. Time and pitch scale modifications of audio signals. In M. Kahrs and K.-H. Brandenburg (eds), *Applications of Digital Signal Processing to Audio and Acoustics*, pp. 279–309. Kluwer, 1998.

[Lee72]   F. F. Lee. Time compression and expansion of speech by the sampling method. *J. Audio Eng. Soc.*, 20(9): 738–742, 1972.

[LJ04]   C. Y. Lin and J. S. R. Jang. A two-phase pitch marking method for TD-PSOLA synthesis. In *8th Int. Conf. Spoken Lang. Process.*, 2004.

[Mas98]   D. C. Massie. Wavetable sampling synthesis. In M. Kahrs and K.-H. Brandenburg (eds), *Applications of Digital Signal Processing to Audio and Acoustics*, pp. 311–341. Kluwer, 1998.

[MC90]   E. Moulines and F. Charpentier. Pitch synchronous waveform processing techniques for text-to speech synthesis using diphones. *Speech Commun.*, 9(5/6): 453–467, 1990.

[McN84]   G. W. McNally. Variable speed replay of digital audio with constant output sampling rate. In *Proc. 76th AES Convention*, Preprint 2137, 1984.

[MEJ86]   J. Makhoul and A. El-Jaroudi. Time-scale modification in medium to low rate speech coding. In *Proc. ICASSP*, pp. 1705–1708, 1986.

[ML95]   E. Moulines and J. Laroche. Non-parametric technique for pitch-scale and time-scale modification of speech. *Speech Commun.*, 16: 175–205, 1995.

[Mol60]   A. Moles. *Les musiques Expérimentales*. Trad. D. Charles. Cercle d'Art Contemporain, 1960.

[MVV06]   W. Mattheyses, W. Verhelst and P. Verhoeve. Robust pitch marking for prosodic modification of spech using TD-PSOLA. In *Proc. IEEE Benelux/DSP Valley Signal Process. Symp.*, 2006.

[Pou54]   J. Poullin. L'apport des techniques d'enregistrement dans la fabraction de matières et formes musicales nouvelles. Applications à la musique concrète. *L'Onde Électrique*, 34(324): 282–291, 1954.

[PR99]   G. Peeters and X. Rodet. SINOLA: A new analysis/synthesis method using spectrum peak shape distortion, phase and reassigned spectrum. In *Proc. ICMC*, pp. 153–156, 1999.

[PS57]   J. Poullin and D. A. Sinclair. *The Application of Recording Techniques to the Production of New Musical Materials and Forms. Application to "Musique Concrète"*. National Research Council of Canada, 1957. Technical Translation TT-646, pp. 1–29.

[Ris98]   J.-C. Risset. Example of the musical use of digital audio effects. In *Proc. DAFX-99 Digital Audio Effects Workshop*, pp. 254–259, 1998.

[Roa96]   C. Roads. *The Computer Music Tutorial*. MIT Press, 1996.

[Roa98]   C. Roads. Micro-sound, history and illusion. In *Proc. DAFX-98 Digital Audio Effects Workshop*, pp. 260–269, 1998.

[RW85]   S. Roucos and A. M. Wilgus. High quality time-scale modification for speech. In *Proc. ICASSP*, pp. 493–496, 1985.

[Sch73]   P. Schaeffer. *La Musique Concrète*. QSJ No 1287, PUF 1973.

[SPLR02]   N. Schnell, G. Peeters, S. Lemouton and X. Rodet. Synthesizing a choir in real-time using pitch synchronous overlap add (PSOLA). In *Proc. 1st IEEE Benelux Workshop Model based Proc. Coding Audio*, 2002.

[Spr55]   A. M. Springer. Ein akustischer Zeitregler. *Gravesaner Blätter*, (1): 32–27, July 1955.

[Spr59]   J. M. Springer. Akustischer Tempo- und Tonlagenregler. *Gravesaner Blätter*, (13): 80, 1959.

[Tru88]   B. Truax. Real-time granular synthesis with a digital signal processor. *Comp. Music J.*, 12(2): 14–26, 1988.

[Tru94]   B. Truax. Discovering inner complexity: time-shifting and transposition with a real-time granulation technique. *Comp. Music J.*, 18(2): 28–38, 1994.

[Tru00a]   B. Truax. http://www.sfu.ca/truax/gran.html. Granular synthesis, 2000.

[Tru00b]   B. Truax. http://www.sfu.ca/truax/gsample.html. Granulation of sampled sounds, 2000.

[VR93]   W. Verhelst and M. Roelands. An overlap-add technique based on waveform similarity (WSOLA) for high quality time-scale modification of speech. In *Proc. ICASSP*, pp. 554–557, 1993.

[WG94]   M. Warstat and T. Görne. *Studiotechnik – Hintergrund und Praxiswissen*. Elektor-Verlag, 1994.

[Whi99]   P. White. *Creative Recording, Effects and Processors*. Sanctuary Publishing, 1999.

7

Time-frequency processing

D. Arfib, F. Keiler, U. Zölzer, V. Verfaille and J. Bonada

7.1 Introduction

This chapter describes the use of time-frequency representations of signals in order to produce transformations of sounds. A very interesting (and intuitive) way of modifying a sound is to make a two-dimensional representation of it, modify this representation in some way and reconstruct a new signal from this representation (see Figure 7.1). Consequently a digital audio effect based on time-frequency representations requires three steps: an analysis (sound to representation), a transformation (of the representation) and a resynthesis (getting back to a sound).

The direct scheme of spectral analysis, transformation and resynthesis will be discussed in Section 7.2. We will explore the modification of the magnitude $|X(k)|$ and phase $\varphi(k)$ of these representations before resynthesis. The analysis/synthesis scheme is termed the *phase vocoder* (see Figure 7.2). The input signal $x(n)$ is multiplied by a sliding window of finite length N, which yields successive windowed signal segments. These are transformed to the spectral domain by FFTs. In this way a time-varying spectrum $X(n,k) = |X(n,k)|e^{j\varphi(n,k)}$ with $k = 0, 1, \ldots, N-1$ is computed for each windowed segment. The short-time spectra can be modified or transformed for a digital audio effect. Then each modified spectrum is applied to an IFFT and windowed in the time domain. The windowed output segments are overlapped and added yielding the output signal. It is also possible to complete this time-frequency processing by spectral processing, which is dealt with in the next two chapters.

7.2 Phase vocoder basics

The concepts of short-time Fourier analysis and synthesis have been widely described in the literature [Por76, Cro80, CR83]. We will briefly summarize the basics and define our notation of terms for application to digital audio effects.

DAFX: Digital Audio Effects, Second Edition. Edited by Udo Zölzer.
© 2011 John Wiley & Sons, Ltd. Published 2011 by John Wiley & Sons, Ltd.

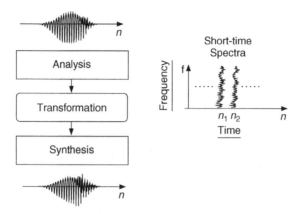

Figure 7.1   Digital audio effects based on analysis, transformation and synthesis (resynthesis).

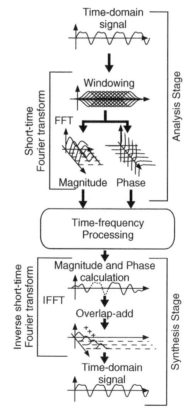

Figure 7.2   Time-frequency processing based on the phase vocoder: analysis, transformation and synthesis.

The short-time Fourier transform (STFT) of the signal $x(n)$ is given by

$$X(n, k) = \sum_{m=-\infty}^{\infty} x(m)h(n - m)W_N^{mk}, \quad k = 0, 1, \ldots, N - 1 \tag{7.1}$$

$$W_N = e^{-j2\pi/N} \tag{7.2}$$

$$= X_R(n, k) + jX_I(n, k) = |X(n, k)| \cdot e^{j\varphi(n,k)}. \tag{7.3}$$

$X(n, k)$ is a complex number and represents the magnitude $|X(n, k)|$ and phase $\varphi(n, k)$ of a time-varying spectrum with frequency bin (index) $0 \le k \le N - 1$ and time index n. Note that the summation index is m in (7.1). At each time index n the signal $x(m)$ is weighted by a finite length window $h(n - m)$. Thus the computation of (7.1) can be performed by a finite sum over m with an FFT of length N. Figure 7.3 shows the input signal $x(m)$ and the sliding window $h(n - m)$ for three time indices of n. The middle plot shows the finite length windowed segments $x(m) \cdot h(n - m)$. These segments are transformed by the FFT, yielding the short-time spectra $X(n, k)$ given by (7.1). The lower two rows in Figure 7.3 show the magnitude and phase spectra of the corresponding time segments.

7.2.1   Filter bank summation model

The computation of the time-varying spectrum of an input signal can also be interpreted as a parallel bank of N bandpass filters, as shown in Figure 7.4, with impulse responses and Fourier transforms given by

$$h_k(n) = h(n)W_N^{-nk}, \quad k = 0, 1, \ldots, N - 1 \tag{7.4}$$

$$H_k(e^{j\omega}) = H(e^{j(\omega - \omega_k)}), \quad \omega_k = \frac{2\pi}{N}k. \tag{7.5}$$

Each bandpass signal $y_k(n)$ is obtained by filtering the input signal $x(n)$ with the corresponding bandpass filter $h_k(n)$. Since the bandpass filters are complex-valued, we get complex-valued output signals $y_k(n)$, which will be denoted by

$$y_k(n) = \tilde{X}(n, k) = |X(n, k)| \cdot e^{j\tilde{\varphi}(n,k)}. \tag{7.6}$$

These filtering operations are performed by the convolutions

$$y_k(n) = \sum_{m=-\infty}^{\infty} x(m)h_k(n - m) = \sum_{m=-\infty}^{\infty} x(m)h(n - m)W_N^{-(n-m)k} \tag{7.7}$$

$$= W_N^{-nk} \sum_{m=-\infty}^{\infty} x(m)W_N^{mk}h(n - m) = W_N^{-nk}X(n, k). \tag{7.8}$$

From (7.6) and (7.8) it is important to notice that

$$\tilde{X}(n, k) = W_N^{-nk}X(n, k) = W_N^{-nk}|X(n, k)|e^{j\varphi(n,k)} \tag{7.9}$$

$$\tilde{\varphi}(n, k) = \frac{2\pi k}{N}n + \varphi(n, k). \tag{7.10}$$

Based on Equations (7.7) and (7.8) two different implementations are possible, as shown in Figure 7.4. The first implementation is the so-called complex baseband implementation according to (7.8). The baseband signals $X(n, k)$ (short-time Fourier transform) are computed by modulation of $x(n)$ with W_N^{nk} and lowpass filtering for each channel k. The modulation of $X(n, k)$ by W_N^{-nk} yields the bandpass signal $\tilde{X}(n, k)$. The second implementation is the so-called complex bandpass

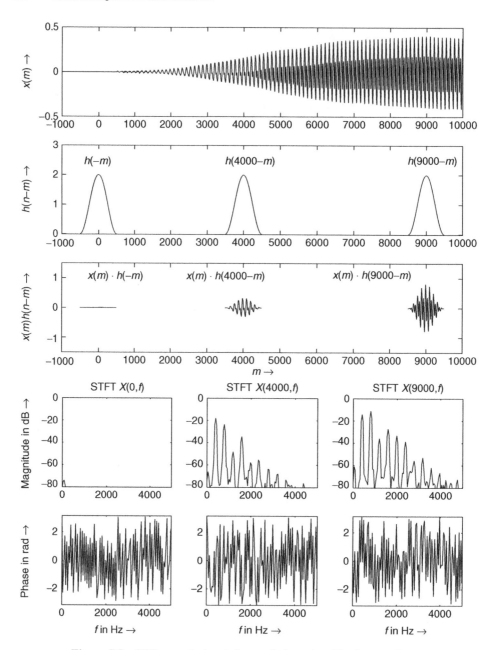

Figure 7.3   Sliding analysis window and short-time Fourier transform.

implementation, which filters the input signal with $h_k(n)$ given by (7.4), as shown in the lower left part of Figure 7.4. This implementation leads directly to the complex-valued bandpass signals $\tilde{X}(n,k)$. If the equivalent baseband signals $X(n,k)$ are necessary, they can be computed by multiplication with W_N^{nk}. The operations for the modulation by W_N^{nk} yielding $X(n,k)$ and back modulation by W_N^{-nk} (lower left part of Figure 7.4) are only shown to point out the equivalence of both implementations.

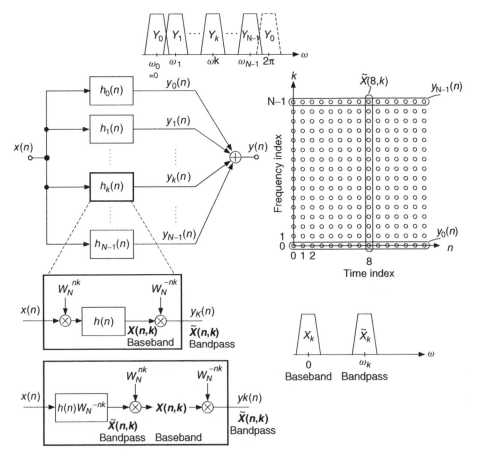

Figure 7.4 Filter bank description of the short-time Fourier transform. Two implementations of the kth channel are shown in the lower left part. The discrete-time and discrete-frequency plane is shown in the right part. The marked bandpass signals $y_k(n)$ are the horizontal samples $\tilde{X}(n, k)$. The different frequency bands Y_k corresponding to each bandpass signal are shown on top of the filter bank. The frequency bands for the baseband signal $X(n, k)$ and the bandpass signal $\tilde{X}(n, k)$ are shown in the lower right part.

The output sequence $y(n)$ is the sum of the bandpass signals according to

$$y(n) = \sum_{k=0}^{N-1} y_k(n) = \sum_{k=0}^{N-1} \tilde{X}(n, k) = \sum_{k=0}^{N-1} X(n, k) W_N^{-nk}. \tag{7.11}$$

The output signals $y_k(n)$ are complex-valued sequences $\tilde{X}(n, k)$. For a real-valued input signal $x(n)$ the bandpass signals satisfy the property $y_k(n) = \tilde{X}(n, k) = \tilde{X}^*(n, N - k) = y_{N-k}^*(n)$. For a channel stacking with $\omega_k = \frac{2\pi k}{N}$ we get the frequency bands shown in the upper part of Figure 7.4. The property $\tilde{X}(n, k) = \tilde{X}^*(n, N - k)$, together with the channel stacking can be used for the formulation of real-valued bandpass signals (real-valued kth channel)

$$\hat{y}_k(n) = \tilde{X}(n, k) + \tilde{X}(n, N - k) = \tilde{X}(n, k) + \tilde{X}^*(n, k) \tag{7.12}$$

$$= |X(n, k)| \cdot \left[e^{j\tilde{\varphi}(n,k)} + e^{-j\tilde{\varphi}(n,k)} \right] \tag{7.13}$$

$$= 2|X(n,k)| \cdot \cos[\tilde{\varphi}(n,k)]$$

$$\text{for } k = 1, \ldots, N/2 - 1. \tag{7.14}$$

This leads to

$$\hat{y}_0(n) = y_0(n), \quad k = 0 \tag{7.15}$$

dc channel

$$\hat{y}_k(n) = \underbrace{2|X(n,k)|}_{A(n,k)} \cdot \cos\underbrace{[\omega_k n + \varphi(n,k)]}_{\tilde{\varphi}(n,k)}, \quad k = 1, \ldots, N/2 - 1 \tag{7.16}$$

bandpass channels

$$\hat{y}_{N/2}(n) = y_{N/2}(n), \quad k = N/2 \tag{7.17}$$

highpass channel.

Besides a dc and a highpass channel we have $N/2 - 1$ cosine signals with fixed frequencies ω_k and time-varying amplitude and phase. This means that we can add real-valued output signals $\hat{y}_k(n)$ to yield the output signal

$$y(n) = \sum_{k=0}^{N/2} \hat{y}_k(n). \tag{7.18}$$

This interpretation offers analysis of a signal by a filter bank, modification of the short-time spectrum $\tilde{X}(n,k)$ on a sample-by-sample basis and synthesis by a summation of the bandpass signals $y_k(n)$. Due to the fact that the baseband signals are bandlimited by the lowpass filter $h(n)$, a sampling rate reduction can be performed in each channel to yield $X(sR,k)$, where only every Rth sample is taken and s denotes the new time index. This leads to a short-time transform $X(sR,k)$ with a hop size of R samples. Before the synthesis upsampling and interpolation filtering have to be performed [CR83].

7.2.2 Block-by-block analysis/synthesis model

A detailed description of a phase vocoder implementation using the FFT can be found in [Por76, Cro80, CR83]. The analysis and synthesis implementations are precisely described in [(CR83, p. 318, Figure 7.19 and 7.19 p. 321, Figure 7.20)]. A simplified analysis and synthesis implementation, where the window length is less or equal to the FFT length, were proposed in [Cro80]. The analysis and synthesis algorithm and the discrete-time and discrete-frequency plane are shown in Figure 7.5. The analysis algorithm [Cro80] is given by

$$X(sR_a,k) = \sum_{m=-\infty}^{\infty} x(m)h(sR_a - m)W_N^{mk} \tag{7.19}$$

$$= W_N^{sR_a k} \sum_{m=-\infty}^{\infty} x(m)h(sR_a - m)W_N^{-(sR_A-m)k} \tag{7.20}$$

$$= W_N^{sR_a k} \cdot \tilde{X}(sR_a,k) \tag{7.21}$$

$$= X_R(sR_a,k) + jX_I(sR_a,k) = |X(sR_a,k)| \cdot e^{j\varphi(sR_a,k)} \tag{7.22}$$

$$k = 0, 1, \ldots, N - 1,$$

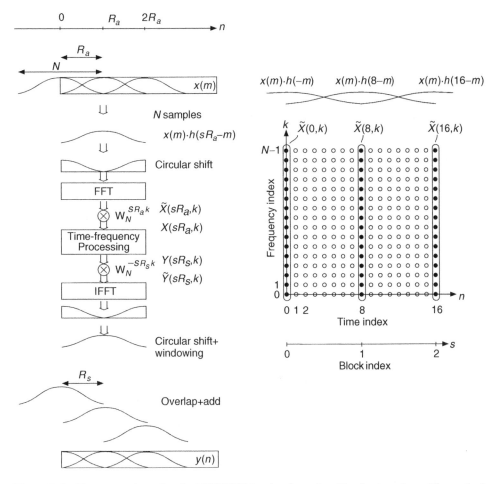

Figure 7.5 Phase vocoder using the FFT/IFFT for the short-time Fourier transform. The analysis hop size R_a determines the sampling of the two-dimensional time-frequency grid. Time-frequency processing allows the reconstruction with a synthesis hop size R_s.

where the short-time Fourier transform is sampled every R_a samples in time and s denotes the time index of the short-time transform at the decimated sampling rate. This means that the time index is now $n = sR_a$, where R_a denotes the analysis hop size. The analysis window is denoted by $h(n)$. Notice that $X(n, k)$ and $\tilde{X}(n, k)$ in the FFT implementation can also be found in the filter bank approach. The circular shift of the windowed segment before the FFT and after the IFFT is derived in [CR83] and provides a zero-phase analysis and synthesis regarding the center of the window. Further details will be discussed in the next section. Spectral modifications in the time-frequency plane can now be done, which yields $Y(sR_s, k)$, where R_s is the synthesis hop size. The synthesis algorithm [Cro80] is given by

$$y(n) = \sum_{s=-\infty}^{\infty} f(n - sR_s)y_s(n - sR_s) \tag{7.23}$$

$$\text{with} \quad y_s(n) = \frac{1}{N} \sum_{k=0}^{N-1} \left[W_N^{-sR_s k} Y(sR_s, k) \right] W_N^{-nk},$$

where $f(n)$ denotes the synthesis window. Finite length signals $y_s(n)$ are derived from inverse transforms of short-time spectra $Y(sR_s, k)$. These short-time segments are weighted by the synthesis window $f(n)$ and then added by the overlap-add procedure given by (7.23) (see Figure 7.5).

7.3   Phase vocoder implementations

This section describes several phase vocoder implementations for digital audio effects. A useful representation is the time-frequency plane where one displays the values of the magnitude $|X(n, k)|$ and phase $\tilde{\varphi}(n, k)$ of the $\tilde{X}(n, k)$ signal. If the sliding Fourier transform is used as an analysis scheme, this graphical representation is the combination of the spectrogram, which displays the magnitude values of this representation, and the *phasogram*, which displays the phase. However, phasograms are harder to read when the hop size is not small. Figure 7.6 shows a spectrogram and a phasogram which correspond to the discrete-time and discrete-frequency plane achieved by a filter bank (see Figure 7.4) or a block-by-block FFT analysis (see Figure 7.5) described in the previous section. In the horizontal direction a line represents the output magnitude $|X(n, k)|$ and the phase $\tilde{\varphi}(n, k)$ of the kth analysis bandpass filter over the time index n. In the vertical direction a line represents the magnitude $|X(n, k)|$ and phase $\tilde{\varphi}(n, k)$ for a fixed time index n, which corresponds to a short-time spectrum over frequency bin k at the center of the analysis window located at time index n. The spectrogram in Figure 7.6 with frequency range up to 2 kHz shows five horizontal rays over the time axis, indicating the magnitude of the harmonics of the analyzed sound segment. The phasogram shows the corresponding phases for all five horizontal rays $\tilde{\varphi}(n, k)$, which rotate according to the frequencies of the five harmonics. With a hop size of one we get a visible tree structure. For a larger hop size we get a sampled version, where the tree structure usually disappears.

The analysis and synthesis part can come from the filter bank summation model (see basics), in which case the resynthesis part consists in summing sinusoids, whose amplitudes and frequencies are coming from a parallel bank of filters. The analysis part can also come from a sliding FFT algorithm, in which case it is possible to perform the resynthesis with either a summation of sinusoids or an IFFT approach.

7.3.1   Filter bank approach

From a musician's point of view the idea behind this technique is to represent a sound signal as a sum of sinusoids. Each of these sinusoids is modulated in amplitude and frequency. They represent filtered versions of the original signal. The manipulation of the amplitudes and frequencies of these individual signals will produce a digital effect, including time stretching or pitch shifting.

One can use a filter bank, as shown in Figure 7.7, to split the audio signal into several filtered versions. The sum of these filtered versions reproduces the original signal. For a perfect reconstruction the sum of the filter frequency responses should be unity. In order to produce a digital audio effect, one needs to alter the intermediate signals that are analytical signals consisting of real and imaginary parts (double lines in Figure 7.7). The implementation of each filter can be performed by a heterodyne filter, as shown in Figure 7.8.

The implementation of a stage of a heterodyne filter consists of a complex-valued oscillator with a fixed frequency ω_k, a multiplier and an FIR filter. The multiplication shifts the spectrum of the sound, and the FIR filter limits the width of the frequency-shifted spectrum. This heterodyne filtering can be used to obtain intermediate analytic signals, which can be put in the form

$$X(n, k) = \left[x(n) \cdot \mathrm{e}^{-j\omega_k n}\right] * h(n) = X_R(n, k) + jX_I(n, k) \tag{7.24}$$

$$= |X(n, k)|\mathrm{e}^{j\varphi(n,k)} \tag{7.25}$$

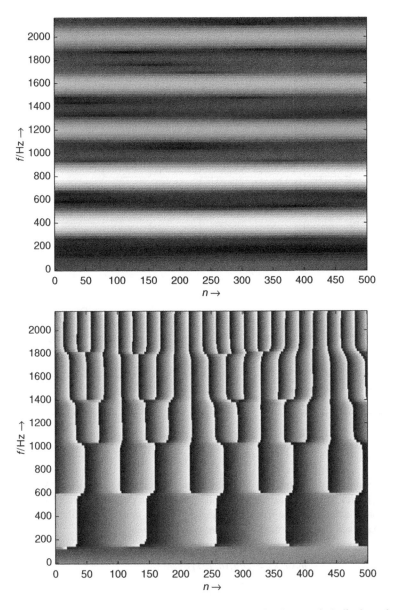

Figure 7.6 Magnitude $|X(n, k)|$ (upper plot) and phase $\tilde{\varphi}(n, k)$ (lower plot) display of a sliding Fourier transform with a hop size $R_a = 1$ or a filter-bank analysis approach. For the upper display the grey value (black $= 0$ and white $=$ maximum amplitude) represents the magnitude range. In the lower display the phase values are in the range $-\pi \leq \tilde{\varphi}(n, k) \leq \pi$.

$$X_R(n, k) = |X(n, k)| \cos(\varphi(n, k)) \tag{7.26}$$

$$X_I(n, k) = |X(n, k)| \sin(\varphi(n, k)). \tag{7.27}$$

The difference from classical bandpass filtering is that here the output signal is located in the baseband. This representation leads to a slowly varying phase $\varphi(n, k)$ and the derivation of the

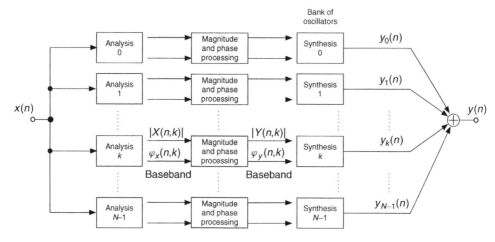

Figure 7.7   Filter-bank implementation.

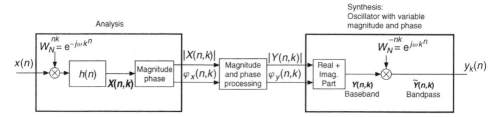

Figure 7.8   Heterodyne-filter implementation.

phase is a measure of the frequency deviation from the center frequency ω_k. A sinusoid $x(n) = \cos[\omega_k n + \varphi_0]$ with frequency ω_k can be written as $x(n) = \cos[\tilde{\varphi}(n)]$, where $\tilde{\varphi}(n) = \omega_k n + \varphi_0$. The derivation of $\tilde{\varphi}(n)$ gives the frequency $\omega_k = \frac{d\tilde{\varphi}(n)}{dn}$. The derivation of the phase $\tilde{\varphi}(n, k)$ at the output of a bandpass filter is termed the *instantaneous frequency* given by

$$\omega_i(n, k) = 2\pi f_i(n, k)/f_S \tag{7.28}$$

$$= \frac{d}{dn}\tilde{\varphi}(n, k) \tag{7.29}$$

$$= \omega_k + \frac{d}{dn}\varphi(n, k) \tag{7.30}$$

$$= \omega_k + \varphi(n, k) - \varphi(n - 1, k) \tag{7.31}$$

$$\Rightarrow f_i(n, k) = \left(\frac{k}{N} + \frac{\varphi(n, k) - \varphi(n - 1, k)}{2\pi} \right) \cdot f_S. \tag{7.32}$$

The instantaneous frequency can be described in a musical way as the frequency of the filter output signal in the filter-bank approach. The phase of the baseband output signal is $\varphi(n, k)$ and the phase of the bandpass output signal is $\tilde{\varphi}(n, k) = \omega_k n + \varphi(n, k)$ (see Figure 7.8). As soon as we have the instantaneous frequencies, we can build an oscillator bank and eventually change the amplitudes and frequencies of this bank to build a digital audio effect. The recalculation of the phase from a modified instantaneous frequency is done by computing the phase according to

$$\tilde{\varphi}(n, k) = \tilde{\varphi}(0, k) + \int_0^{nT} 2\pi f_i(\tau, k)\mathrm{d}\tau. \tag{7.33}$$

The result of the magnitude and phase processing can be written as $Y(n, k) = |Y(n, k)|e^{j\varphi_y(n,k)}$, which is then used as the magnitude and phase for the complex-valued oscillator running with frequency ω_k. The output signal is then given by

$$\tilde{Y}(n, k) = |Y(n, k)|e^{j\varphi_y(n,k)} \cdot e^{j\omega_k n} \tag{7.34}$$

$$= Y(n, k) \cdot e^{j\omega_k n} = \left[Y_R(n, k) + jY_I(n, k)\right] \cdot e^{j\omega_k n}. \tag{7.35}$$

The resynthesis of the output signal can then be performed by summing all the individual back-shifted signals (oscillator bank) according to

$$y(n) = \sum_{k=0}^{N-1} \tilde{Y}(n, k) = \sum_{k=0}^{N-1} Y(n, k) \cdot e^{j\Omega_k n} \tag{7.36}$$

$$= \sum_{k=0}^{N/2} A(n, k) \cos\left[\omega_k n + \varphi_y(n, k)\right], \tag{7.37}$$

where (7.37) was already introduced by (7.18). The modification of the phases and frequencies for time stretching and pitch shifting needs further explanation and will be treated in a following subsection.

The following M-file 7.1 shows a filter-bank implementation with heterodyne filters, as shown in Figure 7.8 (see also Figure 7.4).

M-file 7.1 (VX_het_nothing.m)

```
% VX_het_nothing.m    [DAFXbook, 2nd ed., chapter 7]
clear; clf
%===== This program (i) implements a heterodyne filter bank,
%===== then (ii) filters a sound through the filter bank
%===== and (iii) reconstructs a sound

%----- user data -----
fig_plot    = 0;    % use any value except 0 or [] to plot figures
s_win       = 256;  % window size
n_channel   = 128;  % nb of channels
s_block     = 1024; % computation block size (must be a multiple of s_win)
[DAFx_in, FS] = wavread('la.wav');

%----- initialize windows, arrays, etc -----
window   = hanning(s_win, 'periodic');
s_buffer = length(DAFx_in);
DAFx_in  = [DAFx_in; zeros(s_block,1)]/max(abs(DAFx_in)); % 0-pad & normalize
DAFx_out = zeros(length(DAFx_in),1);
X        = zeros(s_block, n_channel);
z        = zeros(s_win-1, n_channel);
```

```
%----- initialize the heterodyn filters -----
t   = (0:s_block-1)';
het = zeros(s_block,n_channel);
for k=1:n_channel
  wk       = 2*pi*i*(k/s_win);
  het(:,k) = exp(wk*(t+s_win/2));
  het2(:,k) = exp(-wk*t);
end

%----- displays the phase of the filter -----
if(fig_plot)
  colormap(gray); imagesc(angle(het)'); colorbar;
  axis('xy'); xlabel('n \rightarrow'); ylabel('k \rightarrow');
  title('Heterodyn filter bank: initial \phi(n,k)'); pause;
end

tic
%UUUUUUUUUUUUUUUUUUUUUUUUUUUUUUUUUUUUUUUUUUUU
pin  = 0;
pend = length(DAFx_in) - s_block;
while pin<pend
  grain = DAFx_in(pin+1:pin+s_block);
%==========================================
  %----- filtering through the filter bank -----
  for k=1:n_channel
    [X(:,k), z(:,k)] = filter(window, 1, grain.*het(:,k), z(:,k));
  end
  X_tilde = X.*het2;
  %----- drawing -----
  if(fig_plot)
    imagesc(angle(X_tilde')); axis('xy'); colorbar;
    xlabel('n \rightarrow'); ylabel('k \rightarrow');
    txt = sprintf('Heterodyn filter bank: \\phi(n,k),t=%6.3f s',(pin+1)/FS);
    title(txt); drawnow;
  end
  %----- sound reconstruction -----
  res = real(sum(X_tilde,2));
%==========================================
  DAFx_out(pin+1:pin+s_block) = res;
  pin = pin + s_block;
end
%UUUUUUUUUUUUUUUUUUUUUUUUUUUUUUUUUUUUUUUUUUUU
toc

%----- listening and saving the output -----
DAFx_out = DAFx_out(n_channel+1:n_channel+s_buffer) / max(abs(DAFx_out));
soundsc(DAFx_out, FS);
wavwrite(DAFx_out, FS, 'la_het_nothing.wav');
```

M-file 7.2 demonstrates the second-filter bank implementation with complex-valued bandpass filters, as shown in Figure 7.4.

M-file 7.2 (VX_filter_nothing.m)

```
% VX_filter_nothing.m     [DAFXbook, 2nd ed., chapter 7]
clear; clf

%===== This program (i) performs a complex-valued filter bank
%===== then (ii) filters a sound through the filter bank
%===== and (iii) reconstructs a sound

%----- user data -----
fig_plot    = 0;    % use any value except 0 or [] to plot figures
s_win       = 256;  % window size
nChannel    = 128;  % nb of channels
n1          = 1024; % block size for calculation
[DAFx_in,FS] = wavread('la.wav');

%----- initialize windows, arrays, etc -----
window   = hanning(s_win, 'periodic');
L        = length(DAFx_in);
DAFx_in  = [DAFx_in; zeros(n1,1)] / max(abs(DAFx_in)); % 0-pad & normalize
DAFx_out = zeros(length(DAFx_in),1);
X_tilde  = zeros(n1,nChannel);
z        = zeros(s_win-1,nChannel);

%----- initialize the complex-valued filter bank -----
t    = (-s_win/2:s_win/2-1)';
filt = zeros(s_win, nChannel);
for k=1:nChannel
  wk       = 2*pi*i*(k/s_win);
  filt(:,k) = window.*exp(wk*t);
end

if(fig_plot), colormap(gray); end

tic
%UUUUUUUUUUUUUUUUUUUUUUUUUUUUUUUUUUUUUUUUUUUUUUU
pin  = 0;
pend = length(DAFx_in) - n1;
while pin<pend
  grain = DAFx_in(pin+1:pin+n1);
%===========================================
  %----- filtering -----
  for k=1:nChannel
    [X_tilde(:,k),z(:,k)] = filter(filt(:,k),1,grain,z(:,k));
  end
  if(fig_plot)
    imagesc(angle(X_tilde')); axis('xy'); colorbar;
    xlabel('n \rightarrow'); ylabel('k \rightarrow');
    txt = sprintf('Complex-valued fil. bank: \\phi(n,k), t=%6.3f s', (pin+1)/FS);
    title(txt); drawnow;
  end
    %----- sound reconstruction -----
  res = real(sum(X_tilde,2));
%===========================================
  DAFx_out(pin+1:pin+n1) = res;
  pin = pin + n1;
  end
%UUUUUUUUUUUUUUUUUUUUUUUUUUUUUUUUUUUUUUUUUUUUUUU
toc
```

```
%----- listening and saving the output -----
DAFx_out = DAFx_out(nChannel+1:nChannel+L) / max(abs(DAFx_out));
soundsc(DAFx_out, FS);
wavwrite(DAFx_out, FS, 'la_filter_nothing.wav');
```

7.3.2   Direct FFT/IFFT approach

The FFT algorithm also calculates the values of the magnitudes and phases within a time frame, allowing a shorter calculation time. So many analysis-synthesis algorithms use this transform. There are different ways to interpret a sliding Fourier transform, and consequently to invent a method of resynthesis starting from this time-frequency representation. The first one is to apply the inverse FFT on each short-time spectrum and use the overlap-add method to reconstruct the signal. The second one is to consider a horizontal line of the time-frequency representation (constant frequency versus time) and to reconstruct a filtered version for each line. The third one is to consider each point of the time-frequency representation and to make a sum of small grains called *gaborets*. In each interpretation one must test the ability of obtaining a perfect reconstruction if one does not modify the representation. Another important fact is the ability to provide effect implementations that do not have too many artifacts when one modifies on purpose the values of the sliding FFT, especially in operations such as time stretching or filtering.

We now describe the direct FFT/IFFT approach. A time-frequency representation can be seen as a series of overlapping FFTs with or without windowing. As the FFT is invertible, one can reconstruct a sound by adding the inverse FFT of a vertical line (constant time versus frequency), as shown in Figure 7.9.

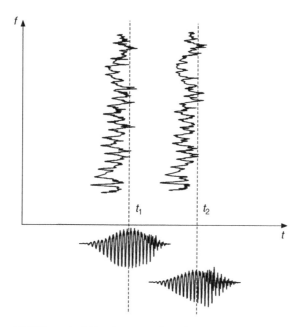

Figure 7.9   FFT and IFFT: vertical line interpretation. At two time instances two spectra are used to compute two time segments.

A perfect reconstruction can be achieved, if the sum of the overlapping windows is unity (see Figure 7.10). A modification of the FFT values can produce time aliasing, which can be avoided

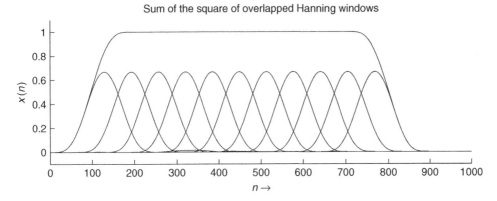

Figure 7.10   Sum of small windows.

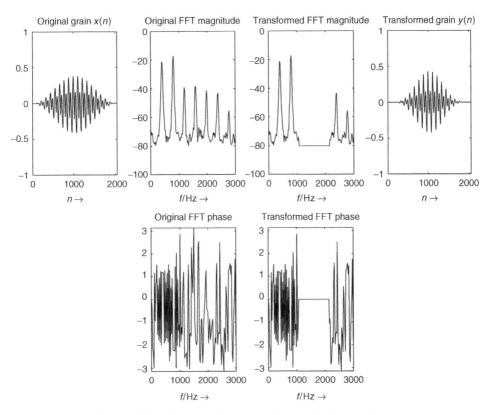

Figure 7.11   Sound windowing, FFT modification and IFFT.

by either zero-padded windows or using windowing after the inverse FFT. In this case the product of the two windows has to be unity. An example is shown in Figure 7.11. This implementation will be used most frequently in this chapter.

The following M-file 7.3 shows a phase vocoder implementation based on the direct FFT/IFFT approach, where the routine itself is given two vectors for the sound, a window and a hop size.

M-file 7.3 (VX_pv_nothing.m)

```
% VX_pv_nothing.m    [DAFXbook, 2nd ed., chapter 7]
%===== this program implements a simple phase vocoder
clear; clf

%----- user data -----
fig_plot      = 0;      % use any value except 0 or [] to plot figures
n1            = 512;    % analysis step [samples]
n2            = n1;     % synthesis step [samples]
s_win         = 2048;   % window size [samples]
[DAFx_in, FS] = wavread('la.wav');

%----- initialize windows, arrays, etc -----
w1            = hanning(s_win, 'periodic'); % input window
w2            = w1;     % output window
L             = length(DAFx_in);
DAFx_in       = [zeros(s_win, 1); DAFx_in; ...
  zeros(s_win-mod(L,n1),1)] / max(abs(DAFx_in));   % 0-pad & normalize
DAFx_out      = zeros(length(DAFx_in),1);

tic
%UUUUUUUUUUUUUUUUUUUUUUUUUUUUUUUUUUUUUUUUUUUU
pin  = 0;
pout = 0;
pend = length(DAFx_in) - s_win;

while pin<pend
  grain = DAFx_in(pin+1:pin+s_win).* w1;
%=========================================
  f     = fft(fftshift(grain));  % FFT
  r     = abs(f);                % magnitude
  phi   = angle(f);              % phase
  ft    = (r.* exp(i*phi));      % reconstructed FFT
  grain = fftshift(real(ifft(ft))).*w2;
% =========================================
  DAFx_out(pout+1:pout+s_win) = ...
     DAFx_out(pout+1:pout+s_win) + grain;
  pin  = pin + n1;
  pout = pout + n2;
end
%UUUUUUUUUUUUUUUUUUUUUUUUUUUUUUUUUUUUUUUUUUUU
toc
%----- listening and saving the output -----
% DAFx_in  = DAFx_in(s_win+1:s_win+L);
DAFx_out = DAFx_out(s_win+1:s_win+L) / max(abs(DAFx_out));
soundsc(DAFx_out, FS);
wavwrite(DAFx_out, FS, 'la_pv_nothing.wav');
```

The kernel algorithm performs successive FFTs, inverse FFTs and overlap-add of successive grains. The key point of the implementations is how to go from the FFT representation, where the time origin is at the beginning of the window, to the phase vocoder representation used in Section 7.2, either in its filter-bank description or its block-by-block approach.

The first problem we have to solve is the fact that the time origin for an FFT is on the left of the window. We would like to have it centered, so that, for example, the FFT of a centered impulse would be zero phase. This is done by a circular shift of the signal, which is a commutation of the first and second part of the buffer. The discrete-time Fourier transform of $\hat{x}(n) = x(n - N/2)$ is $\hat{X}(e^{j\omega}) = e^{-j\omega\frac{N}{2}} X(e^{j\omega})$. With $\omega_k = \frac{2\pi}{N}k$ the discrete Fourier transform gives $\hat{X}(k) = e^{-j\frac{2\pi}{N}k\frac{N}{2}} X(k)$, which is equivalent to $\hat{X}(k) = (-1)^k X(k)$. The circular shift in time domain can be achieved by multiplying the result of the FFT by $(-1)^k$. With this circular shift, the output of the FFT is equivalent to a filter bank, with zero phase filters. When analyzing a sine wave, the display of the values of the phase $\tilde{\varphi}(n, k)$ of the time-frequency representation will follow the phase of the sinusoid. When analyzing a harmonic sound, one obtains a tree with successive branches corresponding to every harmonic (top of Figure 7.12).

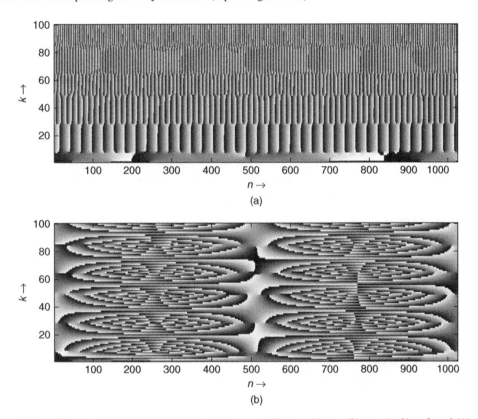

Figure 7.12   Different phase representations: (a) $\tilde{\varphi}(n, k)$ and (b) $\varphi(n, k) = \tilde{\varphi}(n, k) - 2\pi mk/N$.

If we want to take an absolute value as the origin of time, we have to switch to the notation used in Section 7.2. We have to multiply the result of the FFT by W_N^{mk}, where m is the time sample in the middle of the FFT and k is the number of the bin of the FFT. In this way the display of the phase $\varphi(n, k)$ (bottom of Figure 7.12) corresponds to a frequency which is the difference between the frequency of the analyzed signal (here a sine wave) delivered by the FFT and the analyzing frequency (the center of the bin). The phase $\varphi(n, k)$ is calculated as $\varphi(n, k) = \tilde{\varphi}(n, k) - 2\pi mk/N$ (N length of FFT, k number of the bin, m time index).

7.3.3   FFT analysis/sum of sinusoids approach

Conversely, one can read a time-frequency representation with horizontal lines, as shown in Figure 7.13. Each point on a horizontal line can be seen as the convolution of the original signal

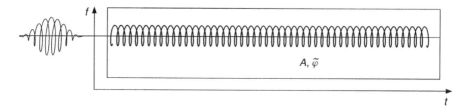

Figure 7.13   Filter-bank approach: horizontal line interpretation.

with an FIR filter, whose filter coefficients have been given by (7.4). The filter-bank approach is very close to the heterodyne-filter implementation. The difference comes from the fact that for heterodyne filtering the complex exponential is running with time and the sliding FFT is considering for each point the same phase initiation of the complex exponential. It means that the heterodyne filter measures the phase deviation between a cosine and the filtered signal, and the sliding FFT measures the phase with a time origin at zero.

The reconstruction of a sliding FFT on a horizontal line with a hop size of one is performed by filtering of this line with the filter corresponding to the frequency bin (see Figure 7.13). However, if the analysis hop size is greater than one, we need to interpolate the magnitude values $|X(n, k)|$ and phase values $\tilde{\varphi}(n, k)$. Phase interpolation is based on phase unwrapping, which will be explained in Section 7.3.5. Combining phase interpolation with linear interpolation of the magnitudes $|X(n, k)|$ allows the reconstruction of the sound by the addition of a bank of oscillators, as given in (7.37).

M-file 7.4 illustrates the interpolation and the sum of sinusoids. Starting from the magnitudes and phases taken from a sliding FFT the synthesis implementation is performed by a bank of oscillators. It uses linear interpolation of the magnitudes and phases.

M-file 7.4 (VX_bank_nothing.m)

```
% VX_bank_nothing.m    [DAFXbook, 2nd ed., chapter 7]
%===== This program performs an FFT analysis and oscillator bank synthesis
clear; clf

%----- user data -----
n1          = 200;   % analysis step [samples]
n2          = n1;    % synthesis step [samples]
s_win       = 2048;  % window size [samples]
[DAFx_in, FS] = wavread('la.wav');

%----- initialize windows, arrays, etc -----
w1    = hanning(s_win, 'periodic'); % input window
w2    = w1;    % output window
L     = length(DAFx_in);
DAFx_in = [zeros(s_win, 1); DAFx_in; ...
   zeros(s_win-mod(L,n1),1)] / max(abs(DAFx_in)); % 0-pad & normalize
DAFx_out = zeros(length(DAFx_in),1);
ll    = s_win/2;
omega = 2*pi*n1*[0:ll-1]'/s_win;
phi0  = zeros(ll,1);
r0    = zeros(ll,1);
psi   = zeros(ll,1);
grain = zeros(s_win,1);
res   = zeros(n2,1);
```

```
tic
%UUUUUUUUUUUUUUUUUUUUUUUUUUUUUUUUUUUUUUUUUUUUU
pin  = 0;
pout = 0;
pend = length(DAFx_in) - s_win;

while pin<pend
  grain = DAFx_in(pin+1:pin+s_win).* w1;
%===============================================
  fc  = fft(fftshift(grain)); % FFT
  f   = fc(1:11);             % positive frequency spectrum
  r   = abs(f);               % magnitudes
  phi = angle(f);             % phases
  %----- unwrapped phase difference on each bin for a n2 step
  delta_phi = omega + princarg(phi-phi0-omega);
  %----- phase and magnitude increment, for linear
  %      interpolation and reconstruction -----
  delta_r   = (r-r0)/n1;    % magnitude increment
  delta_psi = delta_phi/n1; % phase increment
  for k=1:n2 % compute the sum of weighted cosine
     r0       = r0 + delta_r;
     psi      = psi + delta_psi;
     res(k) = r0'*cos(psi);
  end
  %----- for next time -----
  phi0 = phi;
  r0   = r;
  psi  = princarg(psi);
% ===============================================
  DAFx_out(pout+1:pout+n2) = DAFx_out(pout+1:pout+n2) + res;
  pin  = pin + n1;
  pout = pout + n2;
end
%UUUUUUUUUUUUUUUUUUUUUUUUUUUUUUUUUUUUUUUUUUUUU
toc

%----- listening and saving the output -----
% DAFx_in = DAFx_in(s_win+1:s_win+L);
DAFx_out = DAFx_out(s_win/2+n1+1:s_win/2+n1+L) / max(abs(DAFx_out));
soundsc(DAFx_out,FS);
wavwrite(DAFx_out, FS, 'la_bank_nothing.wav');
```

7.3.4   Gaboret approach

The idea of the "gaboret approach" is the reconstruction of a signal from a time-frequency representation with the sum of "gaborets" weighted by the values of the time-frequency representation [AD93]. The shape of a gaboret is a windowed exponential (see Figure 7.14), which can be given by $g_{\omega_k}(n) = \mathrm{e}^{-j\omega_k n} g_\alpha(n)$. The approach is based on the Gabor transform, which is a short-time Fourier transform with the smallest time-frequency window, namely a Gaussian function $g_\alpha(n) = \frac{1}{\sqrt{2\pi\alpha}} e^{-\frac{n^2}{2\alpha}}$ with $\alpha > 0$. The discrete-time Fourier transform of $g_\alpha(n)$ is again a Gaussian function in the Fourier domain. The gaboret approach is very similar to the wavelet transform [CGT89, Chu92]: one does not consider time or frequency as a privileged axis and one point of the time-frequency plane is the scalar product of the signal with a small gaboret. Further details

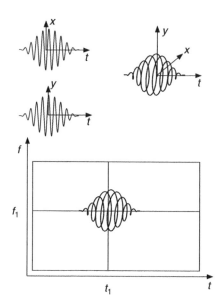

Figure 7.14 Gaboret approach: the upper left part shows real and imaginary values of a gaboret and the upper right part shows a possible 3D repesentation with axes t, x and y. The lower part shows a gaboret associated to a specific point of a time-frequency representation (for every point we can generate a gaboret in the time domain and then make the sum of all gaborets).

can be found in [QC93, WR90]. The reconstruction from a time-frequency representation is the sum of gaborets weighted by the values of this time-frequency plane according to

$$y(n) = \sum_{s=-\infty}^{\infty} \sum_{k=0}^{N-1} Y(sR_s, k) f(n - sR_s) W_N^{-nk}. \tag{7.38}$$

Although this point of view is totally equivalent to windowing plus FFT/IFFT plus windowing, it allows a good comprehension of what happens in case of modification of a point in the plane.

The reconstruction of one single point of a time-frequency representation yields a gaboret in the time domain, as shown in Figure 7.15. Then a new time-frequency representation of this gaboret is computed. We get a new image, which is the called the *reproducing kernel* associated with the transform. This new time-frequency representation is different from the single point of the original time-frequency representation.

So a time-frequency representation of a real signal has some constraints: each value of the time-frequency plane must be the convolution of the neighborhood by the *reproducing kernel* associated with the transformation. This means that if an image (time-frequency representation) is not valid and if we force the reconstruction of a sound by the weighted summation of gaborets, the time-frequency representation of this transformed sound will be in a different form than the initial time-frequency representation. There is no way to avoid this and the beautiful art of making good transforms often relies on the ability to provide "quasi-valid" representations [AD93].

This *reproducing kernel* is only a 2 D extension of the well-known problem of windowing: we find the shape of the FFT of the window around one horizontal ray. But it brings new aspects. When we have two spectral lines, their time-frequency representations are blurred and, when summed, appear as beats. Illustrative examples are shown in Figure 7.16. The shape of the *reproducing kernel*

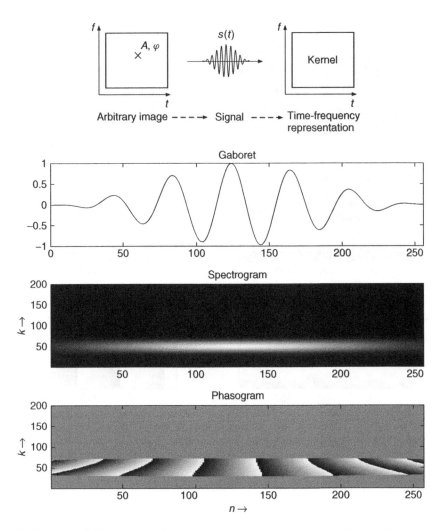

Figure 7.15 Reproducing kernel: the lower three plots represent the forced gaboret and the reproducing kernel consisting of spectrogram and phasogram. (Note: phase values only make sense when the magnitude is not too small.)

depends on the shape of the window and is the key point for differences in representations between different windows. The matter of finding spectral lines starting from time-frequency representations is the subject of Chapter 10. Here we only consider the fact that any signal can be generated as the sum of small gaborets. Frequency estimations in bins are obviously biased by the interaction between rays and additional noise.

The following M-file 7.5 demonstrates the gaboret analysis and synthesis approach.

M-file 7.5 (VX_gab_nothing.m)

```
% VX_gab_nothing.m    [DAFXbook, 2nd ed., chapter 7]
%==== This program performs signal convolution with gaborets
clear; clf
```

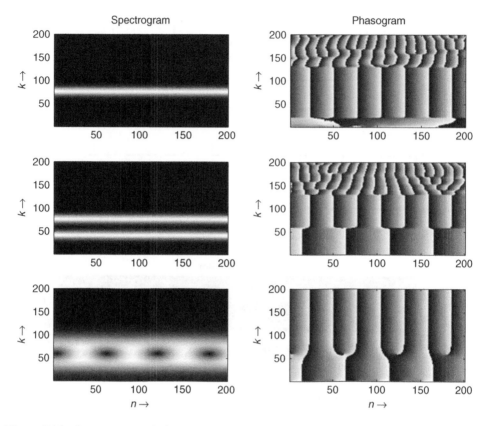

Figure 7.16 Spectrogram and phasogram examples: (a) upper part: the effect of the reproducing kernel is to thicken the line and giving a rotating phase at the frequency of the sinusoid; (b) middle part: for two sinusoids we have two lines with two rotations, if the window is large; (c) lower part: for two sinusoids with a shorter window the two lines mix and we can see beating.

```
%----- user data -----
n1            = 128;   % analysis step [samples]
n2            = n1;    % synthesis step [samples]
s_win         = 512;   % window size [samples]
[DAFx_in, FS] = wavread('la.wav');

%----- initialize windows, arrays, etc -----
window   = hanning(s_win, 'periodic'); % input window
nChannel = s_win/2;
L        = length(DAFx_in);
DAFx_in  = [zeros(s_win, 1); DAFx_in; ...
   zeros(s_win-mod(L,n1),1)] / max(abs(DAFx_in));
DAFx_out = zeros(length(DAFx_in),1); % 0-pad & normalize

%----- initialize calculation of gaborets -----
t   = (-s_win/2:s_win/2-1);
gab = zeros(nChannel,s_win);
for k=1:nChannel
   wk        = 2*pi*i*(k/s_win);
   gab(k,:) = window'.*exp(wk*t);
```

```
end

tic
%UUUUUUUUUUUUUUUUUUUUUUUUUUUUUUUUUUUUUUUUUUUUUUUUU
pin  = 0;
pout = 0;
pend = length(DAFx_in) - s_win;

while pin<pend
  grain = DAFx_in(pin+1:pin+s_win);
%===========================================
  %----- complex vector corresponding to a vertical line
  vec = gab*grain;
  %----- reconstruction from the vector to a grain
  res = real(gab'*vec);
% ===========================================
  DAFx_out(pout+1:pout+s_win) = DAFx_out(pout+1:pout+s_win) + res;
  pin  = pin + n1;
  pout = pout + n2;
  end
%UUUUUUUUUUUUUUUUUUUUUUUUUUUUUUUUUUUUUUUUUUUUUUUUU
toc

%----- listening and saving the output -----
% DAFx_in  = DAFx_in(s_win+1:s_win+L);
DAFx_out = DAFx_out(s_win+1:s_win+L) / max(abs(DAFx_out));
soundsc(DAFx_out, FS);
wavwrite(DAFx_out, FS, 'la_gab_nothing.wav');
```

7.3.5 Phase unwrapping and instantaneous frequency

For the tasks of phase interpolation and instantaneous frequency calculation, for every frequency bin k we need a phase unwrapping algorithm. Starting from Figure 7.4 we perform unwrapping of

$$\tilde{\varphi}(n,k) = \underbrace{\frac{2\pi k}{N}}_{\omega_k} n + \varphi(n,k)$$

by unwrapping $\varphi(n,k)$ and adding the phase variation given by $\omega_k n$ for all k, as already shown by (7.10). We also need a special function which puts an arbitrary radian phase value into the range $[-\pi, \pi]$. We will call this function *principle argument* [GBA00], which is defined by the expression $y = \mathrm{princarg}[2\pi m + \varphi_x] = \varphi_x$, where $-\pi < \varphi_x \le \pi$ and m is an integer number. The corresponding MATLAB® function is shown in Figure 7.17.

M-file 7.6 (princarg.m)

```
function phase = princarg(phase_in)
% This function puts an arbitrary phase value into ]-pi,pi] [rad]
phase = mod(phase_in + pi,-2*pi) + pi;
```

The phase computations are based on the phase values $\tilde{\varphi}(sR_a, k)$ and $\tilde{\varphi}((s+1)R_a, k)$, which are the results of the FFTs of two consecutive frames. These phase values are shown in Figure 7.18. We now consider the phase values regardless of the frequency bin k. If a stable sinusoid with

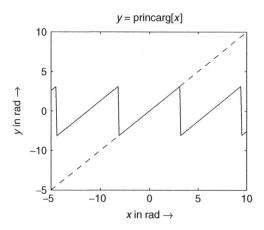

Figure 7.17   Principle argument function (**MATLAB** code and illustrative plot).

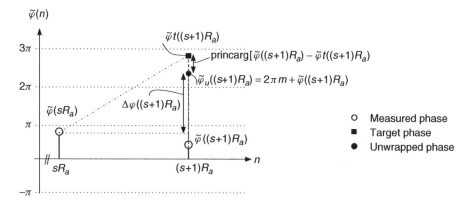

Figure 7.18   Basics of phase computations for frequency bin k.

frequency ω_k exists, we can compute a target phase $\tilde{\varphi}_t((s+1)R_a)$ from the previous phase value $\tilde{\varphi}(sR_a)$ according to

$$\tilde{\varphi}_t((s+1)R_a) = \tilde{\varphi}(sR_a) + \omega_k R_a. \tag{7.39}$$

The unwrapped phase

$$\tilde{\varphi}_u((s+1)R_a) = \tilde{\varphi}_t((s+1)R_a) + \tilde{\varphi}_d((s+1)R_a) \tag{7.40}$$

is computed by the target phase $\tilde{\varphi}_t((s+1)R_a)$ plus a deviation phase $\tilde{\varphi}_d((s+1)R_a)$. This deviation phase can be computed by the measured phase $\tilde{\varphi}((s+1)R_a)$ and the target phase $\tilde{\varphi}_t((s+1)R_a)$ according to

$$\tilde{\varphi}_d((s+1)R_a) = \text{princarg}\left[\tilde{\varphi}((s+1)R_a) - \tilde{\varphi}_t((s+1)R_a)\right]. \tag{7.41}$$

Now we formulate the unwrapped phase (7.40) with the deviation phase (7.41), which leads to the expression

$$\tilde{\varphi}_u((s+1)R_a) = \tilde{\varphi}_t((s+1)R_a) + \text{princarg}\left[\tilde{\varphi}((s+1)R_a) - \tilde{\varphi}_t((s+1)R_a)\right]$$

$$= \tilde{\varphi}(sR_a) + \omega_k R_a + \text{princarg}\left[\tilde{\varphi}((s+1)R_a) - \tilde{\varphi}(sR_a) - \omega_k R_a\right].$$

From the previous equation we can derive the unwrapped phase difference

$$\Delta\varphi((s+1)R_a) = \tilde{\varphi}_u((s+1)R_a) - \tilde{\varphi}(sR_a)$$

$$= \omega_k R_a + \text{princarg}\left[\tilde{\varphi}((s+1)R_a) - \tilde{\varphi}(sR_a) - \omega_k R_a\right] \qquad (7.42)$$

between two consecutive frames. From this unwrapped phase difference we can calculate the instantaneous frequency for frequency bin k at time instant $(s+1)R_a$ by

$$f_i((s+1)R_a) = \frac{1}{2\pi}\frac{\Delta\varphi((s+1)R_a)}{R_a} f_S. \qquad (7.43)$$

The **MATLAB** instructions for the computation of the unwrapped phase difference given by (7.42) for every frequency bin k are given here:

```
omega     = 2*pi*n1*[0:l1-1]' / s_win;
% l1       = N/2 % with N length of the FFT
% n1       = R_a
delta_phi = omega + princarg(phi - phi0 - omega);
```

The term `phi` represents $\tilde{\varphi}((s+1)R_a)$ and `phi0` the previous phase value $\tilde{\varphi}(sR_a)$. In this manner `delta_phi` represents the unwrapped phase variation $\Delta\varphi((s+1)R_a)$ between two successive frames for every frequency bin k.

7.4   Phase vocoder effects

The following subsections will describe several modifications of a time-frequency representation before resynthesis in order to achieve audio effects. Most of them use the FFT analysis followed by either a summation of sinusoids or an IFFT synthesis, which is faster or more adapted to the effect. But all implementations give equivalent results and can be used for audio effects. Figure 7.19 provides a summary of those effects, with their relative operation(s) and the perceptual attribute(s) that are mainly modified.

7.4.1   Time-frequency filtering

Filtering a sound can be done with recursive (IIR) or non-recursive (FIR) filters. However, a musician would like to define or even to draw a frequency response which represents the gain for each frequency band. An intuitive way is to use a time-frequency representation and attenuate certain zones, by multiplying the FFT result in every frame by a filtering function in the frequency domain. One must be aware that in that case we are making a circular convolution (during the FFT–inverse FFT process), which leads to time aliasing, as shown in Figure 7.20. The alternative and exact technique for using time-frequency representations is the design of an FIR impulse response from the filtering function. The convolution of the signal segment $x(n)$ of length N with the impulse response of the FIR filter of length $N+1$ leads to $2N$-point sequence $y(n) = x(n) * h(n)$. This time-domain convolution or filtering can be performed more efficiently in the

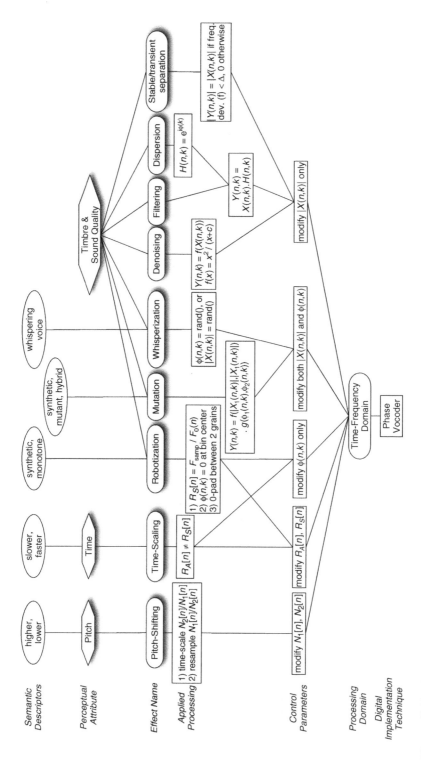

Figure 7.19 Summary of time-frequency domain digital audio effects, with their relative operations and the perceptual attributes that are mainly modified.

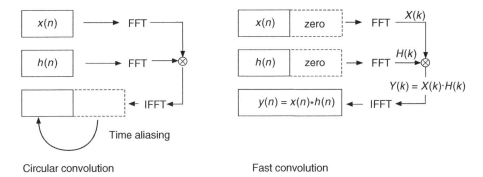

Figure 7.20 Circular convolution and fast convolution.

frequency domain by multiplication of the corresponding FFTs $Y(k) = X(k) \cdot H(k)$. This technique is called *fast convolution* (see Figure 7.20) and is performed by the following steps:

(1) Zero-pad the signal segment $x(n)$ and the impulse response $h(n)$ up to length $2N$.

(2) Take the $2N$-point FFT of these two signals.

(3) Perform multiplication $Y(k) = X(k) \cdot H(k)$ with $k = 0, 1, \ldots, 2N - 1$.

(4) Take the $2N$-point IFFT of $Y(k)$, which yields $y(n)$ with $n = 0, 1, \ldots, 2N - 1$.

Now we can work with successive segments of length N of the original signal (which is equivalent to using a rectangular window), zero-pad each segment up to the length $2N$ and perform the fast convolution with the filter impulse response. The results of each convolution are added in an overlap-add procedure, as shown in Figure 7.21. The algorithm can be summarized as:

(1) Start from an FIR filter of length $N + 1$, zero pad it to $2N$ and take its FFT $\Rightarrow H(k)$.

(2) Partition the signal into segments $x_i(n)$ of length N and zero-pad each segment up to length $2N$.

(3) For each zero-padded segment $s_i(n)$ perform the FFT $X_i(k)$ with $k = 0, 1, \ldots, 2N - 1$.

(4) Perform the multiplication $Y_i(k) = X_i(k) \cdot H(k)$.

(5) Take the inverse FFT of these products $Y_i(k)$.

(6) Overlap-add the convolution results (see Figure 7.21).

The following M-file 7.7 demonstrates the FFT filtering algorithm.

M-file 7.7 (VX_filter.m)

```
% VX_filter.m    [DAFXbook, 2nd ed., chapter 7]
%===== This program performs time-frequency filtering
%===== after calculation of the fir (here band pass)

clear; clf

%----- user data -----
fig_plot        = 0;       % use any value except 0 or [] to plot figures
s_FIR           = 1280;    % length of the fir [samples]
```

```
s_win       = 2*s_FIR; % window size [samples] for zero padding
[DAFx_in, FS] = wavread('la.wav');

%----- initialize windows, arrays, etc -----
L           = length(DAFx_in);
DAFx_in    = [DAFx_in; zeros(s_win-mod(L,s_FIR),1)] ...
   / max(abs(DAFx_in));                % 0-pad & normalize
DAFx_out = zeros(length(DAFx_in)+s_FIR,1);
grain      = zeros(s_win,1);           % input grain
vec_pad    = zeros(s_FIR,1);      % padding array

%----- initialize calculation of fir -----
x           = (1:s_FIR);
fr          = 1000/FS;
alpha       = -0.002;
fir         = (exp(alpha*x).*sin(2*pi*fr*x))'; % FIR coefficients
fir2        = [fir; zeros(s_win-s_FIR,1)];
fcorr       = fft(fir2);

%----- displays the filter' simpulse response -----
if(fig_plot)
  figure(1); clf;
  subplot(2,1,1); plot(fir); xlabel('n [samples] \rightarrow');
  ylabel('h(n) \rightarrow'); axis tight;
  title('Impulse response of the FIR')
  subplot(2,1,2);
  plot((0:s_FIR-1)/s_FIR*FS, 20*log10(abs(fft(fftshift(fir)))));
  xlabel('k \rightarrow'); ylabel('|F(n,k)| / dB \rightarrow');
  title('Magnitude spectrum of the FIR'); axis([0 s_FIR/2, -40, 50])
  pause
end

tic
%UUUUUUUUUUUUUUUUUUUUUUUUUUUUUUUUUUUUUUUUUUUUU
pin  = 0;
pout = 0;
pend = length(DAFx_in) - s_FIR;

while pin<pend
  grain = [DAFx_in(pin+1:pin+s_FIR); vec_pad];
%==========================================
  ft    = fft(grain) .* fcorr;
  grain = (real(ifft(ft)));
%==========================================
  DAFx_out(pin+1:pin+s_win) = ...
    DAFx_out(pin+1:pin+s_win) + grain;
  pin   = pin + s_FIR;
end
%UUUUUUUUUUUUUUUUUUUUUUUUUUUUUUUUUUUUUUUUUUUUU
toc

%----- listening and saving the output -----
% DAFx_in  = DAFx_in(s_win+1:s_win+L);
DAFx_out = DAFx_out / max(abs(DAFx_out));
soundsc(DAFx_out, FS);
wavwrite(DAFx_out, FS, 'la_filter.wav');
```

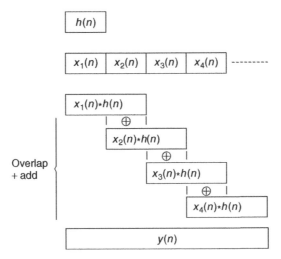

Figure 7.21   FFT filtering.

The design of an N-point FIR filter derived from frequency-domain specifications is a classical problem of signal processing. A simple design algorithm is the frequency sampling method [Zöl05].

7.4.2   Dispersion

When a sound is transmitted over telecommunications lines, some of the frequency bands are delayed. This spreads a sound in time, with some components of the signal being delayed. It is usually considered a default in telecommunications, but can be used musically. This dispersion effect is especially significant on transients, where the sound loses its coherence, but can also *blur* the steady-state parts. Actually, this is what happens with the phase vocoder when time scaling and if the phase is not locked. Each frequency bin coding the same partial has a different phase unfolding and then frequency, and the resulting phase of the synthesized partial may differ from the one in the original sound, resulting in dispersion.

A dispersion effect can be simulated by a filter, especially an FIR filter, whose frequency response has a frequency-dependent time delay. The only change to the previous program is to change the calculation of the FIR vector `fir`. We will now describe several filter designs for a dispersion effect.

Design 1 As an example, a linear chirp signal is a sine wave with linearly increasing frequency and has the property of having a time delay proportional to its frequency. A mathematical definition of a linear chirp signal starting from frequency zero and going to frequency f_1 during time t_1 is given by

$$\text{Chirp}(t) = \sin(\alpha t^2) \text{ with } \alpha = \pi \frac{f_1}{t_1}. \tag{7.44}$$

Sampling of this chirp signal yields the coefficients for an FIR filter. Time-frequency representations of a linear and an exponential chirp signal are shown in Figure 7.22a.

Design 2 It is also possible to numerically approximate a chirp by integrating an arbitrary frequency function of time. In this case the **MATLAB** function `cumsum` can be used to calculate the phase $\varphi(n) = \int_0^{nT} 2\pi f(\tau) d\tau + \varphi(0)$ as the integral of the time-dependent frequency $f(t)$.

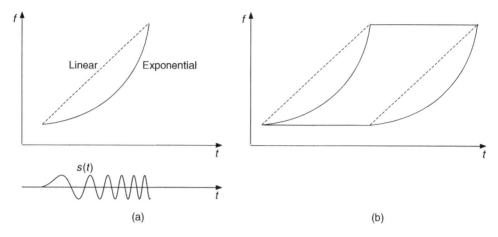

Figure 7.22 Time-frequency representations: (a) linear/exponential chirp signal and (b) time-frequency warping for the linear/exponential chirp.

A linear chirp with 300 samples can be computed by the **MATLAB** instructions:

```
n    = 300;
x    = (1:n)/n;
f0   = 50;
f1   = 4000;
freq = 2*pi * (f0+(f1-f0)*x) / 44100;
fir  = (sin(cumsum(freq)))';
```

and an exponential chirp by

```
n    = 300;
x    = (1:n)/n;
f0   = 50;
f1   = 4000;
rap  = f1/f0;
freq = (2*pi*f0/44100) * (rap.^x);
fir  = (sin(cumsum(freq)))';
```

Any other frequency function $f(t)$ can be used for the calculation of `freq`.

Design 3 Nevertheless these chirp signals deliver the frequency as a function of time delay. We would be more likely to define the time delay as a function of frequency. This is only possible with the previous technique if the function is monotonous. Thus in a more general case we can use the phase information of an FFT as an indication of the time delay corresponding to a frequency bin: the phase of a delayed signal $x(n - M)$, which has a discrete Fourier transform $X(k)e^{-jM\frac{2\pi k}{N}}$ with $k = 0, 1, \ldots, N/2$, is $\varphi(k) = -M\frac{2\pi k}{N}$, where M is the delay in samples, k is the number of the frequency bin and N is the length of the FFT.

A variable delay for each frequency bin can be achieved by replacing the fixed value M (the delay of each frequency bin) by a function $M(k)$, which leads to $X(k)e^{-jM(k)\frac{2\pi k}{N}}$. For example, a linearly increasing time delay for each frequency bin is given by $M(k) = M \cdot \frac{k}{N}$ with $k = 0, 1, \ldots, N/2 - 1$. The derivation of the FIR coefficients can be achieved by performing an IFFT of the positive part of the spectrum and then taking the real part of the resulting complex-valued coefficients. With this technique a linear chirp signal centered around the middle of the window can be computed by the following **MATLAB** instructions:

```
M    = 300;
WLen = 1024;
mask = [1; 2*ones(WLen/2-1,1); 1 ; zeros(WLen/2-1,1)];
fs   = M*(0:WLen/2)' / WLen; % linear increasing delay
teta = [-2*pi*fs.*(0:WLen/2)'/WLen ; zeros(WLen/2-1,1)];
f2   = exp(i*teta);
fir  = fftshift(real(ifft(f2.*mask)));
```

It should be noted that this technique can produce time aliasing. The length of the FIR filter will be greater than M. A proper choice of N is needed, for example $N > 2M$.

Design 4 A final technique is to draw an arbitrary curve on a time-frequency representation, which is an invalid image, and then resynthesize a signal by forcing a reconstruction, for example, by using a summation of gaborets. Then we can use this reconstructed signal as the impulse response of the FIR filter. If the curve displays the dispersion of a filter, we get a dispersive filter.

In conclusion, we can say that dispersion, which is a filtering operation, can be perceived as a delay operation. This leads to a warping of the time-frequency representation, where each horizontal line of this representation is delayed according to the dispersion curve (see Figure 7.22b).

7.4.3   Time stretching

Time-frequency scaling is one of the most interesting and difficult tasks that can be assigned to time-frequency representations: changing the time scale independently of the "frequency content." For example, one can change the rhythm of a song without changing its pitch, or conversely transpose a song without any time change. Time stretching is not a problem that can be stated outside of the perception: we know, for example, that a sum of two sinusoids is equivalent to a product of a carrier and a modulator. Should time stretching of this signal still be a sum of two sinusoids or the same carrier with a lower modulation? This leads us to the perception of tremolo tones or vibrato tones. One generally agrees that tremolos and vibratos under 10 Hz are perceived as such and those over are perceived as a sum of sinusoids. Another example is the exponential decay of sounds produced by percussive gesture (percussions, plucked strings, etc.): should the time-scaled version of such a sound have a natural exponential decay? When time scaling without modeling such aspects, the decay is stretched too, so the exponential decay is modified, potentially resulting in non-physically realistic sounds. A last example is voice (sung or spoken): the perception of some consonants is modified into others when the sound is time scaled, highlighting the fact that it can be interesting to refine such models by modeling the sound content and using non-linear or adaptive processing. Right now, we explain straight time stretching with time-frequency representations and constant control parameters.

One technique has already been evaluated in the time domain (see PSOLA in Section 6.3.3). Here we will deal with another technique in the time-frequency domain using the phase vocoder implementations of Section 7.3. There are two implementations for time-frequency scaling by the "traditional" phase vocoder. Historically, the first one uses a bank of oscillators, whose amplitudes and frequencies vary over time. If we can manage to model a sound by the sum of sinusoids, time stretching and pitch shifting can be performed by expanding the amplitude and frequency functions. The second implementation uses the sliding Fourier transform as the model for resynthesis: if we can manage to spread the image of a sliding FFT over time and calculate new phases, then we can reconstruct a new sound with the help of inverse FFTs. Both of these techniques rely on phase interpolation, which need an unwrapping algorithm at the analysis stage, or equivalently an instantaneous frequency calculation, as introduced in Section 7.3.5.

The time-stretching algorithm mainly consists of providing a synthesis grid which is different from the analysis grid, and to find a way to reconstruct a signal from the values on this grid. Though it is possible to use any stretching factor, we will here only deal with the case where we use an integer both for the analysis hop size R_a, and for the synthesis hop size R_s.

As seen in Section 7.3, changing the values and their coordinates on a time-frequency representation is generally not a valid operation, in the sense that the resulting representation is not the sliding Fourier transform of a real signal. However, it is always possible to force the reconstruction of a sound from an arbitrary image, but the time-frequency representation of the signal issued from this forced synthesis will be different from what was expected. The goal of a good transformation algorithm is to find a strategy that preserves the time-stretching aspect without introducing too many artifacts.

The classical way of using a phase vocoder for time stretching is to keep the magnitude unchanged and to modify the phase in such a way that the instantaneous frequencies are preserved. Providing that the grid is enlarged from an analysis hop size R_a to a synthesis hop size R_s, this means that the new phase values must satisfy $\Delta\psi(k) = \frac{R_s}{R_a}\Delta\varphi(k)$ (see Figure 7.23). Once the grid is filled with these values one can reconstruct a signal using either the filter-bank approach or the block-by-block IFFT approach.

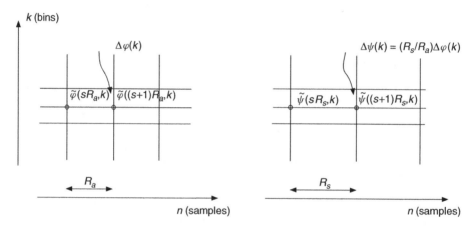

Figure 7.23 Time-stretching principle: analysis with hop size R_a gives the time-frequency grid shown in the left part, where $\Delta\varphi(k) = \tilde{\varphi}((s+1)R_a, k) - \tilde{\varphi}(sR_a, k)$ denotes the phase difference between the unwrapped phases. The synthesis is performed from the modified time-frequency grid with hop size R_s and the phase difference $\Delta\psi(k) = \tilde{\psi}((s+1)R_s, k) - \tilde{\psi}(sR_s, k)$, which is illustrated in the right part.

Filter-bank approach (sum of sinusoids)

In the FFT analysis/sum of sinusoids synthesis approach, we calculate the instantaneous frequency for each bin and integrate the corresponding phase increment in order to reconstruct a signal as the weighted sum of cosines of the phases. However, here the hop size for the resynthesis is different from the analysis. Therefore the following steps are necessary:

(1) Calculate the phase increment per sample by $d\psi(k) = \Delta\varphi(k)/R_a$.

(2) For the output samples of the resynthesis integrate this value according to $\tilde{\psi}(n+1, k) = \tilde{\psi}(n, k) + d\psi(k)$.

(3) Sum the intermediate signals which yields $y(n) = \sum_{k=0}^{N/2} A(n, k) \cos(\tilde{\psi}(n, k))$ (see Figure 7.24).

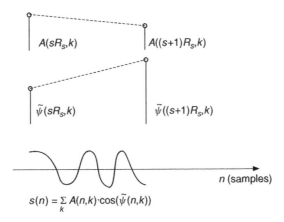

$$s(n) = \sum_{k} A(n,k) \cdot \cos(\tilde{\psi}(n,k))$$

Figure 7.24 Calculation of time-frequency samples. Given the values of A and $\tilde{\psi}$ on the representation grid, we can perform linear interpolation with a hop size between two successive values on the grid. The reconstruction is achieved by a summation of weighted cosines.

A complete **MATLAB** program for time stretching is given by M-file 7.8.

M-file 7.8 (VX_tstretch_bank.m)

```
% VX_tstretch_bank.m      [DAFXbook, 2nd ed., chapter 7]
%===== This program performs time stretching
%===== using the oscillator bank approach
clear; clf
%----- user data -----
n1            = 256;  % analysis step increment [samples]
n2            = 512;  % synthesis step increment [samples]
s_win         = 2048; % analysis window length [samples]
[DAFx_in, FS] = wavread('la.wav');
%----- initialize windows, arrays, etc -----
tstretch_ratio = n2/n1
w1          = hanning(s_win, 'periodic'); % analysis window
w2          = w1;            % synthesis window
L           = length(DAFx_in);
DAFx_in  = [zeros(s_win, 1); DAFx_in; ...
   zeros(s_win-mod(L,n1),1)] / max(abs(DAFx_in)); % 0-pad & normalize
DAFx_out = zeros(s_win+ceil(length(DAFx_in)*tstretch_ratio),1);
grain       = zeros(s_win,1);
ll          = s_win/2;
omega       = 2*pi*n1*[0:ll-1]'/s_win;
phi0        = zeros(ll,1);
r0          = zeros(ll,1);
psi         = zeros(ll,1);
res         = zeros(n2,1);
%UUUUUUUUUUUUUUUUUUUUUUUUUUUUUUUUUUUUUUUUUUUUUUU
pin  = 0;
pout = 0;
```

```
pend = length(DAFx_in)-s_win;
while pin<pend
  grain = DAFx_in(pin+1:pin+s_win).* w1;
%===========================================
  fc  = fft(fftshift(grain));
  f   = fc(1:l1);
  r   = abs(f);
  phi = angle(f);
  %----- calculate phase increment per block -----
  delta_phi = omega + princarg(phi-phi0-omega);
  %----- calculate phase & mag increments per sample -----
  delta_r   = (r-r0) / n2;    % for synthesis
  delta_psi = delta_phi / n1; % derived from analysis
  %----- computing output samples for current block -----
  for k=1:n2
    r0  = r0 + delta_r;
    psi = psi + delta_psi;
    res(k) = r0'*cos(psi);
  end
  %----- values for processing next block -----
  phi0 = phi;
  r0   = r;
  psi  = princarg(psi);
% ===========================================
%  DAFx_out(pout+1:pout+n2) = DAFx_out(pout+1:pout+n2)+res;
  DAFx_out(pout+1:pout+n2) = res;
  pin  = pin + n1;
  pout = pout + n2;
end
%UUUUUUUUUUUUUUUUUUUUUUUUUUUUUUUUUUUUUUUUUUUUU
%----- listening and saving the output -----
% DAFx_in = DAFx_in(s_win+1:s_win+L);
DAFx_out=DAFx_out(s_win/2+n1+1:length(DAFx_out))/max(abs(DAFx_out));
soundsc(DAFx_out, FS);
wavwrite(DAFx_out, FS, 'la_tstretch_bank.wav');
```

This program first extracts a series of sound segments called grains. For each grain the FFT is computed to yield a magnitude and phase representation every n1 samples (n1 is the analysis hop size R_a). It then calculates a sequence of n2 samples (n2 is the synthesis hop size R_s) of the output signal by interpolating the values of r and calculating the phase psi in such a way that the instantaneous frequency derived from psi is equal to the one derived from phi. The unwrapping of the phase is then done by calculating (phi-phi0-omega), putting it in the range $[-\pi, \pi]$ and again adding omega. A phase increment per sample d_psi is calculated from delta_phi/n1. The calculation of the magnitude and phase at the resynthesis is done in the loop for k=1:n2 where r and psi are incremented by d_r and d_psi. The program uses the vector facility of **MATLAB** to calculate the sum of the cosine of the angles weighted by magnitude in one step. This gives a buffer res of n2 output samples which will be inserted into the DAFx_out signal.

Block-by-block approach (FFT/IFFT)

Here we follow the FFT/IFFT implementation used in Section 7.3, but the hop size for resynthesis is different from the analysis. So we have to calculate new phase values in order to preserve the instantaneous frequencies for each bin. This is again done by calculating an unwrapped phase difference for each frequency bin, which is proportional to $\frac{R_s}{R_a}$. We also have to take care of some implementation details, such as the fact that the period of the window has to be equal to the length of the FFT (this is not the case for the standard **MATLAB** functions). The synthesis hop size should at least allow a minimal overlap of windows, or should be a submultiple of it. It is suggested to use overlap values of at least 75% (i.e., $R_a \leq n_1/4$). The following M-file 7.9 demonstrates the block-by-block FFT/IFFT implementation.

M-file 7.9 (VX_tstretch_real_pv.m)

```
% VX_tstretch_real_pv.m    [DAFXbook, 2nd ed., chapter 7]
%===== This program performs time stretching
%===== using the FFT-IFFT approach, for real ratios
clear; clf

%----- user data -----
n1          = 200;      % analysis step [samples]
n2          = 512;      % synthesis step ([samples]
s_win       = 2048;     % analysis window length [samples]
[DAFx_in,FS] = wavread('la.wav');

%----- initialize windows, arrays, etc -----
tstretch_ratio = n2/n1
w1          = hanning(s_win, 'periodic'); % analysis window
w2          = w1;       % synthesis window
L           = length(DAFx_in);
DAFx_in     = [zeros(s_win, 1); DAFx_in; ...
    zeros(s_win-mod(L,n1),1)] / max(abs(DAFx_in));
DAFx_out = zeros(s_win+ceil(length(DAFx_in)*tstretch_ratio),1);
omega       = 2*pi*n1*[0:s_win-1]'/s_win;
phi0        = zeros(s_win,1);
psi         = zeros(s_win,1);

tic
%UUUUUUUUUUUUUUUUUUUUUUUUUUUUUUUUUUUUUUUUUUUUUUUU
pin  = 0;
pout = 0;
pend = length(DAFx_in)-s_win;
while pin<pend
  grain = DAFx_in(pin+1:pin+s_win).* w1;
%==========================================
  f     = fft(fftshift(grain));
  r     = abs(f);
  phi   = angle(f);
  %---- computing input phase increment ----
  delta_phi = omega + princarg(phi-phi0-omega);
  %---- computing output phase increment ----
  psi   = princarg(psi+delta_phi*tstretch_ratio);
  %---- comouting synthesis Fourier transform & grain ----
  ft    = (r.* exp(i*psi));
  grain = fftshift(real(ifft(ft))).*w2;
  % plot(grain);drawnow;
% ==========================================
  DAFx_out(pout+1:pout+s_win) = ...
    DAFx_out(pout+1:pout+s_win) + grain;
  %----- for next block -----
  phi0 = phi;
```

```
  pin  = pin + n1;
  pout = pout + n2;
end
%UUUUUUUUUUUUUUUUUUUUUUUUUUUUUUUUUUUUUUUUUUUU
toc

%----- listening and saving the output -----
%DAFx_in  = DAFx_in(s_win+1:s_win+L);
DAFx_out = DAFx_out(s_win+1:length(DAFx_out))/max(abs(DAFx_out));
soundsc(DAFx_out, FS);
wavwrite(DAFx_out, FS, 'la_tstretch_noint_pv.wav');
```

This program is much faster than the preceding one. It extracts grains of the input signal by windowing the original signal DAFx_in, makes a transformation of these grains and overlap-adds these transformed grains to get a sound DAFx_out. The transformation consists of performing the FFT of the grain and computing the magnitude and phase representation r and phi. The unwrapping of the phase is then done by calculating (phi-phi0-omega), putting it in the range $[-\pi, \pi]$ and again adding omega. The calculation of the phase psi of the transformed grain is then achieved by adding the phase increment delta_phi multiplied by the stretching factor ral to the previous unwrapped phase value. As seen before, this is equivalent to keeping the same instantaneous frequency for the synthesis as is calculated for the analysis. The new output grain is then calculated by an inverse FFT, windowed again and overlap-added to the output signal.

Hints and drawbacks As we have noticed, phase vocoding can produce artifacts. It is important to know them in order to face them.

(1) Changing the phases before the IFFT is equivalent to using an all pass filter whose Fourier transform contains the phase correction that is being applied. If we do not use a window for the resynthesis, we can ensure the circular convolution aspect of this filtering operation. We will have discontinuities at the edges of the signal buffer. So it is necessary to use a synthesis window.

(2) Nevertheless, even with a resynthesis window (also called *tapering window*) the circular aspect still remains: the result is the aliased version of an infinite IFFT. A way to counteract this is to choose a zero-padded window for analysis and synthesis.

(3) Shape of the window: one must ensure that a perfect reconstruction is given with a ratio $\frac{R_s}{R_a}$ equal to one (no time stretching). If we use the same window for analysis and synthesis, the sum of the square of the windows, regularly spaced at the resynthesis hope size, should be one.

(4) For a Hanning window without zero-padding the hop size R_s has to be a divisor of $N/4$.

(5) Hamming and Blackman windows provide smaller side lobes in the Fourier transform. However, they have the inconvenience of being non-zero at the edges, so that no tapering is done by using these windows alone. The resynthesis hop size should be a divisor of $N/8$.

(6) Truncated Gaussian windows, which are good candidates, provide a sum that always has oscillations, but which can be below the level of perception.

Phase dispersion An important problem is the difference of phase unwrapping between different bins, which is not solved by the algorithms we presented: the unwrapping algorithm of the analysis gives a phase that is equal to the measured phase modulo 2π. So the unwrapped phase is equal to the measured phase plus a term that is a multiple of 2π. This second term is not the same for every bin. Because of the multiplication by the time-stretching ratio, there is a dispersion of the phases. One cannot even ensure that two identical successive sounds will be treated in the same way. This is in fact the main drawback of the phase vocoder and its removal is treated in several publications [QM98, Fer99, LD99a, Lar03, Röb03, Röb10].

Phase-locked vocoder

One of the most successful approaches to reduce the phase dispersion was proposed in [LD99a]. If we consider the processed sound to be mostly composed of quasi-sinusoidal components, then we can approximate its spectrum as the sum of the complex convolution of each of those components by the analysis window transform (this will be further explained in the spectral processing chapter). When we transform the sound, for instance time stretching it, the phase of those quasi-sinusoidal components has to propagate accordingly. What is really interesting here is that for each sinusoid the effect of the phase propagation on the spectrum is nothing more than a constant phase rotation of all the spectral bins affected by it. This method is referred to as phase-locked vocoder, since the phase of each spectral bin is locked to the phase of one spectral peak.

Starting from the previous M-file, we need to add the following steps to the processing loop:

(1) Find spectral peaks. A good tradeoff is to find local maxima in a predefined frequency range, for instance considering two bins around each candidate. This helps to minimize spurious peaks as well as to reduce the likelihood of identifying analysis window transform side-lobes as spectral peaks.

(2) Connect current peaks to previous frame peaks. The simplest approach is to choose the closest peak in frequency.

(3) Propagate peaks. A simple but usually effective strategy is to consider that peaks evolve linearly in frequency.

(4) Rotate equally all bins assigned to each spectral peak. The assignment can be performed by segmenting the spectrum into frequency regions delimited by the middle bin between consecutive peaks. An alternative is to set the segment boundaries to the bin with minimum amplitude between consecutive peaks.

Furthermore, the code can be optimized taking into account that the spectrum of a real signal is hermitic, so that we do only need to process the first half of the spectrum. A complete **MATLAB** program for time stretching using the phase-locked vocoder is given by M-file 7.10.

M-file 7.10 (VX_tstretch_real_pv_phaselocked.m)

```
% VX_tstretch_real_pv_phaselocked.m   [DAFXbook, 2nd ed., chapter 7]
%===== this program performs real ratio time stretching using the
%===== FFT-IFFT approach, applying spectral peak phase-locking
clear; clf

%----- user data -----
n1          = 256;    % analysis step [samples]
n2          = 300;    % synthesis step ([samples]
s_win       = 2048;   % analysis window length [samples]
[DAFx_in,FS] = wavread('la.wav');

%----- initialize windows, arrays, etc -----
tstretch_ratio = n2/n1
hs_win      = s_win/2;
w1          = hanning(s_win, 'periodic'); % analysis window
```

```
w2          = w1;    % synthesis window
L           = length(DAFx_in);
DAFx_in     = [zeros(s_win, 1); DAFx_in; ...
  zeros(s_win-mod(L,n1),1)] / max(abs(DAFx_in));
DAFx_out    = zeros(s_win+ceil(length(DAFx_in)*tstretch_ratio),1);
omega       = 2*pi*n1*[0:hs_win]'/s_win;
phi0        = zeros(hs_win+1,1);
psi         = zeros(hs_win+1,1);
psi2        = psi;
nprevpeaks = 0;

tic
%UUUUUUUUUUUUUUUUUUUUUUUUUUUUUUUUUUUUUUUUUUUU
pin  = 0;
pout = 0;
pend = length(DAFx_in) - s_win;
while pin<pend
   grain = DAFx_in(pin+1:pin+s_win).* w1;
   %==========================================
   f     = fft(fftshift(grain));
   %---- optimization: only process the first 1/2 of the spectrum
   f     = f(1:hs_win+1);
   r     = abs(f);
   phi   = angle(f);
   %---- find spectral peaks (local maxima) ----
   peak_loc = zeros(hs_win+1,1);
   npeaks = 0;
   for b=3:hs_win-1
     if ( r(b)>r(b-1) && r(b)>r(b-2) && r(b)>r(b+1) && r(b)>r(b+2) )
       npeaks = npeaks+1;
       peak_loc(npeaks) = b;
       b = b + 3;
     end
   end
   %---- propagate peak phases and compute spectral bin phases
   if (pin==0) % init
     psi = phi;
   elseif (npeaks>0 && nprevpeaks>0)
     prev_p = 1;
     for p=1:npeaks
       p2 = peak_loc(p);
       %---- connect current peak to the previous closest peak
       while (prev_p < nprevpeaks && abs(p2-prev_peak_loc(prev_p+1)) ...
           < abs(p2-prev_peak_loc(prev_p)))
         prev_p = prev_p+1;
       end
       p1 = prev_peak_loc(prev_p);
       %---- propagate peak's phase assuming linear frequency
       %---- variation between connected peaks p1 and p2
       avg_p = (p1 + p2)*.5;
       pomega = 2*pi*n1*(avg_p-1.)/s_win;
       % N.B.: avg_p is a 1-based indexing spectral bin
       peak_delta_phi = pomega + princarg(phi(p2)-phi0(p1)-pomega);
       peak_target_phase = princarg(psi(p1) + peak_delta_phi*tstretch_ratio);
       peak_phase_rotation = princarg(peak_target_phase-phi(p2));
       %---- rotate phases of all bins around the current peak
       if (npeaks==1)
```

```
        bin1 = 1; bin2 = hs_win+1;
      elseif (p==1)
        bin1 = 1; bin2 = hs_win+1;
      elseif (p==npeaks)
        bin1 = round((peak_loc(p-1)+p2)*.5);
        bin2 = hs_win+1;
      else
        bin1 = round((peak_loc(p-1)+p2)*.5)+1;
        bin2 = round((peak_loc(p+1)+p2)*.5);
      end
      psi2(bin1:bin2) = princarg(phi(bin1:bin2) + peak_phase_rotation);
    end
    psi = psi2;
  else
    delta_phi = omega + princarg(phi-phi0-omega);
    psi       = princarg(psi+delta_phi*tstretch_ratio);
  end

  ft    = (r.^ exp(i*psi));
  %---- reconstruct whole spectrum (it is hermitic!)
  ft    = [ ft(1:hs_win+1) ; conj(ft(hs_win:-1:2)) ];
  grain = fftshift(real(ifft(ft))).*w2;
  % plot(grain);drawnow;
  % =========================================
  DAFx_out(pout+1:pout+s_win) = ...
    DAFx_out(pout+1:pout+s_win) + grain;
  %---- store values for next frame ----
  phi0  = phi;
  prev_peak_loc = peak_loc;
  nprevpeaks    = npeaks;
  pin   = pin + n1;
  pout  = pout + n2;
end
%UUUUUUUUUUUUUUUUUUUUUUUUUUUUUUUUUUUUUUUUUUUU
toc

%----- listening and saving the output -----
%DAFx_in  = DAFx_in(s_win+1:s_win+L);
DAFx_out = DAFx_out(s_win+1:length(DAFx_out))/max(abs(DAFx_out));
soundsc(DAFx_out, FS);
wavwrite(DAFx_out, FS, 'la_tstretch_noint_pv_phaselocked.wav');
```

Integer ratio time stretching

When the time-stretching ratio is an integer (e.g., time stretching by 200%, 300%), the unwrapping is no longer necessary in the algorithm, because the 2π modulo relation is still preserved when the phase is multiplied by an integer. The key point here is that we can make a direct multiplication of the analysis phase to get the phase for synthesis. So in this case it is more obvious and elegant to use the following algorithm, given by M-file 7.11.

M-file 7.11 (VX_tstretch_int_pv.m)

```
% VX_tstretch_int_pv.m    [DAFXbook, 2nd ed., chapter 7]
%===== This program performs integer ratio time stretching
```

```
%===== using the FFT-IFFT approach
clear; clf

%----- user data -----
n1          = 64;      % analysis step [samples]
n2          = 512;     % synthesis step ([samples]
s_win       = 2048;    % analysis window length [samples]
[DAFx_in,FS] = wavread('la.wav');

%----- initialize windows, arrays, etc -----
tstretch_ratio = n2/n1
w1          = hanning(s_win, 'periodic'); % analysis window
w2          = w1;      % synthesis window
L           = length(DAFx_in);
DAFx_in     = [zeros(s_win, 1); DAFx_in; ...
    zeros(s_win-mod(L,n1),1)] / max(abs(DAFx_in));
DAFx_out    = zeros(s_win+ceil(length(DAFx_in)*tstretch_ratio),1);
omega       = 2*pi*n1*[0:s_win-1]'/s_win;
phi0        = zeros(s_win,1);
psi         = zeros(s_win,1);

tic
%UUUUUUUUUUUUUUUUUUUUUUUUUUUUUUUUUUUUUUUUUUUUUU
pin  = 0;
pout = 0;
pend = length(DAFx_in)-s_win;

while pin<pend
  grain = DAFx_in(pin+1:pin+s_win) .* w1;
%=============================================
  f     = fft(fftshift(grain));
  r     = abs(f);
  phi   = angle(f);
  ft    = (r .* exp(i*tstretch_ratio*phi));
  grain = fftshift(real(ifft(ft))) .*w2;
% =============================================
  DAFx_out(pout+1:pout+s_win) = ...
    DAFx_out(pout+1:pout+s_win) + grain;
  pin   = pin + n1;
  pout  = pout + n2;
end
%UUUUUUUUUUUUUUUUUUUUUUUUUUUUUUUUUUUUUUUUUUUUUU
toc

%----- listening and saving the output -----
% DAFx_in  = DAFx_in(s_win+1:s_win+L);
DAFx_out = DAFx_out(s_win+1:length(DAFx_out))/max(abs(DAFx_out));
soundsc(DAFx_out, FS);
wavwrite(DAFx_out, FS, 'la_stretch_int_pv.wav');
```

7.4.4 Pitch shifting

Pitch shifting is different from frequency shifting: a frequency shift is an addition to every frequency (i.e., the magnitude spectrum is shifted), while pitch shifting is the multiplication of every frequency by a transposition factor (i.e., the magnitude spectrum is scaled). Pitch shifting can be directly linked

Figure 7.25   Resampling of a time-stretching algorithm.

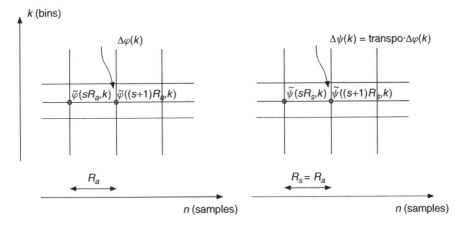

Figure 7.26   Pitch shifting with the filter-bank approach: the analysis gives the time-frequency grid with analysis hop size R_a. For the synthesis the hop size is set to $R_s = R_a$ and the phase difference is calculated according to $\Delta\psi(k) = \texttt{transpo}\ \Delta\varphi(k)$.

to time stretching. Resampling a time-stretched signal with the inverse of the time-stretching ratio performs pitch shifting and going back to the initial duration of the signal (see Figure 7.25). There are, however, alternative solutions which allow the direct calculation of a pitch-shifted version of a sound.

Filter-bank approach (sum of sinusoids)

In the time-stretching algorithm using the sum of sinusoids (see Section 7.3) we have an evaluation of instantaneous frequencies. As a matter of fact transposing all the instantaneous frequencies can lead to an efficient pitch-shifting algorithm. Therefore the following steps have to be performed (see Figure 7.26):

(1) Calculate the phase increment per sample by $d\varphi(k) = \Delta\varphi(k)/R_a$.

(2) Multiply the phase increment by the transposition factor $\texttt{transpo}$ and integrate the modified phase increment according to $\tilde{\psi}(n+1, k) = \tilde{\psi}(n, k)+ \texttt{transpo}\ \cdot\Delta\varphi(k)/R_a$.

(3) Calculate the sum of sinusoids: when the transposition factor is greater than one, keep only frequencies under the Nyquist frequency bin $N/2$. This can be done by taking only the $\texttt{N/(2*transpo)}$ frequency bins.

The following M-file 7.12 is similar to the program given by M-file 7.8 with the exception of a few lines: the definition of the hop size and the resynthesis phase increment have been changed.

M-file 7.12 (VX_pitch_bank.m)

```
% VX_pitch_bank.m    [DAFXbook, 2nd ed., chapter 7]
%===== This program performs pitch shifting
%===== using the oscillator bank approach
clear; clf

%----- user data -----
n1         = 512;     % analysis step [samples]
pit_ratio  = 1.2      % pitch-shifting ratio
s_win      = 2048;    % analysis window length [samples]
[DAFx_in,FS] = wavread('la.wav');

%----- initialize windows, arrays, etc -----
w1         = hanning(s_win, 'periodic'); % analysis window
w2         = w1;     % synthesis window
L          = length(DAFx_in);
DAFx_in    = [zeros(s_win, 1); DAFx_in; ...
   zeros(s_win-mod(L,n1),1)] / max(abs(DAFx_in));
DAFx_out = zeros(length(DAFx_in),1);
grain      = zeros(s_win,1);
hs_win     = s_win/2;
omega      = 2*pi*n1*[0:hs_win-1]'/s_win;
phi0       = zeros(hs_win,1);
r0         = zeros(hs_win,1);
psi        = phi0;
res        = zeros(n1,1);

tic
%UUUUUUUUUUUUUUUUUUUUUUUUUUUUUUUUUUUUUUUUUUU
pin  = 0;
pout = 0;
pend = length(DAFx_in)-s_win;

while pin<pend
  grain = DAFx_in(pin+1:pin+s_win).* w1;
%=========================================
  fc  = fft(fftshift(grain));
  f   = fc(1:hs_win);
  r   = abs(f);
  phi = angle(f);
  %---- compute phase & mangitude increments ----
  delta_phi = omega + princarg(phi-phi0-omega);
  delta_r   = (r-r0)/n1;
  delta_psi = pit_ratio*delta_phi/n1;
  %---- compute output buffer ----
  for k=1:n1
    r0      = r0 + delta_r;
    psi     = psi + delta_psi;
    res(k)  = r0' * cos(psi);
  end
  %---- store for next block ----
  phi0 = phi;
  r0   = r;
  psi  = princarg(psi);
% plot(res);pause;
% =========================================
```

```
DAFx_out(pout+1:pout+n1) = DAFx_out(pout+1:pout+n1) + res;
pin  = pin + n1;
pout = pout + n1;
end
%UUUUUUUUUUUUUUUUUUUUUUUUUUUUUUUUUUUUUUUUU
toc

%----- listening and saving the output -----
% DAFx_in = DAFx_in(s_win+1:s_win+L);
DAFx_out = DAFx_out(hs_win+n1+1:hs_win+n1+L) / max(abs(DAFx_out));
soundsc(DAFx_out, FS);
wavwrite(DAFx_out, FS, 'la_pitch_bank.wav');
```

The program is derived from the time-stretching program using the oscillator-bank approach in a straightforward way: this time the hop size for analysis and synthesis are the same, and a pitch transpose argument `pit` must be defined. This argument will be multiplied by the phase increment `delta_phi/n1` derived from the analysis to get the phase increment `d_psi` in the calculation loop. This means of course that we consider the pitch transposition as fixed in this program, but easy changes may be done to make it vary with time.

Block-by-block approach (FFT/IFFT)

The regular way to deal with pitch shifting using this technique is first to resample the whole output once computed, but this can alternatively be done by resampling the result of every IFFT and overlapping with a hop size equal to the analysis one (see Figure 7.27). Providing that R_s is a divider of N (FFT length), which is quite a natural way for time stretching (to ensure that the sum of the square of windows is equal to one), one can resample each IFFT result to a length of $N\frac{R_a}{R_s}$ and overlap with a hop size of R_a. Another method of resampling is to use the property of the inverse FFT: if $R_a < R_s$, we can take an IFFT of length $N\frac{R_a}{R_s}$ by taking only the first bins of the initial FFT. If $R_a > R_s$, we can zero pad the FFT, before the IFFT is performed. In each of these cases the result is a resampled grain of length $N\frac{R_a}{R_s}$.

The following M-file 7.13 implements pitch shifting with integrated resampling according to Figure 7.27. The M-file is similar to the program given by M-file 7.11, except for the definition of the hop sizes and the calculation for the interpolation.

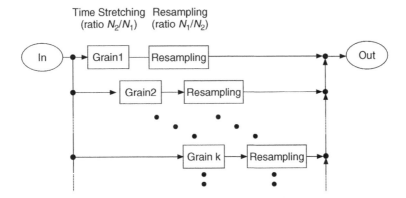

Figure 7.27 Pitch shifting with integrated resampling: for each grain time stretching and resampling are performed. An overlap-add procedure delivers the output signal.

M-file 7.13 (VX_pitch_pv.m)

```
% VX_pitch_pv.m    [DAFXbook, 2nd ed., chapter 7]
%===== This program performs pitch shifting
%===== using the FFT/IFFT approach
clear; clf

%----- user data -----
n2          = 512;    % synthesis step [samples]
pit_ratio   = 1.2     % pitch-shifting ratio
s_win       = 2048;   % analysis window length [samples]
[DAFx_in,FS] = wavread('flute2');

%----- initialize windows, arrays, etc -----
n1        = round(n2 / pit_ratio);     % analysis step [samples]
tstretch_ratio = n2/n1;
w1        = hanning(s_win, 'periodic'); % analysis window
w2        = w1;    % synthesis window
L         = length(DAFx_in);
DAFx_in   = [zeros(s_win, 1); DAFx_in; ...
   zeros(s_win-mod(L,n1),1)] / max(abs(DAFx_in));
DAFx_out = zeros(length(DAFx_in),1);
omega     = 2*pi*n1*[0:hs_win-1]'/s_win;
phi0      = zeros(s_win,1);
psi       = zeros(s_win,1);

%----- for linear interpolation of a grain of length s_win -----
lx   = floor(s_win*n1/n2);
x    = 1 + (0:lx-1)'*s_win/lx;
ix   = floor(x);
ix1  = ix + 1;
dx   = x - ix;
dx1  = 1 - dx;


tic
%UUUUUUUUUUUUUUUUUUUUUUUUUUUUUUUUUUUUUUUUUUUUU
pin  = 0;
pout = 0;
pend = length(DAFx_in)-s_win;

while pin<pend
  grain = DAFx_in(pin+1:pin+s_win).* w1;
%============================================
  f     = fft(fftshift(grain));
  r     = abs(f);
  phi   = angle(f);
  %---- computing phase increment ----
  delta_phi = omega + princarg(phi-phi0-omega);
  phi0  = phi;
  psi   = princarg(psi+delta_phi*tstretch_ratio);
  %---- synthesizing time scaled grain ----
  ft    = (r.* exp(i*psi));
  grain = fftshift(real(ifft(ft))).*w2;
  %----- interpolating grain -----
  grain2 = [grain;0];
  grain3 = grain2(ix).*dx1+grain2(ix1).*dx;
```

```
%  plot(grain);drawnow;
%  =================================================
   DAFx_out(pout+1:pout+lx) = DAFx_out(pout+1:pout+lx) + grain3;
   pin    = pin + n1;
   pout   = pout + n1;
   end
%UUUUUUUUUUUUUUUUUUUUUUUUUUUUUUUUUUUUUUUUUUUUUU
toc

%----- listening and saving the output -----
% DAFx_in  = DAFx_in(s_win+1:s_win+L);
DAFx_out = DAFx_out(s_win+1:s_win+L) / max(abs(DAFx_out));
soundsc(DAFx_out, FS);
wavwrite(DAFx_out, FS, 'flute2_pitch_pv.wav');
```

This program is adapted from the time-stretching program using the FFT/IFFT approach. Here the grain is linearly interpolated before the reconstruction. The length of the interpolated grain is now `lx` and will be overlapped and added with a hop size of `n1` identical to the analysis hop size. In order to speed up the calculation of the interpolation, four vectors of length `lx` are precalculated outside the main loop, which give the necessary parameters for the interpolation (`ix`, `ix1`, `dx` and `dx1`). As stated previously, the linear interpolation is not necessarily the best one, and will surely produce some foldover when the pitch-shifting factor is greater than one. Other interpolation schemes can be inserted instead. Further pitch-shifting techniques can be found in [QM98, Lar98, LD99b].

7.4.5 Stable/transient components separation

This effect extracts "stable components" from a signal by selecting only points of the time-frequency representation that are considered as "stable in frequency" and eliminating all the other grains. Basic ideas can be found in [SL94]. From a musical point of view, one would think about getting only sine waves, and leave aside all the transient signals. However, this is not so: even with pure noise, the time-frequency analysis reveals some zones where we can have stable components. A pulse will also give an analysis where the instantaneous frequencies are the ones of the analyzing system and are very stable. Nevertheless this idea of separating a sound into two complementary sounds is indeed a musically good one. The result can be thought of as an "etherization" of the sound for the stable one, and a "fractalization" for the transient one.

The algorithm for components separation is based on instantaneous frequency computation. The increment of the phase per sample for frequency bin k can be derived as

$$d\varphi(sR_a, k) = [\tilde{\varphi}(sR_a, k) - \tilde{\varphi}((s-1)R_a, k)]/R_a. \tag{7.45}$$

We will now sort out those points of a given FFT that give

$$d\varphi(sR_a, k) - d\varphi((s-1)R_a, k) < df, \tag{7.46}$$

where df is a preset value. From (7.45) and (7.46) we can derive the condition

$$\tilde{\varphi}(sR_a, k) - 2\tilde{\varphi}((s-1)R_a, k) + \tilde{\varphi}((s-2)R_a, k) < df R_a. \tag{7.47}$$

From a geometrical point of view we can say that the value $\tilde{\varphi}(sR_a, k)$ should be in an angle $df R_a$ around the expected target value $\tilde{\varphi}_t(sR_a, k)$, as shown in Figure 7.28.

It is important to note that the instantaneous frequencies may be out of the range of frequencies of the bin itself. The reconstruction performed by the inverse FFT takes only bins that follow this

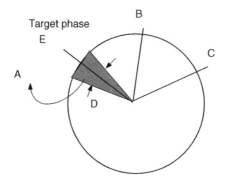

Figure 7.28 Evaluation of stable/unstable grains.

condition. In other words, only gaborets that follow the "frequency stability over time" condition are kept during the reconstruction. The following M-file 7.14 follows this guideline.

M-file 7.14 (VX_stable.m)

```
% VX_stable.m   [DAFXbook, 2nd ed., chapter 7]
%===== this program extracts the stable components of a signal
clear; clf

%----- user data -----
test         = 0.4
n1           = 256;    % analysis step [samples]
n2           = n1;     % synthesis step [samples]
s_win        = 2048;   % analysis window length [samples]
[DAFx_in,FS] = wavread('redwheel.wav');

%----- initialize windows, arrays, etc -----
w1        = hanning(s_win, 'periodic'); % analysis window
w2        = w1;     % synthesis window
L         = length(DAFx_in);
DAFx_in   = [zeros(s_win, 1); DAFx_in; ...
  zeros(s_win-mod(L,n1),1)] / max(abs(DAFx_in));
DAFx_out  = zeros(length(DAFx_in),1);
devcent   = 2*pi*n1/s_win;
vtest     = test * devcent;
grain     = zeros(s_win,1);
theta1    = zeros(s_win,1);
theta2    = zeros(s_win,1);

tic
%UUUUUUUUUUUUUUUUUUUUUUUUUUUUUUUUUUUUUUUUUUUUU
pin  = 0;
pout = 0;
pend = length(DAFx_in)-s_win;

while pin<pend
  grain = DAFx_in(pin+1:pin+s_win) .* w1;
%==========================================
  f     = fft(fftshift(grain));
  theta = angle(f);
```

```
  dev     = princarg(theta - 2*theta1 + theta2);
%   plot(dev);drawnow;
    %---- set to 0 magnitude values below 'test' threshold
    ft      = f.*(abs(dev) < vtest);
    grain   = fftshift(real(ifft(ft))).*w2;
    theta2 = theta1;
    theta1 = theta;
% ==========================================
  DAFx_out(pout+1:pout+s_win) = ...
     DAFx_out(pout+1:pout+s_win) + grain;
  pin  = pin + n1;
  pout = pout + n2;
end
%UUUUUUUUUUUUUUUUUUUUUUUUUUUUUUUUUUUUUUUUUU
toc

%----- listening and saving the output -----
% DAFx_in = DAFx_in(s_win+1:s_win+L);
DAFx_out = DAFx_out(s_win+1:s_win+L) / max(abs(DAFx_out));
soundsc(DAFx_out, FS);
wavwrite(DAFx_out, FS, 'redwheel_stable.wav');
```

So the algorithm for extraction of stable components performs the following steps:

(1) Calculate the instantaneous frequency by making the derivative of the phase along the time axis.

(2) Check if this frequency is within its "stable range."

(3) Use the frequency bin or not for the reconstruction.

The value of vtest is particularly important because it determines the level of the selection between stable and unstable bins.

The algorithm for transient components extraction is the same, except that we keep only bins where the condition (7.47) is not satisfied. So only two lines have to be changed according to

```
test = 2                 % new value for test threshold
...
ft = f*(abs(dev)>vtest); % new condition
```

In order to enhance the unstable grains the value vtest is usually higher for the transient extraction.

7.4.6   Mutation between two sounds

The idea is to calculate an arbitrary time-frequency representation from two original sounds and to reconstruct a sound from it. Some of these spectral mutations (see Figure 7.29) give a flavor of cross-synthesis and morphing, a subject that will be discussed later, but are different from it, because here the effect is only incidental, while in cross-synthesis hybridization of sounds is the primary objective. Further ideas can be found in [PE96]. There are different ways to calculate a new combined magnitude and phase diagram from the values of the original ones. As stated in Section 7.3, an arbitrary image is not valid in the sense that it is not the time-frequency representation of a sound, which means that the result will be musically biased by the resynthesis scheme that we must use. Usually phases and magnitudes are calculated in an independent way,

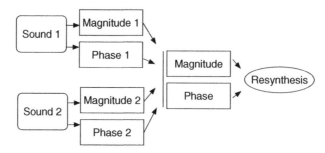

Figure 7.29   Basic principle of spectral mutations.

so that many combinations are possible. Not all of them are musically relevant, and the result also depends upon the nature of the sounds that are combined.

The following M-file 7.15 performs a mutation between two sounds where the magnitude is coming from one sound and the phase from the other. Then only a few lines need to be changed to give different variations.

M-file 7.15 (VX_mutation.m)

```
% VX_mutation.m  [DAFXbook, 2nd ed., chapter 7]
%===== this program performs a mutation between two sounds,
%===== taking the phase of the first one and the modulus
%===== of the second one, and using:
%===== w1 and w2 windows (analysis and synthesis)
%===== WLen is the length of the windows
%===== n1 and n2: steps (in samples) for the analysis and synthesis

clear; clf

%----- user data -----
n1             = 512;
n2             = n1;
WLen           = 2048;
w1             = hanningz(WLen);
w2             = w1;
[DAFx_in1,FS]  = wavread('x1.wav');
DAFx_in2       = wavread('x2.wav');

%----- initializations -----
L              = min(length(DAFx_in1),length(DAFx_in2));
DAFx_in1       = [zeros(WLen, 1); DAFx_in1; ...
   zeros(WLen-mod(L,n1),1)] / max(abs(DAFx_in1));
DAFx_in2       = [zeros(WLen, 1); DAFx_in2; ...
   zeros(WLen-mod(L,n1),1)] / max(abs(DAFx_in2));
DAFx_out       = zeros(length(DAFx_in1),1);

tic
%UUUUUUUUUUUUUUUUUUUUUUUUUUUUUUUUUUUUUUUUUUUUUUU
pin  = 0;
pout = 0;
pend = length(DAFx_in1) - WLen;

while pin<pend
```

```
    grain1 = DAFx_in1(pin+1:pin+WLen).* w1;
    grain2 = DAFx_in2(pin+1:pin+WLen).* w1;
%===========================================
    f1     = fft(fftshift(grain1));
    r1     = abs(f1);
    theta1 = angle(f1);
    f2     = fft(fftshift(grain2));
    r2     = abs(f2);
    theta2 = angle(f2);
    %----- the next two lines can be changed according to the effect
    r      = r1;
    theta  = theta2;
    ft     = (r.* exp(i*theta));
    grain  = fftshift(real(ifft(ft))).*w2;
%  ==========================================
    DAFx_out(pout+1:pout+WLen) = ...
      DAFx_out(pout+1:pout+WLen) + grain;
    pin    = pin + n1;
    pout   = pout + n2;
end
%UUUUUUUUUUUUUUUUUUUUUUUUUUUUUUUUUUUUUUUUUUUU
toc

%----- listening and saving the output -----
%DAFx_in = DAFx_in(WLen+1:WLen+L);
DAFx_out = DAFx_out(WLen+1:WLen+L) / max(abs(DAFx_out));
soundsc(DAFx_out, FS);
wavwrite(DAFx_out, FS, 'r1p2.wav');
```

Possible operations on the magnitude are:

(1) Multiplication of the magnitudes `r=r1.*r2` (so it is an addition in the dB scale). This corresponds to a logical "AND" operation, because one keeps all zones where energy is located.

(2) Addition of the magnitude: the equivalent of a logical "OR" operation. However, this is different from mixing, because one only operates on the magnitude according to `r=r1+r2`.

(3) Masking of one sound by the other is performed by keeping the magnitude of one sound if the other magnitude is under a fixed or relative threshold.

Operations on phase are really important for combinations of two sounds. Phase information is very important to ensure the validity (or quasivalidity) of time-frequency representations, and has an influence on the quality:

(1) One can keep the phase from only one sound while changing the magnitude. This is a strong cue for the pitch of the resulting sound (`theta=theta2`).

(2) One can add the two phases. In this case we strongly alter the validity of the image (the phase turns with a mean double speed). We can also double the resynthesis hop size `n2=2*n1`.

(3) One can take an arbitrary combination of the two phases, but one should remember that phases are given modulo 2π (except if they have been unwrapped).

(4) Design of an arbitrary variation of the phases.

As a matter of fact, these mutations are very experimental, and are very near to the construction of a true arbitrary time-frequency representation, but with some cues coming from the analysis of different sounds.

7.4.7   Robotization

This technique puts zero phase values on every FFT before reconstruction. The effect applies a fixed pitch onto a sound. Moreover, as it forces the sound to be periodic, many erratic and random variations are converted into robotic sounds. The sliding FFT of pulses, where the analysis is taken at the time of these pulses will give a zero phase value for the phase of the FFT. This is a clear indication that putting a zero phase before an IFFT resynthesis will give a fixed pitch sound. This is reminiscent of the PSOLA technique, but here we do not make any assumption on the frequency of the analyzed sound and no marker has to be found. So zeroing the phase can be viewed from two points of view:

(1) The result of an IFFT is a pulse-like sound and summing such grains at regular intervals gives a fixed pitch.

(2) This can also be viewed as an effect of the reproducing kernel on the time-frequency representation: due to fact that the time-frequency representation now shows a succession of vertical lines with zero values in between, this will lead to a comb-filter effect during resynthesis.

The following M-file 7.16 demonstrates the *robotization effect*.

M-file 7.16 (VX_robot.m)

```
% VX_robot.m    [DAFXbook, 2nd ed., chapter 7]
%===== this program performs a robotization of a sound
clear; clf

%----- user data -----
n1          = 441;    % analysis step [samples]
n2          = n1;     % synthesis step [samples]
s_win       = 1024;   % analysis window length [samples]
[DAFx_in,FS] = wavread('redwheel.wav');

%----- initialize windows, arrays, etc -----
w1          = hanning(s_win, 'periodic'); % analysis window
w2          = w1;     % synthesis window
L           = length(DAFx_in);
DAFx_in     = [zeros(s_win, 1); DAFx_in; ...
  zeros(s_win-mod(L,n1),1)] / max(abs(DAFx_in));
DAFx_out = zeros(length(DAFx_in),1);

tic
%UUUUUUUUUUUUUUUUUUUUUUUUUUUUUUUUUUUUUUUUUUUUUUUUU
pin  = 0;
pout = 0;
pend = length(DAFx_in)-s_win;
while pin<pend
  grain = DAFx_in(pin+1:pin+s_win) .* w1;
%=========================================
    f       = fft(grain);
    r       = abs(f);
```

```
  grain = fftshift(real(ifft(r))).*w2;
% ============================================
  DAFx_out(pout+1:pout+s_win) = ...
    DAFx_out(pout+1:pout+s_win) + grain;
  pin  = pin + n1;
  pout = pout + n2;
end
%UUUUUUUUUUUUUUUUUUUUUUUUUUUUUUUUUUUUUUUUUUUU
toc

%----- listening and saving the output -----
% DAFx_in = DAFx_in(s_win+1:s_win+L);
DAFx_out = DAFx_out(s_win+1:s_win+L) / max(abs(DAFx_out));
soundsc(DAFx_out, FS);
wavwrite(DAFx_out, FS, 'redwheel_robot.wav');
```

This is one of the shortest programs we can have, however its effect is very strong. The only drawback is that the n1 value in this program has to be an integer. The frequency of the robot is Fs/n1, where Fs is the sampling frequency. If the hop size is not an integer value, it is possible to use an interpolation scheme in order to dispatch the grain of two samples. This may happen if the hop size is calculated directly from a fundamental frequency value. An example is shown in Figure 7.30.

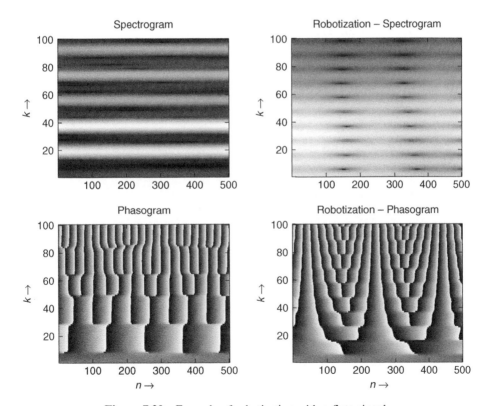

Figure 7.30   Example of robotization with a flute signal.

7.4.8 Whisperization

If we deliberately impose a random phase on a time-frequency representation, we can have a different behavior depending on the length of the window: if the window is quite large (for example, 2048 for a sampling rate of 44100 Hz), the magnitude will represent the behavior of the partials quite well and changes in phase will produce an uncertainty over the frequency. But if the window is small (e.g., 64 points), the spectral envelope will be enhanced and this will lead to a whispering effect. The M-file 7.17 implements the *whisperization effect*.

M-file 7.17 (VX_whisper.m)

```
% VX_whisper.m    [DAFXbook, 2nd ed., chapter 7]
%===== This program makes the whisperization of a sound,
%===== by randomizing the phase
clear; clf

%----- user data -----
s_win       = 512;     % analysis window length [samples]
n1          = s_win/8; % analysis step [samples]
n2          = n1;      % synthesis step [samples]
[DAFx_in,FS] = wavread('redwheel.wav');

%----- initialize windows, arrays, etc -----
w1        = hanning(s_win, 'periodic'); % analysis window
w2        = w1;      % synthesis window
L         = length(DAFx_in);
DAFx_in   = [zeros(s_win, 1); DAFx_in; ...
  zeros(s_win-mod(L,n1),1)] / max(abs(DAFx_in));
DAFx_out = zeros(length(DAFx_in),1);

tic
%UUUUUUUUUUUUUUUUUUUUUUUUUUUUUUUUUUUUUUUUUUUU
pin  = 0;
pout = 0;
pend = length(DAFx_in) - s_win;
while pin<pend
  grain = DAFx_in(pin+1:pin+s_win).* w1;
%===========================================
  f     = fft(fftshift(grain));
  r     = abs(f);
  phi   = 2*pi*rand(s_win,1);
  ft    = (r.* exp(i*phi));
  grain = fftshift(real(ifft(ft))).*w2;
% ===========================================
  DAFx_out(pout+1:pout+s_win) = ...
    DAFx_out(pout+1:pout+s_win) + grain;
  pin   = pin + n1;
  pout  = pout + n2;
end
%UUUUUUUUUUUUUUUUUUUUUUUUUUUUUUUUUUUUUUUUUUUU
toc

%----- listening and saving the output -----
% DAFx_in = DAFx_in(s_win+1:s_win+L);
DAFx_out = DAFx_out(s_win+1:s_win+L) / max(abs(DAFx_out));
```

```
soundsc(DAFx_out, FS);
wavwrite(DAFx_out, FS, 'whisper2.wav');
```

It is also possible to make a random variation of the magnitude and keep the phase. An example is shown in Figure 7.31. This gives another way to implement whisperization, which can be achieved by the following **MATLAB** kernel:

```
%=============================================
    f     = fft(fftshift(grain));
    r     = abs(f).*randn(lfen,1);
    phi   = angle(f);
    ft    = (r.* exp(i*phi));
    grain = fftshift(real(ifft(ft))).*w2;
%=============================================
```

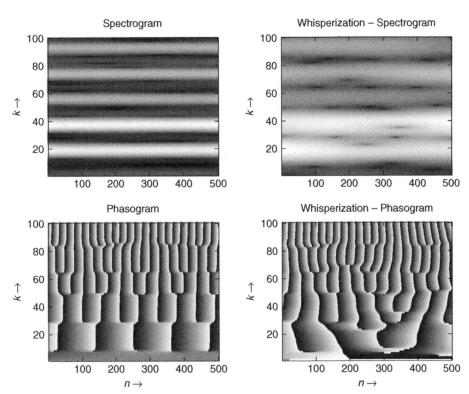

Figure 7.31   Example of whisperization with a flute signal.

7.4.9   Denoising

A musician may want to emphasize some specific areas of a spectrum and lower the noise within a sound. Though this is achieved more perfectly by the use of a sinusoidal model (see Chapter 10), another approach is the use of denoising algorithms. The algorithm we describe uses a non-linear spectral subtraction technique [Vas96]. Further techniques can be found in [Cap94]. A time-frequency analysis and resynthesis are performed, with an extraction of the magnitude and phase information. The phase is kept as it is, while the magnitude is processed in such a way

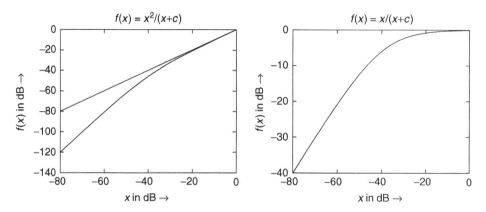

Figure 7.32   Non-linear function for a noise gate.

that it keeps the high-level values while attenuating the lower ones, in such a way as to attenuate the noise. This can also be seen as a bank of noise gates on different channels, because on each bin we perform a non-linear operation. The denoised magnitude vector $X_d(n, k) = f(X(n, k))$ of the denoised signal is then the output of a noise gate with a non-linear function $f(x)$. A basic example of such a function is $f(x) = x^2/(x + c)$, which is shown in Figure 7.32. It can also be seen as the multiplication of the magnitude vector by a correction factor $x/(x + c)$. The result of such a waveshaping function on the magnitude spectrum keeps the high values of the magnitude and lowers the small ones. Then the phase of the initial signal is reintroduced and the sound is reconstructed by overlapping grains with the help of an IFFT. The following M-file 7.18 follows this guideline.

M-file 7.18 (VX_denoise.m)

```
% VX_denoise.m   [DAFXbook, 2nd ed., chapter 7]
%===== This program makes a denoising of a sound
clear; clf

%----- user data -----
n1            = 512;    % analysis step [samples]
n2            = n1;     % synthesis step [samples]
s_win         = 2048;   % analysis window length [samples]
[DAFx_in,FS]  = wavread('redwheel.wav');

%----- initialize windows, arrays, etc -----
w1          = hanning(s_win, 'periodic'); % analysis window
w2          = w1;      % synthesis window
L           = length(DAFx_in);
DAFx_in     = [zeros(s_win, 1); DAFx_in; ...
   zeros(s_win-mod(L,n1),1)] / max(abs(DAFx_in));
DAFx_out = zeros(length(DAFx_in),1);
hs_win      = s_win/2;
coef     = 0.01;
freq     = (0:1:299)/s_win*44100;

tic
%UUUUUUUUUUUUUUUUUUUUUUUUUUUUUUUUUUUUUUUUUUUUUUUUU
```

```
pin  = 0;
pout = 0;
pend = length(DAFx_in) - s_win;

while pin<pend
  grain = DAFx_in(pin+1:pin+s_win).* w1;
%=============================================
  f     = fft(grain);
  r     = abs(f)/hs_win;
  ft    = f.*r. / (r+coef);
  grain = (real(ifft(ft))).*w2;
% =============================================
  DAFx_out(pout+1:pout+s_win) = ...
    DAFx_out(pout+1:pout+s_win) + grain;
  pin  = pin + n1;
  pout = pout + n2;
end
%UUUUUUUUUUUUUUUUUUUUUUUUUUUUUUUUUUUUUUUUUUUU
toc
%----- listening and saving the output -----
% DAFx_in  = DAFx_in(s_win+1:s_win+L);
DAFx_out = DAFx_out(s_win+1:s_win+L);
soundsc(DAFx_out, FS);
wavwrite(DAFx_out, FS, 'x1_denoise.wav');
```

An example is shown in Figure 7.33. It is of course possible to introduce different noise-gate functions instead of the simple ones we have chosen. For instance, the formulation

```
ft = f.*r. / (r+coef);
```

can be replaced by the following one:

```
ft = f.*r. / max(r,coef);
```

With the first formulation, a bias is introduced to the magnitude of each frequency bin, whereas in the second formulaiton, the bias is only introduced for frequency bins that are actually denoised.

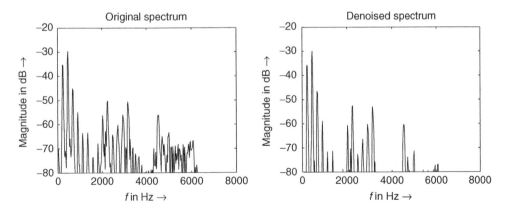

Figure 7.33 The left plot shows the windowed FFT of a flute sound. The right plot shows the same FFT after noise gating each bin using the r/(r+coef) gating function with $c = 0.01$.

Denoising in itself has many variations depending on the application:

(1) Denoising from a tape recorder usually starts from the analysis of a noisy sound coming from a recording of silence. This gives a gaboret for the noise shape, so that the non-linear function will be different for each bin, and can be zero under this threshold.

(2) The noise level can be estimated in a varying manner. For example, one can estimate a noise threshold which can be spectrum dependent. This usually involves spectral estimation techniques (with the help of LPC or cepstrum), which will be seen later.

(3) One can also try to evaluate a level of noise on successive time instances in order to decrease pumping effects.

(4) In any case, these algorithms involve non-linear operations and as such can produce artifacts. One of them is the existence of small grains that remain outside the silence unlike the previous noise (spurious components). The other artifact is that noise can sometimes be a useful component of a sound and will be suppressed as undesirable noise.

7.4.10   Spectral panning

Another sound transformation is to place sound sources in various physical places, which can be simulated in stereophonic sound by making use of azimuth panning. But what happens when trying to split the sound components? Then, each bin of the spectrum can be separately positioned using panning. Even better, by making use of the information from a phase-locked vocoder, one may put all frequency bins of the same component in the same angular position, avoiding the positioning artefacts that result from two adjacent bins that are coding for the same component and that would be otherwise placed in two different positions (the auditory image then being in the two places).

The Blumlein law [Bla83] for each sound sample is adapted to each frequency bin as

$$\sin\theta(n,k) = \frac{g_L(n,k) - g_R(n,k)}{g_L(n,k) + g_R(n,k)} \sin\theta_l \,, \tag{7.48}$$

where $g_L(n,k)$ and $g_L(n,k)$ are the time- and frequency-bin-varying gains to be applied to the left and right stereo channels, $\theta(n,k)$ is the angle of the virtual source position, and θ_l is the angle formed by each loudspeaker with the frontal direction. In the simple case where $\theta_l = 45°$ the output spectra are given by

$$X_L(n,k) = \frac{\sqrt{2}}{2}(\cos\theta(n,k) + \sin\theta(n,k)) \cdot X(n,k) \tag{7.49}$$

$$X_R(n,k) = \frac{\sqrt{2}}{2}(\cos\theta(n,k) - \sin\theta(n,k)) \cdot X(n,k). \tag{7.50}$$

A basic example is shown in Figure 7.34. Only the magnitude spectrum is modified: the phase of the initial signal is used unmodified, because this version of azimuth panning only modifies the gains, but not the fundamental frequency. This means that such effect does not simulate the Doppler effect. The stereophinc sound is then reconstructed by overlapping grains with the help of an IFFT. The following M-file 7.19 follows this guideline.

M-file 7.19 (VX_specpan.m)

```
% VX_specpan.m  [DAFXbook, 2nd ed., chapter 7]
%===== This program makes a spectral panning of a sound
clear; clf
```

```
%----- user data -----
fig_plot    = 1;    % use any value except 0 or [] to plot figures
n1          = 512;  % analysis step [samples]
n2          = n1;   % synthesis step [samples]
s_win       = 2048; % analysis window length [samples]
[DAFx_in,FS] = wavread('redwheel.wav');

%----- initialize windows, arrays, etc -----
w1       = hanning(s_win, 'periodic'); % analysis window
w2       = w1;       % synthesis window
L        = length(DAFx_in);
DAFx_in  = [zeros(s_win, 1); DAFx_in; ...
  zeros(s_win-mod(L,n1),1)] / max(abs(DAFx_in));
DAFx_out = zeros(length(DAFx_in),2);
hs_win   = s_win/2;
coef     = sqrt(2)/2;
%---- control: clipped sine wave with a few periods; in [-pi/4;pi/4]
theta    = min(1,max(-1,2*sin((0:hs_win)/s_win*200))).' * pi/4;
% %---- control: rough left/right split at Fs/30 ~ 1470 Hz
% theta    = (((0:hs_win).'/2 < hs_win/30)) * pi/2 - pi/4;
%---- preserving phase symmetry ----
theta    = [theta(1:hs_win+1); flipud(theta(1:hs_win-1))];

%---- drawing panning function ----
if (fig_plot)
  figure;
  plot((0:hs_win)/s_win*FS/1000, theta(1:hs_win+1));
  axis tight; xlabel('f / kHz \rightarrow');
  ylabel('\theta / rad \rightarrow');
  title('Spectral panning angle as a function of frequency')
end
tic
%UUUUUUUUUUUUUUUUUUUUUUUUUUUUUUUUUUUUUUUUUUUUUUU
pin  = 0;
pout = 0;
pend = length(DAFx_in) - s_win;

while pin<pend
    grain = DAFx_in(pin+1:pin+s_win).* w1;
%===========================================
    f       = fft(grain);
    %---- compute left and right spectrum with Blumlein law at 45°
    ftL     = coef * f .* (cos(theta) + sin(theta));
    ftR     = coef * f .* (cos(theta) - sin(theta));
    grainL = (real(ifft(ftL))).*w2;
    grainR = (real(ifft(ftR))).*w2;
% ===========================================
    DAFx_out(pout+1:pout+s_win,1) = ...
        DAFx_out(pout+1:pout+s_win,1) + grainL;
    DAFx_out(pout+1:pout+s_win,2) = ...
        DAFx_out(pout+1:pout+s_win,2) + grainR;
    pin  = pin + n1;
    pout = pout + n2;
end
%UUUUUUUUUUUUUUUUUUUUUUUUUUUUUUUUUUUUUUUUUUUUUUU
toc
%----- listening and saving the output -----
```

```
% DAFx_in  = DAFx_in(s_win+1:s_win+L);
DAFx_out = DAFx_out(s_win+1:s_win+L,:) / max(max(abs(DAFx_out)));
soundsc(DAFx_out, FS);
wavwrite(DAFx_out, FS, 'x1_specpan.wav');
```

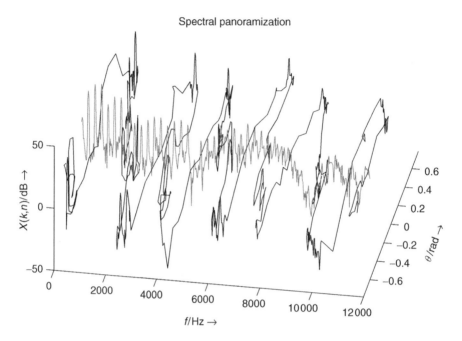

Figure 7.34 Spectral panning of the magnitude spectrum of a single frame, using a wave form as the panning angle. Each frequency bin of the original STFT $X(n, k)$ (centered with $\theta = 0$, in gray) is panoramized with constant power.

Spectral panning offers many applications, which are listed to show the variety of possibilities:

(1) Pseudo-source separation when combined with a multi-pitch detector.

(2) Arbitrary panning when the $\theta(n, k)$ value is not related to the spectral content of the sound.

(3) Vomito effect, when the azimuth angles are refreshed too often (i.e., every frame at a 50 Hz rate), the fast motions of sound also implies timbre modulations (as the amplitude modulation has a frequency higher than 20 Hz), both of which result in some unpleasant effects for the listener.

7.5 Conclusion

The starting point of this chapter was the computation of a time-frequency representation of a sound, to manipulate this representation and reproduce a sound. At first sight this may appear as an easy task, but we have seen that the basis for this time-frequency processing needs a careful description of the fundamentals, because the term 'vocoder' can cover different implementations. We also explained that the arbitrary manipulation of time-frequency representations renders images in a way that they are no longer time-frequency representations of "real" sounds. This phenomenon leads to artifacts, which cannot be avoided.

Digital audio effects described in this chapter only perform manipulations of these time-frequency representations. These effects exclude the extraction of resonances, which will be the subject of the next chapter, and high-level processing such as the extraction of sinusoids and noise. For example, the mentioned bank of filters does not assume any parametric model of the sound. Nevertheless such effects are numerous and diverse. Some of them have brought new solutions to well-known techniques such as filtering. Pitch shifting and time stretching have shown their central place in the phase vocoder approach, which is another implementation possibility independent of the time-segment processing approach from the previous chapter. Their was a clear need for a clarification of the phase vocoder approach in this domain. Though it has been known for years, we have provided a general framework and simple implementations upon which more complex effects may be built. Some of them can reduce the phasiness of the process or perform special high-level processing on transients. Other digital audio effects have been described that fit well under the name "mutations." They are based on modifying the magnitude and phase of one or two time-frequency representations. They put a special flavor on sounds, which musicians characterize as granulation, robotization, homogenization, purification, metallization and so on. Once again, the goal of this chapter is to give a general framework and unveil some of the basic implementations of these alterations of sound, which can be extended to more complex modifications at will.

As a final remark, one can say that no digital audio effect, and time-frequency processing in particular, would exist without a sound. Only a good adaptation of the sound with the effect can give rise to musical creativity. This is the reason why some of the basic algorithms presented put in the hands of creative musicians and artists can give better results than much more complex algorithms in the hands of conventional persons.

References

[AD93]   D. Arfib and N. Delprat. Musical transformations using the modification of time-frequency images. *Comp. Music J.*, 17(2): 66–72, 1993.

[Bla83]   J. Blauert. *Spatial Hearing: the Psychophysics of Human Sound Localization*. MIT Press, 1983.

[Cap94]   O. Cappé. Elimination of the musical noise phenomenon with the ephraim and malah noise suppressor. *IEEE Trans. Acoust. Speech Signal Process.*, 2: 345–349, 1994.

[CGT89]   J. M. Combes, A. Grossmann, and Ph. Tchamitchan (eds). *Wavelets. Time Frequency Methods and Phase Space*, 2nd edition. Springer-Verlag, 1989.

[Chu92]   C. H. Chui. *An Introduction to Wavelets*. Academic Press, 1992.

[CR83]   R. E. Crochiere and L. R. Rabiner. *Multirate Digital Signal Processing*. Prentice-Hall, 1983.

[Cro80]   R. E. Crochiere. A weighted overlap-add method of short-time fourier analysis/synthesis. *IEEE Trans. Acoust. Speech Signal Process.*, 281(1): 99–102, 1980.

[Fer99]   A. J. S. Ferreira. An odd-DFT based approach to time-scale expansion of audio signals. *IEEE Trans. Speech Audio Process.*, 7(4): 441–453, 1999.

[GBA00]   A. De Götzen, N. Bernadini, and D. Arfib. Traditional (?) implementations of a phase vocoder: The tricks of the trade. In *Proc. DAFX-00 Conference on Digital Audio Effects*, pp. 37–43, 2000.

[Lar98]   J. Laroche. Time and pitch scale modifications of audio signals. In M. Kahrs and K.-H. Brandenburg (eds), *Applications of Digital Signal Processing to Audio and Acoustics*, pp. 279–309. Kluwer, 1998.

[Lar03]   J. Laroche. Frequency-domain techniques for high quality voice modification. In *Proc. 6th DAFX-03 Conf. Digital Audio Effects*, pp. 328–332, 2003.

[LD99a]   J. Laroche and M. Dolson. Improved phase vocoder time-scale modification of audio. *IEEE Trans. Speech Audio Process.*, 7(3): 323–332, 1999.

[LD99b]   J. Laroche and M. Dolson. New phase-vocoder techniques for real-time pitch shifting, chorusing, harmonizing, and other exotic audio modifications. *J. Audio Eng. Soc.*, 47(11): 928–936, 1999.

[PE96]   L. Polansky and T. Erbe. Spectral mutation in soundhack. *Comp. Music J.*, 20(1): 92–101, Spring 1996.

[Por76]   M. R. Portnoff. Implementation of the digital phase vocoder using the fast fourier transform. *IEEE Trans. Acoust. Speech Signal Process.*, 24(3): 243–248, 1976.

[QC93]   S. Quian and D. Chen. Discrete gabor transform. *IEEE Trans. Signal Process.*, 41(7): 2429–2438, 1993.

[QM98]   T. F. Quatieri and R. J. McAulay. Audio signal processing based on sinusoidal analysis/synthesis. In M. Kahrs and K.-H. Brandenburg (eds), *Applications of Digital Signal Processing to Audio and Acoustics*, pp. 343–416. Kluwer, 1998.

[Röb03]   A. Röbel. A new approach to transient processing in the phase vocoder. In *Proc. 6th DAFX-03 Conf. Digital Audio Effects*, pp. 344–349, 2003.

[Röb10]   A. Röbel. A shape-invariant phase vocoder for speech transformation. In *Proc. 13th DAFX-10 Conf. Digital Audio Effects*, pp. 298–305, 2010.

[SL94]   Z. Settel and C. Lippe. Real-time musical applications using the FFT-based resynthesis. In *Proc. Int. Comp. Music Conf.*, 1994.

[Vas96]   S. V. Vaseghi. *Advanced Signal Processing and Digital Noise Reduction*. Wiley & Teubner, 1996.

[WR90]   J. Wexler and S. Raz. Discrete gabor expansions. *Signal Process.*, 21(3): 207–220, 1990.

[Zöl05]   U. Zölzer. *Digital Audio Signal Processing*, 2nd edition. John Wiley & Sons, Ltd, 2005.

8

Source-filter processing

D. Arfib, F. Keiler, U. Zölzer and V. Verfaille

8.1 Introduction

Time – frequency representations give the evolution over time of a spectrum calculated from temporal frames. The notion of the spectral envelope extracted from such representations mostly comes from the voice production and recognition system: the voice production uses vocal chords as an excitation and the mouth and nose as a resonator system or anti-resonator. Voiced signals (vowels) produce a harmonic spectrum on which a spectral envelope is superimposed. This fact about voice strongly influences our way of recognizing other sounds, whether because of the ear or the brain; we are looking for such a spectral envelope as a cue to the identification or classification of sounds. This excitation-resonance model is also called source-filter model in the literature. Thus we can understand why the *vocoding* effect, which is the cross-synthesis of a musical instrument with voice, is so attractive for the ear and so resistant to approximations. We will make use of a source-filter model for an audio signal and modify this model in order to achieve different digital audio effects.

However, the signal-processing problem of extracting a spectral envelope from a spectrum is generally badly conditioned. If the sound is purely harmonic we could say that the spectral envelope is the curve that passes through the points related to these harmonics. This leaves two open questions: how to retrieve these exact values of these harmonics, and what kind of interpolation scheme should we use for the completion of the curve in-between these points? But, more generally, if the sound contains inharmonic partials or a noisy part, this definition no longer holds and the notion of a spectral envelope is then completely dependent on the definition of what belongs to the excitation and what belongs to the resonance. In a way it is more a "envelope-recognition" problem than a "signal-processing" one.

With this in mind we will state that a spectral envelope is a smoothing of a spectrum, which tends to leave aside the spectral line structure while preserving the general form of the spectrum.

DAFX: Digital Audio Effects, Second Edition. Edited by Udo Zölzer.
© 2011 John Wiley & Sons, Ltd. Published 2011 by John Wiley & Sons, Ltd.

To provide source-filter sound transformation, two different steps are performed:

(1) Estimate the spectral envelope

(2) Perform the source-filter separation, and sound-filter combination after transformation of one or the other.

There are three techniques with many variants which can be used for both steps:

(1) The **channel vocoder** uses frequency bands and performs estimations of the amplitude of the signal inside these bands and thus the spectral envelope.

(2) **Linear prediction** estimates an all-pole filter that matches the spectral content of a sound. When the order of this filter is low, only the formants are taken, hence the spectral envelope.

(3) **Cepstrum** techniques perform smoothing of the logarithm of the FFT spectrum (in decibels) in order to separate this curve into its slowly varying part (the spectral envelope) and its quickly varying part (the source signal).

For each of these techniques, we will describe the fundamental algorithms in Section 8.2 which allow the calculation of the spectral envelope and the source signal in a frame-oriented approach, as shown in Figure 8.1. Then transformations are applied to the spectral envelope and/or the source signal and a synthesis procedure reconstructs the output sound. Some basic transformations are introduced in Section 8.3. The separation of a source and a filter is only one of the features we can extract from a sound, or more precisely from a time-frequency representation.

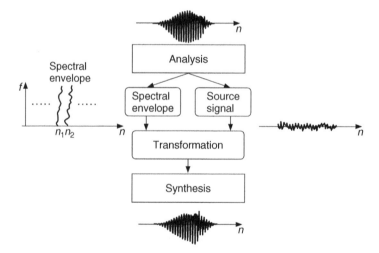

Figure 8.1 Spectral processing based on time-varying spectral envelopes and source signals. The analysis performs a source and filter separation.

8.2 Source-filter separation

Digital audio effects based on source-filter processing extract the spectral envelope and the source (excitation) signal from an input signal, as shown in Figure 8.2. The input signal is whitened by the filter $1/H_1(z)$, which is derived from the spectral envelope of the input signal. In signal-processing terms, the spectral envelope is given by the magnitude response $|H_1(f)|$ or its logarithm $\log|H_1(f)|$ in dB. This leads to extraction of the source signal $e_1(n)$ which can be further processed, for example, by time-stretching or pitch-shifting algorithms. The processed source signal is then

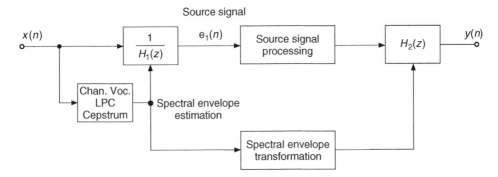

Figure 8.2 Spectrum estimation (Channel vocoder, Linear Predictive Coding or Cepstrum) and source-signal extraction for individual processing.

finally filtered by $H_2(z)$. This filter is derived from the modified spectral envelope of the input signal or another source signal.

8.2.1 Channel vocoder

If we filter a sound with a bank of bandpass filters and calculate the RMS value for each bandpass signal, we can obtain an estimation of the spectral envelope (see Figure 8.3). The parameters of

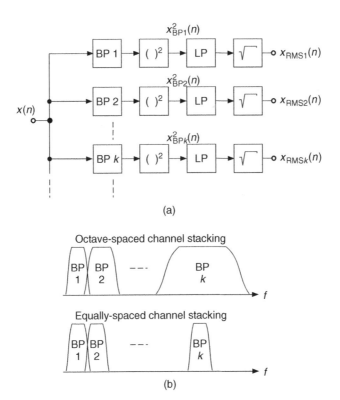

Figure 8.3 (a) Channel vocoder and (b) frequency stacking.

the filters for each channel will of course affect the precision of the measurement, as well as the delay between the sound input and the spectral calculation. The RMS calculation parameters are also a compromise between good definition and an acceptable delay and trail effect. The spectral estimation is valid around the center frequency of the filters. Thus the more channels there are, the more frequency points of the spectral envelope are estimated. The filter bank can be defined on a linear scale, in which case every filter of the filter bank can be equivalent in terms of bandwidth. It can also be defined on a logarithmic scale. In this case, this approach is more like an "equalizer system" and the filters, if given in the time domain, are scaled versions of a mother filter.

The channel-vocoder algorithm shown in Figure 8.3 works in the time domain. There is, however, a possible derivation where it is possible to calculate the spectral envelope from the FFT spectrum, thus directly from the time-frequency representations. A channel can be represented in the frequency domain, and the energy of an effective channel filter can be seen as the sum of the elementary energies of each bin weighted by this channel filter envelope. The amplitude coming out of this filter is then the square root of these energies.

In the case of filters with equally spaced channel stacking (see Figure 8.3b), it is even possible to use a short-cut for the calculation of this spectral envelope: the spectral envelope is the square root of the filtered version of the squared amplitudes. This computation can be performed by a circular convolution $Y(k) = \sqrt{|X(k)|^2 * w(k)}$ in the frequency domain, where $w(k)$ may be a Hanning window function. The circular convolution is accomplished by another FFT/IFFT filtering algorithm. The result is a spectral envelope, which is a smoothing of the FFT values. An example is shown in Figure 8.4.

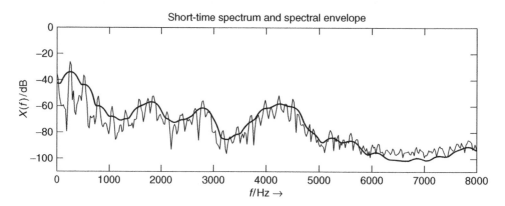

Figure 8.4 Spectral envelope computation with a channel vocoder.

The following M-file 8.1 defines channels in the frequency domain and calculates the energy in dB inside successive channels of that envelope.

M-file 8.1 (UX_specenv.m)

```
s_win = 2048;
w     = hanning(s_win, 'periodic');
buf   = y(offset:offset+s_win-1).*w;
f     = fft(buf)/(s_win/2);
freq  = (0:1:s_win-1)/s_win*44100;
flog  = 20*log10(0.00001+abs(f));
%---- frequency window ----
nob   = input('number of bins must be even = ');
w     = hanning(nob, 'periodic');
```

```
w1      = hanning(nob, 'periodic');
w1      = w1./sum(w1);
f_channel = [zeros((s_win-nob)/2,1); w1; zeros((s_win-nob)/2,1)];
%---- FFT of frequency window ----
fft_channel = fft(fftshift(f_channel));
f2      = f.*conj(f); % Squared FFT values
%---- circular convolution by FFT-Multiplication-IFFT ----
energy  = real(ifft(fft(f2).*fft_channel));
flog_rms = 10*log10(abs(energy)); % 10 => combination with sqrt operation
%---- plot result ----
subplot(2,1,1); plot(freq,flog,freq,flog_rms);
ylabel('X(f)/dB');
xlabel('f/Hz \rightarrow'); axis([0 8000 -110 0]);
title('Short-time spectrum and spectral envelope');
```

The program starts with the calculation of the FFT of a windowed frame, where w is a Hanning window in this case. The vector y contains the sound and a buffer buf contains a windowed segment. In the second part of this program fchannel represents the envelope of the channel with a FFT representation. Here it is a Hanning window of width nob, which is the number of frequency bins. The calculation of the weighted sum of the energies inside a channel is performed by a convolution calculation of the energy pattern and the channel envelope. Here, we use a circular convolution with an FFT-IFFT algorithm to easily retrieve the result for all channels. In a way it can be seen as a smoothing of the energy pattern. The only parameter is the envelope of the channel filter, hence the value of nob in this program. The fact that it is given in bins and that it should be even is only for the simplification of the code. The bandwidth is given by $\text{nob}\cdot\frac{f_S}{N}$ (N is the length of the FFT).

8.2.2 Linear predictive coding (LPC)

One way to estimate the spectral envelope of a sound is directly based on a simple sound-production model. In this model, the sound is produced by passing an excitation source (source signal) through a synthesis filter, as shown in Figure 8.5. The filter models the resonances and has therefore only poles. Thus, this all-pole filter represents the spectral envelope of the sound. This model works well for speech, where the synthesis filter models the human vocal tract, while the excitation source consists of pulses plus noise [Mak75]. For voiced sounds the periodicity of the pulses determines the pitch of the sound, while for unvoiced sounds the excitation is noise-like.

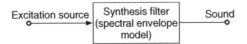

Figure 8.5   Sound production model: the synthesis filter represents the spectral envelope.

The retrieval of the spectral envelope from a given sound at a given time is based on the estimation of the all-pole synthesis filter mentioned previously. This approach is widely used for speech coding and is called linear predictive coding (LPC) [Mak75, MG76].

Analysis/Synthesis structure

In LPC the current input sample $x(n)$ is approximated by a linear combination of past samples of the input signal. The prediction of $x(n)$ is computed using an FIR filter by

$$\hat{x}(n) = \sum_{k=1}^{p} a_k x(n-k),$$

(8.1)

where p is the *prediction order* and a_k are the prediction coefficients. The difference between the original input signal $x(n)$ and its prediction $\hat{x}(n)$ is evaluated by

$$e(n) = x(n) - \hat{x}(n) = x(n) - \sum_{k=1}^{p} a_k x(n-k). \tag{8.2}$$

The difference signal $e(n)$ is called *residual* or *prediction error* and its calculation is depicted in Figure 8.6 where the transversal (direct) FIR filter structure is used.

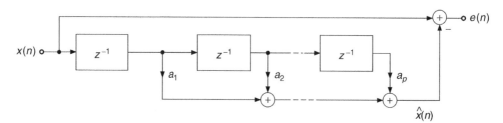

Figure 8.6 Transversal FIR filter structure for the prediction-error calculation.

With the z-transform of the *prediction filter*

$$P(z) = \sum_{k=1}^{p} a_k z^{-k}, \tag{8.3}$$

Equation (8.2) can be written in the z-domain as

$$E(z) = X(z) - \hat{X}(z) = X(z)[1 - P(z)]. \tag{8.4}$$

Figure 8.7(a) illustrates the last equation. The illustrated structure is called *feed-forward prediction* where the prediction is calculated in the forward direction from the input signal.

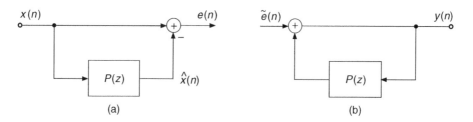

Figure 8.7 LPC structure with feed-forward prediction: (a) analysis, (b) synthesis.

Defining the *prediction error filter* or *inverse filter*

$$A(z) = 1 - P(z) = 1 - \sum_{k=1}^{p} a_k z^{-k}, \tag{8.5}$$

the prediction error is obtained as

$$E(z) = X(z)A(z). \tag{8.6}$$

The sound signal is recovered by using the *excitation signal* $\tilde{e}(n)$ as input to the all-pole filter

$$H(z) = \frac{1}{A(z)} = \frac{1}{1 - P(z)}.$$ (8.7)

This yields the output signal

$$Y(z) = \tilde{E}(z) \cdot H(z),$$ (8.8)

where $H(z)$ can be realized with the FIR filter $P(z)$ in a feedback loop, as shown in Figure 8.7(b). If the residual $e(n)$, which is calculated in the analysis stage, is fed directly into the synthesis filter, the input signal $x(n)$ will be ideally recovered.

The IIR filter $H(z)$ is termed *synthesis filter* or *LPC filter* and represents the spectral model – except for a gain factor – of the input signal $x(n)$. As mentioned previously, this filter models the time-varying vocal tract in the case of speech signals.

With optimal filter coefficients, the residual energy is minimized. This can be exploited for efficient coding of the input signal where the quantized residual $\tilde{e}(n) = Q\{e(n)\}$ is used as excitation to the LPC filter.

Figure 8.8 shows an example where for a short block of a speech signal an LPC filter of order $p = 50$ is computed. In the left plot the time signal is shown, while the right plot shows both the spectra of the input signal and of the LPC filter $H(z)$. In this example the autocorrelation method is used to calculate the LPC coefficients. The MATLAB® code for this example is given by M-file 8.2 (the used function `calc_lpc` will be explained later).

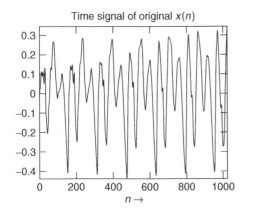
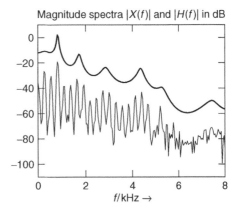

Figure 8.8 LPC example for the female utterance "la" with prediction order $p = 50$, original signal and LPC filter.

M-file 8.2 (figure8_08.m)

```
N      = 1024;    % block length
Nfft   = 1024;    % FFT length
p      = 50;      % prediction order
n1     = n0+N-1;  % end index

[xin,Fs] = wavread(fname,[n0 n1]);
x        = xin(:,1)';    % row vecor of left channel
win      = hamming(N)';  % window for input block
```

```
a = calc_lpc(x.*win,p); % calculate LPC coeffs
% a = [1, -a_1, -a_2,..., -a_p]

Omega  = (0:Nfft-1)/Nfft*Fs/1000; % frequencies in kHz
offset = 20*log10(2/Nfft);        % spectrum offset in dB
A = 20*log10(abs(fft(a,Nfft)));
H = -A+offset;
X = 20*log10(abs(fft(x.*win,Nfft)));
X = X+offset;

n = 0:N-1;
```

Calculation of the filter coefficients

To find an all-pole filter which models a considered sound well, different approaches may be taken. Some common methods compute the filter coefficients from a block of the input signal $x(n)$. These methods are namely the autocorrelation method [Mak75, Orf90], the covariance method [Mak75, MG76], and the Burg algorithm [Mak77, Orf90]. Since both the autocorrelation method and the Burg algorithm compute the lattice coefficients, they are guaranteed to produce stable synthesis filters, while the covariance method may yield unstable filters.

Now we briefly describe the autocorrelation method, which minimizes the energy of the prediction error $e(n)$. With the prediction error $e(n)$ defined in (8.2), the prediction error energy is[1]

$$E_p = E\left\{e^2(n)\right\}. \tag{8.9}$$

Setting the partial derivatives of E_p with respect to the filter coefficients a_i ($i = 1, \ldots, p$) to zero leads to

$$\frac{\partial E_p}{\partial a_i} = 2E\left\{e(n) \cdot \frac{\partial e(n)}{\partial a_i}\right\} \tag{8.10}$$

$$= -2E\left\{e(n)x(n-i)\right\} \tag{8.11}$$

$$= -2E\left\{\left[x(n) - \sum_{k=1}^{p} a_k x(n-k)\right]x(n-i)\right\} = 0 \tag{8.12}$$

$$\Leftrightarrow \sum_{k=1}^{p} a_k E\left\{x(n-k)x(n-i)\right\} = E\left\{x(n)x(n-i)\right\}. \tag{8.13}$$

Equation (8.13) is a formulation of the so-called *normal equations* [Mak75]. The autocorrelation sequence for a block of length N is defined by

$$r_{xx}(i) = \sum_{n=i}^{N-1} u(n)u(n-i) \tag{8.14}$$

where $u(n) = x(n) \cdot w(n)$ is a windowed version of the considered block $x(n)$, $n = 0, \ldots, N - 1$. Normally a Hamming window is used [O'S00]. The expectation values in (8.13) can be replaced

---

[1] With the expectation value $E\{\cdot\}$.

by their approximations using the autocorrelation sequence, which gives the normal equations[2]

$$\sum_{k=1}^{p} a_k r_{xx}(i-k) = r_{xx}(i) \quad , i = 1, \ldots, p. \tag{8.15}$$

The filter coefficients a_k $(k = 1, \ldots, p)$, which model the spectral envelope of the used segment of $x(n)$ are obtained by solving the normal equations. An efficient solution of the normal equations is performed by the Levinson – Durbin recursion [Mak75].

As explained in [Mak75], minimizing the residual energy is equivalent to finding a best spectral fit in the frequency domain, if the gain factor is ignored. Thus the input signal $x(n)$ is modeled by the filter

$$H_g(z) = G \cdot H(z) = \frac{G}{1 - \sum_{k=1}^{p} a_k z^{-k}}, \tag{8.16}$$

where G denotes the gain factor. With this modified synthesis filter the original signal is modeled using a white noise excitation with unit variance. For the autocorrelation method the gain factor is defined by [Mak75]

$$G^2 = r_{xx}(0) - \sum_{k=1}^{p} a_k r_{xx}(k), \tag{8.17}$$

with the autocorrelation sequence given in (8.14). Hence the gain factor depends on the energy of the prediction error. If $|H_g(e^{j\Omega})|^2$ models the power spectrum $|X(e^{j\Omega})|^2$, the prediction-error power spectrum is a flat spectrum with $|E(e^{j\Omega})|^2 = G^2$. The inverse filter $A(z)$ to calculate the prediction error is therefore also called the "whitening filter" [Mak75]. The **MATLAB** code of the function calc_lpc for the calculation of the prediction coefficients and the gain factor using the autocorrelation method is given by M-file 8.3.

M-file 8.3 (calc_lpc.m)

```
% function [a,g] = calc_lpc(x,p) [DAFXbook, 2nd ed., chapter 8]
% ===== This function computes LPC coeffs via autocorrelation method
%         Similar to MATLAB function "lpc"
% !!! IMPORTANT: function "lpc" does not work correctly with MATLAB 6!
% Inputs:
%    x: input signal
%    p: prediction order
% Outputs:
%    a: LPC coefficients
%    g: gain factor
% (c) 2002 Florian Keiler
function [a,g] = calc_lpc(x,p)

R = xcorr(x,p);          % autocorrelation sequence R(k) with k=-p,..,p
R(1:p) = [];             % delete entries for k=-p,..,-1
if norm(R)~=0
    a = levinson(R,p);   % Levinson-Durbin recursion
%    a = [1, -a_1, -a_2,..., -a_p]
else
```

---

[2] The multiplication of the expectation values by the block length N does not have any effect on the normal equations.

```
      a = [1, zeros(1,p)];
end
R = R(:)'; a = a(:)';     % row vectors
g = sqrt(sum(a.*R));      % gain factor
```

Notice that normally the **MATLAB** function `lpc` can be used, but it does not show the expected behavior for an input signal with zeros. M-file 8.3 fixes this problem and returns coefficients $a_k = 0$ in this case.

Figure 8.9 shows the prediction error and the estimated spectral envelope for the input signal shown in Figure 8.8. It can clearly be noticed that the prediction error has strong peaks occurring with the period of the fundamental frequency of the input signal. We can make use of this property of the prediction error signal for computing the fundamental frequency. The fundamental frequency and its pitch period can deliver pitch marks for PSOLA time-stretching or pitch-shifting algorithms, or other applications. The corresponding **MATLAB** code is given by M-file 8.4.

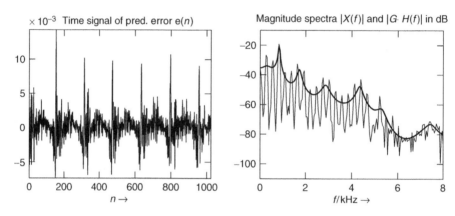

Figure 8.9 LPC example for the female utterance "la" with prediction order $p = 50$, prediction error and spectral envelope.

M-file 8.4 (figure8_09.m)

```
Nfft  = 1024; % FFT length
p     = 50; %prediction order
n1    = n0+N-1; %end index
pre   = p; %filter order= no. of samples required before n0

[xin,Fs] = wavread(fname,[n0-pre n1]);
xin = xin(:,1)';
win = hamming(N)';
x   = xin((1:N)+pre); % block without pre-samples

[a,g] = calc_lpc(x.*win,p); % calculate LPC coeffs and gain
% a = [1, -a_1, -a_2,..., -a_p]
g_db = 20*log10(g) % gain in dB

ein = filter(a,1,xin); % pred. error
e   = ein((1:N)+pre); % without pre-samples
Gp  = 10*log10(sum(x.^2)/sum(e.^2)) % prediction gain

Omega  = (0:Nfft-1)/Nfft*Fs/1000; % frequencies in kHz
offset = 20*log10(2/Nfft); % offset of spectrum in dB
```

```
A    = 20*log10(abs(fft(a,Nfft)));
H_g  = -A+offset+g_db; % spectral envelope
X    = 20*log10(abs(fft(x.*win,Nfft)));
X    = X+offset;

n    =  0:N-1;
figure(1)
clf
subplot(221)
plot(n,e)
title('time signal of pred. error e(n)')
xlabel('n \rightarrow')
axis([0 N-1 -inf inf])

subplot(222)
plot(Omega,X); hold on
plot(Omega,H_g,'r','Linewidth',1.5); hold off
title('magnitude spectra |X(f)| and |G\cdot H(f)| in dB')
xlabel('f/kHz \rightarrow')
axis([0 8 -inf inf])
```

Thus for the computation of the prediction error over the complete block length, additional samples of the input signal are required. The calculated prediction error signal $e(n)$ is equal to the source or excitation which has to be used as input to the synthesis filter $H(z)$ to recover the original signal $x(n)$. For this example the prediction gain, defined as

$$G_p = \frac{\sum_{n=0}^{N-1} x^2(n)}{\sum_{n=0}^{N-1} e^2(n)}, \tag{8.18}$$

has the value 38 dB, and the gain factor is $G = -23$ dB.

Figure 8.10 shows spectra of LPC filters at different filter orders for the same signal block as in Figure 8.8. The bottom line shows the spectrum of the signal segment where only frequencies below 8 kHz are depicted. The other spectra in this plot show the results using the autocorrelation method with different prediction orders. For clarity reasons these spectra are plotted with different

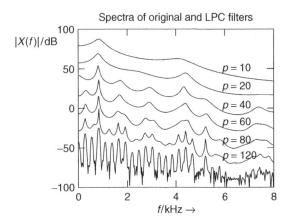

Figure 8.10 LPC filter spectra for different prediction orders for the female utterance "la."

offsets. It is obvious that for an increasing prediction order the spectral model gets better although the prediction gain only increases from 36.6 dB ($p = 10$) to 38.9 dB ($p = 120$).

In summary, the LPC method delivers a source-filter model and allows the determination of pitch marks or the fundamental frequency of the input signal.

8.2.3   Cepstrum

The cepstrum (backward spelling of "spec") method allows the estimation of a spectral envelope starting from the FFT values $X(k)$ of a windowed frame $x(n)$. Zero padding and Hanning, Hamming or Gaussian windows can be used, depending on the number of points used for the spectral envelope estimation. An introduction to the basics of cepstrum-based signal processing can be found in [OS75]. The cepstrum is calculated from the discrete Fourier transform

$$X(k) = \sum_{n=0}^{N-1} x(n) W_N^{kn} = |X(k)| e^{j\varphi_x(k)}, \quad k = 0, 1, \ldots, N - 1 \tag{8.19}$$

by taking the logarithm

$$\hat{X}(k) = \log X(k) = \log |X(k)| + j\varphi_x(k) \tag{8.20}$$

and performing an IFFT of $\hat{X}(k)$, which yields the *complex cepstrum*

$$\hat{x}(n) = \frac{1}{N} \sum_{k=0}^{N-1} \hat{X}(k) W_N^{-kn}. \tag{8.21}$$

The *real cepstrum* is derived from the real part of (8.20) given by

$$\hat{X}_R(k) = \log |X(k)| \tag{8.22}$$

and performing an IFFT of $\hat{X}_R(k)$, which leads to the *real cepstrum*

$$c(n) = \frac{1}{N} \sum_{k=0}^{N-1} \hat{X}_R(k) W_N^{-kn}. \tag{8.23}$$

Since $\hat{X}_R(k)$ is an even function, the inverse discrete Fourier transform of $\hat{X}_R(k)$ gives an even function $c(n)$, which is related to the complex cepstrum $\hat{x}(n)$ by $c(n) = \frac{\hat{x}(n) + \hat{x}(-n)}{2}$.

Figure 8.11 illustrates the computational steps for the computation of the spectral envelope from the real cepstrum. The real cepstrum $c(n)$ is the IFFT of the logarithm of the magnitude of FFT of the windowed sequence $x(n)$. The lowpass window for weighting the cepstrum $c(n)$ is

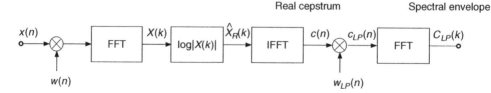

Figure 8.11   Spectral-envelope computation by cepstrum analysis.

derived in [OS75] and is given by

$$w_{LP}(n) = \begin{cases} 1 & n = 0, N_1 \\ 2 & 1 \leq n < N_1 \\ 0 & N_1 < n \leq N - 1. \end{cases} \tag{8.24}$$

with $N_1 \leq N/2$.

The FFT of the windowed cepstrum $c_{LP}(n)$ yields the spectral envelope

$$C_{LP}(k) = \text{FFT}\left[c_{LP}(n)\right], \tag{8.25}$$

which is a smoothed version of the spectrum $X(k)$ in dB. An illustrative example is shown in Figure 8.12. Notice that the first part of the cepstrum $c(n)$ ($0 \leq n \leq 150$) is weighted by the "lowpass window," yielding $c_{LP}(n)$. The IFFT of $c_{LP}(n)$ results in the spectral envelope $C(f)$ in dB, as shown in the lower right plot. The "highpass part" of the cepstrum $c(n)$ ($150 < n \leq 1024$) represents the source signal, where the first peak at $n = 160$ represents the pitch period T_0 (in samples) of the fundamental frequency $f_0 = 44100 \text{ Hz}/160 = 275, 625 \text{ Hz}$. Notice also, although the third harmonic is higher than the fundamental frequency, as can be seen in the spectrum of the segment, the cepstrum method allows the estimation of the pitch period of the fundamental frequency by searching for the time index of the first highly significant peak value

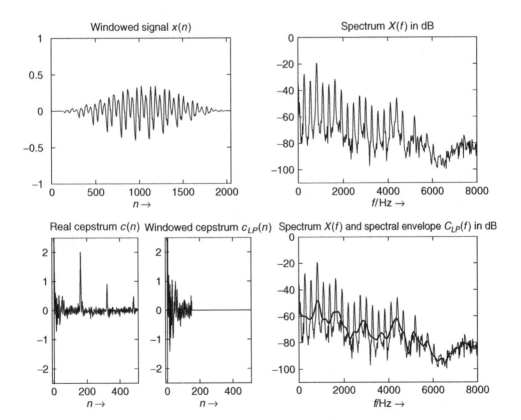

Figure 8.12 Windowed signal segment, spectrum (FFT length $N = 2048$), cepstrum, windowed cepstrum ($N_1 = 150$) and spectral envelope.

in the cepstrum $c(n)$ after the "lowpass" part can be considered to have vanished. The following M-file 8.5 demonstrates briefly the way a spectral envelope can be calculated via the real cepstrum.

M-file 8.5 (UX_specenvceps.m)

```
% N1: cut quefrency
WLen = 2048;
w    = hanning(WLen, 'periodic');
buf  = y(offset:offset+WLen-1).*w;
f    = fft(buf)/(WLen/2);
flog = 20*log10(0.00001+abs(f));
subplot(2,1,1); plot(flog(1:WLen/2));

N1   = input('cut value for cepstrum');
cep  = ifft(flog);
cep_cut = [cep(1); 2*cep(2:N1); cep(N1+1); zeros(WLen-N1-1,1)];
flog_cut = real(fft(cep_cut));
subplot(2,1,2); plot(flog_cut(1:WLen/2));
```

In this program cep represents the cepstrum (hence the IFFT of the log magnitude of the FFT). The vector cep_cut is the version of the cepstrum with all values over the cut index set to zero. Here, we use a programming short-cut: we also remove the negative time values (hence the second part of the FFT) and use only the real part of the inverse FFT. The time indices n of the cepstrum $c(n)$ are also denoted as "quefrencies." The vector flog_cut is a smoothed version of flog and represents the spectral envelope derived by the cepstrum method. The only input value for the spectral envelope computation is the cut variable. This variable cut is homogeneous to a time in samples, and should be less than the period of the analyzed sound.

Source-filter separation

The cepstrum method allows the separation of a signal $y(n) = x(n) * h(n)$, which is based on a source and filter model, into its source signal $x(n)$ and its impulse response $h(n)$. The discrete-time Fourier transform $Y(e^{j\omega}) = X(e^{j\omega}) \cdot H(e^{j\omega})$ is the product of two spectra: one representing the filter frequency response $H(e^{j\omega})$ and the other one the source spectrum $X(e^{j\omega})$. Decomposing the complex values in terms of the magnitude and phase representation, one can make the strong assumption that the filter frequency response will be real-valued and the phase will be assigned to the source signal.

The key point here is to use the mathematical property of the logarithm $\log(a \cdot b) = \log(a) + \log(b)$. The real cepstrum method will perform a spectral-envelope estimation based on the magnitude according to

$$|Y(e^{j\omega})| = |X(e^{j\omega})| \cdot |H(e^{j\omega})|$$

$$\log|Y(e^{j\omega})| = \log|X(e^{j\omega})| + \log|H(e^{j\omega})|.$$

In musical terms separating $\log|X(e^{j\omega})|$ from $\log|H(e^{j\omega})|$ is to keep the slow variation of $\log|Y(e^{j\omega})|$ as a filter and the rapid ones as a source. In terms of signal processing we would like to separate the low frequencies of the signal $\log|Y(e^{j\omega})|$ from the high frequencies (see Figure 8.13).

The separation of source and filter can be achieved by weighting the cepstrum $c(n) = c_x(n) + c_h(n)$ with two window functions, namely the "lowpass window" $w_{LP}(n)$ and the complementary "highpass window" $w_{HP}(n)$. This weighting yields $c_x(n) = c(n) \cdot w_{HP}(n)$ and $c_h(n) = c(n) \cdot w_{LP}(n)$. The low time values (low "quefrencies") for lowpass filtering $\log|Y(e^{j\omega})|$ give $\log|H(e^{j\omega})|$ (spectral envelope in dB) and the high time values (higher

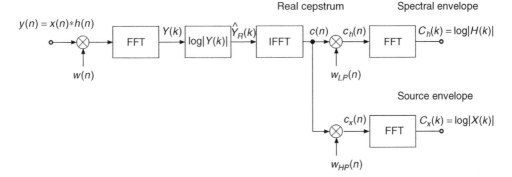

Figure 8.13 Separating source and filter.

"quefrencies") for highpass filtering yield $\log|X(e^{j\omega})|$ (source estimation). The calculation of $\exp(\log|H(e^{j\omega})|)$ gives the magnitude response $|H(e^{j\omega})|$. From this magnitude transfer function we can compute a zero-phase filter impulse response according to

$$h(n) = \text{IFFT}\left[|H(k)|\right]. \tag{8.26}$$

The cepstrum method has a very good by-product. The combination of the highpass filtered version of the cepstrum and the initial phases from the FFT gives a spectrum that can be considered as the source spectrum in a source-filter model. This helps in designing audio effects based on such a source-filter model. The source signal $x(n)$ can be derived from the calculation of $\exp(C_x(k)) = |X(k)|$ and the initial phase taken from $Y(k) = |Y(k)|e^{j\varphi_y(k)}$ by performing the IFFT of $|X(k)|e^{j\varphi_y(k)}$ according to

$$x(n) = \text{IFFT}\left[X(k)e^{j\varphi_y(k)}\right]. \tag{8.27}$$

For finding a good threshold between low and high quefrencies, one can make use of the fact that quefrencies are time variables, and whenever the sound is periodic, the cepstrum shows a periodicity corresponding to the pitch. Hence this value is the upper quefrency or upper time limit for the spectral envelope. A low value will smoothen the spectral envelope, while a higher value will include some of the harmonic or partial peaks in the spectral envelope.

Hints and drawbacks

- "Lowpass filtering" is performed by windowing (zeroing values over a "cut quefrency"). This operation corresponds to filtering in the frequency domain with a $\frac{\sin(f)}{f}$ behavior. An alternative version is to use a smooth transition instead of an abrupt cut in the cepstrum domain.

- The cepstrum method will give a spectral estimation that smoothes the instantaneous spectrum. However, log values can go to $-\infty$ for a zero value in the FFT. Though this rarely happens with sounds coming from the real world, where the noise level prevents such values, a good prevention is the limitation of the log value. In our implementation the addition of a small value 0.00001 to the FFT values limits the lower log limit to -100 dB. Once again, an alternative to this bias applied to all values consists in truncating instead. Then, the following line from **MATLAB** code 8.5

```
flog=20*log10(0.00001+abs(f));
```

becomes

```
flog=20*log10(max(0.00001,abs(f)));
```

The artifact is not the same, as the spectrum shape is no more shifted, but clipped when below the threshold value.

- Though the *real cepstrum* is widely used, it is also possible to use the *complex cepstrum* to perform an estimation of the spectral envelope. In this case the spectral envelope will be defined by a complex FFT.

The spectral envelope estimation with the cepstrum has at least the three following limitations:

- The spectral envelope does not exactly link the spectral peaks (approximation): the spectral envelope estimated being a smoothing of the spectrum, nothing implies that the spectral envelope obtained should have the exact same values as the frequency peaks when it crosses them. And in fact, this does not happen.

- The spectral envelope has a behavior which depends on the choice of the cut-off quefrency (and number of cepstral coefficients): for too small values of the cut-off quefrency, the envelope becomes too smooth, whereas for too high values, the envelope follows the spectrum too much, showing anti-resonances between spectral peaks. Another situation where the cepstrum is not efficient is for high-pitched sounds: the number of spectral peaks is too small for the algorithm to perform well, and the resulting envelope may show erratic oscillations. In fact, the cut-off quefrency should be related to the signal's fundamental frequency, which is not necessarily known at that point in the algorithm.

- The spectral envelope is poorly estimated for high-pitched sounds, since the number of partials is small and widely spaced and the algorithm performs smoothing.

For those reasons, alternatives are needed to enhance the computation of spectral envelopes with the cepstrum, such as the iterative cepstrum and the discrete cepstrum. These two alternative techniques also provide cepstral coefficients that can then be used in the same way as the traditional cepstrum in order to perform source-filter separation and transformation.

Iterative cepstrum

In order to enhance the computation of the spectral envelope, it is possible to use an iterative algorithm which calculates only the positive difference between the instantaneous spectrum and the estimated spectral envelope in each step. The principle is explained by Laroche in [Lar95, Lar98]: We first compute $E_m(n, k)$ the initial spectral envelope of $X(n, k)$ by the standard cepstrum technique (step $m = 0$). Then, we apply an iterative procedure, which for step m does the following:

(1) Compute the positive difference between spectrum and spectral envelope $X_m(n, k) = \max(0, X(n, k) - E_m(n, k))$

(2) Compute the spectral envelope $E_{m+1}(n, k)$ by cepstrum using the $X_m(n, k)$ spectrum

(3) Stop when $|X_m(n, k) - E_{m+1}(n, k)| < \Delta$ (with Δ a given threshold).

The spectral envelope is finally given by $E_{m+1}(n, k)$.

While other refinements of the real cepstrum technique for estimating the spectral envelope (such as the discrete cepstrum) require the sound to be harmonic, the iterative cepstrum is similar to the real cepstrum technique: it works for any type of sound. Second, it improves it by providing a smooth envelope that goes through spectral peaks, provided that the threshold Δ is small and the maximum number of iterations is high. Because of the iterative procedure, the computation complexity is much higher, and increases exponentially as Δ decreases. The following **MATLAB** code 8.6 implements this iterative technique.

M-file 8.6 (UX_iterative_cepstrum.m)

```
% function [env,source] = iterative_cepstrum(FT,NF,order,eps,niter,Delta)
% [DAFXbook, 2nd ed., chapter 8]
% ==== This function computes the spectral enveloppe using the iterative
%       cepstrum method
% Inputs:
%    - FT [NF*1 | complex]     Fourier transform X(NF,k)
%    - NF [1*1 | int]          number of frequency bins
%    - order [1*1 | float]     cepstrum truncation order
%    - eps [1*1 | float]       bias
%    - niter [1*1 | int]       maximum number of iterations
%    - Delta [1*1 | float]     spectral envelope difference threshold
% Outputs:
%    - env [NFx1 | float]      magnitude of spectral enveloppe
%    - source [NFx1 | complex] complex source
function [env,source] = iterative_cepstrum(FT,NF,order,eps,niter,Delta)

%---- use data ----
fig_plot = 0;

%---- drawing ----
if(fig_plot), SR = 44100; freq = (0:NF-1)/NF*SR; figure(3); clf; end

%---- initializing ----
Ep = FT;

%---- computing iterative cepstrum ----
for k=1:niter
  flog     = log(max(eps,abs(Ep)));
  cep      = ifft(flog);        % computes the cepstrum
  cep_cut  = [cep(1)/2; cep(2:order); zeros(NF-order,1)];
  flog_cut = 2*real(fft(cep_cut));
  env      = exp(flog_cut);     % extracts the spectral shape
  Ep       = max(env, Ep);      % get new spectrum for next iteration
  %---- drawing ----
  if(fig_plot)
    figure(3); % clf  %uncomment to not superimpose curves
    subplot(2,1,1); hold on
    plot(freq, 20*log10(abs(FT)), 'k')
    h = plot(freq, 20*log10(abs(env)), 'k');
    set(h, 'Linewidth', 1, 'Color', 0.5*[1 1 1])
    xlabel('f / Hz \rightarrow'); ylabel('\rho(f) / d \rightarrow')
    title('Original spectrum and its enveloppe')
    axis tight; ax = axis; axis([0 SR/5 ax(3:4)])
    drawnow
  end
  %---- convergence criterion ----
  if(max(abs(Ep)) <= Delta), break; end
end

%---- computing source from enveloppe ----
source = FT ./ env;
```

Discrete cepstrum

The discrete-cepstrum technique by Galas and Rodet [GR90] can only be used for harmonic sounds. It requires a peak-picking algorithm first (best suited after additive analysis, see Spectral Processing Chapter 10), from which it computes an exact spectral envelope which links the maximum peaks. From the spectrum $X(n, k)$ of the current frame L amplitudes $a(n, l)$ and corresponding frequencies $f(n, l)$ at the peaks in the spectrum are estimated. The cepstral coefficients are then derived so that the frequency response $\overline{F}(f)$ fits those $\{a(n, l), f(n, l)\}$ values for $l = 1, \ldots, L$. From a cepstral viewpoint, we look for the coefficients $c(n), n = 0, \ldots, N$ of a real cepstrum, which corresponding frequency response $\overline{F}(f)$ minimizes the criterion

$$\epsilon(n) = \sum_{l=1}^{L} w(l) \| \log a(n, l) - \log |\overline{F}(f)| \|^2 \tag{8.28}$$

with $w(l), l = 1, \cdots, L$ a series of weights related to each partial harmonic. Note that a logarithmic scale is used (it can either be $20 \log_{10}$, $\log_{10}$ or $\log$) to ensure the constraint is related to the magnitude spectrum in dB.

Since the values of $\overline{F}(f_l)$ are from a symmetric spectrum (real signal), its Fourier transform can be reduced to a zero-phase cosine sum given by

$$\overline{F}(f) = c(0) + 2 \sum_{i=1}^{N} c(i) \cdot \cos(2\pi f i). \tag{8.29}$$

The quantity ϵ we need to minimize can then be reformulated in matrix form according to

$$\epsilon = \|\mathbf{a} - \mathbf{Mc}\|_W^2 = (\mathbf{a} - \mathbf{Mx})^T \mathbf{W} (\mathbf{a} - \mathbf{Mc}) \tag{8.30}$$

with the following notations:

$$\mathbf{a} = \begin{bmatrix} \log a(n, 1) \\ log a(n, 2) \\ \vdots \\ \log a(n, L) \end{bmatrix} \tag{8.31}$$

$$\mathbf{M} = \begin{bmatrix} 1 & 2\cos(2\pi f_1) & 2\cos(4\pi f_1) & \cdots & 2\cos(2N\pi f_1) \\ 1 & 2\cos(2\pi f_2) & 2\cos(4\pi f_2) & \cdots & 2\cos(2N\pi f_2) \\ \vdots & \vdots & \vdots & & \vdots \\ 1 & 2\cos(2\pi f_L) & 2\cos(4\pi f_L) & \cdots & 2\cos(2N\pi f_L) \end{bmatrix} \tag{8.32}$$

$$\mathbf{c} = \begin{bmatrix} c(0) \\ c(1) \\ \vdots \\ c(L) \end{bmatrix} \tag{8.33}$$

$$\mathbf{W} = \begin{bmatrix} w(1) & 0 & \cdots & 0 \\ 0 & \log w(2) & \cdots & 0 \\ \vdots & \vdots & \ddots & \vdots \\ 0 & 0 & \cdots & \log w(L) \end{bmatrix}. \tag{8.34}$$

The cepstral coefficient vector **c** can be estimated by

$$\mathbf{c} = \left(\mathbf{M}^T \mathbf{W} \ \mathbf{M}\right)^{-1} \mathbf{M}^T \mathbf{W} \ \mathbf{a}.$$ (8.35)

The following **MATLAB** code 8.7 implements the discrete cepstrum computation.

M-file 8.7 (UX_discrete_cepstrum_basic.m)

```
% function cep = discrete_cepstrum_basic(F, A, order)
% [DAFXbook, 2nd ed., chapter 8]
% ==== This function computes the discrete spectrum regardless of
%       matrix conditionning and singularity.
% Inputs:
%    - A [1*L | float]        harmonic partial amplitudes
%    - F [1*L | float]        harmonic partial frequencies
%    - order [1*1 | int]      number of cepstral coefficients
% Outputs:
%    - cep [1xorder | float]  cepstral coefficients
function cep = discrete_cepstrum_basic(F, A, order)

%---- initialize matrices and vectors
L = length(A);
M = zeros(L,order+1);
M = zeros(L,L);
R = zeros(order+1,1);
W = zeros(L,L);

for i=1:L
  M(i,1) = 0.5;
  for k=2:order+1
    M(i,k) = cos(2*pi*(k-1)*F(i));
  end
  W(i,i) = 1; % weights = 1 by default
end
M = 2.*M;

%---- compute the solution, regardless of matric conditioning
Mt = transpose(M);
MtWMR = Mt * W * M;
cep = inv(MtWMR) * Mt * W * log(A);
```

Generally, the $\mathbf{M}^T \mathbf{W} \mathbf{M}$ matrix is poorly conditioned or even singular, when there are a smaller number of constraints than parameters L. Since L corresponds to the number of harmonic peaks in the spectrum, it can be quite small for high-pitched sounds, resulting in such problems. Two improvements will be introduced.

Regularized discrete cepstrum

The criterion error ϵ, as given in (8.28), may be replaced by a composite that balances between the constraint equation $\epsilon(n)$ and a regularization criterion, which computes the energy of the spectral envelope derivative [CLM95]. This regularization criterion is expressed as $\int_0^1 \left[\frac{d \log |F(n,f)|}{df} \right]^2 df$.

The new criterion is then given as

$$\epsilon_{reg}(n) = (1 - \lambda)\epsilon(n) + \lambda \left(\int_0^1 \left[\frac{\mathrm{d} \log |F(n, f)|}{\mathrm{d}f} \right]^2 \mathrm{d}f \right) \tag{8.36}$$

(NB: in [CLM95], there is no $(1 - \lambda)$ coefficient for the first term.) From there, it is then easy to show that

$$\left(\int_0^1 \left[\frac{\mathrm{d} \log |F(n, f)|}{\mathrm{d}f} \right]^2 \mathrm{d}f \right) = \mathbf{c}^T \mathbf{R} \mathbf{c} \tag{8.37}$$

with $\mathbf{R}$ the diagonal matrix which elements are $8\pi^2[0, 1, 2^2, 3^3, ..., L^2]$. From this, we can derive the solution given by

$$\mathbf{c} = \left(\mathbf{M}^T \mathbf{W} \mathbf{M} + \frac{\lambda}{1 - \lambda} \mathbf{R} \right)^{-1} \mathbf{M}^T \mathbf{W} \, \mathbf{a}. \tag{8.38}$$

This formulation only differs from [CLM95] by the ratio $\frac{\lambda}{1-\lambda}$, because we prefer to use a value of $\lambda \in [0, 1[$. The corresponding M-file 8.8 shows the implementation.

M-file 8.8 (UX_discrete_cepstrum_reg.m)

```
% function cep = discrete_cepstrum_reg(F, A, order, lambda)
% [DAFXbook, 2nd ed., chapter 8]
% ==== This function computes the discrete spectrum using a
%        regularization function
% Inputs:
%    - A [1*L | float]      harmonic partial amplitudes
%    - F [1*L | float]      harmonic partial frequencies
%    - order [1*1 | int]    number of cepstral coefficients
%    - lambda [1*2 | float] weighting of the perturbation, in [0,1[
% Output:
%    - cep [1*order | float] cepstral coefficients
function cep = discrete_cepstrum_reg(F, A, order, lambda)

%---- reject incorrect lambda values
if lambda>=1 | lambda <0
  disp('Error: lambda must be in [0,1[')
  cep = [];
  return;
end

%---- initialize matrices and vectors
L = length(A);
M = zeros(L,order+1);
R = zeros(order+1,1);
for i=1:L
  M(i,1) = 1;
  for k=2:order+1
    M(i,k) = 2 * cos(2*pi*(k-1)*F(i));
  end
end

%---- initialize the R vector values
```

```
coef = 8*(pi^2);
for k=1:order+1
  R(k,1) = coef * (k-1)^2;
end

%---- compute the solution
Mt = transpose(M);
MtMR = Mt*M + (lambda/(1.-lambda))*diag(R);
cep = inv(MtMR) * Mt*log(A);
```

Less strict and jittered envelope

A second improvement to relax the constraint consists in adding a number of random points around the peaks, and increasing the smoothing criterion. Then, the spectral envelope is more attracted to the region of the spectral peaks, but does not have to go through them exactly. The following **MATLAB** code 8.9 implements this random discrete cepstrum computation.

M-file 8.9 (UX_discrete_cepstrum_random.m)

```
% function cep = discrete_cepstrum_random(F, A, order, lambda, Nrand, dev)
% [DAFXbook, 2nd ed., chapter 8]
% ==== This function computes the discrete spectrum using multiples of each
%       peak to which a small random amount is added, for better smoothing.
% Inputs:
%   - A [1*L | float]        harmonic partial amplitudes
%   - F [1*L | float]        harmonic partial frequencies
%   - order [1*1 | int]      number of cepstral coefficients
%   - lambda [1v2 | float]   weighting of the perturbation, in [0,1[
%   - Nrand [1*1 | int]      nb of random points generated per (Ai,Fi) pair
%   - dev  1*2 | float]      deviation of random points, with Gaussian
% Outputs:
%   - cep [1*order |à float] cepstral coefficients
function cep = discrete_cepstrum_random(F, A, order, lambda, Nrand, dev)

if lambda>=1 | lambda <0 % reject incorrect lambda values
  disp('Error: lambda must be in [0,1[')
  cep = [];
  return;
end

%---- generate random points ----
L = length(A);
new_A = zeros(L*Nrand,1);
new_F = zeros(L*Nrand,1);
for k=1:L
  sigA = dev * A(k);
  sigF = dev * F(k);
  for l=1:L
    new_A((l-1)*Nrand+1) = A(l);
    new_F((l-1)*Nrand+1) = F(l);
    for n=1:Nrand
      new_A((l-1)*Nrand+n+1) = random('norm', A(l), sigA);
      new_F((l-1)*Nrand+n+1) = random('norm', F(l), sigF);
    end
  end
end
```

```
%---- initialize matrices and vectors
L = length(new_A);
M = zeros(L,order+1);
R = zeros(order+1,1);
for i=1:L
  M(i,1) = 1;
  for k=2:order+1
    M(i,k) = 2 * cos(2*pi*(k-1)*new_F(i));
  end
end
%---- initialize the R vector values
coef = 8*(pi^2);
for k=1:order+1,
  R(k,1) = coef * (k-1)^2;
end
%---- compute the solution
Mt = transpose(M);
MtMR = Mt*M + (lambda/(1.-lambda))*diag(R);
cep = inv(MtMR) * Mt*log(new_A);
```

In conclusion, the cepstrum method allows both the separation of the audio signal into a source signal and a filter (spectral envelope) and, as a by-product, the estimation of the fundamental frequency, which has been published in [Nol64] and later reported in [Sch99]. Various refinements exist, such as the iterative cepstrum and the discrete cepstrum with an increasing computational complexity.

8.3 Source-filter transformations

8.3.1 Vocoding or cross-synthesis

The term vocoder has different meanings. One is "voice-coding" and refers directly to speech synthesis. Another meaning for this term is the phase vocoder, which refers to the short-time Fourier transform, as discussed in Section 7.2. The last meaning is the one of the musical instrument named the *Vocoder* and this is what this paragraph is about: vocoding or cross-synthesis.

This effect takes two sound inputs and generates a third one which is a combination of the two input sounds. The general idea is to combine two sounds by "spectrally shaping" the first sound by the second one and preserving the pitch of the first sound. A variant and improvement are the removal of the spectral envelope of the initial sound (also called whitening) before filtering with the spectral envelope of the second one. This implies the ability to extract a spectral envelope evolving with time and to apply it to a signal.

Although spectral estimation is well represented by its amplitude versus frequency representation, most often it is the filter representation that can be a help in the application of this spectral envelope: the channel vocoder uses the weighted sum of filtered bandpass signals, the LPC calculates an IIR filter, and even the cepstrum method can be seen as a circular convolution with an FIR filter. As this vocoding effect is very important and can give different results depending on the technique used, we will introduce these three techniques applied to the vocoding effect.

Channel vocoder

This technique uses two banks of filters provided by the channel vocoder (see Figure 8.14), as well as the RMS (root mean square) values associated with these channels. For each channel the

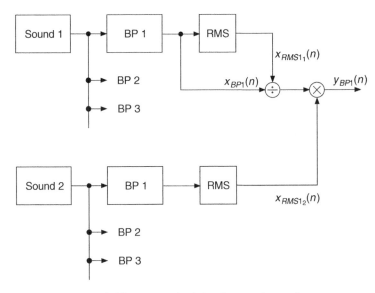

Figure 8.14 Basic principle of spectral mutations.

bandpass signal is divided by the RMS value of this channel, and then multiplied by the RMS value of the other sound. The mathematical operation is given by

$$y_{BP_i}(n) = x_{BP_i}(n) \cdot \frac{x_{RMSi_2}(n)}{x_{RMSi_1}(n)}, \tag{8.39}$$

where $x_{RMSi_1}(n)$ and $x_{RMSi_2}(n)$ represent the RMS values in channel i for the two sounds. One should be careful with the division. Of course divisions by zero should be avoided, but there should also be a threshold for avoiding the amplification of noise. This works well when sound 2 has a strong spectral envelope, for example, a voice. The division by $x_{RMSi_1}(n)$ can be omitted or replaced by just modifying the amplitude of each band. Sound 1 can also be a synthetic sound (pulse, sawtooth, square).

The following M-file 8.10 demonstrates a cross-synthesis between two sounds based on the channel vocoder implemented by IIR filters.

M-file 8.10 (UX_cross_synthesis_CV.m)

```
% UX_cross_synthesis_CV.m    [DAFXbook, 2nd ed., chapter 8]
% ==== This function performs a cross-synthesis with channel vocoder
clear

%----- setting user data -----
[DAFx_in_sou,FS] = wavread('moore_guitar'); % signal for source extraction
DAFx_in_env      = wavread('toms_diner');   % signal for spec. env. extraction
ly       = min(length(DAFx_in_sou), length(DAFx_in_env)); % min signal length
DAFx_out = zeros(ly,1);      % result signal
r        = 0.99;             % sound output normalizing ratio
lp       = [1, -2*r, +r*r];  % low-pass filter used
epsi     = 0.00001;

%----- init bandpass frequencies
f0 = 10;                 % start freq in Hz
f0 = f0/FS *2;           % normalized freq
```

```
fac_third = 2^(1/3);   % freq factor for third octave
K   = floor(log(1/f0) / log(fac_third));  % number of bands

%----- performing the vocoding or cross synthesis effect -----
fprintf(1, 'band number (max. %i):\n', K);
tic
for k=1:K
  fprintf(1, '%i ', k);
  f1 = f0 * fac_third;            % upper freq of bandpass
  [b, a] = cheby1(2, 3, [f0 f1]); % Chebyshev-type 1 filter design
  f0 = f1;                        % start freq for next band
  %-- filtering the two signals --
  z_sou   = filter(b, a, DAFx_in_sou);
  z_env   = filter(b, a, DAFx_in_env);
  rms_env = sqrt(filter(1, lp, z_env.*z_env)); % RMS value of sound 2
  rms_sou = sqrt(epsi+filter(1, lp, z_sou.*z_sou));  % with whitening
% rms_sou = 1.;                             % without whitening
  DAFx_out = DAFx_out + z_sou.*rms_env./rms_sou; % add result to output buffer
end
fprintf(1, '\n');
toc

%----- playing and saving output sound -----
soundsc(DAFx_out, FS)
DAFx_out_norm = r * DAFx_out/max(abs(DAFx_out)); % scale for wav output
wavwrite(DAFx_out_norm, FS, 'CrossCV')
```

This program performs bandpass filtering inside a loop. Precisely, Chebychev type 1 filters are used, which are IIR filters with a ripple of 3 dB in the passband. The bandwidth is chosen as one-third of an octave, hence the 0.005 to 0.0063 window relative to half of the sampling rate in **MATLAB**'s definition. Then sound 1 and sound 2 are filtered, and the RMS value of the filtered sound 2 is extracted: $z2$ is squared, filtered by a two pole filter on the x axis, and its square root is taken. This RMS2 value serves as a magnitude amplifier for the $z1$ signal, which is the filtered version of sound 1. This operation is repeated every one-third of an octave by multiplying the frequency window, which is used for the definition of the filter, by 1.26 (3rd root of 2). A whitening process can be introduced by replacing line $rms1 = 1.;$ with $rms1 = epsi + norm(filter(1, lp, z1.*z1), 2);$. A small value $epsi$ (0.0001) is added to RMS1 to avoid division by zero. If $epsi$ is greater, the whitening process is attenuated. Thus this value can be used as a control for whitening.

Linear prediction

Cross-synthesis between two sounds can also be performed using the LPC method [Moo79, KAZ00]. One filter removes the spectral envelope of the first sound and the spectral envelope of the second sound is used to filter the excitation signal of the first sound, as shown in Figure 8.15.

The following M-file 8.11 performs cross-synthesis based on the LPC method. The prediction coefficients of sound 1 are used for an FIR filter to whiten the original sound. The prediction coefficients of sound 2 are used in the feedback path of a synthesis filter, which performs filtering of the excitation signal of sound 1 with the spectral envelope derived from sound 2.

M-file 8.11 (UX_cross_synthesis_LPC.m)

```
% UX_cross_synthesis_LPC.m   [DAFXbook, 2nd ed., chapter 8]
% ==== This function performs a cross-synthesis with LPC
clear;
```

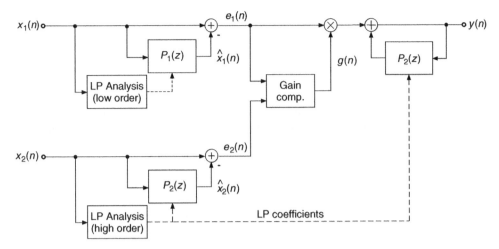

Figure 8.15 Cross-synthesis with LPC.

```
%----- user data -----
[DAFx_in_sou, FS] = wavread('moore_guitar.wav');  % sound 1: source/excitation
DAFx_in_env    = wavread('toms_diner.wav');        % sound 2: spectral env.
long           = 400;        % block length for calculation of coefficients
hopsize        = 160;        % hop size (is 160)
env_order      = 20          % order of the LPC for source signal
source_order   = 6           % order of the LPC for excitation signal
r              = 0.99;       % sound output normalizing ratio

%----- initializations -----
ly = min(length(DAFx_in_sou), length(DAFx_in_env));
DAFx_in_sou = [zeros(env_order, 1); DAFx_in_sou; ...
  zeros(env_order-mod(ly,hopsize),1)] / max(abs(DAFx_in_sou));
DAFx_in_env = [zeros(env_order, 1); DAFx_in_env; ...
  zeros(env_order-mod(ly,hopsize),1)] / max(abs(DAFx_in_env));
DAFx_out = zeros(ly,1);      % result sound
exc      = zeros(ly,1);      % excitation sound
w        = hanning(long, 'periodic');  % window
N_frames = floor((ly-env_order-long)/hopsize); % number of frames

%----- Perform ross-synthesis -----
tic
for j=1:N_frames
  k        = env_order + hopsize*(j-1);      % offset of the buffer
  %!!! IMPORTANT: function "lpc" does not give correct results for MATLAB 6 !!!
  [A_env, g_env] = calc_lpc(DAFx_in_env(k+1:k+long).*w, env_order);
  [A_sou, g_sou] = calc_lpc(DAFx_in_sou(k+1:k+long).*w, source_order);
  gain(j) = g_env;
  ae       = - A_env(2:env_order+1); % LPC coeff. of excitation
  for n=1:hopsize
    excitation1   = (A_sou/g_sou) * DAFx_in_sou(k+n:-1:k+n-source_order);
    exc(k+n)      = excitation1;
    DAFx_out(k+n) = ae * DAFx_out(k+n-1:-1:k+n-env_order)+g_env*excitation1;
  end
end
toc

%----- playing and saving output signal -----
DAFx_out      = DAFx_out(env_order+1:length(DAFx_out)) / max(abs(DAFx_out));
```

```
soundsc(DAFx_out, FS)
DAFx_out_norm = r * DAFx_out/max(abs(DAFx_out)); % scale for wav output
wavwrite(DAFx_out_norm, FS, 'CrossLPC')
```

Cepstrum

Signal processing based on cepstrum analysis is also called homomorphic signal processing [OS75, PM96]. We have seen that we can derive the spectral envelope (in dB) with the cepstrum technique. Reshaping a sound is achieved by whitening (filtering) a sound with the inverse spectral envelope $1/|H_1(f)|$ and then filtering with the spectral envelope $|H_2(f)|$ of the second sound (see Figure 8.16). The series connection of both filters leads to a transfer function $H_2(f)/H_1(f)$. By taking the logarithm according to $\log|H_2(f)|/|H_1(f)| = \log|H_2(f)| - \log|H_1(f)|$, the filtering operation is based on the difference of the two spectral envelopes. The first spectral envelope performs the whitening by inverse filtering and the second spectral envelope introduces the formants. The inverse filtering of the input sound 1 and subsequent filtering with spectral envelope of sound 2 can be performed in one step by the fast convolution technique.

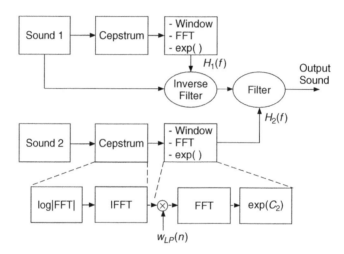

Figure 8.16 Basic principle of homomorphic cross-synthesis. The spectral envelopes of both sounds are derived by the cepstrum method.

Here we present the core of a program given by M-file 8.12 that uses the spectral envelope of a sound (number 2) superimposed on a sound (number 1). Though musically very effective, this first program does not do any whitening of sound 1.

M-file 8.12 (UX_cross_synthesis_cepstrum.m)

```
% UX_cross_synthesis_cepstrum.m    [DAFXbook, 2nd ed., chapter 8]
% ==== This function performs a cross-synthesis with cepstrum
clear all; close all

%----- user data -----
% [DAFx_sou, SR] = wavread('didge_court.wav');  % sound 1: source/excitation
% DAFx_env       = wavread('la.wav');            % sound 2: spectral enveloppe
[DAFx_sou, SR] = wavread('moore_guitar.wav'); % sound 1: source/excitation
DAFx_env  = wavread('toms_diner.wav');          % sound 2: spectral enveloppe
```

```
s_win      = 1024;    % window size
n1         = 256;     % step increment
order_sou  = 30;      % cut quefrency for sound 1
order_env  = 30;      % cut quefrency for sound 2
r          = 0.99;    % sound output normalizing ratio

%----- initialisations -----
w1          = hanning(s_win, 'periodic');  % analysis window
w2          = w1;                  % synthesis window
hs_win      = s_win/2;             % half window size
grain_sou   = zeros(s_win,1);      % grain for extracting source
grain_env   = zeros(s_win,1);      % grain for extracting spec. enveloppe
pin         = 0;                   % start index
L           = min(length(DAFx_sou),length(DAFx_env));
pend        = L - s_win;           % end index
DAFx_sou    = [zeros(s_win, 1); DAFx_sou; ...
  zeros(s_win-mod(L,n1),1)] / max(abs(DAFx_sou));
DAFx_env    = [zeros(s_win, 1); DAFx_env; ...
  zeros(s_win-mod(L,n1),1)] / max(abs(DAFx_env));
DAFx_out    = zeros(L,1);

%----- cross synthesis -----
while pin<pend
  grain_sou = DAFx_sou(pin+1:pin+s_win).* w1;
  grain_env = DAFx_env(pin+1:pin+s_win).* w1;
  %=============================================
  f_sou       = fft(grain_sou);           % FT of source
  f_env       = fft(grain_env)/hs_win;    % FT of filter
  %---- computing cepstrum ----
  flog        = log(0.00001+abs(f_env));
  cep         = ifft(flog);               % cepstrum of sound 2
  %---- liftering cepstrum ----
  cep_cut     = zeros(s_win,1);
  cep_cut(1:order_sou) = [cep(1)/2; cep(2:order_sou)];
  flog_cut    = 2*real(fft(cep_cut));
  %---- computing spectral enveloppe ----
  f_env_out = exp(flog_cut);              % spectral shape of sound 2
  grain     = (real(ifft(f_sou.*f_env_out))).*w2; % resynthesis grain
  % =========================================
  DAFx_out(pin+1:pin+s_win) = DAFx_out(pin+1:pin+s_win) + grain;
  pin       = pin + n1;
end

%----- listening and saving the output -----
% DAFx_in = DAFx_in(s_win+1:s_win+L);
DAFx_out = DAFx_out(s_win+1:length(DAFx_out)) / max(abs(DAFx_out));
soundsc(DAFx_out, SR);
DAFx_out_norm = r * DAFx_out/max(abs(DAFx_out)); % scale for wav output
wavwrite(DAFx_out_norm, SR, 'CrossCepstrum')
```

In this program n1 represents the analysis step increment (or hop size), and grain_sou and grain_env windowed buffers of DAFx_in_sou and DAFx_in_env. f_sou is the FFT of grain_sou and f_env is the spectral envelope derived from the FFT of grain_env. Although this algorithm performs a circular convolution, which theoretically introduces time aliasing, the resulting sound does not have artifacts.

Whitening `DAFx_in_sou` before processing it with the spectral envelope of `DAFx_in_env` can be done in a combined step: we calculate the spectral envelope of `DAFx_in_sou` and subtract it (in dB) from the spectral envelope of `DAFx_in_env`. The following code lines given by M-file 8.13 perform a whitening of `DAFx_in_sou` and a cross-synthesis with `DAFx_in_env`.

M-file 8.13 (UX_cross_synthesis_cepstrum_whitening.m)

```
%===========================================
f_sou     = fft(grain_sou);            % FT of source
f_env     = fft(grain_env)/hs_win;     % FT of filter
%---- computing cepstra ----
flog_sou       = log(0.00001+abs(f_sou));
cep_sou        = ifft(flog_sou);       % cepstrum of sound 1 / source
flog_env       = log(0.00001+abs(f_env));
cep_env        = ifft(flog_env);       % cepstrum of sound 2 / env.
%---- liftering cepstra ----
cep_cut_env    = zeros(s_win,1);
cep_cut_env(1:order_env) = [cep_env(1)/2; cep_env(2:order_env)];
flog_cut_env   = 2*real(fft(cep_cut_env));
cep_cut_sou    = zeros(s_win,1);
cep_cut_sou(1:order_sou) = [cep_sou(1)/2; cep_sou(2:order_sou)];
flog_cut_sou   = 2*real(fft(cep_cut_sou));
%---- computing spectral enveloppe ----
f_env_out = exp(flog_cut_env - flog_cut_sou);   % whitening with source
grain     = (real(ifft(f_sou.*f_env_out))).*w2; % resynthesis grain
% ==========================================
```

In this program `flog_cut_sou` and `flog_cut_env` represent (in dB) the spectral envelopes derived from `grain_sou` and `grain_env` for a predefined cut quefrency. Recall that this value is given in samples. It should normally be below the pitch period of the sound, and the lower it is, the more smoothed the spectral envelope will be.

8.3.2   Formant changing

This effect produces a "Donald Duck" voice without any alteration of the fundamental frequency. It can be used for performing an alteration of a sound whenever there is a formant structure. However, it can also be used in conjunction with pitch-shifted sounds for recovering a natural formant structure (see Section 8.3.4).

The musical goal is to remove the spectral envelope from one sound and to impose another one, which is a warped version of the first one, as shown in Figure 8.17, where the signal processing is also illustrated. This means that we have to use a spectral correction that is a ratio of the two spectral envelopes. In this way the formants, if there are any, are changed according to this warping function. For example, a transposition of the spectral envelope by a factor of two will give a "Donald Duck" effect without time stretching. This effect can also be seen as a particular case of cross-synthesis, where the modifier comes from an interpolated version of the original sound. Though transposition of the spectral envelope is classical, other warping functions can be used.

From a signal-processing point of view the spectral correction for formant changing can be seen in the frequency domain as $H_2(f)/H_1(f)$. First divide by the spectral envelope $H_1(f)$ of the input sound and then multiply by the frequency scaled spectral envelope $H_2(f)$. In the cepstrum domain the operation $H_2(f)/H_1(f)$ leads to the subtraction $C_2(f) - C_1(f)$, where $C(f) = \log|H(f)|$. When using filters for time-domain processing, the transfer function is $H_2(f)/H_1(f)$ (see Figure 8.17). We will shortly describe three different methods for the estimation of the two spectral envelopes.

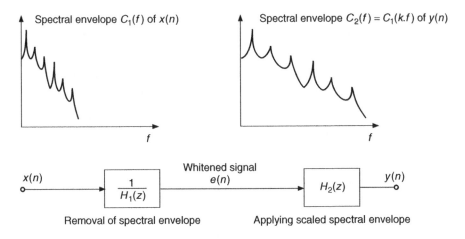

Figure 8.17 Formant changing by frequency scaling the spectral envelope and time-domain processing.

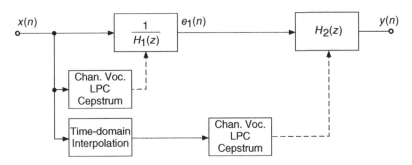

Figure 8.18 Formant changing by time-domain processing.

Interpolation of the input signal

The spectral envelopes $C_1(f)$ and $C_2(f)$, or filters $H_1(f)$ and $H_2(f)$ can be obtained by different techniques. If $C_2(f)$ is a frequency-scaled version of $C_1(f)$, one can calculate the spectral envelope $C_2(f)$ from the analysis of a transposed version of the initial signal, as shown in Figure 8.18. The transposed version is obtained by time-domain interpolation of the input signal. The channel vocoder, LPC and the cepstrum method, allow the estimation of either the spectral envelope or the corresponding filter. One must take care to keep synchronicity between the two signals. This can be achieved by changing the hop size according to this ratio. The algorithm works as follows:

- Whitening: filter the input signal with frequency response $\frac{1}{H_1(f)}$ or subtract the input spectral envelope $C_1(f) = \log|H_1(f)|$ from the log of the input magnitude spectrum.

- The filter $H_1(f)$ or the spectral envelope $C_1(f)$ is estimated from the input signal.

- Formant changing: apply the filter with frequency response $H_2(f)$ to the whitened signal or add the spectral envelope $C_2(f) = \log|H_2(f)|$ to the whitened log of the input magnitude spectrum.

- The filter $H_2(f)$ or the spectral envelope $C_2(f)$ is estimated from the interpolated input signal.

Formant changing based on the cepstrum analysis is shown in Figure 8.19. The spectral correction is calculated from the difference of the log values of the FFTs, of both the input signal and the interpolated input signal. This log difference is transformed to the cepstrum domain, lowpass weighted and transformed back by the exponential to the frequency domain. Then, the filtering of the input signal with the spectral correction filter $H_2(z)/H_1(z)$ is performed in the frequency domain. This fast convolution is achieved by multiplication of the corresponding Fourier transforms of the input signal and the spectral correction filter. The result is transformed back to the time domain by an IFFT yielding the output signal. An illustrative example is shown in Figure 8.20. The M-file 8.14 demonstrates this technique.

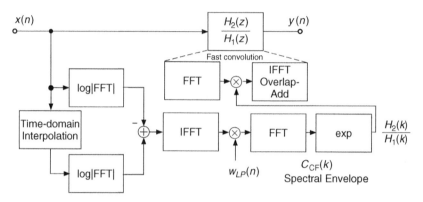

Figure 8.19 Formant changing by frequency-domain processing: cepstrum analysis, spectral correction filter computation and fast convolution.

M-file 8.14 (UX_fmove_cepstrum.m)

```
% UX_fmove_cepstrum.m    [DAFXbook, 2nd ed., chapter 8]
% ==== This function performs a formant warping with cepstrum
clear; clf;
%----- user data -----
fig_plot = 0;      % use any value except 0 or [] to plot figures
[DAFx_in, SR] = wavread('la.wav'); % sound file
warping_coef  = 2.0;
n1       = 512;   % analysis hop size
n2       = n1;    % synthesis hop size
s_win    = 2048;  % window length
order    = 50;    % cut quefrency
r        = 0.99;  % sound output normalizing ratio
%----- initializations -----
w1       = hanning(s_win, 'periodic'); % analysis window
w2       = w1;                % synthesis window
hs_win   = s_win/2;          % half window size
L        = length(DAFx_in);  % signal length
DAFx_in  = [zeros(s_win, 1); DAFx_in; ...
   zeros(s_win-mod(L,n1),1)] / max(abs(DAFx_in)); % 0-pad + normalize
DAFx_out = zeros(L,1);       % output signal
t        = 1 + floor((0:s_win-1)*warping_coef); % apply the warping
lmax     = max(s_win,t(s_win));
```

```
tic
%UUUUUUUUUUUUUUUUUUUUUUUUUUUUUUUUUUUUUUUUUUU
pin  = 0;
pout = 0;
pend = L - s_win;
if(fig_plot)
  pin  = 6500;
  pend = pin + s_win;
end
while pin<pend
   grain  = DAFx_in(pin+1:pin+s_win).* w1;
%============================================
   f      = fft(grain)/hs_win;         % spectrum of grain
   flogs  = 20*log10(0.00001+abs(f));  % log|X(k)|

   grain1 = DAFx_in(pin+t).* w1;       % linear interpolation of grain
   f1     = fft(grain1)/hs_win;        % spectrum of interpolated grain
   flogs1 = 20*log10(0.00001 + abs(f1)); % log|X1(k)|
   flog   = log(0.00001+abs(f1)) - log(0.00001+abs(f));
   cep    = ifft(flog);                % cepstrum
   cep_cut = [cep(1)/2; cep(2:order); zeros(s_win-order,1)];

   corr   = exp(2*real(fft(cep_cut))); % spectral shape
   grain  = (real(ifft(f.*corr))).*w2;

   fout   = fft(grain);
   flogs2 = 20*log10(0.00001+abs(fout));

   %----- figures for real-time spectral shape up to SR/2 -----
   if(fig_plot)
     range = (1:hs_win/2);
     subplot(3,1,1);  plot((range)*SR/s_win, flogs(range));
     title('a) original spectrum'); drawnow;
     subplot(3,1,2);  plot((range)*SR/s_win, flogs1(range));
     title('b) spectrum of time-scaled signal');
     subplot(3,1,3);  plot((range)*SR/s_win, flogs2(range));
     title('c) formant changed spectrum');
     xlabel('f in Hz \rightarrow');
     drawnow
   end
% ============================================
   DAFx_out(pout+1:pout+s_win) = DAFx_out(pout+1:pout+s_win) + grain;
   pin  = pin + n1;
   pout = pout + n2;
end
%UUUUUUUUUUUUUUUUUUUUUUUUUUUUUUUUUUUUUUUUUUU
toc
%----- listening and saving the output -----
soundsc(DAFx_out, SR);
DAFx_out_norm = r * DAFx_out/max(abs(DAFx_out)); % scale for wav output
wavwrite(DAFx_out_norm, SR, 'la_fmove.wav');
```

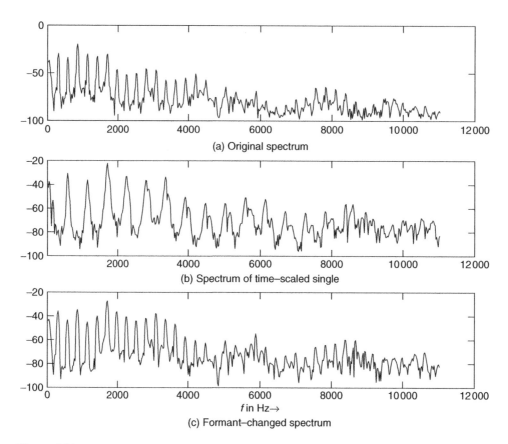

Figure 8.20 Example of formant changing: the upper plot shows the input spectrum and the middle plot the spectrum of the interpolated signal. The lower plot shows the result of the formant-changing operation, where the spectral envelope of the interpolated spectrum can be noticed.

Interpolation or scaling of the spectral envelope

The direct warping is also possible, for example, by using the interpolation of the spectral envelope derived from a cepstrum technique: $C_2(f) = C_1(k \cdot f)$ or $C_2(f/k) = C_1(f)$. There are, however, numerical limits: the cepstrum method uses an FFT and frequencies should be below half of the sampling frequency. Thus, if the transposition factor is greater than one, we will get only a part of the initial envelope. If the transposition factor is less than one, we will have to zero-pad the rest of the spectral envelope to go up to half of the sampling frequency. The block diagram for the algorithm using the cepstrum analysis method is shown in Figure 8.21. The following M-file 8.15 demonstrates this method.

M-file 8.15 (UX_fomove_cepstrum.m)

```
% UX_fomove_cepstrum.m   [DAFXbook, 2nd ed., chapter 8]
% ==== This function performs a formant warping with cepstrum
clear; clf;
```

```
%----- user data -----
fig_plot = 0;      % use any value except 0 or [] to plot figures
[DAFx_in, SR] = wavread('la.wav'); % sound file
warping_coef  = 2.0
n1        = 512;   % analysis hop size
n2        = n1;    % synthesis hop size
s_win     = 2048;  % window length
order     = 50;    % cut quefrency
r         = 0.99;  % sound output normalizing ratio

%----- initializations -----
w1        = hanning(s_win,  'periodic'); % analysis window
w2        = w1;                 % synthesis window
hs_win    = s_win/2;           % half window size
L         = length(DAFx_in); % signal length
DAFx_in   = [zeros(s_win, 1); DAFx_in; ...
   zeros(s_win-mod(L,n1),1)] / max(abs(DAFx_in)); % 0-pad + normalize
DAFx_out = zeros(L,1);
x0        = floor(min((1+(0:hs_win)/warping_coef), 1+hs_win));
          % apply the warping
x         = [x0, x0(hs_win:-1:2)];% symmetric extension

tic
%UUUUUUUUUUUUUUUUUUUUUUUUUUUUUUUUUUUUUUUUUUUUUU
pin  = 0;
pout = 0;
pend = L - s_win;

while pin<pend
   grain = DAFx_in(pin+1:pin+s_win).* w1;
%=========================================
   f     = fft(grain)/hs_win;
   flog  = log(0.00001+abs(f));
   cep   = ifft(flog);
   cep_cut  = [cep(1)/2; cep(2:order); zeros(s_win-order,1)];
   %---- flog_cut1|2 =  spectral shapes before/after formant move
   flog_cut1 = 2*real(fft(cep_cut));
   flog_cut2 = flog_cut1(x);
   corr  = exp(flog_cut2-flog_cut1);
   grain = (real(ifft(f.*corr))).*w2;
% =========================================
   DAFx_out(pout+1:pout+s_win) = DAFx_out(pout+1:pout+s_win) + grain;
   pin  = pin + n1;
   pout = pout + n2;
end
%UUUUUUUUUUUUUUUUUUUUUUUUUUUUUUUUUUUUUUUUUUUUUU
toc

%----- listening and saving the output -----
soundsc(DAFx_out, SR);
DAFx_out_norm = r * DAFx_out/max(abs(DAFx_out)); % scale for wav output
wavwrite(DAFx_out_norm, SR, 'la_fomove.wav');
```

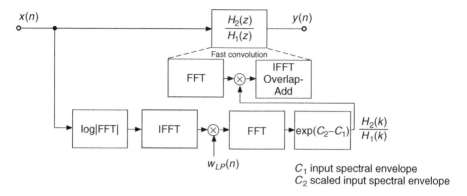

Figure 8.21   Formant changing by scaling the spectral envelope.

Direct warping of filters

A direct warping of the spectral envelope filter $H_1(z)$ to $H_2(z)$ is also possible. The warping of a filter transfer function can be performed by the allpass function $z^{-1} \rightarrow \frac{z^{-1}-\alpha}{1-\alpha z^{-1}}$. Substituting z^{-1} in the transfer function $H_1(z)$ by $\frac{z^{-1}-\alpha}{1-\alpha z^{-1}}$ yields the warped transfer function $H_2(z)$. Further details on warping can be found in Chapter 11 and in [Str80, LS81, HKS+00].

8.3.3   Spectral interpolation

Spectral interpolation means that instead of mixing two sounds, we mix their excitation signals independently of their spectral envelopes, as shown in Figure 8.22. If we have the decomposition of sound grains in the frequency domain according to $E(f) \cdot H(f)$, where $E(f)$ represents the Fourier transform of the excitation and $H(f)$ is the spectral envelope ($H(f) = \exp[C(f)]$), we

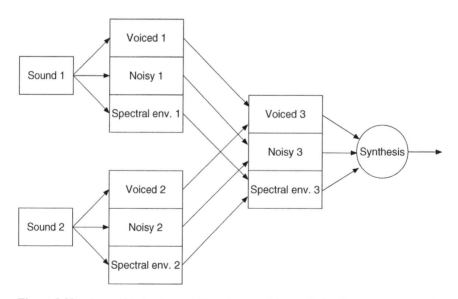

Figure 8.22   A possible implementation of spectral interpolation between two sounds.

can perform spectral interpolation between two sounds by mixing according to

$$Y(f) = [e_1 E_1(f) + e_2 E_2(f)] \cdot [c_1 H_1(f) + c_2 H_2(f)]. \tag{8.40}$$

The excitation grains and the spectral envelopes are added. This transformed representation is then used for the resynthesis operation. We introduce cross-terms by this method, which musically means that the excitation source of one sound also influences the spectral envelope of the second and conversely. For regular mixing of two sounds the result would be $k_1 E_1(f) \cdot H_1(f) + k_2 E_2(f) \cdot H_2(f)$. The M-file 8.16 performs time-varying spectral interpolation between two sounds. We go from a first sound to another one by independently mixing the sources and resonances of these two sounds.

M-file 8.16 (UX_spectral_interp.m)

```
% UX_spectral_interp.m    [DAFXbook, 2nd ed., chapter 8]
% ==== This function performs a spectral interpolation with cepstrum
%
% k: spectral mix, calculated at every step in this example, as
%     starts with gain=0 for sound 1 and gain=1 for sound 2
%     finishes with gain=1 for sound 1 and gain=0 for sound 2
%     so we move from sound 1 to sound 2
clear;

%----- user data -----
[DAFx_in1,SR] = wavread('claire_oubli_voix.WAV');  % sound 1
DAFx_in2 = wavread('claire_oubli_flute.WAV'); % sound 2
n1       = 512;              % analysis hop size
n2       = n1;              % synthesis hop size
s_win    = 2048;            % window length
w1       = hanning(s_win, 'periodic'); % analysis window
w2       = w1;              % synthesis window
cut      = 50              % cut-off quefrency

%----- initializations -----
L        = min(length(DAFx_in1), length(DAFx_in2));
DAFx_in1 = [zeros(s_win, 1); DAFx_in1; ...
   zeros(s_win-mod(L,n1),1)] / max(abs(DAFx_in1)); % 0-pad + norm
DAFx_in2 = [zeros(s_win, 1); DAFx_in2; ...
   zeros(s_win-mod(L,n1),1)] / max(abs(DAFx_in2)); % 0-pad + norm
DAFx_out = zeros(length(DAFx_in1),1);

tic
%UUUUUUUUUUUUUUUUUUUUUUUUUUUUUUUUUUUUUUUUUUUUUUU
pin  = 0;
pout = 0;
pend = L - s_win;
while pin<pend
    %---- k factor (spectral mix) wich varies between 0 and 1
    k       = pin / pend;
    kp      = 1 - k;
    %---- extracting input grains
    grain1 = DAFx_in1(pin+1:pin+s_win) .* w1;
    grain2 = DAFx_in2(pin+1:pin+s_win) .* w1;
%==========================================
    %---- computing spectral shape of sound 1
    f1     = fft(fftshift(grain1));
```

```
flog   = log(0.00001+abs(f1));
cep    = fft(flog);
cep_coupe   = [cep(1)/2; cep(2:cut); zeros(s_win-cut,1)];
flog_coupe1 = 2*real(ifft(cep_coupe));
spec1 = exp(flog_coupe1);
%---- computing spectral shape of sound 2
f2     = fft(fftshift(grain2));
flog   = log(0.00001+abs(f2));
cep    = fft(flog);
cep_coupe   = [cep(1)/2; cep(2:cut); zeros(s_win-cut,1)];
flog_coupe2 = 2*real(ifft(cep_coupe));
spec2 = exp(flog_coupe2);
%----- interpolating the spectral shapes in dBs
spec   = exp(kp*flog_coupe1+k*flog_coupe2);
%----- computing the output spectrum and grain
ft     = (kp*f1./spec1+k*f2./spec2).*spec;
grain = fftshift(real(ifft(ft))).*w2;
%============================================
   DAFx_out(pout+1:pout+s_win) = DAFx_out(pout+1:pout+s_win) + grain;
   pin    = pin + n1;
   pout   = pout + n2;
end
%UUUUUUUUUUUUUUUUUUUUUUUUUUUUUUUUUUUUUUUUUUU
toc

%----- listening and saving the output -----
% DAFx_in = DAFx_in1(s_win+1:s_win+L);
DAFx_out = DAFx_out(s_win+1:s_win+L) / max(abs(DAFx_out));
soundsc(DAFx_out, SR);
wavwrite(DAFx_out, SR, 'spec_interp.wav');
```

Spectral interpolation is the first step towards morphing, a term borrowed from the visual domain but with a much more ambiguous meaning in the audio domain. Time synchronization between the two sounds has to be taken into account. The matter of pitch interpolation should be different from the mixing of excitation signals as it is presented here. Morphing usually relies on high-level attributes and spectral interpolation and follows more complicated schemes, such as shown in Figure 8.22. Advanced methods will be discussed in Chapter 10.

8.3.4   Pitch shifting with formant preservation

In Chapter 6, we saw some pitch-shifting algorithms which transpose the entire spectrum, and consequently the spectral envelope. This typically alters the voice giving a "Donald Duck" or "barrel" feeling. For pitch shifting a sound without changing its articulation, i.e., its formant structure, one has to keep the spectral envelope of the original sound.

Inverse formant move plus pitch shifting

A possible way to remove the artifacts is to perform a formant move in the inverse direction of the pitch shifting. This process can be inserted into a FFT/IFFT-based pitch-shifting algorithm before the reconstruction, as shown in Figure 8.23. For this purpose we have to calculate a correction function for this formant move.

The following algorithm (see M-file 8.17) is based on the pitch-shifting algorithm described in Chapter 7 (see Section 7.4.4). The only modification is a formant move calculation before the

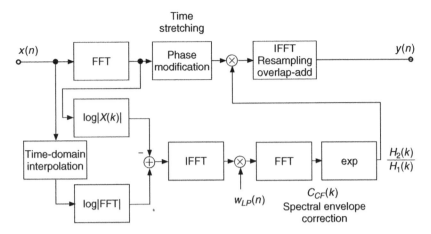

Figure 8.23 Pitch shifting with formant preservation: the pitch shifting is performed in the frequency domain.

reconstruction of every individual grain, which will be overlapped and added. For the formant move calculation, a crude interpolation of the analysis grain is performed, in order to recover two spectral envelopes: the one of the original grain and the one of its pitch-transposed version. From these two spectral envelopes the correction factor is computed (see previous section) and applied to the magnitude spectrum of the input signal before the reconstruction of the output grain (see Figure 8.23).

M-file 8.17 (UX_pitch_pv_move.m)

```
% UX_pitch_pv_move.m    [DAFXbook, 2nd ed., chapter 7]
% ==== This function performs a ptch-shifting that preserves
%      the spectral enveloppe
clear;

%----- user data -----
[DAFx_in, SR] = wavread('la.wav'); % sound file
n1      = 512;  % analysis hop size
                % try n1=400 (pitch down) or 150 (pitch up)
n2      = 256;  % synthesis hop size
                % keep it a divisor of s_win (256 is pretty good)
s_win   = 2048; % window length
order   = 50;   % cut quefrency
coef    = 0.99;   % sound output normalizing ratio

%----- initializations -----
w1        = hanning(s_win, 'periodic'); % analysis window
w2        = w1;   % synthesis window
tscal     = n2/n1;  % time-scaling ratio
s_win2    = s_win/2;
L         = length(DAFx_in);
DAFx_in   = [zeros(s_win, 1); DAFx_in; ...
   zeros(s_win-mod(L,n1),1)] / max(abs(DAFx_in)); % 0-pad + norm
%-- for phase unwrapping
omega     = 2*pi*n1*[0:s_win-1]'/s_win;
phi0      = zeros(s_win,1);
```

```
psi       = zeros(s_win,1);
%-- for linear interpolation of a grain of length s_win
lx        = floor(s_win*n1/n2);
DAFx_out = zeros(lx+length(DAFx_in),1);
x         = 1 + (0:lx-1)'*s_win/lx;
ix        = floor(x);
ix1       = ix + 1;
dx        = x - ix;
dx1       = 1 - dx;
warp      = n1/n2    % warpinf coefficient, = 1/tscal
t         = 1 + floor((0:s_win-1)*warp);
lmax      = max(s_win,t(s_win))

tic
%UUUUUUUUUUUUUUUUUUUUUUUUUUUUUUUUUUUUUUUUUUUU
pin    = 0;
pout   = 0;
pend   = L - lmax;

while pin<pend
   grain    = DAFx_in(pin+1:pin+s_win).* w1;
%==========================================
   f        = fft(fftshift(grain));
   r        = abs(f);
   phi      = angle(f);
   %---- unwrapping the phase ----
   delta_phi = omega + princarg(phi-phi0-omega);
   phi0     = phi;
   psi      = princarg(psi+delta_phi*tscal);
   %---- moving formant ----
   grain1   = DAFx_in(pin+t) .* w1;
   f1       = fft(grain1)/s_win2;
   flog     = log(0.00001+abs(f1))-log(0.00001+abs(f));
   cep      = ifft(flog);
   cep_cut = [cep(1)/2; cep(2:order); zeros(s_win-order,1)];
   corr     = exp(2*real(fft(cep_cut))); % correction enveloppe
   %---- spec env modif.: computing output FT and grain ----
   ft       = (r.* corr.* exp(i*psi));
   grain    = fftshift(real(ifft(ft))).*w2;
   %---- pitch-shifting: interpolating output grain -----
   grain2   = [grain;0];
   grain3   = grain2(ix).*dx1+grain2(ix1).*dx;
   % plot(grain);drawnow;
%==========================================
   DAFx_out(pout+1:pout+lx) = DAFx_out(pout+1:pout+lx) + grain3;
   pin      = pin + n1;
   pout     = pout + n1;
end
%UUUUUUUUUUUUUUUUUUUUUUUUUUUUUUUUUUUUUUUUUUUU
toc

%----- listening and saving the output -----
% DAFx_in  = DAFx_in(s_win+1:s_win+L);
DAFx_out = coef * DAFx_out(s_win+1:s_win+L) / max(abs(DAFx_out));
soundsc(DAFx_out, SR);
wavwrite(DAFx_out, SR, 'la_pitch_pv_move.wav');
```

An illustrative example of pitch shifting with formant preservation is shown in Figure 8.24. The spectral envelope is preserved and the pitch is increased by a factor of two.

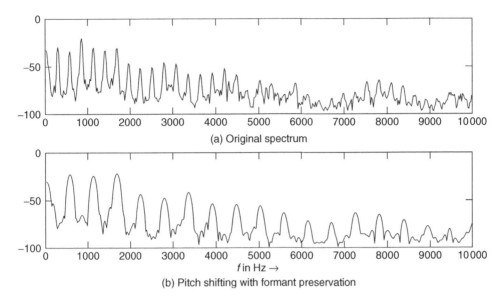

(a) Original spectrum

(b) Pitch shifting with formant preservation

Figure 8.24   Example of pitch shifting with formant preservation.

Resampling plus formant move

It is also possible to combine an interpolation scheme with a formant move inside an analysis-synthesis loop. The block diagram in Figure 8.25 demonstrates this approach. The input segments are interpolated from length N_1 to length N_2. This interpolation or resampling also changes the time duration and thus performs pitch shifting in the time domain. The resampled segment is then applied to an FFT/IFFT-based analysis/synthesis system, where the correction function for the formant move is computed by the cepstrum method. This correction function is based on the input spectrum and the spectrum of the interpolated signal and is computed with the help of the

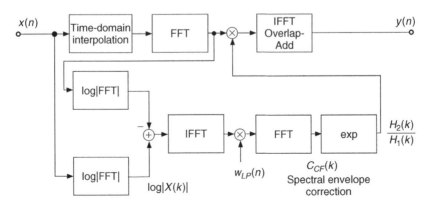

Figure 8.25   Pitch shifting with formant preservation: the pitch shifting is performed in the time domain.

cepstrum technique. Then the correction function is applied to the interpolated input spectrum by the fast convolution technique.

The following M-file 8.18 performs interpolation of successive grains with a ratio given by the two numbers $R_a = $ n1 and $R_s = $ n2 and performs a formant move to recover the original spectral envelope.

M-file 8.18 (UX_interp_move.m)

```
% UX_interp_move.m    [DAFXbook, 2nd ed., chapter 8]
% ==== This function performs a ptch-shifting that preserves
%       the spectral enveloppe
clear;

%----- user data -----
[DAFx_in, SR] = wavread('la.wav'); % sound file
n1      = 400;  % analysis hop size
                % try n1=400 (pitch down) or 150 (pitch up)
n2      = 256;  % synthesis hop size
                % keep it a divisor of s_win (256 is pretty good)
s_win = 2048; % window length
order = 50;   % cut quefrency
coef  = 0.99; % sound output normalizing ratio

%----- initializations -----
w1        = hanning(s_win, 'periodic'); % analysis window
w2        = w1;       % synthesis window
tscal     = n2/n1     % time-scaling ratio
hs_win    = s_win/2; % half window size
L         = length(DAFx_in);
DAFx_in   = [zeros(s_win, 1); DAFx_in; ...
    zeros(s_win-mod(L,n1),1)] / max(abs(DAFx_in)); % 0-pad + norm
%-- for linear interpolation of a grain of length s_win
lx        = floor(s_win*n1/n2);
DAFx_out = zeros(ceil(tscal*length(DAFx_in)),1);
x         = 1 + (0:s_win-1)'*lx/s_win;
ix        = floor(x);
ix1       = ix + 1;
dx        = x - ix;
dx1       = 1 - dx;
warp      = n1/n2    % warpinf coefficient, = 1/tscal
lmax      = max(s_win,lx)

tic
%UUUUUUUUUUUUUUUUUUUUUUUUUUUUUUUUUUUUUUUUUUUUUU
pin  = 0;
pout = 0;
pend = L - lmax;

while pin<pend
%==========================================
    %----- FT of interpolated grain
    grain1  = (DAFx_in(pin+ix).*dx1 + DAFx_in(pin+ix1).*dx).* w1;
    f1      = fft(grain1)/hs_win;
    %----- FT of reference grain, for formant matching
    grain2  = DAFx_in(pin+1:pin+s_win).* w1;
    f2      = fft(grain2)/hs_win;
```

```
%----- correction factor for spectral enveloppe
flog     = log(0.00001+abs(f2))-log(0.00001+abs(f1));
cep      = ifft(flog);
cep_cut  = [cep(1)/2; cep(2:order); zeros(s_win-order,1)];
corr     = exp(2*real(fft(cep_cut)));
%----- so now make the formant move
grain    = fftshift(real(ifft(f1.*corr))).*w2;
% plot(grain);drawnow;
%==========================================
    DAFx_out(pout+1:pout+s_win) = DAFx_out(pout+1:pout+s_win) + grain;
    pin     = pin + n1;
    pout    = pout + n2;
end
%UUUUUUUUUUUUUUUUUUUUUUUUUUUUUUUUUUUUUUUU
toc

%----- listening and saving the output -----
% DAFx_in = DAFx_in(s_win+1:s_win+L);
DAFx_out = coef * DAFx_out(s_win+1:length(DAFx_out)) / max(abs(DAFx_out));
soundsc(DAFx_out, SR);
wavwrite(DAFx_out, SR, 'la_interp_move.wav');
```

Resampling of the excitation signal

Instead of moving the formants, an alternative technique is to calculate an excitation signal by removing the spectral envelope, to process the excitation signal by a pitch shifting algorithm and to filter the pitch shifted excitation signal with the original spectral envelope. LPC algorithms can be used for this approach. Figure 8.26 shows a block diagram of pitch shifting with formant preservation using the LPC method. First, a predictor is computed and the predictor is used for the inverse filtering of the input signal, which yields the excitation signal. Then the excitation signal is applied to a pitch shifting algorithm and the output signal is filtered with the synthesis filter $H_1(z)$. The processing steps can be performed completely in the time domain. The pitch shifting is achieved by first time stretching and subsequent resampling.

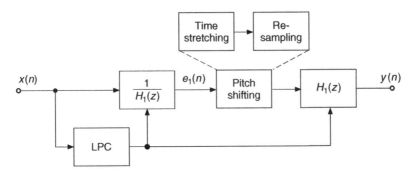

Figure 8.26 Pitch shifting with formant preservation with the LPC method.

8.4 Conclusion

The central topic of this chapter is the division of the audio signal into its source signal and a time-varying filter derived from the spectral envelope of the signal. These two features are individually processed before synthesis of an output signal. The source-filter model of an audio signal, originally a basic technique for speech processing, allows the implementation of several digital audio effects based on these two global features of an audio signal and opens up new vistas for experimentation and further research. These global features can either be extracted by time-frequency techniques (FFT/IFFT) and the cepstrum method or time-domain techniques based on linear prediction (LPC). Both techniques deliver a source-filter model of the audio input signal. Beyond it, they allow the extraction of further global features such as pitch or fundamental frequency, and this will be further described in Chapter 9. A further alternative to the source-filter processing presented in this chapter, is the separation of the audio signal into individual components such as sinusoids and noise, which is discussed in Chapter 10.

References

[CLM95] O. Cappé, J. Laroche and E. Moulines. Regularized estimation of cepstrum envelope from discrete frequency points. In *IEEE ASSP Workshop on App. Signal Proces. Audio Acoust.*, pp. 213–216, 1995.

[GR90] T. Galas and X. Rodet. An improved cepstral method for deconvolution of source-filter systems with discrete spectra: Application to musical sounds. In *Proc. Int. Comp. Music Conf. (ICMC'90), Glasgow*, pp. 82–8, 1990.

[HKS+00] A. Härma, M. Karjalainen, L. Savioja, V. Välimäki, U. K. Laine and J. Huopaniemi. Frequency-warped signal processing for audio applications. *J. Audio Eng. Soc.*, 48(11): 1011–1031, 2000.

[KAZ00] F. Keiler, D. Arfib and U. Zölzer. Efficient linear prediction for digital audio effects. In *Proc. DAFX-00 Conf. Digital Audio Effects*, pp. 19–24, 2000.

[Lar95] J. Laroche. *Traitement des Signaux Audio-Fréquences*. Département TSI, Sup'Télécom Paris, 1995.

[Lar98] J. Laroche. Time and pitch scale modification of audio signals. In M. Kahrs and K. Brandenburg (eds), *Applications of Digital Signal Processing to Audio & Acoustics*, pp. 279–309. Kluwer Academic Publishers, 1998.

[LS81] P. Lansky and K. Steiglitz. Synthesis of timbral families by warped linear prediction. *Comp. Music J.*, 5(3): 45–47, 1981.

[Mak75] J. Makhoul. Linear prediction: A tutorial review. *Proc. IEEE*, 63(4): 561–580, 1975.

[Mak77] J. Makhoul. Stable and efficient lattice methods for linear prediction. *IEEE Trans. Acoust. Speech Signal Proc.* ASSP-25(5): 423–428, 1977.

[MG76] J. D. Markel and A. H. Gray. *Linear Prediction of Speech*. Springer-Verlag, 1976.

[Moo79] J. A. Moorer. The use of linear prediction of speech in computer music applications. *J. Audio Eng. Soc.*, 27(3): 134–140, 1979.

[Nol64] A. M. Noll. Short-time spectrum and "cepstrum" techniques for vocal-pitch detection. *J. Acoust. Soc. Am.*, 36(2): 296–302, 1964.

[Orf90] S. J. Orfanidis. *Optimum Signal Processing, An Introduction*, 2nd edition. McGraw-Hill, 1990.

[OS75] A. V. Oppenheim and R. W. Schafer. *Digital Signal Processing*. Prentice-Hall, 1975.

[O'S00] D. O'Shaugnessy. *Speech Communication*, 2nd edition. Addison-Wesley, 2000.

[PM96] J. G. Proakis and D. G. Manolakis. *Digital Signal Processing*. Prentice-Hall, 1996.

[Sch99] M. R. Schroeder. *Computer Speech*. Springer-Verlag, 1999.

[Str80] H. W. Strube. Linear prediction on a warped frequency scale. *J. Acoust. Soc. Am.*, 68(4): 1071–1076, 1980.

9

Adaptive digital audio effects

V. Verfaille, D. Arfib, F. Keiler, A. von dem Knesebeck and U. Zölzer

9.1 Introduction

The idea of controlling a sound transformation according to the musical scene it is displayed in may be as old as the idea of composition. The particular case of adaptive DAFX is when the sound to be transformed is also used as the source of the modification control parameter(s): some information about the sound is then collected and used to modify the sound with a coherent evolution. With such a perspective, adaptive DAFX can be considered as an extension of, or inspired by, composition processes similar to counterpoint. This process can also be compared to what happens in natural physical phenomena, such as the harmonic enrichment happening in brass instruments when the sound level increases. This chapter presents and formalizes the use of adaptive control in order to build new digital audio effects. It presents a general framework that encompasses existing DAFX and opens doors to the development of new and refined DAFX. It is aimed at presenting the adaptive control of effects, describing the steps to build an adaptive effect and explaining the necessary modifications of signal-processing techniques.

Adaptive DAFX can be developed and used with various goals in mind: to provide a high-level control for usual DAFX, to propose new production and/or creative tools by offering new DAFX, or to strengthen the relationship between Fx, control and perception. The control and mapping aspects of adaptive DAFX are important matters. In any DAFX, the control is sometimes part of the effect (e.g., compressor), sometimes part of the mapping (e.g., pitch-shift amount). Also, the gestural control mapping of DAFX is unfortunately often limited to a one-to-one mapping (one gestural parameter is directly mapped to one effect parameter), with the noticeable exception of the GRM Tools [Fav01, INA03], which allow for linear interpolation between presets of N parameters. In order to define a general framework we will look at some famous simple examples of adaptive DAFX. As explained in Section 4.2 the compressor (see Figure 9.1) transforms the input sound

DAFX: Digital Audio Effects, Second Edition. Edited by Udo Zölzer.
© 2011 John Wiley & Sons, Ltd. Published 2011 by John Wiley & Sons, Ltd.

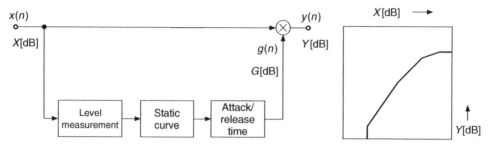

Figure 9.1   Compressor/expander with input/output level relationship.

level to the output sound level according to a gain control signal. The input sound level is mapped depending on a non-linear curve into the control signal with an attack and release time (inducing some hysteresis).

The principle of auto-tuning a musical sound consists in applying a time-varying transposition (or pitch shift), which is controlled by the fundamental frequency of the input signal so that the pitch becomes tuned to a given musical scale (see Figure 9.2). It is also called "pitch discretization to temperate scale" (see Chapter 10), even though it would work for any non-temperature scale too. The auto-tune effect modifies the pitch by applying a f_0-dependent pitch shift, as depicted in Figure 9.2. The output fundamental frequency depends on: (i) the input fundamental frequency, (ii) a non-linear mapping law that applies a discretization of fundamental frequency to the tempered scale (see Figure 9.3), and (iii) a musical scale that may change from time to time depending on the music signature and chord changes.

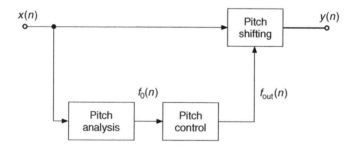

Figure 9.2   Auto-tune.

Some adaptive DAFX have existed and been in use for a long time. They were designed and finely crafted with a specific musical or music production goal. Their properties and design are now used to generalize the adaption principle, allowing one to define several forms of adaptive DAFX and to perform a more systematic investigation of sound-feature control. When extracting sound features, one performs some kind of indirect acquisition of the physical gesture used to produce the sound. Then, the musical gesture conveyed by the sound used to extract features is implicitly used to shape the sound transformation with meaning, because '*the intelligence is* (already) *in the sound signal.*' Such generalizing approach has been helpful to finding new and creative DAFX.

Definition of adaptive DAFX

Adaptive DAFX are made by combining an audio effect with an adaptive control stage. More specifically, adaptive DAFX are defined as audio effects with a time-varying control derived from

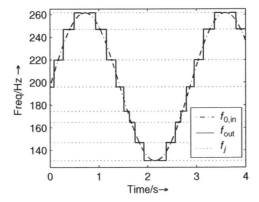

Figure 9.3   Fundamental frequency of an auto-tuned FM sound

sound features[1] transformed into valid control parameter values using specific mapping functions [VA01], as depicted in Figure 9.4. This definition generalizes previous observations of existing adaptive effects (compressor, auto-tune, cross-synthesis), but is also inspired by the combination of an amplitude/pitch follower with a voltage-controlled oscillator [Moo65].

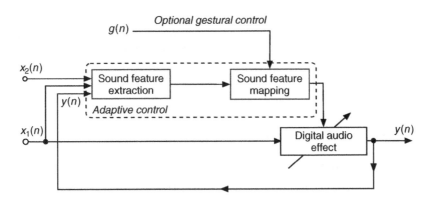

Figure 9.4   Diagram of the adaptive effect. Sound features are extracted from an input signal $x_1(n)$ or $x_2(n)$, or from the output signal $y(n)$. The mapping between sound features and the control parameters of the effect is modified by a gestural control. Figure reprinted with IEEE permission from [VZA06].

Adaptive DAFX are called differently according to the authors, for instance 'dynamic processing' (even though 'dynamic' will mean 'adaptive' for some people, or more generally 'time-varying' without adaptation for other people), 'intelligent effects' [Arf98], 'content-based transformations' [ABL+03], etc. The corresponding acronym to adaptive DAFX is ADAFX. With ADAFX, it is to be noted that the effect name can be non-specific to the sound descriptor (for instance: cross-synthesis, adaptive spectral panning, adaptive time-scaling), but it also can have a control-based name (for instance: auto-tune, compressor). Such names are based on the perceptual effect

---

[1] Recent literature tends to use 'sound descriptors' instead of 'sound features'; both describe the same reality, that is to say parameters that describe the sound signal, and/or some of its statistical, acoustical or perceptual properties.

produced by the signal-processing technique. Generally speaking, ADAFX don't have their control limited to the adaptive part, but rather it is two-fold:

- Adaptive control derived from sound features;

- Gestural control – used for real-time access through input devices.

The mapping laws to transform sound features into DAFX control parameters make use of non-linear warping curves, possibly hysteresis, as well as feature combination (see Section 9.3).

The various forms ADAFX may take depend on the input signal used for feature extraction:

- **Auto-adaptive** effects have their features extracted from the input signal $x_1(n)$. Common examples are compressor/expander, and auto-tune.

- **Adaptive** or **external-adaptive** effects have their features extracted from at least one other input signal $x_2(n)$. An example is cross-ducking, where the sound level of $x_1(n)$ is lowered when the sound level of $x_2(n)$ goes above a given threshold.

- **Feedback adaptive** effects have their features extracted from the output signal $y(n)$; it follows that auto-adaptive and external-adaptive effects are feed-forward-adaptive effects.

- **Cross-adaptive** effects are a combination of at least two external-adaptive effects (not depicted in Figure 9.4); they use at least two input signals $x_1(n)$ and $x_2(n)$. Each signal is processed using the features of another signal as controls. Examples are cross-synthesis and automatic mixing (see Chapter 13).

Note that cross synthesis can be considered as both an external-adaptive effect and a cross-adaptive effect Therefore, the four forms of ADAFX do not provide a good classification of ADAFX since they are not exclusive; they do, however, provide a way to better describe, directly in the effect name, where the sound descriptor come from. The next two sections investigate sound-feature extraction (Section 9.2), and mapping strategies related to adaptive DAFX (Section 9.3).

9.2   Sound-feature extraction

9.2.1   General comments

Sound features are parameters that describe the sound. They are used in a wide variety of applications such as coding, automatic transcription, automatic score following, and analysis-synthesis. As an example, the research field of music information retrieval has been rapidly and increasingly developing during the last ten years, offering various analysis systems and many sound features. A musical sound has some perceptive features that can be extracted from a time-frequency representation. As an example, pitch is a function of time that is very important for musicians, but richness of timbre, inharmonicity, balance between odd and even harmonics, and noise level are other examples of such time-varying parameters. These parameters are global in the sense that they are observations of the sound without any analytical separation of these components, which will be discussed in Chapter 10. They are related to perceptive cues and are based on hearing and psychoacoustics. These global parameters can be extracted from time-frequency or source-filter representations using classical tools of signal processing, where psychoacoustic fundamentals also have to be taken into account. The use of these parameters for digital audio effects is twofold: one can use them inside the effect algorithm itself, or one can use these features as control variables for other effects, which is the purpose of this chapter. Pitch tracking as a source of control is a well-known application. Examples of audio effects using feature extraction inside the algorithm are the correction of tuning, which uses pitch extraction (auto-tune), or even the compression of a sound, which uses amplitude extraction.

Their computation is based on a representation of the sound (for instance a source-filter, a time-frequency or a spectral model), but not necessarily the same as the one used to apply the adaptive effect. This means that the two signal-processing blocks of sound-feature extraction and audio effect may be decorrelated, and the implementation of one may not rely on the implementation of the other, resulting in an increase in CPU use. For this reason, we will present the computation of various sound features, each with various implementations, depending on the model domain. Depending on the application, sound features may require more- or less-accurate computation. For instance, an automatic score-following system must have accurate pitch and rhythm detection. Another example is the evaluation of brightness, acoustical correlate of which is the spectral centroid. Therefore, brightness can either be computed from a psychoacoustic model of brightness [vA85, ZF99], or approximated by the spectral centroid, with an optional correction factor [Bea82], or by the zero-crossing rate or the spectral slope. In the context of adaptive control, any feature can provide good control: depending on its mapping to the effect control parameters, it may provide a transformation that sounds. This is not systematically related to the accuracy of the feature computation, since the feature is extracted and then mapped to a control. For example, a pitch model using the auto-correlation function does not always provide a good pitch estimation; this may be a problem for automatic transcription or auto-tune, but not if it is low-pass filtered and drives the frequency of a tremolo. As already explained in Chapter 1, there is a complex and subjective equation involving the sound to be processed, the audio effect, the mapping, the feature, and the will of the musician. For that reason, no restriction is given *a priori* to existing and eventually redundant features; however, perceptual features seem to be a better starting point when investigating the adaptive control of an effect.

Sound-feature classification

At least six viewpoints can be considered in order to classify the sound features or descriptors: (i) the description level, (ii) the acquisition method, (iii) the integration time, (iv) the type of feature, (v) the causality, and (vi) the computational domain (time or frequency).

Description level   We consider low-level sound features as features that are related to acoustical or signal-processing parameters, whereas high-level sound features are related to sound perception and/or cognition. For instance, sound level, spectral centroid, fundamental frequency, and signal-to-noise ratio are signal/acoustical properties, whereas (perceived) loudness, brightness, pitch, and noisiness are perceptual properties of the sound. Those two categories can be further separated as follows:

- Low level: signal level itself, acoustical properties, without the need for a signal model
  - direct computation, e.g., amplitude by RMS, spectral centroid
  - indirect computation, e.g., using complex computation and sound models (partials' amplitude and frequency)
- High level: perceptual attributes and cognitive descriptions
  - perceptually relevant parameters, but not psychoacoustical models (e.g., jitter and shimmer of harmonics, related to timbral properties)
  - perceptual attributes: pitch, loudness, timbral attributes (brightness, noisiness, roughness), spatial cues, etc.
  - cognitive parameters and expressiveness-related parameters: harmony, vibrato, etc.

There are some relationships between low-level features and perceptual features, as some perceptual features are approximated by some low-level sound features. A non-exhaustive set of sound features [VZA06] shown in Figure 9.5 will contain various sound features that are commonly used for

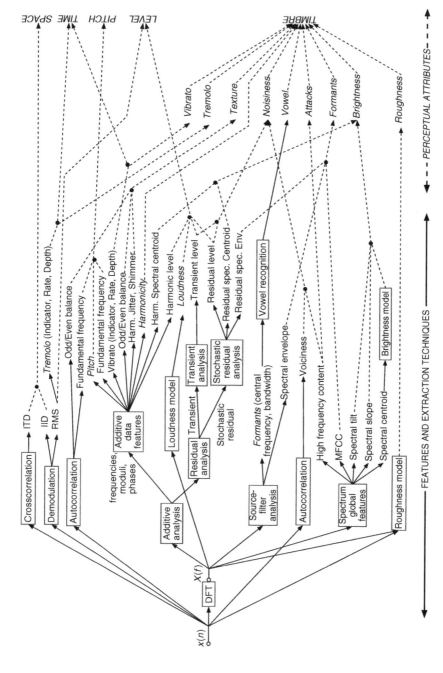

Figure 9.5 Example set of sound features that can be used as control parameters in adaptive effects [VZA06]. The arrow line types indicate the techniques used for extraction (left and plain lines) and the related perceptual attribute (right and dashed lines). Italic words refer to perceptual attributes. Figure reprinted with IEEE permission from [VZA06].

timbre space description (for instance based on MPEG-7 proposals [PMH00]) as well as features computed by perceptual models such as the ones extracted by the PsySound software [Cab99] in an offline (non-real-time) context: pitch, loudness, brightness, roughness, etc. Therefore, the wider the sound-feature set, the more chances we have to grasp the sound information along all perceptual attributes, with a consequent increase in information redundancy.

Acquisition method   Various acquisition and computation methods can be used. A sound feature $f(m)$ can be obtained directly, as is the sound amplitude by RMS. It can also be obtained indirectly, as the derivative:

$$\text{der}_1(m) = f_S \frac{f(m) - f(m-1)}{R_a} \tag{9.1}$$

$$\text{der}_2(m) = f_S \frac{f(m+1) - f(m)}{R_a}, \tag{9.2}$$

with R_a the analysis increment step, f_S the sampling rate. While instantaneous sound features provide information about acoustical or perceptual features, their derivatives inform about the evolution of such features. It can also be obtained indirectly as the integration, the absolute value, the mean of the standard deviation of another parameter. In this latter case, it can be seen as obtained through a given mapping. However, as soon as this new feature has a descriptive meaning, it can also be considered as a new feature.

Integration time   Each parameter is computed and has a meaning only for a given time interval. Due to the time-frequency uncertainty (similar to the Heisenberg principle in quantum mechanics), no sound feature can be considered as really instantaneous, but rather is obtained from a certain number of sound samples, and is then quasi-instantaneous. This remark can also be expanded to samples themselves, as they represent the sound wave of a given time interval with a single value. We will then consider that *quasi-instantaneous* features correspond to parameters extracted from a 512 to 2048 samples of a signal sampled at 44.1 kHz, representing 12–46 ms. *Mid-term* sound features are features derived from the mean, the standard variance, the skewness or the kurtosis (i.e., the four first-order statistical moments) of N values of a parameter using a sliding window, or the beat, loudness. *Long-term* sound features are descriptors based on the signal description, and, for instance, relate to notes, presence/absence of acoustical effects such as vibrato, tremolo, flutter-tonguing. *Very long-term* sound features describe a whole musical excerpt in terms of a sound sequence as seen through music analysis: style, tonality, structure, etc.

The integration time is then related to sound segmentation and region attributes, on which sound feature statistics (mean, standard deviation) are useful. While sound features such as spectral centroid and fundamental frequency can be computed as (almost) instantaneous parameters, there are also sound descriptions that require longer-term estimation and processing. For instance, some loudness perceptual models account for time integration.

Moreover, one may want to segment a note into attack/decay/sustain/release and extract specific features for each section. One may also want to segment a musical excerpt into notes and silences, and then process differently each note, or each sequence of notes, depending on some criterion. This is the case for auto-tune (even though this is somewhat done on-the-fly), swing change (adaptive time-scaling with onset modification depending on the rhythm), etc. Such adaptive segmentation processes may use both low-level and/or high-level features. Note that even in the context of real-time implementation, sound features are not really instantaneous, as they often are computed with a block-by-block approach. Therefore, we need, when describing low-level and high-level features, to indicate their instantaneous and segmental aspects as well. Sound segmentation, which is a common resource in automatic speech-recognition systems, as well as in automatic music-transcription systems, score-following systems, etc., has a central place in ADAFX. Since the late

1990s, music segmentation applications [Ros98] started to use techniques originally developed in the context of speech segmentation [VM90], such as those based on pattern recognition or knowledge-based methodologies.

Type   We may consider at least two main types of sound descriptors: continuous and indicators. *Indicators* are parameters that can take a small and limited number of discrete values, for instance the presence of an acoustical effect (vibrato, tremolo, flutter-tonguing) or the identification of a sung vowel among a subset of five. Conversely, *continuous* features are features that can take any value in a given range, for instance the amplitude with RMS in the interval [0, 1] or the fundamental frequency in the interval [20, 20000] Hz. An intertwined case is the *probability* or *pseudo probability* that is continuous, but can also be used as an indicator as soon as it is coupled with a threshold. The voiciness computed from autocorrelation is such a feature, as it can indicate if the sound is harmonic/voicy or not depending on a continuous value in [0, 1] and a threshold around 0.8. By definition, indicators are higher-level features than continuous descriptors.

Causality   A sound feature can be computed either only from past samples, in which case it is a *causal* process, or from past and future samples, in which case it is an *anti-causal* process. For instance, when considering a time frame, the sound intensity computed by RMS, using the last frame sample as the reference time of the frame will make this computation causal (it can be obtained in real-time), whereas attributing this value to the frame central time will consider this as an anti-causal process. Only causal processing can be performed in real-time (with a latency depending on both the frame size and the computational time), thus limiting the possible real-time applications to the sound features available in real-time.

Time and time-frequency domains   A sound feature directly computed from the wave form uses a time-domain computation, whereas a sound feature computed from the Fourier transform of a time frame uses a frequency-domain computation. We will use this classification. While these six ways to look at sound features inform us about their properties and computation, the next sections will use the perceptual attribute described by the sound feature as a way to organize descriptions of various sound features. As proposed in Section 1.2.2 of Chapter 1, we now present sound features classified according to the perceptual attribute they relate to, namely: loudness, time, pitch, spatial hearing, and timbre.

9.2.2   Loudness-related sound features

Amplitude envelope

One very important feature that can be used for adaptive effects is the amplitude envelope of a sound evolving with time. Even the modulation of a sound by the envelope of another sound is an effect by itself. But more generally the amplitude envelope can be used to control many variables of an effect. Applications of amplitude detection can be found in dynamics processing (see Chapter 4), but can also be integrated into many effects as an external control parameter.

Except for the fact that we want to write a signal as $x(n) = \text{amp}(n) \cdot \text{sig}(n)$, there is no unique definition of an amplitude envelope of a sound. The ear is devised in such a way that slow variations of amplitude (under 10 Hz) are considered as a time envelope while more rapid variations would be heard as a sound. This distinction between an envelope and a signal is known in electroacoustic music as the difference between a 'shape' and a 'matter,' two terms well developed by P. Schaeffer in his *Traité des objets musicaux* [Sch66].

The RMS (root mean square) algorithm has been largely used in Chapter 4 as an amplitude detector based on filtering the squared input samples and taking the square root of the filter output. The RMS value is a good indication of the temporal variation of the energy of a sound, as shown in Figure 9.6. This filtering can also be performed by a FIR filter, and in this case can be inserted into

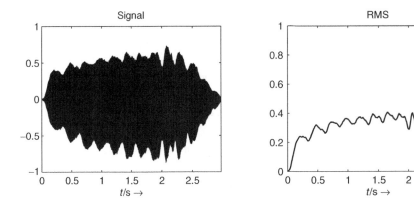

Figure 9.6 Signal and amplitude envelope (RMS value) of the signal.

an FFT/IFFT-based analysis-synthesis scheme for a digital audio effect. The FFT window can be considered a lowpass FIR filter, and one of the reasons for the crucial choice of window size for a short-time Fourier transform is found in the separation between shape and matter: if the window is too short, the envelope will follow rapid oscillations which should not be included. If the window is too large, the envelope will not take into account tremolos which should be included. The following M-file 9.1 calculates the amplitude envelope of a signal according to an RMS algorithm.

M-file 9.1 (UX_rms.m)

```
% Author: Verfaille, Arfib, Keiler, Zölzer
clear; clf
%----- USER DATA -----
[DAFx_in, FS]   = wavread('x1.wav');
hop             = 256;  % hop size between two FFTs
WLen            = 1024; % length of the windows
w               = hanningz(WLen);
%----- some initializations -----
WLen2           = WLen/2;
normW           = norm(w,2);
pft             = 1;
lf              = floor((length(DAFx_in) - WLen)/hop);
feature_rms     = zeros(lf,1);
tic
%=============================================
pin  = 0;
pend = length(DAFx_in) - WLen;

while pin<pend
    grain = DAFx_in(pin+1:pin+WLen).* w;
    feature_rms(pft) = norm(grain,2) / normW;
    pft    = pft + 1;
    pin    = pin + hop;
end
% =============================================
toc
subplot(2,2,1); plot(DAFx_in); axis([1 pend -1 1])
subplot(2,2,2); plot(feature_rms); axis([1 lf -1 1])
```

When using a spectral model, one can separate the amplitude of the sinusoidal component and the amplitude of the residual component. The amplitude of the sinusoidal component is computed for a given frame m as the sum of the amplitude for all L harmonics given by

$$a_{sin,lin}(m) = \sum_{i=1}^{L} a_i(m),$$

(9.3)

with $a_i(m)$ the linear amplitude of the ith harmonic. It can also be expressed in dB as

$$a_{sin,dB}(m) = 20\log_{10}\left(\sum_{i=1}^{L} a_i\right).$$

(9.4)

The amplitude of the residual component is the sum of the absolute values of the residual of one frame, and can also be computed according to

$$a_{res,dB} = 20\log_{10}\left(\sum_{n=0}^{M-1} |x_R(n)|\right)$$

$$= 20\log_{10}\left(\sum_{k=0}^{N-1} |X_R(k)|\right)$$

(9.5)

where $x_R(n)$ is the residual sound, M is the block size, $X_R(k)$ is residual sound spectrum, and N the magnitude spectrum size.

Sound energy

The instantaneous sound energy is the squared amplitude. It can either be derived from the wave form by

$$e_1(n) = [x(n)]^2,$$

(9.6)

from a time-frequency representation for the mth block by

$$e_2(m) = \sum_{k=0}^{N-1} |X(m,k)|^2,$$

(9.7)

or also from a spectral representation by

$$e_3(m) = \sum_{i=1}^{L} [a_i(m)]^2.$$

(9.8)

Loudness

There exist various computational models of loudness, starting from Zwicker's model [ZS65, Zwi77] to various improvements by Zwicker and Fastl [ZF99], Moore and Glasberg [MG96, MGB97], most of them being implemented in the Psysound3[2] [Cab99, Cab00]. Generally speaking, these models consider a critical band in the spectrum, onto which the energy is summed after accounting for frequency masking. More improved models also account for time integration and masking. Since the loudness of a sound depends on the sound level at which it is played, various different loudness curves can be obtained as control curves for adaptive effect control.

Tremolo description

Using a sinusoidal model of the amplitude envelope, one can describe the time evolution of a tremolo in terms of rate or frequency (in Hz), amplitude or depth (in dB), and phase at the start.

---

[2] http://psysound.wikidot.com/

Those parameters can be used as sound features for other purposes. An example is the special sinusoidal model [MR04], when it is used for time-scaling of vibrato sounds, while preserving the vibrato attributes.

9.2.3 Time features: beat detection and tracking

A useful feature for controlling parameters of digital audio effects is the actual tempo or so-called beats-per-minute measure. In a live playing situation usually a drummer or conductor counts the tempo in by hitting his stick, which gives the first precise estimate for the beat. So the beat per minute is known from the very beginning. In a recording situation the first tracks are usually recorded with a so-called click track which is given by the recording system and everything is played in sync to that track. In both situations the beat is detected by simple means of listening and playing in sync to the beat. The beat signal can be used to control effect parameters, such as delay-time settings, speed of parameter modulation, gates for reverb and so on. A variety of beat-synced effects can be found in the Adrenalinn product. In the following, a robust and proven concept based on [BFC05, Fit04, Fit10] will be introduced which offers beat detection and tracking. The beat detection and tracking has a pre-processing stage which separates harmonic and percussive parts for further onset detection of harmonic and percussive signals. The harmonic/percussion separation is based on processing on the spectrogram, making use of median filtering across each frame in frequency direction and across each frequency bin in the time direction (see Figure 9.7).

This separation technique is based on the idea that as a first approximation, broadband noise signals such as drums can be regarded as stable vertical ridges in a spectrogram. Therefore, the

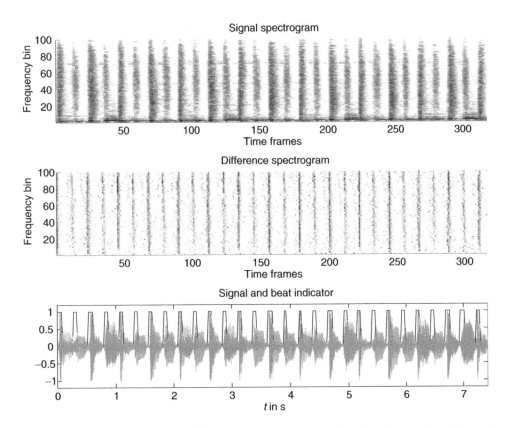

Figure 9.7 Signal spectrogram, difference spectrogram, and time-domain signal and its beat indicators.

presence of narrow band signals, such as the harmonics from a pitched instrument, will result in an increase in energy within a bin over and above that due to the drum instrument, resulting in outliers in the spectrogram frame. These can be removed by the use of a median filter, thereby suppressing the harmonic information within the spectrogram frame. The median filtered frames are stored in a percussion enhanced spectrogram, denoted $P(n, k)$. Similarly, the harmonics of pitched instruments can be regarded as stable horizontal ridges in a spectrogram. In this case, a sudden onset due to a drum or percussion instrument will result in a large increase in energy across time within a given frequency slice. This will again result in outliers in the evolution of the frequency slice with time, which can be removed by median filtering, thereby suppressing percussive events within the frequency bin. The median-filtered frequency slices are then stored in a harmonic-enhanced spectrogram $H(n, k)$. However, as median filtering is a non-linear operation which introduces artifacts into the spectrogram, it is better to use the enhanced spectrograms obtained from median filtering to create masks to be applied to the original spectrogram. This can be done using a Wiener-filtering-based approach, which delivers the harmonic spectrogram

$$\hat{H}(n, k) = X(n, k) \cdot \frac{H^p(n, k)}{H^p(n, k) + P^p(n, k)} \tag{9.9}$$

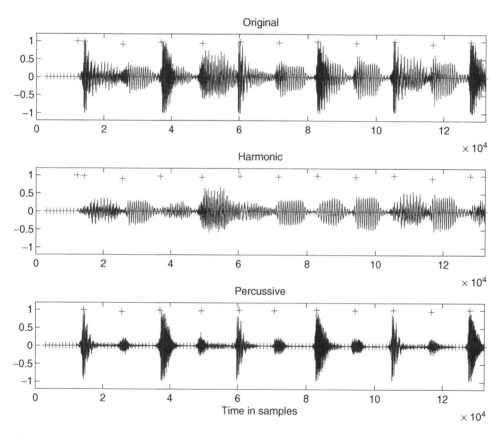

Figure 9.8 Original signal with onset markers, harmonic signal with onset markers, and percussive signal with beat markers.

and the percussive spectrogram

$$\hat{P}(n, k) = X(n, k) \cdot \frac{P^p(n, k)}{H^p(n, k) + P^p(n, k)}. \tag{9.10}$$

These spectrograms can then be inverted to the time domain by the inverse short-time Fourier transform. Beats are then detected by carrying out differentiation between successive frames $X(n, k) - X(n - 1, k)$ and counting the number of frequency bins which have a positive energy change. This is a simple method for detecting the occurrence of a broadband noise signal such as a drum. As this method is not based on the amount of energy in the signal, it can be used to detect low-energy noise-based events. By setting a threshold of how many bins have to be positive before an event is considered to be detected, and by keeping only local maxima in this function, a beat detection function can be obtained. This is illustrated on both the original signal (spectrogram), as well as the separated harmonic and percussion signal (spectrogram) (see Figure 9.8). The following M-file 9.2 shows the harmonic/percussion separation. The code assumes odd length median filters with p as the power to which the separated spectrogram frames are raised when generating masks to be applied to the original spectrogram frame. The output of the percussive separation is then used to generate an onset detection function for use with beat-driven effects.

M-file 9.2 (HPseparation.m)

```
% Author: Derry FitzGerald
%----- user data -----
WLen            =4096;
hopsize         =1024;
lh              =17; % length of the harmonic median filter
lp              =17; % length of the percussive median filter
p               =2;
w1              =hanning(WLen,'periodic');
w2              =w1;
hlh             =floor(lh/2)+1;
th              =2500;
[DAFx_in, FS]   =wavread('filename');
L               = length(DAFx_in);
DAFx_in         = [zeros(WLen, 1); DAFx_in; ...
    zeros(WLen-mod(L,hopsize),1)] / max(abs(DAFx_in));
DAFx_out1 = zeros(length(DAFx_in),1);
DAFx_out2 = zeros(length(DAFx_in),1);

%----- initialisations -----
grain           = zeros(WLen,1);
buffer          = zeros(WLen,lh);
buffercomplex   = zeros(WLen,lh);
oldperframe     = zeros(WLen,1);
onall           = [];
onperc          = [];

tic
%UUUUUUUUUUUUUUUUUUUUUUUUUUUUUUUUUUUUUUUUUUUUUUUUUU
pin  = 0;
pout = 0;
pend = length(DAFx_in)-WLen;

while pin<pend
    grain = DAFx_in(pin+1:pin+WLen) .* w1;
```

```
%===============================================
    fc   = fft(fftshift(grain));
    fa   = abs(fc);
    % remove oldest frame from buffers and add
    % current frame to buffers
    buffercomplex(:,1:lh-1)=buffercomplex(:,2:end);
    buffercomplex(:,lh)=fc;
    buffer(:,1:lh-1)=buffer(:,2:end);
    buffer(:,lh)=fa;
    % do median filtering within frame to suppress harmonic instruments
    Per = medfilt1(buffer(:,hlh),lp);
    % do median filtering on buffer to suppress percussion instruments
    Har = median(buffer,2);
    % use these Percussion and Harmonic enhanced frames to generate masks
    maskHar = (Har.^p)./(Har.^p + Per.^p);
    maskPer = (Per.^p)./(Har.^p + Per.^p);
    % apply masks to middle frame in buffer
    % Note: this is the "current" frame from the point of view of the median
    % filtering
    curframe=buffercomplex(:,hlh);
    perframe=curframe.*maskPer;
    harframe=curframe.*maskHar;
    grain1 = fftshift(real(ifft(perframe))).*w2;
    grain2 = fftshift(real(ifft(harframe))).*w2;
    % onset detection functions
    % difference of frames
    dall=buffer(:,hlh)-buffer(:,hlh-1);
    dperc=abs(perframe)-oldperframe;
    oall=sum(dall>0);
    operc=sum(dperc>0);
    onall = [onall oall];
    onperc = [onperc operc];
    oldperframe=abs(perframe);
%===============================================
    DAFx_out1(pout+1:pout+WLen) = ...
        DAFx_out1(pout+1:pout+WLen) + grain1;
    DAFx_out2(pout+1:pout+WLen) = ...
        DAFx_out2(pout+1:pout+WLen) + grain2;
    pin  = pin + hopsize;
    pout = pout + hopsize;
end
%UUUUUUUUUUUUUUUUUUUUUUUUUUUUUUUUUUUUUUUUUUUUU
toc
% process onset detection function to get beats
[or,oc]=size(onall);
omin=min(onall);
% get peaks
v1 = (onall > [omin, onall(1:(oc-1))]);
% allow for greater-than-or-equal
v2 = (onall >= [onall(2:oc), omin]);
% simple Beat tracking function
omax = onall .* (onall > th).* v1 .* v2;
% now do the same for the percussion onset detection function
% process onset detection function to get beats
[opr,opc]=size(onperc);
opmin=min(onperc);
% get peaks
```

```
p1 = (onperc > [opmin, onperc(1:(opc-1))]);
% allow for greater-than-or-equal
p2 = (onperc >= [onperc(2:opc), opmin]);
% simple Beat tracking function
opmax = onperc .* (onperc > th).* p1 .* p2;
%----- listening and saving the output -----
DAFx_out1 = DAFx_out1((WLen + hopsize*(hlh-1)) ...
                :length(DAFx_out1))/max(abs(DAFx_out1));
DAFx_out2 = DAFx_out2(WLen + (hopsize*(hlh-1)) ...
                :length(DAFx_out2))/max(abs(DAFx_out2));
% soundsc(DAFx_out1, FS);
% soundsc(DAFx_out2, FS);
wavwrite(DAFx_out1, FS, 'ex-percussion.wav');
wavwrite(DAFx_out2, FS, 'ex-harmonic.wav');
```

Avoiding latency and improving the robustness of the detection function can be obtained by using high-order prediction approaches in frame and frequency direction [NZ08] compared to the simple one-frame prediction (difference). Several further features can be derived from such kinds of low-level beat detector [Fit04, UH03, SZST10].

9.2.4 Pitch extraction

The main task of pitch extraction is to estimate a fundamental frequency f_0, which in musical terms is the pitch of a sound segment, and follow the fundamental frequency over the time. We can use this pitch information to control effects like time stretching and pitch shifting based on the PSOLA method, which is described in Chapter 6, but it also plays a major role in sound modeling with spectral models, which is treated extensively in Chapter 10. Moreover, the fundamental frequency can be used as a control parameter for a variety of audio effects based either on time-domain or on frequency-domain processing.

There is no definitive technique for pitch extraction and tracking, and only the bases of existing algorithms will be described here. We will consider pitch extraction both in the frequency domain and in the time domain. An overview and comparison of the presented algorithms can be found in [KZ10]. Most often an algorithm first looks for candidates of a pitch, then selects one and tries to improve the precision of the choice. After the calculation of pitch candidates post-processing, for example, pitch tracking has to be applied. During post-processing the estimation of the fundamental frequency from the pitch candidates can be improved by taking the frequency relationships between the detected candidates into account, which should ideally be multiples of the fundamental frequency.

FFT-based approach

In this subsection we describe the calculation of pitch candidates from the FFT of a signal segment where the phase information is used. This approach is similar to the technique used in the phase vocoder, see Section 7.3. The main structure of the algorithm is depicted in Figure 9.9, where a segment of length N is extracted every R samples and then applied to FFTs.

Considering the calculation of an N-point FFT, the frequency resolution of the FFT is

$$\Delta f = \frac{f_S}{N}, \tag{9.11}$$

with the sampling frequency $f_S = 1/T_S$. From the input signal $x(n)$ we use a block

$$x_1(n) = x(n_0 + n), \quad n = 0, \ldots, N - 1 \tag{9.12}$$

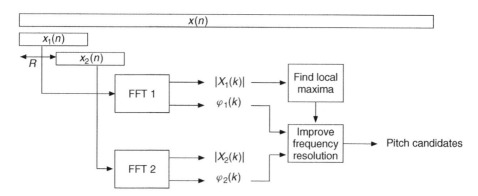

Figure 9.9   FFT-based pitch estimation structure with phase evaluation.

of N samples. After applying an appropriate window, the FFT yields $X_1(k)$ with $k = 0, \ldots, N - 1$. At the FFT index k_0 a local maximum of the FFT magnitude $|X_1(k)|$ is detected. From this FFT maximum, the initial estimate of the fundamental frequency is

$$\tilde{f}_0 = k_0 \cdot \Delta f = k_0 \frac{f_s}{N}. \tag{9.13}$$

The corresponding normalized frequency is

$$\tilde{\Omega}_0 = 2\pi \tilde{f}_0 T_S = k_0 \frac{2\pi}{N}. \tag{9.14}$$

To improve the frequency resolution, the phase information can be used, since for a harmonic signal $x_h(n) = \cos(\Omega_0 n + \varphi_0) = \cos(\phi(n))$ the fundamental frequency can be computed by the derivative

$$\Omega_0 = \frac{\mathrm{d}\phi(n)}{\mathrm{d}n}. \tag{9.15}$$

The derivative can be approximated by computing the phases of two FFTs separated by a hop size of R samples leading to

$$\hat{\Omega}_0 = \frac{\Delta\phi}{R}, \tag{9.16}$$

where $\Delta\phi$ is the phase difference between the two FFTs evaluated at the FFT index k_0. The second FFT of the signal segment

$$x_2(n) = x(n_0 + R + n), \quad n = 0, \ldots, N - 1 \tag{9.17}$$

leads to $X_2(k)$. For the two FFTs, the phases at frequency $\tilde{f}_0$ are given by

$$\varphi_1 = \angle\{X_1(k_0)\} \tag{9.18}$$

$$\varphi_2 = \angle\{X_2(k_0)\}. \tag{9.19}$$

Both phases φ_1 and φ_2 are obtained in the range $[-\pi, \pi]$. We now calculate an 'unwrapped' φ_2 value corresponding to the value of an instantaneous phase, see also Section 7.3.5 and

Figure 7.17. Assuming that the signal contains a harmonic component with a frequency $\tilde{f}_0 = k_0 \cdot \Delta f$, the expected target phase after a hop size of R samples is

$$\varphi_{2t} = \varphi_1 + \tilde{\Omega}_0 R = \varphi_1 + \frac{2\pi}{N} k_0 R. \tag{9.20}$$

The phase error between the unwrapped value φ_2 and the target phase can be computed by

$$\varphi_{2err} = \text{princarg}(\varphi_2 - \varphi_{2t}). \tag{9.21}$$

The function 'princarg' computes the principal phase argument in the range $[-\pi, \pi]$. It is assumed that the unwrapped phase differs from the target phase by a maximum of π. The unwrapped phase is obtained by

$$\varphi_{2u} = \varphi_{2t} + \varphi_{2err}. \tag{9.22}$$

The final estimate of the fundamental frequency is then obtained by

$$\hat{f}_0 = \frac{1}{2\pi} \hat{\Omega}_0 \cdot f_S = \frac{1}{2\pi} \cdot \frac{\varphi_{2u} - \varphi_1}{R} \cdot f_S. \tag{9.23}$$

Normally we assume that the first pitch estimation $\tilde{f}_0$ differs from the fundamental frequency by a maximum of $\Delta f/2$. Thus the maximum amount for the absolute value of the phase error φ_{2err} is

$$\varphi_{2err,max} = \frac{1}{2} \frac{2\pi}{N} R = \frac{R}{N} \pi. \tag{9.24}$$

We should accept phase errors with slightly higher values to have some tolerance in the pitch estimation.

One simple example of an ideal sine wave at a fundamental frequency of 420 Hz at $f_S = 44.1$ kHz analyzed with the FFT length $N = 1024$ using a Hanning window and hop size $R = 1$ leads to the following results: $k_0 = 10$, $\tilde{f}_0 = k_0 \frac{f_S}{N} = 430.66$ Hz, $\varphi_1/\pi = -0.2474$, $\varphi_{2t}/\pi = -0.2278$, $\varphi_2/\pi = -0.2283$, $\hat{f}_0 = 419.9996$ Hz. Thus the original sine frequency is almost ideally recovered by the described algorithm.

Figure 9.10 shows an example of the described algorithm applied to a short signal of the female utterance 'la' analyzed at an FFT length $N = 1024$. The top plot shows the FFT magnitude, the middle plot the estimated pitch, and the bottom plot the phase error φ_{2err} for frequencies up to 1500 Hz. For this example the frequency evaluation is performed for all FFT bins and not only for those with detected magnitude maxima. The circles show the positions of detected maxima in the FFT magnitude. The dashed lines in the bottom plot show the used threshold for the phase error. In this example the first maximum is detected at FFT index $k_0 = 6$, the corresponding bin frequency is 258.40 Hz, and the corrected pitch frequency is 274.99 Hz. Please notice that in this case the magnitude of the third harmonic (at appr. 820 Hz) has a greater value than the magnitude of the fundamental frequency.

M-file 9.3 presents a MATLAB® implementation to calculate the pitch candidates from a block of the input signal.

M-file 9.3 (find_pitch_fft.m)

```
function [FFTidx, Fp_est, Fp_corr] = ...
find_pitch_fft(x, win, Nfft, Fs, R, fmin, fmax, thres)
% [DAFXbook, 2nd ed., chapter 9]
%===== This function finds pitch candidates
%
% Inputs:
```

```
%    x: input signal of length Nfft+R
%    win: window for the FFT
%    Nfft: FFT length
%    Fs: sampling frequency
%    R: FFT hop size
%    fmin, fmax: minumum/ maximum pitch freqs to be detected
%    thres: %omit maxima more than thres dB below the main peak
% Outputs:
%    FFTidx: FFT indices
%    Fp_est: FFT bin frequencies
%    Fp_corr: corrected frequencies

FFTidx  = [];
Fp_est  = [];
Fp_corr = [];
dt      = R/Fs;         % time diff between FFTs
df      = Fs/Nfft;      % freq resolution
kp_min  = round(fmin/df);
kp_max  = round(fmax/df);
x1      = x(1:Nfft);    % 1st block
x2      = x((1:Nfft)+R); % 2nd block with hop size R
[X1, Phi1] = fftdb(x1.*win,Nfft);
[X2, Phi2] = fftdb(x2.*win,Nfft);
X1      = X1(1:kp_max+1);
Phi1    = Phi1(1:kp_max+1);
X2      = X2(1:kp_max+1);
Phi2    = Phi2(1:kp_max+1);
idx     = find_loc_max(X1);
Max     = max(X1(idx));
ii      = find(X1(idx)-Max>-thres);

%----- omit maxima more than thres dB below the main peak -----
idx     = idx(ii);
Nidx    = length(idx);  % number of detected maxima
maxerr  = R/Nfft;       % max phase diff error/pi
                        % (pitch max. 0.5 bins wrong)
maxerr  = maxerr*1.2;   % some tolerance
for ii=1:Nidx
   k        = idx(ii) - 1;         % FFT bin with maximum
   phi1     = Phi1(k+1);           % phase of x1 in [-pi,pi]
   phi2_t   = phi1 + 2*pi/Nfft*k*R; % expected target phase
                                   % after hop size R
   phi2     = Phi2(k+1);           % phase of x2 in [-pi,pi]
   phi2_err = princarg(phi2-phi2_t);
   phi2_unwrap = phi2_t+phi2_err;
   dphi     = phi2_unwrap - phi1;  % phase diff
   if (k>kp_min) & (abs(phi2_err)/pi<maxerr)
      Fp_corr = [Fp_corr; dphi/(2*pi*dt)];
      FFTidx  = [FFTidx; k];
      Fp_est  = [Fp_est; k*df];
   end
end
```

In addition to the algorithm described, the magnitude values of the detected FFT maxima are checked. In the given code those maxima are omitted whose FFT magnitudes are more than thres

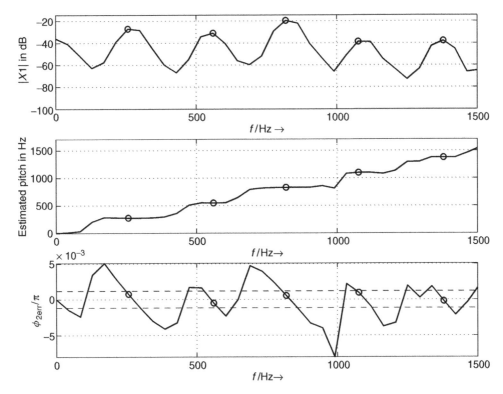

Figure 9.10 Example of pitch estimation of speech signal 'la.'

dB below the global maximum. Typical values for the parameter `thres` lie in the range from 30 to 50. The function `princarg` is given in Figure 7.17. The following function `fftdb` (see M-file 9.4) returns the FFT magnitude in a dB scale and the phase.

M-file 9.4 (`fftdb.m`)

```
function [H, phi]  = fftdb(x, Nfft)
% [DAFXbook, 2nd ed., chapter 9]
%==== This function discards values in FFT bins for which magnitude >Â thresh
if nargin<2
  Nfft = length(x);
end

F      = fft(x,Nfft);
F      = F(1:Nfft/2+1);       % f=0,..,Fs/2
phi    = angle(F);            % phase in [-pi,pi]
F      = abs(F)/Nfft*2;       % normalize to FFT length
%----- return -100 db for F==0 to avoid "log of zero" warnings -----
H      = -100*ones(size(F));
idx    = find(F~=0);
H(idx) = 20*log10(F(idx));    % non-zero values in dB
```

The following function `find_loc_max` (see M-file 9.5) searches for local maxima using the derivative.

M-file 9.5 (`find_loc_max.m`)

```
function [idx, idx0] = find_loc_max(x)
% [DAFXbook, 2nd ed., chapter 9]
%=====  This function finds local maxima in vector x
%  Inputs:
%     x: any vector
%  Outputs:
%     idx : positions of local max.
%     idx0: positions of local max. with 2 identical values
%     if only 1 return value: positions of all maxima

N    = length(x);
dx   = diff(x);              % derivation
                             % to find sign changes from + to -
dx1  = dx(2:N-1);
dx2  = dx(1:N-2);
prod = dx1.*dx2;
idx1 = find(prod<0);         % sign change in dx1
idx2 = find(dx1(idx1)<0);    % only change from + to -
idx  = idx1(idx2)+1;         % positions of single maxima
%----- zeros in dx? => maxima with 2 identical values -----
idx3 = find(dx==0);
idx4 = find(x(idx3)>0);      % only maxima
idx0 = idx3(idx4);
%----- positions of double maxima, same values at idx3(idx4)+1 -----
if nargout==1                % output 1 vector
                             % with positions of all maxima
   idx = sort([idx,idx0]); % (for double max. only 1st position)
end
```

Now we present an example where the algorithm is applied to a signal segment of Suzanne Vega's 'Tom's Diner.' Figure 9.11 shows time-frequency representations of the analysis results. The top plot shows the spectrogram of the signal. The middle plot shows the FFT bin frequencies of detected pitch candidates while the bottom plot shows the corrected frequency values. In the bottom plot the text of the sung words is also shown. In all plots frequencies up to 800 Hz are shown. For the spectrogram an FFT length of 4096 points is used. The pitch-estimation algorithm is performed with an FFT length of 1024 points. This example shows that the melody of the sound can be recognized in the bottom plot of Figure 9.11. The applied algorithm improves the frequency resolution of the FFT shown in the middle plot. To choose the correct pitch among the detected candidates some post-processing is required. Other methods to improve the frequency resolution of the FFT are described in [Can98, DM00, Mar00, Mar98, AKZ99] and in Chapter 10.

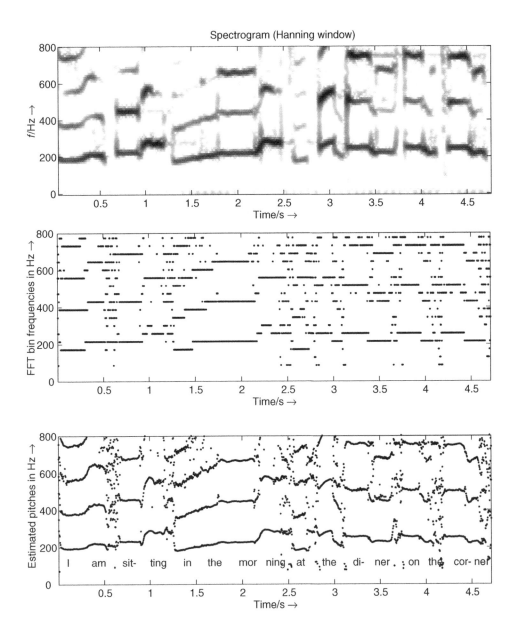

Figure 9.11 Time/frequency planes for pitch estimation example of an excerpt from Suzanne Vega's 'Tom's Diner.' Top: spectrogram, middle: FFT bin frequencies of pitch candidates, bottom: corrected frequency values of pitch candidates.

M-file 9.6 demonstrates a pitch-tracking algorithm in a block-based implementation.

M-file 9.6 (Pitch_Tracker_FFT_Main.m)

```
% Pitch_Tracker_FFT_Main.m      [DAFXbook, 2nd ed., chapter 9]
%===== This function demonstrates a pitch tracking algorithm
%===== in a block-based implementation

%----- initializations -----
fname='Toms_diner';
n0=2000; %start index
n1=210000;

Nfft=1024;
R=1;        % FFT hop size for pitch estimation
K=200;      % hop size for time resolution of pitch estimation
thres=50; % threshold for FFT maxima
% checked pitch range in Hz:
fmin=50;
fmax=800;
p_fac_thres=1.05;  % threshold for voiced detection
                   % deviation of pitch from mean value
win=hanning(Nfft)';% window for FFT
Nx=n1-n0+1+R;      % signal length
blocks=floor(Nx/K);
Nx=(blocks-1)*K+Nfft+R;
n1=n0+Nx;          % new end index
[X,Fs]=wavread(fname,[n0,n1]);
X=X(:,1)';

%----- pitch extraction per block -----
pitches=zeros(1,blocks);
for b=1:blocks
  x=X((b-1)*K+1+(1:Nfft+R));
  [FFTidx, F0_est, F0_corr]= ...
    find_pitch_fft(x,win,Nfft,Fs,R,fmin,fmax,thres);
  if ~isempty(F0_corr)
    pitches(b)=F0_corr(1); % take candidate with lowest pitch
  else
    pitches(b)=0;
  end
end
%----- post-processing -----
L=9;               % odd number of blocks for mean calculation
D=(L-1)/2;         % delay
h=ones(1,L)./L;    % impulse response for mean calculation
%----- mirror beginning and end for "non-causal" filtering -----
p=[pitches(D+1:-1:2),pitches,pitches(blocks-1:-1:blocks-D)];
y=conv(p,h);            % length: blocks+2D+2D
pm=y((1:blocks)+2*D); % cut result

Fac=zeros(1,blocks);
idx=find(pm~=0);        % don't divide by zero
Fac(idx)=pitches(idx)./pm(idx);
ii=find(Fac<1 & Fac~=0);
Fac(ii)=1./Fac(ii);    % all non-zero elements are now > 1
```

```
%----- voiced/unvoiced detection -----
voiced=Fac~=0 & Fac<p_fac_thres;

T=40;                    % time in ms for segment lengths
M=round(T/1000*Fs/K);  % min. number of consecutive blocks
[V,p2]=segmentation(voiced, M, pitches);
p2=V.*p2;               % set pitches to zero for unvoiced

%----- plotting and drawing figure -----
figure(1),clf,
time=(0:blocks-1)*K+1; % start sample of blocks
time=time/Fs;          % time in seconds
t=(0:length(X)-1)/Fs;  % time in sec for original
subplot(211)
plot(t,X),title('original x(n)')
axis([0 max([t,time]) -1.1*max(abs(X)) 1.1*max(abs(X))])
subplot(212)
idx=find(p2~=0);
plot_split(idx,time, p2),title('pitch in Hz');
xlabel('time/s \rightarrow');
axis([0 max([t,time]) .9*min(p2(idx)) 1.1*max(p2(idx))])
```

In the above implementation the post-processing is performed by choosing the lowest pitch candidate in each block. Then the mean pitch of surrounding blocks is computed and compared to the detected pitch. If the deviation from the mean value is higher than a given threshold, this block is considered as 'unvoiced.' Finally a segmentation is performed to get a minimum number of consecutive blocks that are voiced/unvoiced (to avoid very short segments). M-file 9.7 presents an implementation for the segmentation.

M-file 9.7 (segmentation.m)

```
function [V,pitches2] = segmentation(voiced, M, pitches)
% function [V,pitches2] = segmentation(voiced, M, pitches)
%    [DAFXbook, 2nd ed., chapter 9]
%===== This function implements the pitch segmentation
%
% Inputs:
%    voiced:    original voiced/unvoiced detection
%    M:         min. number of consecutive blocks with same voiced flag
%    pitches:   original pitches
% Outputs:
%    V:         changed voiced flag
%    pitches2:  changed pitches

blocks=length(voiced); % get number of blocks
pitches2=pitches;
V=voiced;
Nv=length(V);

%%%%%%%%%%% step1: eliminate too short voiced segments:
V(Nv+1)=~V(Nv);  % change at end to get length of last segment
dv=[0, diff(V)]; % derivative
idx=find(dv~=0); % changes in voiced
di=[idx(1)-1,diff(idx)];  % segment lengths
```

```
v0=V(1);          % status of 1st segment
k0=1;
ii=1; % counter for segments, idx(ii)-1 is end of segment
if v0==0
  k0=idx(1); % start of voiced
  ii=ii+1;   % first change voiced to unvoiced
end
while ii<=length(idx);
  L=di(ii);
  k1=idx(ii)-1;    % end of voiced segment
  if L<M
    V(k0:k1)=zeros(1,k1-k0+1);
  end
  if ii<length(idx)
    k0=idx(ii+1); % start of next voiced segment
  end
  ii=ii+2;
end

%%%%%%%%%% step2: eliminate too short unvoiced segments:
V(Nv+1)=~V(Nv);              % one more change at end
dv=[0, diff(V)];
idx=find(dv~=0);            % changes in voiced
di=[idx(1)-1,diff(idx)];   % segment lengths
if length(idx)>1            % changes in V
  v0=V(1);                 % status of 1st segment
  k0=1;
  ii=1;    % counter for segments, idx(ii)-1 is end of segment
  if v0==0
    k0=idx(2); % start of unvoiced
    ii=ii+2;   % first change unvoiced to voiced
  end
  while ii<=length(idx);
    L=di(ii);
    k1=idx(ii)-1;    % end of unvoiced segment
    if L<M
      if k1<blocks % NOT last unvoiced segment
        V(k0:k1)=ones(1,k1-k0+1);
        % linear pitch interpolation:
        p0=pitches(k0-1);
        p1=pitches(k1+1);
        N=k1-k0+1;
        pitches2(k0:k1)=(1:N)*(p1-p0)/(N+1)+p0;
      end
    end
    if ii<length(idx)
      k0=idx(ii+1); % start of next unvoiced segment
    end
    ii=ii+2;
  end
end

V=V(1:Nv); % cut last element
```

The `plot_split` function is given by M-file 9.8.

M-file 9.8 (plot_split.m)

```
function plot_split(idx, t, x)
% function plot_split(idx, t, x)    [DAFXbook, 2nd ed., chapter 9]
%===== This function plots the segmented pitch curve
%   Inputs:
%      idx: vector with positions of vector x to be plotted
%      t: time indexes
%      x is segmented into parts

di=diff(idx);
L=length(di);

n0=1;
pos_di=find(di>1);
ii=1; % counter for pos_di

hold off
while ii<=length(pos_di) %n0<=length(x)
  n1=pos_di(ii);
  plot(t(idx(n0:n1)),x(idx(n0:n1)))
  hold on
  n0=n1+1;
  ii=ii+1;
end

n1=length(idx);
plot(t(idx(n0:n1)),x(idx(n0:n1)))
hold off
```

The result of the pitch-tracking algorithm is illustrated in Figure 9.12. The bottom plot shows the pitch over time calculated using the block-based FFT approach.

Any FFT-based pitch estimator can be improved by detecting the harmonic structure of the sound. If the harmonics of the fundamental frequency are detected, the greatest common divisor of these harmonic frequencies can be used in the estimation of the fundamental frequency [O'S00, p. 220]. M.R. Schroeder mentions for speech processing in [Sch99, p. 65], 'the pitch problem was finally laid to rest with the invention of cepstrum pitch detectors' [Nol64]. The cepstrum technique allows the estimation of the pitch period directly from the cepstrum sequence $c(n)$. Schroeder also suggested a 'harmonic product spectrum' [Sch68] to improve the fundamental frequency estimation, which sometimes outperforms the cepstrum method [Sch99, p. 65]. A further improvement of the pitch estimates can be achieved by applying a peak-continuation algorithm to the detected pitches of adjacent frames, which is described in Chapter 10.

General remarks on time-domain pitch extraction

In the time domain the task of pitch extraction leads us to find the corresponding *pitch period*. The pitch period is the time duration of one period. With the fundamental frequency f_0 (to be detected) the pitch period is given by

$$T_0 = \frac{1}{f_0}. \tag{9.25}$$

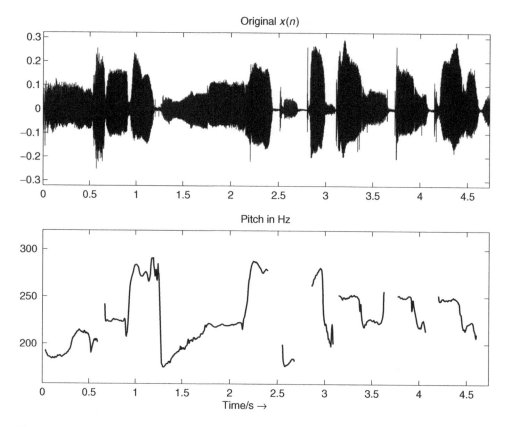

Figure 9.12 Pitch over time from the FFT with phase vocoder approach for a signal segment of Suzanne Vega's 'Tom's Diner.'

For a discrete-time signal sampled at $f_S = \frac{1}{T_S}$ we have to find the *pitch lag* M, which is the number of samples in one period. The pitch period is $T_0 = M \cdot T_S$, which leads to

$$M = \frac{T_0}{T_S} = \frac{f_S}{f_0}. \tag{9.26}$$

Since only integer-valued pitch lags can be detected, we have a certain frequency resolution in detecting the fundamental frequency dependent on f_0 and f_S. Now we are assuming the case of $\tilde{M} = M + 0.5$ where $\tilde{M}$ is the detected integer pitch lag. The detected fundamental frequency is $\tilde{f}_0 = \frac{f_S}{\tilde{M}}$ instead of the exact pitch $f_0 = \frac{f_S}{M}$. The frequency error factor is in this case

$$\alpha(f_0) = \frac{f_0}{\tilde{f}_0} = \frac{\tilde{M}}{M} = 1 + \frac{0.5}{M} = 1 + 0.5\frac{f_0}{f_S}. \tag{9.27}$$

With the halftone factor $\alpha_{ht} = \sqrt[12]{2}$ and setting $\alpha(f_0) = \alpha_{ht}^x$, the frequency error in halftones is

$$x = \frac{\ln \alpha(f_0)}{\ln \alpha_{ht}}. \tag{9.28}$$

Figure 9.13 shows the frequency error both as factor $\alpha(f_0)$ and as percentage of halftones for pitches in the range from 50 to 5000 Hz at the sampling frequency $f_S = 44.1$ kHz. The maximum

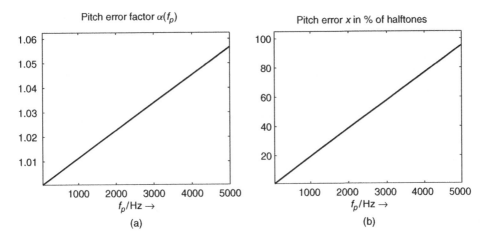

Figure 9.13 Resolution of time-domain pitch detection at $f_S = 44.1$ kHz, (a) frequency error factor, (b) pitch error in percentage of a halftone.

frequency error is approximately 6%, or one halftone, for pitches up to 5000 Hz. For a fundamental frequency of 1000 Hz the frequency error is only 20% of a halftone which is reasonably accurate precision.

Normally the pitch estimation in the time domain is performed in three steps [O'S00, p. 218]:

(1) Segmentation of the input signal into overlapping blocks and pre-processing of each block, for example lowpass filtering (see segmentation shown in Figure 9.9).

(2) Basic pitch estimation algorithm applied to the pre-processed block.

(3) Post-processing for an error correction of the pitch estimates and smoothing of pitch trajectories.

Auto-correlation and LPC

The auto-correlation sequence can also be used to detect the pitch period of a signal segment. First, we present different definitions of autocorrelation sequences:

- Using one block

$$r_{xx}(m) = \sum_{n=m}^{N-1} x(n)x(n-m) \qquad (9.29)$$

- Using one windowed block

$$r_{xx}(m) = \sum_{n=m}^{N-1} u(n)u(n-m), \qquad (9.30)$$

with $u(n) = x(n) \cdot w(n)$ (window function $w(n)$)

- and Using the exact signal, thus using samples preceding the considered block

$$\tilde{r}_{xx}(m) = \sum_{n=0}^{N-1} x(n)x(n-m). \qquad (9.31)$$

Notice, that in the definitions given by (9.29)–(9.31) no normalization to the block length N is applied.

Figure 9.14 shows the three different auto-correlation sequences for an excerpt of the speech signal "la." Here the same input signal is used as in Figure 9.10. In this example the pitch lag corresponding to the fundamental frequency is $M = 160$ samples, and thus at the third maximum of the auto-correlation. Normally we expect the first maximum in the auto-correlation at the pitch lag. But sometimes, as in this example, the first maximum in the auto-correlation function is not at this position. In general, the auto-correlation has maxima at the pitch lag M and at its multiples, since, for a periodic signal, the same correlation occurs if comparing the signal with the same signal delayed by multiples of the pitch period. Since, in the example of Figures 9.10 and 9.14, the third harmonic is more dominant than the fundamental frequency, the first maximum in the auto-correlation is located at $M/3$. Conversely there can be a higher peak in the auto-correlation after the true pitch period.

Often the prediction error of an LPC analysis contains peaks spaced by the pitch period, see Figure 8.9. Thus it might be promising to try to estimate the pitch period from the prediction error

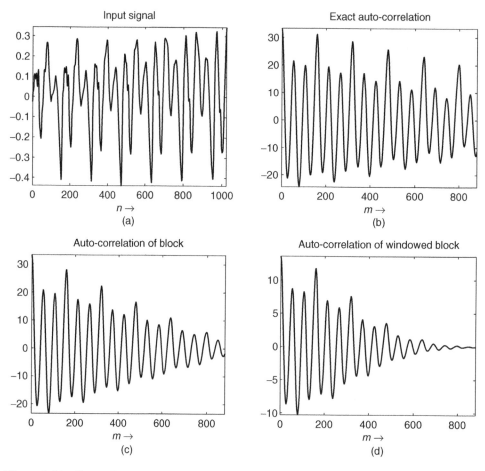

Figure 9.14 Comparison between different autocorrelation computations for speech signal 'la.': (a) input block $x(n)$, (b) exact auto-correlation $\tilde{r}_{xx}(m)$, (c) standard auto-correlation $r_{xx}(m)$ using block, (d) standard auto-correlation $r_{xx}(m)$ using windowed block.

instead of using the original signal. The SIFT algorithm [Mar72], which has been developed for voice, is based on removing the spectral envelope by inverse filtering in a linear prediction scheme. But in some cases it is not possible to estimate the pitch period from the prediction error, because the linear prediction has removed all pitch redundancies from the signal. Figure 9.15 compares two excerpts of a speech signal where the input block (top) and the auto-correlations of both the input signal (middle) and the prediction error (bottom) are shown. An LPC analysis of order $p = 8$ using the auto-correlation method has been applied.

For the example presented in subplots (a)–(c) the pitch period can be well detected in the auto-correlation of the prediction error (same excerpt as in Figures 9.10 and 9.14). For the other excerpt presented in subplots (d)–(f) it is not possible to detect the pitch in the auto-correlation of the prediction error while the auto-correlation of the input signal has a local maximum at the correct pitch period. Notice that in the plots of the auto-correlation sequences only time-lag ranges from 29 to 882 are shown. This corresponds to pitch frequencies from 1500 down to 50 Hz at sampling frequency 44.1 kHz.

Another time-domain method for the extraction of the fundamental frequency is based on 'center clipping' the input signal and subsequent auto-correlation analysis [Son68]. First, the input signal is bandlimited by a lowpass filter. If the filter output signal exceeds a certain threshold $\pm c$ the operation $x_{clip}(n) = x(n) \mp c$ is performed, otherwise $x_{clip}(n) = 0$ [RS78, Son68]. The result of this pre-processing is illustrated in Figure 9.16. The auto-correlation sequence $r_{xx}(m)$ of the center-clipped signal $x_{clip}(n)$ shows a strong positive peak at the time lag of the pitch period.

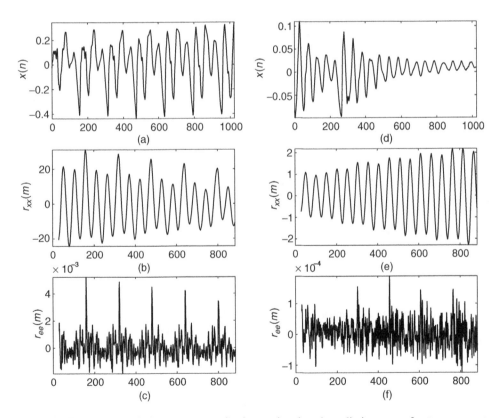

Figure 9.15 Auto-correlation sequences for input signal and prediction error for two excerpts of the speech signal 'la.' Input signals (a, d), auto-correlation of input (b, e), auto-correlation of prediction error (c, f).

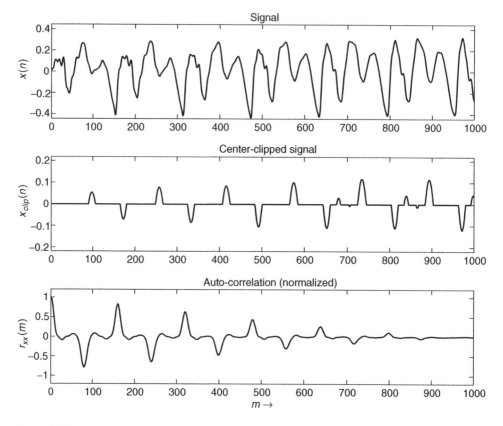

Figure 9.16 Center clipping and subsequent auto-correlation analysis: input signal, lowpass filtered, and center-clipped signal (notice the time delay) and auto-correlation.

Narrowed correlation: the YIN algorithm

Another way to determine the periodicity of a signal is to calculate the sum of differences of a time frame with its shifted version analogous to the ACF. The average magnitude difference function (AMDF) [RSC+74] is defined as

$$d(l) = \frac{1}{N} \sum_{n=0}^{N-1} |x(n) - x(n - l)|. \tag{9.32}$$

The function properties are similar to the ACF, but the AMDF shows dips at the lags of high correlation instead of peaks like the ACF does. De Cheveigné [dCK02] defined the difference function as sum of squared differences

$$d_t(l) = \sum_{n=1}^{N-1} (x(n) - x(n + l))^2. \tag{9.33}$$

The ACF and the difference function are both sensitive to amplitude changes of the time signal. An increasing amplitude of the time signal leads to higher peaks at later lags for the ACF and lower dips for the difference function respectively. To avoid this a cumulative normalization is

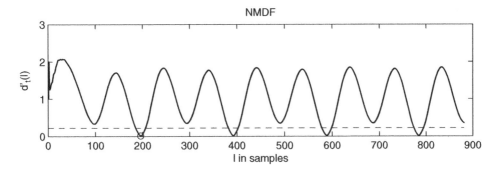

Figure 9.17 YIN algorithm: normalized mean difference function (NDMF) for a signal segment of Suzanne Vega's 'Tom's Diner.'

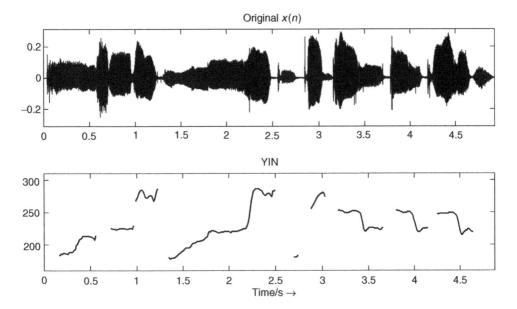

Figure 9.18 Pitch over time from the YIN algorithm for a signal segment of Suzanne Vega's 'Tom's Diner.'

applied to average the current lag value with the previous values. The result is the normalized mean difference function (NMDF) defined as

$$
d'_t(l) = \begin{cases} 1, & l = 0 \\ \dfrac{d_t(l)}{\frac{1}{l}\sum\limits_{n=1}^{l} d_t(n)}, & \text{else.} \end{cases}
\tag{9.34}
$$

The NMDF starts at a value of 1 and drops below 1 only where the current lag value is below the average of all previous lags. This allows one to define a threshold, which a local minimum $d'_t(l)$ has to fall below in order to consider it as a valid pitch candidate (see figure 9.17). To increase the frequency resolution of the YIN algorithm the local minima of $d'_t(l)$ can be refined by parabolic interpolation with their neighboring lag values. The minimum of the parabola is used as the refined

lag value. The result of the presented pitch-tracking algorithm is illustrated in Figure 9.18. The
bottom plot shows the pitch over time calculated using the YIN algorithm.

M-file 9.9 (yinDAFX.m)

```
function pitch = yinDAFX(x,fs,f0min,hop)
% function pitch = yinDAFX(x,fs,f0min,hop)
% Author: Adrian v.d. Knesebeck
% determines the pitches of the input signal x at a given hop size
%
% input:
% x         input signal
% fs        sampling frequency
% f0min     minimum detectable pitch
% hop       hop size
%
% output:
% pitch     pitch frequencies in Hz at the given hop size

% initialization
yinTolerance = 0.22;
taumax = round(1/f0min*fs);
yinLen = 1024;
k = 0;

% frame processing
for i = 1:hop:(length(x)-(yinLen+taumax))
    k=k+1;
    xframe = x(i:i+(yinLen+taumax));
    yinTemp = zeros(1,taumax);
    % calculate the square differences
        for tau=1:taumax
            for j=1:yinLen
                yinTemp(tau) = yinTemp(tau) + (xframe(j) - xframe(j+tau))^2;
            end
        end

    % calculate cumulated normalization
        tmp = 0;
        yinTemp(1) = 1;
        for tau=2:taumax
            tmp = tmp + yinTemp(tau);
            yinTemp(tau) = yinTemp(tau) *(tau/tmp);
        end

    % determine lowest pitch
      tau=1;
      while(tau<taumax)
          if(yinTemp(tau) < yinTolerance)
              % search turning point
              while (yinTemp(tau+1) < yinTemp(tau))
                  tau = tau+1;
              end
              pitch(k) = fs/tau;
              break
          else
```

```
            tau = tau+1;
        end
    % if no pitch detected
    pitch(k) = 0;
    end
end
end
```

Long-term prediction (LTP)

A further method of estimating the fundamental frequency is based on long-term prediction. A common approach to remove pitch-period redundancies from a signal is to use a short FIR prediction filter after a delay line of M samples, where M is the pitch lag [KA90]. Thus the long-term prediction error or residual is given by

$$d(n) = x(n) - \sum_{k=0}^{q} b_k x(n - M - k), \tag{9.35}$$

where the order $q + 1$ is normally in the range $\{1, 2, 3\}$ [KA90]. Considering the case of a one-tap filter, the residual simplifies to

$$d(n) = x(n) - b_0 \cdot x(n - M), \tag{9.36}$$

which is shown in Figure 9.19.

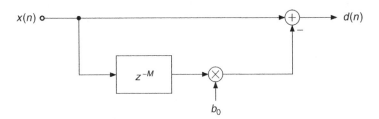

Figure 9.19   Long-term prediction with a one-tap filter.

For minimizing the energy of $d(n)$ over one block of length N we set the derivative with respect to b_0 to zero. This leads to the optimal filter coefficient

$$b_0 = \frac{\tilde{r}_{xx}(M)}{r_{xx0}(M)}, \tag{9.37}$$

with $\tilde{r}_{xx}(m)$ as defined in (9.31) and

$$r_{xx0}(m) = \sum_{n=0}^{N-1} x^2(n - m), \tag{9.38}$$

which is the energy of a block delayed by m samples. Setting this solution into (9.36) leads to the error energy

$$E_d = \sum_{n=0}^{N-1} x^2(n) - r_{xx,norm}(M) \tag{9.39}$$

dependent on M with

$$r_{xx,norm}(m) = \frac{\tilde{r}_{xx}^2(m)}{r_{xx0}(m)}. \tag{9.40}$$

Figure 9.20 shows an example where the input signal shown in Figure 9.15(a) is used. The top plot shows the exact autocorrelation $\tilde{r}_{xx}(m)$, the middle plot shows the normalized autocorrelation $r_{xx,norm}(m)$, and the bottom plot shows the LTP coefficient $b_0(m)$ dependent on the lag m.

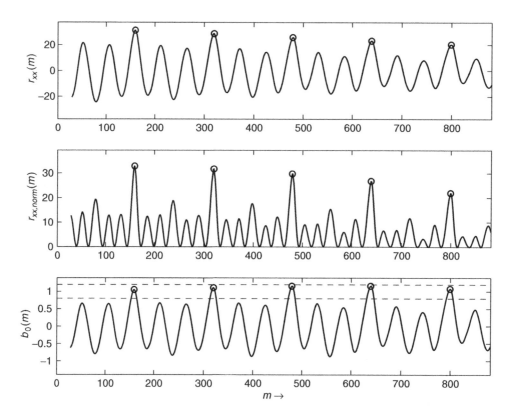

Figure 9.20   Auto-correlation, normalized auto-correlation and LTP coefficient dependent on lag m for excerpt from the speech signal 'la.' The circles show the pitch lag candidates, the dashed lines the accepted b_0 values.

In $r_{xx,norm}(m)$ the lag $m = M$ has to be found where $r_{xx,norm}(m)$ is maximized to minimize the residual energy. Considering one block of length N, the numerator of (9.40) is the squared auto-correlation, while the denominator is the energy of the block delayed by M samples. The function $r_{xx,norm}(m)$ therefore represents a kind of normalized auto-correlation sequence with only positive values. If used for the detection of the pitch period, $r_{xx,norm}(m)$ does not need to have a global maximum at $m = M$, but it is expected to have a local maximum at that position.

To find candidates of the pitch lag M, first local maxima in $r_{xx,norm}(m)$ are searched. In a second step, from these maxima only those ones are considered where the auto-correlation $\tilde{r}_{xx}(m)$ is positive valued. The function $r_{xx,norm}(m)$ also has maxima at positions where $\tilde{r}_{xx}(m)$ has minima. In a third step the $b_0(m)$ values are considered. The value of the coefficient b_0 is close to one for voiced sounds and close to zero for noise-like sounds [JN84, p. 315]. Thus the value of b_0 can serve as a quality check for the estimate of the computed pitch lag.

In the example in Figure 9.20, b_0 values in the range $0.8, \ldots 1.2$ are accepted. This range is shown by the dashed lines in the bottom plot. The circles represent the positions of pitch-lag candidates. Thus, at these positions $r_{xx,norm}(m)$ has a local maximum, $\tilde{r}_{xx}(m)$ is positive valued, and $b_0(m)$ lies in the described range. In this example, the first pitch lag candidate corresponds to the pitch of the sound segment.

The described algorithm for the computation of pitch-lag candidates from a signal block is implemented by the following M-file 9.10.

M-file 9.10 (find_pitch_ltp.m)

```
function [M,Fp] = find_pitch_ltp(xp, lmin, lmax, Nblock, Fs, b0_thres)
% function [M,Fp] = find_pitch_ltp(xp, lmin, lmax, Nblock, Fs, b0_thres)
%     [DAFXbook, 2nd ed., chapter 9]
%===== This function computes the pitch lag candidates from a signal block
%
% Inputs:
%       xp       : input block including lmax pre-samples
%                    for correct autocorrelation
%       lmin     : min. checked pitch lag
%       lmax     : max. checked pitch lag
%       Nblock   : block length without pre-samples
%       Fs       : sampling freq.
%       b0_thres : max b0 deviation from 1
%
% Outputs:
%    M: pitch lags
%    Fp: pitch frequencies

lags  = lmin:lmax;        % tested lag range
Nlag  = length(lags);     % no. of lags
[rxx_norm, rxx, rxx0] = xcorr_norm(xp, lmin, lmax, Nblock);


%----- calc. autocorr sequences -----
B0    = rxx./rxx0;        % LTP coeffs for all lags
idx   = find_loc_max(rxx_norm);
i     = find(rxx(idx)>0); % only max. where r_xx>0
idx   = idx(i);           % indices of maxima candidates
i     = find(abs(B0(idx)-1)<b0_thres);

%----- only max. where LTP coeff is close to 1 -----
idx   = idx(i);           % indices of maxima candidates

%----- vectors for all pitch candidates: -----
M     = lags(idx);
M     = M(:);             % pitch lags
Fp    = Fs./M;
Fp    = Fp(:);            % pitch freqs
```

The function `find_loc_max` is given in Section 9.2.4. The function `xcorr_norm` to compute the auto-correlation sequences is given by M-file 9.11.

M-file 9.11 (`xcorr_norm.m`)

```
function [rxx_norm, rxx, rxx0] = xcorr_norm(xp, lmin, lmax, Nblock)
% function [rxx_norm, rxx, rxx0] = xcorr_norm(xp, lmin, lmax, Nblock)
%     [DAFXbook, 2nd ed., chapter 9]
%===== This function computes the normalized autocorrelation
%  Inputs:
%     xp: input block
%     lmin: min of tested lag range
%     lmax: max of tested lag range
%     Nblock: block size
%
%  Outputs:
%     rxx_norm: normalized autocorr. sequence
%     rxx: autocorr. sequence
%     rxx0: energy of delayed blocks

%----- initializations -----
x        = xp((1:Nblock)+lmax); % input block without pre-samples
lags     = lmin:lmax;           % tested lag range
Nlag     = length(lags);        % no. of lags

%----- empty output variables -----
rxx      = zeros(1,Nlag);
rxx0     = zeros(1,Nlag);
rxx_norm = zeros(1,Nlag);

%----- computes autocorrelation(s) -----
for l=1:Nlag
    ii      = lags(l);          % tested lag
    rxx0(l) = sum(xp((1:Nblock)+lmax-lags(l)).^2);
    %----- energy of delayed block
    rxx(l)  = sum(x.*xp((1:Nblock)+lmax-lags(l)));
end
rxx_norm=rxx.^2./rxx0;          % normalized autocorr. sequence
```

The performance of the function `xcorr_norm` is quite slow in **MATLAB**. The computation speed can be improved if using a C-MEX function. Thus the function is implemented in C and a 'MEX' file is created with the C compiler (on Windows systems the MEX file is a dll). In this example the computation speed is improved by a factor of approximately 50, if using the MEX file instead of the **MATLAB** function.

The described LTP algorithm may also be applied to the prediction error of a linear prediction approach. Figure 9.21 compares LTP applied to original signals and their prediction errors. In this example the same signal segments are used as in Figure 9.15. The circles denote the detected global maxima in the normalized auto-correlation. For the first signal shown in plots (a)–(c) the computed LTP coefficients are $b_{0x} = 1.055$ for the input signal and $b_{0e} = 0.663$ for the prediction error. The LTP coefficients for the second signal are $b_{0x} = 0.704$ and $b_{0e} = 0.141$, respectively. As in Figure 9.15, the pitch estimation from the prediction error works well for the first signal while this approach fails for the second signal. For the second signal the value of the LTP coefficient indicates that the prediction error is noise-like.

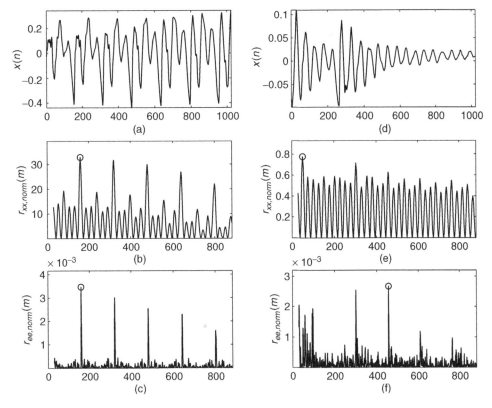

Figure 9.21 Normalized auto-correlation sequences for input signal and prediction error for two excerpts of the speech signal 'la.' Input signals (a, d), normalized auto-correlation of input (b, e), normalized auto-correlation of prediction error (c, f).

Figure 9.22 shows the detected pitch-lag candidates and the corresponding frequencies over time for a signal segment of Suzanne Vega's 'Tom's Diner.' It is the same example as presented in Figure 9.11 where also a spectrogram of this sound signal is given. The top plot of Figure 9.22 shows the detected pitch-lag candidates computed by the LTP algorithm applied to the input signal. The parameter b0_thres is set to 0.3, thus b_0 values in the range $0.7, \ldots, 1.3$ are accepted. The corresponding pitch frequencies in the bottom plot are computed by $f_p = f_S/M$ (see (9.26)).

In the top plot of Figure 9.22 the lowest detected pitch lag normally corresponds to the pitch of the signal frame. The algorithm detects other candidates at multiples of this pitch lag. In some parts of this signal (for example, between 3 and 4 s) the third harmonic of the real pitch is more dominant than the fundamental frequency. In these parts the lowest detected pitch lag is not the one to be chosen. In this time-domain approach the precision of the detected pitch lags can be improved if the greatest common divisor of the pitch-lag candidates is used. The algorithm computes only integer-valued pitch-lag candidates. LTP with a higher precision (non-integer pitch lag M) is presented in [LVKL96, KA90]. As in the FFT-based approach a post-processing should be applied to choose one of the detected candidates for each frame. For a more reliable pitch estimation both time and frequency domain approaches may be combined.

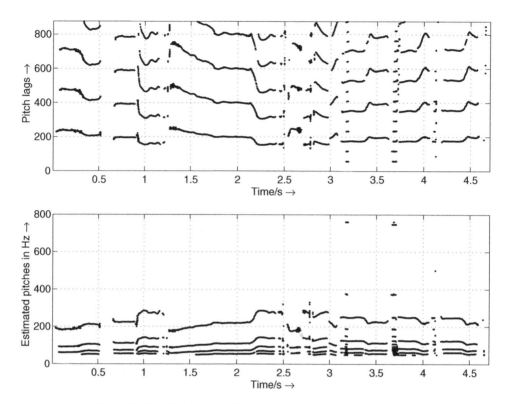

Figure 9.22   Pitch-lag candidates and corresponding frequencies.

The following M-file 9.12 presents an implementation of a pitch tracker based on the LTP approach.

M-file 9.12 (`Pitch_Tracker_LTP.m`)

```
% Pitch_Tracker_LTP.m    [DAFXbook, 2nd ed., chapter 9]
%===== This function demonstrates a pitch tracker based
%===== on the Long-Term Prediction

%----- initializations -----
fname='Toms_diner';
n0=2000; % start index
n1=210000;
K=200;   % hop size for time resolution of pitch estimation
N=1024;  % block length
% checked pitch range in Hz:
fmin=50;
fmax=800;
b0_thres=.2;    % threshold for LTP coeff
p_fac_thres=1.05; % threshold for voiced detection
                % deviation of pitch from mean value

[xin,Fs]=wavread(fname,[n0 n0]); %get Fs
% lag range in samples:
```

```
lmin=floor(Fs/fmax);
lmax=ceil(Fs/fmin);
pre=lmax;      % number of pre-samples
if n0-pre<1
  n0=pre+1;
end
Nx=n1-n0+1; % signal length
blocks=floor(Nx/K);
Nx=(blocks-1)*K+N;
[X,Fs]=wavread(fname,[n0-pre n0+Nx]);
X=X(:,1)';

pitches=zeros(1,blocks);
for b=1:blocks
  x=X((b-1)*K+(1:N+pre));
  [M, F0]=find_pitch_ltp(x, lmin, lmax, N, Fs, b0_thres);
  if ~isempty(M)
    pitches(b)=Fs/M(1); % take candidate with lowest pitch
  else
    pitches(b)=0;
  end
end

%----- post-processing -----
L=9;                % number of blocks for mean calculation
if mod(L,2)==0     % L is even
  L=L+1;
end
D=(L-1)/2;       % delay
h=ones(1,L)./L;  % impulse response for mean calculation
% mirror start and end for "non-causal" filtering:
p=[pitches(D+1:-1:2), pitches, pitches(blocks-1:-1:blocks-D)];
y=conv(p,h);             % length: blocks+2D+2D
pm=y((1:blocks)+2*D); % cut result

Fac=zeros(1,blocks);
idx=find(pm~=0); % don't divide by zero
Fac(idx)=pitches(idx)./pm(idx);
ii=find(Fac<1 & Fac~=0);
Fac(ii)=1./Fac(ii); % all non-zero element are now > 1
% voiced/unvoiced detection:
voiced=Fac~=0 & Fac<p_fac_thres;

T=40;                    % time in ms for segment lengths
M=round(T/1000*Fs/K); % min. number of blocks in a row
[V,p2]=segmentation(voiced, M, pitches);
p2=V.*p2;  % set pitches to zero for unvoiced

figure(1),clf;
time=(0:blocks-1)*K+1; % start sample of blocks
time=time/Fs;          % time in seconds
t=(0:length(X)-1)/Fs; % time in sec for original
subplot(211)
plot(t, X),title('original x(n)');
axis([0 max([t,time]) -1.1*max(abs(X)) 1.1*max(abs(X))])

subplot(212)
```

```
idx=find(p2~=0);
plot_split(idx,time, p2),title('pitch in Hz');
xlabel('time/s \rightarrow');
axis([0 max([t,time]) .9*min(p2(idx)) 1.1*max(p2(idx))])
```

The result of the presented pitch-tracking algorithm is illustrated in Figure 9.23. The bottom plot shows the pitch over time calculated using the LTP method. In comparison to the FFT-based approach in Figure 9.12, the FFT approach performs better in the regions where unvoiced parts occur. The described approach performs well for singing-voice examples. The selection of the post-processing strategy depends on the specific sound or signal.

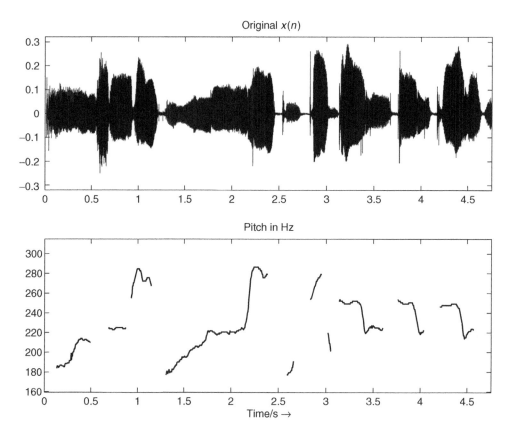

Figure 9.23 Pitch over time using the long-term prediction method for a signal segment of Suzanne Vega's 'Tom's Diner.'

9.2.5 Spatial hearing cues

Spatial hearing relates to source localization (in terms of distance, azimuth, elevation), motion (Doppler), and directivity, as well as to the room effect (reverberation, echo). Computational models that perform auditory scene analysis (ASA) rely on both inter-aural intensity (IID) and inter-aural time (ITD) differences [Bla83] in order to estimate the source azimuth. Elevation and distance are more difficult to estimate, as they involve modeling knowing or estimating the head-related transfer function. While it is quite complex matter to properly deconvolve a signal in order to remove its reverberation, the same deconvolution techniques can perform a bit better to estimate a room echo. In any case, spatial-related sound features extracted from ASA software are good starting points for building an adaptive control that depends on spatial attributes.

9.2.6   Timbral features

Timbre is the most complex perceptual attribute for sound analysis. Here is a reminder of some of the sound features related to timbre:

- Brightness, correlated to spectral centroid [MWdSK95] – itself related to spectral slope, zero-crossing rate, and high frequency content [MB96] – and computed with various models [Cab99].

- Quality and noisiness, correlated to signal-to-noise ratio and to voiciness.

- Texture, related to jitter and shimmer of partials/harmonics [DT96a] (resulting from a statistical analysis of the partials' frequencies and amplitudes), to the balance of odd/even harmonics (given as the peak of the normalized auto-correlation sequence situated half way between the first- and second-highest peak values [AKZ02a]) and to harmonicity.

- Formants and especially vowels for the voice [Sun87] extracted from the spectral envelope; the spectral envelope of the residual; and the mel-frequency critical bands (MFCC), perceptual correlate of the spectral envelope.

Again, specialized software for computing perceptual models of timbre parameters are also good sources of sound features. For instance, PsySound performs the computation of brightness and roughness models, among others. For implementation purposes, sound features will be described by the family of signal-processing technique/domain used to compute them.

Auto-correlation features

We can extract important features from the auto-correlation sequence of a windowed signal: an estimation of the harmonic/non-harmonic content of a signal, the odd/even harmonics ratio in the case of harmonic sounds, and a voiced/unvoiced part in a speech signal. Several algorithms which determine whether a speech frame is voiced or unvoiced are known from speech research [Hes83]. Voiced/unvoiced detection is used either for speech recognition or for synthesis. For digital audio effects, such a feature is useful as a control parameter for an adaptive audio effect. The first peak value of the normalized auto-correlation sequence $r_{xx}(m)$ for $m > 0$ is a good indicator of the unvoiced or voiced part of a signal, as shown in Figure 9.24. When sounds are harmonic, the first auto-correlation peak $(m > 0)$ on the abscissa corresponds to the pitch period of this sound. The value of this peak will be maximum if the sound is harmonic and minimum if the sound is noisy. If a window is used, which gives a better estimate for pitch extraction, this peak value will not go to one, but will be weighted by the auto-correlation of the two windows. This first peak value will be denoted pv at m_0 and is a good indication of voiced/noisy parts in a spoken or sung voice [BP89]. From then, voiciness is defined as the ratio between the amplitude of the first peak $m > 0$ divided by the auto-correlation for $m = 0$, which is the signal amplitude

$$\text{voiciness}(m) = \frac{pv}{r_{xx}(0)} = \frac{r_{xx}(m_0/2)}{r_{xx}(0)}. \tag{9.41}$$

In the case of harmonic sounds, it can be noted that the odd/even harmonics ratio can also be retrieved from the value at half of the time lag of the first peak. The percentage of even harmonics

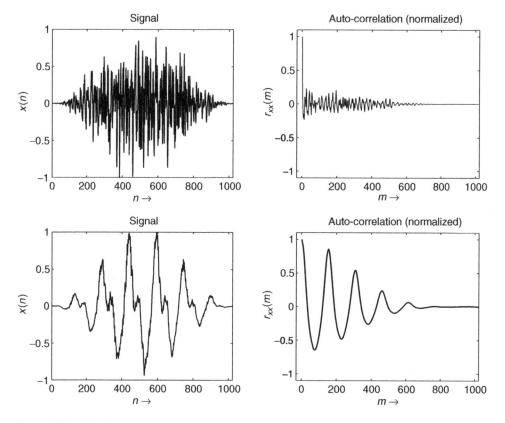

Figure 9.24 Unvoiced (upper part) and voiced (lower part) signals and the corresponding auto-correlation sequence $r_{xx}(m)$.

amplitudes is given as

$$\text{even}(m) = \frac{r_{xx}(m_0/2)}{r_{xx}(0)}. \tag{9.42}$$

An alternative computation of the auto-correlation sequence can be performed in the frequency domain [OS75]. Normally, the auto-correlation is computed from the power spectrum $|X(k)|^2$ of the input signal by $r_{xx}(m) = \text{IFFT}\left[|X(k)|^2\right]$. Here, we perform the IFFT of the magnitude $|X(k)|$ (square root of the power spectrum), which is computed from the FFT of a windowed signal. This last method is illustrated by the following M-file 9.13 that leads to a curve following the voiced/unvoiced feature, as shown in Figure 9.25.

M-file 9.13 (UX_voiced.m)

```
% UX_voiced.m

% feature_voice is a measure of the maximum of the second peak
% of the acf
clear;clf
%----- USER DATA -----
[DAFx_in, FS]  = wavread('x1.wav');
```

```
hop             = 256;  % hop size between two FFTs
WLen            = 1024; % length of the windows
w               = hanningz(WLen);
%----- some initializations -----
WLen2           = WLen/2;
tx              = (1:WLen2+1)';
normW           = norm(w,2);
coef            = (WLen/(2*pi));
pft             = 1;
lf              = floor((length(DAFx_in) - WLen)/hop);
feature_voiced  = zeros(lf,1);
tic
%==========================================
pin  = 0;
pend = length(DAFx_in) - WLen;

while pin<pend
    grain     = DAFx_in(pin+1:pin+WLen).* w;
    f         = fft(grain)/WLen2;
    f2        = real(ifft(abs(f)));
    f2        = f2/f2(1);
    [v,i1]    = min(f2(1:WLen2)>0.);
    f2(1:i1)  = zeros(i1,1);
    [v,imax]  = max(f2(1:WLen2));
    feature_voiced(pft) = v;
    pft       = pft + 1;
    pin       = pin + hop;
end
% ==========================================
toc
subplot(2,1,1)
plot(feature_voiced)
```

A particular way to use this feature is the construction of an adaptive time-stretching effect, where the stretching ratio α depends on this feature according to a mapping function $\alpha = 8^{pv}$ (see Figure 9.26). The time-stretching ratio will vary from 1 to 8, depending on the evolution of pv over time. A threshold detector can help to force this ratio to 1 in the case of silence. This leads to great improvements over regular time-stretching algorithms.

Center of gravity of a spectrum (spectral centroid)

An important feature of a sound is the evolution of the 'richness of harmonics' over time. It has been clearly pointed out at the beginning of computer music that sounds synthesized with a fixed waveform give only static sounds, and that the sound's harmonic content must evolve with time to give a lively sound impression. So algorithmic methods of synthesis have used this variation: additive synthesis uses the balance between harmonics or partials, waveshaping or FM synthesis use an index which changes the richness by the strength of the components.

A good indication of the instantaneous richness of a sound can be measured by the center of gravity of its spectrum, as depicted in Figure 9.27. A sound with a fixed pitch, but with stronger harmonics has a higher center of gravity. It should be noted here that this center of gravity is linked to the pitch of the sound, and that this should be taken into account during the use of this feature. Thus, a good indicator of the instantaneous richness of a sound can be the ratio of the center of gravity divided by the pitch.

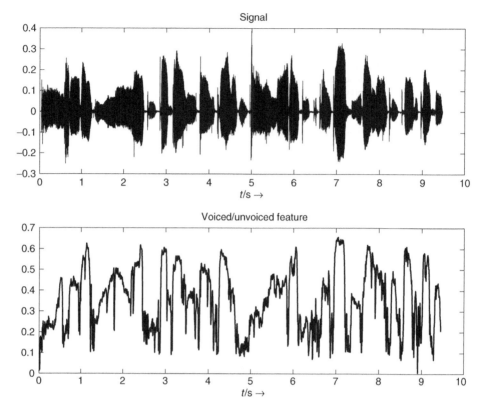

Figure 9.25 Vocal signal and the 'voiced/unvoiced' feature $pv(n)$.

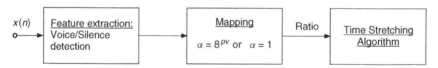

Figure 9.26 Adaptive time stretching based on auto-correlation feature.

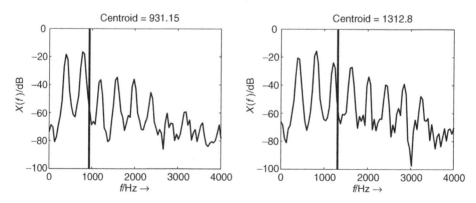

Figure 9.27 Center of gravity of a spectrum as a good indicator of the richness of a harmonic sound.

A straightforward method of calculating this centroid can be achieved inside an FFT/IFFT-based analysis-synthesis scheme. The spectral centroid is at the center of the spectral energy distribution and can be calculated by

$$\text{centroid}_a = \frac{\sum_{k=0}^{N/2} k \cdot |X(k)|}{\sum_{k=0}^{N/2} |X(k)|}. \tag{9.43}$$

The centroid is defined by the ratio of the sum of the magnitudes multiplied by the corresponding frequencies divided by the sum of the magnitudes and it is also possible to use the square of the magnitudes

$$\text{centroid}_e = \frac{\sum_{k=0}^{N/2} k \cdot |X(k)|}{\sum_{k=0}^{N/2} |X(k)|^2}. \tag{9.44}$$

Another method working in the time domain makes use of the property of the derivative of a sinusoid which gives $\frac{d}{dn} A_k \sin(\Omega_k n) = A_k \Omega_k \cdot \cos(\Omega_k n)$ with $\Omega_k = 2\pi \frac{f_k}{f_S}$. If we can express the input signal by a sum of sinusoids according to

$$x(n) = \sum_{k=0}^{N/2-1} A_k \sin(\Omega_k n), \tag{9.45}$$

the derivative of the input signal leads to

$$\frac{dx(n)}{dn} = \sum_{k=0}^{N/2-1} A_k \Omega_k \cos(\Omega_k n). \tag{9.46}$$

The spectral centroid can then be computed according to (9.43) by the ratio of the RMS value of the derivative of the input signal divided by the RMS value of the input signal itself. The derivative of the discrete-time input signal $x(n)$ can be approximated by $\Delta x(n) = x(n) - x(n-1)$. The described time-domain method is quite effective because it does not need any FFT and is suitable for real-time applications. The following M-file 9.14 illustrates these possibilities.

M-file 9.14 (UX_centroid.m)

```
% UX_centroid.m
[DAFXbook, 2nd ed., chapter 9]
% feature_centroid1 and 2 are centroids
% calculate by two different methods
clear;clf
%----- USER DATA -----
[DAFx_in, FS]   = wavread('x1.wav');
hop             = 256;  % hop size between two FFTs
WLen            = 1024; % length of the windows
w               = hanningz(WLen);
%----- some initializations -----
WLen2           = WLen/2;
tx              = (1:WLen2+1)';
normW           = norm(w,2);
coef            = (WLen/(2*pi));
pft             = 1;
lf              = floor((length(DAFx_in) - WLen)/hop);
feature_rms     = zeros(lf,1);
```

```
feature_centroid   = zeros(1f,1);
feature_centroid2 = zeros(1f,1);
tic
%==============================================
pin  = 0;
pend = length(DAFx_in) - WLen;

while pin<pend
    grain                  = DAFx_in(pin+1:pin+WLen).* w;
    feature_rms(pft)       = norm(grain,2) / normW;
    f                      = fft(grain)/WLen2;
    fx                     = abs(f(tx));
    feature_centroid(pft)  = sum(fx.*(tx-1)) / sum(fx);
    fx2                    = fx.*fx;
    feature_centroid2(pft) = sum(fx2.*(tx-1)) / sum(fx2);
    grain2                 = diff(DAFx_in(pin+1:pin+WLen+1)).* w;
    feature_deriv(pft)     = coef * norm(grain2,2) / norm(grain,2);
    pft                    = pft + 1;
    pin                    = pin + hop;
end
% ==============================================
toc
subplot(4,1,1); plot(feature_rms); xlabel('RMS')
subplot(4,1,2); plot(feature_centroid); xlabel('centroid 1')
subplot(4,1,3); plot(feature_centroid2); xlabel('centroid 2')
subplot(4,1,4); plot(feature_deriv); xlabel('centroid 3')
```

For each method the center of gravity is calculated in frequency bins. Figure 9.28 illustrates the results for each method. It can be seen at the end of a flute sound that the centroid parameter is very important: the variations of the centroid are quite independent of the RMS values of the signal. The centroid takes some time to oscillate and then is maintained until the end of the sound. An alternative has been proposed, so that the centroid tends to 0 when the sound intensity level also tends to 0. It consists of adding a constant of small value in the centroid denominator [Bea82]:

$$\text{centroid}_{a,2} = \frac{\sum_{k=0}^{N/2} k \cdot |X(k)|}{c_0 + \sum_{k=0}^{N/2} |X(k)|}. \tag{9.47}$$

An artifact of this computation is that it alway biases the centroid value from the usual formulation one, whereas the following computation only biases for low signal intensity levels:

$$\text{centroid}_{a,2} = \frac{\sum_{k=0}^{N/2} k \cdot |X(k)|}{\max(c_0, \sum_{k=0}^{N/2} |X(k)|)}. \tag{9.48}$$

A digital effect which relies on the spectral centroid feature is the mimicking of a natural sound by a synthetic one. As an example, we can use a waveshaping synthesis method. This method calculates a synthetic sound by distorting a sine wave with the help of a waveshaping function (also called nonlinear transfer function) and multiplying the result by an amplitude variation (see Figure 9.29). The waveshaping function is usually a polynomial, because this function can be calculated with the aim of having a fixed output spectrum [Arf79, Bru79]. So apart from the pitch

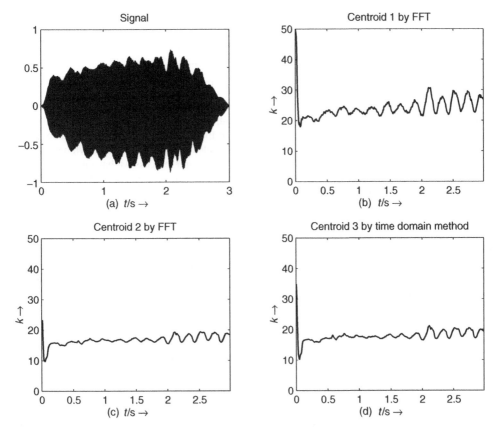

Figure 9.28 Spectral centroid computation in frequency and time domain. Plots (b)–(d) show the centroids in bins, where the corresponding tone pitch is given by $f_k = \frac{k}{N} f_S$ (with FFT length N and sampling frequency f_S).

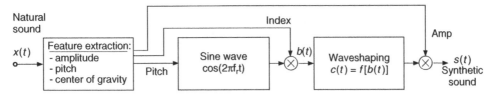

Figure 9.29 Mimicking with waveshaping.

of the sine wave, this method relies on the evolution of two parameters: the amplitude of the sine wave, which is called the 'index' because the sine wave is used as an input to the waveshaping function, and an amplitude factor, which is used as an amplitude envelope. If we extract the centroid and the RMS evolution from a natural sound, as well as the pitch, we can compute an index proportional to the ratio of the centroid towards the pitch (this proportional factor, apart from a necessary normalization, drives the general brightness of the sound) and an amplitude factor proportional to the extracted RMS feature. Thus we obtain a synthetic sound that retains some characteristics of the initial sound and is given by

$$s(t) = amp \cdot f \left[index \cdot \cos(2\pi f_r t) \right] \tag{9.49}$$

$$f_r = pitch, \quad index = coef \cdot \frac{centroid}{pitch}, \quad amp = rms.$$

The mimicking is improved when the waveshaping function is calculated for the spectrum at one point of the initial sound. Two other further improvements can be added: an amplitude normalization factor due to the fact that the index should only change the centroid and not the amplitude, and a correcting factor for the index due to the fact that the index and centroid of the synthetic sound have no reason to be in a linear relationship. But even the simple process we have described gives a variety of allotropic sounds which all resemble the original in some way, but are purely harmonic and do not contain any noisy components.

Features from harmonic partials

Once a spectral model of a harmonic sound is computed, various sound features can be extracted from the harmonic partial amplitude and frequency, apart from the harmonic centroid we have already presented. The relative percentage of amplitude or energy of the even and odd harmonics can be computed as

$$\% A_{even}(m) = \frac{\sum_{l=1}^{L/2} a_{2l}(m)}{\sum_{l=1}^{L} a_l(m)} \tag{9.50}$$

$$\% A_{odd}(m) = \frac{\sum_{l=0}^{L/2} a_{2l+1}(m)}{\sum_{l=1}^{L} a_l(m)}. \tag{9.51}$$

These features are called *even/odd harmonic ratios*. Such computation is more accurately than the one proposed with the auto-correlation function, because the latter computes the amplitude of even harmonics relative to the whole sound amplitude, not only that of the harmonic partials. Alternatives are the ratio of odd versus even harmonics and the ratio of even versus odd harmonics.

The *tristimulus* is a timbral descriptor that was derived for sounds as an equivalent of the color attributes for vision [PJ82]. It is computed by

$$T_1(m) = \frac{a_1(m)}{\sum_{l=1}^{L} a_l(m)} \tag{9.52}$$

$$T_2(m) = \frac{\sum_{l=2}^{4} a_l(m)}{\sum_{l=1}^{L} a_l(m)} \tag{9.53}$$

$$T_3(m) = \frac{\sum_{l=5}^{L} a_l(m)}{\sum_{l=1}^{L} a_l(m)}. \tag{9.54}$$

From these equations, it follows that $T_1(m)$ describes the strength of fundamental amplitude compared to all harmonics. $T_2(m)$ describes how strong are the middle frequency harmonics and $T_3(m)$ describes how strong are the higher harmonic amplitudes. As for the spectral centroid, it can be modified using energies instead of amplitudes, and truncating the denominator for low-level signals, in which case the tristimuli becomes:

$$\overline{T}_1(m) = \frac{(a_1(m))^2}{\max\left(\varepsilon, \sum_{l=1}^{L} (a_l(m))^2 \right)} \tag{9.55}$$

$$\overline{T}_2(m) = \frac{\sum_{l=2}^{4} (a_l(m))^2}{\max\left(\varepsilon, \sum_{l=1}^{L} (a_l(m))^2\right)} \qquad (9.56)$$

$$\overline{T}_3(m) = \frac{\sum_{l=5}^{L} (a_l(m))^2}{\max\left(\varepsilon, \sum_{l=1}^{L} (a_l(m))^2\right)}. \qquad (9.57)$$

9.2.7   Statistical features

As an example, Dubnov [DT96b] has obtained the classification of instrumental timbres on a 2-D map by using skew and kurtosis. These features can help in defining the texturization of a sound. The texture of a sound is very difficult to evaluate: why a trumpet does not sound like a string does not rely only on a spectral richness. The way the individual components are synchronized or not is an important key for defining a texture. Many other features can be extracted from a sound [HB98, RDS+99, DH00], just to mention a few from a very active field of research.

9.3   Mapping sound features to control parameters

9.3.1   The mapping structure

While recent studies define specific strategies of mapping for gestural control of sound synthesizers [Wan02] or audio effects [WD00], some mapping strategies for ADAFX were specifically derived from the three-layer mapping that uses a perceptive layer [ACKV02, AV03, VWD06], which is shown in Figure 9.30. To convert sound features $f_i(n), i = 1, ..., M$ into effect control parameters $c_j(n), j = 1, ..., N$, we use an M-to-N explicit mapping scheme[3] divided into two stages: sound-feature combination and control-signal conditioning (see Figure 9.30).

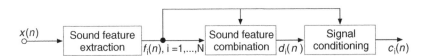

Figure 9.30   Mapping structure between sound features and one effect control $c_i(n)$: sound features are first combined, and then conditioned in order to provide a valid control to the effect. Figure reprinted with IEEE permission from [VZA06].

The sound features may often vary rapidly and with a constant sampling rate (synchronous data), whereas the gestural controls used in sound synthesis vary less frequently and sometimes in an asynchronous mode. For that reason, we chose sound features for direct control of the effect and optional gestural control for modifications of the mapping between sound features and effect control parameters [VWD06], thus providing navigation by interpolation between presets.

Defining a clear mapping structure offers a higher level of control and generalizes any effect: with adaptive control (remove the gestural control level), with gestural control (remove the adaptive control), or with both controls. Sound features are either short-term or long-term features; therefore they may have different and well-identified roles in the proposed mapping structure. Short-term features (e.g., energy, instantaneous pitch or loudness, voiciness, spectral centroid) provide a continuous adaptive control with a high rate that we consider equivalent to a modification gesture [Cad99] and useful as inputs (left horizontal arrows in Figures 9.31 and 9.32). Long-term features

---

[3] M is the number of features we use, usually between 1 and 5; N is the number of effect control parameters, usually between 1 and 20.

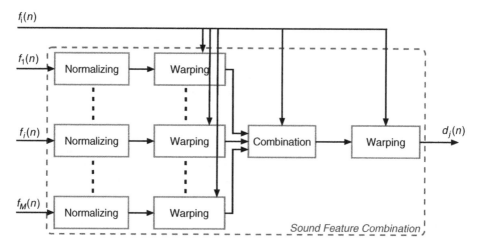

Figure 9.31 Feature combination, first stage of the sound-feature mapping. $f_i(n), i = 1, ..., M$ are the sound features, and $d_j(n), j = 1, ..., N$ are the combined features. Figure reprinted with IEEE permission from [VZA06].

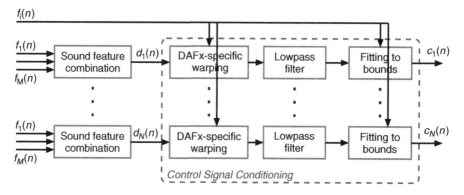

Figure 9.32 Signal conditioning, the second stage of the sound feature mapping. $c_i(n), n = 1, ..., N$ are the effect controls derived from sound features $f_i(n), i = 1, ..., M$. The DAFx-specific warping and the fitting to boundaries can be controlled by other sound features. Figure reprinted with IEEE permission from [VZA06].

computed after signal segmentation (e.g., vibrato, roughness, duration, note pitch, or loudness) are often used for content-based transformations [ABL$^+$03]. They provide a sequential adaptive control with a low rate that we consider equivalent to a selection gesture, and that is useful for control of the mapping (upper vertical arrows in Figures 9.31 and 9.32).

9.3.2 Sound-feature combination

The first stage combines several features, as depicted in Figure 9.31. First, all the features are normalized in [0, 1] for unsigned values features and in [−1, 1] for signed value features. Second, a warping function – a transfer function that is not necessarily linear – can then be applied: a truncation of the feature in order to select an interesting part, low pass filtering, a scale change (from linear to exponential or logarithmic), or any non-linear transfer function. Parameters of the warping function can also be derived from sound features (for example the truncation boundaries). Third, the feature combination is done by linear combination, except when weightings are derived from other sound features. Fourth and finally, a warping function can also be applied to the feature combination output in order to symmetrically provide modifications of features before and after combination.

9.3.3   Control-signal conditioning

Conditioning a signal consists of modifying the signal so that its behavior fits to pre-requisites in terms of boundaries and variation type. It is usually used to protect hardware from an input signal. The second mapping stage conditions the effect control signal $d_i(n)$ coming out from the feature combination box, as shown in Figure 9.32, so that it fits the required behavior of the effect controls. It uses three steps: an effect-specific warping, a low pass filter and scaling. First, the specific warping is effect dependent. It may consist of quantizing the pitch curve to the tempered scale (auto-tune effect), quantizing the control curve of the delay time (adaptive granular delay, cf. Section 9.4.6), or modifying a time-warping ratio varying with time in order to preserve the signal length (cf. Section 9.4.2). Second, the low pass filter ensures the suitability of the control signal for the selected application. Third and last, the control signal is scaled to the effect control boundaries given by the user, that are eventually adaptively controlled. When necessary, the control signal, sampled at the block rate is resampled to the audio sampling rate f_S.

9.4   Examples of adaptive DAFX

As explained in this chapter's introduction, several effects already made use of adaptive control a long time before recent studies tended to generalize this concept to all audio effects [VA01, ABL+03]. Such effects were developed for technical or musical purposes, as answers to specific needs (e.g., auto-tune, compressor, cross-synthesis). Using the framework presented in this chapter, we can now ride on the adaptive wave, and present old and new adaptive effects in terms of: their form, the sound features that are used, the mapping of sound features to effect control parameters, the modifications of implementation techniques that are required, and the perceptual effect of the ADAFX.

9.4.1   Adaptive effects on loudness

Adaptive sound-level change

By controlling the sound level from a sound feature, we perform an amplitude modulation with a signal which is not monosinusoidal. This generalizes compressor/expander, noise gate/limiter, and cross-duking, which all are specific cases in terms of sound-feature extraction and mapping. Adaptive amplitude modulation controlled by $c(n)$ provides the following signal

$$y(n) = x(n) \cdot (1 + c(n)). \tag{9.58}$$

By deriving $c(n)$ from the sound-intensity level, one obtains compressor/expander and noise gate/limiter. By using the voiciness $v(n) \in [0, 1]$ and a $c(n) = (1 - \cos[\pi v(n)]) / 2$ mapping law, one obtains a 'voiciness gate,' which is a timbre effect that removes voicy sounds and leaves only noisy sounds (which differs from the de-esser [DZ02] that mainly removes the 's'). Adaptive sound-level change is also useful for attack modification of instrumental and electroacoustic sounds (differently from compressor/expander), thus modifying loudness and timbre. If using a computational model of perceived loudness, one can make a feedforward adaptive loudness change, that tries to reach a target loudness by means of iterative computations on the output loudness depending on the gain applied.

Adaptive tremolo

A tremolo, of monosinusoidal amplitude modulation, is an effect for which either the rate (or modulation frequency $f_m(n)$) and the depth $d(n)$, or both, can be derived from sound features. The time-varying amplitude modulation is then expressed using a linear scale

$$c(n) = d(n) \cdot \sin\left(2\pi \frac{f_m(n)}{f_S} n\right),$$ (9.59)

where f_S the audio sampling rate. It may also be expressed using a logarithmic scale according to

$$c_{dB}(m) = 10^{d(m)\left(\sin\left(2\pi \frac{f_m(n)}{f_S} n\right) - 1\right)/40}.$$ (9.60)

The modulation function is sinusoidal, but may be replaced by any other periodic function (e.g., triangular, exponential, logarithmic or other). The real-time implementation only requires an oscillator, a warping function, and an audio rate control. Adaptive tremolo allows for a more natural tremolo that accelerates/slows down (which also sounds like a rhythm modification) and emphasizes or de-emphasizes, depending on the sound content (which is perceived as a loudness modification). Figure 9.33 shows an example where the fundamental frequency $f_0(m) \in [780, 1420]$ Hz and the sound-intensity level $a(m) \in [0, 1]$ are mapped to the control rate and the depth according to the following mapping rules

$$f_m(m) = 1 + 13 \cdot \frac{1420 - f_0(m)}{1420 - 780}$$ (9.61)

$$d(m) = 100 \cdot a(m).$$ (9.62)

9.4.2   Adaptive effects on time

Adaptive time-warping

Time-warping is non-linear time-scaling. This non-real-time processing uses a time-scaling ratio $\gamma(m)$ that varies with m the block index. The sound is then alternatively locally time-expanded when $\gamma(m) > 1$, and locally time-compressed when $\gamma(m) < 1$. The adaptive control is provided with the input signal (feedforward adaption). The implementation can be achieved either using a constant analysis step increment R_A and a time-varying synthesis step increment $R_S(m)$, or using a time-varying $R_A(m)$ and constant R_S, thus providing more implementation efficiency. In the latter case, the recursive formulae of the analysis time index t_A and the synthesis time index t_S are given by

$$t_A(m) = t_A(m-1) + R_A(m-1)$$ (9.63)

$$t_S(m) = t_S(m-1) + R_S,$$ (9.64)

with the analysis step increment according to

$$R_A(m-1) = \gamma(t_A(m-1)) \cdot R_S.$$ (9.65)

Adaptive time-warping provides improvement to the usual time-scaling, for example by minimizing the timbre modification. It allows for time-scaling with attack preservation when using an attack/transient detector to vary the time-scaling ratio [Bon00, Pal03].

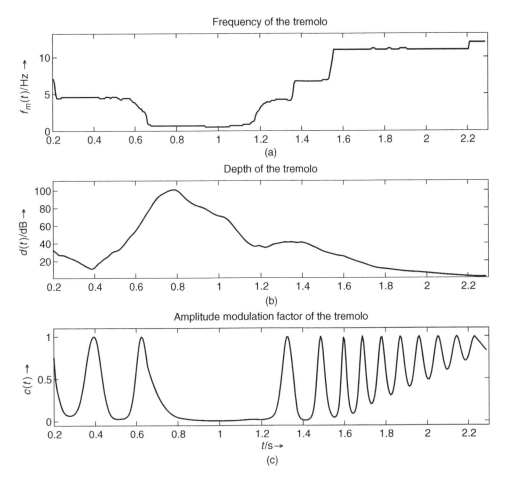

Figure 9.33 Control curves for the adaptive tremolo: (a) frequency $f_m(n)$ is derived from the fundamental frequency, as in Equation (9.61); (b) depth $d(m)$ is derived from the signal intensity level, as in Equation (9.62); (c) the amplitude modulation curve is computed with a logarithmic scale, as in Equation (9.60). Figure reprinted with IEEE permission from [VZA06].

Using auto-adaptive time-warping, we can apply fine changes in duration. A first example consists of time-compressing the gaps and time-expanding the sounding parts: the time-warping ratio γ is computed from the intensity level $a(n) \in [0, 1]$ using a mapping law such as $\gamma(n) = 2^{a(n)-a_0}$, with a_0 as a threshold. A second example consists of time-compressing the voicy parts and time-expanding the noisy parts of a sound, using the mapping law $\gamma(n) = 2^{v(n)-v_0}$, with $v(n) \in [0, 1]$ the voiciness and v_0 the voiciness threshold. When used for local changes of duration, it provides modifications of timbre and expressiveness by modifying the attack, sustain and decay durations. Using cross-adaptive time-warping, time-folding of sound A is slowed down or sped up depending on the sound B content. Generally speaking, adaptive time-warping allows for a re-interpretation of recorded sounds, for modifications of expressiveness (music) and perceived emotion (speech). Unfortunately, there is a lack of knowledge of and investigation into the link between sound features and their mapping to the effect control on one side, and the modifications of expressiveness on the other side.

Adaptive time-warping that preserves signal length

When applying time-warping with adaptive control, the signal length is changed. To preserve the original signal length, we must evaluate the length of the time-warped signal according to the adaptive control curve. Then, a specific mapping function is applied to the time-warping ratio γ so that it verifies the synchronization constraint.

Synchronization constraint Time indices in Equations (9.63) and (9.64) are functions that depend on γ and m as given by

$$t_A(m) = \sum_{l=1}^{m} \gamma(t_A(l-1)) R_S \tag{9.66}$$

$$t_S(m) = m \, R_S, \quad 1 \le m \le M. \tag{9.67}$$

The analysis signal length $L_A = \sum_{l=1}^{M} \gamma(t_A(l-1)) \, R_S$ differs from the synthesis signal length $L_S = M R_S$. This is no more the case for $\tilde{\gamma}$ verifying the synchronization constraint

$$M = \sum_{l=1}^{M} \tilde{\gamma}(t_A(l-1)). \tag{9.68}$$

Three synchronization schemes The constraint ratio $\tilde{\gamma}(t_A(m))$ can be derived from γ by:

(1) Addition as

$$\tilde{\gamma}_1(t_A(m)) = \gamma(t_A(m)) + 1 - \frac{\sum_{l=1}^{M} \gamma(t_A(l-1))}{M} \tag{9.69}$$

(2) By multiplication as

$$\tilde{\gamma}_2(t_A(m)) = \gamma(t_A(m)) \cdot M / \sum_{l=1}^{M} \gamma(t_A(l-1)) \tag{9.70}$$

(3) By exponential weighting $\tilde{\gamma}_3(t_A(m)) = \left[\gamma(t_A(m))\right]^{\gamma_3}$, with γ_3 the iterative solution[4] of

$$\gamma_3 = \arg\min_p \left| \frac{\sum_{l=1}^{M} \left[\gamma(t_A(l-1))\right]^p}{M} - 1 \right|. \tag{9.71}$$

An example is provided in Figure 9.34. Each of these modifications imposes a specific behavior on the time-warping control. For example, the exponential weighting is the only synchronization technique that preserves the locations where the signal has to be time-compressed or expanded: $\tilde{\gamma} > 1$ when $\gamma > 1$ and $\tilde{\gamma} < 1$ when $\gamma < 1$.

Synchronization that preserves γ boundaries However, none of these three synchronization schemes ensure to preserve $\gamma_{\min}$ and $\gamma_{\max}$, the boundaries of γ as given by the user. A solution consists in using the clipping function

$$\overline{\gamma}(p) = \begin{cases} \tilde{\gamma}_i(p) & \text{if } \tilde{\gamma}_i(p) \in [\gamma_{\min}; \gamma_{\max}] \\ \gamma_{\min} & \text{if } \tilde{\gamma}_i(p) < \gamma_{\min} \\ \gamma_{\max} & \text{if } \tilde{\gamma}_i(p) > \gamma_{\max} \end{cases}. \tag{9.72}$$

---

[4] There is no analytical solution, so an iterative scheme is necessary.

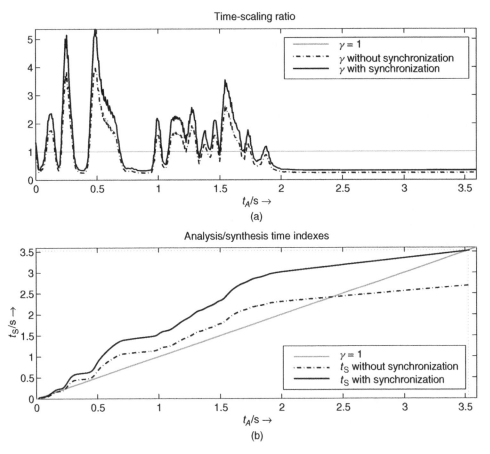

Figure 9.34 (a) The time-warping ratio γ is derived from the amplitude (RMS) as $\gamma(m) = 2^{4(a(m)-0.5)} \in [0.25, 4]$ (dashed line), and modified by the multiplication ratio $\gamma_m = 1.339$ (solid line). (b) The analysis time index $t_A(m)$ is computed according to Equation (9.63), verifying the synchronization constraint of Equation (9.68).

The iterative solution $\overline{\overline{\gamma}}_i$ that both preserves the synchronization constraint of Equation (9.68) and the initial boundaries can be derived as

$$\overline{\overline{\gamma}}_i = \arg\min_{\overline{\gamma_i}} \left| \frac{\sum_{l=1}^{M} \overline{\gamma}_i(t_A(l-1))}{M} - 1 \right|,$$
(9.73)

where $i = 1, 2, 3$ respectively denotes addition, multiplication, and exponential weighting. The adaptive time-warping that preserves the signal length can be used for various things, among which expressiveness change (slight modifications of a solo improvisation that still sticks to the beat), a more natural chorus (when combined with adaptive pitch-shifting), or a swing change.

Swing change

Adaptive time-warping that preserves the signal length provides groove change when giving several synchronization points [VZA06]. When time-scaling is controlled by an analysis from a beat tracker, synchronization points can be beat-dependent and then the swing can be changed [GFB03] by displacing one every two beats either to make them even (binary rhythm) of uneven with the rule of thumb 2/3 and 1/3 (ternary rhythm). This effect modifies time and rhythm.

Time-scaling that preserves the vibrato and tremolo

Adaptive time-scaling also allows for time-scaling sounds with vibrato, for instance when combined with adaptive pitch-shifting controlled by a vibrato estimator: vibrato is removed, the sound is time-scaled, and vibrato with same frequency and depth is applied [AD98]. Using the special sinusoidal model [MR04], both vibrato (often modeled and reduced as frequency modulation) and tremolo (amplitude modulation) can be preserved by applying the resampling of control parameters on the partials of partials. This allows one to time-scale the portion of the sound which would be considered as 'sustained,' while leaving untouched the attack and release.

9.4.3 Adaptive effects on pitch

Adaptive pitch-shifting

Using any of the techniques proposed for the usual pitch-shifting with formant preservation (PSOLA, phase vocoder combined with source-filter separation, and additive model), adaptive pitch-shifting can be performed in real time, with its pitch-shift ratio $\rho(m)$ defined in the middle of the block as

$$\rho(m) = \frac{F_{0,\text{out}}(m)}{F_{0,\text{in}}(m)} \tag{9.74}$$

where $F_{0,\text{in}}(m)$ (resp. $F_{0,\text{out}}(m)$) denotes the fundamental frequency of the input (resp. the output) signal. The additive model allows for varying pitch-shift ratios, since the synthesis can be made sample by sample in the time domain [MQ86]. The pitch-shifting ratio is then interpolated sample by sample between two blocks. PSOLA allows for varying pitch-shifting ratios as long as one performs at the block level and performs energy normalization during the overlap-add technique. The phase vocoder technique has to be modified in order to permit that two overlap-added blocks have the same pitch-shifting ratio for all the samples they share, thus avoiding phase cancellation of overlap-added blocks. First, the control curve must be low pass filtered to limit the pitch-shifting ratio variations. In doing so, we can consider that the spectral envelope does not vary inside a block, and then use the source-filter decomposition to resample only the source. Second, the variable sampling rate $F_A(m)$ implies a variable length of the synthesis block $N_S(m) = N_A/\rho(m)$ and so a variable energy of the overlap-added synthesis signal. The solution we chose consists in imposing a constant synthesis block size $N_c = N_U/\max \rho(m)$, either by using a variable analysis block size $N_A(m) = \rho(m)N_U$ and then $N_S = N_U$, or by using a constant analysis block size $N_A = N_U$ and post-correcting the synthesis block x_{ps} according to

$$y(n) = x_{ps}(n) \cdot \frac{h_{N_c}(n)}{w_{N(m)}(n)}, \tag{9.75}$$

where h is the Hanning window, $N(m) = 1 + \sum_{l=2}^{N_A} \rho(l)$ is the number of samples of the synthesis block m, $x_{ps}(n)$ is the resampled and formant-corrected block $n = 1, ..., N(m)$, w is the warped analysis window defined for $n = 1, ..., N(m)$ as $w_{N(m)}(n) = h(\sum_{l=1}^{n} \rho_s(l))$, and $\rho_s(n)$ is the pitch-shifting ratio $\rho(m)$ resampled at the signal sampling rate F_A.

A musical application of adaptive pitch-shifting is adaptive detuning, obtained by adding to a signal its pitch-shifted version with a lower than a quarter-tone ratio (this also modifies timbre). For instance, adaptive detuning can be controlled by the amplitude as $\rho(n) = 2^{0.25 \cdot a(n)}$, where louder sounds are the most detuned. Adaptive pitch-shifting allows for melody change when controlled by long-term features such as the pitch of each note of a musical sentence [GPAH03]. The auto-tune is a feedback-adaptive pitch-shifting effect, where the pitch is shifted so that the processed sound reaches a target pitch. Adaptive pitch-shifting is also useful for intonation change, as explained below.

Harmonizer

As it will be further explained in Chapter 10, a vocal chorus can be harmonized by adding pitch-shifted versions of a voice sound. These pitch-shifted versions are tuned to one given target degree in the current musical scale, so that chords of voices are obtained. This is very similar to the auto-tune (feedback-adaptive effect), except that the target pitch is not the pitch in the scale which is nearest the original pitch, but a pitch with a specific relation to the original voice pitch. This effect, combined with other effects such as auto-tune, reverberation, etc., has been widely used in recent products such as the Vocaloid by Yamaha, and the VoiceOne by TC Helicon.

Adaptive intonation change

Intonation is the pitch information contained in prosody of human speech. It is composed of the macro-intonation and the micro-intonation [Cri82]. To compute these two components, the fundamental frequency $F_{0,in}(m)$ is segmented over time. Its local mean $\overline{F_{0,in}^{loc}}$ is the macro-intonation structure for a given segment, and the remainder $\Delta F_{0,in}(m) = F_{0,in}(m) - \overline{F_{0,in}^{loc}}$ is the micro-intonation structure,[5] as shown in Figure 9.35. This yields the following decomposition of the input fundamental frequency

$$F_{0,in}(m) = \overline{F_{0,in}^{loc}} + \Delta F_{0,in}(m). \tag{9.76}$$

The adaptive intonation change is a non-real-time effect that modifies the fundamental frequency trends by deriving (α, β, γ) from sound features, using the decomposition

$$F_{0,out}(m) = \gamma \overline{F_{0,in}} + \alpha(\overline{F_{0,in}^{loc}} - \overline{F_{0,in}}) + \beta \Delta F_{0,in}(m), \tag{9.77}$$

where $\overline{F_{0,in}}$ is the mean of $F_{0,in}$ over the whole signal [AV03]. One can independently control the mean fundamental frequency (γ e.g., controlled by the first formant frequency), the macro-intonation structure (α e.g., controlled by the second formant frequency) and the micro-intonation structure (β e.g., controlled by the intensity level $a(m)$); as well as strengthen ($\alpha \geq 1$ and $\beta \geq 1$), flatten ($0 \leq \alpha < 1$ and $0 \leq \beta < 1$), or inverse ($\alpha < 0$ and $\beta < 0$) an intonation, thus modifying the voice ambitus, but also the whole expressiveness of speech, similarly to people from different countries speaking a foreign language with different accents.

9.4.4 Adaptive effects on timbre

The perceptual attribute of timbre offers the widest category of audio effects, among which voice morphing [DGR95, CLB+00] and voice conversion, spectral compressor (also known as Contrast [Fav01]), automatic vibrato (with both frequency and amplitude modulation [ABLS02]), martianization [VA02], adaptive spectral tremolo, adaptive equalizer, and adaptive spectral warping [VZA06].

---

[5] In order to avoid rapid pitch-shifting modifications at the boundaries of voiced segments, the local mean of unvoiced segments is modified as the linear interpolation between its bound values (see Figure 9.35.(b)). The same modification is applied to the remainder (micro-intonation).

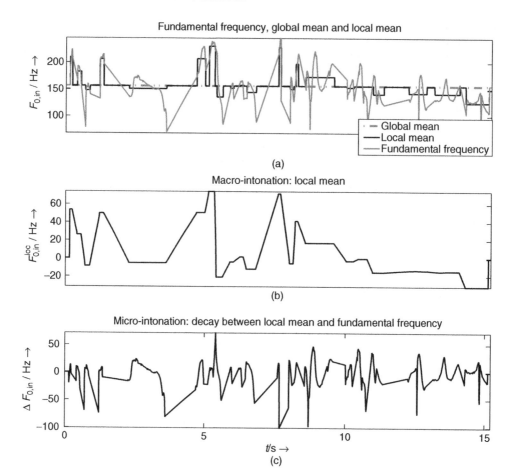

Figure 9.35 Intonation decomposition using an improved voiced/unvoiced mask. (a) Fundamental frequency $F_{0,\text{in}}(m)$, global mean $\overline{F_{0,\text{in}}}$ and local mean $\overline{F_{0,\text{in}}^{loc}}$. (b) Macro-intonation $\overline{F_{0,\text{in}}^{loc}}$ with linear interpolation between voiced segments. (c) Micro-intonation $\Delta F_{0,\text{in}}(m)$ with the same linear interpolation.

Adaptive equalizer

This effect is obtained by applying a time-varying equalizing curve $H_i(m,k)$, which is constituted of N_q filter gains of a constant-Q filter bank. In the frequency domain, we extract a feature vector of length N denoted[6] $f_i(m,\bullet)$ from the STFT $X_i(m,k)$ of each input channel i (the sound being mono or multi-channel). This vector feature $f_i(m,\bullet)$ is then mapped to $H_i(m,\bullet)$, for example by averaging its values in each of the constant-Q segments, or by taking only the N_q first values of $f_i(m,\bullet)$ as the gains of the filters. The equalizer output STFT is then

$$Y_i(m,k) = H_i(m,k) \cdot X_i(m,k). \tag{9.78}$$

If $H_i(m,k)$ varies too rapidly, the perceived effect is not varying equalizer/filtering, but ring modulation of partials, and potentially phasing. To avoid this, we low pass filter $H_i(\bullet,k)$ in time

---

[6] The notation $f_i(m,\bullet)$ corresponds to the frequency vector made of $f_i(m,k), k = 1,...,N$.

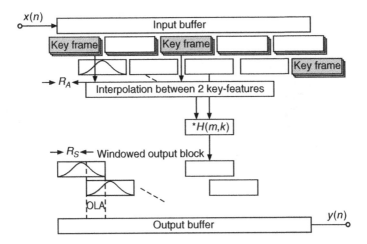

Figure 9.36 Block-by-block processing of adaptive equalizer. The equalizer curve is derived from a vector feature that is low pass filtered in time, using interpolation between key frames. Figure reprinted with IEEE permission from [VZA06].

[VD04], with L the down sampling ratio, $F_I = F_B/L$ the equalizer control sampling rate, and F_B the block sampling rate. This is obtained by linear interpolation between two key vectors denoted C_{P-1} and C_P (see Figure 9.36). For each block position m, $PL \leq m \leq (P+1)L$, the vector feature $f_i(m, \bullet)$ is given by

$$f_i(m, k) = \alpha(m) \cdot C_{P-1}(m, k)$$
$$+ (1 - \alpha(m)) \cdot C_P(m, k), \tag{9.79}$$

with $\alpha(m) = (m - PL)/L$ the interpolation ratio. Real-time implementation requires the extraction of a fast-computing key vector $C_P(m, k)$, such as the samples buffer $C_P(m, k) = x(PLR_A + k)$, or the spectral envelope $C_P(m, k) = E(PL, k)$. However, non-real-time implementations allow for using more computationally expensive features, such as a harmonic comb filter, thus providing an odd/even harmonics balance modification.

Adaptive spectral warping

Harmonicity is adaptively modified when using spectral warping with an adaptive warping function $W(m, k)$. The STFT magnitude is computed by

$$|Y(m, k)| = |X(m, W(m, k))| \tag{9.80}$$

The warping function is given by

$$W(m, k) = C_1(m) \cdot C_2(m, k) + (1 - C_1(m)) \cdot k \tag{9.81}$$

and varies in time according to two control parameters: a vector $C_2(m, k) \in [1, N]$, $k = 1, ..., N$ (e.g., the spectral envelope E or its cumulative sum) which is the maximum warping function, and an interpolation ratio $C_1(m) \in [0, 1]$ (e.g., the energy, the voiciness), which determines the warping depth. An example is shown in Figure 9.37, with $C_2(m, k)$ derived from the spectral

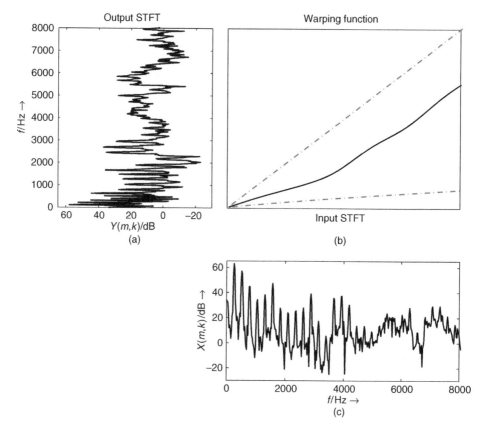

Figure 9.37 A-spectral warping: (a) output STFT, (b) warping function derived from the cumulative sum of the spectral envelope, (c) Input STFT. The warping function gives to any frequency bin the corresponding output magnitude. The spectrum is then non-linearly scaled according to the warping-function slope p: compressed for $p < 1$ and expanded for $p > 1$. The dashed lines represent $W(m, k) = C_2(m, k)$ and $W(m, k) = k$. Figure reprinted with IEEE permission from [VZA06].

envelope $E(m, k)$ as

$$C_2(m, k) = k - (N - 1) \cdot \frac{\sum_{l=2}^{k} E(m, l)}{\sum_{l=2}^{N} E(m, l)}.$$ (9.82)

This mapping provides a monotonous curve, and prevents the spectrum folding over. Adaptive spectral warping allows for dynamically changing the harmonicity of a sound. When applied only to the source, it allows for better in-harmonizing of voice or a musical instrument since formants are preserved.

9.4.5 Adaptive effects on spatial perception

Adaptive panning

Usually, panning requires the use of both a modification of left and right intensity levels and delays. In order to avoid the Doppler effect, delays are not taken into account in this example. With adaptive control, the azimuth angle $\theta(n) \in [-\frac{\pi}{4}, \frac{\pi}{4}]$ varies in time according to sound features. A constant power panning with the Blumlein law [Bla83] gives the following gains

$$L_l(n) = \frac{\sqrt{2}}{2} (\cos \theta(n) + \sin \theta(n)) \tag{9.83}$$

$$L_r(n) = \frac{\sqrt{2}}{2} (\cos \theta(n) - \sin \theta(n)). \tag{9.84}$$

A sinusoidal control $\theta(n) = \sin(2\pi f_{pan} n / F_A)$ with $f_{pan} > 20$ Hz is not heard anymore as a motion, but as a ring modulation (with a phase decay of $\pi/2$ between the two channels). With more complex motions obtained from sound feature control, this effect does not appear because the motion is not sinusoidal and varies most of the time under 20 Hz. The fast motions cause a stream segregation effect [Bre90], and the coherence in time between the sound motion and the sound content gives the illusion of splitting a monophonic sound into several sources. An example consists of panning synthetic trumpet sounds (obtained by frequency-modulation techniques [Cho71]) with an adaptive control derived from brightness, which is a strong perceptual indicator of brass timbre [Ris65], given by

$$\theta(n) = \pi \cdot \frac{cgs(n)}{fs} - \frac{\pi}{4}. \tag{9.85}$$

Low-brightness sounds are left panned, whereas high brightness sounds are right panned. Brightness of trumpet sounds evolves differently during notes, attack and decay, implying that the sound attack moves fast from left to right, whereas the sound decay moves slowly from right to left. This adaptive control then provides a spatial spreading effect.

Adaptive spectral panning

Panning in the spectral domain allows for intensity panning by modifying the left and right spectrum magnitudes as well as for time delays by modifying the left and right spectrum phases. Using the phase vocoder, we only use intensity panning in order to avoid the Doppler effect, thus requiring slow motions of sound. To each frequency bin of the input STFT $X(m, k)$ we attribute a position given by the panning angle $\theta(m, k)$ derived from sound features. The resulting gains for left and right channels are then

$$L_l(m, k) = \frac{\sqrt{2}}{2} (\cos \theta(m, k) + \sin \theta(m, k)) \tag{9.86}$$

$$L_r(m, k) = \frac{\sqrt{2}}{2} (\cos \theta(m, k) - \sin \theta(m, k)). \tag{9.87}$$

In this way, each frequency bin of the input STFT is panned separately from its neighbors (see Figure 9.38): the original spectrum is then split across the space between two loudspeakers. To avoid a phasiness effect due to the lack of continuity of the control curve between neighboring frequency bins, a smooth control curve is needed, such as the spectral envelope. In order to control the variation speed of the spectral panning, $\theta(m, k)$ is computed from a time-interpolated value of a control vector (see the adaptive equalizer, Section 9.4.4). This effect adds envelopment to the sound when the panning curve is smoothed. Otherwise, the signal is split into virtual sources having more or less independent motions and speeds. In the case the panning vector $\theta(m, \bullet)$ is derived from the magnitude spectrum with a multi-pitch tracking technique, it allows for source separation. When derived from the voiciness $v(m)$ as $\theta(m, k) = \frac{\pi v(m) \cdot (2k - N - 1)}{4(N-1)}$, the sound localization varies between a point during attacks and a wide spatial spread during steady state, simulating width variations of the sound source.

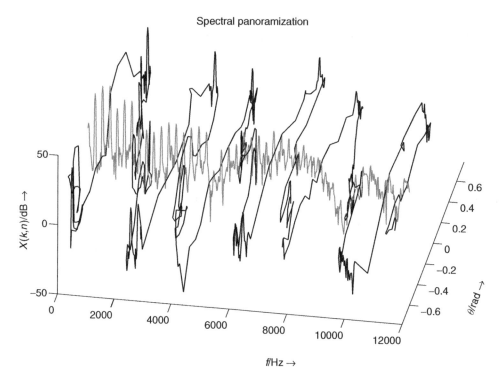

Figure 9.38   Frequency-space domain for the adaptive spectral panning (in black). Each frequency bin of the original STFT $X(m, k)$ (centered with $\theta = 0$, in gray) is panned with constant power. The azimuth angles are derived from sound features as $\theta(m, k) = x(mR_A - N/2 + k) \cdot \pi/4$. Figure reprinted with IEEE permission from [VZA06].

Spatialization

Both adaptive panning and adaptive spectral panning can be extended to 3-D sound projection, using techniques such as VBAP techniques, and so on. For instance, the user defines a trajectory (for example an ellipse), onto which the sound moves, with adaptive control on the position, the speed, or the acceleration. Concerning the position control, the azimuth can depend on the chroma $a(n) = \frac{\pi \log_2 F_0(n)}{6}$, splitting the sounds into a spatial chromatic scale. The speed control adaptively depending on voiciness as $\dot{x}(n) = (1 - v(n))$ allows for the sound to move only during attacks and silences; conversely, an adaptive control of speed given as $\dot{x}(n) = v(n)$ allows for the sound to move only during steady states, and not during attacks and silences.

9.4.6   Multi-dimensional adaptive effects

Various adaptive effects affect several perceptual attributes simultaneously: adaptive resampling modifies time, pitch and timbre; adaptive ring modulation modifies only harmonicity when combined to formant preservation, and harmonicity and timbre when combined with formants modifications [VD04]; gender change combines pitch-shifting and adaptive formant-shifting [ABLS01, ABLS02] to transform a female voice into a male voice, and vice versa. We now present two other multi-dimensional adaptive effects: adaptive robotization, which modifies pitch and timbre, and adaptive granular delay, which modifies spatial perception and timbre.

Adaptive robotization

Adaptive robotization changes expressiveness on two perceptual attributes, namely intonation (pitch) and roughness (timbre), and allows the transformation a human voice into an expressive robot voice [VA01]. This consists of zeroing the phase $\varphi(m, k)$ of the grain STFT $X(m, k)$ at a time index given by sound features: $Y(m, k) = |X(m, k)|$, and zeroing the signal between two blocks [VA01, AKZ02b]. The synthesis time index $t_S(m) = t_A(m)$ is recursively given as

$$t_S(m) = t_S(m - 1) + R_S(m). \tag{9.88}$$

The step increment $R_S(m) = \frac{F_A}{F_0(m)}$ is also the period of the robot voice, i.e., the inverse of the robot fundamental frequency to which sound features are mapped (e.g., the spectral centroid as $F_0(m) = 0.01 \cdot cgs(m)$, in Figure 9.39). Its real-time implementation implies the careful use of a circular buffer, in order to allow for varying window and step increments. Both the harmonic and the noisy part of the sound are processed, and formants are locally preserved for each block. However, the energy of the signal is not preserved, due to the zero-phasing, the varying step increment, and the zeroing process between two blocks, resulting in a pitch and modifying the

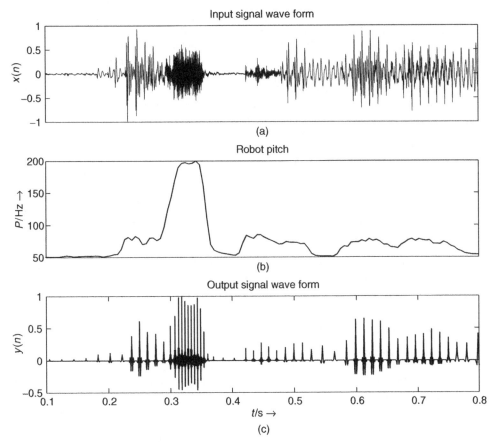

Figure 9.39 Robotization with a 512 samples block. (a) Input signal wave form. (b) $F_0 \in$ [50, 200] Hz derived from the spectral centroid as $F_0(m) = 0.01 \cdot cgs(m)$. (c) A-robotized signal wave form before amplitude correction. Figure reprinted with IEEE permission from [VZA06].

loudness of noisy content. An annoying buzz sound is then perceived, and can be easily removed by reducing the loudness modification. After zeroing the phases, the synthesis grain is multiplied by the ratio of analysis to synthesis intensity level computed on the current block m given by

$$y_{norm}(n) = y(n) \cdot \frac{a_x(m)}{a_y(m)}, n \in [m - N/2, m + N/2]. \tag{9.89}$$

A second adaptive control is given by the block size $N(m)$ and allows for changing the robot roughness: the lower the block length, the higher the roughness. At the same time, it allows preservation of the original pitch (e.g., $N \geq 1024$) or removal (e.g., $N \leq 256$), with an ambiguity in between. This is due to the fact that zero phasing a small block creates a main peak in the middle of the block and implies amplitude modulation (and then roughness). Inversely, zero phasing a large block creates several additional peaks in the window, the periodicity of the equally spaced secondary peaks being responsible for the original pitch.

Adaptive granular delay

This effect consists of applying delays to sound grains, with constant grain size N and step increment R_A [VA01], and varying delay gain $g(m)$ and/or delay time $\tau(m)$ derived from sound features (see Figure 9.40). In non-real-time applications, any delay time is possible, even fractional delay times [LVKL96], since each grain repetition is overlapped and added into a buffer. However, real-time implementations require limiting the number of delay lines, and so forth, to quantize delay time and delay gain control curves to a limited number of values. In our experience, 10 values for the delay gain and 30 for the delay time is a good minimum configuration, yielding 300 delay lines.

In the case where only $g(m)$ varies, the effect is a combination between delay and timbre morphing (spatial perception and timbre). For example, when applying this effect to a plucked string sound and controlling the gain with a voiciness feature as $g(m) = 0.5 \cdot (1 + \cos(-\pi v(m)))$, the attacks are repeated a much longer time than the sustain part. With the complementary mapping $g(m) = 0.5 \cdot (1 + \cos(\pi(1 - v(m))))$, the attacks rapidly disappear from the delayed version, whereas the sustain part is still repeated.

In the case where only $\tau(m)$ varies, the effect is a kind of granular synthesis with adaptive control, where grains collapse in time, thus implying modifications of time, timbre, and loudness. With a delay time derived from voiciness $\tau(m) = v(m)$ (in seconds), attack and sustain parts of a plucked string sound have different delay times, so sustain parts may be repeated before the attack with repetitions going on, as depicted Figure 9.40: not only are time and timbre are modified, but also loudness, since the grain superposition is uneven.

Adaptive granular delay is a perfect example of how the creative modification of an effect with adaptive control offers new sound transformation possibilities. It also shows how the frontiers between the perceptual attributes modified by the effect may be blurred.

9.4.7 Concatenative synthesis

The concept of concatenative synthesis is already in use for speech synthesis. An overview of this technique for audio processing can be found in [Sch07]. From an audio effects point of view it is an adaptive audio effect, which is controlled by low-level and high-level features extracted from the incoming audio signal and then uses sound snippets from a database to resynthesize a similar input audio. Figure 9.41 shows the functional units of such a signal-processing scheme. Sound features are derived from a block-by-block analysis scheme, which are then used for the selection of sound units from a sound database which possess similar sound features. These selected sound units are then used in a concatenative synthesis to reconstruct an audio signal. The concatenative synthesis can be performed by all time- and frequency-domain techniques discussed inside the DAFx book.

Input sound

1st delay line

2nd delay line

3rd delay line

4th delay line

Sum of delay lines

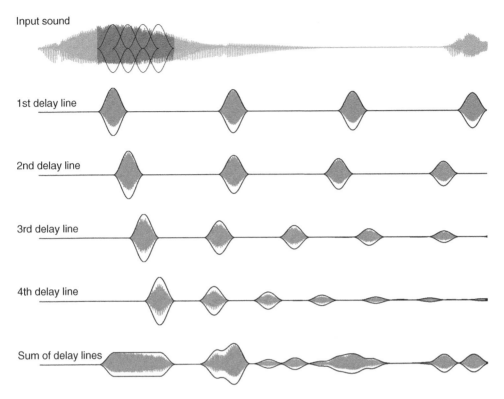

Figure 9.40 Illustration of the adaptive granular delay: each grain is delayed, with feedback gain $g(m) = a(m)$ and delay time $\tau(m) = 0.1 \cdot a(m)$ both derived from intensity level. Since the intensity level of the four first grains is going down, the gains $(g(m))^n$ and delay times $n\tau(m)$ of the repetitions are also going down with n, resulting in a granular time-collapsing effect. Figure reprinted with IEEE permission from [VZA06].

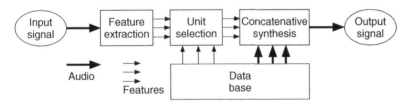

Figure 9.41 Concatenative synthesis using feature extraction, unit selection and concatenation based on a sound database.

The following M-file 9.15 shows the main processing steps for a concatenative singing resynthesis used in [FF10]. The script only presents the minimum number of features for singing resynthesis. It extracts energy, pitch, and LPC frequency response (no pitch smoothing or complex phonetic information) and searches for the best audio frame with a similar pitch. It uses the chosen frame, changes its gain to get a similar energy, and adds it to the output (no phase alignment or pitch changing). Further improvements and refinements are introduced in [FF10].

M-file 9.15 (SampleBasedResynthesis.m)

```
function out=SampleBasedResynthesis(audio)
% out = SampleBasedResynthesis(audio)
% Author: Nuno Fonseca (nuno.fonseca@ipleiria.pt)
%
% Resynthesizes the input audio, but using frames from an internal
% sound library.
%
% input:      audio signal
%
% output:     resynthesized audio signal

    %%%%%%%%%%%%%%%%%%%%%%%%%%%%%%%%%%%%%%%
    % Variables
    sr=44100;              % sample rate
    wsize=1024;            % window size
    hop=512;               % hop size
    window=hann(wsize);    % main window function
    nFrames=GetNumberOfFrames(audio,wsize,hop); % number of frames

    %%%%%%%%%%%%%%%%%%%%%%%%%%%%%%%%%%%%%%%%
    % Feature extraction (Energy, Pitch, Phonetic)
    disp('Feature extraction');
    % Get Features from input audio
    % Get Energy
    disp('- Energy (input)');
    energy=zeros(1,nFrames);
    for frame=1:nFrames
        energy(frame)=sumsqr(GetFrame(audio,frame,wsize,hop).*window);
    end
    % Get Pitch
    disp('- Pitch (input)');
    pitch=yinDAFX(audio,sr,160,hop);
    nFrames=min(nFrames,length(pitch));
    % Get LPC Freq Response
    disp('- Phonetic info (input)');
    LpcFreqRes=zeros(128,nFrames);
    window2=hann(wsize/4);
    audio2=resample(audio,sr/4,sr);
    for frame=1:nFrames
        temp=lpc(GetFrame(audio2,frame,wsize/4,hop/4).*window2,12);
        temp(find(isnan(temp)))=0;
        LpcFreqRes(:,frame)=20*log10(eps+abs(freqz(1,temp,128)));
    end

    % Load lib and extract information
    disp('- Loading sound library');
    lib=wavread('InternalLib.wav');
    disp('- Pitch (lib)');
    pitchLib=yinDAFX(lib,sr,160,hop);
    notesLib=round(note(pitchLib));
    disp('- Phonetic info (lib)');
    libLpcFreqRes=zeros(128,GetNumberOfFrames(lib,wsize,hop));
    audio2=resample(lib,sr/4,sr);
    for frame=1:GetNumberOfFrames(lib,wsize,hop)
        temp=lpc(GetFrame(audio2,frame,wsize/4,hop/4).*window2,12);
        temp(find(isnan(temp)))=0;
```

```
            libLpcFreqRes(:,frame)=20*log10(eps+abs(freqz(1,temp,128))));
    end
    %%%%%%%%%%%%%%%%%%%%%%%%%%%%%%%%%%%%%%%%%%%%%%%%%%%%%%%%%%%%
    % Unit Selection
    disp('Unit Selection');
    chosenFrames=zeros(1,nFrames);
    for frame=1:nFrames
        % From all frames with the same musical note
        % the system chooses the more similar one
        temp=LpcFreqRes(:,frame);
        n=round(note(pitch(frame)));
        indexes=find(notesLib==n);
        if(length(indexes)==0)
            n=round(note(0));
            indexes=find(notesLib==n);
        end
        [distance,index]=min(dist(temp',libLpcFreqRes(:,indexes)));
        chosenFrames(frame)=indexes(index);
    end
    %%%%%%%%%%%%%%%%%%%%%%%%%%%%%%%%%%%%%%%%%%%%%%%%%%%%%%%%%%%%
    % Synthesis
    disp('Synthesis');
    out=zeros(length(audio),1);
    for frame=1:nFrames
        % Gets the frame from the sound lib., change its gain to have a
        % similar energy, and adds it to the output buffer.
        buffer=lib((chosenFrames(frame)-1)*hop+1:(chosenFrames(frame)-1)...
            *hop+wsize).*window;
        gain=sqrt(energy(frame)/sumsqr(buffer));
        out((frame-1)*hop+1:(frame-1)*hop+wsize)=out((frame-1)...
            *hop+1:(frame-1)*hop+wsize)+ buffer*gain;
    end
end

%%%%%%%%%%%%%%%%%%%%%%%%%%%%%%%%%%%%%%%%%%%%%%%%%%%%%%%%%%%%%%%%%%%%%%%%%%%%
%% Auxiliary functions

% Get number of frames
function out=GetNumberOfFrames(data,size,hop)
    out=max(0,1+floor((length(data)-size)/hop));
end

% Get Frame, starting at frame 1
function out=GetFrame(data,index,size,hop)
    if(index<=GetNumberOfFrames(data,size,hop))
        out=data((index-1)*hop+1:(index-1)*hop+size);
    else
        out=[];
    end
end

% Convert frequency to note (MIDI value)
function out=note(freq)
    out=12*log(abs(freq)/440)/log(2)+69;
end
```

9.5   Conclusions

From existing simple effects such as the compressor and auto-tune, we presented a general framework for adaptive DAFX using sound features as control parameters. Such adaptive control can rely on any type of sound features that are extracted from various representations of sound: samples, STFT, spectrum, source and filter. Indeed, previously described techniques such as the phase vocoder, source-filter models, and spectral models do allow for both the representation of the sound and for the extraction of further global features such as pitch or fundamental frequency, which can be estimated by the cepstrum method or auto-correlation techniques applied to the input directly or the extracted source signal. Further global features such as amplitude envelope, spectral centroid, and auto-correlation features (voiced/unvoiced detection) have been introduced, which can be estimated by simple time-domain or by advanced time-frequency techniques.

References

[ABL+03]   X. Amatriain, J. Bonada, A. Loscos, J. L. Arcos, and V. Verfaille. Content-based Transformations. *J. New Music Res.*, 32(1): 95–114, 2003.

[ABLS01]   X. Amatriain, J. Bonada, A. Loscos, and X. Serra. Spectral modeling for higher-level sound transformations. In *MOSART Workshop Curr. Res. Dir. Comp. Music, IUA-UPF*, 2001.

[ABLS02]   X. Amatriain, J. Bonada, A. Loscos, and X. Serra. Spectral processing. In U. Zölzer (ed.), *DAFX - Digital Audio Effects*, pp. 373–438. J. Wiley & Sons, Ltd, 2002.

[ACKV02]   D. Arfib, J.-M. Couturier, L. Kessous, and V. Verfaille. Strategies of mapping between gesture parameters and synthesis model parameters using perceptual spaces. *Org. Sound*, 7(2): 135–52, 2002.

[AD98]   D. Arfib and N. Delprat. Selective transformations of sound using time-frequency representations: An application to the vibrato modification. In *104th Conv. Audio Eng. Soc.*, 1998.

[AKZ99]   R. Althoff, F. Keiler, and U. Zölzer. Extracting sinusoids from harmonic signals. In *Proc. DAFX-99 Digital Audio Effects Workshop*, pp. 97–100, 1999.

[AKZ02a]   D. Arfib, F. Keiler, and U. Zölzer. Source-filter processing. In U. Zölzer (ed.), *DAFX - Digital Audio Effects*, pp. 299–372. J. Wiley & Sons, Ltd, 2002.

[AKZ02b]   D. Arfib, F. Keiler, and U. Zölzer. Time-frequency processing. In U. Zölzer (ed.), *DAFX - Digital Audio Effects*, pp. 237–97. J. Wiley & Sons, Ltd, 2002.

[Arf79]   D. Arfib. Digital synthesis of complex spectra by means of multiplication of non linear distorted sine waves. *J. Audio Eng. Soc.*, 27: 757–768, 1979.

[Arf98]   D. Arfib. Des Courbes et des Sons. In *Recherches et Applications en Informatique Musicale*, pp. 277–86. Hermès, 1998.

[AV03]   D. Arfib and V. Verfaille. Driving pitch-shifting and time-scaling algorithms with adaptive and gestural techniques. In *Proc. Int. Conf. on Digital Audio Effects (DAFx-03)*, pp. 106–11, 2003.

[Bea82]   J. W. Beauchamp. Synthesis by spectral amplitude and "brightness" matching of analyzed musical instrument tones. *J. Audio Eng. Soc.*, 30(6): 396–406, 1982.

[BFC05]   D. Barry, D. FitzGerald, and E. Coyle. Drum source separation using percussive feature detection and spectral modulation. In *Proc. IEE Irish Signals Syst. Conf.*, pp. 217–220, 2005.

[Bla83]   J. Blauert. *Spatial Hearing: the Psychophysics of Human Sound Localization*. MIT Press, 1983.

[Bon00]   J. Bonada. Automatic technique in frequency domain for near-lossless time-scale modification of audio. In *Proc. Int. Comp. Music Conf. (ICMC'00)*, 2000.

[BP89]   J. C. Brown and M S. Puckette. Calculation of a narrowed autocorrelation function. *J. Ac. Soc. Am.*, 85: 1595–601, 1989.

[Bre90]   A. Bregman. *Auditory Scene Analysis*. MIT Press, 1990.

[Bru79]   M. Le Brun. Digital waveshaping synthesis. *J. Audio Eng. Soc.*, 27(4): 250–265, April 1979.

[Cab99]   D. Cabrera. PsySound: a computer program for psychoacoustical analysis. In *Proc. Australian Ac. Soc. Conf.*, pp. 47–53, 1999.

[Cab00]   D. Cabrera. PsySound 2: Psychoacoustical software for Macintosh PPC. Technical report, 2000.

[Cad99]   C. Cadoz. Musique, geste, technologie. In H. Genevois and R. de Vivo, (eds), *Les Nouveaux Gestes de la Musique*, pp. 47–92. Parenthèses, 1999.

[Can98]   P. Cano. Fundamental frequency estimation in the SMS analysis. In *Proc. DAFX-98 Digital Audio Effects Workshop*, pp. 99–102, 1998.

[Cho71]   J. Chowning. The synthesis of complex audio spectra by means of frequency modulation. *J. Audio Eng. Soc.*, 21: 526–34, 1971.

[CLB⁺00]   P. Cano, A. Loscos, J. Bonada, M. de Boer, and X. Serra. Voice morphing system for impersonating in karaoke applications. In *Proc. Int. Comp. Music Conf. (ICMC'00)*, pp. 109–12, 2000.

[Cri82]   A. Di Cristo. *Prolégomènes à L'étude de L'intonation*. Editions du CNRS, 1982.

[dCK02]   A. de Cheveigné and H. Kawahara. Yin, a fundamental frequency estimator for speech and music. *J. Acoust. Soc. Am.*, 111(4): 1917–1930, 2002.

[DGR95]   P. Depalle, G. Garcia, and X. Rodet. Reconstruction of a castrato voice: Farinelli's voice. In *Proc. IEEE Workshop Appl. Digital Signal Proces. Audio Acoust.*, 1995.

[DH00]   M. Desainte-Catherine and P. Hanna. Statistical approach for sounds modeling. In *Proc. DAFX-00 Conf. Digital Audio Effects*, pp. 91–96, 2000.

[DM00]   M. Desainte-Catherine and S. Marchand. High-precision Fourier analysis of sounds using signal derivatives. *J. Audio Eng. Soc.*, 48(7/8): 654–667, 2000.

[DT96a]   S. Dubnov and N. Tishby. Testing for gaussianity and non linearity in the sustained portion of musical sounds. In *Proc. Journées Informatique Musicale (JIM'96)*, 1996.

[DT96b]   S. Dubnov and N. Tishby. Testing for gaussianity and non-linearity in the sustained portion of musical sounds. In *Proc. Journées Informatique Musicale*, 1996.

[DZ02]   P. Dutilleux and U. Zölzer. Nonlinear processing. In U. Zölzer (ed), *DAFX - Digital Audio Effects*, pp. 93–135. J. Wiley & Sons, Ltd, 2002.

[Fav01]   E. Favreau. Phase vocoder applications in GRM tools environment. In *Proc. COST-G6 Workshop on Digital Audio Effects (DAFx-01)*, pp. 134–7, 2001.

[FF10]   N. Fonseca and A. Ferreira. Singing voice resynthesis using vocal sound libraries. In *Proc. of the 13th Int. Conf. on Digital Audio Effects (DAFx-10)*, pp. 322–325, 2010.

[Fit04]   D. FitzGerald. *Automatic drum transcription and source separation*. PhD thesis, Dublin Institute of Technology, 2004.

[Fit10]   D. FitzGerald. Harmonic/percussive separation using median filtering. In *Proc. of the 13th Int. Conf. on Digital Audio Effects (DAFx-10)*, pp. 217–220, Graz, Austria, 2010.

[GFB03]   F. Gouyon, L. Fabig, and J. Bonada. Rhythmic expressiveness transformations of audio recordings: swing modifications. In *Proc. Int. Conf. on Digital Audio Effects (DAFx-03)*, pp. 94–99, 2003.

[GPAH03]   E. Gómez, G. Peterschmitt, X. Amatriain, and P. Herrera. Content-based melodic transformations of audio material for a music processing application. In *Proc. Int. Conf. on Digital Audio Effects (DAFx-03)*, 2003.

[HB98]   P. Herrera and J. Bonada. Vibrato extraction and parameterization in the spectral modeling synthesis framework. In *Proc. DAFX-98 Digital Audio Effects Workshop*, pp. 107–110, 1998.

[Hes83]   W. Hess. *Pitch Determination of Speech Signals*. Springer-Verlag, 1983.

[INA03]   INA-GRM. GRM Tools, 2003.

[JN84]   N. S. Jayant and P. Noll. *Digital Coding of Waveforms*. Prentice-Hall, 1984.

[KA90]   P. Kroon and B. S. Atal. Pitch predictors with high temporal resolution. In *Proc. ICASSP*, pp. 661–664, 1990.

[KZ10]   A. von dem Knesebeck and U. Zölzer. Comparison of pitch trackers for real-time guitar effects. In *Proc. 13th Int. Conf. on Digital Audio Effects (DAFx-10)*, pp. 266–269, 2010.

[LVKL96]   T. I. Laakso, V. Välimäki, M. Karjalainen, and U. K. Laine. Splitting the unit delay. *IEEE Signal Proces. Mag.*, 13: 30–60, 1996.

[Mar72]   J. D. Markel. The SIFT algorithm for fundamental frequency estimation. *IEEE Trans. Audio Electroacoust.*, 20(5): 367–377, 1972.

[Mar98]   S. Marchand. Improving spectral analysis precision with enhanced phase vocoder using signal derivatives. In *Proc. DAFX-98 Digital Audio Effects Workshop*, pp. 114–118, 1998.

[Mar00]   S. Marchand. *Sound models for computer music*. PhD thesis, University of Bordeaux, 2000.

[MB96]   P. Masri and A. Bateman. Improved modelling of attack transients in music analysis-resynthesis. In *Proc. Int. Comp. Music Conf. (ICMC'96)*, pp. 100–3, 1996.

[MG96]   B. C. J. Moore and B. R. Glasberg. A revision of Zwicker's loudness model. *Acta Acust. United AC*, 82: 3335–45, 1996.

[MGB97]   B. C. J. Moore, B. R. Glasberg, and T. Baer. A model for the prediction of thresholds, loudness, and partial loudness. *J. Audio Eng. Soc.*, 45(4): 224–40, 1997.

[Moo65]   R. Moog. A voltage-controlled low-pass, high-pass filter for audio signal processing. In *17th Annual AES Meeting*, Preprint 413, 1965.

[MQ86]   R. J. McAulay and T. F. Quatieri. Speech analysis/synthesis based on a sinusoidal representation. *IEEE Trans. Acoust. Speech, Signal Proces.*, 34(4): 744–54, 1986.

[MR04]   S. Marchand and M. Raspaud. Enhanced time-stretching using order-2 sinusoidal modeling. In *Proc. Int. Conf. Digital Audio Effects (DAFx-04)*, pp. 76–82, 2004.

[MWdSK95]   S. McAdams, S. Winsberg, G. de Soete, and J. Krimphoff. Perceptual scaling of synthesized musical timbres: common dimensions, specificities, and latent subject classes. *Psychol. Res.*, 58: 177–92, 1995.

[Nol64]   A. M. Noll. Short-time spectrum and "cepstrum" techniques for vocal-pitch detection. *J. Acoust. Soc. Am.*, 36(2): 296–302, 1964.

[NZ08]   F. X. Nsabimana and U. Zölzer. Audio signal decomposition for pitch and time scaling. In *3rd Int. Symp. Commun. Control Signal Proces.*, pp. 1285–1290, 2008.

[OS75]   A. V. Oppenheim and R. W. Schafer. *Digital Signal Processing*. Prentice-Hall, 1975.

[O'S00]   D. O'Shaugnessy. *Speech Communication*, 2nd edition. Addison-Wesley, 2000.

[Pal03]   G. Pallone. *Dilatation et transposition sous contraintes perceptives des signaux audio: application au transfert cinéma-vidéo*. PhD thesis, University of Aix-Marseille III, 2003.

[PJ82]   H. Pollard and E. Jansson. A tristimulus method for the specification of musical timbre. *Acta Acust. United AC*, 51: 162–71, 1982.

[PMH00]   G. Peeters, S. McAdams, and P. Herrera. Instrument sound description in the context of MPEG-7. In *Proc. Int. Comp. Music Conf. (ICMC'00)*, 2000.

[RDS+99]   S. Rossignol, P. Depalle, J. Soumagne, X. Rodet, and J.-L. Colette. Vibrato: detection, estimation, extraction, modification. In *Proc. DAFX-99 Digital Audio Effects Workshop*, pp. 175–179, 1999.

[Ris65]   J.-C. Risset. Computer study of trumpet tones. *J. Ac. Soc. Am.*, 33: 912, 1965.

[Ros98]   S. Rossignol. Feature extraction and temporal segmentation of acoustic signals. In *Proc. Int. Comp. Music Conf.*, 1998.

[RS78]   L. R. Rabiner and R. W. Schafer. *Digital Processing of Speech Signals*. Prentice-Hall, 1978.

[RSC+74]   M. Ross, H. Shaffer, A. Cohen, R. Freudberg, and H. Manley. Average magnitude difference function pitch extractor. *IEEE Trans. Acoust. Speech Signal Proces.*, 22(5): 353–362, 1974.

[Sch66]   P. Schaeffer. *Traité des Objets Musicaux*. Seuil, 1966.

[Sch68]   M. R. Schroeder. Period histogram and product spectrum: New methods for fundamental-frequency measurement. *J. Acoust. Soc. Am.*, 43(4): 829–834, 1968.

[Sch99]   M. R. Schroeder. *Computer Speech*. Springer-Verlag, 1999.

[Sch07]   D. Schwarz. Corpus-Based Concatenative Synthesis. *IEEE Signal Proces. Mag.*, 24(2): 92–104, 2007.

[Son68]   M. M. Sondhi. New methods of pitch extraction. *IEEE Trans. on Audio Electroacoust.*, 16(2): 262–266, 1968.

[Sun87]   J. Sundberg. *The Science of the Singing Voice*. Northern Illinois University Press, 1987.

[SZST10]   A. Spich, M. Zanoni, A. Sarti, and S. Tubaro. Drum music transcription using prior subspace analysis and pattern recognition. In *Proc. 13th Int. Conf. Digital Audio Effects (DAFx-10)*, pp. 233–237, 2010.

[UH03]   C. Uhle and J. Herre. Estimation of tempo, micro time and time signature from percussive music. In *Proc. 6th Int. Conf. Digital Audio Effects (DAFx-03)*, pp. 84–89, 2003.

[vA85]   W. von Aures. Der sensorische wohlklang als funktion psychoakustischer empfindungsgröfsen. *Acustica*, 58: 282–90, 1985.

[VA01]   V. Verfaille and D. Arfib. ADAFx: Adaptive digital audio effects. In *Proc. COST-G6 Workshop on Digital Audio Effects (DAFx-01)*, pp. 10–4, 2001.

[VA02]   V. Verfaille and D. Arfib. Implementation strategies for adaptive digital audio effects. In *Proc. Int. Conf. Digital Audio Effects (DAFx-02)*, pp. 21–6, 2002.

[VD04]   V. Verfaille and Ph. Depalle. Adaptive effects based on STFT, using a source-filter model. In *Proc. Int. Conf. Digital Audio Effects (DAFx-04)*, pp. 296–301, 2004.

[VM90]   E. Vidal and A. Marzal. A review and new approaches for automatic segmentation of speech signals. In L. Torres, E. Masgrau, and M. A. Lagunas (eds), *Signal Processing V: Theories and Applications*, pp. 43–53. Elsevier Science Publishers, 1990.

[VWD06]   V. Verfaille, M. M. Wanderley, and Ph. Depalle. Mapping Strategies for Gestural Control of Adaptive Digital Audio Effects. *J. New Music Res.*, 35(1): 71–93, 2006.

[VZA06]   V. Verfaille, U. Zölzer, and D. Arfib. Adaptive digital audio effects (A-DAFx): A new class of sound transformations. *IEEE Trans. Audio Speech Lang. Proc.*, 14(5): 1817–1831, 2006.

[Wan02]   M. M. Wanderley. Mapping strategies in real-time computer music. *Org. Sound*, 7(2), 2002.

[WD00]   M. M. Wanderley and P. Depalle. Gesturally controlled digital audio effects. In *Proc. COST-G6 Workshop Digital Audio Effects (DAFx-00)*, pp. 165–9, 2000.

[ZF99]   E. Zwicker and H. Fastl. *Psychoacoustics: Facts and Models*. Springer-Verlag, Berlin, 1999.

[ZS65]   E. Zwicker and B. Scharf. A model of loudness summation. *Psychol. Rev.*, 72: 3–26, 1965.

[Zwi77]   E. Zwicker. Procedure for calculating loudness of temporally variable sounds. *J. Ac. Soc. Am.*, 62(3): 675–82, 1977.

10

Spectral processing

J. Bonada, X. Serra, X. Amatriain and A. Loscos

10.1 Introduction

In the context of this book, we are looking for representations of sound signals and signal-processing systems that can give us ways to design sound transformations for a variety of musical applications and contexts. It should have been clear throughout the book that several points of view have to be considered, including a mathematical, and thus objective, perspective, and a perceptual, and thus mainly subjective, standpoint. Both points of view are necessary to fully understand the concept of sound effects and to be able to use the described techniques in practical situations.

The mathematical and signal-processing points of view are straightforward to present, which does not mean easy, since the language of the equations and of flow diagrams is suitable for them. However, the top-down implications are much harder to express due to the huge number of variables involved and to the inherent perceptual subjectivity of the music-making process. This is clearly one of the main challenges of the book and the main reason for its existence.

The use of a spectral representation of a sound yields a perspective that is sometimes closer to the one used in a sound-engineering approach. By understanding the basic concepts of frequency-domain analysis, we are able to acquire the tools to use a large number of effects processors and to understand many types of sound-transformation systems. Moreover, as frequency-domain analysis is a somewhat similar process to the one performed by the human hearing system, it yields fairly intuitive intermediate representations.

The basic idea of spectral processing is that we can analyze a sound to obtain alternative frequency-domain representations, which can then be transformed and inverted to produce new sounds (see Figure 10.1). Most of the approaches start by developing an analysis/synthesis system from which the input sound is reconstructed without any perceptual loss of sound quality. The techniques described in Chapter 7 are clear examples of this approach. Then the main issues are what is the intermediate representation and what parameters are available for applying the desired transformations.

Perceptual or musical concepts such as timbre or pitch are clearly related to the spectral characteristics of a sound. Even some common processes for sound effects are better explained

---

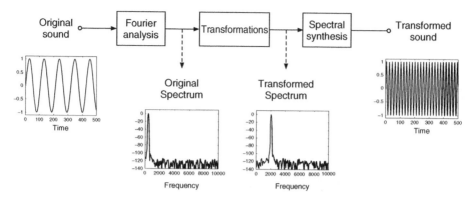

Figure 10.1 Block diagram of a simple spectral-processing framework.

using a frequency-domain representation. We usually think on the frequency axis when we talk about equalizing, filtering, pitch shifting, harmonizing... In fact, some of them are specific to this signal-processing approach and do not have an immediate counterpart on the time domain. On the other hand, most (but not all) of the sound effects presented in this book can be implemented in the frequency domain.

Another issue is whether or not this approach is the most efficient, or practical, for a given application. The process of transforming a time-domain signal into a frequency-domain representation is, by itself, not an immediate step. Some parameters are difficult to adjust and force us to make several compromises. Some settings, such as the size of the analysis window, have little or nothing to do with the high-level approach we intend to favor, and require the user to have a basic signal-processing understanding.

In that sense, when we talk about higher-level spectral processing we are thinking of an intermediate analysis step in which relevant features are extracted, or computed, from the spectrum. These relevant features should be much closer to a musical or high-level approach. We can then process the features themselves, as shown in Figure 10.2, or even apply transformations that keep some of the features unchanged. For example, we can extract the fundamental frequency and the spectral shape from a sound and then modify the fundamental frequency without affecting the shape of the spectrum.

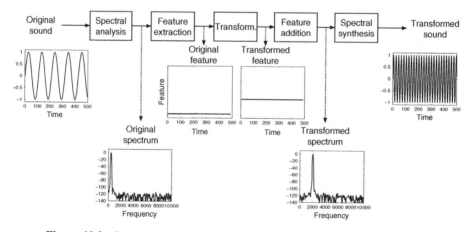

Figure 10.2 Block diagram of a higher-level spectral-processing framework.

Assuming the fact that there is no single representation and processing system optimal for everything, our approach will be to present a set of complementary spectral models that can be combined to cover the largest possible set of sounds and musical applications.

Having set the basis of the various spectral models, we will then give the details of the implementation techniques used both for their analysis and synthesis processes, providing MATLAB® code to implement a complete analysis-synthesis framework.

In the final section we will present a set of basic audio effects and their implementation based on the analysis-synthesis framework just introduced. **MATLAB** code is provided for all of them.

10.2   Spectral models

The most common approach for converting a time-domain signal into its frequency-domain representation is the short-time fourier transform (STFT), which can be expressed by the following equation

$$X_l(k) = \sum_{n=0}^{N-1} w(n)x(n+lH) e^{-j\omega_k n}, \tag{10.1}$$

where $X_l(k)$ is the complex spectrum of a given time frame, $x(n)$ is the input sound, $e^{-j\omega_k n}$ is a complex sinusoid with frequency ω_k expressed in radians, $w(n)$ is the analysis window, l is the frame number, k is the frequency index, n is the time index, H is the time index hop size, and N is the FFT size.

The STFT results in a general technique from which we can implement loss less analysis/synthesis systems. Many sound-transformation systems are based on direct implementations of the basic algorithm, and several examples have already been presented in previous chapters.

In this chapter, we extend the STFT framework by presenting higher-level modeling of the spectral data obtained with it. There are many spectral models based on the STFT that have been developed for sound and music signals and that fulfill different compromises and applications. The decision as to which one to use in a particular situation is not an easy one. The boundaries are not clear and there are compromises to take into account, such as: (1) sound fidelity, (2) flexibility, (3) coding efficiency, and (4) computational requirements. Ideally, we want to maximize fidelity and flexibility while minimizing memory consumption and computational requirements. The best choice for maximum fidelity and minimum computation time is the direct implementation of the STFT that, anyhow, yields a rather inflexible representation and inefficient coding scheme.

Here we introduce two different spectral models: sinusoidal and sinusoidal plus residual. These models represent an abstraction level higher than the STFT and from them, but with different compromises, we can identify and extract higher-level information on a musical sound, such as: harmonics, fundamental frequency, spectral shape, vibrato, or note boundaries. These models bring the spectral representation closer to our perceptual understanding of a sound. The complexity of the analysis will depend on the sound to be analyzed and the transformation desired. The benefits of going to this higher level of analysis are enormous and open up a wide range of new musical applications.

10.2.1   Sinusoidal model

Using the STFT representation, the sinusoidal model is a step towards a more flexible representation while compromising both sound fidelity and computing time. It is based on modeling the time-varying spectral characteristics of a sound as sums of time-varying sinusoids. The sound $s(t)$ is modeled by

$$s(t) = \sum_{r=1}^{R} A_r(t) \cos[\theta_r(t)], \tag{10.2}$$

where $A_r(t)$ and $\theta_r(t)$ are the instantaneous amplitude and phase of the rth sinusoid, respectively, and R is the number of sinusoids [MQ86, SS87].

To obtain a sinusoidal representation from a sound, an analysis is performed in order to estimate the instantaneous amplitudes and phases of the sinusoids. This estimation is generally done by first computing the STFT of the sound, as described in Chapter 7, then detecting the spectral peaks (and measuring the magnitude, frequency and phase of each one), and finally organizing them as time-varying sinusoidal tracks. We can then reconstruct the original sound using additive synthesis.

The sinusoidal model yields a quite general analysis/synthesis technique that can be used in a wide range of sounds and offers a gain in flexibility compared with the direct STFT implementation.

10.2.2   Sinusoidal plus residual model

The sinusoidal plus residual model can cover a wide *compromise space* and can in fact be seen as the generalization of both the STFT and the sinusoidal models. Using this approach, we can decide what part of the spectral information is modeled as sinusoids and what is left as STFT. With a good analysis, the sinusoidal plus residual representation is very flexible, while maintaining a good sound fidelity, and the representation is quite efficient. In this approach, the sinusoidal representation is used to model only the stable partials of a sound. The residual, or its approximation, models what is left, which should ideally be a stochastic component. This model is less general than either the STFT or the sinusoidal representations, but it results in an enormous gain in flexibility [Ser89, SS90, Ser96]. One of its main drawbacks is that it is not suitable for transient signals, thus several extensions have been proposed to tackle these (e.g., [VM98, VM00]). The sound $s(t)$ is modeled in the continuous domain by

$$s(t) = \sum_{r=1}^{R} A_r(t) \cos[\theta_r(t)] + e(t), \tag{10.3}$$

where $A_r(t)$ and $\theta_r(t)$ are the instantaneous amplitude and phase of the rth sinusoid, R is the number of sinusoids and $e(t)$ is the residual component. The sinusoidal plus residual model assumes that the sinusoids are stable partials of the sound with a slowly changing amplitude and frequency. With this restriction, we are able to add major constraints to the detection of sinusoids in the spectrum and we might omit the detection of the phase of each peak. For many sounds the instantaneous phase that appears in the equation can be taken to be the integral of the instantaneous frequency $\omega_r(t)$, and therefore satisfies

$$\theta_r(t) = \int_0^t \omega_r(\tau) \, d\tau, \tag{10.4}$$

where $\omega_r(t)$ is the frequency in radians, and r is the sinusoid number. When the sinusoids are used to model only the stable partials of the sound, we refer to this part of the sound as the deterministic component.

Within this model we can either leave the residual signal $e(t)$ to be the difference between the original sound and the sinusoidal component, resulting in an identity system, or we can assume that $e(t)$ is a stochastic signal. In this case, the residual can be described as filtered white noise

$$e(t) = \int_0^t h(t, \tau) u(\tau) \, d\tau, \tag{10.5}$$

where $u(t)$ is white noise and $h(t, \tau)$ is the response of a time-varying filter to an impulse at time t. That is, the residual is modeled by the time-domain convolution of white noise with a time-varying frequency-shaping filter.

The identification of the sinusoids is done by adding restrictions to a standard sinusoidal analysis approach. Then the residual is obtained by subtracting the sinusoids from the original sound. The residual can also be considered a stochastic signal and thus represent it with a noise-filter model. We can then reconstruct the original sound using additive synthesis for the sinusoidal component and subtractive synthesis for the residual component.

The sinusoidal plus residual model yields a more general analysis/synthesis framework than the one obtained with a sinusoidal model and it has some clear advantages for specific applications and types of sounds. It has also led to other different spectral models that still share some of its basic principles [DQ97, FHC00, VM00].

10.3   Techniques

In this section we present and discuss a set of implementations of the different spectral models, building one implementation on top of another and making sure that each implementation is self-contained, thus being useful for some applications. Each implementation is an analysis/synthesis system that has as input a monophonic sound, $x(n)$, plus a set of parameters, and outputs a synthesized sound, $y(n)$. If the parameters are set correctly and the input sound used is adequate for the model, the output sound should be quite close, from a perceptual point of view, to the input sound. We start with an implementation of the STFT, which should yield a mathematical input-ouput identity for any sound. On top of that we build an analysis/synthesis system based on detecting the spectral peaks, and we extend it to implement a simple sinusoidal model. The following system implements a sinusoidal model with a harmonic constraint, thus only working for pseudo-harmonic sounds. We then include the residual analysis, thus implementing a harmonic plus residual model. Finally we assume that the residual is stochastic and implement a harmonic plus stochastic residual model.

10.3.1   Short-time fourier transform

Figure 10.3 shows the general block diagram of an analysis/sysnthesis system based on the STFT.

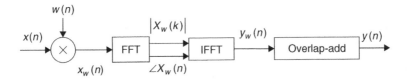

Figure 10.3   Block diagram of an analysis/synthesis system based on the STFT.

In order to use the STFT as a basis for the other spectral models we have to pay special attention to a number of issues related to the windowing process, specifically zero-phase windowing, the size and type of the analysis window, and the overlap-add process that is performed in the inverse transform process.

Below is the **MATLAB** code that implements a complete analysis/synthesis system based on the STFT.

M-file 10.1 (stft.m)

```
function y = stft(x, w, N, H)
% Authors: J. Bonada, X. Serra, X. Amatriain, A. Loscos
% Analysis/synthesis of a sound using the short-time Fourier transform
% x: input sound, w: analysis window (odd size), N: FFT size, H: hop size
```

```
% y: output sound
M = length(w);                            % analysis window size
N2 = N/2+1;                               % size of positive spectrum
soundlength = length(x);                  % length of input sound array
hM = (M-1)/2;                             % half analysis window size
pin = 1+hM;        % initialize sound pointer in middle of analysis window
pend = soundlength-hM;                    % last sample to start a frame
fftbuffer = zeros(N,1);                   % initialize buffer for FFT
yw = zeros(M,1);                          % initialize output sound frame
y = zeros(soundlength,1);                 % initialize output array
w = w/sum(w);                             % normalize analysis window
while pin<pend
    %-----analysis-----%
    xw = x(pin-hM:pin+hM).*w(1:M);        % window the input sound
    fftbuffer(:) = 0;                     % reset buffer
    fftbuffer(1:(M+1)/2) = xw((M+1)/2:M); % zero-phase window in fftbuffer
    fftbuffer(N-(M-1)/2+1:N) = xw(1:(M-1)/2);
    X = fft(fftbuffer);                   % compute FFT
    mX = 20*log10(abs(X(1:N2)));   % magnitude spectrum of positive frequencies
    pX = unwrap(angle(X(1:N2)));   % unwrapped phase spect. of positive freq.
    %-----synthesis-----%
    Y = zeros(N,1);                       % initialize output spectrum
    Y(1:N2) = 10.^(mX/20).*exp(i.*pX);    % generate positive freq.
    Y(N2+1:N) = 10.^(mX(N2-1:-1:2)/20).*exp(-i.*pX(N2-1:-1:2));
                                          % generate neg.freq.
    fftbuffer = real(ifft(Y));            % inverse FFT
    yw(1:(M-1)/2) = fftbuffer(N-(M-1)/2+1:N); % undo zero-phase window
    yw((M+1)/2:M) = fftbuffer(1:(M+1)/2);
    y(pin-hM:pin+hM) = y(pin-hM:pin+hM) + H*yw(1:M);   % overlap-add
    pin = pin+H;                          % advance sound pointer
end
```

In this code we step through the input sound x, performing the FFT and the inverse-FFT on each frame. This operation involves selecting a number of samples from the sound signal and multiplying their value by a windowing function. The number of samples taken in every processing step is defined by the window size. It is a crucial parameter, especially if we take into account that the number of spectral samples that the DFT will yield at its output, corresponds to half the number of samples plus one of its input spread over half of the original sampling rate. We will not go into the details of the DFT mathematics that lead to this property, but it is very important to note that the longer the window, the more frequency resolution we will have. On the other hand, it is almost immediate to see the drawback of taking very long windows: the loss of temporal resolution. This phenomenon is known as the time vs. frequency resolution trade-off (see Figure 10.4). A more specific limitation of the window size has to do with choosing windows with odd sample lengths in order to guarantee even symmetry about the origin.

The type of window used also has a very strong effect on the qualities of the spectral representation we will obtain. At this point we should remember that a time-domain multiplication (as the one done between the signal and the windowing function), becomes a frequency-domain convolution between the Fourier transforms of each of the signals (see Figure 10.5). One may be tempted to forget about deciding on these matters and apply no window at all, just taking M samples from the signal and feeding them to the chosen FFT algorithm. Even in that case, though, a rectangular window is being used, so the spectrum of the signal is being convolved with the transform of a rectangular pulse, a *sinc-like* function.

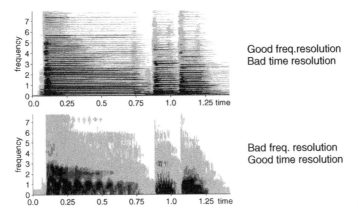

Figure 10.4   Time vs. frequency resolution trade-off.

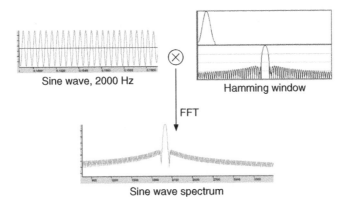

Figure 10.5   Effect of applying a window in the time domain.

Two features of the transform of the window are especially relevant to whether a particular function is useful or not: the width of the main lobe, and the main to highest side lobe relation. The main lobe bandwidth is expressed in bins (spectral samples) and, in conjunction with the window size, defines the ability to distinguish two sinusoidal peaks (see Figure 10.6). The following formula expresses the relation that the window size, M, the main lobe bandwidth, B_s, and the sampling rate, f_s, should meet in order to distinguish two sinusoids of frequencies f_k and f_{k+1}:

$$M \geq B_s \frac{f_s}{|f_{k+1} - f_k|}. \tag{10.6}$$

The amplitude relation between the main and the highest side lobe explains the amount of distortion a peak will receive from surrounding partials. It would be ideal to have a window with an extremely narrow main lobe and a very high main to secondary lobe relation. However, the inherent trade-off between these two parameters forces a compromise to be made.

Common windows that can be used in the analysis step are: rectangular, triangular, Kaiser-Bessel, Hamming, Hanning and Blackman-Harris. In the **MATLAB** code supplied, the user provides the analysis window, $w(n)$, to use as the input parameter.

One may think that a possible way of overcoming the time/frequency trade-off is to add zeros at the extremes of the windowed signals to increase the frequency resolution, that is, to have the

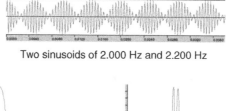

Two sinusoids of 2.000 Hz and 2.200 Hz

Spectrum with a small window   Spectrum with a larger window

Figure 10.6   Effect of the window size in distinguishing between two sinusoids.

FFT size N larger than the window size M. This process is known as zero-padding and it represents an interpolation in the frequency domain. When we zero-pad a signal before the DFT process, we are not adding any information to its frequency representation, given that we are not adding any new signal samples. We will still not distinguish the sinusoids if Equation (10.6) is not satisfied, but we are indeed increasing the frequency resolution by adding intermediate interpolated bins. With zero-padding we are able to use sizes of windows that are not powers of two (requirement for using many FFT algorithm implementations) and we also obtain smoother spectra, which helps in the peak detection process, as later explained.

A final step before computing the FFT of the input signal is the circular shift already described in previous chapters. This data centering on the origin guarantees the preservation of zero-phase conditions in the analysis process.

Once the spectrum of a frame has been computed, the window must move to the next position in the input signal in order to take the next set of samples. The distance between the centers of two consecutive windows is known as hop size, H. If the hop size is smaller than the window size, we will be including some overlap, that is, some samples will be used more than once in the analysis process. In general, the more overlap, the smoother the transitions of the spectrum will be across time, but that is a computationally expensive process. The window type and the hop must be chosen in such a way that the resulting envelope adds approximately to a constant, following the equation

$$A_w(m) = \sum_{n=-\infty}^{\infty} w(m - nH) \approx \text{constant.} \tag{10.7}$$

A measure of the deviation of A_w from a constant is the difference between the maximum and minimum values for the envelope as a percentage of the maximum value. This measure is referred to as the amplitude deviation of the overlap factor. Variables should be chosen so as to keep this factor around or below 1%

$$d_w = 100 \times \frac{\max_w [A_w(m)] - \min_w [A_w(m)]}{\max_w [A_w(m)]}. \tag{10.8}$$

After the analysis process we reverse every single step done until now, starting by computing the inverse FFT of every spectrum. If A_w is equal to a constant the output signal, $y(n)$, will be identical to the original signal, $x(n)$. Otherwise an amplitude deviation is manifested in the output sound, creating an audible distortion if the modulation is big enough.

A solution to the distortion created by the overlap-add process is to divide the output signal by the envelope A_w. If some window overlap exists, this operation surely removes any modulation coming from the window overlap process. However, this does not mean that we can apply any combination of parameters. Dividing by small numbers should be generally avoided, since noise coming from numerical errors can be greatly boosted and introduce undesired artifacts at synthesis. In addition, we have to be especially careful at beginning and end sections of the processed audio, since A_w will have values around zero. The following code implements a complete STFT analysis/synthesis system using this approach.

M-file 10.2 (stftenv.m)

```
function y = stftenv(x, w, N, H)
% Authors: J. Bonada, X. Serra, X. Amatriain, A. Loscos
% Analysis/synthesis of a sound using the short-time Fourier transform
% x: input sound, w: analysis window (odd size), N: FFT size, H: hop size
% y: output sound
M = length(w);                          % analysis window size
N2 = N/2+1;                             % size of positive spectrum
soundlength = length(x);               % length of input sound array
hM = (M-1)/2;                          % half analysis window size
pin = 1+hM;          % initialize sound pointer in middle of analysis window
pend = soundlength-hM;                 % last sample to start a frame
fftbuffer = zeros(N,1);                % initialize buffer for FFT
yw = zeros(M,1);                       % initialize output sound frame
y = zeros(soundlength,1);              % initialize output array
yenv = y;                             % initialize window overlap envelope
w = w/sum(w);                         % normalize analysis window
while pin<pend
    %-----analysis-----%
    xw = x(pin-hM:pin+hM).*w(1:M);     % window the input sound
    fftbuffer(:) = 0;                  % reset buffer
    fftbuffer(1:(M+1)/2) = xw((M+1)/2:M);  % zero-phase window in fftbuffer
    fftbuffer(N-(M-1)/2+1:N) = xw(1:(M-1)/2);
    X = fft(fftbuffer);                % compute FFT
    mX = 20*log10(abs(X(1:N2)));       % magnitude spectrum of positive frequencies
    pX = unwrap(angle(X(1:N2)));       % unwrapped phase spect. of positive freq.
    %-----synthesis-----%
    Y = zeros(N,1);                    % initialize spectrum
    Y(1:N2) = 10.^(mX/20).*exp(i.*pX);  % generate positive freq.
    Y(N2+1:N) = 10.^(mX(N2-1:-1:2)/20).*exp(-i.*pX(N2-1:-1:2));
                                       % generate neg.freq.
    fftbuffer = real(ifft(Y));         % inverse FFT
    yw(1:(M-1)/2) = fftbuffer(N-(M-1)/2+1:N);  % undo zero-phase window
    yw((M+1)/2:M) = fftbuffer(1:(M+1)/2);
    y(pin-hM:pin+hM) = y(pin-hM:pin+hM) + yw(1:M);  % output signal overlap-add
    yenv(pin-hM:pin+hM) = yenv(pin-hM:pin+hM) + w;  % window overlap-add
    pin  = pin+H;                      % advance sound pointer
end
yenvth = max(yenv)*0.1;                % envelope threshold
yenv(find(yenv<yenvth)) = yenvth;
y = y./yenv;
```

The STFT process provides a suitable frequency-domain representation of the input signal. It is a far from trivial process and it is dependent on some low-level parameters closely related to the signal-processing domain. A little theoretical knowledge is required to understand the process, but we will also need practice to obtain the desired results for a given application.

10.3.2 Spectral peaks

The sinusoidal model assumes that each spectrum of the STFT representation can be explained by the sum of a small number of sinusoids. Given enough frequency resolution, and thus, enough points in the spectrum, the spectrum of a sinusoid can be identified by its shape. Theoretically, a sinusoid that is stable both in amplitude and in frequency, a partial of the sound, has a well-defined frequency representation: the transform of the analysis window used to compute the Fourier transform. It should be possible to take advantage of this characteristic to distinguish partials from other frequency components. However, in practice this is rarely the case, since most natural sounds are not perfectly periodic and do not have nicely spaced and clearly defined peaks in the frequency domain. There are interactions between the different components, and the shapes of the spectral peaks cannot be detected without tolerating some mismatch. Only some instrumental sounds (e.g., the steady-state part of an oboe sound) are periodic enough and sufficiently free from prominent noise components that the frequency representation of a stable sinusoid can be recognized easily in a single spectrum (see Figure 10.7). A practical solution is to detect as many peaks as possible, with some small constraints, and delay the decision of what is a *well-behaved* partial to the next step in the analysis: the peak-continuation algorithm.

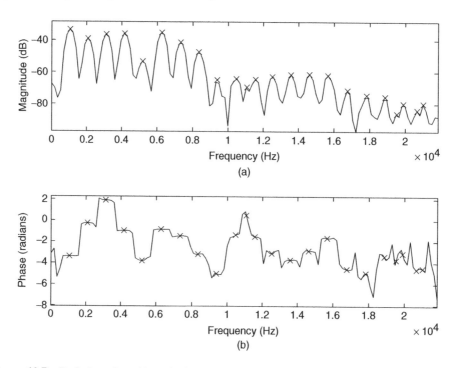

Figure 10.7 Peak detection: (a) peaks in magnitude spectrum; (b) peaks in the phase spectrum.

A *peak* is defined as a local maximum in the magnitude spectrum, and the only practical constraints to be made in the peak search are to have a local maximum over a certain frequency range and to have an amplitude greater than a given threshold.

Due to the sampled nature of the spectrum returned by the FFT, each peak is accurate only to within half a sample. A spectral sample represents a frequency interval of f_s/N Hz, where f_s is the sampling rate and N is the FFT size. Zero-padding in the time domain increases the number of spectral samples per Hz and thus increases the accuracy of the simple peak detection (see previous section). However, to obtain frequency accuracy on the level of 0.1% of the distance from the top of an ideal peak to its first zero crossing (in the case of a rectangular window), the zero-padding factor required is 1000.

Here we include a modified version of the STFT code in which we only use the spectral peak values to perform the inverse-FFT.

M-file 10.3 (stpt.m)

```
function y = stpt(x, w, N, H, t)
% Authors: J. Bonada, X. Serra, X. Amatriain, A. Loscos
% Analysis/synthesis of a sound using the peaks
% of the short-time Fourier transform
% x: input sound, w: analysis window (odd size), N: FFT size, H: hop size,
% t: threshold in negative dB, y: output sound
M = length(w);                          % analysis window size
N2 = N/2+1;                             % size of positive spectrum
soundlength = length(x);               % length of input sound aray
hM = (M-1)/2;                          % half analysis window size
pin = 1+hM;        % initialize sound pointer at the middle of analysis window
pend = soundlength-hM;                 % last sample to start a frame
fftbuffer = zeros(N,1);                % initialize buffer for FFT
yw = zeros(M,1);                        % initialize output sound frame
y = zeros(soundlength,1);              % initialize output array
w = w/sum(w);                          % normalize analysis window
sw = hanning(M);                       % synthesis window
sw = sw./sum(sw);
while pin<pend
    %-----analysis-----%
    xw = x(pin-hM:pin+hM).*w(1:M);      % window the input sound
    fftbuffer(:) = 0;                   % reset buffer
    fftbuffer(1:(M+1)/2) = xw((M+1)/2:M);   % zero-phase fftbuffer
    fftbuffer(N-(M-1)/2+1:N) = xw(1:(M-1)/2);
    X = fft(fftbuffer);                 % compute the FFT
    mX = 20*log10(abs(X(1:N2)));        % magnitude spectrum of positive frequencies
    pX = unwrap(angle(X(1:N2)));        % unwrapped phase spectrum
    ploc = 1 + find((mX(2:N2-1)>t) .* (mX(2:N2-1)>mX(3:N2)) ...
          .* (mX(2:N2-1)>mX(1:N2-2)));   % peaks
    pmag = mX(ploc);                    % magnitude of peaks
    pphase = pX(ploc);                  % phase of peaks
    %-----synthesis-----%
    Y = zeros(N,1); % initialize output spectrum
    Y(ploc) = 10.^(pmag/20).*exp(i.*pphase);    % generate positive freq.
    Y(N+2-ploc) = 10.^(pmag/20).*exp(-i.*pphase); % generate negative freq.
    fftbuffer = real(ifft(Y));          % real part of the inverse FFT
    yw((M+1)/2:M) = fftbuffer(1:(M+1)/2);   % undo zero phase window
    yw(1:(M-1)/2) = fftbuffer(N-(M-1)/2+1:N);
    y(pin-hM:pin+hM) = y(pin-hM:pin+hM) + H*N*sw.*yw(1:M);    % overlap-add
    pin  = pin+H;                       % advance sound pointer
end
```

This code is mostly the same as the one used for the STFT, with the addition of a peak-detection step based on a magnitude threshold, that is, we only detect peaks whose magnitude is greater than a magnitude threshold specified by the user. Then, in the synthesis stage, the spectrum used to compute the inverse-FFT has values only at the bins of the peaks, and the rest have zero magnitude. It can be shown that each of these isolated bins is precisely the transform of a stationary sinusoid (of the frequency corresponding to the bin) multiplied by a rectangular window. Therefore, we smooth the resulting signal frame with a synthesis window, $sw(n)$, to have smoother overlap-add behavior. Nevertheless, this implementation of a sinusoidal model is very simple and thus it is not appropriate for most applications. The next implementation is much more useful.

10.3.3 Spectral sinusoids

In order to improve the implementation of the sinusoidal model, we have to use more refined methods for estimating the sinusoidal parameters and we have to implement an accurate synthesis of time-varying sinusoids. The diagram of the complete system is shown in Figure 10.8.

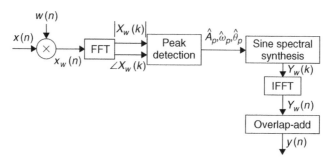

Figure 10.8 Block diagram of an analysis/synthesis system based on the sinusoidal model.

An efficient spectral interpolation scheme to better measure peak frequencies and magnitudes is to zero-pad only enough so that quadratic (or other simple) spectral interpolation, by using samples immediately surrounding the maximum-magnitude sample, suffices to refine the estimate to 0.1% accuracy. This is illustrated in Figure 10.9, where magnitudes are expressed in dB.

For a spectral peak located at bin k_p, let us define $\alpha = X_w^{dB}(k_p - 1)$, $\beta = X_w^{dB}(k_p)$ and $\gamma = X_w^{dB}(k_p + 1)$. The center of the parabola in bins is $\hat{k}_p = k_p + (\alpha - \gamma)/2(\alpha - 2\beta + \gamma)$, and the estimated amplitude $\hat{a}_p = \beta - (\alpha - \gamma)^2/8(\alpha - 2\beta + \gamma)$. Then the phase value of the peak is

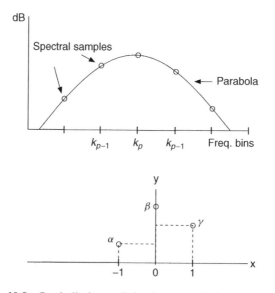

Figure 10.9 Parabolic interpolation in the peak-detection process.

measured by reading the value of the unwrapped phase spectrum at the position resulting from the frequency of the peak. This is a good first approximation, but it is still not the ideal solution, since significant deviations in amplitude and phase can be found even in the case of simple linear frequency modulations.

Here we include the code to perform the parabolic interpolation on the spectral peaks:

M-file 10.4 (peakinterp.m)

```
function [iploc, ipmag, ipphase] = peakinterp(mX, pX, ploc)
% Authors: J. Bonada, X. Serra, X. Amatriain, A. Loscos
% Parabolic interpolation of spectral peaks
% mX: magnitude spectrum, pX: phase spectrum, ploc: locations of peaks
% iploc, ipmag, ipphase: interpolated values
% note that ploc values are assumed to be between 2 and length(mX)-1
val = mX(ploc);                                 % magnitude of peak bin
lval = mX(ploc-1);                              % magnitude of bin at left
rval= mX(ploc+1);                               % magnitude of bin at right
iploc = ploc + .5*(lval-rval)./(lval-2*val+rval); % center of parabola
ipmag = val-.25*(lval-rval).*(iploc-ploc);      % magnitude of peaks
ipphase = interp1(1:length(pX),pX,iploc,'linear'); % phase of peaks
```

In order to decide whether a peak is a partial or not, it is sometimes useful to have a measure of how close its shape is to the ideal sinusoidal peak. With this idea in mind, different techniques have been used to improve the estimation of the spectral peak parameters [DH97]. More sophisticated methods make use of the spectral shape details and derive descriptors to distinguish between sinusoidal peaks, sidelobes and noise (e.g., [ZRR07]). Several other approaches target amplitude and frequency modulated sinusoids and are able to estimate their modulation parameters (e.g., [MB10]).

Peak continuation

Once the spectral peaks of a frame have been detected, a peak-continuation algorithm can organize the peaks into frequency trajectories, where each trajectory models a time-varying sinusoid (see Figure 10.10).

Several strategies have been explored during the last decades with the aim of connecting the sinusoidal components in the best possible way. McAulay and Quatieri proposed a simple sinusoidal continuation algorithm based on finding, for each spectral peak, the closest one in frequency in the next frame [MQ86]. Serra added to the continuation algorithm a set of frequency guides used to create sinusoidal trajectories [Ser89]. The frequency guide values were obtained from the peak values and their context, such as surrounding peaks and fundamental frequency. In the case of harmonic sounds, these guides were initialized according to the harmonic series of the estimated fundamental frequency. The trajectories were computed by assigning to each guide the closest peak in frequency.

There are peak-continuation methods based on hidden Markov models, which seem to be very valuable for tracking partials in polyphonic signals and complex inharmonic tones, for instance [DGR93]. Another interesting approach proposed by Peeters is to use a non-stationary sinusoid model, with linearly varying amplitude and frequency [Pee01]. Within that framework, the continuation algorithm focuses on the continuation of the value and first derivative for both amplitude and frequency polynomial parameters, combined with a measure of sinusoidality. Observation and transitions probabilities are defined, and a Viterbi algorithm is proposed for computing the sinusoidal trajectories.

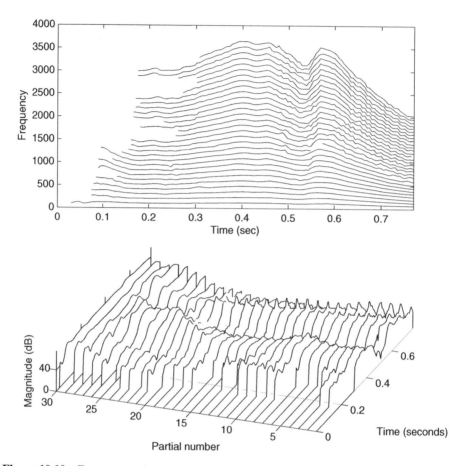

Figure 10.10   Frequency trajectories resulting from the sinusoidal analysis of a vocal sound.

Sinusoidal synthesis

Once all spectral peaks are identified and ordered, we can start the synthesis part, thus generating the sinusoids that correspond to the connected peaks. The sinusoids can be generated in the time domain with additive synthesis, controlling the instantaneous frequency and amplitude of a bank of oscillators, as shown in Figure 10.11. For this case, we define synthesis frames $d^l(m)$ as the segments determined by consecutive analysis times. For each synthesis frame, the instantaneous amplitude $\hat{A}^l(m)$ of an oscillator is obtained by linear interpolation of the surrounding amplitude estimations,

$$\hat{A}^l(m) = \hat{A}^{l-1} + \frac{\left(\hat{A}^l - \hat{A}^{l-1}\right)}{H} m, \tag{10.9}$$

where $m = 0, 1, \ldots, H - 1$ is the time sample within the frame.

The instantaneous phase is taken to be the integral of the instantaneous frequency, where the instantaneous radian frequency $\hat{\omega}^l(m)$ is obtained by linear interpolation,

$$\hat{\omega}^l(m) = \hat{\omega}^{l-1} + \frac{\left(\hat{\omega}^l - \hat{\omega}^{l-1}\right)}{H} m, \tag{10.10}$$

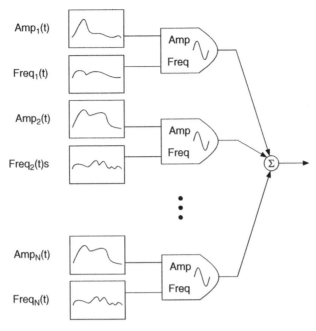

Figure 10.11   Additive synthesis block diagram.

and the instantaneous phase is

$$\hat{\theta}^l (m) = \hat{\theta}^{l-1} (H - 1) + \sum_{s=0}^{m} \hat{\omega}^l (s). \tag{10.11}$$

Finally, the synthesis equation of a frame becomes

$$d^l (m) = \sum_{r=1}^{R^l} \hat{A}_r^l (m) \cos \left[\hat{\theta}_r^l (m) \right], \tag{10.12}$$

where r is the oscillator index and R^l the number of sinusoids existing on the lth frame. The output sound $d (n)$ is obtained by adding all frame segments together,

$$d (n) = \sum_{l=0}^{L-1} d^l (n - lH). \tag{10.13}$$

A much more efficient implementation of additive synthesis, where the instantaneous phase is not preserved, is based on the inverse-FFT [RD92]. While this approach loses some of the flexibility of the traditional oscillator-bank implementation, especially the instantaneous control of frequency and magnitude, the gain in speed is significant. This gain is based on the fact that a stationary sinusoid in the frequency domain is a *sinc-type* function, the transform of the window used, and on these functions not all the samples carry the same amplitude relevance. A sinusoid can be approximated in the spectral domain by computing the samples of the main lobe of the window transform, with the appropriate magnitude, frequency and phase values. We can then synthesize as many sinusoids as we want by adding these main lobes into the FFT buffer and performing an IFFT to obtain the resulting time-domain signal. By an overlap-add process we then get the time-varying characteristics of the sound.

The synthesis frame rate is completely independent of the analysis one. In the implementation using the IFFT we want to have a frame rate high enough so as to preserve the temporal characteristics of the sound. As in all short-time-based processes we have the problem of having to make a compromise between time and frequency resolution. The window transform should have the fewest possible significant bins since this will be the number of points used to generate per sinusoid. A good window choice is the Blackman-Harris 92 dB (BH92) because its main lobe includes most of the energy. However, the problem is that such a window does not overlap perfectly to a constant in the time domain without having to use very high overlap factors, and thus very high frame rates. A solution to this problem is to undo the effect of the window by dividing the result of the IFFT by it (in the time domain) and applying an appropriate overlapping window (e.g., triangular) before performing the overlap-add process. This gives a good time-frequency compromise. However, it is desirable to use a hop-size significantly smaller than half the synthesis window length, so an overlap greater than 50%. Otherwise, large gains are applied at the window edges, which might introduce undesired artifacts at synthesis. This is illustrated in Figure 10.12, where a triangular window is used. Note that for a 50% overlap ($Ns = 1024$, $H = 512$) the gain at the window edges reaches values greater than 150.

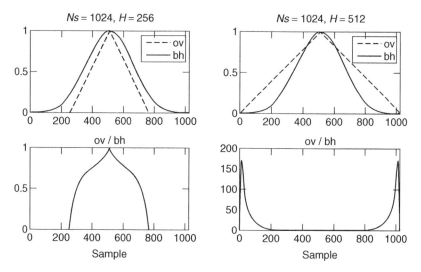

Figure 10.12 Overlapping strategy based on dividing by the synthesis window and multiplying by an overlapping window. Undesired artifacts can be introduced at synthesis if the overlap is not significantly greater than 50%.

The zero-centered BH92 window is defined as

$$w_{BH92}(n) = 0.35875 + 0.48829\cos\left(\frac{2\pi n}{N}\right) + 0.14128\cos\left(\frac{4\pi n}{N}\right) +$$

$$+ 0.01168\cos\left(\frac{6\pi n}{N}\right), \tag{10.14}$$

where N is the window length. Since each cosine function is the sum of two complex exponentials, then its transform can be expressed by a sum of rectangular window transforms (or Dirichlet kernels) shifted to the cosine (positive and negative) frequencies. The following **MATLAB** code implements the computation of the Blackman-Harris 92 dB transform, which will be used to generate sinusoids in the spectral domain:

M-file 10.5 (genbh92lobe.m)

```
function y = genbh92lobe(x)
% Authors: J. Bonada, X. Serra, X. Amatriain, A. Loscos
% Calculate transform of the Blackman-Harris 92dB window
% x: bin positions to compute (real values)
% y: transform values
N = 512;
f = x*pi*2/N;                                    % frequency sampling
df = 2*pi/N;
y = zeros(size(x));                              % initialize window
consts = [.35875, .48829, .14128, .01168];       % window constants
for m=0:3
    y = y + consts(m+1)/2*(D(f-df*m,N)+D(f+df*m,N));  % sum Dirichlet kernels
end
y = y/N/consts(1);                               % normalize
end

function y = D(x,N)
% Calculate rectangular window transform (Dirichlet kernel)
y = sin(N*x/2)./sin(x/2);
y(find(y~=y))=N;                                 % avoid NaN if x==0
end
```

Once we can generate a single sinusoid in the frequency domain, we can also generate a complete complex spectrum of a series of sinusoids from their frequency, magnitude and phase values.

M-file 10.6 (genspecsines.m)

```
function Y = genspecsines(ploc, pmag, pphase, N)
% Authors: J. Bonada, X. Serra, X. Amatriain, A. Loscos
% Compute a spectrum from a series of sine values
% iploc, ipmag, ipphase: sine locations, magnitudes and phases
% N: size of complex spectrum
% Y: generated complex spectrum of sines
Y =zeros(N,1); % initialize output spectrum
hN = N/2+1;                            % size of positive freq. spectrum
for i=1:length(ploc);                 % generate all sine spectral lobes
  loc = ploc(i);                      % location of peak (zero-based indexing)
                                      % it should be in range ]0,hN-1[
  if (loc<=1||loc>=hN-1) continue; end; % avoid frequencies out of range
  binremainder = round(loc)-loc;
  lb = [binremainder-4:binremainder+4]'; % main lobe (real value) bins to read
  lmag = genbh92lobe(lb)*10.^(pmag(i)/20); % lobe magnitudes of the
                                      % complex exponential
  b = 1+[round(loc)-4:round(loc)+4]'; % spectrum bins to fill
                                      % (1-based indexing)
  for m=1:9
      if (b(m)<1)                     % peak lobe crosses DC bin
          Y(2-b(m)) = Y(2-b(m)) + lmag(m)*exp(-1i*pphase(i));
      elseif (b(m)>hN)                % peak lobe crosses Nyquist bin
          Y(2*hN-b(m)) = Y(2*hN-b(m)) + lmag(m)*exp(-1i*pphase(i));
      else                            % peak lobe in positive freq. range
          Y(b(m)) = Y(b(m)) + lmag(m)*exp(1i*pphase(i)) ...
                  + lmag(m)*exp(-1i*pphase(i))*(b(m)==1||b(m)==hN);
      end
  end
  Y(hN+1:end) = conj(Y(hN-1:-1:2));   % fill the rest of the spectrum
end
```

In this code we place each sinusoid in its spectral location with the right amplitude and phase. What complicates the code a bit is the inclusion of special conditions when spectral lobe values cross the DC or the Nyquist bin locations.

Now that we have an improved implementation for detecting and synthesizing sinusoids we can implement a complete analysis/synthesis system based on this sinusoidal model.

M-file 10.7 (sinemodel.m)

```
function y = sinemodel(x, w, N, t)
% Authors: J. Bonada, X. Serra, X. Amatriain, A. Loscos
% Analysis/synthesis of a sound using the sinusoidal model
% x: input sound, w: analysis window (odd size), N: FFT size,
% t: threshold in negative dB, y: output sound
M = length(w);                          % analysis window size
Ns= 1024;                               % FFT size for synthesis (even)
H = 256;                                % analysis/synthesishop size
N2= N/2+1;                              % size of positive spectrum
soundlength = length(x);               % length of input sound array
hNs = Ns/2;                            % half synthesis window size
hM = (M-1)/2;                          % half analysis window size
pin = max(hNs+1,1+hM); % initialize sound pointer to middle of analysis window
pend = soundlength-max(hNs,hM);        % last sample to start a frame
fftbuffer = zeros(N,1);               % initialize buffer for FFT
y = zeros(soundlength,1);              % initialize output array
w = w/sum(w);                          % normalize analysis window
sw = zeros(Ns,1);
ow = triang(2*H-1);                    % overlapping window
ovidx = Ns/2+1-H+1:Ns/2+H;            % overlap indexes
sw(ovidx) = ow(1:2*H-1);
bh = blackmanharris(Ns);              % synthesis window
bh = bh ./ sum(bh);                   % normalize synthesis window
sw(ovidx) = sw(ovidx) ./ bh(ovidx);
while pin<pend
    %-----analysis-----%
    xw = x(pin-hM:pin+hM).*w(1:M);     % window the input sound
    fftbuffer(:) = 0;                  % reset buffer
    fftbuffer(1:(M+1)/2) = xw((M+1)/2:M);  % zero-phase window in fftbuffer
    fftbuffer(N-(M-1)/2+1:N) = xw(1:(M-1)/2);
    X = fft(fftbuffer);                % compute the FFT
    mX = 20*log10(abs(X(1:N2)));       % magnitude spectrum of positive frequencies
    pX = unwrap(angle(X(1:N/2+1)));    % unwrapped phase spectrum
    ploc = 1 + find((mX(2:N2-1)>t) .* (mX(2:N2-1)>mX(3:N2)) ...
            .* (mX(2:N2-1)>mX(1:N2-2)));  % find peaks
    [ploc,pmag,pphase] = peakinterp(mX,pX,ploc);  % refine peak values
    %-----synthesis-----%
    plocs = (ploc-1)*Ns/N;             % adapt peak locations to synthesis FFT
    Y = genspecsines(plocs,pmag,pphase,Ns);  % generate spec sines
    yw = fftshift(real(ifft(Y)));      % time domain of sinusoids
    y(pin-hNs:pin+hNs-1) = y(pin-hNs:pin+hNs-1) + sw.*yw(1:Ns);  % overlap-add
    pin = pin+H;                       % advance the sound pointer
end
```

The basic difference from the analysis/synthesis implementation based on spectral peaks is in the improvement of the peak detection using a parabolic interpolation, peakinterp, and on the implementation of the synthesis part. We now have a real additive synthesis section, which is completely independent of the analysis part. Thus it is no longer an FFT transform followed by its inverse-FFT transform. We could have implemented an additive synthesis in the time domain, but instead we have implemented an additive synthesis in the frequency domain, using the IFFT. We have fixed the synthesis FFT-size, 1204, and hop-size, 256, and they are independent of the analysis window type, window size and FFT size, which are defined by the user as input parameters of the function and are set depending on the sound to be processed. Since this method generates stationary sinusoids, there is no need to estimate the instantaneous phase or to interpolate the sinusoidal parameters, and therefore we can omit the peak-continuation algorithm. This would not be the case if we wanted to apply transformations.

10.3.4   Spectral harmonics

A very useful constraint to be included in the sinusoidal model is to restrict the sinusoids to being harmonic partials, thus to assume that the input sound is monophonic and harmonic. With this constraint it should be possible to identify the fundamental frequency, F_0, at each frame, and to have a much more compact and flexible spectral representation.

Given this restriction and the set of spectral peaks of a frame, with magnitude and frequency values for each one, there are many possible F_0 estimation strategies, none of them perfect, e.g., [Hes83, MB94, Can98]. An obvious approach is to define F_0 as the common divisor of the harmonic series that best explains the spectral peaks found in a given frame. For example, in the two-way mismatch procedure proposed by Maher and Beauchamp the estimated F_0 is chosen as to minimize discrepancies between measured peak frequencies and the harmonic frequencies generated by trial values of F_0. For each trial F_0, mismatches between the harmonics generated and the measured peak frequencies are averaged over a fixed subset of the available peaks. This is a basic idea on top of which we can add features and tune all the parameters for a given family of sounds.

Many trade-offs are involved in the implementation of a F_0 detection system and every application will require a clear design strategy. For example, the issue of real-time performance is a requirement with strong design implications. We can add context-specific optimizations when knowledge of the signal is available. Knowing, for instance, the frequency range of the F_0 of a particular sound helps both the accuracy and the computational cost. Then, there are sounds with specific characteristics, like in a clarinet, where the even partials are softer than the odd ones. From this information, we can define a set of rules that will improve the performance of the estimator used.

In the framework of many spectral models there are strong dependencies between the fundamental-frequency detection step and many other analysis steps. For example, choosing an appropriate window for the Fourier analysis will facilitate detecting the fundamental frequency and, at the same time, getting a good fundamental frequency will assist other analysis steps, including the selection of an appropriate window. Thus, it could be designed as a recursive process.

The following **MATLAB** code implements the two-way mismatch algorithm for fundamental frequency detection:

M-file 10.8 (`f0detectiontwm.m`)

```
function f0 = f0detectiontwm(mX, fs, ploc, pmag, ef0max, minf0, maxf0)
% Authors: J. Bonada, X. Serra, X. Amatriain, A. Loscos
% Fundamental frequency detection function
% mX: magnitude spectrum, fs: sampling rate, ploc, pmag: peak loc and mag,
% ef0max: maximim error allowed, minf0: minimum f0, maxf0: maximum f0
% f0: fundamental frequency detected in Hz
N = length(mX)*2;                    % size of complex spectrum
nPeaks = length(ploc);               % number of peaks
f0 = 0;                              % initialize output
if(nPeaks>3)             % at least 3 peaks in spectrum for trying to find f0
  nf0peaks = min(50,nPeaks);         % use a maximum of 50 peaks
  [f0,f0error] = TWM(ploc(1:nf0peaks),pmag(1:nf0peaks),N,fs,minf0,maxf0);
  if (f0>0 && f0error>ef0max)        % limit the possible error by ethreshold
    f0 = 0;
  end
end;
```

```
function [f0, f0error] = TWM (ploc, pmag, N, fs, minf0, maxf0)
% Two-way mismatch algorithm (by Beauchamp&Maher)
% ploc, pmag: peak locations and magnitudes, N: size of complex spectrum
% fs: sampling rate of sound, minf0: minimum f0, maxf0: maximum f0
% f0: fundamental frequency detected, f0error: error measure
pfreq = (ploc-1)/N*fs;                     % frequency in Hertz of peaks
[zvalue,zindex] = min(pfreq);
if (zvalue==0)                             % avoid zero frequency peak
  pfreq(zindex) = 1;
  pmag(zindex) = -100;
end
ival2 = pmag;
[Mmag1,Mloc1] = max(ival2);                % find peak with maximum magnitude
ival2(Mloc1) = -100;                       % clear max peak
[Mmag2,Mloc2]= max(ival2);                 % find second maximum magnitude peak
ival2(Mloc2) = -100;                       % clear second max peak
[Mmag3,Mloc3]= max(ival2);                 % find third maximum magnitude peak
nCand = 3;                  % number of possible f0 candidates for each max peak
f0c = zeros(1,3*nCand);                    % initialize array of candidates
f0c(1:nCand)=(pfreq(Mloc1)*ones(1,nCand))./((nCand+1-(1:nCand))); % candidates
f0c(nCand+1:nCand*2)=(pfreq(Mloc2)*ones(1,nCand))./((nCand+1-(1:nCand)));
f0c(nCand*2+1:nCand*3)=(pfreq(Mloc3)*ones(1,nCand))./((nCand+1-(1:nCand)));
f0c = f0c((f0c<maxf0)&(f0c>minf0));        % candidates within boundaries
if (isempty(f0c))                          % if no candidates exit
  f0 = 0; f0error=100;
  return
end
harmonic = f0c;
ErrorPM = zeros(fliplr(size(harmonic)));        % initialize PM errors
MaxNPM = min(10,length(ploc));
for i=1:MaxNPM % predicted to measured mismatch error
  difmatrixPM = harmonic' * ones(size(pfreq))';
  difmatrixPM = abs(difmatrixPM-ones(fliplr(size(harmonic)))*pfreq');
  [FreqDistance,peakloc] = min(difmatrixPM,[],2);
  Ponddif = FreqDistance .* (harmonic'.^(-0.5));
  PeakMag = pmag(peakloc);
  MagFactor = 10.^((PeakMag-Mmag1)./20);
  ErrorPM = ErrorPM+(Ponddif+MagFactor.*(1.4*Ponddif-0.5));
  harmonic = harmonic+f0c;
end
ErrorMP = zeros(fliplr(size(harmonic)));        % initialize MP errors
MaxNMP = min(10,length(pfreq));
for i=1:length(f0c)                 % measured to predicted mismatch error
  nharm = round(pfreq(1:MaxNMP)/f0c(i));
  nharm = (nharm>=1).*nharm + (nharm<1);
  FreqDistance = abs(pfreq(1:MaxNMP) - nharm*f0c(i));
  Ponddif = FreqDistance.* (pfreq(1:MaxNMP).^(-0.5));
  PeakMag = pmag(1:MaxNMP);
  MagFactor = 10.^((PeakMag-Mmag1)./20);
  ErrorMP(i) = sum(MagFactor.*(Ponddif+MagFactor.*(1.4*Ponddif-0.5)));
end
Error = (ErrorPM/MaxNPM) + (0.3*ErrorMP/MaxNMP);  % total errors
[f0error, f0index] = min(Error);                  % get the smallest error
f0 = f0c(f0index);                                % f0 with the smallest error
```

There also exist many time-domain methods for estimating the fundamental frequency. It is worth mentioning the Yin algorithm, which offers excellent performance in many situations [CK02]. It is based on finding minima in the cumulative mean normalized difference function

$d'(\tau)$, defined as

$$d(\tau) = \sum_{j=t+1}^{t+W} (x(j) - x(j+\tau))^2 \tag{10.15}$$

$$d'(\tau) = \begin{cases} 1 & if\ \tau = 0 \\ \frac{\tau \cdot d(\tau)}{\sum_{j=1}^{\tau} d(j)} & otherwise, \end{cases} \tag{10.16}$$

where x is the input signal, τ is the lag time, and W is the window size. Ideally, this function exhibits local minima at lag times corresponding to the fundamental period and its multiples. More refinements are described in the referenced article, although here we will only implement the basic procedure.

The following **MATLAB** code implements a simplified version of the Yin algorithm for fundamental frequency detection. We have included some optimizations in the calculations, such as performing sequential cumulative sums by adding and subtracting, respectively, the new and initial samples, or using the `xcorr` **MATLAB** function.

M-file 10.9 (`f0detectionyin.m`)

```
function f0 = f0detectionyin(x,fs,ws,minf0,maxf0)
% Authors: J. Bonada, X. Serra, X. Amatriain, A. Loscos
% Fundamental frequency detection function
% x: input signal, fs: sampling rate, ws: integration window length
% minf0: minimum f0, maxf0: maximum f0
% f0: fundamental frequency detected in Hz
maxlag = ws-2;                          % maximum lag
th = 0.1;                               % set threshold
d = zeros(maxlag,1);                    % init variable
d2 = zeros(maxlag,1);                   % init variable
% compute d(tau)
x1 = x(1:ws);
cumsumx = sum(x1.^2);
cumsumx1 = cumsumx;
xy = xcorr(x(1:ws*2),x1);
xy = xy(ws*2+1:ws*3-2);
for lag=0:maxlag-1
    d(1+lag) = cumsumx + cumsumx1 - 2*xy(1+lag);
    cumsumx1 = cumsumx1 - x(1+lag).^2 + x(1+lag+ws+1)^2;
end
cumsum = 0;
% compute d'(tau)
d2(1) = 1;
for lag=1:maxlag-1
    cumsum = cumsum + d(1+lag);
    d2(1+lag) = d(1+lag)*lag./cumsum;
end
% limit the search to the target range
minf0lag = 1+round(fs./minf0);          % compute lag corresponding to minf0
maxf0lag = 1+round(fs./maxf0);          % compute lag corresponding to maxf0
if (maxf0lag>1 && maxf0lag<maxlag)
    d2(1:maxf0lag) = 100;               % avoid lags shorter than maxf0lag
end
if (minf0lag>1 && minf0lag<maxlag)
    d2(minf0lag:end) = 100;            % avoid lags larger than minf0lag
end
% find the best candidate
mloc = 1 + find((d2(2:end-1)<d2(3:end)).*(d2(2:end-1)<d2(1:end-2)));  % minima
```

```
candf0lag = 0;
if (length(mloc)>0)
    I = find(d2(mloc)<th);
    if (length(I)>0)
        candf0lag = mloc(I(1));
    else
        [Y,I2] = min(d2(mloc));
        candf0lag = mloc(I2);
    end
    candf0lag = candf0lag;                  % this is zero-based indexing
    if (candf0lag>1 & candf0lag<maxlag)
        % parabolic interpolation
        lval = d2(candf0lag-1);
        val = d2(candf0lag);
        rval= d2(candf0lag+1);
        candf0lag = candf0lag + .5*(lval-rval)./(lval-2*val+rval);
    end
end
ac = min(d2);
f0lag = candf0lag-1;                         % convert to zero-based indexing
f0 = fs./f0lag;                              % compute candidate frequency in Hz
if (ac > 0.2)                                % voiced/unvoiced threshold
    f0 = 0;                                  % set to unvoiced
end
```

When a relevant fundamental frequency is identified, we can decide to what harmonic number each of the peaks belongs and thus restrict the sinusoidal components to be only the harmonic ones. The diagram of the complete system is shown in Figure 10.13.

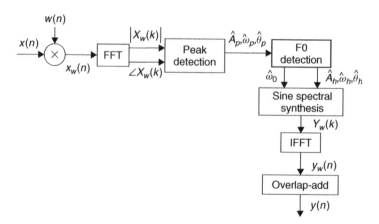

Figure 10.13 Block diagram of an analysis/synthesis system based on the harmonic sinusoidal model.

We can now add these steps into the implementation of the sinusoidal model represented in the previous section to implement a system that works just for harmonic sounds. Next is the complete **MATLAB** code for it.

M-file 10.10 (harmonicmodel.m)

```
function y = harmonicmodel(x, fs, w, N, t, nH, minf0, maxf0, f0et, maxhd)
% Authors: J. Bonada, X. Serra, X. Amatriain, A. Loscos
% Analysis/synthesis of a sound using the sinusoidal harmonic model
```

```
% x: input sound, fs: sampling rate, w: analysis window (odd size),
% N: FFT size (minimum 512), t: threshold in negative dB,
% nH: maximum number of harmonics, minf0: minimum f0 frequency in Hz,
% maxf0: maximim f0 frequency in Hz,
% f0et: error threshold in the f0 detection (ex: 5),
% maxhd: max. relative deviation in harmonic detection (ex: .2)
% y: output sound
M = length(w);                          % analysis window size
Ns= 1024;                               % FFT size for synthesis
H = 256;                                % hop size for analysis and synthesis
N2 = N/2+1;                             % size postive spectrum
soundlength = length(x);                % length of input sound array
hNs = Ns/2;                             % half synthesis window size
hM = (M-1)/2;                           % half analysis window size
pin = max(hNs+1,1+hM);   % initialize sound pointer to middle of analysis window
pend = soundlength-max(hNs,hM);                     % last sample to start a frame
fftbuffer = zeros(N,1);                 % initialize buffer for FFT
y = zeros(soundlength+Ns/2,1);          % output sound
w = w/sum(w);                           % normalize analysis window
sw = zeros(Ns,1);
ow = triang(2*H-1);                     % overlapping window
ovidx = Ns/2+1-H+1:Ns/2+H;             % overlap indexes
sw(ovidx) = ow(1:2*H-1);
bh = blackmanharris(Ns);                % synthesis window
bh = bh ./ sum(bh);                     % normalize synthesis window
sw(ovidx) = sw(ovidx) ./ bh(ovidx);
while pin<pend
  %-----analysis-----%
  xw = x(pin-hM:pin+hM).*w(1:M);        % window the input sound
  fftbuffer(:) = 0;                     % reset buffer
  fftbuffer(1:(M+1)/2) = xw((M+1)/2:M); % zero-phase window in fftbuffer
  fftbuffer(N-(M-1)/2+1:N) = xw(1:(M-1)/2);
  X = fft(fftbuffer);                   % compute the FFT
  mX = 20*log10(abs(X(1:N2)));          % magnitude spectrum
  pX = unwrap(angle(X(1:N/2+1)));       % unwrapped phase spectrum
  ploc = 1 + find((mX(2:N2-1)>t) .* (mX(2:N2-1)>mX(3:N2)) ...
                 .* (mX(2:N2-1)>mX(1:N2-2)));           % find peaks
  [ploc,pmag,pphase] = peakinterp(mX,pX,ploc);          % refine peak values
  f0 = f0detectiontwm(mX,fs,ploc,pmag,f0et,minf0,maxf0);  % find f0
  hloc = zeros(nH,1);                   % initialize harmonic locations
  hmag = zeros(nH,1)-100;               % initialize harmonic magnitudes
  hphase = zeros(nH,1);                 % initialize harmonic phases
  hf = (f0>0).*(f0.*(1:nH));            % initialize harmonic frequencies
  hi = 1;                               % initialize harmonic index
  npeaks = length(ploc);               % number of peaks found
  while (f0>0 && hi<=nH && hf(hi)<fs/2) % find harmonic peaks
    [dev,pei] = min(abs((ploc(1:npeaks)-1)/N*fs-hf(hi)));      % closest peak
    if ((hi==1 || ~any(hloc(1:hi-1)==ploc(pei))) && dev<maxhd*hf(hi))
      hloc(hi) = ploc(pei);             % harmonic locations
      hmag(hi) = pmag(pei);             % harmonic magnitudes
      hphase(hi) = pphase(pei);         % harmonic phases
    end
    hi = hi+1;                          %increase harmonic index
  end
  hloc(1:hi-1) = (hloc(1:hi-1)~=0).*((hloc(1:hi-1)-1)*Ns/N); % synth. locs
  %-----synthesis-----%
  Yh = genspecsines(hloc(1:hi-1),hmag,hphase,Ns);       % generate sines
  yh = fftshift(real(ifft(Yh)));        % sines in time domain
  y(pin-hNs:pin+hNs-1) = y(pin-hNs:pin+hNs-1) + sw.*yh(1:Ns);   % overlap-add
  pin = pin+H;                          % advance the input sound pointer
end
```

The basic differences from the previous implementation of the sinusoidal model are the detection of the F_0 using the function f0detectiontwm, and the detection of the harmonic peaks by first generating a perfect harmonic series from the identified F_0 and then searching the closest peaks for each harmonic value. This is a very simple implementation of a peak-continuation algorithm, but generally works for clean recordings of harmonic sounds. The major possible problem in using this implementation is in failing to detect the correct F_0 for a given sound, causing the complete system to fail.

In the previous analysis/synthesis code we used the two-way mismatch algorithm, but we could perfectly use the Yin algorithm instead. A substantial difference between both is that whereas the first one operates on the spectra information, Yin receives a time-domain segment as input. If we prefer to use Yin, we can replace the line where f0detectiontwm was called in the previous code for the following ones. Note that the window length, yinws, has to be larger than the period corresponding to the minimum fundamental frequency to estimate.

M-file 10.11 (callyin.m)

```
% Authors: J. Bonada, X. Serra, X. Amatriain, A. Loscos
yinws = round(fs*0.015);       % using approx. a 15 ms window for yin
yinws = yinws+mod(yinws,2);    % make it even
yb = pin-yinws/2;
ye = pin+yinws/2+yinws;
if (yb<1 || ye>length(x))      % out of boundaries
    f0 = 0;
else
    f0 = f0detectionyin(x(yb:ye),fs,yinws,minf0,maxf0);
end
```

10.3.5   Spectral harmonics plus residual

Once we have identified the harmonic partials of a sound, we can subtract them from the original signal and obtain a residual component. This subtraction can be done either in the time domain or in the frequency domain. A time-domain approach requires first to synthesize a time signal from the sinusoidal trajectories, while if we stay in the frequency domain, we can perform the subtraction directly in the already computed magnitude spectrum. For the time-domain subtraction, the phases of the original sound have to be preserved in the synthesized signal, thus we have to use a type of additive synthesis with which we can control the instantaneous phase. This is a type of synthesis that is computationally quite expensive. On the other hand, the sinusoidal subtraction in the spectral domain is in many cases computationally simpler, and can give similar results, in terms of accuracy, as the time-domain implementation. We have to understand that the sinusoidal information obtained from the analysis is very much under-sampled, since for every sinusoid we only have the value at the tip of the peaks, and thus we have to re-generate all the spectral samples that belong to the sinusoidal peak to be subtracted.

Once we have, either the residual spectrum or the residual time signal, it is useful to study it in order to check how well the partials of the sound were subtracted and therefore analyzed. If partials remain in the residual, the possibilities for transformations will be reduced, since these are not adequate for typical residual models. In this case, we should re-analyze the sound until we get a good residual, free of harmonic partials. Ideally, for monophonic signals, the resulting residual should be as close as possible to a stochastic signal.

The first step in obtaining the residual is to synthesize the sinusoids obtained as the output of the harmonic analysis. For a time-domain subtraction (see Figure 10.14) the synthesized signal will reproduce the instantaneous phase and amplitude of the partials of the original sound with a bank of oscillators. Different approaches are possible for computing the instantaneous phase, for instance

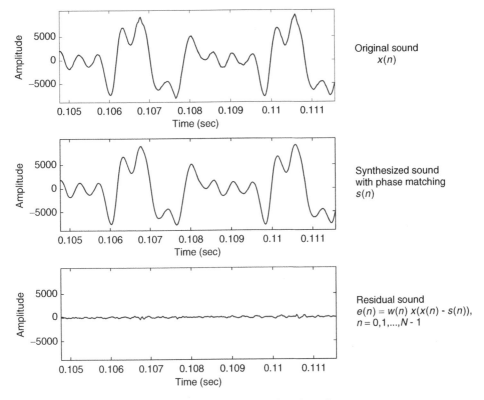

Figure 10.14   Time-domain subtraction.

[MQ86], thus being able to synthesize one frame which goes smoothly from the previous to the current frame with each sinusoid accounting for both the rapid phase changes (frequency) and the slowly varying phase changes. However, an efficient implementation can also be obtained by frequency-domain subtraction, where a spectral representation of stationary sinusoids is generated [RD92].

Next is an implementation of a complete system using a harmonic plus residual model and based on subtracting the harmonic component in the frequency domain (see the diagram in Figure 10.15).

M-file 10.12 (hprmodel.m)

```
function [y,yh,yr] = hprmodel(x,fs,w,N,t,nH,minf0,maxf0,f0et,maxhd)
% Authors: J. Bonada, X. Serra, X. Amatriain, A. Loscos
% Analysis/synthesis of a sound using the sinusoidal harmonic model
% x: input sound, fs: sampling rate, w: analysis window (odd size),
% N: FFT size (minimum 512), t: threshold in negative dB,
% nH: maximum number of harmonics, minf0: minimum f0 frequency in Hz,
% maxf0: maximim f0 frequency in Hz,
% f0et: error threshold in the f0 detection (ex: 5),
% maxhd: max. relative deviation in harmonic detection (ex: .2)
% y: output sound, yh: harmonic component, yr: residual component
M = length(w);              % analysis window size
Ns = 1024;                  % FFT size for synthesis
H = 256;                    % hop size for analysis and synthesis
N2 = N/2+1;                 % half-size of spectrum
```

```
soundlength = length(x);                    % length of input sound array
hNs = Ns/2;                                 % half synthesis window size
hM = (M-1)/2;                               % half analysis window size
pin = max(hNs+1,1+hM);    % initialize sound pointer to middle of analysis window
pend = soundlength-max(hM,hNs);             % last sample to start a frame
fftbuffer = zeros(N,1);                     % initialize buffer for FFT
yh = zeros(soundlength+Ns/2,1);             % output sine component
yr = zeros(soundlength+Ns/2,1);             % output residual component
w = w/sum(w);                               % normalize analysis window
sw = zeros(Ns,1);
ow = triang(2*H-1);                         % overlapping window
ovidx = Ns/2+1-H+1:Ns/2+H;                  % overlap indexes
sw(ovidx) = ow(1:2*H-1);
bh = blackmanharris(Ns);                    % synthesis window
bh = bh ./ sum(bh);                         % normalize synthesis window
wr = bh;                                    % window for residual
sw(ovidx) = sw(ovidx) ./ bh(ovidx);
while pin<pend
    %-----analysis-----%
    xw = x(pin-hM:pin+hM).*w(1:M);          % window the input sound
    fftbuffer(:) = 0;                       % reset buffer
    fftbuffer(1:(M+1)/2) = xw((M+1)/2:M);   % zero-phase window in fftbuffer
    fftbuffer(N-(M-1)/2+1:N) = xw(1:(M-1)/2);
    X = fft(fftbuffer);                     % compute the FFT
    mX = 20*log10(abs(X(1:N2)));            % magnitude spectrum
    pX = unwrap(angle(X(1:N/2+1)));         % unwrapped phase spectrum
    ploc = 1 + find((mX(2:N2-1)>t) .* (mX(2:N2-1)>mX(3:N2)) ...
                    .* (mX(2:N2-1)>mX(1:N2-2)));        % find peaks
    [ploc,pmag,pphase] = peakinterp(mX,pX,ploc);        % refine peak values
    f0 = f0detectiontwm(mX,fs,ploc,pmag,f0et,minf0,maxf0);  % find f0
    hloc = zeros(nH,1);                     % initialize harmonic locations
    hmag = zeros(nH,1)-100;                 % initialize harmonic magnitudes
    hphase = zeros(nH,1);                   % initialize harmonic phases
    hf = (f0>0).*(f0.*(1:nH));              % initialize harmonic frequencies
    hi = 1;                                 % initialize harmonic index
    npeaks = length(ploc);                  % number of peaks found
    while (f0>0 && hi<=nH && hf(hi)<fs/2)   % find harmonic peaks
        [dev,pei] = min(abs((ploc(1:npeaks)-1)/N*fs-hf(hi)));   % closest peak
        if ((hi==1 || ~any(hloc(1:hi-1)==ploc(pei))) && dev<maxhd*hf(hi))
            hloc(hi) = ploc(pei);           % harmonic locations
            hmag(hi) = pmag(pei);           % harmonic magnitudes
            hphase(hi) = pphase(pei);       % harmonic phases
        end
        hi = hi+1;                          % increase harmonic index
    end
    hloc(1:hi-1) = (hloc(1:hi-1)~=0).*((hloc(1:hi-1)-1)*Ns/N);  % synth. locs
    ri= pin-hNs;                            % input sound pointer for residual analysis
    xr = x(ri:ri+Ns-1).*wr(1:Ns);          % window the input sound
    Xr = fft(fftshift(xr));                 % compute FFT for residual analysis
    %-----synthesis-----%
    Yh = genspecsines(hloc(1:hi-1),hmag,hphase,Ns);        % generate sines
    Yr = Xr-Yh;                             % get the residual complex spectrum
    yhw = fftshift(real(ifft(Yh)));         % sines in time domain using inverse FFT
    yrw = fftshift(real(ifft(Yr)));         % residual in time domain using inverse FFT
    yh(ri:ri+Ns-1) = yh(ri:ri+Ns-1)+yhw(1:Ns).*sw;   % overlap-add for sines
    yr(ri:ri+Ns-1) = yr(ri:ri+Ns-1)+yrw(1:Ns).*sw;   % overlap-add for residual
    pin = pin+H;                            % advance the sound pointer
end
y= yh+yr;                                   % sum sines and residual
```

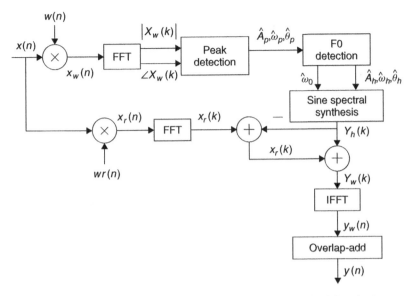

Figure 10.15 Block diagram of the harmonic plus residual analysis/synthesis system.

In order to subtract the harmonic component from the original sound in the frequency domain we have added a parallel FFT analysis of the input sound, with an analysis window which is the same than the one used in the synthesis step. Thus we can get a residual spectrum, Xres, and by simply computing its inverse FFT we obtain the time-domain residual. The synthesized signal, $y(n)$, is the sum of the harmonic and residual components. The function also returns the harmonic and residual components as separate signals.

10.3.6   Spectral harmonics plus stochastic residual

Once we have a decomposition of a sound into harmonic and residual components, from the residual signal we can continue our modeling strategy towards a more compact and flexible representation. When the harmonics have been well identified and subtracted the residual can be considered a stochastic signal ready to be parameterized. To model, or parameterize, the relevant parts of the residual component of a musical sound, such as the bow noise in stringed instruments or the breath noise in wind instruments, we need good time resolution and we can give up some of the frequency resolution required for modeling the harmonic component. Given the window requirements for the STFT analysis the harmonic component cannot maintain the sharpness of the attacks, because, even if a high frame rate is used we are forced to use a long enough window, and this size determines most of the time resolution. However, once the harmonic subtraction has been done, the temporal resolution to analyze the residual component can be improved by using a different analysis window (see Figure 10.16).

Since the harmonic analysis has been performed using long windows, the subtraction of the harmonic component generated from that analysis might result in smearing of the sharp discontinuities, like note attacks, which remain in the residual component. We can *fix* this smearing effect of the residual and try to preserve the sharpness of the attacks of the original sound. For example, the resulting time-domain residual can be compared with the original waveform and its amplitude re-scaled whenever the residual has a greater energy than the original waveform. Then the stochastic analysis is performed on this modified residual. We can also compare the synthesized harmonic signal with the original sound and whenever this signal has a greater energy than the

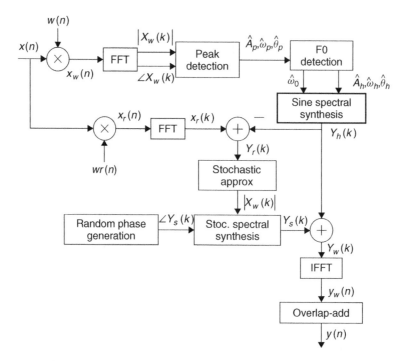

Figure 10.16 Block diagram of an analysis/synthesis system based on a harmonic plus stochastic model.

original waveform it means that a smearing of the harmonic component has been produced. This can be fixed a bit by scaling the amplitudes of the harmonic analysis in the corresponding frame using the difference between the original sound and the harmonic signal.

Residual analysis

One of the underlying assumptions of the sinusoidal plus residual model is that the residual is a stochastic signal. Such an assumption implies that the residual is fully described by its amplitude and its general frequency characteristics (see Figure 10.17). It is unnecessary to keep either the instantaneous phase or the exact spectral shape information. Based on this, a frame of the stochastic residual can be completely characterized by a filter, i.e., this filter encodes the amplitude and general frequency characteristics of the residual. The representation of the residual in the overall sound will be a sequence of these filters, i.e., a time-varying filter.

The filter design problem is generally solved by performing some sort of curve fitting in the magnitude spectrum of the current frame [Str80, Sed88]. Standard techniques are: spline interpolation [Cox71], the method of least squares [Sed88], or straight-line approximations.

One way to carry out the line-segment approximation is to step through the magnitude spectrum and find local maxima in each of several defined sections, thus giving equally spaced points in the spectrum that are connected by straight lines to create the spectral envelope. The number of points gives the accuracy of the fit, and that can be set depending on the sound complexity. Other options are to have unequally spaced points, for example, logarithmically spaced, or spaced according to other perceptual criteria.

Another practical alternative is to use a type of least squares approximation called linear predictive coding, LPC [Mak75, MG75]. LPC is a popular technique used in speech research

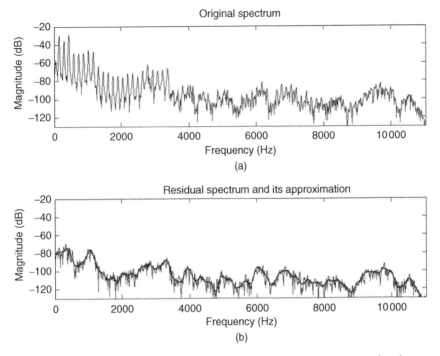

Figure 10.17 (a) Original spectrum. (b) Residual spectrum and approximation.

for fitting an nth-order polynomial to a magnitude spectrum. For our purposes, the line-segment approach is more flexible than LPC, and although LPC results in less analysis points, the flexibility is considered more important. For a comprehensive collection of different approximation techniques of the residual component see [Goo97].

Residual synthesis

From the stochastic model, parameterization of the residual component, we can synthesize a signal that should preserve the perceptually relevant characteristic of the residual signal. Like the sinusoidal synthesis, this synthesis can either be done in the time or in the frequency domains. Here we present a frequency-domain implementation. We generate a complete complex spectrum at each synthesis frame from the magnitude spectral envelope that approximated the residual.

The synthesis of a stochastic signal from the residual approximation can be understood as the generation of noise that has the frequency and amplitude characteristics described by the spectral magnitude envelopes. The intuitive operation is to filter white noise with these frequency envelopes, that is, performing a time-varying filtering, which is generally implemented by the time-domain convolution of white noise with the impulse response corresponding to the spectral envelope of a frame. We can instead approximate it in the frequency domain (see Figure 10.18) by creating a magnitude spectrum from the estimated envelope, or its transformation, and generating a random phase spectrum with new values at each frame in order to avoid periodicity.

Once the harmonic and stochastic spectral components have been generated, we can compute the IFFT of each one, and add the resulting time-domain signals. A more efficient alternative is to directly add the spectrum of the residual component to that of the sinusoids. However, in this case we need to worry about windows. In the process of generating the noise spectrum there has not been any window applied, since the data was added directly into the spectrum without any

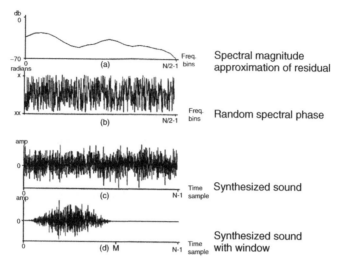

Figure 10.18   Stochastic synthesis.

smoothing consideration, but in the sinusoidal synthesis we have used a Blackman-Harris 92 dB, which is undone in the time domain after the IFFT. Therefore we should apply the same window in the noise spectrum before adding it to the sinusoidal spectrum. Convolving the transform of the Blackman-Harris 92 dB by the noise spectrum accomplishes this, and there is only the need to use the main lobe of the window since that includes most of its energy. This is implemented quite efficiently because it only involves a few bins and the window is symmetric. Then we can use a single IFFT for the combined spectrum. Finally in the time domain we undo the effect of the Blackman-Harris 92 dB and impose the triangular window. By an overlap-add process we combine successive frames to get the time-varying characteristics of the sound. In the implementation shown later on this is not done in order to be able to output the two components separately and thus be able to hear the harmonic and the stochastic components of the sound.

Several other approaches have been used for synthesizing the output of a sinusoidal plus stochastic analysis. These techniques, though, include modifications to the model as a whole. For instance, [FHC00] proposes to link the stochastic components to each sinusoid by using stochastic modulation to spread spectral energy away from the sinusoid's center frequency. With this technique each partial has an extra parameter, the bandwidth coefficient, which sets the balance between noise and sinusoidal energy.

Below is the code of a complete system using a harmonic plus stochastic model:

M-file 10.13 (hpsmodel.m)

```
function [y,yh,ys] = hpsmodel(x,fs,w,N,t,nH,minf0,maxf0,f0et,maxhd,stocf)
% Authors: J. Bonada, X. Serra, X. Amatriain, A. Loscos
% Analysis/synthesis of a sound using the sinusoidal harmonic model
% x: input sound, fs: sampling rate, w: analysis window (odd size),
% N: FFT size (minimum 512), t: threshold in negative dB,
% nH: maximum number of harmonics, minf0: minimum f0 frequency in Hz,
% maxf0: maximim f0 frequency in Hz,
% f0et: error threshold in the f0 detection (ex: 5),
% maxhd: max. relative deviation in harmonic detection (ex: .2)
% stocf: decimation factor of mag spectrum for stochastic analysis
% y: output sound, yh: harmonic component, ys: stochastic component
M = length(w);   % analysis window size
Ns = 1024;                        % FFT size for synthesis
```

```
H = 256;                              % hop size for analysis and synthesis
N2 = N/2+1;                           % half-size of spectrum
soundlength = length(x);             % length of input sound array
hNs = Ns/2;                           % half synthesis window size
hM = (M-1)/2;                         % half analysis window size
pin = max(hNs+1,1+hM);   % initialize sound pointer to middle of analysis window
pend = soundlength-max(hM,hNs);         % last sample to start a frame
fftbuffer = zeros(N,1);              % initialize buffer for FFT
yh = zeros(soundlength+Ns/2,1);      % output sine component
ys = zeros(soundlength+Ns/2,1);      % output residual component
w = w/sum(w);                         % normalize analysis window
sw = zeros(Ns,1);
ow = triang(2*H-1);                   % overlapping window
ovidx = Ns/2+1-H+1:Ns/2+H;           % overlap indexes
sw(ovidx) = ow(1:2*H-1);
bh = blackmanharris(Ns);              % synthesis window
bh = bh ./ sum(bh);                   % normalize synthesis window
wr = bh;                              % window for residual
sw(ovidx) = sw(ovidx) ./ bh(ovidx);
sws = H*hanning(Ns)/2;                % synthesis window for stochastic
while pin<pend
  %-----analysis-----%
  xw = x(pin-hM:pin+hM).*w(1:M);     % window the input sound
  fftbuffer(:) = 0;                  % reset buffer
  fftbuffer(1:(M+1)/2) = xw((M+1)/2:M); % zero-phase window in fftbuffer
  fftbuffer(N-(M-1)/2+1:N) = xw(1:(M-1)/2);
  X = fft(fftbuffer);                % compute the FFT
  mX = 20*log10(abs(X(1:N2)));       % magnitude spectrum
  pX = unwrap(angle(X(1:N/2+1)));    % unwrapped phase spectrum
  ploc = 1 + find((mX(2:N2-1)>t) .* (mX(2:N2-1)>mX(3:N2)) ...
               .* (mX(2:N2-1)>mX(1:N2-2)));     % find peaks
  [ploc,pmag,pphase] = peakinterp(mX,pX,ploc);     % refine peak values
  f0 = f0detectiontwm(mX,fs,ploc,pmag,f0et,minf0,maxf0);  % find f0
  hloc = zeros(nH,1);                % initialize harmonic locations
  hmag = zeros(nH,1)-100;            % initialize harmonic magnitudes
  hphase = zeros(nH,1);              % initialize harmonic phases
  hf = (f0>0).*(f0.*(1:nH));         % initialize harmonic frequencies
  hi = 1;                            % initialize harmonic index
  npeaks = length(ploc);             % number of peaks found
  while (f0>0 && hi<=nH && hf(hi)<fs/2)  % find harmonic peaks
    [dev,pei] = min(abs((ploc(1:npeaks)-1)/N*fs-hf(hi)));    % closest peak
    if ((hi==1 || ~any(hloc(1:hi-1)==ploc(pei))) && dev<maxhd*hf(hi))
      hloc(hi) = ploc(pei);          % harmonic locations
      hmag(hi) = pmag(pei);          % harmonic magnitudes
      hphase(hi) = pphase(pei);      % harmonic phases
    end
    hi = hi+1;                       % increase harmonic index
  end
  hloc(1:hi-1) = (hloc(1:hi-1)~=0).*((hloc(1:hi-1)-1)*Ns/N);  % synth. locs
  ri= pin-hNs;                       % input sound pointer for residual analysis
  xr = x(ri:ri+Ns-1).*wr(1:Ns);      % window the input sound
  Xr = fft(fftshift(xr));            % compute FFT for residual analysis
  Yh = genspecsines(hloc(1:hi-1),hmag,hphase,Ns);        % generate sines
  Yr = Xr-Yh;                        % get the residual complex spectrum
  mYr = abs(Yr(1:Ns/2+1));           % magnitude spectrum of residual
  mYsenv = decimate(mYr,stocf);      % decimate the magnitude spectrum
  %-----synthesis-----%
  mYs = interp(mYsenv,stocf);           % interpolate to original size
  roffset = ceil(stocf/2)-1;            % interpolated array offset
  mYs = [ mYs(1)*ones(roffset,1); mYs(1:Ns/2+1-roffset) ];
  pYs = 2*pi*rand(Ns/2+1,1);            % generate phase random values
  mYs1 = [mYs(1:Ns/2+1); mYs(Ns/2:-1:2)];  % create magnitude spectrum
  pYs1 = [pYs(1:Ns/2+1); -1*pYs(Ns/2:-1:2)]; % create phase spectrum
```

```
Ys = mYs1.*cos(pYs1)+1i*mYs1.*sin(pYs1);    % compute complex spectrum
yhw = fftshift(real(ifft(Yh)));             % sines in time domain using IFFT
ysw = fftshift(real(ifft(Ys)));             % stoc. in time domain using IFFT
yh(ri:ri+Ns-1) = yh(ri:ri+Ns-1)+yhw(1:Ns).*sw;   % overlap-add for sines
ys(ri:ri+Ns-1) = ys(ri:ri+Ns-1)+ysw(1:Ns).*sws;  % overlap-add for stoch.
pin = pin+H;                                % advance the sound pointer
end
y= yh+ys; % sum sines and stochastic
```

This code extends the implementation of the harmonic plus residual with the approximation of the residual and the synthesis of a stochastic signal. It first approximates the residual magnitude spectrum using the function `decimate` from **MATLAB**. This function resamples a data array at a lower rate after lowpass filtering and using a decimation factor, `stocf`, given by the user. At synthesis a complete magnitude spectrum is generated by interpolating the approximated envelope using the function `interp`. This is a **MATLAB** function that re-samples data at a higher rate using lowpass interpolation. The corresponding phase spectrum is generated with a random number generator, the function `rand`. The output signal, y(n), is the sum of the harmonic and the stochastic components.

10.4   Effects

In this section we introduce a set of effects and transformations that can be added to some of the analysis-synthesis frameworks that have just been presented. To do that we first need to change a few things on the implementations given above in order to make them suitable for incorporating the code for the transformations. We have to add new variables to handle the synthesis data and for controlling effects. Other modifications in the code are related to peak continuation and phase propagation. We first focus on the sinusoidal plus residual model, and next we will use the harmonic-based model.

10.4.1   Sinusoidal plus residual

In the implementation of the sinusoidal plus residual model presented, now we use different variables for analysis and synthesis parameters and keep a history of the last frame values. This is required for continuing analysis spectral peaks and propagating synthesis phases. The peak continuation implementation is really simple: each current frame peak is connected to the closest peak in frequency of the last frame. The phase propagation is also straightforward: it assumes that the frequency of connected peaks evolves linearly between consecutive frames. Note that when computing the residual we have to be careful to subtract the analysis sinusoids (not the synthesis ones) to the input signal. Another significant change is that here we use the parameter `maxnS` to limit the number of sinusoids. With that restriction, peaks found are sorted by energy and only the first `maxnS` are taken into account.

M-file 10.14 (spsmodel.m)

```
function [y,yh,ys] = spsmodel(x,fs,w,N,t,maxnS,stocf)
% Authors: J. Bonada, X. Serra, X. Amatriain, A. Loscos
% Analysis/synthesis of a sound using the sinusoidal harmonic model
% x: input sound, fs: sampling rate, w: analysis window (odd size),
% N: FFT size (minimum 512), t: threshold in negative dB,
% maxnS: maximum number of sinusoids,
% stocf: decimation factor of mag spectrum for stochastic analysis
% y: output sound, yh: harmonic component, ys: stochastic component
M = length(w);                      % analysis window size
```

```
Ns = 1024;                              % FFT size for synthesis
H = 256;                                % hop size for analysis and synthesis
N2 = N/2+1;                             % half-size of spectrum
soundlength = length(x);                % length of input sound array
hNs = Ns/2;                            % half synthesis window size
hM = (M-1)/2;                          % half analysis window size
pin = max(hNs+1,1+hM);   % initialize sound pointer to middle of analysis window
pend = soundlength-max(hM,hNs);         % last sample to start a frame
fftbuffer = zeros(N,1);                % initialize buffer for FFT
yh = zeros(soundlength+Ns/2,1);        % output sine component
ys = zeros(soundlength+Ns/2,1);        % output residual component
w = w/sum(w);                          % normalize analysis window
sw = zeros(Ns,1);
ow = triang(2*H-1);                     % overlapping window
ovidx = Ns/2+1-H+1:Ns/2+H;              % overlap indexes
sw(ovidx) = ow(1:2*H-1);
bh = blackmanharris(Ns);                % synthesis window
bh = bh ./ sum(bh);                     % normalize synthesis window
wr = bh;                                % window for residual
sw(ovidx) = sw(ovidx) ./ bh(ovidx);
sws = H*hanning(Ns)/2;                   % synthesis window for stochastic
lastysloc = zeros(maxnS,1);              % initialize synthesis harmonic locations
ysphase = 2*pi*rand(maxnS,1);            % initialize synthesis harmonic phases
fridx = 0;
while pin<pend
    %-----analysis-----%
    xw = x(pin-hM:pin+hM).*w(1:M);       % window the input sound
    fftbuffer = fftbuffer*0;             % reset buffer;
    fftbuffer(1:(M+1)/2) = xw((M+1)/2:M);  % zero-phase window in fftbuffer
    fftbuffer(N-(M-1)/2+1:N) = xw(1:(M-1)/2);
    X = fft(fftbuffer);                  % compute the FFT
    mX = 20*log10(abs(X(1:N2)));         % magnitude spectrum
    pX = unwrap(angle(X(1:N/2+1)));      % unwrapped phase spectrum
    ploc = 1 + find((mX(2:N2-1)>t) .* (mX(2:N2-1)>mX(3:N2)) ...
                 .* (mX(2:N2-1)>mX(1:N2-2)));        % find peaks
    [ploc,pmag,pphase] = peakinterp(mX,pX,ploc);      % refine peak values
    % sort by magnitude
    [smag,I] = sort(pmag(:),1,'descend');
    nS = min(maxnS,length(find(smag>t)));
    sloc = ploc(I(1:nS));
    sphase = pphase(I(1:nS));
    if (fridx==0)
        % update last frame data for first frame
        lastnS = nS;
        lastsloc = sloc;
        lastsmag = smag;
        lastsphase = sphase;
    end
    % connect sinusoids to last frame lnS (lastsloc,lastsphase,lastsmag)
    sloc(1:nS) = (sloc(1:nS)~=0).*((sloc(1:nS)-1)*Ns/N);  % synth. locs
    lastidx = zeros(1,nS);
    for i=1:nS
      [dev,idx] = min(abs(sloc(i) - lastsloc(1:lastnS)));
      lastidx(i) = idx;
    end
    ri= pin-hNs;                         % input sound pointer for residual analysis
    xr = x(ri:ri+Ns-1).*wr(1:Ns);        % window the input sound
    Xr = fft(fftshift(xr));              % compute FFT for residual analysis
    Xh = genspecsines(sloc,smag,sphase,Ns);  % generate sines
    Xr = Xr-Xh;                          % get the residual complex spectrum
    mXr = 20*log10(abs(Xr(1:Ns/2+1)));   % magnitude spectrum of residual
    mXsenv = decimate(max(-200,mXr),stocf);  % decimate the magnitude spectrum
                                         % and avoid -Inf
```

```
%-----synthesis data-----%
ysloc = sloc;                            % synthesis locations
ysmag = smag(1:nS);                      % synthesis magnitudes
mYsenv = mXsenv;                         % synthesis residual envelope
%-----transformations-----%
%-----synthesis-----%
if (fridx==0)
    lastysphase = ysphase;
end
if (nS>lastnS)
    lastysphase = [ lastysphase ; zeros(nS-lastnS,1) ];
    lastysloc = [ lastysloc ; zeros(nS-lastnS,1) ];
end
ysphase = lastysphase(lastidx(1:nS)) + 2*pi*( ...
         lastysloc(lastidx(1:nS))+ysloc)/2/Ns*H; % propagate phases
lastysloc = ysloc;
lastysphase = ysphase;
lastnS = nS;                             % update last frame data
lastsloc = sloc;                         % update last frame data
lastsmag = smag;                         % update last frame data
lastsphase = sphase;                     % update last frame data
Yh = genspecsines(ysloc,ysmag,ysphase,Ns); % generate sines
mYs = interp(mYsenv,stocf);              % interpolate to original size
roffset = ceil(stocf/2)-1;               % interpolated array offset
mYs = [ mYs(1)*ones(roffset,1); mYs(1:Ns/2+1-roffset) ];
mYs = 10.^(mYs/20);                      % dB to linear magnitude
pYs = 2*pi*rand(Ns/2+1,1);       % generate phase spectrum with random values
mYs1 = [mYs(1:Ns/2+1); mYs(Ns/2:-1:2)]; % create complete magnitude spectrum
pYs1 = [pYs(1:Ns/2+1); -1*pYs(Ns/2:-1:2)]; % create complete phase spectrum
Ys = mYs1.*cos(pYs1)+1i*mYs1.*sin(pYs1); % compute complex spectrum
yhw = fftshift(real(ifft(Yh)));     % sines in time domain using inverse FFT
ysw = fftshift(real(ifft(Ys)));     % stochastic in time domain using IFFT
yh(ri:ri+Ns-1) = yh(ri:ri+Ns-1)+yhw(1:Ns).*sw;  % overlap-add for sines
ys(ri:ri+Ns-1) = ys(ri:ri+Ns-1)+ysw(1:Ns).*sws; % overlap-add for stochastic
pin = pin+H;                             % advance the sound pointer
fridx = fridx+1;
end
y= yh+ys;                                % sum sines and stochastic
```

Now we have an implementation of the sinusoidal plus residual model ready to be used for sound transformations. In order to use the different effects we just have to add the code of the effect after the line %-----transformations-----%.

Filtering

Filters are probably the paradigm of a classical effect. In our implementation of filtering we take advantage of the sinusoidal plus residual model, which allows us to modify the amplitude of any partial present in the sinusoidal component.

For example, we can implement a band pass filter defined by (x, y) points where x is the frequency value in Hertzs and y is the amplitude factor to apply (see Figure 10.19). In the example code given below, we define a band pass filter which supreses sinusoidal frequencies not included in the range [2100 3000].

M-file 10.15 (spsfiltering.m)

```
% Authors: J. Bonada, X. Serra, X. Amatriain, A. Loscos
%----- filtering -----%
Filter=[    0  2099 2100 3000 3001 fs/2;   % Hz
         -200  -200    0    0 -200 -200 ]; % db
ysmag = ysmag+interp1(Filter(1,:),Filter(2,:),ysloc/Ns*fs);
```

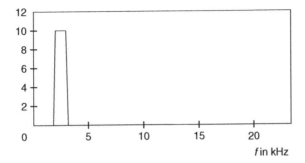

Figure 10.19 Bandpass filter with arbitrary resolution.

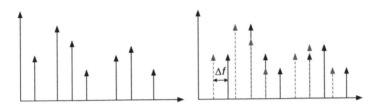

Figure 10.20 Frequency shift of the partials.

Frequency shifting

In this example we introduce a frequency shift factor to all the partials of our sound (see Figure 10.20). Note, though, that if the input sound is harmonic, then adding a constant to every partial produces a sound that will be inharmonic.

M-file 10.16 (spsfrequencyshifting.m)

```
% Authors: J. Bonada, X. Serra, X. Amatriain, A. Loscos
%-----frequency shift-----%
fshift = 100;
ysloc = (ysloc>0).*(ysloc + fshift/fs*Ns); % frequency shift in Hz
```

Frequency stretching

Another effect we can implement following this same idea is to add a stretching factor to the frequency of every partial. The relative shift of every partial will depend on its original partial index, following the formula:

$$f_i = f_i \cdot f_{stretch}^{(i-1)}. \tag{10.17}$$

Figure 10.21 illustrates this frequency stretching.

M-file 10.17 (spsfrequencystretching.m)

```
%Authors: J. Bonada, X. Serra, X. Amatriain, A. Loscos
%-----frequency stretch-----%
fstretch = 1.1;
ysloc = ysloc .* (fstretch.^[0:length(ysloc)-1]');
```

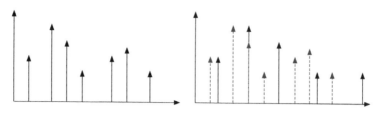

Figure 10.21   Frequency stretching.

Frequency scaling

In the same way, we can scale all the partials multiplying them by a given scaling factor. Note that this effect will act as a pitch shifter without timbre preservation.

M-file 10.18 (spsfrequencyscaling.m)

```
% Authors: J. Bonada, X. Serra, X. Amatriain, A. Loscos
%-----frequency scale-----%
fscale = 1.2;
ysloc = ysloc*fscale;
```

Time scaling

Time scaling is trickier and we have to modify some aspects of the main processing loop. We now use two different variables for the input and output times (pin and pout). The idea is that the analysis hop size will not be constant, but will depend on the time-scaling factor, while the synthesis hop size will be fixed. If the sound is played slower (time expansion), then the analysis hop size will be smaller and pin will be incremented by a smaller amount. Otherwise, when the sound is played faster (time compression), the hop size will be larger. Instead of using a constant time-scaling factor, here we opt for a more flexible approach by setting a mapping between input and output time. This allows, for instance, easy alignment of two audio signals by using synchronization onset times as the mapping function.

The following code sets the input/output time mapping. It has to be added at the beginning of the function. In this example, the sound is time expanded by a factor of 2.

M-file 10.19 (spstimemappingparams.m)

```
% Authors: J. Bonada, X. Serra, X. Amatriain, A. Loscos
%-----time mapping-----%
timemapping = [ 0  1;                         % input time (sec)
                0  2 ];                        % output time (sec)
timemapping = timemapping *soundlength/fs;
outsoundlength = 1+round(timemapping(2,end)*fs); % length of output sound
```

Since the output and input durations may be different, we have to change the creation of the output signal variables so that they match the output duration.

M-file 10.20 (spstimemappinginit.m)

```
% Authors: J. Bonada, X. Serra, X. Amatriain, A. Loscos
yh = zeros(outsoundlength+Ns/2,1);            % output sine component
ys = zeros(outsoundlength+Ns/2,1);            % output residual component
```

Finally, we modify the processing loop. Note the changes in the last part, where the synthesis frame is added to the output vectors yh and ys. Note also that pin is computed from the synthesis time pout by interpolating the time-mapping function.

M-file 10.21 (spstimemappingprocess.m)

```
% Authors: J. Bonada, X. Serra, X. Amatriain, A. Loscos
poutend = outsoundlength-hNs;                % last sample to start a frame
pout = pin;
minpin = 1+max(hNs,hM);
maxpin = min(length(x)-max(hNs,hM)-1);
fridx = 0;
while pout<poutend
  pin = round( interp1(TM(2,:),TM(1,:),pout/fs,'linear','extrap') * fs );
  pin = max(minpin,pin);
  pin = min(maxpin,pin);
  %-----analysis-----%
  (...)
  ro = pout-hNs;                             % output sound pointer for overlap
  yh(ro:ro+Ns-1) = yh(ro:ro+Ns-1)+yhw(1:Ns).*sw;  % overlap-add for sines
  ys(ro:ro+Ns-1) = ys(ro:ro+Ns-1)+ysw(1:Ns).*sws; % overlap-add for stochastic
  pout = pout+H;                             % advance the sound pointer
  fridx = fridx+1;
end
y= yh+ys;                                    % sum sines and stochastic
```

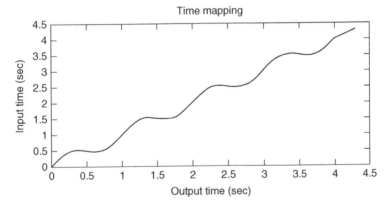

Figure 10.22 Complex time mapping.

With the proposed time-mapping control we can play the input sound in forward or reverse directions at any speed, or even freeze it. The following mapping uses a sinusoidal function to combine all these possibilities (see Figure 10.22). When applied to the *fairytale.wav* audio example, it produces a really funny result.

M-file 10.22 (spstimemappingcomplex.m)

```
% Authors: J. Bonada, X. Serra, X. Amatriain, A. Loscos
tm = 0.01:0.01:.93;
timemapping = [  0 tm+0.05*sin(8.6*pi*tm) 1 ;  % input time --> keep end value
                 0 tm                     1 ]; % output time
timemapping = timemapping*length(x)/fs;
```

10.4.2 Harmonic plus residual

We will now use the harmonic plus residual model and also modify the implementation above. We use different variables for analysis and synthesis parameters and we keep a history of the last frame values. As before, phase propagation is implemented assuming linear frequency evolution of harmonics. Peak continuation, however, works differently: we just connect the closest peaks to each predicted harmonic frequency. In addition, we add the modifications required to able to perform time scaling. When we apply effects to harmonic sounds, sometimes we perceive the output harmonic and residual components to be somehow unrelated, in a way that loses part of the cohesion found in the original sound. Applying a comb filter to the residual determined by the synthesis fundamental frequency helps to merge both components and perceive them as a single entity. We have added such filter to the code below. Note also that the Yin algorithm is used by default when computing the fundamental frequency.

On the other hand, we can go a step further by implementing several transformations in the same code, and adding the corresponding control parameters as function arguments. This has the advantage that we can easily combine transformations to achieve more complex effects. Moreover, as we will see, this is great for generating several outputs with different effects to be concatenated or played simultaneously.

M-file 10.23 (hpsmodelparams.m)

```
function [y,yh,ys] = hpsmodelparams(x,fs,w,N,t,nH,minf0,maxf0,f0et,...
                                maxhd,stocf,timemapping)
% Authors: J. Bonada, X. Serra, X. Amatriain, A. Loscos
% Analysis/synthesis of a sound using the sinusoidal harmonic model
% x: input sound, fs: sampling rate, w: analysis window (odd size),
% N: FFT size (minimum 512), t: threshold in negative dB,
% nH: maximum number of harmonics, minf0: minimum f0 frequency in Hz,
% maxf0: maximim f0 frequency in Hz,
% f0et: error threshold in the f0 detection (ex: 5),
% maxhd: max. relative deviation in harmonic detection (ex: .2)
% stocf: decimation factor of mag spectrum for stochastic analysis
% timemapping: mapping between input and output time (sec)
% y: output sound, yh: harmonic component, ys: stochastic component
if length(timemapping)==0                % argument not specified
    timemapping =[   0 length(x)/fs;     % input time
                     0 length(x)/fs ];   % output time
end
M = length(w);                           % analysis window size
Ns = 1024;                               % FFT size for synthesis
H = 256;                                 % hop size for analysis and synthesis
N2 = N/2+1;                              % half-size of spectrum
hNs = Ns/2;                              % half synthesis window size
hM = (M-1)/2;                            % half analysis window size
fftbuffer = zeros(N,1);                  % initialize buffer for FFT
outsoundlength = 1+round(timemapping(2,end)*fs);     % length of output sound
yh = zeros(outsoundlength+Ns/2,1);       % output sine component
ys = zeros(outsoundlength+Ns/2,1);       % output residual component
w = w/sum(w);                            % normalize analysis window
sw = zeros(Ns,1);
ow = triang(2*H-1);                      % overlapping window
ovidx = Ns/2+1-H+1:Ns/2+H;              % overlap indexes
sw(ovidx) = ow(1:2*H-1);
bh = blackmanharris(Ns);                 % synthesis window
bh = bh ./ sum(bh);                      % normalize synthesis window
wr = bh;                                 % window for residual
sw(ovidx) = sw(ovidx) ./ bh(ovidx);
sws = H*hanning(Ns)/2;                   % synthesis window for stochastic
lastyhloc = zeros(nH,1);                 % initialize synthesis harmonic locations
```

```
yhphase = 2*pi*rand(nH,1);              % initialize synthesis harmonic phases
poutend = outsoundlength-max(hM,H);     % last sample to start a frame
pout = 1+max(hNs,hM);                   % initialize sound pointer to middle of analysis window
minpin = 1+max(hNs,hM);
maxpin = min(length(x)-max(hNs,hM)-1);
while pout<poutend
  pin = round( interp1(timemapping(2,:),timemapping(1,:),pout/fs,'linear',...
                'extrap') * fs );
  pin = max(minpin,pin);
  pin = min(maxpin,pin);
  %-----analysis-----%
  xw = x(pin-hM:pin+hM).*w(1:M);        % window the input sound
  fftbuffer(:) = 0;                     % reset buffer
  fftbuffer(1:(M+1)/2) = xw((M+1)/2:M); % zero-phase window in fftbuffer
  fftbuffer(N-(M-1)/2+1:N) = xw(1:(M-1)/2);
  X = fft(fftbuffer);                   % compute the FFT
  mX = 20*log10(abs(X(1:N2)));          % magnitude spectrum
  pX = unwrap(angle(X(1:N/2+1)));       % unwrapped phase spectrum
  ploc = 1 + find((mX(2:N2-1)>t) .* (mX(2:N2-1)>mX(3:N2)) ...
               .* (mX(2:N2-1)>mX(1:N2-2)));     % find peaks
  [ploc,pmag,pphase] = peakinterp(mX,pX,ploc);  % refine peak values
  yinws = round(fs*0.0125);            % using approx. a 12.5 ms window for yin
  yinws = yinws+mod(yinws,2);          % make it even
  yb = pin-yinws/2;
  ye = pin+yinws/2+yinws;
  if (yb<1 || ye>length(x))            % out of boundaries
     f0 = 0;
  else
     f0 = f0detectionyin(x(yb:ye),fs,yinws,minf0,maxf0); % compute f0
  end
  hloc = zeros(nH,1);                  % initialize harmonic locations
  hmag = zeros(nH,1)-100;              % initialize harmonic magnitudes
  hphase = zeros(nH,1);                % initialize harmonic phases
  hf = (f0>0).*(f0.*(1:nH));           % initialize harmonic frequencies
  hi = 1;                              % initialize harmonic index
  npeaks = length(ploc);              % number of peaks found
  while (f0>0 && hi<=nH && hf(hi)<fs/2) % find harmonic peaks
    [dev,pei] = min(abs((ploc(1:npeaks)-1)/N*fs-hf(hi)));   % closest peak
    if ((hi==1 || ~any(hloc(1:hi-1)==ploc(pei))) && dev<maxhd*hf(hi))
      hloc(hi) = ploc(pei);            % harmonic locations
      hmag(hi) = pmag(pei);            % harmonic magnitudes
      hphase(hi) = pphase(pei);        % harmonic phases
    end
    hi = hi+1;                         % increase harmonic index
  end
  hloc(1:hi-1) = (hloc(1:hi-1)~=0).*((hloc(1:hi-1)-1)*Ns/N);   % synth. locs
  ri= pin-hNs;                         % input sound pointer for residual analysis
  xr = x(ri:ri+Ns-1).*wr(1:Ns);        % window the input sound
  Xr = fft(fftshift(xr));              % compute FFT for residual analysis
  Xh = genspecsines(hloc(1:hi-1),hmag,hphase,Ns);     % generate sines
  Xr = Xr-Xh;                          % get the residual complex spectrum
  mXr = 20*log10(abs(Xr(1:Ns/2+1)));   % magnitude spectrum of residual
  mXsenv = decimate(max(-200,mXr),stocf); % decimate the magnitude spectrum
                                       % and avoid -Inf
  %-----synthesis data-----%
  yhloc = hloc;                        % synthesis harmonics locs
  yhmag = hmag;                        % synthesis harmonic amplitudes
  mYsenv = mXsenv;                     % synthesis residual envelope
  yf0 = f0;                            % synthesis f0
  %-----transformations-----%
  %-----synthesis-----%
  yhphase = yhphase + 2*pi*(lastyhloc+yhloc)/2/Ns*H;   % propagate phases
  lastyhloc = yhloc;
```

```
Yh = genspecsines(yhloc,yhmag,yhphase,Ns);      % generate sines
mYs = interp(mYsenv,stocf);                      % interpolate to original size
roffset = ceil(stocf/2)-1;                       % interpolated array offset
mYs = [ mYs(1)*ones(roffset,1); mYs(1:Ns/2+1-roffset) ];
mYs = 10.^(mYs/20);                              % dB to linear magnitude
if (f0>0)
    mYs = mYs .* cos(pi*[0:Ns/2]'/Ns*fs/yf0).^2;  % filter residual
end
fc = 1+round(500/fs*Ns);                         % 500 Hz
mYs(1:fc) = mYs(1:fc) .* ([0:fc-1]'/(fc-1)).^2;  % HPF
pYs = 2*pi*rand(Ns/2+1,1);          % generate phase spectrum with random values
mYs1 = [mYs(1:Ns/2+1); mYs(Ns/2:-1:2)]; % create complete magnitude spectrum
pYs1 = [pYs(1:Ns/2+1); -1*pYs(Ns/2:-1:2)]; % create complete phase spectrum
Ys = mYs1.*cos(pYs1)+1i*mYs1.*sin(pYs1);    % compute complex spectrum
yhw = fftshift(real(ifft(Yh)));          % sines in time domain using IFFT
ysw = fftshift(real(ifft(Ys)));          % stochastic in time domain using IFFT
ro= pout-hNs;                            % output sound pointer for overlap
yh(ro:ro+Ns-1) = yh(ro:ro+Ns-1)+yhw(1:Ns).*sw;  % overlap-add for sines
ys(ro:ro+Ns-1) = ys(ro:ro+Ns-1)+ysw(1:Ns).*sws; % overlap-add for stochastic
pout = pout+H;                           % advance the sound pointer
end
y= yh+ys;                                % sum sines and stochastic
```

In the previous code the phase of each partial is propagated independently using the estimated frequencies. This has two disadvantages: (a) inaccuracies in frequency estimation add errors to the phase propagation that are accumulated over time; (b) the phase information of the input signal is not used, so its phase behavior will not be transferred to the output signal. In many cases, this results not only in a loss of presence and definition, often referred to as *phasiness*, but also makes the synthetic signal to sound artificial, especially at low pitches and transitions. This issue is very much related to the concept of shape invariance, which we introduce next.

Although we focus the following discussion on the human voice, it can be generalized to many musical instruments and sound-production systems. In a simplified model of voice production, a train of impulses at the pitch rate excites a resonant filter (i.e., the vocal tract). According to this model, a speaker or singer changes the pitch of his voice by modifying the rate at which those impulses occur. An interesting observation is that the shape of the time-domain waveform signal around the impulse onsets is roughly independent of the pitch, but it depends mostly on the impulse response of the vocal tract. This characteristic is called *shape invariance*. In terms of frequency domain, this shape is related to the amplitude, frequency and phase values of the harmonics at the impulse onset times. A given processing technique will be shape invariant if it preserves the phase coherence between the various harmonics at estimated pulse onsets. Figure 10.23 compares the results of a time-scaling transformation using shape-variant and -invariant methods.

Several algorithms have been proposed in the literature regarding the harmonic phase-coherence for both phase-vocoder and sinusoidal modeling (for example [DiF98, Lar03]). Most of them are based on the idea of defining pitch-synchronous input and output onset times and reproducing at the output onset times the phase relationship existing in the original signal at the input onset times. Nevertheless, in order to obtain the best sound quality, it is desirable that for speech signals those detected onsets match the actual glottal pulse onsets [Bon08].

The following code uses this idea to implement a shape-invariant transformation. It should be inserted in the previous code after the line where synthesis phases are propagated, just at the beginning of the %-----synthesis-----% section.

M-file 10.24 (shapeinvariance.m)

```
% Authors: J. Bonada, X. Serra, X. Amatriain, A. Loscos
% shape invariance:
% assume pulse onsets to match zero phase of the fundamental
```

```
% and ideal harmonic distribution
pos = mod(hphase(1),2*pi)/2/pi;          % input normalized period position
ypos = mod(yhphase(1),2*pi)/2/pi;        % output normalized period position
yhphase = hphase + (ypos-pos)*2*pi*[1:length(yhloc)]';
```

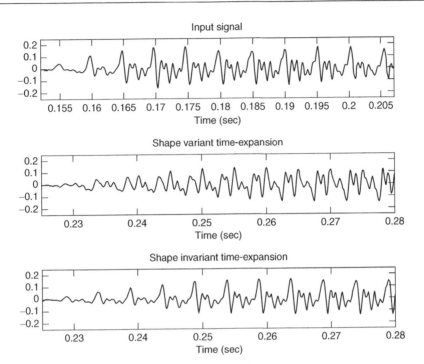

Figure 10.23 Shape-variant and -invariant transformations. In this example the input signal is time-expanded by a factor of 1.5.

Harmonic filtering

As shown, a filter does not need to be characterized by a traditional transfer function, but a more complex filter can be defined. For example, the following code filters out the even partials of the input sound. If applied to a sound with a broadband spectrum, like a vocal sound, it will convert it to a clarinet-like sound.

M-file 10.25 (hpsmodelharmfiltering.m)

```
% Authors: J. Bonada, X. Serra, X. Amatriain, A. Loscos
%-----voice to clarinet-----%
yhloc(2:2:end)=0; % set to zero the frequency of even harmonics
                  % so that they won't be synthesized
```

Pitch discretization

An interesting effect can be accomplished by forcing the pitch to take the nearest frequency value of the temperate scale. It is indeed a very particular case of pitch transposition, where the pitch is quantified to one of the 12 semitones into which an octave is divided. This effect is widely used on vocal sounds for dance music and is many times referred to with the misleading name of the vocoder effect.

M-file 10.26 (hpsmodelpitchdisc.m)

```
% Authors: J. Bonada, X. Serra, X. Amatriain, A. Loscos
%-----pitch discretization to temperate scale-----%
if (f0>0) % it has harmonics
  nst = round(12*log2(f0/55));      % closest semitone
  discpitch = 55*2^(nst/12);        % discretized pitch
  fscale = discpitch/f0 ;           % pitch transposition factor
  yf0 = f0*fscale;                  % synthesis f0
  yhloc = yhloc*fscale;
end
```

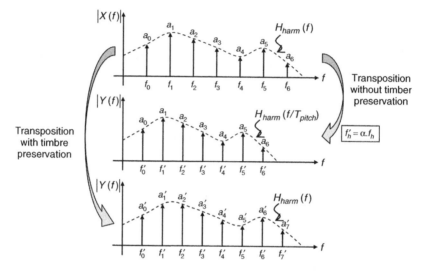

Figure 10.24 Pitch transposition. The signal whose transform is represented in the top view is transposed to a lower pitch. The middle view shows the result when only harmonic frequencies are modified, whereas in the bottom view representation both harmonic frequencies and amplitudes have been modified so that the timbre is preserved.

Pitch transposition with timbre preservation

Pitch transposition is the scaling of all the partials of a sound by the same multiplying factor. An undesirable effect is obtained if the amplitude of partials is not modified. In that case, the timbre is scaled as well, producing the typical *Mickey Mouse* effect. This undesired effect can be avoided using the analysis harmonic spectral envelope, which is obtained from the interpolation of the harmonic amplitude values. Then, when synthesizing, we compute harmonic amplitudes interpolating this same envelope at their scaled frequency position. This is illustrated in Figure 10.24, where α is the frequency scaling factor, and H_{harm} the harmonic spectral envelope.

M-file 10.27 (transpositionpreservingtimbre.m)

```
% Authors: J. Bonada, X. Serra, X. Amatriain, A. Loscos
%-----pitch transposition and timbre scaling-----%
fscale = 0.9;
yhloc = yhloc*fscale;            % scale harmonic frequencies
yf0 = f0*fscale;                 % synthesis fundamental frequency
```

```
% harmonics
if (f0>0)
  thloc = interp1( timbremapping(2,:), timbremapping(1,:), ...
                  yhloc/Ns*fs) / fs*Ns; % mapped harmonic freqs.
  idx = find(hloc>0 & hloc<Ns*.5);        % harmonic indexes in frequency range
  yhmag = interp1([0; hloc(idx); Ns],[hmag(1); hmag(idx); hmag(end)],thloc);
                                        % interpolated envelope
end
% residual
  % frequency (Hz) of the last  coefficient
  frescoef = fs/2*length(mYsenv)*stocf/length(mXr);
  % mapped coef. indexes
  trescoef = interp1( timbremapping(2,:), timbremapping(1,:), ...
            min(fs/2,[0:length(mYsenv)-1]'/(length(mYsenv)-1)*frescoef) );
  % interpolated envelope
  mYsenv = interp1([0:length(mYsenv)-1],mYsenv, ...
                  trescoef/frescoef*(length(mYsenv)-1));
```

Vibrato and tremolo

Vibrato and tremolo are common effects used with different kinds of acoustical instruments, including the human voice. Both are low-frequency modulations: vibrato is applied to the frequency and tremolo to the amplitude of the partials. Note, though, that in this particular implementation, both effects share the same modulation frequency. The control parameters are expressed in perceptually meaning units so to ease an intuitive manipulation.

M-file 10.28 (hpsmodelvibandtrem.m)

```
% Authors: J. Bonada, X. Serra, X. Amatriain, A. Loscos
%-----vibrato and tremolo-----%
if (f0>0)
  vtf = 5;                            % vibrato-tremolo frequency in Hz
  va  = 50;                           % vibrato depth in cents
  td  = 3;                            % tremolo depth in dB
  sfscale = fscale*2^(va/1200*sin(2*pi*vtf*pin/fs));
  yhloc = yhloc*sfscale;              % synthesis harmonic locs
  yf0 = f0*sfscale;                   % synthesis f0
  idx = find(hloc>0 & hloc<Ns*.5);
  yhmag = interp1([0; hloc(idx); Ns],[ hmag(1); hmag(idx); ...
                  hmag(end) ],yhloc);  % interpolated envelope
  yhmag = yhmag + td*sin(2*pi*vtf*pin/fs); % tremolo
end
```

Timbre scaling

This is a very common, but still exciting transformation. The character of a voice changes significantly when timbre is scaled. Compressing the timbre produces deeper voices, whereas expanding it generates thinner and more female or childish-sounding utterances. Also, with the appropriate parameters, we can convincingly sound like a different person. In the following implementation, we define the timbre scaling with a mapping function between input and output frequencies. This is a very flexible and intuitive way of controlling the effect, and it is found in several voice transformation plug-ins that work in real time. In the following example, the low-frequency band of the spectrum (up to 5Khz) is compressed, so that deeper voices are generated. Note that the same timbre frequency mapping is applied to harmonic and residual components, although it would be straightforward to use separate controls.

M-file 10.29 (hpsmodeltimbrescaling.m)

```
% Authors: J. Bonada, X. Serra, X. Amatriain, A. Loscos
%-----timbre scaling-----%
timbremapping = [ 0  5000  fs/2;   % input frequency
                  0  4000  fs/2 ]; % output frequency
% harmonics
if (f0>0)
  thloc = interp1( timbremapping(2,:), timbremapping(1,:), ...
                  yhloc/Ns*fs) / fs*Ns; % mapped harmonic freqs.
  idx = find(hloc>0 & hloc<Ns*.5); % harmonic indexes in frequency range
  yhmag = interp1([0; hloc(idx); Ns],[hmag(1); hmag(idx); hmag(end)],thloc);
  % interpolated envelope
end
% residual
  % frequency (Hz) of the last  coefficient
  frescoef = fs/2*length(mYsenv)*stocf/length(mXr);
  % mapped coef. indexes
  trescoef = interp1( timbremapping(2,:), timbremapping(1,:), ...
            min(fs/2,[0:length(mYsenv)-1]'/(length(mYsenv)-1)*frescoef) );
  % interpolated envelope
  mYsenv = interp1([0:length(mYsenv)-1],mYsenv, ...
                  trescoef/frescoef*(length(mYsenv)-1));
```

Roughness

Although roughness is sometimes thought of as a symptom of some kind of vocal disorder [Chi94], this effect has been widely used by singers in order to resemble the voices of famous performers (Louis Armstrong or Tom Waits, for example). In this elemental approximation, we accomplish a similar effect by just applying a gain to the residual component of our analysis.

M-file 10.30 (hpsmodelroughness.m)

```
% Authors: J. Bonada, X. Serra, X. Amatriain, A. Loscos
%-----roughness-----%
if f0>0
        mYsenv = mXsenv + 12; % gain factor applied to the residual (dB)
end
```

10.4.3 Combined effects

By combining *basic* effects like the ones presented, we are able to create more complex effects. Especially we are able to step higher in the level of abstraction and get closer to what a naive user could ask for in a sound-transformation environment, such as: imagine having a gender control on a vocal processor... Next we present some examples of those transformations.

Gender change

Using some of the previous effects we can change the gender of a vocal sound. In the following example we want to convert a male voice into a female one. Female fundamental frequencies are typically higher than male ones, so we first apply a pitch transposition upwards. Although we could apply any transposition factors, one octave is a common choice, especially for singing, since then background music does not need to be transposed as well. A second required transformation is timbre scaling, more concretely timbre expansion. The reason is that females typically have shorter vocal tracts than males, which results in higher formant (i.e., resonance) frequencies.

It is also interesting to consider a shift in the spectral shape, especially if we want to generate convincing female singing of certain specific musical styles such as opera. The theoretical explanation is that trained female opera singers move the formants along with the fundamental, especially in the high pitch range, to avoid the fundamental being higher than the first formant frequency, which would result in a loss of intelligibility and effort efficiency. Although not implemented in the following code, this feature can be simply added by subtracting the frequency shift value in Hz to the variable `thloc` and limiting resulting values to the sound frequency range.

M-file 10.31 (hpsmodeltranspandtimbrescaling.m)

```
% Authors: J. Bonada, X. Serra, X. Amatriain, A. Loscos
%-----pitch transposition and timbre scaling-----%
yhloc = yhloc*fscale;              % scale harmonic frequencies
yf0 = f0*fscale;                   % synthesis fundamental frequency
% harmonics
if (f0>0)
  thloc = interp1( timbremapping(2,:), timbremapping(1,:), ...
                  yhloc/Ns*fs) / fs*Ns; % mapped harmonic freqs.
  idx = find(hloc>0 & hloc<Ns*.5);      % harmonic indexes in frequency range
  yhmag = interp1([0; hloc(idx); Ns],[hmag(1); hmag(idx); hmag(end)],thloc);
                                   % interpolated envelope
end
% residual
  % frequency (Hz) of the last  coefficient
  frescoef = fs/2*length(mYsenv)*stocf/length(mXr);
  % mapped coef. indexes
  trescoef = interp1( timbremapping(2,:), timbremapping(1,:), ...
            min(fs/2,[0:length(mYsenv)-1]'/(length(mYsenv)-1)*frescoef) );
  % interpolated envelope
  mYsenv = interp1([0:length(mYsenv)-1],mYsenv, ...
                  trescoef/frescoef*(length(mYsenv)-1));
```

Next, we have to add the effect controls `fscale` and `timbremapping` to M-file 10.23 as function arguments, as shown below.

M-file 10.32 (hpsmodelparamscall.m)

```
% Authors: J. Bonada, X. Serra, X. Amatriain, A. Loscos
function [y,yh,ys] =
  hpsmodelparams(x,fs,w,N,t,nH,minf0,maxf0,f0et,maxhd,stocf,timemapping,...
                fscale,timbremapping)
(...)
```

And finally we can call the function with appropriate parameters for generating the male to female gender conversion.

M-file 10.33 (maletofemale.m)

```
% Authors: J. Bonada, X. Serra, X. Amatriain, A. Loscos
%-----male to female-----%
[x,fs] = wavread('basket.wav');
w=[blackmanharris(1024);0];
fscale = 2;
timbremapping = [ 0  4000  fs/2;  % input frequency
                  0  5000  fs/2 ]; % output frequency
[y,yh,yr] = hpsmodelparams(x,fs,w,2048,-150,200,100,400,1,.2,10,...
                [],fscale,timbremapping);
```

Now it is straightforward to apply other gender conversions, just modifying the parameters and calling the function again.

M-file 10.34 (maletochild.m)

```
% Authors: J. Bonada, X. Serra, X. Amatriain, A. Loscos
%-----male to child-----%
[x,fs] = wavread('basket.wav');
w=[blackmanharris(1024);0];
fscale = 2;
timbremapping = [ 0   3600  fs/2;   % input frequency
                  0   5000  fs/2 ]; % output frequency
[y,yh,yr] = hpsmodelparams(x,fs,w,2048,-150,200,100,400,1,.2,10,...
                           [],fscale,timbremapping);
```

M-file 10.35 (femaletomale.m)

```
% Authors: J. Bonada, X. Serra, X. Amatriain, A. Loscos
%-----female to male-----%
[x,fs] = wavread('meeting.wav');
w=[blackmanharris(1024);0];
fscale = 0.5;
timbremapping = [ 0   5000  fs/2;   % input frequency
                  0   4000  fs/2 ]; % output frequency
[y,yh,yr] = hpsmodelparams(x,fs,w,2048,-150,200,100,400,1,.2,10,...
                           [],fscale,timbremapping);
```

Adding even more transformations we can achieve more sophisticated gender changes. For instance, an exaggerated vibrato applied to speech helps to emulate the fundamental instability typical of an old person. Note that vibrato parameters and the corresponding transformation have to be added to the hpsmodelparams function.

M-file 10.36 (genderchangetoold.m)

```
% Authors: J. Bonada, X. Serra, X. Amatriain, A. Loscos
%-----change to old-----%
[x,fs] = wavread('fairytale.wav');
w=[blackmanharris(1024);0];
fscale = 2;
timbremapping = [ 0   fs/2;   % input frequency
                  0   fs/2 ]; % output frequency
vtf = 6.5;                    % vibrato-tremolo frequency in Hz
va  = 400;                    % vibrato depth in cents
td  = 3;                      % tremolo depth in dB
[y,yh,yr] = hpsmodelparams(x,fs,w,4096,-150,200,50,600,2,.3,1,...
                           [],fscale,timbremapping,vtf,va,td);
```

Harmonizer

In order to create the effect of harmonizing vocals, we can add pitch-shifted versions of the original voice (with the same or different timbres) and force them to be in tune with the accompanying melodies. In this example we generate two voices: a more female-sounding singer a major third upwards, and a more male-sounding vocalization a perfect fourth downwards. Then we add all of them together. The method is very simple and actually generates voices that behave too similarly. More natural results could be obtained by adding random variations in timing and tuning to the different voices.

M-file 10.37 (harmonizer.m)

```
% Authors: J. Bonada, X. Serra, X. Amatriain, A. Loscos
[x,fs]=wavread('tedeum2.wav');
w=[blackmanharris(1024);0];
% female voice
fscale = 2^(4/12); % 4 semitones upwards
timbremapping = [ 0  4000  fs/2;   % input frequency
                  0  5000  fs/2 ]; % output frequency
[y,yh,yr] = hpsmodelparams(x,fs,w,2048,-150,200,100,400,1,.2,10,...
                           [],fscale,timbremapping);
% male voice
fscale = 2^(-5/12); % 5 semitones downwards
timbremapping = [ 0  5000  fs/2;   % input frequency
                  0  4000  fs/2 ]; % output frequency
[y2,yh2,yr2] = hpsmodelparams(x,fs,w,2048,-150,200,100,400,1,.2,10,...
                              [],fscale,timbremapping);
% add voices
l = min([length(x) length(y) length(y2) ]);
ysum = x(1:l)+y(1:l)+y2(1:l);
```

Choir

We can simulate a choir from a single vocalization by generating many clones of the input voice. It is important that each clone has slightly different characteristics, such as different timing, timbre and tuning. We can use the same function `hpsmodelparams` used before. However, as it is, pitch transposition is a constant, so we would get too similar fundamental behaviors. This can be easily improved by allowing the `fscale` parameter to be a vector with random transposition factors. Using the following code to compute the transposition parameter before performing pitch transposition and timbre scaling solves the problem. It has to be inserted in the %-----transformations---
--% section of M-file 10.23, and the transformation parameters have to be added to the function header, as in M-file 10.32.

M-file 10.38 (hpsmodeltranspositionenv.m)

```
% Authors: J. Bonada, X. Serra, X. Amatriain, A. Loscos
%-----pitch transposition and timbre scaling-----%
if (size(fscale,1)>1) % matrix
    cfscale = interp1(fscale(1,:),fscale(2,:),pin/fs,'spline','extrap');
    yhloc = yhloc*cfscale;                  % synthesis harmonic locs
    yf0 = f0*cfscale;                       % synthesis fundamental frequency
else
    yhloc = yhloc*fscale;                   % scale harmonic frequencies
    yf0 = f0*fscale;                        % synthesis fundamental frequency
end
% harmonics
if (f0>0)
  thloc = interp1( timbremapping(2,:), timbremapping(1,:), ...
                yhloc/Ns*fs) / fs*Ns; % mapped harmonic freqs.
  idx = find(hloc>0 & hloc<Ns*.5);          % harmonic indexes in frequency range
  yhmag = interp1([0; hloc(idx); Ns],[ hmag(1); hmag(idx); hmag(end) ],thloc);
                                            % interpolated envelope
end
% residual
  % frequency (Hz) of the last  coefficient
  frescoef = fs/2*length(mYsenv)*stocf/length(mXr);
  % mapped coef. indexes
```

```
trescoef = interp1( timbremapping(2,:), timbremapping(1,:), ...
             min(fs/2,[0:length(mYsenv)-1]'/(length(mYsenv)-1)*frescoef) );
% interpolated envelope
mYsenv = interp1([0:length(mYsenv)-1],mYsenv, ...
             trescoef/frescoef*(length(mYsenv)-1));
```

Now we have all the ingredients ready for generating the choir. In the following example we generate up to 15 voices, each one with random variations, which are added to the original one afterwards. For improving the transformation, each clone is added to a random panning position within a stereo output.

M-file 10.39 (choir.m)

```
% Authors: J. Bonada, X. Serra, X. Amatriain, A. Loscos
[x,fs]=wavread('tedeum.wav');
w=[blackmanharris(2048);0];
dur = length(x)/fs;
fn = ceil(dur/0.2);
fscale = zeros(2,fn);
fscale(1,:) = [0:fn-1]/(fn-1)*dur;
tn = ceil(dur/0.5);
timemapping = zeros(2,tn);
timemapping(1,:) = [0:tn-1]/(tn-1)*dur;
timemapping(2,:) = timemapping(1,:);
ysum = [ x x ]; % make it stereo
for i=1:15 % generate 15 voices
  disp([ ' processing ',num2str(i) ]);
  fscale(2,:) = 2.^(randn(1,fn)*30/1200);
  timemapping(2,2:end-1) = timemapping(1,2:end-1) + ...
                     randn(1,tn-2)*length(x)/fs/tn/6;
  timbremapping = [ 0 1000:1000:fs/2-1000   fs/2;
   0 (1000:1000:fs/2-1000).*(1+.1*randn(1,length(1000:1000:fs/2-1000))) fs/2];
  [y,yh,yr] = hpsmodelparams(x,fs,w,2048,-150,200,100,400,1,.2,10,...
                     timemapping,fscale,timbremapping);
  pan = max(-1,min(1,randn(1)/3.)); % [0,1]
  l = cos(pan*pi/2);%.^2;
  r = sin(pan*pi/2);%1-l;
  ysum = ysum + [l*y(1:length(x)) r*y(1:length(x))];
end
```

Note that this code is not optimized, there are a lot of redundant computations. An obvious way to improve it would be to first analyze the whole input sound, and then to use the analysis data to synthesize each of the clone voices. Nevertheless, there is no limit in the number of clone voices.

Morphing

Morphing is a transformation with which, out of two or more elements, we can generate new ones with hybrid properties. With different names, and using different signal-processing techniques, the idea of audio morphing is well known in the computer music community (Serra, 1994; Tellman, Haken, Holloway, 1995; Osaka, 1995; Slaney, Covell, Lassiter. 1996; Settel, Lippe, 1996). In most of these techniques, the morph is based on the interpolation of sound parameterizations resulting from analysis/synthesis techniques, such as the short-time fourier transform (STFT), linear predictive coding (LPC) or sinusoidal models (see Cross Synthesis and Spectral Interpolation in Sections 8.3.1 and 8.3.3 respectively).

In the following **MATLAB** code we introduce a morphing algorithm based on the interpolation of the harmonic and residual components of two sounds. In our implementation, we provide three interpolation factors that independently control the fundamental frequency, the harmonic timbre and the residual envelope. Playing with those control parameters we can smoothly go from one sound to the other, or combine characteristics of both.

M-file 10.40 (hpsmodelmorph.m)

```
function [y,yh,ys] = hpsmodelmorph(x,x2,fs,w,N,t,nH,minf0,maxf0,f0et,...
                            maxhd,stocf,f0intp,htintp,rintp)
% Authors: J. Bonada, X. Serra, X. Amatriain, A. Loscos
% Morph between two sounds using the harmonic plus stochastic model
% x,x2: input sounds, fs: sampling rate, w: analysis window (odd size),
% N: FFT size (minimum 512), t: threshold in negative dB,
% nH: maximum number of harmonics, minf0: minimum f0 frequency in Hz,
% maxf0: maximim f0 frequency in Hz,
% f0et: error threshold in the f0 detection (ex: 5),
% maxhd: max. relative deviation in harmonic detection (ex: .2)
% stocf: decimation factor of mag spectrum for stochastic analysis,
% f0intp: f0 interpolation factor,
% htintp: harmonic timbre interpolation factor,
% rintp: residual interpolation factor,
% y: output sound, yh: harmonic component, ys: stochastic component
if length(f0intp)==1
    f0intp =[ 0       length(x)/fs;     % input time
              f0intp f0intp      ];     % control value
end
if length(htintp)==1
    htintp =[ 0       length(x)/fs;     % input time
              htintp htintp      ];     % control value
end
if length(rintp)==1
    rintp =[ 0       length(x)/fs;      % input time
             rintp rintp         ];     % control value
end
M = length(w);                          % analysis window size
Ns = 1024;                              % FFT size for synthesis
H = 256;                                % hop size for analysis and synthesis
N2 = N/2+1;                             % half-size of spectrum
soundlength = length(x);                % length of input sound array
hNs = Ns/2;                             % half synthesis window size
hM = (M-1)/2;                           % half analysis window size
pin = 1+max(hNs,hM);    % initialize sound pointer to middle of analysis window
pend = soundlength-max(hM,hNs);         % last sample to start a frame
fftbuffer = zeros(N,1);                 % initialize buffer for FFT
yh = zeros(soundlength+Ns/2,1);         % output sine component
ys = zeros(soundlength+Ns/2,1);         % output residual component
w = w/sum(w);                           % normalize analysis window
sw = zeros(Ns,1);
ow = triang(2*H-1);                     % overlapping window
ovidx = Ns/2+1-H+1:Ns/2+H;              % overlap indexes
sw(ovidx) = ow(1:2*H-1);
bh = blackmanharris(Ns);                % synthesis window
bh = bh ./ sum(bh);                     % normalize synthesis window
wr = bh;                                % window for residual
sw(ovidx) = sw(ovidx) ./ bh(ovidx);
sws = H*hanning(Ns)/2;                  % synthesis window for stochastic
lastyhloc = zeros(nH,1);                % initialize synthesis harmonic locs.
yhphase = 2*pi*rand(nH,1);              % initialize synthesis harmonic phases
minpin2 = max(H+1,1+hM);                % minimum sample value for x2
maxpin2 = min(length(x2)-hM-1);         % maximum sample value for x2
```

```
while pin<pend
    %-----first sound analysis-----%
    [f0,hloc,hmag,mXsenv] = hpsanalysis(x,fs,w,wr,pin,M,hM,N,N2,Ns,hNs,...
                                    nH,t,f0et,minf0,maxf0,maxhd,stocf);
    %-----second sound analysis-----%
    pin2 = round(pin/length(x)*length(x2)); % linear time mapping between inputs
    pin2 = min(maxpin2,max(minpin2,pin2));
    [f02,hloc2,hmag2,mXsenv2] = hpsanalysis(x2,fs,w,wr,pin2,M,hM,N,N2,Ns,hNs,...
                                    nH,t,f0et,minf0,maxf0,maxhd,stocf);
    %-----morph-----%
    cf0intp = interp1(f0intp(1,:),f0intp(2,:),pin/fs);  % get control value
    chtintp = interp1(htintp(1,:),htintp(2,:),pin/fs);  % get control value
    crintp = interp1(rintp(1,:),rintp(2,:),pin/fs);     % get control value
    if (f0>0 && f02>0)
        outf0 = f0*(1-cf0intp) + f02*cf0intp;           % both inputs are harmonic
        yhloc = [1:nH]'*outf0/fs*Ns;            % generate synthesis harmonic serie
        idx = find(hloc>0 & hloc<Ns*.5);
        yhmag = interp1([0;hloc(idx);Ns], [hmag(1);hmag(idx);hmag(end)],yhloc);
                                                % interpolated envelope
        idx2 = find(hloc2>0 & hloc2<Ns*.5);
        yhmag2 = interp1([0; hloc2(idx2); Ns],...
                [hmag2(1);hmag2(idx2);hmag2(end)],yhloc); % interpolated envelope
        yhmag = yhmag*(1-chtintp) + yhmag2*chtintp;       % timbre morphing
    else
        outf0 = 0;                                      % remove harmonic content
        yhloc = hloc.*0;
        yhmag = hmag.*0;
    end
    mYsenv = mXsenv*(1-crintp) + mXsenv2*crintp;
    %-----synthesis-----%
    yhphase = yhphase + 2*pi*(lastyhloc+yhloc)/2/Ns*H; % propagate phases
    lastyhloc = yhloc;
    Yh = genspecsines(yhloc,yhmag,yhphase,Ns);     % generate sines
    mYs = interp(mYsenv,stocf);                        % interpolate to original size
    roffset = ceil(stocf/2)-1;                         % interpolated array offset
    mYs = [ mYs(1)*ones(roffset,1); mYs(1:Ns/2+1-roffset) ];
    mYs = 10.^(mYs/20);                                % dB to linear magnitude
    pYs = 2*pi*rand(Ns/2+1,1);          % generate phase spectrum with random values
    mYs1 = [mYs(1:Ns/2+1); mYs(Ns/2:-1:2)]; % create complete magnitude spectrum
    pYs1 = [pYs(1:Ns/2+1); -1*pYs(Ns/2:-1:2)]; % create complete phase spectrum
    Ys = mYs1.*cos(pYs1)+1i*mYs1.*sin(pYs1);   % compute complex spectrum
    yhw = fftshift(real(ifft(Yh)));               % sines in time domain using IFFT
    ysw = fftshift(real(ifft(Ys)));        % stochastic in time domain using IFFT
    ro = pin-hNs;                          % output sound pointer for overlap
    yh(ro:ro+Ns-1) = yh(ro:ro+Ns-1)+yhw(1:Ns).*sw;  % overlap-add for sines
    ys(ro:ro+Ns-1) = ys(ro:ro+Ns-1)+ysw(1:Ns).*sws; % overlap-add for stochastic
    pin = pin+H;                               % advance the sound pointer
end
y= yh+ys;                               % sum sines and stochastic
end


function [f0,hloc,hmag,mXsenv] = hpsanalysis(x,fs,w,wr,pin,M,hM,N,N2,...
                                Ns,hNs,nH,t,f0et,minf0,maxf0,maxhd,stocf)
    xw = x(pin-hM:pin+hM).*w(1:M);              % window the input sound
    fftbuffer = zeros(N,1);                     % initialize buffer for FFT
    fftbuffer(1:(M+1)/2) = xw((M+1)/2:M);       % zero-phase window in fftbuffer
    fftbuffer(N-(M-1)/2+1:N) = xw(1:(M-1)/2);
    X = fft(fftbuffer);                         % compute the FFT
    mX = 20*log10(abs(X(1:N2)));                % magnitude spectrum
    pX = unwrap(angle(X(1:N/2+1)));             % unwrapped phase spectrum
    ploc = 1 + find((mX(2:N2-1)>t) .* (mX(2:N2-1)>mX(3:N2)) ...
                .* (mX(2:N2-1)>mX(1:N2-2)));    % find peaks
    [ploc,pmag,pphase] = peakinterp(mX,pX,ploc);   % refine peak values
```

```
f0 = f0detectiontwm(mX,fs,ploc,pmag,f0et,minf0,maxf0);      % find f0
hloc = zeros(nH,1);                      % initialize harmonic locations
hmag = zeros(nH,1)-100;                  % initialize harmonic magnitudes
hphase = zeros(nH,1);                    % initialize harmonic phases
hf = (f0>0).*(f0.*(1:nH));               % initialize harmonic frequencies
hi = 1;                                  % initialize harmonic index
npeaks = length(ploc);                   % number of peaks found
while (f0>0 && hi<=nH && hf(hi)<fs/2)     % find harmonic peaks
  [dev,pei] = min(abs((ploc(1:npeaks)-1)/N*fs-hf(hi)));   % closest peak
  if ((hi==1 || ~any(hloc(1:hi-1)==ploc(pei))) && dev<maxhd*hf(hi))
    hloc(hi) = ploc(pei);                % harmonic locations
    hmag(hi) = pmag(pei);                % harmonic magnitudes
    hphase(hi) = pphase(pei);            % harmonic phases
  end
  hi = hi+1;                             % increase harmonic index
end
hloc(1:hi-1) = (hloc(1:hi-1)~=0).*((hloc(1:hi-1)-1)*Ns/N); % synth. locs
ri = pin-hNs;                     % input sound pointer for residual analysis
xr = x(ri:ri+Ns-1).*wr(1:Ns);    % window the input sound
Xr = fft(fftshift(xr));          % compute FFT for residual analysis
Xh = genspecsines(hloc(1:hi-1),hmag,hphase,Ns);       % generate sines
Xr = Xr-Xh;                      % get the residual complex spectrum
mXr = 20*log10(abs(Xr(1:Ns/2+1)));    % magnitude spectrum of residual
mXsenv = decimate(max(-200,mXr),stocf);  % decimate the magnitude spectrum
end
```

Compared to the previous code M-file 10.23, we added a second analysis section followed by the morph section. For simplicity, we put the analysis in a separate function, and removed the time-scaling transformation. Besides, we constrained the morph of the deterministic component to frames where both input signals have pitch. Otherwise, the deterministic part is muted. Note also that if the sounds have different durations, the audio resulting from the morphing will have the duration of the input.

The next code performs a morph between a soprano and a violin, where the timbre of the violin is applied to the voice.

M-file 10.41 (morphvocalviolin.m)

```
% Authors: J. Bonada, X. Serra, X. Amatriain, A. Loscos
[x,fs]=wavread('soprano-E4.wav');
[x2,fs]=wavread('violin-B3.wav');
w=[blackmanharris(1024);0];
f0intp = 0;
htintp = 1;
rintp = 0;
[y,yh,ys] = hpsmodelmorph(x,x2,fs,w,2048,-150,200,100,400,1500,1.5,10,...
                          f0intp,htintp,rintp);
```

In this other example we use time-varying functions to control the morph so that we smoothly change the characteristics from the voice to the violin.

M-file 10.42 (morphvocalviolin2.m)

```
% Authors: J. Bonada, X. Serra, X. Amatriain, A. Loscos
[x,fs]=wavread('soprano-E4.wav');
[x2,fs]=wavread('violin-B3.wav');
```

```
w=[blackmanharris(1024);0];
dur = (length(x)-1)/fs;
f0intp = [ 0 dur; 0 1];
htintp = [ 0 dur; 0 1];
rintp = [ 0 dur; 0 1];
[y,yh,ys] = hpsmodelmorph(x,x2,fs,w,2048,-150,200,100,400,1500,1.5,10,...
                          f0intp,htintp,rintp);
```

10.5   Conclusions

In this chapter, we have shown how the use of spectral models based on a sinusoidal plus residual decomposition can lead to new and interesting sound effects and transformations. We have also seen that it is not easy nor immediate to get a good spectral representation of a sound, so the use of this kind of approach needs to be carefully considered, bearing in mind the application and the type of sounds we want to process.

For example, most of the techniques here presented work well only on monophonic sounds and some rely on the pseudo-harmonicity of the input signal.

Nevertheless, the use of spectral models for musical processing has not been around too long and it has already proven useful for many applications, such as the ones presented in this chapter. Under many circumstances, spectral models based on the sinusoidal plus residual decomposition offer much more flexibility and processing capabilities than more immediate representations of the sound signal.

In general, higher-level sound representations offer more flexibility at the cost of a more complex and time-consuming analysis process. It is important to remember that the model of the sound we choose will surely have a great effect on the kind of transformations we will be able to achieve and on the complexity and efficiency of our implementation. Hopefully, the reading of this chapter, and the book as a whole, will guide the reader in taking the right decision in order to get the desired results.

References

[Bon08] J. Bonada. Wide-band harmonic sinusoidal modeling. In *Proc. 11th Int. Conf. Digital Audio Effects (DAFx-08)*, 2008.

[Can98] P. Cano. Fundamental frequency estimation in the SMS analysis. In *Proc. DAFX-98 Digital Audio Effects Workshop*, pp. 99–102, 1998.

[Chi94] D. G. Childers. Measuring and modeling vocal source-tract interaction. *IEEE Trans. Biomed. Eng.*, 41(7): 663–671, 1994.

[CK02]   A. Cheveigné and H. Kawahara. YIN, A fundamental frequency estimator for speech and music. *J. Acoust. Soc. Am.*, 111(4): 1917–1930, 2002.

[Cox71] M. G. Cox. An algorithm for approximating convex functions by means of first-degree splines. *Comp. J.*, 14: 272–275, 1971.

[DGR93] Ph. Depalle, G. Garcia and X. Rodet. Analysis of sound for additive synthesis: tracking of partials using Hidden Markov models. In *Proc. Int. Comp. Music Conf.*, pp. 94–97, 1993.

[DH97]   Ph. Depalle and T. Hélie. Extraction of spectral peak parameters using a short-time Fourier transform modeling and no sidelobe windows. In *Proc. 1997 IEEE Workshop Appl. Signal Process. Audio Acoust.*, pp. 298–231, 1997.

[DiF98] R. DiFederico. Waveform preserving time stretching and pitch shifting for sinusoidal models of sound. In *Proc. DAFX-98 Digital Audio Effects Workshop*, 1998.

[DQ97]   Y. Ding and X. Qian. Sinusoidal and residual decomposition and residual modeling of musical tones using the QUASAR signal model. In *Proc. Int. Comp. Music Conf.*, pp. 35–42, 1997.

[FHC00] K. Fitz, L. Haken, and P. Christensen. A new algorithm for bandwidth association in bandwidth-enhanced additive sound modeling. In *Proc. Int. Com. Music Conf.*, pp. 384–387, 2000.

[Goo97]   M. Goodwin. *Adaptative signal models: Theory, algorithms and audio applications*. PhD thesis, University of California, Berkeley, 1997.

[Hes83]   W. Hess. *Pitch Determination of Speech Signals*. Springer-Verlag, 1983.

[Lar03]   J. Laroche. Frequency-domain techniques for high-quality voice modification. In *Proc. 6th Int. Conf Digital Audio Effects (DAFx-03)*, 2003.

[Mak75]   J. Makhoul. Linear prediction: a tutorial review. *Proce IEEE*, 63(4): 561–580, 1975.

[MB94]   R. C. Maher and J. W. Beauchamp. Fundamental frequency estimation of musical signals using a two-way mismatch procedure. *J. Acoust. Soc. Am.*, 95(4): 2254–2263, 1994.

[MB10]   S. Musevic and J. Bonada. Comparison of non-stationary sinusoid estimation methods using reassignment and derivatives. In *Proc. Sound Music Computing Conf*. 2010.

[MG75]   J. D. Markel and A. H. Gray. *Linear Prediction of Speech*. Springer-Verlag, 1975.

[MQ86]   R. J. McAulay and T. F. Quatieri. Speech analysis/synthesis based on a sinusoidal representation. *IEEE Trans Acoustics Speech Signal Process*, 34(4): 744–754, 1986.

[Pee01]   G. Peeters. *Modéles et modification du signal sonore adaptès á ses caractéristiques locales*. PhD thesis, spécialité Acoustique Traitement du signal et Informatique Appliqués à la Musique, Universite Paris 6, 2001.

[RD92]   X. Rodet and Ph. Depalle. Spectral envelopes and inverse FFT synthesis. *Proc. 93rd AES Conve*. AES Preprint No. 3393 (H-3), 1992.

[Sed88]   R. Sedgewick. *Algorithms*. Addison-Wesley, 1988.

[Ser89]   X. Serra. *A System for Sound Analysis/Transformation/Synthesis based on a Deterministic plus Stochastic Decomposition*. PhD thesis, Stanford University, 1989.

[Ser96]   X. Serra. Musical sound modeling with sinusoids plus noise. In G. De Poli, A. Picialli, S. T. Pope, and C. Roads (eds), *Musical Signal Processing*, pp. 91–122, Swets & Zeitlinger Publishers, 1996.

[SS87]   J. O. Smith and X. Serra. PARSHL: an analysis/synthesis program for non-harmonic sounds based on a sinusoidal representation. In *Proc. Int. Comp. Music Conf*., pp. 290–297, 1987.

[SS90]   X. Serra and J. Smith. Spectral modeling synthesis: a sound analysis/synthesis system based on a deterministic plus stochastic decomposition. *Comp. Music J*., 14(4): 12–24, 1990.

[Str80]   J. Strawn. Approximation and syntactic analysis of amplitude and frequency functions for digital sound synthesis. *Comp. Music J*., 4(3): 3–24, 1980.

[VM98]   T. S. Verma and T. H. Y. Meng. Time scale modification using a sines+transients+noise signal model. In *Proc. DAFX-98 Digital Audio Effects Workshop*, pp. 49–52, 1998.

[VM00]   T. S. Verma and T. H. Y. Meng. Extending spectral modeling synthesis with transient modeling synthesis. *Comp. Music J*., 24(2): 47–59, 2000.

[ZRR07]   M. Zivanovic, A. Röbel and X. Rodet. Adaptive threshold determination for spectral peak classification. In *Proc. 10th Int. Conf. Digital Audio Effects (DAFx-07)*, 2007.

11

Time and frequency-warping musical signals

G. Evangelista

11.1   Introduction

In this chapter we describe interesting audio effects that can be obtained by deforming the time and/or the frequency axis. Whilst discrete-time warping techniques were introduced in 1965 [Bro65], their interest in musical applications is fairly recent. Time warping aims at deforming the waveform or the envelope of the signal, while frequency warping modifies its spectral content, e.g., by transforming a harmonic signal into an inharmonic one or vice versa. The effects obtained by warping often increase the richness of the signal by introducing detuning or fluctuation of the waveform. The sounds from natural instruments like piano and drums already possess this property. The wave propagation in stiff strings and membranes can actually be explained in terms of frequency warping. By warping these sounds one can enhance or reduce their natural features. Even uninteresting synthetic sounds such as pulse trains may be transformed into interesting sounds by warping. Frequency warping is amenable to a time-varying version that allows us to introduce dynamic effects such as vibrato, tremolo and Flatterzunge in flute.

The quality of warping ultimately depends on the warping map, i.e., on the function describing the deformation of the time or frequency axis. Time and frequency warping are flexible techniques that give rise to a tremendous amount of possibilities, most of which are at present still unexplored from a musical point of view. By choosing the proper map one can actually morph the sound of an instrument into that produced by another instrument.

This chapter is divided into two main sections. In the first section we describe the time- and frequency-warping operations and derive algorithms for computing these effects, including recent advances in approximation. In the second section we illustrate some of their musical applications based on examples and case studies.

DAFX: Digital Audio Effects, Second Edition. Edited by Udo Zölzer.
© 2011 John Wiley & Sons, Ltd. Published 2011 by John Wiley & Sons, Ltd.

11.2   Warping

11.2.1   Time warping

Suppose that we want to change the shape of a periodic waveform $s(t)$ by moving the amplitude values attained by the signal to other time instants. One can achieve this by plotting the signal on an elastic sheet and by stretching and/or compressing the sheet at different points along its horizontal direction. The waveshape appears as if the original time axis had been deformed. Instants of time that were equidistant now have a different time distribution. This deformation of the time axis called time warping is characterized by a warping map $\theta(t)$, mapping points of the original t-axis onto points of the transformed axis. An example of time warping a sinewave is shown in Figure 11.1. The figure is obtained by plotting the original signal along the ordinates and transforming time instants into new time instants via the warping map, obtaining the signal plotted along the abscissa axis. Notice that to one point in the original signal there can correspond more points in the warped signal. These points are obtained by joining time instants of the original signal to points on the warping characteristic $\theta(t)$ using horizontal lines. The corresponding warped time instants are the value(s) of the abscissa corresponding to these intersection point(s). The time-warped signal is obtained by plotting the corresponding amplitude values at the new time instants along the abscissa. In this example the signal $\sin(\theta(t))$ may be interpreted as a phase modulation of the original sinewave. Time warping a signal composed of a superposition of sinewaves is equivalent to phase modulating each of the component sinewaves and adding them together. By time warping we alter not only the waveshape, but also the period of the signal. Clearly, the map is an effective modulo of the period of the signal, that is, the map $\theta(t)$ and the map

$$\theta_0(t) = \operatorname{rem}(\theta(t), T),$$

where $\operatorname{rem}(x, T)$ denotes the remainder of the integer division of x by T, have the same net effect on a T-periodic signal. More generally, we can time warp an arbitrary, aperiodic signal $s(t)$ via an arbitrary map, obtaining a signal

$$s_{tw}(t) = s(\theta(t))$$

whose waveshape and envelope may be completely different from the starting signal. If the map is invertible, i.e., one-to-one, then

$$s_{tw}(\theta^{-1}(t)) = s(t),$$

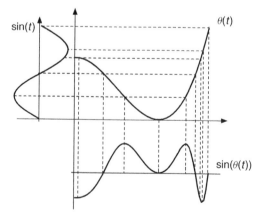

Figure 11.1   Time warping a sinewave by means of an arbitrary map $\theta(t)$.

that is, at time $\tau = \theta^{-1}(t)$ the time-warped signal attains the same amplitude value as that attained by the starting signal at time t.

Time-warping transformations are useful for musical applications, e.g., for morphing a sound into a new one in the time domain.

11.2.2 Frequency warping

Frequency warping is the frequency-domain counterpart of time warping. Given a signal whose discrete-time Fourier transform (DTFT) is $S(\omega)$, we form the signal $s_{fw}(t)$ whose DTFT is

$$S_{fw}(\omega) = S(\theta(\omega)).$$

That is, the frequency spectrum of the frequency-warped signal agrees with that of the starting signal at frequencies that are displaced by the map $\theta(\omega)$. If the map is invertible, then

$$S_{fw}(\theta^{-1}(\omega)) = S(\omega).$$

The frequency-warped signal is obtained by computing the inverse DTFT of the warped frequency spectrum. In order to obtain a real warped signal from a real signal, the warping map must have odd parity, i.e.,

$$\theta(-\omega) = -\theta(\omega).$$

In order to illustrate the features of frequency warping, consider a periodic signal $s(t)$ whose frequency spectrum peaks at integer multiples of the fundamental frequency ω_0. The frequency spectrum of the warped signal will peak at frequencies

$$\widehat{\omega}_k = \theta^{-1}(k\omega_0).$$

The situation is illustrated in Figure 11.2, where the original harmonic frequencies are represented by dots along the ordinate axis. The warped frequencies are obtained by drawing horizontal lines from the original set of frequencies to the graph of $\theta(\omega)$ and by reading the corresponding values of the abscissa. As a result, harmonically related partials are mapped onto non-harmonically related ones. Furthermore, if the frequency-warping map is not monotonically increasing, one obtains effects analogous to the foldover of frequencies. This is similar to that which is obtained from a phase vocoder in which the frequency bands are scrambled in the synthesis of the signal. However,

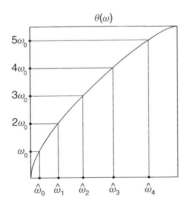

Figure 11.2 Frequency warping of a periodic signal: transformation of the harmonics into inharmonic partials.

the resolution and flexibility of the frequency-warping method are generally much higher than that of the scrambled phase vocoder.

Energy preservation and unitary frequency warping

By frequency warping a signal one dilates or shrinks portions of its frequency spectrum. As a result, the areas under the spectral characteristics are affected. Perceptually this results in an amplification of certain bands and an attenuation of other bands. This is depicted in Figure 11.3 where the original narrow band spectrum of Figure 11.3(a) is dilated, obtaining the dotted curve shown in Figure 11.3(b). In order to circumvent this problem, which causes an alteration of the relative energy levels of the spectrum, one should perform an equalization aimed at reducing the amplitude of dilated portions and increasing that of shrunk portions of the spectrum. Mathematically this is simply achieved, in the case where the warping map is increasing, by scaling the magnitude square of the DTFT of the warped signal by the derivative of the warping map. In fact, the energy in an arbitrary band $[\omega_0, \omega_1]$ is

$$E_{[\omega_0, \omega_1]} = \frac{1}{2\pi} \int_{\omega_0}^{\omega_1} |S(\omega)|^2 \, d\omega.$$

By the simple change of variable $\omega = \theta(\Omega)$ in the last integral we obtain

$$E_{[\omega_0, \omega_1]} = \frac{1}{2\pi} \int_{\Omega_0 = \theta^{-1}(\omega_0)}^{\Omega_1 = \theta^{-1}(\omega_1)} |S(\theta(\Omega))|^2 \frac{d\theta}{d\Omega} d\Omega = \frac{1}{2\pi} \int_{\Omega_0}^{\Omega_1} \left| \widetilde{S}_{fw}(\Omega) \right|^2 d\Omega, \qquad (11.1)$$

where

$$\widetilde{S}_{fw}(\omega) = \sqrt{\frac{d\theta}{d\omega}} S(\theta(\omega)) \qquad (11.2)$$

is the DTFT of the scaled frequency warped signal. Equation (11.1) states the energy preservation property of the scaled warped signal in any band of the spectrum: the energy in any band $[\omega_0, \omega_1]$ of the original signal equals the energy of the warped signal in the warped band $[\theta^{-1}(\omega_0), \theta^{-1}(\omega_1)]$. Thus, the scaled frequency warping is a unitary operation on signals.

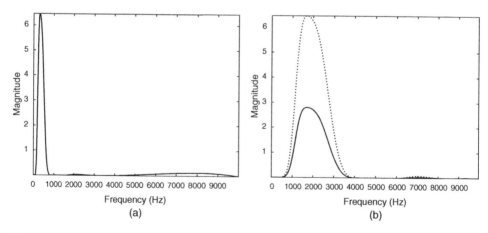

Figure 11.3 Frequency warping a narrow-band signal: (a) original frequency spectrum; (b) frequency-warped spectrum (dotted line) and scaled frequency-warped spectrum (solid line).

11.2.3   Algorithms for warping

In Sections 11.2.1 and 11.2.2 we explored basic methods for time warping in the time domain and frequency warping in the frequency domain, respectively. However, one can derive time- and frequency-warping algorithms in crossed domains. It is easy to realize that time and frequency warping are dual operations. Once a time-domain algorithm for frequency warping is determined, then a frequency-domain algorithm for time warping will work the same way. This section contains an overview of techniques for computing frequency warping. The same techniques can be used for time warping in the dual domain. We start from the basic maps using the Fourier transform and end up with time-varying warping using allpass chains in dispersive delay lines.

Frequency warping by means of FFT

A simple way to implement the frequency-warping operation on finite length discrete-time signals is via the FFT algorithm. Let

$$S\left(\frac{2\pi m}{N}\right) = \sum_{n=0}^{N-1} s(n)e^{-j\frac{2\pi nm}{N}}$$

denote the DFT of a length N signal $s(n)$. Consider a map $\theta(\omega)$ mapping the interval $[-\pi, \pi]$ onto itself and extend $\theta(\omega)$ outside this interval by letting

$$\theta(\omega + 2k\pi) = \theta(\omega) + 2k\pi, \ k \text{ integer}.$$

The last requirement is necessary in order to guarantee that the warped discrete-time signal has a 2π-periodic Fourier transform

$$S_{fw}(\omega + 2k\pi) = S(\theta(\omega + 2k\pi)) = S(\theta(\omega) + 2k\pi) = S(\theta(\omega)) = S_{fw}(\omega),$$

i.e., $S_{fw}(\omega)$ is the Fourier transform of a discrete-time signal. In order to obtain the frequency-warped signal we would need to compute $S\left(\theta\left(\frac{2\pi m}{N}\right)\right)$ and then perform the inverse Fourier transform. However, from the DFT we only know $S(\omega)$ at integer multiples of $\frac{2\pi}{N}$. The map $\theta(\omega)$ is arbitrary and $\theta\left(\frac{2\pi m}{N}\right)$ is not necessarily a multiple of $\frac{2\pi}{N}$. However, we may approximate $\theta\left(\frac{2\pi m}{N}\right)$ with the nearest integer multiple of $\frac{2\pi}{N}$, i.e., we can define the quantized map

$$\theta_q\left(\frac{2\pi m}{N}\right) = \frac{2\pi}{N}\text{round}\left[\theta\left(\frac{2\pi m}{N}\right)\frac{N}{2\pi}\right].$$

The values $S\left(\theta_q\left(\frac{2\pi m}{N}\right)\right)$ are known from the DFT of the signal and we can compute the approximated frequency-warped signal by means of the inverse DFT:

$$s_{fw}(n) \approx \frac{1}{N}\sum_{m=0}^{N-1} S\left(\theta_q\left(\frac{2\pi m}{N}\right)\right)e^{j\frac{2\pi nm}{N}}.$$

The diagram of the frequency-warping algorithm via FFT is shown in Figure 11.4. If the warping map is an increasing function, one can introduce the equalization factor as in (11.2) simply

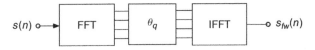

Figure 11.4   Frequency warping by means of FFT: schematic diagram.

by multiplying $S\left(\theta_q\left(\frac{2\pi m}{N}\right)\right)$ by the factor $\sqrt{\dfrac{\mathrm{d}\theta}{\mathrm{d}\omega}}\bigg|_{\omega=\frac{2\pi m}{N}}$ before processing with the IFFT block. The FFT algorithm for warping is rather efficient, with a complexity proportional to $N \log N$. However, it has some drawbacks. The quantization of the map introduces distortion in the desired frequency spectrum, given by repetitions of the same value in phase and magnitude at near frequencies. These sum almost coherently and are perceived as beating components that have a slow amplitude decay. In frequency-warping signals one must pay attention to the fact that the warped version of a finite-length signal is not necessarily finite length. In the FFT-warping algorithm, components that should lie outside the analysis interval are folded back into it causing some echo artifacts. Furthermore, even if the original warping map is one-to-one, the quantized map is not and the warping effect cannot be undone without losses. The influence of the artifacts introduced by the FFT-warping algorithms may be reduced by zero-padding the original signal in order to obtain a larger value of N and, at the same time, a smaller quantization step for θ, at the expense of an increased computational cost.

Dispersive delay lines

In order to derive alternate algorithms for frequency warping [Bro65, OJ72], consider the DTFT (11.2) of the scaled frequency-warped version of a causal signal $s(n)$,

$$\widetilde{S}_{fw}(\omega) = \sqrt{\frac{\mathrm{d}\theta}{\mathrm{d}\omega}} S(\theta(\omega)) = \sqrt{\frac{\mathrm{d}\theta}{\mathrm{d}\omega}} \sum_{n=0}^{\infty} s(n)\mathrm{e}^{-jn\theta(\omega)}. \tag{11.3}$$

The last formula is obtained by considering the DTFT of the signal $s(n)$, replacing ω with $\theta(\omega)$ and multiplying by $\sqrt{\frac{\mathrm{d}\theta}{\mathrm{d}\omega}}$. The warped signal $\widetilde{s}_{fw}(k)$ is obtained from the inverse DTFT of $\widetilde{S}_{fw}(\omega)$:

$$\widetilde{s}_{fw}(k) = \mathrm{IDTFT}\left[\widetilde{S}_{fw}(\omega)\right](k) = \sum_{n=0}^{\infty} s(n)\mathrm{IDTFT}\left[\sqrt{\frac{\mathrm{d}\theta}{\mathrm{d}\omega}}\mathrm{e}^{-jn\theta(\omega)}\right](k). \tag{11.4}$$

Defining the sequences $\lambda_n(k)$ as follows,

$$\lambda_n(k) = \mathrm{IDTFT}\left[\sqrt{\frac{\mathrm{d}\theta}{\mathrm{d}\omega}}\mathrm{e}^{-jn\theta(\omega)}\right](k) = \frac{1}{2\pi}\int_{-\pi}^{+\pi}\sqrt{\frac{\mathrm{d}\theta}{\mathrm{d}\omega}}\mathrm{e}^{j[k\omega - n\theta(\omega)]}\mathrm{d}\omega \tag{11.5}$$

we can put (11.4) in the form

$$\widetilde{s}_{fw}(k) = \sum_{n=0}^{\infty} s(n)\lambda_n(k). \tag{11.6}$$

If we find a way of generating the sequences $\lambda_n(k)$, then we have a new algorithm for frequency warping, which consists of multiplying these sequences by the signal samples and adding the result. From (11.5) we have an easy way for accomplishing this since

$$\Lambda_n(\omega) = \mathrm{DTFT}[\lambda_n](\omega) = \Lambda_{n-1}(\omega)\mathrm{e}^{-j\theta(\omega)}, \tag{11.7}$$

with

$$\Lambda_0(\omega) = \sqrt{\frac{\mathrm{d}\theta}{\mathrm{d}\omega}}.$$

Notice that the term $\mathrm{e}^{-j\theta(\omega)}$ has magnitude 1 and corresponds to an allpass filter. The sequence $\lambda_0(k)$ may be generated as the impulse response of the filter $\sqrt{\frac{\mathrm{d}\theta}{\mathrm{d}\omega}}$. The sequence $\lambda_n(k)$ is obtained

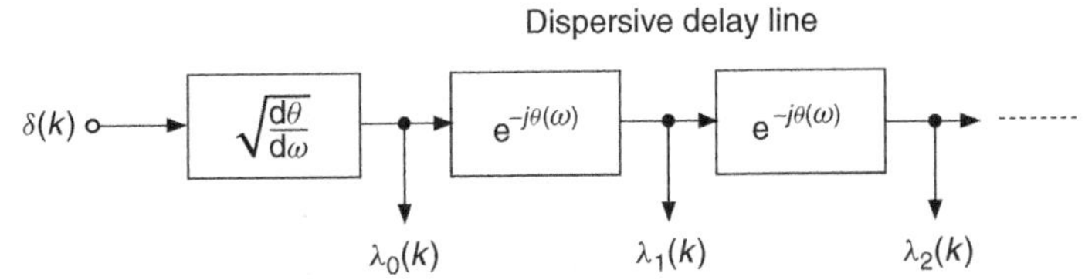

Dispersive delay line

Figure 11.5 Dispersive delay line for generating the sequences $\lambda_n(k)$.

by filtering $\lambda_{n-1}(k)$ through the allpass filter $e^{-j\theta(\omega)}$. This can be realized in the structure of Figure 11.5 for computing the sequences $\lambda_n(k)$ as the impulse responses of a chain of filters. In order to perform warping it suffices to multiply each of the outputs by the corresponding signal sample and sum these terms together. The structure is essentially a delay line in which the elementary delays are replaced by allpass filters. Each of these filters introduces a frequency dependent group delay

$$\tau_G(\omega) = \frac{d\theta}{d\omega}.$$

The result is reminiscent of propagation of light in dispersive media where speed depends on frequency. For this reason this structure is called a dispersive delay line. What happens if we input a generic signal $y(k)$ to the dispersive delay line? The outputs $\widehat{y}_n(k)$ are computed as the convolution of the input signal by the sequences $\lambda_n(k)$,

$$y(k) * \lambda_n(k) = \sum_r y(k-r)\lambda_n(r).$$

As a special case, for $k = 0$ and choosing as input the signal $s(k) = y(-k)$, which is the time-reversed version of $y(k)$, we obtain

$$\widehat{y}_n(0) = \sum_r s(r)\lambda_n(r).$$

The last equation should be compared with (11.6) to notice that the summation is now over the argument $\lambda_n(r)$. However, we can define the transposed sequences

$$\lambda_r^T(n) \equiv \lambda_n(r),$$

and write

$$\widehat{y}_n(0) = \sum_r s(r)\lambda_r^T(n). \tag{11.8}$$

From (11.5) we have

$$\lambda_r^T(n) = \text{IDTFT}\left[\sqrt{\frac{d\theta}{d\omega}}e^{-jn\theta(\omega)}\right](r) = \frac{1}{2\pi}\int_{-\pi}^{+\pi}\sqrt{\frac{d\theta}{d\omega}}e^{j[r\omega - n\theta(\omega)]}d\omega. \tag{11.9}$$

Suppose that the map $\theta(\omega)$ has odd parity, is increasing and maps π onto π. Then we can perform in (11.9) the same change of variable $\Omega = \theta(\omega)$ as in (11.1) to obtain

$$\lambda_r^T(n) = \frac{1}{2\pi}\int_{-\pi}^{+\pi}\sqrt{\frac{d\theta^{-1}}{d\omega}}e^{j[n\omega - r\theta^{-1}(\omega)]}d\omega.$$

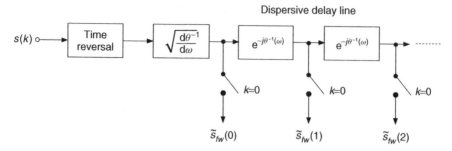

Figure 11.6   Computational structure for frequency warping.

As a result,

$$\Lambda_r^T(\omega) = \sqrt{\frac{d\theta^{-1}}{d\omega}} e^{jr\theta^{-1}(\omega)},$$

hence the transposed sequences $\lambda_r^T(n)$ have the same form as the sequences $\lambda_r(n)$ except that they are based on the inverse map $\theta^{-1}(\omega)$. Consequently, (11.8) is a formula for unwarping the signal. Furthermore, by exchanging the roles of $\theta(\omega)$ and $\theta^{-1}(\omega)$, (11.8) is also a valid algorithm for warping. The corresponding structure is shown in Figure 11.6. The input signal is time reversed, then fed to the $\sqrt{\frac{d\theta^{-1}}{d\omega}}$ filter and to the dispersive delay line. The output of each filter is collected at time $k = 0$ by means of switches closing at that instant to form the scaled frequency-warped sequence $\tilde{s}_{fw}(n)$. The structures in Figures 11.5 and 11.6 still present some computational problems. In general, the transfer functions involved are not rational. Furthermore, an infinite number of filters is needed for computing the transform. One can show that the only one-to-one map implementable by a rational transfer function is given by the phase of the first-order allpass filter

$$A(z) = \frac{z^{-1} - b}{1 - bz^{-1}}, \tag{11.10}$$

where $-1 < b < 1$. By varying the real parameter b in the allowed range, one obtains the family of Laguerre curves shown in Figure 11.7. The curves with a negative value of the parameter are the inverses of those with a positive value, i.e., the inverse mapping $\theta^{-1}(\omega)$ corresponds to a sign reversal of the parameter. One can show that for causal signals the derivative $\sqrt{\frac{d\theta^{-1}}{d\omega}}$ can be replaced by the filter

$$\Lambda_0^T(z) = \frac{\sqrt{1-b^2}}{1 + bz^{-1}}.$$

The structure in Figure 11.6 includes a time-reversal block and switches closing at time zero. It is clear that for a finite-length N signal one can equivalently form the signal $s(N - n)$ and close the switches at time $k = N$. Furthermore, by inspection of the structure, the required number M of allpass filters is approximately given by N times the maximum group delay, i.e.,

$$M \approx N \frac{1 + |b|}{1 - |b|}.$$

A larger number of sections would contribute little or nothing to the output signal.

The main advantage of the time-domain algorithm for warping is that the family of warping curves is smooth and does not introduce artifacts, as opposed to the FFT-based algorithm illustrated in the above. Furthermore, the effect can be undone and structures for unwarping signals are obtained by the identical structure for warping provided that we reverse the sign of the parameter.

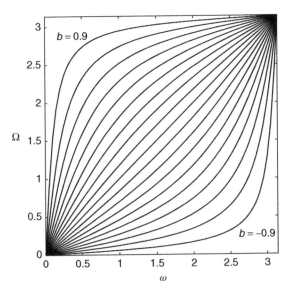

Figure 11.7   The family of Laguerre warping maps.

In fact, the frequency-warping algorithm corresponds to the computation of an expansion over an orthogonal basis, giving rise to the Laguerre transform. Next we provide a simple MATLAB® function implementing the structure of Figure 11.6. The following M-file 11.1 gives a simple implementation of the Laguerre transform.

M-file 11.1 (lagt.m)

```
function y=lagt(x,b,M)
% Author: G. Evangelista
% computes M terms of the Laguerre transform y of the input x
% with Laguerre parameter b
N=length(x);
x=x(N:-1:1);      % time reverse input
% filter by normalizing filter lambda_0
yy=filter(sqrt(1-b^2),[1,b],x);
y(1)=yy(N);       % retain the last sample only
for k=2:M
% filter the previous output by allpass
 yy=filter([b,1],[1,b],yy);
 y(k)=yy(N);      % retain the last sample only
end
```

11.2.4   Short-time warping and real-time implementation

The frequency-warping algorithm based on the Laguerre transform illustrated in Section 11.2.3 is not ideally suited to real-time implementation. Besides the computational cost, which is of the order of N^2, each output sample depends on every input sample. Another drawback is that with a long signal the frequency-dependent delays cumulate to introduce large delay differences between high and low frequencies. As a result, the time organization of the input signal is destroyed by frequency warping. This can also be seen from the computational structure in Figure 11.6, where subsignals pertaining to different frequency regions of the spectrum travel with different speeds along the dispersive delay line. At sampling time some of these signals have reached the end of the line, whilst other are left behind. For example, consider the Laguerre transform of a signal $s(n)$ windowed by a length N window $h(n)$ shifted on the interval $rM, ..., rM + N - 1$. According to (11.6) we obtain

$$\tilde{s}_{fw}^{(r)}(k) = \sum_{n=rM}^{rM+N-1} h(n - rM)s(n)\lambda_n(k) = \sum_{n=0}^{N-1} x^{(r)}(n)\lambda_{n+rM}(k), \qquad (11.11)$$

where

$$x^{(r)}(n) = h(n)s(n + rM).$$

The DTFT of (11.11) yields

$$\widetilde{S}_{fw}^{(r)}(\omega) = e^{-jrM\theta(\omega)} \sum_{n=0}^{N-1} x^{(r)}(n)\Lambda_n(\omega) = e^{-jrM\theta(\omega)} \Lambda_0(\omega)X^{(r)}(\theta(\omega)). \qquad (11.12)$$

From this we can see that the spectral contribution of the signal supported on $rM, ..., rM + N - 1$ is delayed, in the warped signal, by the term $e^{-jM\theta(\omega)}$, which introduces a largely dispersed group delay $M\tau_G(\omega)$. Approximations of the warping algorithm are possible in which windowing is applied in order to compute a short-time Laguerre transform (STLT) and, at the same time, large frequency-dependent delay terms are replaced by constant delays. In order to derive the STLT algorithm, consider a window $w(n)$ satisfying the perfect overlap-add condition

$$\sum_{r=-\infty}^{+\infty} w(n - rL) = 1, \qquad (11.13)$$

where $L \leq N$ is an integer. This condition says that the superposition of shifted windows adds up to one. If $\tilde{s}_{fw}(n)$ denotes the Laguerre transform (11.6) of the signal $s(n)$, then we have identically,

$$\tilde{s}_{fw}(k) = \sum_{r=-\infty}^{+\infty} w(k - rL)\tilde{s}_{fw}(k) = \sum_{r=-\infty}^{+\infty} \sum_{n=0}^{+\infty} s(n)w(k - rL)\lambda_n(k). \qquad (11.14)$$

By taking the DTFT of both sides of (11.14) one can show that

$$\widetilde{S}_{fw}(\omega) = \sum_{r=-\infty}^{+\infty} e^{-jrL\omega} \frac{1}{2\pi} \int_{-\pi}^{+\pi} \Lambda_0(\Omega)S(\theta(\Omega)) W(\omega - \Omega)e^{jrL\Omega}d\Omega. \qquad (11.15)$$

On the other hand, from (11.12) a delay compensated version of $\widetilde{S}_{fw}^{(r)}(\omega)$ is

$$\widehat{S}_{fw}^{(r)}(\omega) = e^{-jr(L\omega - M\theta(\omega))}\widetilde{S}_{fw}^{(r)}(\omega) = e^{-jrL\omega}\Lambda_0(\omega)X^{(r)}(\theta(\omega)), \qquad (11.16)$$

which is the DTFT of the sequence

$$\widehat{s}_{fw}^{(r)}(k) = \sum_{n=0}^{N-1} h(n)s(n + rM)\lambda_n(k - rL). \qquad (11.17)$$

This equation defines the short-time Laguerre transform (STLT) of the signal $s(n)$. In order to select the proper integer M we need to study the term $X^{(r)}(\theta(\omega))$. One can show that

$$X^{(r)}(\theta(\omega)) = \frac{1}{2\pi} \int_{-\pi}^{+\pi} S(\Omega) H(\theta(\omega) - \Omega) e^{jrM\Omega} d\Omega. \tag{11.18}$$

We would like to approximate the integral in (11.15) by $\Lambda_0(\omega) X^{(r)}(\theta(\omega))$. Suppose that $H(\omega)$ is an unwarped version of $W(\omega)$, i.e., that

$$H(\omega) = \frac{d\theta^{-1}(\omega)}{d\omega} W(\theta^{-1}(\omega)) = \left|\Lambda_0^T(\omega)\right|^2 W(\theta^{-1}(\omega)). \tag{11.19}$$

By performing in (11.18) the change of variable $\Omega = \theta(\omega) + \theta(\alpha - \omega)$ we obtain

$$X^{(r)}(\theta(\omega)) = \frac{1}{2\pi} \int_{-\pi}^{+\pi} S(\theta(\omega) - \theta(\omega - \alpha)) W(\omega - \alpha) e^{jrM(\theta(\omega) - \theta(\omega - \alpha))} d\alpha. \tag{11.20}$$

Since $W(\omega)$ is a lowpass function, only the terms for $\alpha \approx \omega$ contribute to the last integral. Therefore, from (11.16) and (11.20) we conclude that the superposition of delay-compensated versions of $\widetilde{S}_{fw}^{(r)}(\omega)$ can be approximated as follows,

$$\widehat{S}_{fw}(\omega) = \sum_{r=-\infty}^{+\infty} \widehat{S}_{fw}^{(r)}(\omega) \approx \sum_{r=-\infty}^{+\infty} e^{-jrL\omega} \frac{1}{2\pi} \int_{-\pi}^{+\pi} \Lambda_0(\alpha) S(\theta(\alpha)) W(\omega - \alpha) e^{jrM\theta(\alpha)} d\alpha. \tag{11.21}$$

Equation (11.21) should be compared with (11.15). A linear approximation of $\theta(\alpha)$ is

$$\theta(\alpha) = \theta'(0)\alpha + O(\alpha^3) = \frac{1+b}{1-b}\alpha + O(\alpha^3). \tag{11.22}$$

One can show that this is a fairly good approximation for $|\alpha| < \frac{1-b}{2}\pi$. In this frequency range, if we select

$$M \approx \frac{1-b}{1+b} L \tag{11.23}$$

then

$$\widehat{S}_{fw}(\omega) \approx \widetilde{S}_{fw}(\omega),$$

i.e., the overlap-add of STLT components well approximates the Laguerre transform. In other words, an approximate scheme for computing the Laguerre transform consists of taking the Laguerre transform of overlapping signal frames windowed by the unwarped window $h(n)$ and overlap-adding the result, as shown in Figure 11.9. This method allows for a real-time implementation of frequency warping via the Laguerre transform. It relies on the linear approximation (11.22) of the phase of the allpass, valid for the low-frequency range. An important issue is the choice of the window $w(n)$. Many classical windows, e.g., rectangular, triangular, etc., satisfy condition (11.13). However, (11.21) is a close approximation of the Laguerre transform only if the window sidelobes are sufficiently attenuated. Furthermore, the unwarped version (11.19) of the window can be computed via a Laguerre transform with the normalizing filter $\Lambda_0^T(\omega)$ removed. In principle $h(n)$ has infinite length. However, the inverse Laguerre transform of a lowpass window $w(n)$ has essential length

$$N \approx \left. \frac{d\theta^{-1}}{d\omega} \right|_{\omega=0} N_w = \frac{1-b}{1+b} N_w.$$

In order to avoid artifacts in the multiplication of the signal by the window, we are interested in windows whose Laguerre transform essentially is a dilated or stretched version of the window itself. This property turns out to be approximately well satisfied by the Hanning window

$$w(n) = \begin{cases} \frac{1}{2}\left(1 - \cos\frac{2\pi n}{N_w}\right) & n = 0, 1, ..., N_w - 1 \\ 0 & \text{otherwise} \end{cases}.$$

The choice of the length N_w is arbitrary. Furthermore, the Hanning window satisfies (11.13) for any L integer submultiple of N_w. Long windows tend to better approximate pure frequency warping. However, both response time and computational complexity increase with the length of the window. Moreover, the time-organization destruction effect is more audible using extremely long windows. The integer L controls the overlap $N_w - L$ of the output warped frames. When warping with a positive value of the parameter b one should select a considerable overlap, e.g., $N_w = 5L$, in order to avoid amplitude distortion of the high-frequency components, which, in this case, are more concentrated in the Laguerre domain, as shown in Figure 11.8. Finally, the integer M fixing the input frames overlap is obtained by rounding the right-hand side of (11.23). Next we provide a simple M-file 11.2 implementing frequency warping by means of STLT overlap-add. The function gives a simple implementation of frequency warping via short-time Laguerre transform.[1]

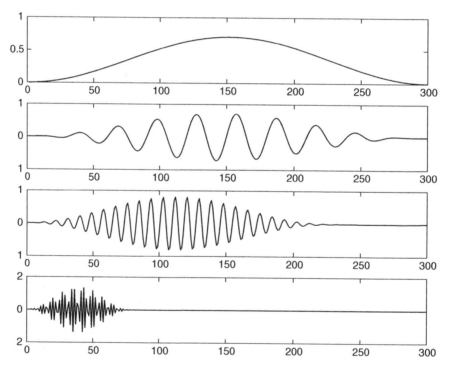

Figure 11.8 Short-time warping: different length of warped signals from low to high frequencies (top to bottom).

---

[1] The function lugtun is the same as lagt reported in Section 11.2.3, except that the line yy = filter (sqrt(1-b ^ 2),[1,b],x); is replaced by the line yy = x; in order to compute the non-normalized Laguerre transform.

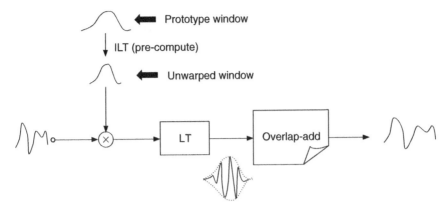

Figure 11.9 Block diagram of the approximate algorithm for frequency warping via overlap-add of the STLT components. The block LT denotes the Laguerre transform and ILT its inverse.

M-file 11.2 (winlagt.m)

```
function sfw=winlagt(s,b,Nw,L)
% Author: G. Evangelista
% Frequency warping via STLT of the signal s with parameter b,
% output window length Nw and time-shift L
w=L*(1-cos(2*pi*(0:Nw-1)/Nw))/Nw;      % normalized Hanning window
N=ceil(Nw*(1-b)/(1+b));                % length of unwarped window h
M=round(L*(1-b)/(1+b));                % time-domain window shift
h=lagtun(w,-b,N); h=h(:)               % unwarped window
Ls=length(s);                          % pad signal with zeros
K=ceil((Ls-N)/M);                      % to fit an entire number
s=s(:); s=[s ; zeros(N+K\ast M-Ls,1)]; % of windows
Ti=1; To=1;                            % initialize I/O pointers
Q=ceil(N*(1+abs(b))/(1-abs(b)));       % length of Laguerre transform
sfw=zeros(Q,1);                        % initialize output signal
for k=1:K
 yy=lagt(s(Ti:Ti+N-1).*h,b,Q);         % Short-time Laguerre transf.
 sfw(To:end)=sfw(To:end)+yy;           % overlap-add STLT
 Ti=Ti+M;To=To+L;                      % advance I/O signal pointers
 sfw=[sfw; zeros(L,1)];                % zero pad for overlap-add
end
```

11.2.5   Vocoder-based approximation of frequency warping

A major drawback of the short-time Laguerre-transform-based algorithm for warping described in Section 11.2.4 is that the warping map approximation (11.22) is only valid in the low-frequency range. This results in a choice of window length (11.23) that is satisfactory only in this range, generating artifacts for wideband signals. Moreover, the warping map $\theta(\omega)$ is still constrained to follow one of the Laguerre curves in Figure 11.7.

An alternate approximate algorithm for frequency warping [EC07] can be derived from the STFT based time-frequency representation of the discrete time signal $s(n)$,

$$s(n) = \sum_{q=0}^{M-1} \sum_{r} S_{q,r} g_{q,r}(n),$$
(11.24)

where

$$g_{q,r}(n) = g(n - rN)e^{j\frac{2\pi}{M}qn},$$
(11.25)

for $q = 0, 1, \ldots, M - 1$ and $r \in \mathbf{Z}$, are overlapping time-shifted and frequency-modulated windows and

$$S_{q,r} = \sum_{n} x(n)g_{q,r}^*(n)$$
(11.26)

are the STFT coefficients of the signal. The integer M controls the frequency resolution and is here constrained to an integer multiple $M = KN$ of the time-shift integer N, for some integer K. If the window g has finite length M, then the factor K determines the number of windows that have non-zero overlap in each length N segment. Intuitively, each narrow-band component of the time-frequency representation intercepts only a small portion of the warping map θ, which makes a local linear approximation possible.

The analysis and synthesis real windows $g(n)$ in (11.26) and (11.24) are identical as we assume that

$$\sum_{r} g^2(n - rN) = \frac{1}{M}$$
(11.27)

for perfect reconstruction. For our purposes, $g(n)$ can be identified with the sine window

$$g(n) = \sqrt{\frac{2}{KM}} \sin\left(\frac{\pi n}{M}\right),$$
(11.28)

in which case the following Parseval relationship holds true,

$$\sum_{q=0}^{M-1} \sum_{r} |S_{q,r}|^2 = \|s\|^2.$$
(11.29)

Taking the DTFT of both sides of (11.24) yields

$$S(\omega) = \sum_{q=0}^{M-1} \sum_{r} S_{q,r} G_{q,r}(\omega),$$
(11.30)

where

$$G_{q,r}(\omega) = e^{-jrN\left(\omega - \frac{2\pi q}{M}\right)} G\left(\omega - \frac{2\pi q}{M}\right).$$
(11.31)

As a result, the DTFT of the warped signal $S_{fw}(\omega) = S(\theta(\omega))$ can be obtained from (11.30) by replacing the DTFT of the shifted-modulated windows $G_{q,r}(\omega)$ with the warped windows

$$\tilde{G}_{q,r}(\omega) = e^{-jrN\left(\theta(\omega) - \frac{2\pi q}{M}\right)} G\left(\theta(\omega) - \frac{2\pi q}{M}\right).$$
(11.32)

Since the window is a low pass function, the warped windows (11.32) are essentially non-zero only for ω in the neighborhood of the roots of the equation $\theta(\omega) = \frac{2\pi q}{M}$. If the map θ is invertible, a first order Taylor series approximation about the unique roots $\omega_q = \theta^{-1}\left(\frac{2\pi q}{M}\right)$ is then justified:

$$\theta(\omega) \approx \theta(\omega_q) + \theta'(\omega_q)(\omega - \omega_q) = \frac{2\pi q}{M} + \beta_q(\omega - \omega_q),\tag{11.33}$$

where

$$\beta_q = \theta'(\omega_q) = \theta'\left(\theta^{-1}\left(\frac{2\pi q}{M}\right)\right) = \left(\frac{d\theta^{-1}}{d\omega}\bigg|_{\omega = \frac{2\pi q}{M}}\right)^{-1}.\tag{11.34}$$

Considering (11.33) for each synthesis band results in the locally linear approximation of the warping map shown in Figure 11.10.

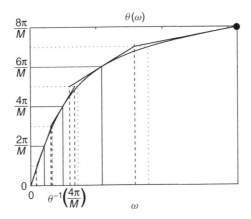

Figure 11.10 Locally linear approximation of warping map: center bands (solid lines) and band edges (dotted lines).

In the same approximation we have

$$\tilde{G}_{q,r}(\omega) \approx e^{-jrN\beta_q(\omega - \omega_q)} G(\beta_q(\omega - \omega_q)).\tag{11.35}$$

Like several other windows, the sine window $g(n)$ is obtained by sampling a continuous time function $g^{(a)}(t)$, so that $g(n) = g^{(a)}(n)$. In that case, one can show [EC07] that

$$\tilde{g}_{q,r}(n) \approx \frac{e^{j\omega_q n}}{\beta_q} g^{(a)}\left(\frac{n - r\beta_q N}{\beta_q}\right),\tag{11.36}$$

which is a scaled, shifted and modulated version of the original window. For a unitary warping operation (see Section 11.2.2) the window (11.36) must be further multiplied by a factor $\sqrt{\beta_q}$, which is the square root of the derivative of the map evaluated at the point ω_q.

Since the shift factor $\beta_q N$ is not necessarily an integer, the computation is greatly simplified if $\beta_q N$ is rounded to the nearest integer N_q. The resulting quantization error of the time-shift steps

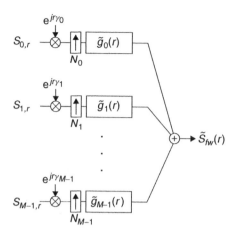

Figure 11.11   Synthesis filter bank structure for computing approximate frequency warping from STFT analysis coefficients.

is negligible for sufficiently large N. Similarly, the window length $\beta_q M = \beta_q K N$ can be rounded to the integer $M_q = K N_q$. In this case, the approximated computation of frequency warping from the STFT $S_{q,r}$ of the signal $s(n)$ can be performed by means of the multirate filter bank shown in Figure 11.11, where

$$\tilde{g}_q(n) = \tilde{g}_{q,0}(n), \tag{11.37}$$

with phase factors $\gamma_q = N_q \omega_q$.

The modulating frequencies of the impulse responses of the various channels of the filter bank are not harmonically related and the window length is channel dependent. Therefore, while the analysis coefficients can be obtained by frame-by-frame FFT, the approximate warping synthesis structure cannot be implemented in an efficient FFT-based computational scheme. In the operation count per number of samples, the synthesis filter bank has linear complexity. If the signal is real and if the warping map has odd symmetry, then only the first half of the complex filter-bank sections need to be computed, the output being formed by taking the real part.

With the given time-frequency approximate warping algorithm, real-time operation is only possible if $N_q \geq N$ for any q. This constraint is satisfied if $\theta'(\omega) \geq 1$ for any ω. In fact, in the multirate structure in Figure 11.11 each channel operates at a different rate regulated by the upsampling factor N_q. When $N_q < N$ the synthesis structure produces fewer samples than those required by the STFT analysis block. In this case, the output lags behind the input and real-time operation is ruled out. In synthesis applications the map and the input pitch can both be suitably scaled to guarantee real-time operation. In audio effects applications, in order to compute warping in real-time, interpolation or prediction of the STFT data must be introduced in those channels where the warping map has $\theta'(\omega) < 1$, similarly to that often introduced in real-time pitch-shifters when the pitch is shifted upwards.

The artifacts introduced by the vocoder approximation of frequency warping are much less severe than the ones introduced with short-time Laguerre transform, both numerically and perceptually, as measured with PEAQ quality index. The main problems arise from the quantization of time-shift step and window length, especially in conjunction with flatter portions of the warping map (small derivative). These problems are mitigated by using proportionally larger values of M and N. Increasing the overlap does not improve quality.

11.2.6   Time-varying frequency warping

Suppose that each frequency-dependent delay element in the structure of Figure 11.5 has its own phase characteristics $\theta_k(\omega)$ and suppose that we remove the scaling filter. Accordingly, the outputs of the structure are the sequences

$$\psi_n(k) = a_1(k) * a_2(k) * \ldots * a_n(k),$$

with $\psi_0(k) = \delta(k)$, obtained by convolving the impulse responses $a_m(k)$ of the allpass filters

$$A_m(z) = \frac{z^{-1} - b_m}{1 - b_m z^{-1}}.$$

Hence the z-transforms of the sequences $\psi_n(k)$ are

$$\Phi_n(z) = \prod_{k=1}^{n} \frac{z^{-1} - b_m}{1 - b_m z^{-1}}$$

and their DTFT is

$$\Phi_n(\omega) = \prod_{k=1}^{n} e^{-j\theta_k(\omega)} = e^{-j\Theta_n(\omega)},$$

where

$$\Theta_n(\omega) = \sum_{k=1}^{n} \theta_k(\omega)$$

is the sign-reversed cumulative phase of the first n delay elements. By multiplying each signal sample $s(n)$ by the corresponding sequence $\varphi_n(k)$ we obtain the signal

$$s_{tvfw}(k) = \sum_{n=0}^{+\infty} s(n)\varphi_n(k),$$

whose DTFT is

$$S_{tvfw}(\omega) = \sum_{n=0}^{+\infty} s(n)e^{-j\Theta_n(\omega)}.$$

Note that this is an important generalization of (11.3) in which the phase terms are not integer multiples of each other. In the special case where all the delays are equal we have $\theta_k(\omega) = \theta(\omega)$ and $\Theta_n(\omega) = n\theta(\omega)$. If we suppose that the delays are equal in runs of N, then signals of finite length N, supported on the intervals $(r-1)N, \ldots, rN - 1$ are frequency warped according to distinct characteristics. For the same reason, signal samples falling in these intervals are differently warped. Portions of the signal falling in two adjacent intervals are warped in a mixed way. More generally, one can have a different delay for each signal sample. This results in a time-varying frequency warping [EC99, EC00]. From a musical point of view one is often interested in slow and oscillatory variations of the Laguerre parameter, as we will discuss in Section 11.3. It is possible to derive a computational structure for time-varying warping analogous to that reported in Figure 11.6. This is obtained by considering the sequences $\psi_n(k)$ whose z-transforms satisfy the following recurrence:

$$\Psi_0(z) = \frac{1}{1 - b_1 z^{-1}}$$

$$\Psi_n(z) = H_n(z)\Psi_{n-1}(z),$$

where

$$H_n(z) = \frac{1 - b_n b_{n+1}}{1 - b_{n-1} b_n} \frac{z^{-1} - b_{n-1}}{1 - b_{n+1} z^{-1}}$$

and $b_0 = 0$. This set of sequences plays the same role as the transposed sequences (11.9) in the Laguerre expansion. However, the sequences $\varphi_n(k)$ and $\psi_n(k)$ are not orthogonal, rather, they are biorthogonal, i.e.,

$$\sum_{k=0}^{+\infty} \varphi_n(k) \psi_m(k) = \delta(n - m).$$

Consequently, our time-varying frequency-warping scheme is not a unitary transform of the signal, hence it does not verify the energy preservation property (11.1). However, one can show that this is a complete representation of signals. Hence the time-varying frequency warping is an effect that can be undone without storing the original signal. The modified structure for computing time-varying frequency warping is reported in Figure 11.12. In order to preserve the same direction of warping as in the fixed parameter Laguerre transform, the sign of the parameter sequence must be reversed, which is equivalent to exchanging the roles of $\theta_n(\omega)$ and $\theta_n^{-1}(\omega)$. The inverse structure can be derived in terms of a tapped dispersive delay line based on $\Phi_n(\omega)$ with the warped signal samples used as tap weights. Next we provide a simple M-file 11.3 implementing the structure of Figure 11.12. The function gives a simple implementation of the variable parameter generalized Laguerre transform.

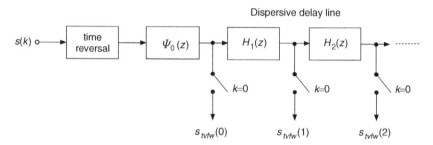

Figure 11.12   Structure for computing time-varying frequency warping via generalized Laguerre transform with variable parameter.

M-file 11.3 (lagtbvar.m)

```
function y=lagtbvar(x,b,M)
% Author: G. Evangelista
% computes coefficients y of biorthogonal Laguerre expansion of x
% using variable parameters b(k) where b is a length M array
N=length(x);
yy=x(N:-1:1);                  % time reverse input
y=zeros(1,M);
yy=filter(1,[1, b(1)],yy);     % filter by psi_0(z)
y(1)=yy(N);                    % retain the last sample only
% filter by H_1(z)(unscaled, b to -b)
yy=filter([0,1],[1, b(2)],yy);
y(2)=yy(N)*(1-b(1)*b(2));      % retain the last sample only and scale
for k=3:M
  % filter by H_(k-1)(z)(unscaled, b to -b)
  yy=filter([b(k-2),1],[1, b(k)],yy);
  y(k)=yy(N)*(1-b(k-1)*b(k));  % retain the last sample only and scale
end
```

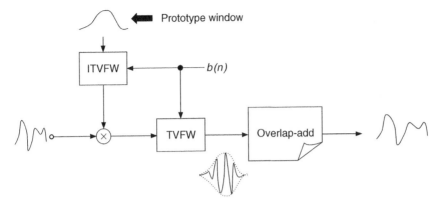

Figure 11.13 Block diagram of the approximate algorithm for time-varying frequency warping. The blocks TVFW and ITVFW respectively denote time-varying frequency warping and its inverse.

Time-varying frequency warping has a fast approximate algorithm whose block diagram is reported in Figure 11.13. The scheme is similar to the overlap-add method derived for the Laguerre transform and is shown in Figure 11.9. However, due to the time-varying aspect, the inverse time-varying warping of the prototype window must be computed for each input frame.

An extension of the vocoder-based frequency-warping algorithm discussed in Section 11.2.5 for handling the time-varying case is available [E08], which works under the assumption that the warping map is constant in each time interval of N samples. Since changes in the warping map are audible only over time intervals larger than 25 ms, this constraint on the update rate is not too severe.

11.3   Musical uses of warping

In this section we describe a few applications of warping in music. As already pointed out, many aspects and properties of warping musical signals are still to be explored and many results of this section may be deemed as experimental. Applications that will be discussed range from accurate pitch-shifting of inharmonic sources and inharmonization of harmonic sources, to feature and transient extraction, vibrato editing and morphing.

11.3.1   Pitch-shifting inharmonic sounds

The sounds from a large class of instruments are inherently inharmonic. The spacing of the frequencies of the partials is not uniform. In piano sounds, in the low register, the displacement of the partials from the harmonics becomes more and more apparent as we move towards the lower end of the keyboard. In Figure 11.14 we report data ($\times$ marks) extracted from a low-pitch piano tone (≈ 27 Hz). These represent the differences between the frequency of a partial and that of the next one. If the sound were harmonic, one should observe a flat distribution of points aligned on the pitch frequency. On the contrary, one observes that the spacing between the partials increases with the order of the overtones. The distribution of the partials can be closely matched to the derivative of a Laguerre curve. This can be obtained by means of an optimization of the parameter b in (11.10). It turns out that the absolute value of the optimum Laguerre parameter decreases as we move from lower to higher tones. This means that the warping curve becomes more and more linear, as can be seen from Figure 11.7. By frequency warping the original piano tone with the inverse of the fitted Laguerre map one transforms the originally inharmonic partials into a set of

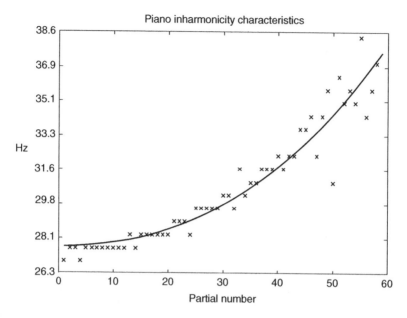

Figure 11.14 Inharmonicity characteristics of a 27 Hz piano tone: data are marked by x and the solid curve represents the optimum Laguerre difference curve fitting the data.

harmonic partials. As a result of warping the fundamental frequency, the pitch of the resulting tone will be higher. Vice versa, by warping by a Laguerre map with a small positive value of the parameter one decreases pitch and increases the degree of inharmonicity. This gives us a method for pitch-shifting piano tones that is particularly accurate in matching the inharmonicity of lower tones. Given a piano tone one can determine the value and the sign of the warping parameter in order to transform it to a lower or higher tone. Specifically, suppose that the fundamental frequency is f_0 and that the desired frequency is $\widehat{f}_0$. In terms of the normalized frequency ω, with a sampling rate f_S, we have, respectively, $\omega_0 = \frac{2\pi f_0}{f_S}$ and $\widehat{\omega}_0 = \frac{2\pi \widehat{f}_0}{f_S}$. As remarked in Section 11.2.2 the new normalized fundamental frequency after warping is $\widehat{\omega}_0 = \theta^{-1}(\omega_0)$. One can show that

$$\theta^{-1}(\omega) = 2 \arctan\left(\frac{1-b}{1+b} \tan \frac{\omega}{2}\right),$$

hence we can determine the required value of b as follows:

$$b = \frac{\tan \frac{\pi f_0}{f_S} - \tan \frac{\pi \widehat{f}_0}{f_S}}{\tan \frac{\pi f_0}{f_S} + \tan \frac{\pi \widehat{f}_0}{f_S}}. \tag{11.38}$$

For inharmonic sounds, pitch-shifting by frequency warping is more accurate than conventional algorithms based on proportional scaling of fundamental frequency and overtones. In fact, the warping characteristics can be ultimately justified by means of a physical model of stiff strings or membranes [VS94,TEC97]. It is quite striking that the Laguerre characteristics match those of piano tones for a large range. Therefore one obtains accurate pitch-shifting and the inharmonicity law by pure frequency warping. Otherwise one should resort to a combination of conventional

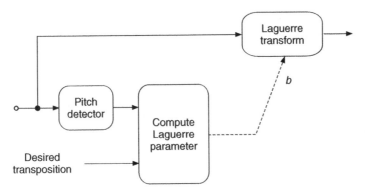

Figure 11.15 Block diagram of inharmonic sounds pitch shifter.

pitch-shifting and warping. The block diagram of a pitch shifter for inharmonic sounds based on the Laguerre transform is shown in Figure 11.15. Frequency warping can also be used in conjunction with proportional pitch-shifting algorithms to pitch-shift harmonic signals. These techniques usually yield a rational alteration of the pitch and one needs to improve their resolution. Also, ratios other than simple ratios with small integers in both numerator and denominator are costly from a computational point of view. By frequency warping the proportionally pitch-shifted signal with a small absolute value of the warping parameter one can introduce a small incremental pitch-shifting operation, which, when added to the rational pitch-shifting operation, provides a pitch closer or equal to the desired pitch. At the same time, the inharmonicity introduced is not perceptually relevant due to the small value of the warping parameter.

11.3.2 Inharmonizer

Among the new effects introduced by frequency warping is the inharmonizer. This effect is obtained by frequency warping an original harmonic sound with a large absolute value ($\simeq 0.5$) of the parameter. The resulting sound is enriched by inharmonic partials, maps of the original harmonic partials, as discussed in Section 11.2.2. Notice that both pitch and duration of the original sound are altered by warping. In fact, frequency warping stretches or shrinks the width of the peaks centered on the partial frequencies. As a result, the amplitude envelopes of the partials are altered. In the first approximation they are simply time-scaled. In order to restore the original pitch and duration one can resort to resampling techniques. At conventional sampling rates (20–44 kHz) the fundamental frequency of a large class of sounds from natural instruments falls into the low-frequency portion of the axis. In that region the warping map is approximately linear with coefficients which are the derivative of the map in $\omega = 0$. This is also the amount by which the duration of the signal is scaled. This makes it possible to achieve pitch and duration rescaling by a single resampling operation. In many cases the inharmonizer effect introduces interesting detuning of the higher partials, transforming, for example, a trumpet sound into a bell-like sound or a guitar sound into a piano-like sound.

The inharmonizer can also be used in physical model synthesis, e.g., as a Karplus–Strong post-processing block, in order to model inharmonicity due to dispersive propagation in stiff media [TEC04]. In that case, the synthesis block can be implemented with elementary delays instead of a long chain of allpass filters. Moreover, using the vocoder-based warping algorithm of Section 11.2.5, one can achieve higher flexibility in the choice of the warping map in order to match physical dispersion characteristics.

11.3.3   Comb filtering + warping and extraction of excitation signals in inharmonic sounds

As previously pointed out, by frequency warping the original piano tone with the inverse of the fitted Laguerre map, one transforms the originally inharmonic partials into a set of harmonic partials. This property can be exploited in order to extract the hammer noise from piano sounds. In fact, the audible effect of the hammer noise lies in areas of the frequency spectrum that are not masked by the partials, i.e., in between the partials. It is easy to build a comb filter based on the harmonics of the transformed piano sound. In fact, given a narrow-band lowpass filter with frequency response $H(\omega)$, the frequency response $H(\omega P)$, where P is the period of the signal expressed in number of samples, is a comb filter adjusted to the harmonics. This filter is obtained by inserting $P - 1$ zeros in the filter coefficients. Likewise, if $G(\omega)$ is a high pass filter, the filter $G(\omega P)$ will select all the frequency bands that lie in between the harmonics. In order to obtain the piano hammer noise it suffices to unwarp the signal in order to regularize the partials into harmonics, determine the transformed pitch, filter with $G(\omega P)$ and apply frequency warping to re-obtain the inharmonic distribution. In the present case it is more convenient to pre-warp the filters rather than the signals. However, in a more general setting where the inharmonic signal components are analyzed by means of pitch-synchronous wavelets [Eva93, Eva94], which include downsampling operations, it can be shown that it is more convenient to warp the signal [EC97, EC98a, EC98b]. The block diagram of a tuned warped comb filter is shown in Figure 11.16.

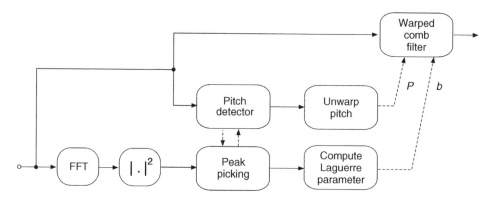

Figure 11.16 Block diagram of tuned warped comb structure for extracting partials or excitation noise from inharmonic sounds.

11.3.4   Vibrato, glissando, trill and flatterzunge

Vibrato can be generated by means of time-varying frequency warping, by using an oscillating sequence of parameters b with low amplitude and frequency. For small values of the warping parameter, the warping curve only slightly deviates from the linear map and the harmonic structure of the signal is essentially preserved, while pitch-shifting is the only perceptually relevant effect. This is especially true when the parameter law is oscillatory so that the harmonics fluctuate around their original frequency. This allows us to introduce dynamic pitch fluctuations in natural or synthetic sounds, which can be directly controlled by the warping parameter sequence according to Equation (11.38). In particular, one can use a sinusoidal LFO as a control parameter generator to insert very natural vibrato. Both the frequency and amplitude of the oscillator can be changed at will, i.e., to synchronize the effect on the amplitude envelope of the signal or to include random fluctuations. Trill and rapid fluctuations of the pitch can be obtained by means of a square wave

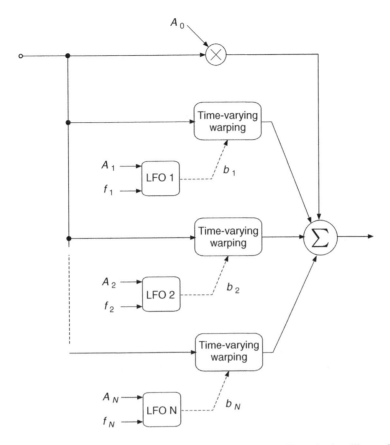

Figure 11.17   Block diagram for computing vibrato, trill, chorus-like, phasing-like or flange-like effects. For Flatterzunge we add random noise to the LFOs. For glissando the LFOs are replaced by envelope generators.

LFO. By mixing pitch-modulated versions of the sound with the original signal one can obtain effects similar to phasing, flanging and chorusing. By frequency warping a flute sound using random noise or random amplitude square wave as parameter sequences one obtains interesting effects typical of Flatterzunge. As another example, glissando can be inserted by means of an increasing or decreasing sequence of parameters. A general structure based on mixed independent time-varying warping channels for computing the above effects is shown in Figure 11.17. In much the same way, one can edit sounds containing vibrato or any pitch modulation in order to reduce or remove this effect. It suffices to extract the pitch fluctuation law from the sound by means of a pitch detection algorithm or by tracking the partials in the spectrogram of the sound. From this law one can obtain the law of variation of the parameter b and by applying the time-varying frequency-warping algorithm with a reversed sign sequence of parameters, one can counteract the pitch modulation effect [EC00].

11.3.5   Morphing

Accurate spectral morphing requires arbitrary maps of the frequency axis in order to transform the partials of one sound into the partials of another sound. The FFT warping algorithm illustrated in Section 11.2.3 can be employed with simplicity to perform this task. However, since invertibility

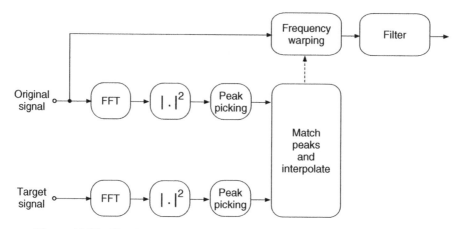

Figure 11.18 Simple diagram for computing morphing via frequency warping.

is not an issue, versions of the Laguerre transform based on higher-order allpass filters can be employed as well. In order to determine the suitable warping map one can use a peak-picking algorithm in the frequency domain to detect the partials of both the original and desired sound. Simple morphing examples can be computed using the structure shown in Figure 11.18. A set of points on an initial-final frequency plane is determined, which can be interpolated to produce a smooth warping curve. As an example one can eliminate the even harmonics in a voiced sound by mapping these onto odd harmonics. Realistic morphing also requires amplitude scaling of the partials. This corresponds to a simple filtering operation on the signal. Morphing can also be performed as a dynamic operation by means of time-varying frequency warping using a sequence of maps.

11.4 Conclusion

In this chapter we introduced a class of digital audio effects based on frequency-warping techniques of recent interest in musical applications. The deformation of the frequency axis, whether static or dynamic, introduces a new point of view and new tools for processing sounds. This transformation allows us to insert or edit vibrato, trill, Flatterzunge and glissando, adding controlled expression to static sounds. Harmonic sounds can be mapped into inharmonic sounds, introducing fine partial detuning to color them. Frequency warping also provides a concerned or model-based method for pitch-shifting inherently inharmonic sounds such as piano and drums sounds. Mixing independent time-varying warping channels achieves interesting generalizations of flanging, chorusing and phasing effects. An efficient algorithm based on the short-time Laguerre transform makes frequency warping computable in real-time. Since frequency warping is at present fairly unexploited in musical contexts we encourage musicians and sound engineers to experiment with this appealing technique.

References

[Bro65] P. W. Broome. Discrete orthonormal sequences. *J. Assoc. Comput. Machinery*, 12(2): 151–168, 1965.

[E08]   G. Evangelista. Modified phase vocoder scheme for dynamic frequency warping. In *Proc. IEEE 3rd Int. Symp. Commun. Control Signal Process. (ISCCSP 2008)*, pp. 1291–1296, 2008.

[EC97]   G. Evangelista and S. Cavaliere. Analysis and regularization of inharmonic sounds via pitch-synchronous frequency warped wavelets. In *Proc. Int. Comp. Music Conf.*, pp. 51–54, 1997.

[EC98a] G. Evangelista and S. Cavaliere. Discrete frequency warped wavelets: theory and applications. *IEEE Trans. Signal Process.*, special issue on Theory and Applications of Filter Banks and Wavelets, 46(4): 874–885, 1998.

[EC98b] G. Evangelista and S. Cavaliere. Frequency warped filter banks and wavelet transform: a discrete-time approach via Laguerre expansions. *IEEE Trans. Signal Proc.*, 46(10): 2638–2650, 1998.

[EC99] G. Evangelista and S. Cavaliere. Time-varying frequency warping: results and experiments. In *Proc. DAFX-99 Digital Audio Effects Workshop*, pp. 13–16, 1999.

[EC07] G. Evangelista and S. Cavaliere. Real-time and efficient algorithms for frequency warping based on local approximations of warping operators. In *Proc. Digital Audio Effects Conf. (DAFx '07)*, pp. 269–276, 2007.

[EC00] G. Evangelista and S. Cavaliere. Audio effects based on biorthogonal time-varying frequency warping. *EURASIP J. Appl. Signal Process.*, 1(1): 27–35, 2001.

[Eva93] G. Evangelista. Pitch synchronous wavelet representations of speech and music signals. *IEEE Trans. Signal Process.*, special issue on Wavelets and Signal Processing, 41(12): 3313–3330, 1993.

[Eva94] G. Evangelista. Comb and multiplexed wavelet transforms and their applications to signal processing. *IEEE Trans. Signal Process.*, 42(2): 292–303, 1994.

[OJ72] A. V. Oppenheim and D. H. Johnson. Discrete representation of signals. *Proc. IEEE*, 60: 681–691, 1972.

[TEC04] I. Testa, G. Evangelista and S. Cavaliere. Physically inspired models for the synthesis of stiff strings with dispersive waveguides. *EURASIP J. Appl. Signal Process.* special issue on Model-Based Sound Synthesis. 2004(7): 964–977, 2004.

[TEC97] I. Testa, G. Evangelista and S. Cavaliere. A physical model of stiff strings. In *Proc. Inst. Acoust. (Internat. Symp. on Music and Acoustics, ISMA'97)*, vol. 19: Part 5 (1997) Book 1, pp. 219–224, Edinburgh, 1997.

[VS94] S. A. Van Duyne and J. O. Smith. A simplified approach to modeling dispersion caused by stiffness in strings and plates. In *Proc. Int. Comp. Music Conf.*, pp. 407–410, 1994.

12

Virtual analog effects

V. Välimäki, S. Bilbao, J. O. Smith, J. S. Abel, J. Pakarinen and D. Berners

12.1 Introduction

Virtual analog effects are a consequence of the ongoing digitization of all equipment used in music production. Various digital methods to imitate the warm or lo-fi sound qualities that remind listeners of analog times are covered in this chapter. In particular, many algorithms presented in this chapter are physical models of audio effect boxes that have been traditionally analog electronic or electromechanical devices, such as voltage-controlled filters and spring reverberation units. Some algorithms, for instance the telephone sound effect, are signal models, which produce analog-sounding results without analog circuit analysis. Almost all algorithms are nonlinear and produce distortion. A few virtual analog effects, such as the wah-wah filter, phase, and vintage valve amplifier simulation, are also mentioned elsewhere in this book.

The following virtual analog effect processing techniques are reviewed in this chapter. Section 12.2 discusses virtual analog filters. We start with second- and higher-order filters, which include nonlinear elements, and proceed to equalizers and filter-based effect-processing algorithms. Models for valve amplifiers are reviewed in Section 12.3. Simulation of spring and plate reverberations units is described in Section 12.4. Section 12.5 focuses on simulation of vintage tape-based echo units. Finally, Section 12.6 gives an introduction to audio antiquing, which refers to the transformation of clean, modern audio files into ancient-sounding analog recordings.

12.2 Virtual analog filters

12.2.1 Nonlinear resonator

Analog filters used in music technology are not strictly speaking linear, because at high signal levels they produce distortion. One attempt to include this phenomenon in digital filters has been described by Rossum [Ros92]. He proposed inserting a saturating nonlinearity in the feedback path of a second-order all-pole filter, see Figure 12.1. In this case, the clipper is a symmetrical hard limiter. With this modification, the filter behaves a lot like an analog filter. It produces harmonic distortion and compression when the input signal level is high. Furthermore, its resonance frequency changes when the filter is overloaded, as pointed out in [Ros92]. This technique was used in the E-mu EMAX II sampler, which appeared in 1989. It is an early example of a virtual analog filter used in commercial products.

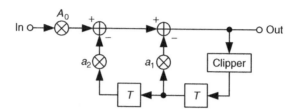

Figure 12.1   A digital resonant filter with a nonlinear element in its feedback path [Ros92].

A MATLAB® implementation of Rossum's nonlinear resonator is given in M-file 12.1. The filter coefficients A_0, a_1, and a_2 are computed as in a conventional digital resonator, see, e.g., [Ste96]. In the following examples, we set the resonance frequency to 1 kHz and the bandwidth to 20 Hz. The sampling rate is $f_S = 44.1$ kHz. The saturation limit of the clipper is set to 1.0.

When the amplitude of the input signal is 1.0, no distortion occurs, because the signal level at the input of the first state variable (unit delay) does not exceed the saturation level. However, when the input amplitude is larger than the saturation limit, the filter compresses and distorts the signal. At the same time aliasing occurs, since all distortion components above the Nyquist limit get mirrored back to the audio band. To avoid this, it would be necessary run the filter at a higher sample rate.

Figure 12.2 shows two examples of the power spectrum of the output signal of the nonlinear resonator, when the input signal is a white-noise sequence. In Figure 12.2(a) the random samples are uniformly distributed between −1.0 and 1.0, while in Figure 11.2(b) they are distributed between −40 and 40. Again, the limit has been set to 1.0. In Figure 12.2(a) the peak in the power spectrum appears at 1000 Hz, as expected, and the −3 dB bandwidth is 20 Hz. However, in Figure 12.2(b), the center frequency has changed: It is now about 1030 Hz. Additionally, the bandwidth is wider than before, about 70 Hz. These phenomena are caused by the saturating nonlinear element, as explained in [Ros92].

M-file 12.1 (nlreson.m)

```
function y = nlreson(fc, bw, limit, x)
% function y = nlreson(fc, bw, limit, x)
% Authors: Välimäki, Bilbao, Smith, Abel, Pakarinen, Berners
%
% Parameters:
% fc = center frequency (in Hz)
% bw = bandwidth of resonance (in Hz)
% limit = saturation level
% x = input signal
fs = 44100;  % Sampling rate
R = 1 - pi*(bw/fs);  % Calculate pole radius
costheta = ((1+(R*R))/(2*R))*cos(2*pi*(fc/fs)); % Cosine of pole angle
a1 = -2*R*costheta;  % Calculate first filter coefficient
a2 = R*R;  % Calculate second filter coefficient
```

```
A0 = (1 - R*R)*sin(2*pi*(fc/fs)); % Scale factor
y = zeros(size(x)); % Allocate memory for output signal
w1 = 0; w2 = 0; % Initialize state variables (unit delays)
y(1) = A0*x(1); % The first input sample goes right through
w0 = y(1); % Input to the saturating nonlinearity
for n = 2:length(x); % Process the rest of input samples
    if y(n-1) > limit, w0 = limit; % Saturate above limit
    elseif y(n-1) < -limit, w0 = - limit; % Saturate below limit
    else w0 = y(n-1);end % Otherwise do nothing
    w2 = w1; % Update the second state variable
    w1 = w0; % Update the first state variable
    y(n) = A0*x(n) - a1*w1 - a2*w2; % Compute filter output
end
```

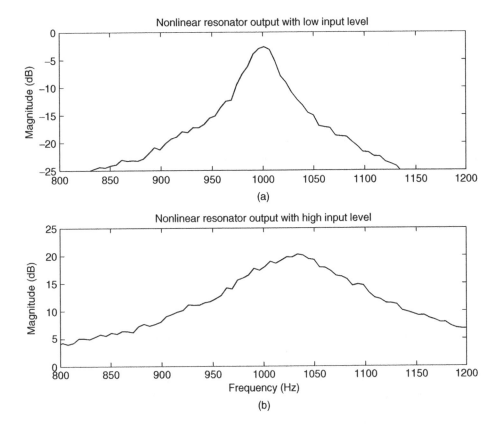

Figure 12.2 Power spectrum of the output signal when the input signal is (a) a low-level and (b) a high-level white-noise sequence.

12.2.2 Linear and nonlinear digital models of the Moog ladder filter

Next we discuss a well-known analog filter originally proposed by Robert Moog for his synthesizer designs [Moo65]. The filter consists of four one-pole filters in cascade and a global negative feedback loop. The structure is called a ladder filter because of the way in which the one-pole filter sections are cascaded. The filter includes a feedback gain factor k, which may be varied between

0 and 4. This unusual choice of range comes from the fact that at the cut-off frequency the gain of each filter section is 1/4. When $k = 4.0$, the Moog filter oscillates at its cut-off frequency (i.e., self-oscillates). The Moog ladder filter is also famous for its uncoupled control of the resonance (Q value) and the corner frequency, which are directly adjusted by the feedback gain k and the cut-off frequency parameters, respectively.

Stilson and Smith [SS96] have considered various methods of converting the Moog ladder filter into a corresponding digital filter. They found that standard transforms, the bilinear and the backward difference transform, yield a structure containing a delay-free path from input to output. To solve this problem, an ad-hoc unit delay may be inserted into the feedback loop. Figure 12.3 shows the resulting filter structure with the extra unit delay. Since the one-pole filters remain first-order filters in the digital implementation, but there is now an extra unit delay, the overall system becomes a fifth-order filter.

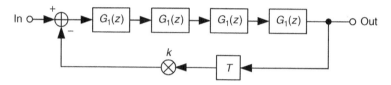

Figure 12.3   The digital Moog filter structure proposed in [SS96].

Another complication in the discretization of the Moog filter is that the constant-Q control of the corner frequency is lost. This happens with both the bilinear and the backward difference transform, which place the zeros of the first-order filter at different locations. Stilson and Smith have found a useful compromise first-order filter that has largely independent control of the Q value with corner frequency:

$$G_1(z) = \frac{1+p}{1.3} \frac{1+0.3z^{-1}}{1+pz^{-1}}, \tag{12.1}$$

where $0 \leq p \leq 1$ is the pole location. It can be determined conveniently from the normalized cut-off frequency f_c (in Hz),

$$p = \frac{f_c}{f_S}. \tag{12.2}$$

However, this relation is accurate only when the cut-off frequency is not very high (below 2 kHz or so), and otherwise the actual corner frequency of the filter will be higher than expected. A fourth-order polynomial correction to the pole location has been presented in [VH06]. The Q value of the digital Moog filter proposed by Stilson and Smith [SS96] also deviates slightly from constant at large Q values, but this error may be negligible, since humans are not very sensitive to variations in Q [SS96].

Several alternative versions of the digital Moog filter have been proposed over the years. Wise has shown that a cascade of digital allpass filters can be used to realize a filter with a similar behavior [Wis98]. Fontana has derived a simulation of the Moog filter, which avoids the extra delay in the feedback loop [Fon07]. Instead, Fontana directly solves the contribution of the states of first-order lowpass filters to the output signal. This algorithm requires more operations than the version that was described above, because divisions are involved. However, it is likely to be a more faithful simulation of the Moog ladder filter, since the structure is in principle identical to the analog prototype system.

Other researchers have considered the nonlinear behavior of the Moog filter. It is well known that the transistors used in analog filters softly saturate the signal, when the signal level becomes high. Huovilainen [Huo04] first derived a physically correct nonlinear model for the Moog filter, including the nonlinear behavior of all transistors involved. The model contains five instantaneous nonlinear functions in a feedback loop, one for each first-order section and one for the feedback. It was then found that oversampling by a factor of two at least is necessary to reduce aliasing when nonlinear functions are used [Huo04]. The structure self-oscillates when the feedback gain is 1.0. The feedback gain can even be larger than that; the nonlinear functions prevent the system from becoming unstable. The nonlinear functions also provide amplitude compression, because large signal values are limited by each of them.

Figure 12.4 shows a simplified version of Huovilainen's nonlinear Moog filter model, in which only one nonlinear function is used [VH06]. The ideal form of the nonlinear function in this case is the hyperbolic tangent function [Huo04]. In real-time implementations this would usually be implemented using a look-up table. Alternatively, another similar smoothly saturating function, such as a third-order polynomial, can be used instead. A **MATLAB** implementation of the simplified nonlinear Moog filter is given in M-file 12.2.

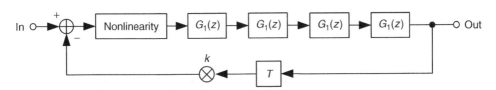

Figure 12.4   A simplified nonlinear Moog filter structure proposed in [VH06].

The simplified nonlinear Moog filter may sound slightly different from the full model. However, they share many common features, such as the ability to self-oscillate (when the resonance parameter is set to a value larger than 1) and similar compression characteristics. The latter feature is demonstrated in Figure 12.5, in which a so-called overtone sweep has been generated by filtering a sawtooth signal using three different digital versions of the Moog filter (the signals were published in the *Computer Music Journal DVD* in 2006 as demonstrations related to [VH06]). The resonant frequency of the filters slowly decreases with time. In Figure 12.5(a), the signal level increases every time the resonance frequency coincides with one of the harmonics of the signal. However, the nonlinear compression decreases these amplitude variations in Figures 12.5(b) and (c). There are minor differences between the two signals, but the output signal envelopes of the two nonlinear models are fairly similar.

M-file 12.2 (moogvcf.m)

```
function [out,out2,in2,g,h0,h1] = moogvcf(in,fc,res)
% function [out,out2,in2,g,h0,h1] = moogvcf(in,fc,res)
% Authors: Välimäki, Bilbao, Smith, Abel, Pakarinen, Berners
% Parameters:
% in = input signal
% fc= cutoff frequency (Hz)
% res = resonance (0...1 or larger for self-oscillation)
fs = 44100;  % Input and output sampling rate
fs2 = 2*fs;  % Internal sampling rate
% Two times oversampled input signal:
in = in(:); in2 = zeros(1,2*length(in)); in2(1:2:end) = in;
h = fir1(10,0.5); in2 = filter(h,1,in2);  % Anti-imaging filter
Gcomp = 0.5;  % Compensation of passband gain
g = 2*pi*fc/fs2;  % IIR feedback coefficient at fs2
Gres = res;  % Direct mapping (no table or polynomial)
```

```
h0 = g/1.3; h1 = g*0.3/1.3; % FIR part with gain g
w = [0 0 0 0 0]; % Five state variables
wold = [0 0 0 0 0]; % Previous states (unit delays)
out = zeros(size(in)); out2 = zeros(size(in2));
for n = 1:length(in2),
    u = in2(n) - 4*Gres*(wold(5) - Gcomp*in2(n)); % Input and feedback
    w(1) = tanh(u); % Saturating nonlinearity
    w(2) = h0*w(1) + h1*wold(1) + (1-g)*wold(2); % First IIR1
    w(3) = h0*w(2) + h1*wold(2) + (1-g)*wold(3); % Second IIR1
    w(4) = h0*w(3) + h1*wold(3) + (1-g)*wold(4); % Third IIR1
    w(5) = h0*w(4) + h1*wold(4) + (1-g)*wold(5); % Fourth IIR1
    out2(n) = w(5); % Filter output
    wold = w; % Data move (unit delays)
end
out2 = filter(h,1,out2); % Antialiasing filter at fs2
out = out2(1:2:end); % Decimation by factor 2 (return to original fs)
```

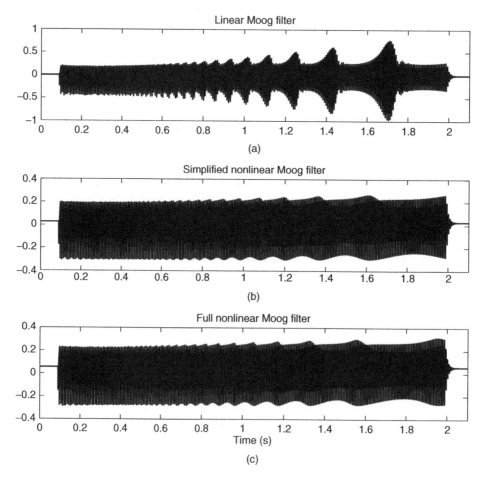

Figure 12.5 Sawtooth signal filtered with three Moog filter models: (a) the linear Stilson – Smith model of Figure 12.3, (b) the simplified nonlinear model of Figure 12.4, and (c) the full nonlinear model [Huo04].

12.2.3 Tone stack

As another useful example of a virtual analog filter, a three-channel equalizing filter used in electric guitar and bass amplifiers is presented. This so-called tone stack has the following linear third-order transfer function,

$$H_{\text{tone}}(z) = \frac{B_0 + B_1 z^{-1} + B_2 z^{-2} + B_3 z^{-3}}{A_0 + A_1 z^{-1} + A_2 z^{-2} + A_3 z^{-3}}. \tag{12.3}$$

Yeh has derived the parameter values for this digital tone stack model [YS06, Yeh09]. The equations can be seen in the M-file 12.3 below. Three parameters (top, mid, and low), which all affect several filter coefficients, can be varied to adjust the filter's magnitude response.

Figure 12.6 shows examples of magnitude responses with different parameter settings. Figure 12.6(a), (b), and (c) present the variations in the low-, middle-, and high-frequency regions, respectively. Note that the parameters are not strictly independent, but they all affect the filter gain in the middle range (see, for example, the magnitude response around 1 kHz). Furthermore, the neutral setting (low = mid = top = 0.5) does not yield a flat response, see dashed lines in Figure 12.6. This filter has its own character.

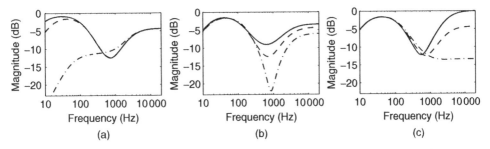

Figure 12.6 Magnitude responses of the tone stack filter model with the following parameters: (a) low = 0 (dash-dot line), low = 0.5 (dashed line), low = 1 (solid line), (b) mid = 0 (dash-dot line), mid = 0.5 (dashed line), mid = 1 (solid line), (c) top = 0 (dash-dot line), top = 0.5 (dashed line), top = 1 (solid line). The rest of the parameters are set to 0.5 in each case.

M-file 12.3 (bassman.m)

```
function [y,B0,B1,B2,B3,A0,A1,A2,A3] = bassman(low, mid, top, x)
% function [y,B0,B1,B2,B3,A0,A1,A2,A3] = bassman(low, mid, top, x)
% Authors: Välimäki, Bilbao, Smith, Abel, Pakarinen, Berners
%
% Parameters:
% low = bass level
% mid = noise level
% top = treble level
% x = input signal
fs = 44100;  % Sample rate
C1 = 0.25*10^-9;C2 = 20*10^-9;C3 = 20*10^-9;  % Component values
R1 = 250000;R2 = 1000000;R3 = 25000;R4 = 56000;  % Component values
% Analog transfer function coefficients:
b1 = top*C1*R1 + mid*C3*R3 + low*(C1*R2 + C2*R2) + (C1*R3 + C2*R3);
b2 = top*(C1*C2*R1*R4 + C1*C3*R1*R4) - mid^2*(C1*C3*R3^2 + C2*C3*R3^2) ...
     + mid*(C1*C3*R1*R3 + C1*C3*R3^2 + C2*C3*R3^2) ...
     + low*(C1*C2*R1*R2 + C1*C2*R2*R4 + C1*C3*R2*R4) ...
```

```
      + low*mid*(C1*C3*R2*R3 + C2*C3*R2*R3) ...
      + (C1*C2*R1*R3 + C1*C2*R3*R4 + C1*C3*R3*R4);
b3 = low*mid*(C1*C2*C3*R1*R2*R3 + C1*C2*C3*R2*R3*R4) ...
      - mid^2*(C1*C2*C3*R1*R3^2 + C1*C2*C3*R3^2*R4) ...
      + mid*(C1*C2*C3*R1*R3^2 + C1*C2*C3*R3^2*R4) ...
      + top*C1*C2*C3*R1*R3*R4 - top*mid*C1*C2*C3*R1*R3*R4 ...
      + top*low*C1*C2*C3*R1*R2*R4;
a0 = 1;
a1 = (C1*R1 + C1*R3 + C2*R3 + C2*R4 + C3*R4) + mid*C3*R3 ...
      + low*(C1*R2 + C2*R2);
a2 = mid*(C1*C3*R1*R3 - C2*C3*R3*R4 + C1*C3*R3^2 + C2*C3*R3^2) ...
      + low*mid*(C1*C3*R2*R3 + C2*C3*R2*R3) ...
      - mid^2*(C1*C3*R3^2 + C2*C3*R3^2) ...
      + low*(C1*C2*R2*R4 + C1*C2*R1*R2 + C1*C3*R2*R4 + C2*C3*R2*R4) ...
      + (C1*C2*R1*R4 + C1*C3*R1*R4 + C1*C2*R3*R4 + C1*C2*R1*R3 ...
      + C1*C3*R3*R4 + C2*C3*R3*R4);
a3 = low*mid*(C1*C2*C3*R1*R2*R3 + C1*C2*C3*R2*R3*R4) ...
      - mid^2*(C1*C2*C3*R1*R3^2 + C1*C2*C3*R3^2*R4) ...
      + mid*(C1*C2*C3*R3^2*R4 + C1*C2*C3*R1*R3^2 ...
      - C1*C2*C3*R1*R3*R4) + low*C1*C2*C3*R1*R2*R4 + C1*C2*C3*R1*R3*R4;
% Digital filter coefficients:
c = 2*fs;
B0 = -b1*c - b2*c^2 - b3*c^3; B1 = -b1*c + b2*c^2 + 3*b3*c^3;
B2 = b1*c + b2*c^2 - 3*b3*c^3; B3 = b1*c - b2*c^2 + b3*c^3;
A0 = -a0 - a1*c - a2*c^2 - a3*c^3;
A1 = -3*a0 - a1*c + a2*c^2 + 3*a3*c^3;
A2 = -3*a0 + a1*c + a2*c^2 - 3*a3*c^3;
A3 = -a0 + a1*c - a2*c^2 + a3*c^3;
y = filter(B,A,x);   % Output signal
```

12.2.4   Wah-wah filter

The wah-wah filter was introduced in Section 2.4.1. It operates by sweeping a single resonance through the spectrum. Typically this resonance is second-order. Following [Smi08], this section will describe digitization of the "CryBaby" wah-wah filter controlled by footpedal.

Figure 12.7(a), (b), and (c) show the amplitude responses (solid lines) of a CryBaby wah pedal measured at three representative pedal settings (rocked fully backward, middle, and forward). Our goal is to "digitize" the CryBaby by devising a sweeping resonator that audibly matches these three responses when the "wah" variable is 0, 1/2, and 1, respectively. The results of this exercise are shown in dashed lines in 12.7(a)–(c), and the audible quality is excellent.

Based on the measured shape of the amplitude response (a bandpass-resonator characteristic), and knowledge (from circuit schematics) that the bandpass is second-order, the transfer function can be presumed to be of the form

$$H(s) = g \frac{s - \xi}{\left(\frac{s}{\omega_r}\right)^2 + \frac{2}{Q}\left(\frac{s}{\omega_r}\right) + 1}, \tag{12.4}$$

where g is an overall gain factor, ξ is a real zero at or near dc (the other being at infinity), ω_r is the pole resonance frequency, and Q is the so-called "quality factor" of the resonator [Smi07].[1] The measurements reveal that ω_r, Q, and g all vary significantly with pedal angle θ. As discussed in [Smi08], good choices for these functions are as shown in M-file 12.4, where the controlling wah variable is the pedal-angle θ normalized to a [0, 1] range.

---

[1] https://ccrma.stanford.edu/~jos/filters/Quality_Factor_Q.html

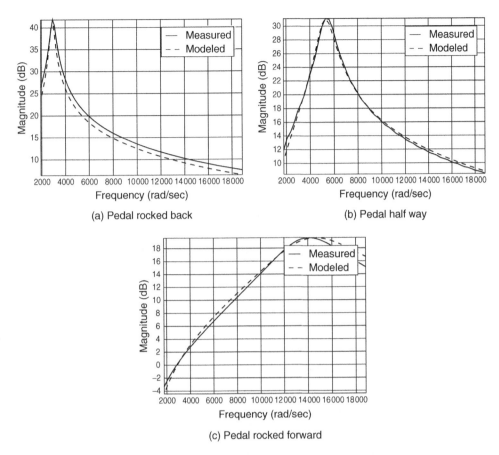

Figure 12.7   Measured (solid) and modeled (dashed) amplitude responses of the CryBaby wah pedal at three different pedal angles [Smi08].

M-file 12.4 (wahcontrols.m)

```
function [g,fr,Q] = wahcontrols(wah)
% Authors: Välimäki, Bilbao, Smith, Abel, Pakarinen, Berners
% function [g,fr,Q] = wahcontrols(wah)
%
% Parameter: wah = wah-pedal-angle normalized to lie between 0 and 1
g  = 0.1*4^wah;        % overall gain for second-order s-plane transfer funct.
fr = 450*2^(2.3*wah);  % resonance frequency (Hz) for the same transfer funct.
Q  = 2^(2*(1-wah)+1);  % resonance quality factor for the same transfer funct.
```

Digitization

Closed-form expressions for digital filter coefficients in terms of (Q, fr, g) based on $z = e^{sT} \approx 1 + sT$ (low-frequency resonance assumed) yield the code shown in M-file 12.5.

M-file 12.5 (wahdig.m)

```
% wahdig.m
% Authors: Välimäki, Bilbao, Smith, Abel, Pakarinen, Berners
```

```
% A = wahdig(fr,Q,fs)
%
% Parameters:
% fr = resonance frequency (Hz)
% Q  = resonance quality factor
% fs = sampling frequency (Hz)
%
% Returned:
% A = [1 a1 a2] = digital filter transfer-function denominator poly

frn = fr/fs;
R = 1 - PI*frn/Q; % pole radius
theta = 2*PI*frn; % pole angle
a1 = -2.0*R*cos(theta); % biquad coeff
a2 = R*R;               % biquad coeff
```

Note that in practice each time-varying coefficient should be smoothed, e.g., by a unity-gain one-pole smoother with pole at $p = 0.999$:

$$H_s(z) = \frac{1 - p}{1 - p\,z^{-1}}. \tag{12.5}$$

Virtual CryBaby results

While the presented wah pedal model sounds very faithful to the original (minus its noise), at low resonance frequencies the loudness is significantly greater than at high resonance frequencies. (This is a characteristic of the original wah pedal.) Therefore, an improvement over the original could be to determine a new scaling function g(wah) that preserves *constant loudness* as much as possible as the pedal varies. A similar effect can be had by applying dynamic range compression to the wah output, as is often done when recording an electric guitar.

A Faust[2] software implementation of the CryBaby wah pedal described in this section is included in the Faust distribution (file effect.lib).

12.2.5 Phaser

The phasing effect was introduced in Section 2.4.2. It operates by sweeping a few "notches" through the input signal spectrum. The notches are created by summing the input signal with a variably phase-shifted version of the input signal, as shown in Figure 12.8. The phase-shifting stages are conventionally first- or second-order *allpass filters* [Smi07].[3]

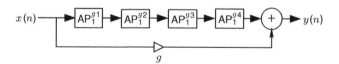

Figure 12.8 Phaser implemented by summing the direct signal with the output of four first-order allpass filters in series (from [Smi10]).

---

[2] http://faust.grame.fr/

[3] https://ccrma.stanford.edu/~jos/filters/Analog_Allpass_Filters.html

In analog hardware, such as the Univibe or MXR phase shifters, the allpass filters are typically first-order. Thus, each analog allpass has a transfer function of the form

$$H_a(s) = -\frac{s - \omega_b}{s + \omega_b}, \qquad (12.6)$$

where we will call ω_b (a real number) the *break frequency* of the allpass.

To create a *virtual analog* phaser, following closely the design of typical analog phasers, we must translate each first-order allpass to the digital domain. In discrete time, the general first-order allpass has the transfer function

$$\mathrm{AP}_1^{g_i}(z) \triangleq -\frac{g_i + z^{-1}}{1 + g_i z^{-1}}. \qquad (12.7)$$

Thus, we wish to "digitize" each first-order allpass by means of a mapping from the s plane to the z plane. There are several ways to accomplish this goal [RG75]. In this case, an excellent choice is the *bilinear transformation*[4] defined by

$$s \;\rightarrow\; c\,\frac{z - 1}{z + 1}, \qquad (12.8)$$

where c is chosen to map one particular analog frequency to a particular digital frequency (other than dc or half the sampling rate, which are always mapped from dc and infinity in the s plane, respectively). In this case, c is well chosen for each section to map the *break frequency* of the section to the corresponding point on the digital frequency axis. The relation between analog frequency ω_a and digital frequency ω_d follows immediately from Equation (12.8):

$$j\omega_a = c\,\frac{e^{j\omega_d T} - 1}{e^{j\omega_d T} + 1} = jc\,\frac{\sin(\omega_d T/2)}{\cos(\omega_d T/2)} = jc\tan(\omega_d T/2). \qquad (12.9)$$

Thus, given a particular desired break-frequency $\omega_a = \omega_d = \omega_b$, we can set

$$c = \omega_b \cot\left(\frac{\omega_b T}{2}\right). \qquad (12.10)$$

The bilinear transform preserves filter order (so we will obtain a first-order digital allpass for each first-order analog allpass), and it always maps a stable analog filter to a stable digital filter. In fact, the entire $j\omega$ axis of the s plane maps to the unit circle of the z plane, giving a one-to-one correspondence between the analog and digital frequency axes. The main error in the bilinear transform is its frequency warping, which is displayed in Equation (12.9). Only dc and one other finite frequency (chosen by setting c) are mapped without any warping error.

Applying the bilinear transformation Equation (12.8) to the first-order analog allpass filter Equation (12.6) gives

$$H_d(z) = H_a\left(c\,\frac{1 - z^{-1}}{1 + z^{-1}}\right) = \frac{c\left(\frac{1 - z^{-1}}{1 + z^{-1}}\right) - \omega_b}{c\left(\frac{1 - z^{-1}}{1 + z^{-1}}\right) + \omega_b} \triangleq \frac{p_d - z^{-1}}{1 - p_d z^{-1}}, \qquad (12.11)$$

where we have denoted the pole of the digital allpass by

$$p_d \triangleq \frac{c - \omega_b}{c + \omega_b} = \frac{1 - \tan(\omega_b T/2)}{1 + \tan(\omega_b T/2)} \approx \frac{1 - \omega_b T/2}{1 + \omega_b T/2} \approx 1 - \omega_b T. \qquad (12.12)$$

---

[4] https://ccrma.stanford.edu/~jos/pasp/Bilinear_Transformation.html

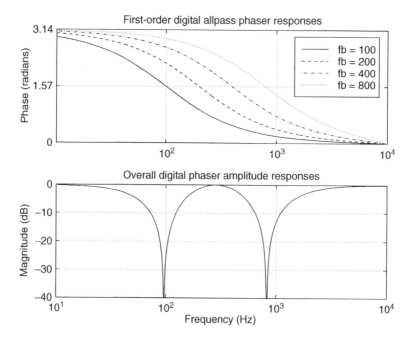

Figure 12.9 (a) Phase responses of first-order digital allpass sections having break frequencies at 100, 200, 400, and 800 Hz. The sampling rate is 20 kHz. (b) Corresponding phaser amplitude response [Smi10].

Figure 12.9 shows the digital phaser response curves. They look almost identical to the analog response curves. While the break frequencies are preserved by construction, the notches have moved slightly, although this is not visible from the plots. An overlay of the total phase of the analog and digital allpass chains is shown in Figure 12.10. We can see that the phase responses of the analog and digital allpass chains diverge visibly only above 9 kHz. The analog phase response approaches zero in the limit as $\omega_a \to \infty$, while the digital phase response reaches zero at half the sampling rate, 10 kHz in this case. This is a good example of when the bilinear transform performs very well to digitize an analog system.

In general, the bilinear transform works well to digitize feedforward analog structures in which the high-frequency warping is acceptable. When frequency warping is excessive, it can be alleviated by the use of *oversampling*; for example, the slight visible deviation in Figure 12.10 below 10 kHz can be largely eliminated by increasing the sampling rate by 15% or so. See digitizing the Moog VCF for an example in which the presence of feedback in the analog circuit leads to a delay-free loop in the digitized system under the bilinear transform [SS96, Sti06]. In such cases it is common to insert an extra unit delay in the loop, which has little effect at low frequencies. See Section 12.2.2. (Stability should then be carefully checked, as it is no longer guaranteed.)

Phasing with second-order allpass filters

While the use of first-order allpass sections is classic for hardware phase shifters, second-order allpass filters, mentioned in Section 2.4.2, are easier to use for generating precisely located notches that are more independently controllable [Smi84].

The architecture of a phaser based on second-order allpasses is identical to that in Figure 12.8, but with each first-order allpass $AP_1^{g_i}$ being replaced by a second-order allpass $AP_2^{R_i,\theta_i}$, where the control parameters R_i and θ_i are given below. As before, the phaser will have a notch wherever

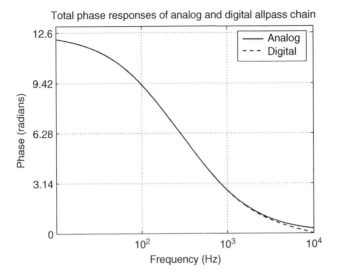

Figure 12.10 Phase response of four first-order allpass sections in series – analog and digital cases overlaid [Smi10].

the phase of the allpass chain passes through π radians (180 degrees). It can be shown that for second-order allpasses notch frequencies occur close to the resonant frequencies of the allpass sections [Smi84]. It is therefore convenient to use allpass sections of the form

$$H(z) = \frac{a_2 + a_1 z^{-1} + z^{-2}}{1 + a_1 z^{-1} + a_2 z^{-2}},\qquad(12.13)$$

where

$$a_1 = -2R\cos(\theta),$$

$$a_2 = R^2,$$

$R < 1$ is the radius of each pole in a complex-conjugate pole pair, and the pole angles are $\pm\theta$. The pole angle $\theta \in (0, \pi)$ can be interpreted as $\theta = \omega_n T$, where ω_n is the desired notch frequency and T is the sampling interval. The pole radius R controls the width of the notch – the closer it is to 1, the narrower the notch (and the more accurate is the tuning parameter θ).

12.3   Circuit-based valve emulation

Digital emulation of valve- or vacuum-tube amplifiers is currently a vibrant area of research with many commercial applications. As explained in a recent review article [PY09], most existing digital valve-emulation methods may roughly be divided into static waveshapers, custom nonlinear filters, and circuit-simulation-based techniques. The first type of these methods, static waveshapers (e.g., [Sul90, Kra91, AS96, Shi96, DMRS98, FC01, MGZ02, Jac03, Ame03, SST07, SM07]), use memoryless nonlinear functions for creating signal distortion and linear filtering before and after the nonlinearity for tuning the magnitude response. Oversampling is usually used to avoid signal aliasing.

12.3.1   Dynamic nonlinearities and impedance coupling

Although the valve component itself is mainly a memoryless device that can in principle be approximated with static nonlinear functions, reactive components (typically capacitors) in the circuit make the nonlinearity act as dynamic. This means that in reality, the shape of the nonlinearity changes according to the input signal and the internal state of the circuit. Custom nonlinear valve emulation filters [Pri91, KI98, GCO+04, KMKH06] simulate this dynamic nonlinearity, for example by creating a feedback loop around the nonlinearity.

Another important phenomenon in real valve circuits is the two-directional impedance coupling between components and different parts of the circuit. This causes, for example, an additional signal-dependent bias variation of a valve circuit when connected to a reactive load, such as a loudspeaker. If the digital valve circuit model uses a unidirectional signal path – as many simple models do – altering some part in the virtual circuit has no effect on the parts earlier in the signal chain. For example, if a linear loudspeaker model is attached to a virtual tube circuit with unidirectional signal flow, the resulting effect will only be a linear filtering according to the transfer characteristics of the loudspeaker, and no coupling effects with the tube circuit will be present. Nonlinear circuit-simulation-based modeling techniques (e.g., [Huo04, Huo05, YS08, YAAS08, Gal08, MS09]) try to incorporate the impedance coupling effect, at least between some parts of the circuit. Traditionally, these methods use Kirchhoff's rules and energy conservation laws to manually obtain the ordinary differential equations (ODEs) that represent the operation of the circuit. The ODEs are then discretized (usually using the bilinear transform), and the system of implicit nonlinear equations is iteratively solved using numerical integration methods, such as the Newton – Raphson or Runge – Kutta.

12.3.2 Modularity

From the digital valve-amplifier designer's point of view, modularity would be a desirable property for the emulator. In an ideal system, it should be easy to edit the circuit topology, for example by graphically altering the circuit schematics, and the sonic results should be immediately available. Enabling full control over the digital circuit construction would allow the emulation of any vintage valve amplifier simply by copying its circuit schematics into the system. Furthermore, it would enable the designer to apply the knowledge of valve-amplifier building tradition into the novel digital models. Note that this would mean that the designer should not be limited by conventional circuit design constraints or even general physical laws in creating a new digital amplifier, so that also purely digital or "abstract" processing techniques could well be used in conjunction. In the late 1990s, several valve circuit models (for example [Ryd95, Lea95, PLBC97, Sju97]) were presented for the SPICE circuit simulator software [QPN+07]. Although these models were modular and able to simulate the full impedance coupling within the whole system, they could not be used as real-time effects due to their intensive computational load. In fact, even over a decade later, these SPICE models are computationally still too heavy to run in real time.

Wave digital filters (WDFs), introduced by Fettweis [Fet86], offer a modular and relatively light approach for real-time circuit simulation. The main difference between WDFs and most other modeling methods is that WDFs represent all signals and states as wave variables and use local discretization for the circuit components. The WDF method will be explained more thoroughly in Section 12.3.3, and a simple nonlinear circuit simulation example using WDFs is presented in Section 12.3.4. The K-method, a state-space approach for the simulation of nonlinear systems has been introduced by Borin and others [BPR00]. This alternative approach for circuit simulation is currently another promising candidate for real-time valve simulation. It should be noted that although state-space models are not inherently modular, a novel technique by Yeh [Yeh09] allows the automatization of the model-building process, so that state-space simulation models may automatically be obtained from a circuit schematics description.

12.3.3 Wave digital filter basics

The basics of WDF modeling are briefly reviewed in the following section. A signal-processing approach has been chosen with less emphasis on the physical modeling aspects, in order to clarify the operation of the modeling example in Section 12.3.4. For a more thorough tutorial on WDFs, see, for example [Fet86, VPEK06].

One-port elements

WDF components connect to each other using ports. Each port has two terminals, one for transporting incoming waves, and one for transporting outgoing waves. Also, each port has an additional parameter, port resistance, which is used in implementing proper impedance coupling between components. The relationship between the Kirchhoff pair (e.g., voltage U and current I) and wave variables A and B is given by

$$\left[\begin{array}{c} A \\ B \end{array} \right] = \left[\begin{array}{cc} 1 + R_p \\ 1 - R_p \end{array} \right] \left[\begin{array}{c} U \\ I \end{array} \right] \Leftrightarrow \left[\begin{array}{c} U \\ I \end{array} \right] = \frac{1}{2} \left[\begin{array}{cc} 1 & 1 \\ 1/R_p & -1/R_p \end{array} \right] \left[\begin{array}{c} A \\ B \end{array} \right], \qquad (12.14)$$

where R_p denotes the port resistance.

Note that this port resistance is purely a computational parameter, and it should not be confused with electrical resistance. Most elementary circuit components can be represented using WDF one-port elements. Some basic circuit components are illustrated together with their WDF one-port counterparts in Figure 12.11. Some other circuit components, such as transformers, cannot be represented as one-port elements, but require a multiport representation, which is out of the scope of this book. The port resistances of the one-port elements in Figure 12.11 can be given as follows:

$$R_p = \begin{cases} R & \text{for resistance,} \\ 1/(2CF_s) & \text{for capacitance,} \\ 2LF_s & \text{for inductance,} \end{cases} \qquad (12.15)$$

where R, C and L are the electrical resistance (Ohms), capacitance (Farads), and inductance (Henrys), respectively, while F_s stands for the sample rate (Hertz). Similar to the WDF resistor, the port resistance of a voltage source is equivalent to the physical resistance.

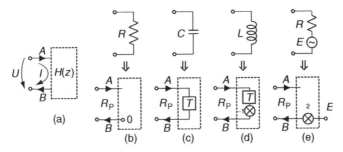

(a)   (b)   (c)   (d)   (e)

Figure 12.11 Basic WDF one-port elements: (a) a generic one-port with voltage U across and current I across the terminals, (b) resistor, (c) capacitor, (d) inductor, (e) voltage source. Here, A represents an incoming wave for each element, while B denotes an outgoing wave. Symbol R_p stands for the port resistance. Figure adapted from [PK10] and reprinted with IEEE permission.

Adaptors

The WDF circuit components connect to each other via adaptors. In practice, the adaptors direct signal routing inside the WDF circuit model, and implement the correct impedance coupling via port resistances. Although the number of ports in an adaptor is not limited in principle, three-port adaptors are typically used, since any N-port adaptor ($N > 3$) can be expressed using a connection of three-port adaptors, so that the whole WDF circuit becomes a binary tree structure [DST03].

There are two types of WDF adaptors: series and parallel, which implement the series and parallel connection between elements, respectively. Furthermore, the port resistance values for the adaptors should be set equal to the port resistances of the elements they are connected to.

Figures 12.12(a) and (b) illustrate the WDF series and parallel adaptors, respectively. Here, the ports have been numbered, for clarity. The outgoing wave B_n at port $n = 1, 2, 3$ of a three-port adaptor can generally be expressed as

$$B_n = \begin{cases} A_n - 2R_n(A_1 + A_2 + A_3)/(R_1 + R_2 + R_3) & \text{for series adaptor,} \\ 2(G_1A_1 + G_2A_2 + G_3A_3)/(G_1 + G_2 + G_3) - A_n & \text{for parallel adaptor,} \end{cases} \quad (12.16)$$

where A_n denotes the incoming wave at port n and $G_n = 1/R_n$ is the inverse of the port resistance R_n.

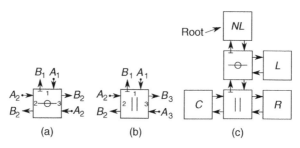

Figure 12.12   WDF three-port serial (a) and parallel (b) adaptors and an example WDF binary tree (c).

Computational scheduling

Figure 12.12(c) depicts an example WDF binary tree, simulating an RLC circuit with a nonlinear resistor (marked NL in the figure). As can be seen, the adaptors act as nodal points connecting the one-port elements together. For this reason, the adaptors in a WDF binary tree are also called nodes, and the one-port elements are called the leaves of the binary tree. When deciding the order of computations, a single one-port element must be chosen as the root of the tree. In Figure 12.12(c), the nonlinear resistor is chosen as the root. When this decision has been made, the WDF simulation starts by first evaluating all the waves propagating from the leaves towards the root. When the incoming wave arrives at the root element, the outgoing wave is computed, and the waves are propagated from the root towards the leaves, after which the process is repeated.

As can be seen in Equation (12.16), the wave leaving the WDF adaptor is given as a function of the incoming waves and port resistances. This poses a problem for the computation schedule discussed above, since in order for the adaptor to compute the waves towards the root, it would also have to know the wave coming from the root at the same time. Interestingly, the port resistances can be used as a remedy. By properly selecting the port resistance for the port facing the root, the wave traveling towards the root can be made independent from the wave traveling away from the root.

For example, if we name the port facing the root element as port number one, and set its port resistance as $R_1 = R_2 + R_3$ if it is a series adaptor (and the inverse port resistance $G_1 = G_2 + G_3$ if it is a parallel adaptor), Equation (12.16) simplifies into

$$B_1 = \begin{cases} -A_2 - A_3 & \text{for series connection} \\ G_2/(G_2 + G_3)A_2 + G_3/(G_2 + G_3)A_3 & \text{for parallel connection} \end{cases} \quad (12.17)$$

for the wave components traveling towards the root. In our example, the port number one would be called adapted, or reflection free, since the outgoing wave does not depend on the incoming (reflected) wave. Such adapted ports are typically denoted with a "T-shaped" ending for the outwards terminal, as illustrated for port number one in Figure 12.12(a) and (b). As Figure 12.12(c) shows, all adapted ports point towards the root.

Since the root element is connected to an adapted port, and the port resistances between the adapted port and the root should be equal, an interesting paradox arises. On one hand, the shared port resistance value should be set as required by the adaptor (for example as the sum of the other port resistances on a series adaptor), but on the other hand, the port resistance should be set as dictated by the root element (for example as a resistance value in Ohms for a resistor). If a resistor is chosen as a root element, the solution is to define the outgoing wave B from the root as [Kar]

$$B = \frac{R - R_\mathrm{p}}{R + R_\mathrm{p}} A, \qquad (12.18)$$

where R is the electrical resistance of the root, R_p is the port resistance set by the adapted port, and A is the wave going into the root element. Since the port resistance of the adapted port is independent of the electrical resistance of the root, the latter can freely be varied during simulation without encountering computability problems. Thus, if the circuit has a nonlinear one-port element, it should be chosen as the root for the WDF tree (since nonlinearity can be seen as parametric variation at a signal rate). For all other leaves, changing the port resistance during simulation is problematic since correct operation would require the port resistance changes to be propagated throughout the whole tree and iterated to correctly set the changed wave values. In practice, however, it is possible to vary the port resistances (i.e., component values) of the leaves without problems, provided that the parametric variation is slow compared to the sampling rate of the system.

Nonlinearities and model initialization

In a nonlinear resistor, the electrical resistance value depends nonlinearly on the voltage over the resistor, and a correct simulation of this implicit nonlinearity requires iterative techniques in general. Note the difference between the earlier discussed global iteration for setting the values of all port resistances, and the local iteration to set only the value of the nonlinear resistor: although the adapted ports remove the need for the former, one should still in principle perform the latter. Since run-time iteration is a computationally intensive operation, a typical practical simplification for avoiding local iteration is to insert an additional unit delay to the system, for example by using the voltage value at the previous time instant when calculating the resistance value. The error caused by this extra delay is usually negligible, provided that the shape of the nonlinearity is relatively smooth, as is the case with typical valve components. Further information on nonlinear WDFs can be found in [SD99, Bil01]. Valve simulation using WDFs was first presented in [KP06], and refined models have been discussed in [PTK09, PK10].

Reactive WDF circuit components should be correctly initialized before the simulation starts. This means that the one-sample memory of inductors and capacitors should be set so that the voltages and currents comply with Kirchhoff's laws. For reactive components that have nonzero initial energy (for example an initially charged capacitor), this can be tricky since the relationship between the stored energy and the wave value inside the memory is not straightforward. However, the correct initialization procedure can still be performed by using Thévenin or Norton equivalents. A practical alternative is to set the memory of reactive WDF components to zero, and let the simulation run for some "warm-up" time before inserting the actual input signal so that a steady operating point is reached and the reactances have been properly charged. In a sense, this is similar to letting a real electric circuit warm up and reach the correct operating point before feeding the input signal.

Remaining challenges in WDF modeling

Although WDFs have many desirable properties in circuit-simulation applications, there are also some open research problems related to them that limit their usability on a large scale. Probably the most severe limitation is that those circuit topologies that do not map onto binary trees are difficult to realize. Such topologies include bridge connections and loop-like structures. Modeling of bridge connections using WDFs is further discussed in [Kar08]. Another limitation is that a WDF binary tree can generally have only a single nonlinear element. If multiple nonlinearities are to be simulated using WDFs, global iteration should be applied for the whole sub-tree connecting the nonlinearities to each other. Alternatively, unit delays can be inserted into the system to enable computability, as done in [PK10], but this may drastically affect the stability of the system in some cases.

12.3.4 Diode circuit model using wave digital filters

This section discusses a WDF representation of a simple valve diode circuit, depicted in Figure 12.13(a). The WDF equivalent of the electric circuit is illustrated in Figure 12.13(b). The simulator algorithm is implemented using object-oriented programming for illustrating the inherent modularity of WDFs. The related code requires a basic understanding of object-oriented programming principles, and is mainly intended to show the possibilities of WDF modeling, rather than trying to provide a computationally efficient implementation. The class files are defined in the M-file 12.6, and the diode circuit model is presented in M-file 12.7. The presented WDF simulator consists of seven classes, three of which are abstract (i.e., they only serve as superclasses to real classes). It must be noted that all the presented classes are shown in a single M-file for compactness although in practice **MATLAB** requires each class to reside in an individual file. In other words, the classes in M-file 12.6 should be split into seven different files in order for the model to run in **MATLAB**.

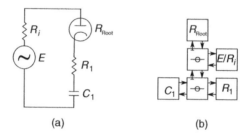

(a)   (b)

Figure 12.13   Electrical (a) and WDF (b) representations of an RC circuit with a vacuum-tube diode. The diode is denoted R_{Root}, since it is realized as a nonlinear resistor as the root element of the binary WDF tree structure.

The first class in M-file 12.6 defines the wdf superclass, which serves as a parent for the other six classes. The wdf class itself is inherited from **MATLAB**'s hgsetget-class, which results in all WDF elements being handle-objects. This means that when object properties (such as wave variable values) are edited, **MATLAB** only modifies the property values, instead of creating entirely new objects. The PortRes property defines the port resistance of a WDF object, and the Voltage method gives the voltage over the element, as defined in Equation (12.14). The next class in M-file 12.6 defines the Adaptor class, which serves as a superclass for three-port series and parallel adaptors. Two properties, KidLeft and KidRight, are defined, which serve as handles to the WDF objects connected to the adaptor.

The ser class defines the WDF series adaptor. The waves traveling up (towards the root) and down (away from the root) are given as properties WU and WD, respectively. The adaptor is realized so that the adapted port always points up, to enable the connection of a nonlinear element at the root. In addition to the class constructor, this class defines two methods, WaveUp and set.WD. The first of these reads the up-going wave according to Equation (12.17), and the second sets the down-going waves for the connected elements according to Equation (12.16). Note that the parallel adaptor is similarly defined and can be found among the supplementary **MATLAB**-files on-line, although it is omitted here for brevity.

The OnePort class in M-file 12.6 serves as a superclass for all one-port WDF elements. It also defines the up- and down-going waves WU and WD and the set.WD-method. This method also updates the internal state, or memory, of a reactive WDF one-port. The last three classes in M-file 12.6 introduce the classes R, C, and V, which represent the WDF resistors, capacitors, and voltage sources, respectively. Note that the class L for implementing a WDF inductor may easily be edited from the C class, although it is not printed here (but included in the associated on-line code).

M-file 12.6 (WDFClasses.m)

```
% WDFclasses.m
% Authors: Välimäki, Bilbao, Smith, Abel, Pakarinen, Berners
%--------------------WDF Class----------------------
classdef WDF < hgsetget % the WDF element superclass
    properties
        PortRes % the WDF port resistance
    end
    methods
            function Volts = Voltage(obj)  % the voltage (V) over a WDF element
                Volts = (obj.WU+obj.WD)/2; % as defined in the WDF literature
            end
    end;
end
%--------------------Adaptor Class----------------------
classdef Adaptor < WDF % the superclass for ser. and par. (3-port) adaptors
    properties
        KidLeft % a handle to the WDF element connected at the left port
        KidRight % a handle to the WDF element connected at the right port
    end;
end
%--------------------Ser Class----------------------
classdef ser < Adaptor % the class for series 3-port adaptors
    properties
        WD % this is the down-going wave at the adapted port
        WU % this is the up-going wave at the adapted port
    end;
    methods
        function obj = ser(KidLeft,KidRight) % constructor function
            obj.KidLeft = KidLeft; % connect the left 'child'
            obj.KidRight = KidRight; % connect the right 'child'
            obj.PortRes = KidLeft.PortRes+KidRight.PortRes; % adapt. port
        end;
        function WU = WaveUp(obj) % the up-going wave at the adapted port
            WU = -(WaveUp(obj.KidLeft)+WaveUp(obj.KidRight)); % wave up
            obj.WU = WU;
        end;
        function set.WD(obj,WaveFromParent) %  sets the down-going wave
            obj.WD = WaveFromParent; % set the down-going wave for the adaptor
            % set the waves to the 'children' according to the scattering rules
            set(obj.KidLeft,'WD',obj.KidLeft.WU-(obj.KidLeft.PortRes/...
            obj.PortRes)*(WaveFromParent+obj.KidLeft.WU+obj.KidRight.WU));
            set(obj.KidRight,'WD',obj.KidRight.WU-(obj.KidRight.PortRes/...
            obj.PortRes)*(WaveFromParent+obj.KidLeft.WU+obj.KidRight.WU));
        end;
    end
end
%--------------------OnePort Class----------------------
classdef OnePort < WDF % superclass for all WDF one-port elements
    properties
        WD % the incoming wave to the one-port element
        WU % the out-going wave from the one-port element
```

```
        end;
        methods
            function obj = set.WD(obj,val) % this function sets the out-going wave
            obj.WD = val;
                if or(strcmp(class(obj),'C'),strcmp(class(obj),'L')) % if react.
                    obj.State = val; % update internal state
                end;
            end;
        end
end
%--------------------R Class----------------------
classdef R < OnePort % a (linear) WDF resistor
        methods
            function obj = R(PortRes) % constructor function
                obj.PortRes = PortRes; % port resistance (equal to el. res.)
            end;
            function WU = WaveUp(obj) % get the up-going wave
                WU = 0; % always zero for a linear WDF resistor
                obj.WU = WU;
            end;
        end
end
%--------------------C Class----------------------
classdef C < OnePort
    properties
        State % this is the one-sample internal memory of the WDF capacitor
    end;
        methods
            function obj = C(PortRes) % constructor function
                obj.PortRes = PortRes; % set the port resistance
                obj.State = 0; % initialization of the internal memory
            end;
            function WU = WaveUp(obj) % get the up-going wave
                WU = obj.State; % in practice, this implements the unit delay
                obj.WU = WU;
            end;
        end
end
%--------------------V Class----------------------
classdef V < OnePort % class for the WDF voltage source (and ser. res.)
    properties
        E % this is the source voltage
    end
        methods
            function obj = V(E,PortRes) % constructor function
                obj.E = E; % set the source voltage
                obj.PortRes = PortRes; % set the port resistance
                obj.WD = 0; % initial value for the incoming wave
            end;
            function WU = WaveUp(obj) % evaluate the outgoing wave
                WU = 2*obj.E-obj.WD; % from the def. of the WDF voltage source
                obj.WU = WU;
            end;
        end
end
```

The actual diode simulation example is printed as M-file 12.7, and will be briefly explained here. M-file 12.7 starts by defining the overall simulation parameters and variables, such as the sample rate, and input and output signals. Next, the WDF elements (resistive voltage source, resistor, and a capacitor) are created, and the WDF is formed as a series connection. The nonlinear resistor is not created as an object, but it is manually implemented in the simulation loop.

The simulation loop starts by reading the input signal as the source voltage for object v1. Next, the WaveUp method is called for the WDF tree, resulting in all up-going waves to be propagated at the root. The valve resistor is modeled as the nonlinear resistance

$$R = 125.56e^{-0.036U} \Omega \qquad (12.19)$$

as a function of the voltage U over the diode. Equation (12.19) was empirically found to be a simple, but fairly accurate simulation of a GZ 34 valve diode. Here, the previous value of the diode voltage is used, in order to avoid the local iteration of the implicit nonlinearity. The wave reflection at the nonlinearity is implemented according to Equation (12.18), and the down-going waves are propagated to the leaves. Finally, the diode voltage is updated for the next time sample, and the output is read as the voltage over the resistor R1. After the simulation loop is finished, the results are illustrated using the plot-commands.

It is important to note, that due to the modularity of the WDFs and the object-oriented nature of the implementation, editing of the simulation circuit is very easy. All that has to be done to simulate a different circuit is to change the one-port element definitions (rows 10-13 in M-file 12.7) and the circuit topology (row 14 in M-file 12.7). In other words, M-files 12.6 and 12.7 define an entire circuit simulation software!

M-file 12.7 (WDFDiodeExample.m)

```
% WDFDiodeExample.m
% Authors: Välimäki, Bilbao, Smith, Abel, Pakarinen, Berners
Fs = 20000; % sample rate (Hz)
N = Fs/10; % number of samples to simulate
gain = 30; % input signal gain parameter
f0 = 100; % excitation frequency (Hz)
t = 0:N-1; % time vector for the excitation
input = gain.*sin(2*pi*f0/Fs.*t); % the excitation signal
output = zeros(1,length(input));
V1 = V(0,1); % create a source with 0 (initial) voltage and 1 Ohm ser. res.
R1 = R(80); % create an 80Ohm resistor
CapVal = 3.5e-5; % the capacitance value in Farads
C1 = C(1/(2*CapVal*Fs)); % create the capacitance
s1 =  ser(V1,ser(C1,R1)); % create WDF tree as a ser. conn. of V1,C1, and R1
Vdiode = 0; % initial value for the voltage over the diode
%% The simulation loop:
for n = 1:N % run each time sample until N
    V1.E = input(n); % read the input signal for the voltage source
    WaveUp(s1); % get the waves up to the root
    Rdiode = 125.56*exp(-0.036*Vdiode); % the nonlinear resist. of the diode
    r = (Rdiode-s1.PortRes)/(Rdiode+s1.PortRes); % update scattering coeff.
    s1.WD = r*s1.WU; % evaluate the wave leaving the diode (root element)
    Vdiode = (s1.WD+s1.WU)/2; % update the diode voltage for next time sample
    output(n) = Voltage(R1); % the output is the voltage over the resistor R1
end;
%% Plot the results
t = (1:length(input))./Fs; % create a time vector for the figure
hi = plot(t,input,'--'); hold on; % plot the input signal, keep figure open
ho = plot(t,output); hold off; % plot output signal, prevent further plots
grid on; % use the grid for clarity
xlabel('Time (s)'); ylabel('Voltage (V)'); % insert x- and y-axis labels
legend([hi ho],'Source voltage E','Voltage over R1'); % insert legend
```

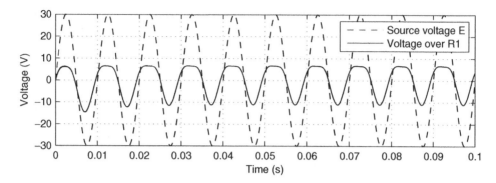

Figure 12.14 Voltage over the tube diode, as plotted by the M-file 12.7. As can be seen, the diode nonlinearity has squashed the positive signal peaks, while charging of the capacitor causes a shift in the local minima.

The output of the WDF model, i.e., the circuit response to a 100 Hz sine signal is illustrated in Figure 12.14. As expected, the positive signal peaks have been squashed since the diode lets forward current pass, reducing the potential difference over the diode. This current also charges the capacitor, reducing the voltage drop for negative signal cycles in the beginning of the simulation. Thus, Figure 12.14 visualizes both the static nonlinearity due to the diode component itself, as well as the dynamic behavior caused by the capacitance. The simulation results were verified using LTSpice simulation for the same circuit. The resulting waveforms were visually identical for both the WDF and LTSpice simulations.

12.4   Electromechanical effects

A rather special family of audio effects consists of those which employ mechanical elements in conjunction with analog electronics – though many classic effects rely on such components (such as, for example, the Leslie speaker, or tape delays), for some problems in the world of virtual analog, an involved treatment of the mechanical part of the effect is necessary, in order to be able to capture the perceptually salient quality of the effect. This is particularly the case for electromechanical artificial reverberation, which exhibits an extremely complex response. Two interesting cases, namely plate and spring reverberation, will be briefly described here.

The attribute of these devices which distinguishes them from other electromechanical effects is that the mechanical components cannot be modelled as "lumped" structurally, a spring or a plate occupies space, and its vibration pattern varies from one point to the next. It is precisely the distributed character of these components which gives these effects their complex sound – and which, at the same time, requires a somewhat different approach to emulation. One must now think of the behavior of the component in terms of various different modes of vibration, or in terms of waves which require finite propagation times, just like real acoustic spaces. Indeed, spring and plate reverbs were originally intended as convenient substitutes for real room reverbs – but developed a loyal audience of their own. Originally, such popularity was probably in spite of this distinction, but as such units have become scarce, convenient digital substitutes for these sometimes bulky and damage-prone units have become sought-after – and make for a fascinating application of virtual analog modeling!

Distributed modeling is seen only rarely in the world of digital audio effects, but plays, of course, a central role in sound synthesis based on physical models of musical instruments – a topic which is too broad to fit into this volume! In this short section, some of the basics of distributed modeling for electromechanical elements are covered, from a high-level perspective, focusing on the nature of the phenomena involved, and some simulation techniques (and in particular, finite difference schemes). It's probably worth mentioning that distributed modeling can be a lot more expensive, in terms of number-crunching, than other analog effect emulation – which is true of any digital reverberation algorithm. But, these days, standard computer hardware is becoming powerful enough to tackle these modeling problems in real-time, or something close to it.

12.4.1   Room reverberation and the 3D wave equation

When looking at artificial reverberation techniques, it's useful to first take a look at the behaviour of real rooms – to understand the ways in which electromechanical effects attempt to emulate this real-world effect, and, more importantly, how they differ!

In air, to a very good approximation, waves travel at a constant speed, here referred to as c. c has a mild dependence on temperature, and is approximately 343 m/s at atmospheric pressure, and near room temperature [FR91]. From a given acoustic point source, waves travel uniformly in all directions (isotropically) at this speed, and there is a reduction in amplitude as the waves spread out. Formally, to a very good approximation, the time evolution of a pressure field in three dimensions may be described by the wave equation,

$$\frac{\partial^2 p}{\partial t^2} = c^2 \nabla^2 p \tag{12.20}$$

where here, $p(x, y, z, t)$ is the pressure at spatial coordinates x, y and z, and at time t. ∇^2 is the 3D Laplacian operator. For more on this equation, see [MI68].

A key concept in all distributed modeling for linear systems is a dispersion relation, relating angular frequency ω (in radians/sec) to a vector wavenumber β (measured in units of m^{-1}) for a wave component of the solution. Such a component will be of the form

$$p(x, t) = e^{j\omega t + \beta \cdot x} \tag{12.21}$$

in 3D, and the dispersion relation for the wave equation above takes the following form,

$$\omega = c|\beta|. \tag{12.22}$$

It turns out to be convenient to use ω and β here, but one could equally well write this relationship in terms of frequency $f = \omega/2\pi$ and wavelength $\lambda = 2\pi/|\beta|$ – the above dispersion relation then becomes the familiar expression $c = \lambda f$. In the case of the wave equation, this expression is of a very simple form; for other systems it will not be, and often, even for a single system, there may be many such relations, which may not be expressible in simple closed form. The dispersion relation, in general, yields a huge amount of information about the behavior of a system which is very important acoustically. When a system's geometry is specified, one can say a great deal not only about acoustic attributes such as echo density and mode density, but also about how much computational power will be required to perform a digital emulation!

Expressions for wave speed as a function of frequency may be derived from a dispersion relation as

$$v_{phase} = \frac{\omega}{|\beta|} \qquad v_{group} = \frac{d\omega}{d|\beta|}, \tag{12.23}$$

where v_{phase} is the phase velocity, or propagation speed of a wave at wavenumber β, and v_{group} is the group, or packet velocity. In the case of rooms, from the dispersion relation given above, these speeds are both c. Such wave propagation is often referred to as non dispersive; all disturbances propagate at the same speed, regardless of wavelength or frequency. In the present case of wave propagation in air, it also implies that waveforms which propagate from one point to another preserve shape, or remain coherent during propagation.

When a given delimited acoustic space is defined, the obvious acoustic effect is that of echoes. For a room with reflective walls, a typical response consists of series of distinct echoes (early reflections) which are perceptually distinct, and which serve as localization cues, followed by increasingly dense late reflections, and, finally when reflections become so dense so as to be not perceptually distinct, a reverberant tail. It is room geometry which gives acoustic responses their characteristic complexity – and this is definitely not the case for plate and spring reverberation, which emulate this response using relatively simple structures.

Digital emulation of 3D acoustic spaces through the direct solution of the wave equation is a daunting task, from the point of view of computational complexity (though it is an active research topic [Bot95, MKMS07], which will surely eventually bear fruit). In fact, by further examination of the dispersion relation one may arrive at bounds on computational cost: for any simulation of the 3D wave equation over a space of volume V, and which is intended to produce an approximation to the response over a band of frequencies from 0 Hz, to $f_s/2$ Hz, for some frequency f_s (i.e., an audio sample rate), the amount of memory required will be approximately

$$N(f_s) \propto V f_s^3/c^3, \tag{12.24}$$

where the constant of proportionality depends on the particular method employed. For $c = 340$, and at at typical audio rate $f_s = 48$ kHz, and for even a moderately sized room ($V = 1000$ m^3), this can be very large indeed – here, for (say) a finite difference scheme $N = 2.8 \times 10^9$! Because arithmetic operations will presumably be performed on all the data, locally, at the audio rate, the operation count will be on the order of $N \times f_s$ flops, which is approaching the petaflop range. For more on the topic of computational complexity estimates in physical audio applications, see [Bil09].

Most reverberation techniques are thus based around perceptual simplifications, as described in detail in Chapter 5. In industrial acoustical applications, methods based on the image source method [AB79] are popular, and rely on simplified models of reflection from surfaces; in audio, feedback delay networks [Puc82, Roc97, JC91], which are very efficient, but not based on direct solution of the 3D wave equation, are commonly employed.

12.4.2   Plates and plate reverberation

Plate reverberation was originally intended as a convenient means of applying a reverberant effect to a recorded sound [Kuh58], long before the advent of digital reverberation. Such effects were extensively researched and eventually commericialized, with the EMT-140 the most successful resulting product. The basic operation of such a unit is relatively simple: a metal plate, normally rectangular, made of steel and supported by a frame is driven by an input signal through an actuator, and outputs are read at a pair of pickups. See Figure 12.15(a). Such a device is often complemented by adjustable absorbing plates which allow for some control over the decay time. The response of a plate is generally quite different from that of room acoustic reverberation – distinct relections are notably absent, and the response as a whole has a smooth noise-like character.

A given plate is characterized by its density ρ, in kg/m^3, Young's modulus E, in kg/s^{2}m, Poisson's ratio ν (dimensionless), and geometrical properties such as its thickness H in m, and its surface area A in m^2, as well as the particular boundary conditions. A typical reverberation unit is constructed from steel, with a thickness of approximately 0.5 mm, and with a surface area of approximately 2 m^2 (other materials and dimensions are also in use – the much smaller EMT 240 unit employs thin gold foil instead of steel). Usually the edges are very nearly free to vibrate, except for at the plate supports. For a sufficiently thin lossless plate, the equation of motion may

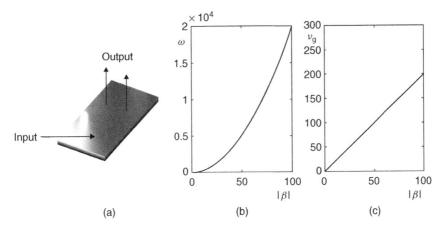

Figure 12.15 (a) A metal plate, driven by an input signal, and from which output(s) are read at distinct locations. (b) Dispersion relation, and (c) group velocity for a thin plate.

be written succinctly as

$$\frac{\partial^2 u}{\partial t^2} = -\kappa^2 \nabla^2 \nabla^2 u, \tag{12.25}$$

where ∇^2 is the 2D Laplacian operator defined, in Cartesian coordinates (x, y), as

$$\nabla^2 = \frac{\partial^2}{\partial x^2} + \frac{\partial^2}{\partial y^2}. \tag{12.26}$$

For more on the physics of plates, see, e.g., [FR91, Gra75, MI68].

The dispersion relation for a plate is very different from that corresponding to wave propagation in air,

$$\omega = \kappa \beta^2, \tag{12.27}$$

where $\kappa = \sqrt{EH^2/(12(1-v^2)\rho)}$. Now, the phase and group velocities are no longer constant,

$$v_{phase} = \kappa \beta = \sqrt{\kappa \omega} \qquad v_{group} = 2\kappa \beta = 2\sqrt{\kappa \omega} \tag{12.28}$$

See Figure 12.15 (b) and (c). As a result, wave propagation is dispersive, and highly so. See Figure 12.16, showing the time evolution of plate displacement in response to a pulse. Notice in particular that the high-frequency components of the pulse travel more quickly than the low-frequency components – and thus the pulse rapidly loses coherence as it travels. Another related distinction between plate and room responses is the mode density, which is roughly constant in the case of the plate, but which increases as the square of frequency for a room. See Figure 12.17.

One may show, as in the case of the wave equation, that for a plate of stiffness parameter κ, and of surface area A, that the amount of memory required will be approximately

$$N(f_s) \propto Af_s/\kappa, \tag{12.29}$$

which, for typical plate materials and geometries ($\kappa = 0.737$, $A = 2$), and at an audio sample rate such as 48 kHz, is not particularly large (here, for a finite difference scheme, $N = 8.29 \times 10^4$). The dependence of memory requirements may be directly related to both the dispersive character

Figure 12.16   Time evolution of plate displacement, with $\kappa = 0.5$, and of aspect ratio 2, in response to a pulse, at times as indicated.

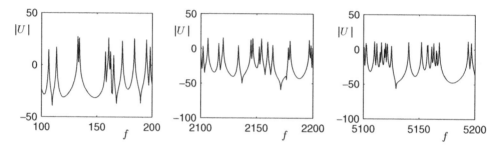

Figure 12.17   Log magnitude spectrum $|U|$ of impulse response of a plate, with $\kappa = 2$, and of aspect ratio 2, over different frequency ranges, as indicated.

of the plate, as well as the constancy of mode density [Bil09]. The operation count will again scale with $N \cdot f_s$ – which, in comparison with full 3D modeling, is in the Gflop range, which is expensive still by today's standards, but not unreasonably so. As such, it is worth looking at how one might design such a simulation through the direct time/space solution of the plate equation.

Case study: Finite difference plate reverberation

The emulation of distributed models, such as plates or springs, requires a different treatment from lumped analog components – probably the best-known distributed modeling techniques in sound synthesis are digital waveguides [Smi10], which are extremely efficient for problems in 1D, but for which such an efficiency advantage does not extend to problems in higher dimensions. Mainstream time-domain numerical simulation techniques (of which finite difference schemes [Str89] are the easiest to understand, and simplest to program) are an attractive alternative. Here, a very simple time-domain finite-difference scheme [Str89] will be presented, based on the direct solution to the equation of motion (12.25) for a thin plate. Finite difference schemes for plates are discussed by various authors (see, e.g., [Szi74]), and have been used in musical acoustics applications [LCM01], as well as in the present case of plate reverberation [Arc08, BAC06, Bil07].

Equation (12.25) describes free vibration of a lossless thin plate. A simple extension to the more realistic case of frequency-independent loss, and where the plate is driven externally (as in a reverberation unit) is

$$\frac{\partial^2 u}{\partial t^2} = -\kappa^2 \nabla^2 \nabla^2 u - 2\sigma \frac{\partial u}{\partial t} + \delta(x - x_i, y - y_i) f(t)/\rho H. \qquad (12.30)$$

Here $\sigma \geq 0$ is a loss parameter – it is related to a global T_{60} reverberation time by $T_{60} = 6 \ln(10)/\sigma$. More realistic (frequency-dependent) models of loss are available [CL01], but the above is sufficient for a simple demonstration of finite difference techniques. $f(t)$ is a force signal in N, assumed known, and applied at the location $x = x_i$, $y = y_i$, where here, δ is a Dirac delta function.

The first step in the design of any audio effect is the choice of a sample rate f_s. In simulation applications, it is more natural to make use of a time step $T = 1/f_s$. Another choice which must be made is that of a spatial grid, at the points of which an approximate solution to a partial differential equation will be computed. In the case of a plate defined over a rectangular domain $x \in [0, L_x]$, and $y \in [0, L_y]$, the obvious choice is a rectangular grid, of spacing X between adjacent points. The grid function $u_{l,m}^n$ then represents an approximation to the solution $u(x, y, t)$ of (12.25), at times $t = nT$, and at locations $x = lX$, and $y = mX$, for integer n, l and m. See Figure 12.18(a). It makes sense to choose X such that the grid spacing divides the side lengths as evenly as possible, i.e., $L_x/X \approx N_x$, $L_y/X \approx N_y$ for some integers N_x and N_y. It is not possible to do this exactly for arbitrary side lengths – to remedy this, one could choose distinct grid spacings X and Y in the x and y directions, but this subtle point will not be explored further here. There are, of course, many other ways of choosing grids, which may or may not be regular – finite element methods [Coo02], for example, are usually designed to operate over unstructured grids, and are suitable for problems in irregular geometries. Consider first the first and second partial time derivatives which appear in (12.25). The simplest finite-difference approximations, δ_t and δ_{tt} may be written as

$$\delta_t u_{l,m}^n = \frac{1}{2T}\left(u_{l,m}^{n+1} - u_{l,m}^{n-1}\right) \approx \frac{\partial u}{\partial t}(x = lX, y = mX, t = nT) \tag{12.31}$$

$$\delta_{tt} u_{l,m}^n = \frac{1}{T^2}\left(u_{l,m}^{n+1} - 2u_{l,m}^n + u_{l,m}^{n-1}\right) \approx \frac{\partial^2 u}{\partial t^2}(x = lX, y = mX, t = nT). \tag{12.32}$$

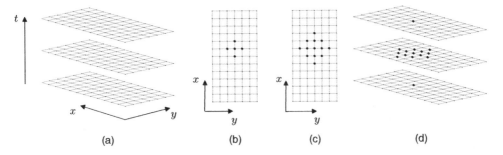

Figure 12.18 (a) Computational grid, defined over Cartesian coordinates x and y, and for time t. (b) Computational footprint of the five-point Laplacian operator, and (c) when applied twice. (d) Computational footprint for the scheme (12.34).

The other operation which must be approximated is the Laplacian ∇^2, as defined in (12.26). Here is the simplest (five-point) choice,

$$\delta_{\nabla^2} u_{l,m}^n = \frac{1}{X^2}\left(u_{l+1,m}^n + u_{l-1,m}^n + u_{l,m+1}^n + u_{l,m-1}^n - 4u_{l,m}^n\right)$$

$$\approx \nabla^2 u(x = lX, y = mX, t = nT), \tag{12.33}$$

see Figure 12.18(b). System (12.30) requires a double application of this operator – see Figure 12.18(c). Near the edges of the domain, this operation appears to require values which lie beyond the edges of the grid – these may be set by applying the appropriate boundary conditions. For a plate reverberation unit, these will be of free type, but in the **MATLAB** example which follows, for simplicity, they have been set to be of a simply supported type (i.e., the plate is constrained at its edges, but able to pivot). A complete treatment of numerical boundary conditions is beyond the scope of the present chapter – see [Bil09] for more information.

A complete scheme for (12.25) then follows as

$$\delta_{tt}u_{l,m}^{n} = -\kappa^2\delta_{\nabla^2}\delta_{\nabla^2}u_{l,m}^{n} - 2\sigma\delta_t u_{l,m}^{n} + \frac{1}{\rho H X^2}\delta_{l_i,m_i}f^n. \tag{12.34}$$

This scheme relies on a discrete delta function δ_{l_i,m_i}, picking out a grid location corresponding to $x = x_i$, and $y = y_i$ (perhaps through truncation), and a sampled input signal f^n. The scheme operates over three time levels, or steps, as shown in (d), and is also explicit – values at the unknown time step $n + 1$ may be written in terms of previously computed values (after expanding out the operator notation above) as

$$(1 + \sigma T)u_{l,m}^{n+1} = 2u_{l,m}^{n} - (1 - \sigma T)u_{l,m}^{n-1} - \mu^2\left(u_{l+2,m}^{n} + u_{l-2,m}^{n} + u_{l,m+2}^{n} + u_{l,m-2}^{n}\right)$$

$$- 2\mu^2\left(u_{l+1,m+1}^{n} + u_{l+1,m-1}^{n} + u_{l-1,m+1}^{n} + u_{l-1,m-1}^{n}\right)$$

$$+ 8\mu^2\left(u_{l+1,m}^{n} + u_{l+1,m}^{n} + u_{l,m+1}^{n} + u_{l,m-1}^{n}\right) - 20\mu^2 u_{l,m}^{n}$$

$$+ \frac{T^2}{\rho H X^2}\delta_{l_i,m_i}f^n, \tag{12.35}$$

where $\mu = \kappa T/X^2$ is a numerical parameter for the scheme. It may be shown that for stability, one must choose

$$\mu \leq 1/4 \tag{12.36}$$

and in fact, in order to reduce artifacts due to numerical dispersion (i.e., additional unwanted dispersive behavior induced by the scheme itself, on top of that inherent to the plate itself), this bound should be satisfied as near to equality as possible. In audio applications, this allows the grid spacing X to be chosen in terms of the sample rate. See [Bil09] for much more on the properties of this scheme.

In implementation, it can be useful to rewrite this scheme in a vector-matrix form. A grid function $u_{l,m}^n$, representing the values of a grid function over a rectangular region, may be rewritten as a column vector $\mathbf{u}^n$, consisting of consecutive "stacked" columns of values over the grid, at time step n. Because the scheme as a whole is linear, and explicit, it must then be possible to rewrite it as the two-step recursion,

$$\mathbf{u}^{n+1} = \mathbf{B}\mathbf{u}^n - \mathbf{C}\mathbf{u}^{n-1} + \mathbf{r}f^n. \tag{12.37}$$

Here, the effects of loss and the spatial difference operators have been consolidated in the (extremely sparse) matrices $\mathbf{B}$ and $\mathbf{C}$, and $\mathbf{r}$ is a column vector which chooses an input location. Output may be drawn from the scheme at a location $x = x_o$, $y = y_o$ by simply reading u_{l_o,m_o}^n at each time step. In vector form, the output y^n may be written as

$$y^n = \mathbf{q}^T\mathbf{u}^n \tag{12.38}$$

for some vector $\mathbf{q}$, which, in the simplest case, will consist of a single value at the readout location.

Below is a very simple **MATLAB** implementation of the plate reverberation algorithm mentioned above – it generates a reverberant output, for a given plate, sample rate, and excitation and readout points. It's not particularly fast (at least in **MATLAB**) – but not extremely slow either!

M-file 12.8 (platerevsimp.m)

```
% platerevsimp.m
% Authors: Välimäki, Bilbao, Smith, Abel, Pakarinen, Berners
% global parameters
```

```
[f, SR] = wavread('bassoon.wav');    % read input soundfile and sample rate
rho = 7850;                          % mass density (kg/m^3)
E = 2e11;                            % Young's modulus (Pa)
nu = 0.3;                            % Poisson's ratio (nondimensional)
H = 0.0005;                          % thickness (m)
Lx = 1;                              % plate side length---x (m)
Ly = 2;                              % plate side length---y (m)
T60 = 8;                             % 60 dB decay time (s)
TF = 1;                              % extra duration of simulation (s)
ep = [0.5 0.4];                      % center location ([0-1,0-1]) nondim.
rp = [0.3 0.7];                      % position of readout([0-1,0-1]) nondim.
% derived parameters
K_over_A = sqrt(E*H^2/(12*rho*(1-nu^2)))/(Lx*Ly);   % stiffness parameter/area
epsilon = Lx/Ly;                     % domain aspect ratio
T = 1/SR;                            % time step
NF = floor(SR*TF)+size(f,1);         % total duration of simulation (samples)
sigma = 6*log(10)/T60;               % loss parameter
% stability condition/scheme parameters
X = 2*sqrt(K_over_A*T);              % find grid spacing, from stability cond.
Nx = floor(sqrt(epsilon)/X);         % number of x-subdivisions/spatial domain
Ny = floor(1/(sqrt(epsilon)*X));     % number of y-subdivisions/spatial domain
X = sqrt(epsilon)/Nx;                % reset grid spacing
ss = (Nx-1)*(Ny-1);                  % total grid size
% generate scheme matrices
Dxx = sparse(toeplitz([-2;1;zeros(Nx-3,1)]));
Dyy = sparse(toeplitz([-2;1;zeros(Ny-3,1)]));
D = kron(speye(Nx-1), Dyy)+kron(Dxx, speye(Ny-1));  DD = D*D/X^4;
B = sparse((2*speye(ss)-K_over_A^2*T^2*DD)/(1+sigma*T));
C = ((1-sigma*T)/(1+sigma*T))*speye(ss);
% generate I/O vectors
rp_index = (Ny-1)*floor(rp(1)*Nx)+floor(rp(2)*Ny);
ep_index = (Ny-1)*floor(ep(1)*Nx)+floor(ep(2)*Ny);
r = sparse(ss,1); r(ep_index) = T^2/(X^2*rho*H);
q = sparse(ss,1); q(rp_index) = 1;
% initialize state variables and input/output
u = zeros(ss,1); u2 = u; u1 = u;
f = [f;zeros(NF-size(f,1),1)];
out = zeros(NF,1);
% main loop
for n=1:NF
    u = B*u1-C*u2+r*f(n);    % difference scheme calculation
    out(n) = q'*u;           % output
    u2 = u1; u1 = u;         % shift data
end
% play input and output
soundsc(f,SR); pause(2); soundsc(out,SR);
```

This example is written to be compact and readable – and many more realistic features which have been omitted could be added in. Among these are:

- Frequency-dependent damping – at the moment the T_{60} is set to be uniform at all frequencies. This could be done directly in the PDE model above, or possibly through introducing a model of a damping plate.

- Boundary conditions are set to be simply supported – allowing the easy generation of difference matrices. These should ideally be set to be free, or going further, to incorporate the effect of point supports.

- Only a single output is generated – multiple outputs (such as stereo, but perhaps more in a virtual environment) should be allowed. Notice that multiple outputs may be generated essentially "for free," as the entire state (**u**) is available.

- Output displacement is taken; in real plate reverberation units, it is rather an acceleration – acceleration can be derived from displacement easily through a double time difference operation.

- Post-processing (analog electronic) and the behavior of the pickup are not modelled.

Information on all these extensions appears in various publications, including those mentioned at the beginning of this section.

12.4.3   Springs and spring reverberation

A helical spring under low tension has long been used as an artificial reverberation device [Ham41, YI63, Sta48]. In most units, the spring is driven through an electromagnetic coupling at one end, and readout is taken via a pickup at the opposite end. Spring reverbs come in a variety of sizes and configurations, sometimes involving multiple springs. A typical set-up is shown in Figure 12.19(a).

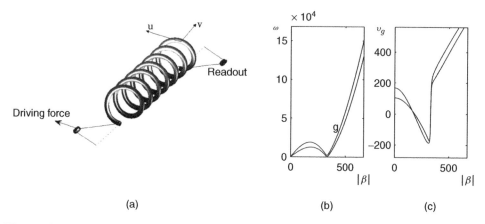

(a)   (b)   (c)

Figure 12.19   (a) A typical spring reverberation configuration, for a spring driven at one end, and with readout taken from the other; longitudinal and transverse motion of the spring are indicated by u and v. (b) Dispersion relations $\omega(\beta)$, and (c) group velocities $v_g(\beta)$.

The physics of helical structures is far more involved than that of the flat plate – see [Wit66, DdV82] for typical models. The important point is that the various types of motion (transverse to the spring, in both polarizations, and longitudinal) are strongly coupled in a way that they are not for a straight wire. A complex combination of relatively coherent wave propagation (leading to echoes) and highly dispersive propagation is present, leading to a characteristic sound which resembles both real room responses, and plate reverbs.

One can garner much useful information from the dispersion relations for a spring, as shown in Figure 12.19(b). For springs of dimensions and composition as found in reverberation devices, there are two relations which lie within the audio range – both correspond to mixtures (wavenumber-dependent!) of longitudinal and transverse motion. Both curves exhibit a "hump" in the low wavenumber range corresponding to a cutoff – for most spring reverb units, this occurs in the range between 2 kHz and 5 kHz. An examination of the group velocities, as shown in Figure 12.19(c) allows for some insight with regard to the behavior of spring responses, an example of which is shown at top in Figure 12.20. In the range of low wavenumbers, the group velocities approach a

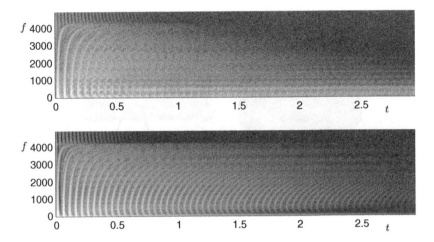

Figure 12.20   Top, spectrogram of a measured spring reverberation response, and bottom, that of a synthetic response produced using a finite difference model.

constant value, and thus dispersion is low at low frequencies, and strong echoes are present. But as the wavenumber increases towards the cutoff, the group velocity decreases, and thus the frequency components of the echoes are distorted increasingly (slowed) near the cutoff. Above the cutoff, the group velocity is much faster, and leads to distorted echoes which recur at a higher rate. Above the cutoff, the response is very similar to transverse motion for a straight bar.

Emulation techniques

As in the case of plate reverberation, there is a variety of techniques available – and as of 2010, physical modeling of springs is still an open research problem. The most rigorous approach, given a partial differential equation model, is again a time-stepping method such as finite differences, which has been used by this author [Bil09, BP10], as well as Parker [Par08] in order to generate synthetic responses. See Figure 12.20(b) for a comparison between a measured response and synthetic output. This approach turns out to be rather expensive, and given that the system is essentially 1D (i.e., for a thin spring, the equations of motion may be written with respect to a single coordinate running along the spring helix), structures based on delay lines and allpass networks are a possibility, and an excellent compromise between physical and perceptual modeling. See, e.g., [ABCS] and [VPA10].

The difficulties here lie in associating such a model with an underlying model in a definitive way. Another approach, as yet unexplored, could be based on the use of a modal decomposition. In other words, given appropriate boundary conditions, one may solve for the modes of vibration of the helix. This is the approach taken in the analysis of helical structures in mainstream applications – see, e.g., [LT01].

12.5   Tape-based echo simulation

12.5.1   Introduction

In this section, we turn our attention to simulating tape echo, focusing on two popular units, the Roland Space Echo, used widely in dub and reggae music, and the Maestro Echoplex, popular among guitarists.

The Echoplex was first released in 1959. Four versions were made, the EP-1 and EP-2 employing tube circuitry, and the EP-3 and EP-4 using solid-state electronics. An EP-4 is shown in

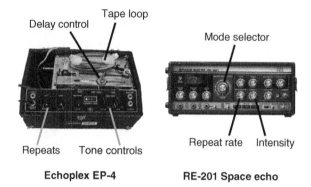

Delay control

Tape loop

Mode selector

Repeats   Tone controls

Repeat rate   Intensity

Echoplex EP-4   **RE-201 Space echo**

Figure 12.21   Maestro Echoplex EP-4 (left) and Roland RE-201 Space Echo (right).

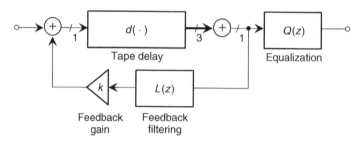

Tape delay

Equalization

Feedback
gain

Feedback
filtering

Figure 12.22   Tape Delay Signal Flow Architecture. The Space Echo provides up to three separate delays which are summed (as shown); the Echoplex features a single delay.

Figure 12.21, and its signal flow architecture in Figure 12.22. Playback and erase heads are fixed on either side of a slot along which the record head is free to move. The record head writes to the moving tape, and the recorded signal is later read as the tape passes by the playback head. Moving the delay control changes the distance between the record and playback heads, and, therefore, the time delay between input and output. With a nominal tape speed of 8 ips, delays roughly in the range of 60 ms to 600 ms are available.

As seen in Figure 12.22, the input signal is delayed and fed back, with the delayed output equalized according to the tone controls. The amount of feedback is controlled by the "Repeats" knob, producing a loop gain k roughly in the range $k \in [0, 2]$. For loop gains less than one, the Echoplex produces a decaying series of echoes. With a loop gain greater than one, sound present in the system will increase in amplitude until saturating, and take on the bandpass spectral quality of the loop filtering, with a rhythmic temporal character determined by the delay setting. When $k > 1$, no input signal is needed to produce an output, as tape hiss and 60 Hz harmonics present in the system will cause the unit to self-oscillate.

The movable record head is capable of producing extreme Doppler shifts [AAS08]. If the delay control is quickly moved away from the playback head, the input may be Doppler shifted down sufficiently that the bias signal appears in the audio band. If the delay control is moved toward the playback head at a rate faster than the tape speed, a high-bandwidth transient will be recorded as the record head slows and is overtaken by the tape.

The Space Echo, released in 1973, is shown in Figure 12.21. It has similar controls to the Echoplex, but uses a variable tape speed controlled by its "Repeat Rate" knob to fix the time delay between the record and playback heads. As shown in Figure 12.23, the Space Echo has three playback heads whose outputs are summed according to the "Mode Selector" to form the delayed output.

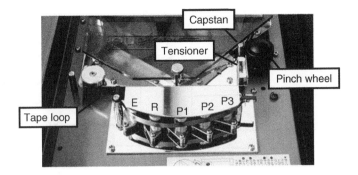

Figure 12.23   Space Echo Tape Transport. The erase (E), record (R), and three playback heads (P1, P2, P3) are shown.

Like the Echoplex, the Space Echo also has a saturating signal path, and a feedback loop gain k ranging from $k \in [0, 2]$ according to "Intensity" control. Noise in the electronics will produce a self-oscillation similar to that of the Echoplex.

The Space Echo and Echoplex may be modeled according to their signal flow architecture, as shown in Figure 12.22. Unlike digital or electronic delays, the mechanics of the tape delay transport produce subtle fluctuations in the time delay which add to the character of the effect. In Section 12.5.2 below, the mechanics of the tape transport are described, and methods for simulating the time-delay trajectory are presented. In Section 12.5.3, details of the signal path are noted, including tape and electronic saturation, and an analysis of the tone control circuit.

12.5.2   Tape transport

Delay trajectories

The tape transport mechanism employed by the Space Echo and Echoplex uses a metal capstan engaged with a rubber pinch wheel to pull the tape past the record and playback heads. As seen in Figure 12.23, the tape is spliced into a loop, and passes through a tensioner before arriving at the pinch wheel and re-entering its cartridge. The various forces acting on the tape produce a tape speed which varies somewhat over time. This varying tape speed results in a fluctuating time delay, which adds to the character of the delayed signal and is important to the time evolution of the sound produced when the feedback gain is greater than 1.0. It should be pointed out that as the tape splice passes by the playback head, a modest dropout is produced.

Figure 12.24 shows the time evolution of the time delays provided by the Space Echo playback head P1 measured at a variety of "Repeat Rate" (i.e., tape speed) settings. The resulting average time delays range from a little over 60 ms to a little over 160 ms. Figure 12.24 also shows the same delay trajectories with their means subtracted and offset for display. Both quasi-periodic and noise-like components are evident. Figure 12.25 shows spectra of the time-delay trajectories of Figure 12.24, plotted on frequency axes normalized according to their respective time delays. The spectra peak at the capstan rotation rate (about 22 Hz for the shortest time delay) and at the pinch-wheel rotation rate (near 3.5 Hz for the shortest time delay).

There are a series of nulls appearing near integer multiples of 15 Hz, and an overall low pass quality to the spectra. This pattern is reminiscent of a sinc function corresponding to a time-domain integration over a 60 ms window.

The 60 ms window length is precisely the (normalized) time delay, and represents the integration of velocity fluctuations as the tape travels between the record and playback heads. Tape speed disturbances completing an integer number of periods (slowing down and speeding up the tape)

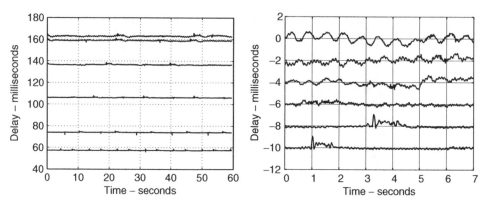

Figure 12.24   Space Echo delay trajectories (left), mean-subtracted trajectories, (offset, right).

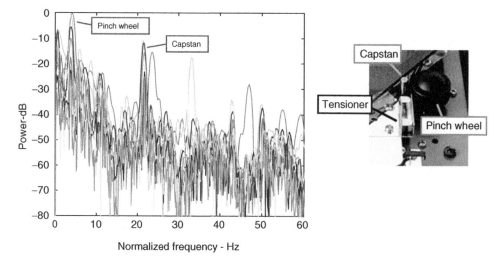

Figure 12.25   Delay trajectory spectra. Spectra of the delay trajectories of Figure 12.24 are plotted on frequency axes scaled to produce a 60 ms nominal delay.

while traveling between the heads will have no effect on the resulting time delay, and therefore, do not appear in the time delay spectra.[5]

Another effect of the integration can be seen in Figure 12.24. Note that the longer the time delay, the longer the integration, and the greater the time-delay fluctuations. In fact, the amplitude of time-delay fluctuations is roughly proportional to the average delay.

In Figure 12.24, transients appear in the two time-delay trajectories offset at −10 ms and −8 ms. These temporary increases in time delay are the result of the tape splice squeezing through the tensioner and then the pinch wheel. The tape is temporarily slowed, and the time delay later temporarily increased. The passage of the splice − about once every nine seconds for the fast tape speed setting, and about every 27 seconds for the slow tape speed setting − is important for creating an evolving sound in the presence of heavy feedback.

---

[5] As an aside, note that if the distance between the record head and the playback head were equal to integer multiples of the capstan and pinch-wheel circumferences, the quasi-periodic time delay trajectory components would be eliminated.

Other factors influence the time-delay trajectory. Compared to the trajectories seen in Figure 12.24, measured using a new tape, the fluctuations when using old tape have a much larger stochastic component.

Delay trajectory physical model

The delay trajectory may be generated using a model of the tape transport mechanics. The angular rotation rate of the capstan ω_c is changed according to its moment of inertia I and applied torques,

$$I\frac{d\omega_c}{dt} = \tau(r) - \mu T\rho_c - \gamma(\theta_p). \tag{12.39}$$

In the above expression, $\tau(r)$ represents the motor torque applied as a function of the Space Echo "Repeat Rate" setting r ($\tau(r)$ is presumed constant for the Echoplex). The term $\mu T\rho_c$ is the torque resulting from the tensioner friction – it is the tape tension T, scaled by the coefficient of friction μ, acting at the capstan radius ρ_c. Rather than applying a constant torque according to $\mu T\rho_c$, a unit-energy noise process is suggested, as this corresponds to the stochastic nature of frictional forces [Ser04].

The torque $\gamma(\theta_p)$ accounts for angular velocity changes due to the periodic deformation of the pinch wheel as it rotates about its axis. The distance between the capstan center and pinch-wheel axle is fixed, and any irregularities in pinch-wheel radius will result in corresponding deformations in the pinch-wheel rubber. Assuming a spring constant k, the energy stored in the pinch-wheel deformation at pinch-wheel angle θ_p is

$$E_s = \frac{1}{2}k\rho_p^2(\theta_p), \tag{12.40}$$

where $\rho_p(\theta_p)$ is the pinch-wheel radius at pinch-wheel rotation angle θ_p. In a time period Δt, the energy stored is

$$\Delta E_s = k\rho_p(\theta_p)\frac{d\rho_p}{d\theta_p}\frac{d\theta_p}{dt}\cdot\Delta t. \tag{12.41}$$

The kinetic energy change ΔE_ω over the same time period is

$$\Delta E_\omega = I\omega_c\frac{d\omega_c}{dt}\cdot\Delta t. \tag{12.42}$$

The pinch-wheel deformation results in a torque that balances the energy changes, $\Delta E_s + \Delta E_\omega = 0$,

$$\gamma(\theta_p) = I\frac{d\omega_c}{dt} = -k\rho_c\frac{d\rho_p}{d\theta_p}, \tag{12.43}$$

where the ratio of the capstan and pinch-wheel radii was substituted for the inverse ratio of their angular velocities. A source of pinch-wheel deformation is an off-center axle, generating a pinch-wheel radius

$$\rho_p(\theta_p) = \rho_0\left[(\cos\theta_p - \beta)^2 + \sin^2\theta\right]^{\frac{1}{2}}, \tag{12.44}$$

where ρ_0 is the pinch-wheel radius, and β is the distance of the pinch-wheel axle from the pinch-wheel center. This pinch-wheel radius generates the sensitivity

$$\frac{d\rho_p}{d\theta_p} = \frac{\rho_0^2\beta\sin\theta_p}{\rho_p(\theta_p)}. \tag{12.45}$$

The time delay $\delta(t)$ between the record and playback heads may be found by integrating the tape speed $v(t)$ until the record head-playback head distance D is achieved,

$$D = \int_{t}^{t+\delta(t)} v(\tau)d\tau, \qquad v(t) = \rho_c \frac{d\theta_c}{dt}, \qquad (12.46)$$

where $v(t)$ is the tape speed produced by the spinning capstan. Compared to the global average tape speed v_0, the tape speed fluctuations $v(t) - v_0$ are small, and the varying time delay may be approximated by

$$\delta(t) \approx \delta_0 - \int_{t}^{t+\delta_0} \frac{v(\tau) - v_0}{v_0} d\tau, \qquad (12.47)$$

where δ_0 is the nominal delay, $\delta_0 = v_0/D$. The time-delay trajectory is therefore the difference between the nominal delay and a running mean of the tape speed fluctuations.

Delay trajectories synthesized using (12.39) and (12.47) are shown in Figure 12.26, along with the corresponding delay fluctuations. A simple tape splice model was included.

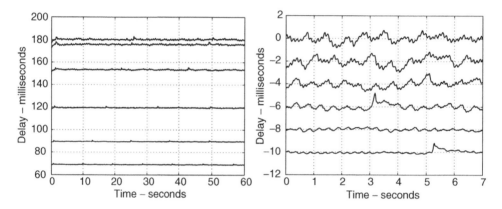

Figure 12.26 Space Echo synthesized delay trajectories (left), mean-subtracted (offset, right).

Delay-trajectory signal model

The fluctuating time delay driving the tape-delay model may be formed without reference to the mechanics of the tape transport. Instead, the observed time-delay trajectory characteristics may be reproduced via a "signal model."

In this approach, the tape delay is formed, as shown in Figure 12.27, by adding the three time-delay trajectory components: a mean delay, as determined by the delay control position for the Echoplex or the "Repeat Rate" for the Space Echo; quasi-periodic processes representing the observed capstan and pinch-wheel harmonics; and a stochastic low-frequency drift. This sum is filtered via a running mean having length equal to the time delay. The pinch-wheel and capstan components are generated by summing sinusoids at integer multiples of the observed capstan and pinch-wheel rotation rates, with amplitudes equal to those seen in the measured time-delay fluctuation spectra. The sinusoid phases are incremented according to their respective measured frequencies, with small low pass, zero-mean noise processes added to the sinusoid phases to introduce observed frequency fluctuations. The low-frequency drift component is formed by filtering white Gaussian noise.

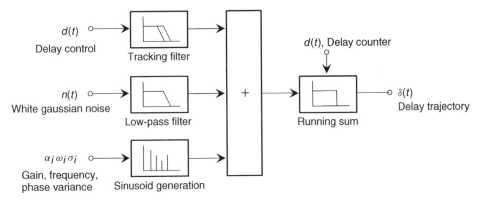

Figure 12.27   Delay trajectory signal model.

Delay control ballistics

As described above, the Space Echo time delay is controlled by adjusting the speed of the motor driving the capstan-pinch wheel assembly; the Echoplex time delay is controlled directly by positioning the record head. In both of these controls, there is a time lag between when the control is moved and when the desired delay is reached. This is seen in Figure 12.28 for the case of the Space Echo having its "Repeat Rate" control quickly adjusted between its slowest and fastest settings.

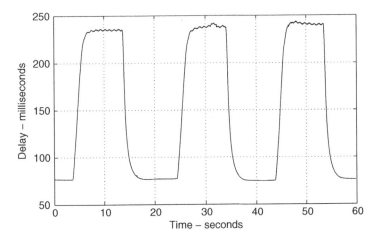

Figure 12.28   Space Echo delay trajectory, stepped "Repeats Rate" control.

The behavior seen in Figure 12.28 is well approximated by a so-called leaky integrator: a target signal v_T is tracked to produce $v(n)$ using a first-order update,

$$v(n) = (1 - \lambda)v_T + \lambda v(n - 1), \tag{12.48}$$

where λ, the "forgetting factor," governs the rate at which the target signal v_T replaces the current estimate $v(n)$. With λ near 0, the target v_T quickly replaces the integrator output $v(n)$, whereas with λ near 1, the integrator output slowly relaxes to the target. Given a time constant τ and sampling rate f_s, the forgetting factor

$$\lambda = e^{-1/\tau f_s} \tag{12.49}$$

will produce a leaky integrator, whose output will be a factor $1 - 1/e$ closer to a constant target signal after a period of time τ.

Referring again to Figure 12.28, the tape speed is seen to relax to its target value with a time constant on the order of 1 second when the target tape speed is greater than the current tape speed. However, when the target tape speed is less than the current tape speed, the time constant is slower at about 2 seconds. This behavior may be captured using different forgetting factors, depending on whether the target tape speed is greater than or less than the current tape speed.

Time-varying delay implementation

For arbitrary interpolated delay-line access, it is convenient to use Lagrange interpolation, since the needed filter coefficients can be calculated inexpensively for any fractional delay [Laa96]. The Lagrange interpolation filter is defined as the FIR filter which models the ideal fractional delay $e^{-j\delta\omega}$ with a maximally flat approximation at DC. In other words, for a fractional delay of δ, the Nth-order Lagrange filter will have a frequency response $H(e^{j\omega})$ which matches $e^{-j\delta\omega}$ and its first N derivatives at $\omega = 0$. Usually, the M-tap Lagrange filter will be used to produce a delay δ such that $M/2 < \delta < M/2 + 1$ for even M.

The ideal fractional delay $e^{-j\delta\omega}$ has nth derivative $(-j)^n\delta^n$ at $\omega = 0$. The Nth-order FIR filter has a frequency response

$$H(e^{j\omega}) = \sum_{n=0}^{N} b_n e^{-j\omega n} \tag{12.50}$$

which has nth derivative

$$(-j)^n b_1 + 2^n(-j)^n b_2 + \cdots + N^n(-j)^n b_n \tag{12.51}$$

at $\omega = 0$. Matching the response and first N derivatives of $H(e^{j\omega})$ at DC to those of the ideal fractional delay defines the filter coefficients b_n for the desired delay δ,

$$\mathbf{V}\vec{b} = \vec{\delta}, \tag{12.52}$$

where $\mathbf{V}$ is the Vandermonde matrix defined by the row $[0 \quad 1 \quad 2 \quad \cdots \quad N]$, $\vec{b}$ is the column of filter coefficients $[b_0 \quad b_1 \quad b_2 \quad \cdots \quad b_N]^T$, and $\vec{\delta} = [1 \quad \delta \quad \delta^2 \quad \cdots \quad \delta^N]^T$. For $N = 3$, we have

$$\begin{bmatrix} 1 & 1 & 1 & 1 \\ 0 & 1 & 2 & 3 \\ 0 & 1 & 4 & 9 \\ 0 & 1 & 8 & 27 \end{bmatrix} \begin{bmatrix} b_0 \\ b_1 \\ b_2 \\ b_3 \end{bmatrix} = \begin{bmatrix} 1 \\ \delta \\ \delta^2 \\ \delta^3 \end{bmatrix}. \tag{12.53}$$

The filter coefficients $\vec{b}$ can be found by inverting $\mathbf{V}$,

$$\vec{b} = \mathbf{V}^{-1}\vec{\delta}. \tag{12.54}$$

For real-time operation, the matrix inversion can be carried out in advance. The product $\mathbf{V}^{-1}\vec{\delta}$ allows efficient calculation of b_n for a given fractional delay δ. As the filter order N increases, the Lagrange interpolator coefficients converge towards a sampled sinc function, which would give ideal bandlimited interpolation.

M-file 12.9 (lagr2.m)

```
% lagr2.m
% Authors: Välimäki, Bilbao, Smith, Abel, Pakarinen, Berners
```

```
% lagr.m -- Lagrange filter design script
fs=44100;
numtaps=8;    %% Make this even, please.
ordvec=[0:numtaps-1]';
VA=flipud(vander(ordvec)');
iVA=inv(VA); %matrix to compute coefs
numplots=16;
for ind=1:numplots
    eta=(ind-1)/(numplots-1);   %% fractional delay
    delay=eta+numtaps/2-1;  %% keep fract. delay between two center taps
    deltavec=(delay*ones(numtaps,1)).^ordvec;
    b=iVA*deltavec;
    [H,w]=freqz(b,1,2000);
    figure(1)
    subplot(2,1,1)
    plot(w*fs/(2*pi),(abs(H)))
    grid on
    hold on
    xlabel('Freq, Hz')
    ylabel('magnitude')
    axis([0 fs/2 0 1.1])
    subplot(2,1,2)
    plot(w*fs/(2*pi),180/pi*unwrap(angle(H)))
    grid on
    hold on
    xlabel('Freq, Hz')
    ylabel('phase')
    xlim([0 fs/2])
end
figure(1)
subplot(2,1,1);hold off;
title('Lagrange Interpolator')
subplot(2,1,2);hold off;
```

12.5.3 Signal path

Recording with AC bias

Magnetic data storage is achieved by exposing magnetic material to an external magnetic field. If the applied field is of sufficient magnitude, residual magnetization of the material will persist after the external field is removed. For a time-varying field applied along a single axis to a magnetic material, the relationship between the applied field and the magnetization of the material will take the hysteretic form shown in Figure 12.29. A demagnetized sample will follow trajectory '1' in the figure if an increasing magnetic field is applied. The magnetization will grow to a maximum M_s for large fields, where M_s is the saturation magnetization for the material. As the applied field is reduced, the magnetization will decrease along trajectory '2' until, at an applied field of zero, the magnetization will be M_r, the remanent magnetization for the material. When the applied field reaches the coercive force $-H_c$, the total magnetization of the sample will once again be zero. If the applied field becomes more negative, the sample will continue to follow trajectory '2'. If, at a later time, the applied field is once again increased, the sample will follow trajectory '3'.

The hysteretic process of Figure 12.29 leads to a highly nonlinear relationship between the applied field and the resultant magnetization. In order to linearize the recording process, an AC bias signal consisting of a high-frequency sinusoid is typically added to the audio signal. The sum of the two signals is passed to a record head which creates a localized magnetic field that is proportional to the current passing through it.

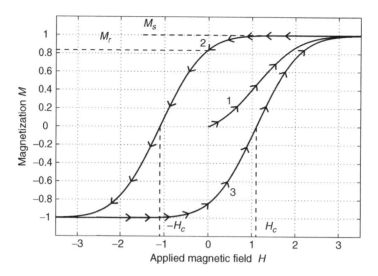

Figure 12.29 Hysteretic magnetization curve, showing saturation magnetization M_s, remanent magnetization M_r, and coercive force H_c.

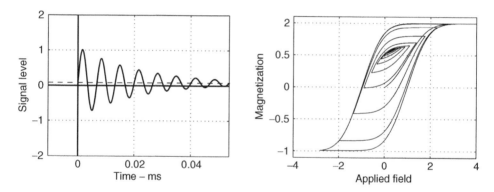

Figure 12.30 Anhysteretic recording. Decaying AC bias signal plus DC offset (left). Magnetization trajectory for decaying signal (right).

When an element of tape moves past the record head, it is exposed to the magnetic field created by the head. As the tape recedes from the head gap, the field applied to the tape becomes progressively weaker through distance, and the tape element experiences a decaying, oscillating magnetic field due to the AC bias. If the audio signal is bandlimited to frequencies much lower than the AC bias frequency, it can be considered quasistatic during the decay of the bias field. For a decaying AC bias signal added to a quasi-DC signal, the field applied to the tape would be as shown on the left of Figure 12.30. This signal produces the magnetization trajectory shown on the right-hand side of the figure. The trajectory spirals inward to a final magnetization which is largely insensitive to the details of the bias signal, and depends only upon the value of the quasi-DC component. In this way, the hysteretic behavior is eliminated, resulting in what is known as the anhysteretic recording process.

In reality, the audio component of the record signal will decay along with the bias signal as the tape element moves out of the recording head gap, producing the signal and magnetization trajectory of Figure 12.31. This is known as the modified anhysteretic recording process [Mal87].

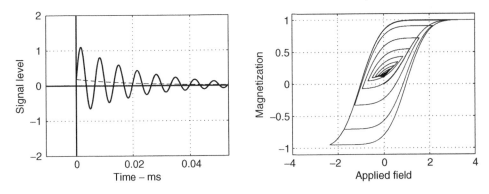

Figure 12.31 Modified anhysteretic recording. Decaying AC bias signal and signal (left). Magnetization trajectory for decaying signal (right).

With the hysteresis eliminated, the record process can be modeled as a memoryless nonlinearity. With proper biasing levels, recordings can be made with very little distortion, as long as levels are kept below M_s. The anhysteretic recording nonlinearity can be approximated by the error function $M = \mathrm{erf}(H)$, shown in Figure 12.32.

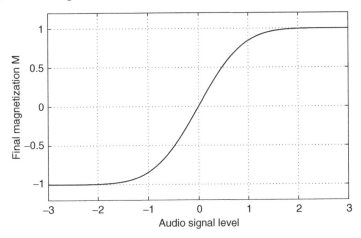

Figure 12.32 Memoryless nonlinearity for anhysteretic recording.

Tape-speed-dependent equalization

For signal reproduction, the tape is dragged across a gapped play-head which detects changes in magnetization as the tape goes by. The head is most sensitive to the space immediately surrounding the gap, but also responds to more distant elements of the tape. The recovered signal can be calculated as the derivative in time of a weighted volume integral over the space surrounding the head. The sensitivity of the head depends upon field direction as well as spatial position. This is reflected by taking a dot product between the tape magnetization and a vector representing the head's (directional) sensitivity as a function of space. The recovered signal s can be expressed as

$$s(t) = \frac{\mathrm{d}}{\mathrm{d}t} \int \vec{M} \cdot \vec{w} \,\mathrm{d}x\,\mathrm{d}y\,\mathrm{d}z \tag{12.55}$$

where $\vec{w}(x, y, z)$ represents the head's sensitivity.

The spatial integration performed by the playback head leads to wavelength-dependent equalization. At high frequencies, the wavelength recorded on tape becomes comparable to the gap width in the head, leading to a sinc-like frequency response; when an integral number of wavelengths fits in the gap, the response is diminished. This effect is called gap loss and takes the form

$$\gamma(k) = \frac{\sin(kg)}{kg} \tag{12.56}$$

where $\gamma(k)$ is the wavelength-dependent gain, k is the wavenumber, and g is the width of the head gap. A related effect happens at low frequencies when the wavelength becomes comparable to the dimension of the head core. This is called the contour effect, and produces what is known as head bump. Both gap loss and the contour effect are influenced by tape speed v, since $k \propto 1/v$. For the Roland Space Echo, since delay times are adjusted by changing the tape speed, the equalization will depend on delay. For the Echoplex, the tape speed is relatively constant, and the equalization will not be affected by delay setting.

Electronics

Equalization is applied electronically before writing to tape, and again after reading back from tape. This is done to maximize the tape's dynamic range, and to minimize the spectral coloration associated with the record/playback process. The equalization at the record head can be measured directly if the AC bias source is temporarily disconnected. The record head itself presents an inductive load over most of the audio band. At low frequencies, the series resistance of the head windings can become dominant. The field applied to tape is proportional to the current through the head, which can be measured directly or calculated from the head voltage if the head impedance is known. In many cases the high-frequency content of the signal is emphasized at the record head. It should be noted that at some frequencies the amplifier circuit will clip before reaching the level required to saturate the tape. This can be observed with both the Space Echo and the Echoplex.

After playback, the signal is equalized to give the desired transfer function, as measured from input to output. For the Space Echo and Echoplex, the overall equalization is relatively flat, and bandlimited. Plots of the equalization as a function of tape speed for the Space Echo are shown in Figure 12.33.

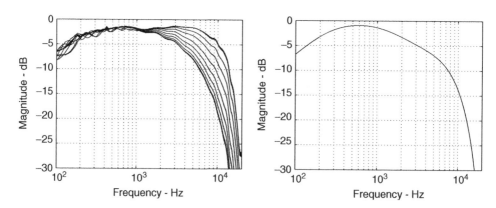

Figure 12.33 Space Echo equalization, various tape speeds (left), Echoplex loop equalization (right).

When in feedback mode, the Space Echo and Echoplex have an overall equalization associated with one trip around the feedback loop. This equalization can be measured by taking spectral ratios between successive echoes of a broadband signal. The loop equalization is the concatenation of parts of the pre-record and post-playback equalization, along with whatever equalization is present in the feedback path. The loop equalization for the Echoplex is plotted in Figure 12.33.

Tone controls

Tone controls are present on both the Space Echo and Echoplex, and affect the output equalization. Neither unit places the tone controls within the feedback loop. The Echoplex tone circuit is as shown in Figure 12.34. In the figure, 'B' refers to the position of the bass tone control, where $B = 1$ for full boost and $B = 0$ for full cut. The marking 'T' indicates the position of the treble control. Measured frequency responses for various control settings are plotted in the same figure.

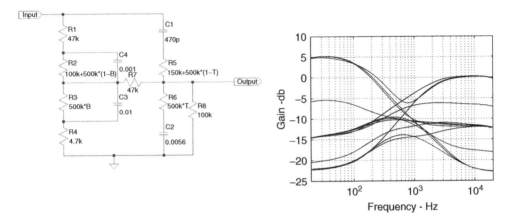

Figure 12.34   Echoplex EP-4 tone circuit and frequency response.

This circuit is related to the Baxandall tone circuit [Bax52] and provides high and low shelving functions. The Baxandall circuit is common in hi-fi and guitar tone stacks. Because of the topology of the circuit, the transfer function cannot be directly computed using series-parallel combinations of the components. However, superposition can be used to decompose the transfer function into two components, each of which can be calculated in a straightforward way. The two superposition components are shown in Figure 12.35.

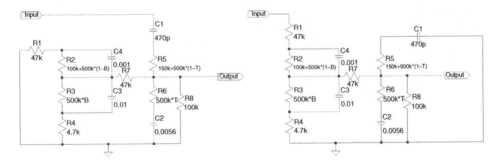

Figure 12.35   Echoplex EP-4 tone circuit superposition components.

The circuit transfer function is identically equal to the sum of the transfer functions of the two superposition components. Because of the topologies of the components, the two transfer functions have the same poles, so that the numerator terms can be added directly. As can be seen, each of the two components can be evaluated directly using series-parallel combinations.

Alternatively, the circuit can be analyzed using the n-extra element theorem (nEET) [Vor02]. Using nEET, the terms of the numerator and denominator of the transfer function can be calculated directly by inspection, using driving-point impedances associated with the reactive components of the circuit.

12.6   Antiquing of audio files

In this section we discuss an algorithm to transform audio files to sound very old. The signal modeling approach is taken here, although the basis of many related algorithms lies in the physical principles of the underlying analog systems [VGKP08].

The antiquing methods introduce simulated degradations to audio signals. They can be divided into two general groups: global and localized degradations [GR98]. Global degradations affect all samples of the audio signal and contain effects such as background noise, wow and flutter, and certain types of nonlinear distortion. Localized degradations affect some signal samples, but not all of them. Examples of such a localized degradation would be the 'clicks' and 'pops' heard on a dusty vinyl record.

Since audio signals are often stereophonic, the first step in audio antiquing is usually to convert the audio signal into the monophonic form. The simplest method, which yields satisfactory results in most cases, is to average the two channels. However, some stereo recordings use special effects, such as time delay or inverted phase between the two channels, and in such cases the simple technique fails. In the worst cases one or more sources in the original signal can be cancelled or be strongly colored, when the channels are added together.

12.6.1   Telephone line effect

The telephone sound is a commonly used effect in music production and in film soundtracks. It is used in movies and TV series to process the actor's voice, when she or he is talking on the phone, but the other person is shown listening. Additionally, it is widely applied to vocals in pop music as a special effect. A straightforward yet fairly realistic audio processing algorithm is given next.

The main component in the telephone sound is its severely limited bandwidth. Even today, telephone systems only transmit signal frequencies between 300 Hz and 3400 Hz. Below and above these cut-off frequencies, the signal energy is greatly suppressed. Figure 12.36 shows the magnitude response of an IIR filter which can be used to model this response. This example filter is a 12th-order Chebyshev type 2 design with cut-off frequencies of 234 Hz and 4300 Hz and a stopband rejection of -40 dB. With these parameters, the -6-dB points are at 300 Hz and 3400 Hz. Applying this filter to a wideband audio signal converts it to a low-bandwidth signal. The sound quality of a musical signal is drastically reduced by this filter. However, there will be no extra disturbances, and voice signals processed like this are perfectly intelligible. Nonetheless, this bandpass filter alone can be used as a simulation of a modern phone.

To obtain a historical telephone sound, it is necessary to add some noise and distortion. For much of the history of the telephone, almost all phone handsets contained a carbon microphone. This is a cheap and robust device, but has problems in sound quality: The output of a carbon microphone is noisy and contains harmonic distortion, which is characterized by a large amount of the second harmonic. This is a consequence of the fact that the resistance of the carbon-button varies in a different manner for positive and negative sound pressures.

The carbon microphone nonlinearity can be modeled with the following asymmetric function [QRO00]:

$$y(n) = \frac{1 - \alpha x(n)}{(1 - \alpha)x(n)},$$ (12.57)

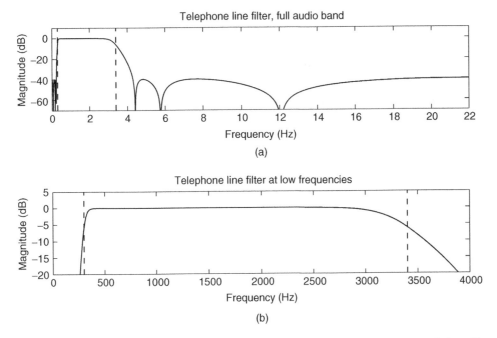

Figure 12.36 Magnitude response of the bandpass filter for telephone sound emulation. The dashed vertical lines indicate the cut-off frequencies 300 Hz and 3400 Hz.

where α determines the amount of nonlinearity when $\alpha > 0$, $x(n)$ is the input signal assumed to vary between -1.0 and 1.0, and $y(n)$ is the output signal. The following simplified nonlinearity can approximately produce the right kind of distortion:

$$y(n) = (1 - \alpha)x(n) + \alpha x^2(n). \qquad (12.58)$$

When α is smaller than about 0.4, this nonlinear function can produce a similar asymmetric nonlinear mapping between input and output samples as a physical model of the carbon-button microphone or empirically measured nonlinear functions [QRO00].

To complete the historical telephone sound emulation, a version of the nonlinear sandwich model proposed by Quatieri *et al.* [QRO00] is proposed in the following. The above instantaneous nonlinearity is placed between two linear filters, as shown in Figure 12.37. The role of the first filter, or pre-filter, is to introduce a wide resonance around 2 kHz [QRO00], and the second filter can be the bandpass filter of Figure 12.36. When the sampling rate of the original signal is 44.1 kHz, the following inverse comb filter can be used as the pre-filter:

$$H_{pre}(z) = 0.90 - 0.75z^{-11}, \qquad (12.59)$$

which introduces an approximately 4-dB amplification at 2 kHz and at its odd multiples (but the peaks at higher frequencies will be suppressed by the post-filter), and 16-dB dips at dc, at 4 kHz, and at its multiples up to 20 kHz.

White or colored noise may be added to the signal to add realism. In Figure 12.37 it is inserted after the nonlinearity. Although white noise is used here, it will still go through the post-filter and will thus turn into colored, bandpass-filtered hiss. M-file 12.10 gives a compact implementation of the full telephone sound model.

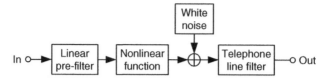

Figure 12.37   Sandwich model for the old telephone sound including the carbon-microphone nonlinearity and a noise source.

M-file 12.10 (phonefx.m)

```
function [y, ylin] = phonefx(alpha, noise, x)
% Authors: Välimäki, Bilbao, Smith, Abel, Pakarinen, Berners
% function [y, ylin] = phonefx(alpha, noise, x)
%
% Parameters:
% alpha = nonlinearity factor (alpha >= 0)
% noise = noise level (e.g. noise = 0.01)
% x = input signal
fs = 44100;  % Sample rate
u = filter([0.9 zeros(1,10) -0.75],1,x);  % Pre-filter
[B,A] = cheby2(6,40,[234/(fs/2) 4300/(fs/2)]);  % Telephone line filter
w = 2*rand(size(x))-1;  % White noise generation
y1 = (1-alpha)*u + alpha*u.^2 ;  % Carbon mic nonlinearity
y2 = y1 + noise*w;    % Add scaled white noise
y = filter(B,A,y2);    % Apply telephone line filter
ylin = filter(B,A,u);  % Linear filtering only (for comparison)
```

12.7   Conclusion

This chapter has focused on virtual analog effects. These digital audio effects are implemented using modern methods, but the aim is to reproduce historical sonorities. In this chapter we have described simulations for various analog filters, tube amplifiers, plate and spring reverberation, tape echo, and an old telephone. Time-domain processing techniques have been applied in all cases. One reason for this is that many algorithms contain nonlinear elements: thus the processing depends on instantaneous sample values and must proceed sample by sample. The nonlinearities, which imitate the behavior of analog components, bring about pleasing distortion and compression, familiar characteristics of nostalgic music equipment.

References

[AAS08]   S. Arnardottir, J. S. Abel, and J. O. Smith. A digital model of the Echoplex tape delay. In *Proceedings of the 125th AES Convention*, Preprint 7649, San Francisco, California, October 2008.

[AB79]   J. Allen and D. Berkley. Image method for efficiently simulating small-room acoustics. *Journal of Acoustical Society of America*, 65(4): 943–950, 1979.

[ABCS]   J. Abel, D. Berners, S. Costello, and J. O. Smith III. Spring reverb emulation using dispersive allpass filters in a waveguide structure. *Presented at the 121st Audio Engineering Society Convention*, San Francisco, California, October, 2006. Preprint 6954.

[Ame03]   D. Amels. System and method for distorting a signal, 2003. US Patent No. 6,611,854 B1. Filed September 22, 2000, issued August 26, 2003.

[Arc08]   K. Arcas. *Simulation numérique d'un réverbérateur à plaque*. PhD thesis, Ecole Nationale Supérieure de Techniques Avancées, Palaiseau, France, 2008.

[AS96]   T. Araya and A. Suyama. Sound effector capable of imparting plural sound effects like distortion and other effects, 1996. US Patent No. 5,570,424. Filed November 24, 1993, issued June 4, 1996.

[BAC06]   S. Bilbao, K. Arcas, and A. Chaigne. A physical model of plate reverberation. In *Proceedings of the IEEE International Conference on Acoustics, Speech, and Signal Processing*, volume 5, pp. 165–168, Toulouse, France, 2006.

[Bax52]   P. Baxandall. Negative-feedback tone control. *Wireless World*, pp. 402–405, October 1952.

[Bil01]   S. Bilbao. *Wave and Scattering Methods for the Numerical Integration of Partial Differential Equations*. PhD thesis, Stanford University, Palo Alto, CA, USA, 2001.

[Bil07]   S. Bilbao. A digital plate reverberation algorithm. *Journal of the Audio Engineering Society*, 55(3): 135–144, 2007.

[Bil09]   S. Bilbao. *Numerical Sound Synthesis: Finite Difference Schemes and Simulation in Musical Acoustics*. John Wiley & Sons, Ltd, Chichester, UK, 2009.

[Bot95]   D. Botteldooren. Finite-difference time-domain simulation of low-frequency room acoustic problems. *Journal of Acoustical Society of America*, 98(6): 3302–3308, 1995.

[BP10]   S. Bilbao and J. Parker. A virtual model of spring reverberation. *IEEE Transactions on Audio, Speech, and Language Processing*, 18(4): 799–808, 2010.

[BPR00]   G. Borin, G. De Poli, and D. Rocchesso. Elimination of delay-free loops in discrete- time models of nonlinear acoustic systems. *IEEE Transactions on Speech and Audio Processing*, 8: 597–605, September 2000.

[CL01]   A. Chaigne and C. Lambourg. Time-domain simulation of damped impacted plates. I Theory and experiments. *Journal of Acoustical Society of America*, 109(4): 1422–1432, 2001.

[Coo02]   R. Cook (ed). *Concepts and Applications of Finite Element Analysis*, 4th edition John Wiley & Sons, Inc., New York, New York, 2002.

[DdV82]   L. Della Pietra and S. della Valle. On the dynamic behaviour of axially excited helical springs. *Meccanica*, 17: 31–43, 1982.

[DMRS98]   M. Doidic, M. Mecca, M. Ryle, and C. Senffner. Tube modeling programmable digital guitar amplification system, 1998. US Patent No. 5,789,689.

[DST03]   G. De Sanctis, A. Sarti, and S. Tubaro. Automatic synthesis strategies for object-based dynamical physical models in musical acoustics. In *Proceedings of the International Conference on Digital Audio Effects*, pp. 219–224, London, England, September 8–11, 2003.

[FC01]   P. Fernández-Cid and F. J. Casajús-Quirós. Distortion of musical signals by means of multiband waveshaping. *Journal of New Music Research*, 30(3): 219–287, 2001.

[Fet86]   A. Fettweis. Wave digital filters: Theory and practice. *Proceedings of the IEEE*, 74(2): 270–327, February 1986.

[Fon07]   F. Fontana. Preserving the structure of the Moog VCF in the digital domain. In *Proceedings of the International Computer Music Conference*, pp. 291–294, Copenhagen, Denmark, August 2007.

[FR91]   N. Fletcher and T. Rossing. *The Physics of Musical Instruments*. Springer-Verlag, New York, New York, 1991.

[Gal08]   M. N. Gallo. Method and apparatus for distortion of audio signals and emulation of vacuum tube amplifiers, 2008. US Patent Application 2008/0218259 A1. Filed March 6, 2007, published September 11, 2008.

[GCO⁺04]   F. Gustafsson, P. Connman, O. Oberg, N. Odelholm, and M. Enqvist. System and method for simulation of non-linear audio equipment. US Patent Application 20040258250, 2004.

[GR98]   S. J. Godsill and P. J. W. Rayner. *Digital Audio Restoration – A Statistical Model Based Approach*. Springer-Verlag, New York, New York, 1998.

[Gra75]   K. Graff. *Wave Motion in Elastic Solids*. Dover, New York, New York, 1975.

[Ham41]   L. Hammond. Electrical musical instrument, February 2, 1941. US Patent 2,230,836.

[Huo04]   A. Huovilainen. Non-linear digital implementation of the Moog ladder filter. In *Proceedings of the International Conference on Digital Audio Effects*, pp. 61–64, Naples, Italy, October 2004.

[Huo05]   A. Huovilainen. Enhanced digital models for analog modulation effects. In *Proceedings of the International Conference on Digital Audio Effects*, pp. 155–160, Madrid, Spain, September 20–22, 2005.

[Jac03]   D. L. Jackson. Method and apparatus for the modeling and synthesis of harmonic distortion, 2003. US Patent No. 6,504,935 B1. Filed August 19, 1998, issued January 7, 2003.

[JC91]   J.-M. Jot and A. Chaigne. Digital delay networks for designing artificial reverberators, 1991. *Presented at the 90th Audio Engineering Society Convention*, Paris, France, February, 1991. Preprint 3030.

[Kar]   M. Karjalainen. BlockCompiler documentation. Unfinished report, available on-line at http: http://www.acoustics.hut.fi/software/BlockCompiler/docu.html.

[Kar08]   M. Karjalainen. Efficient realization of wave digital components for physical modeling and sound synthesis. *IEEE Transactions on Audio, Speech, and Language Processing*, 16(5): 947–956, 2008.

[KI98]   R. Kuroki and T. Ito. Digital audio signal processor with harmonics modification, 1998. US Patent No. 5,841,875. Filed January 18, 1996, issued November 24, 1998.

[KMKH06]   M. Karjalainen, T. Mäki-Patola, A. Kanerva, and A. Huovilainen. Virtual air guitar. *Journal of the Audio Engineering Society*, 54(10): 964–980, October 2006.

[KP06]   M. Karjalainen and J. Pakarinen. Wave digital simulation of a vacuum-tube amplifier. In *Proceedings of the IEEE International Conference on Acoustics, Speech, and Signal Processing*, Toulouse, France, May 15–19, 2006.

[Kra91]   G. Kramer. Digital signal processor for providing timbral change in arbitrary audio and dynamically controlled stored digital audio signals, 1991. US Patent No. 4,991,218 (continuation-in-part of US Pat. 4,868,869). Filed August 24, 1989, issued February 5, 1991.

[Kuh58]   W. Kuhl. The acoustical and technological properties of the reverberation plate. *EBU. Review*, A(49), 1958.

[Laa96]   T. I. Laakso, V. Välimäki, M. Karjalainen, and U. K. Laine. Splitting the unit delay – Tools for fractional delay filter design. *IEEE Signal Processing Magazine*, 13(1): 30–60, January 1996.

[LCM01]   C. Lambourg, A. Chaigne, and D. Matignon. Time-domain simulation of damped impacted plates. II Numerical model and results. *Journal of Acoustical Society of America*, 109(4): 1433–1447, 2001.

[Lea95]   W. M. Leach Jr. SPICE models for Vacuum-Tube Amplifiers. *Journal of the Audio Engineering Society*, 43(3): 117–126, 1995.

[LT01]   J. Lee and D. Thompson. Dynamic stiffness formulation, free vibration, and wave motion of helical springs. *Journal on Sound and Vibration*, 239(2): 297–320, 2001.

[Mal87]   J. Mallinson. *The Foundations of Magnetic Recording*. Academic Press, New York, New York, 1987.

[MGZ02]   S. Möller, M. Gromowski, and U. Zölzer. A measurement technique for highly nonlinear transfer functions. In *Proceedings of the International Conference on Digital Audio Effects*, pp. 203–206, Hamburg, Germany, September 26-28, 2002.

[MI68]   P. Morse and U. Ingard. *Theoretical Acoustics*. Princeton University Press, Princeton, New Jersey, 1968.

[MKMS07]   D. Murphy, A. Kelloniemi, J. Mullen, and S. Shelley. Acoustic modelling using the digital waveguide mesh. *IEEE Signal Processing Magazine*, 24(2): 55–66, 2007.

[Moo65]   R. A. Moog. A voltage-controlled low-pass high-pass filter for audio signal processing. In *Proceedings of the 17th Annual Meeting of the Audio Engineering Society*, October 1965.

[MS09]   J. Macak and J. Schimmel. Nonlinear circuit simulation using time-variant filter. In *Proceedings of the International Conf. Digital Audio Effects*, Como, Italy, September 1-4, 2009.

[Par08]   J. Parker. Spring reverberation: A finite difference approach. *Master's thesis*, University of Edinburgh, 2008.

[PK10]   J. Pakarinen and M. Karjalainen. Enhanced wave digital triode model for real-time tube amplifier emulation. *IEEE Transactions on Audio, Speech, and Language Processing*, 18(4): 738–746, 2010.

[PLBC97]   E. Pritchard, W. M. Leach Jr, F. Broydé, and E. Clavelier. Comments on "Spice Models for Vacuum-Tube Amplifiers" and Author's Replies. *Journal of the Audio Engineering Society*, 45(6): 488–496, 1997.

[Pri91]   E. K. Pritchard. Semiconductor emulation of tube amplifiers, 1991. US Patent No. 4,995,084. Filed March 23, 1998, issued February 19, 1991.

[PTK09]   J. Pakarinen, M. Tikander, and M. Karjalainen. Wave digital modeling of the output chain of a vacuum-tube amplifier. In *Proceedings of the 12th International Conference on Digital Audio Effects (DAFx09)*, Como, Italy, September 1–4, 2009.

[Puc82]   M. Puckette. Designing multichannel reverberators. *Computer Music Journal*, 6(1): 52–65, 1982.

[PY09]   J. Pakarinen and D. T. Yeh. A review of digital techniques for modeling vacuum-tube guitar amplifiers. *Computer Music Journal*, 33(2): 85–100, 2009.

[QPN+07]   T. Quarles, D. Pederson, R. Newton, A. Sangiovanni-Vincentelli, and C. Wayne. The spice page, 2007. Internet article http://bwrc.eecs.berkeley.edu/Classes/IcBook/SPICE/ (checked June 5, 2007).

[QRO00]   T. F. Quatieri, D. A. Reynolds, and G. C. O'Leary. Estimation of handset nonlinearity with application to speaker recognition. *IEEE Transactions on Speech and Audio Processing*, 8(5): 567–584, September 2000.

[RG75]   L. R. Rabiner and B. Gold. *Theory and Application of Digital Signal Processing*. Prentice-Hall, Upper Saddle River, New Jersey, 1975.

[Roc97]   D. Rocchesso. Maximally diffusive yet efficient feedback delay networks for artificial reverberation. *IEEE Signal Processing Letters*, 4(9): 252–255, 1997.

[Ros92]   D. Rossum. Making digital filters sound "analog". In *Proceedings of the International Computer Music Conference*, pp. 30–33, San Jose, CA, October 1992.

[Ryd95]   C. Rydel. Simulation of Electron Tubes with SPICE. In *Proceedings of the 98th AES Convention*, Preprint 3965 (G1), Paris, France, October 25–28, 1995.

[SD99]   A. Sarti and G. De Poli. Toward nonlinear wave digital filters. *IEEE Transactions on Signal Processing*, 47(6): 1654–1668, June 1999.

[Ser04]   S. Serafin. *The sound of friction: real-time models, playability and musical applications*. PhD thesis, Stanford University, 2004.

[Shi96]   M. Shibutani. Distortion circuits for improving distortion effects to audio data, 1996. US Patent No. 5,528,532. Filed June 6, 1995, issued June 18, 1996.

[Sju97]   W. Sjursen. Improved SPICE Model for Triode Vacuum Tubes. *Journal of the Audio Engineering Society*, 45(12): 1082–1088, 1997.

[SM07]   J. Schimmel and J. Misurec. Characteristics of broken-line approximation and its use in distortion audio effects. In *Proceedings of the International Conference on Digital Audio Effects*, pp. 161–164, Bordeaux, France, September 10–15, 2007.

[Smi84]   J. O. Smith. An all-pass approach to digital phasing and flanging. In *Proceedings of the International Computer Music Conference*, pp. 103–109, 1984.

[Smi07]   J. O. Smith III. *Introduction to Digital Filters with Audio Applications*. http://ccrma. stanford.edu/~jos/filters/, September 2007. Online book.

[Smi08]   J. O. Smith III. Virtual electric guitars and effects using Faust and Octave. In *Proceedings of the 6th Int. Linux Audio Conf. (LAC2008)*, 2008. paper and supporting website: http://ccrma.stanford.edu/realsimple/faust_strings/, presentation overheads: http://ccrma-ftp.stanford.edu/~jos/pdf/LAC2008-jos.pdf.

[SS96]   T. Stilson and J. Smith. Analyzing the Moog VCF with considerations for digital implementation. In *Proceedings of the International Computer Music Conference*, pp. 398–401, Hong Kong, China, August 1996.

[Smi10]   J. O. Smith. *Physical Audio Signal Processing: for Virtual Musical Instruments and Digital Audio Effects.*. 2010. On-line version at https://ccrma.stanford.edu/~jos/pasp/.

[SST07]   F. Santagata, A. Sarti, and S. Tubaro. Non-linear digital implementation of a parametric analog tube ground cathode amplifier. In *Proceedings of the International Conference on Digital Audio Effects*, pp. 169–172, Bordeaux, France, September 10–15, 2007.

[Sta48]   J. D. Stack. Sound reverberating device, March 9 1948. US Patent 2,437,445.

[Ste96]   K. Steiglitz. *A Digital Signal Processing Primer with Applications to Digital Audio and Computer Music*. Addison-Wesley, Reading, Massachusetts, 1996.

[Sti06]   T. Stilson. *Efficiently Variable Non-Oversampled Algorithms in Virtual-Analog Music Synthesis – A Root-Locus Perspective*. PhD thesis, Elec. Eng. Dept., Stanford University (CCRMA), June 2006. http://ccrma.stanford.edu/~stilti/.

[Str89]   J. Strikwerda. *Finite Difference Schemes and Partial Differential Equations*. Wadsworth and Brooks/Cole Advanced Books and Software, Pacific Grove, California, 1989.

[Sul90]   C. S. Sullivan. Extending the Karplus-Strong algorithm to synthesize electric guitar timbres with distortion and feedback. *Computer Music Journal*, 14(3): 26–37, fall 1990.

[Szi74]   R. Szilard. *Theory and Analysis of Plates*. Prentice Hall, Englewood Cliffs, New Jersey, 1974.

[VGKP08]   V. Välimäki, S. González, O. Kimmelma, and J. Parviainen. Digital audio antiquing – signal processing methods for imitating the sound quality of historical recordings. *Journal of the Audio Engineering Society*, 56(3): 115–139, March 2008.

[VH06]   V. Välimäki and A. Huovilainen. Oscillator and filter algorithms for virtual analog synthesis. *Computer Music Journal*, 30(2): 19–31, 2006.

[Vor02]   V. Vorpérian. *Fast Analytical Techniques for Electrical and Electronic Circuits*. Cambridge University Press, 2002.

[VPA10]   V. Välimäki, J. Parker, and J. S. Abel. Parametric spring reverberation effect. *Journal of the Audio Engineering Society*, 58(7/8): 547–562, July/August 2010.

[VPEK06]   V. Välimäki, J. Pakarinen, C. Erkut, and M. Karjalainen. Discrete-time modelling of musical instruments. *Reports on Progress in Physics*, 69(1): 1–78, January 2006.

[Wis98]   D. K. Wise. The recursive allpass as a resonance filter. In *Proceedings of the International Computer Music Conference*, Ann Arbor, MI, October 1998.

[Wit66]   W. Wittrick. On elastic wave propagation in helical springs. *International Journal of Mechanical Sciences*, 8: 25–47, 1966.

[YAAS08]   D. T. Yeh, J. S. Abel, A. Vladimirescu, and J. O. Smith. Numerical methods for simulation of guitar distortion circuits. *Computer Music Journal*, 32(2): 23–42, 2008.

[Yeh09]   D. T. Yeh. *Digital Implementation of Musical Distortion Circuits by Analysis and Simulation*. PhD thesis, CCRMA, Elec. Eng. Dept., Stanford University (CCRMA), Palo Alto, CA, USA, June 2009. http:http://ccrma.stanford.edu/dtyeh///ccrma.stanford.edu/~dtyeh/.

[YI63]   A. C. Young and P. It. Artificial reverberation unit, October 8, 1963. US Patent 3,106,610.

[YS06]   D. Yeh and J. O. Smith III. Discretization of the 59 Fender Bassman tone stack. In *Proceedings of the 9th International Conference on Digital Audio Effects (DAFx06)*, September 2006. http://www.dafx.de/.

[YS08]   D. T. Yeh and J. O. Smith. Simulating guitar distortion circuits using wave digital and nonlinear state-space formulations. In *Proceedings of the International Conference on Digital Audio Effects*, pp. 19–26, Espoo, Finland, September 1–4, 2008.

13

Automatic mixing

E. Perez-Gonzalez and J. D. Reiss

13.1 Introduction

Audio mixing is the process of applying a series of signal-processing operations to multiple audio sources and then combining them together to create a sound mixture. In this chapter we will explore signal-processing algorithms which aim to automate this process. The first automatic mixing implementations for live sound can be traced to [Dug75, Dug89]. Here the basic principles of automatic level adjustment for automatic mixing were proposed. This system is able to maintain constant gain structure regardless of the number of active microphone inputs. Decisions on time-domain gain compensation were based on RMS measurements extracted from the signal. A similar system, but based on a mechanical principle called direction-sensitive gating for automatic microphone mixing was developed by [JT84]. Other implementations of automatic microphone mixing such as [Pet78, SBI00] have been implemented, but most of these designs concentrate on level microphone management for speech applications only. Such automatic microphone mixing implementations make use of low-level features, in order to take mixing decisions. In recent years, techniques have been described related to non-real-time automatic-mixing processing algorithms. In [TR09b] an automatic monitor mixing method for deriving fader levels using optimisation is described. In [Kol08] and [BR09] a method that reconstructs mixing parameter values of each channel through analysing a target mixture was proposed. In [Ree00] a method which uses nearest-neighbour optimisation techniques to attempt to recreate expert mixing is derived. [TR09a] presented a method for automatically setting noise-gate parameters for drum recording using optimisation. Finally, some work on perception and automatic detection of frequencies which require equalisation compensation has been performed by [BLS08, BJ09].

In this chapter we will look at current automatic-mixing techniques for real-time digital signal processing that are capable of panning, correcting polarity and time offset problems, enhancing channels, compensating gain and fader level, and a simple self-equalisation algorithm. We will concentrate on automatic-mixing designs for live music mixing as opposed to speech-oriented

DAFX: Digital Audio Effects, Second Edition. Edited by Udo Zölzer.
© 2011 John Wiley & Sons, Ltd. Published 2011 by John Wiley & Sons, Ltd.

microphone systems. Automatic mixing has applications to live sound and music performance, remote mixing, recording and post-production as well as real-time mixing for interactive scenes and games. We will refer to these automatic-mixing digital effect tools as AM-DAFX.

13.2 AM-DAFX

From the point of view of signal flow, a DAFX is a device that takes an un-processed input signal and outputs a processed signal. In most cases the user can control the signal-processing behaviour by manipulating a number of parameters through a graphical user interface. The aim of the user is to manipulate the signal-processing parameters in order to produce the desired transformation of the input signals. Figure 13.1 shows the standard implementation of a DAFX, where $x(n)$ is the input source and $y(n)$ is the output resulting from the signal processing.

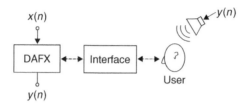

Figure 13.1   Diagram of a DAFX and user.

In an automatic-mixing context we aim to aid or replace the task normally performed by the user. In order to achieve this, some important design objectives should be performed by the AM-DAFX:

(1) The system should comply with all the technical constraints of a mixture, such as avoiding distortion and maintaining adequate dynamic range.

(2) The design should simplify complex mixing tasks while performing at a standard similar to that of an expert user.

(3) For sound-reinforcement applications the system must remain free of undesired acoustic feedback artefacts.

In the case of a system used for live performance mixing, the automatic system must avoid undesired acoustic feedback artefacts at all cost. For this reason several stability solutions have been developed, for example gain shearing [Dug75, Dug89] and self-normalisation techniques [PGR08a, PGR08b]. In most cases these techniques try to prevent acoustic feedback by ensuring a maximum electronic transfer function gain no bigger than unity. This ensures that regardless of the changes in signal-processing parameters the system remains stable.

A diagram depicting a generic AM-DAFX can be seen in Figure 13.2, where $x_e(n)$ is an external source. Our aim is to emulate the user's control parameters. An AM-DAFx is formed of two main sections: the signal-processing section and the side-chain processing portion. The signal-processing algorithm is a standard DAFX processing device and can include a user interface if the AM-DAFX is meant to give visual feedback for its actions. The analysis decision section of the automatic-mixing algorithm is what we will refer as the side-chain processing. The analysis decision-making portion of the automatic mixing tool takes audio from one or more channels together with optional external inputs and outputs the derived control data. The controlling data drives the control parameters back to the signal-processing algorithm.

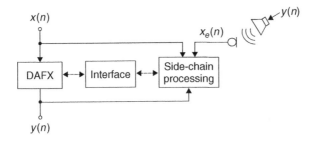

Figure 13.2 Diagram of an AM-DAFX.

The AM-DAFX described herein aims to take objective technical decisions. This is useful for improving the audio engineer's work flow and allowing him to achieve a well-balanced mix in a shorter period of time. The AM-DAFX described in this chapter are not designed to take into account any uncommon mixing practices or to be able to take subjective mixing decisions. In order to optimise the design of AM-DAFX the use of common mixing practices can be used as constraints. Given that the task normally performed by an expert user also involves perceptual considerations, perceptual rules can improve the performance of the algorithms. When combining several basic AM-DAFX tools to emulate the signal flow of a standard mixer, we can achieve a mixture in which the signal-processing flow is comparable to the one performed in a standard mixing situation.

One of the simplest AM-DAFX is the automatic gain control. In a standard digital audio mixer the head amplifier gain control is a simple multiplier which is in charge of ensuring correct analogue to digital conversion. Typically the head amplifier gain is used to scale the signal such that two technical properties are achieved:

(1) The input signal should be scaled in order not to have distortion.

(2) The signal must make optimal use of the dynamic range available.

This involves setting the gain such that the maximum peak values do not overflow the *analogue to digital converter* (ADC), while ensuring that its maximum peak value is as close as possible to 0 dB FS. Figure 13.3 shows the implementation of such an automatic-gain AM-DAFX device, where the input signal-processing section of the algorithm consists of a simple gain controller and an ADC. The side-chain processing corresponds to a simple peak feature measurement performed on the input. Every time the peak input voltage is bigger than the maximum peak value held by the ADC, the input head amplifier gain gets diminished by a step. An equivalent implementation can

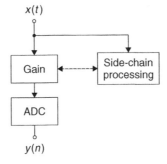

Figure 13.3 Diagram of an automatic gain AM-DAFX.

be achieved by using the overflow flag of the ADC instead of performing a direct measurement over the peak input [PGR09a]. In Figure 13.3 the AM-DAFX side chain extracts a feature from the input signal, taking a decision based on the extracted feature and then outputs control data to perform changes to the desired parameter in the signal-processing portion of the automatic-mixing algorithm. This feature extraction and decision-making process is characteristic of adaptive AM-DAFX.

13.3   Cross-adaptive AM-DAFX

DAFX architectures have been classified by their implementation [Zöl05]: filters, delays, modulators, time-segment processing, time-frequency processing, etc. Similarly, DAFX have also been classified by the perceptual attributes [ABLAV03] which they modify e.g., timbre, delay, pitch, positions or quality. Although these classifications tend to be accurate in many contexts, they are not optimal for understanding the signal-processing control architectures of some more complex effects. More recently, an adaptive digital audio effect (ADAFx) class was proposed [VZA06]. This class uses features extracted from the signals to control the signal-processing process. In terms of their adaptive properties, digital audio effects may be distinguished as follows:

(1) Direct user control: Features are not extracted from input signals so they are non-adaptive. A multi-source extension of this approach is the result of unifying the user interface, for example when linking a stereo equaliser. This provides exactly the same equalisation for the left and right channel using a single user panel. Although the user interface is unified, the output signal processing is independent of the signal content.

(2) Auto-adaptive: Control parameters are based on a feature extracted from the input source. These include, for example, auto tuning, harmonisers, simple single-channel noise gates and compressors.

(3) External-adaptive: The system takes its control processing variable from a different source to the one on which it has been applied. This is the case for ducking effects, side-chain gates and side-chain compressors.

(4) Cross-adaptive effects: Signal processing is the direct result of the analysis of the content of each individual channel with respect to the other channels. The signal processing in such devices is accomplished by inter-source dependency. It is a feedforward cross-adaptive effect if it takes its control variable from the inputs, and it is called a feedback cross-adaptive effect if it takes its control feature from the outputs.

When mixing audio, the user tends to perform signal-processing changes on a given signal source not only because of the source content, but also because there is a simultaneous need to blend it with the content of other sources, so that an overall mix balance is achieved. There is a need to be aware of the relationship between all the sources involved in the audio mixture. Thus, a cross-adaptive effect-processing architecture is ideal for automatic mixing. The general block diagram of a cross-adaptive device is depicted in Figure 13.4. Due to the importance of source inter-relationship in audio mixing for music, we can add another design objective to be performed by the AM-DAFX:

(5) The signal processing of an individual source is the result of the inter-dependent relationships between all involved sources involved.

A cross-adaptive process is characterised by the use of a multi-input multi-output (MIMO) architecture. For the sake of simplicity we will define our MIMO systems in this chapter to have the same number of input and outputs, unless stated. We will identify inputs as $x_m(n)$ and outputs

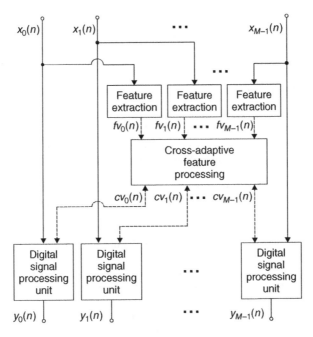

Figure 13.4 General diagram of a cross-adaptive device using side-chain processing.

as $y_m(n)$, where m has a valid range from $0, \ldots, M - 1$ given that M is the maximum number of input sources involved in the signal-processing section of the AM-DAFX. External sources are denoted $x_e(n)$, as in Figure 13.2. During this chapter we will use an architecture that does not make use of feedback. Therefore the side-chain processing inputs will be taken only from the input of the signal-processing section of the AM-DAFX. In a cross-adaptive AM-DAFX the side chain consists of two main sections:

(1) A feature extraction processing section.

(2) A cross-adaptive feature processing block.

The feature extraction vector for all sources, obtained from the feature extraction processing section, will be denoted $f v_m(n)$, where n denotes the discrete time index in samples. The control data vectors for all sources, obtained from the cross-adaptive feature processing block, will be denoted as $cv_m(n)$.

13.3.1   Feature extraction for AM-DAFX

The feature extraction processing block is in charge of extracting a series of features per input channel. The ability to extract the features fast and accurately will determine the ability of the system to perform appropriately in real-time. The better the model for extracting a feature, the better the algorithm will perform. For example, if perceptual loudness is the feature to be extracted, the model of loudness chosen to extract the feature will have a direct impact on the performance of the system. According to their feature usage AM-DAFX can be in one of two forms:

(1) Accumulative: This type of AM-DAFX aim to achieve a converging data value which improves in accuracy with time in proportion to the amount and distribution of data received. The system has no need to continuously update the data control stream, which means that

the accumulative AM-DAFX can operate on systems which are performing real-time signal-processing operations, even if the feature extraction process is non-real-time. The main idea behind accumulative AM-DAFX, as implemented herein, is to obtain the probability mass function of the feature under study and use the most probable solution as the driving feature of the system. In other words we derive the mode, which corresponds to the peak value of the accumulated extracted feature.

(2) Dynamic: This type of AM-DAFX makes use of fast extractable features to drive data-control processing parameters in real-time. An example of such a dynamic system can be a system which uses an RMS feature to ride vocals against background music. Another example can be gain-sharing algorithms for controlling microphones such as the one originally implemented in [Dug75]. Dynamic AM-DAFX do not tend to converge to a static value. A compromise between dynamic and accumulative feature extraction can be achieved by using relatively small accumulative windows with weighted averages.

An important consideration to be taken into account during the feature extraction process is noise. The existence of bleed, crosstalk, self-noise and ambient noise will influence the reliability of the feature extraction. Common methods for obtaining more reliable features include averaging, coherence validation and gating. One of the most common methods used for AM-DAFX is adaptive gating, where the gating threshold adapts according to the existing noise. This method was introduced to automatic mixing applications by [Dug75, Dug89]. It requires an input noise source which is representative of the noise in the system. In the case of a live system a microphone outside of the input source capture area is a good representation of ambient noise. Therefore this microphone signal can be used to derive the adaptive threshold needed to validate the feature.

For accumulative AM-DAFX, variance threshold measures can be used to validate the accuracy of the probability mass function peak value. The choice of feature extraction model will influence the convergence time in order to achieve the desired variance. For this to work appropriately in a system that is receiving an unknown input signal, in real-time, some re-scaling operations must be undertaken. First the probability mass function must always be equal to one. Second, if the maximum dynamic range of the feature is unknown the mass probability function must be re-scaled. In such a case, the axis range should be normalised continuously to unity by dividing all received feature magnitudes by the magnitude of the maximum received input value.

An example of the effects of adaptive gating and re-scaling in an accumulative feature extraction block is shown in Figure 13.5. In this example the feature under study is loudness, which has been extracted from a musical test signal. If no re-scaling and no adaptive gating is used to optimise the loudness mass probability function, the resulting most probable feature value is always 0, as shown in Figure 13.5(a). This is because there is a large amount of low-level noise which biases the loudness measurement. A second test with re-scaling and no adaptive gating is shown in Figure 13.5(b). It can be see that although a Gaussian shape corresponding to the actual loudness can be seen, there are still a large number of data points in the lowest bin of the histogram, causing an erroneous null measurement. When adaptive gating is performed without re-scaling, Figure 13.5(c), the number of zero-bin occurrences is dramatically reduced. Finally, a test consisting of both, re-scaling and adaptive gating, is depicted in Figure 13.5(d). It can be seen that the algorithm is able to correctly identify the most probable feature value. This means that that both adaptive re-scaling and gating must be performed in order to achieve accurate extraction of the most probable feature value.

13.3.2   Cross-adaptive feature processing

The cross-adaptive processing section of the AM-DAFX is in charge of determining the interdependence of the input features in order to output the appropriate control data. These data controls parameters in the signal-processing section of the AM-DAFX. The obtained control parameters are usually interpolated before being sent to the signal-processing portion of the AM-DAFX. This

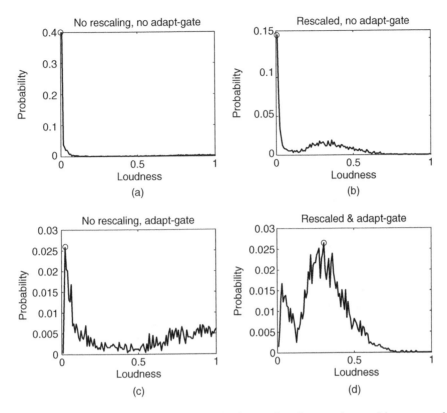

Figure 13.5 Accumulated histograms. The circular marker denotes the resulting accumulated peak loudness value [PGR09a].

can be achieved using a low pass filter that will ensure a smooth interpolation between control data points. The cross-adaptive feature processing can be implemented by a mathematical function that maps the inter-dependence between channels. In many cases constraint rules can be used to narrow the inter-dependency between channels. In order to keep the cross-adaptive processing system stability the overall gain contribution of the resulting control signals can be normalised so that the overall addition of all source control gains is equal to unity. The cross-adaptive function is unique for every design, and has to be individually derived according to the aim of the AM-DAFX.

13.4   AM-DAFX implementations

In this section we will describe the major steps needed to implement five different AM-DAFX. The resulting audio signal processing is the direct result of the analysis of the inter-relationship between input sources. The systems described are intended to be used for real-time signal processing. They can be implemented individually or cascaded together in order to implement an automatic audio mixer suitable for live audio mixing of music.

13.4.1   Source enhancer

In audio mixing a common process is to enhance a source by making it more prominent. A way to achieve enhancement is by incrementing the gain of a source $x_\mu(n)$ with respect of the other input sources. Performing such an action could introduce acoustic feedback or distortion if the gain needed is too large. For this reason the preferred action is to lower the gain of all sources, except for the one in need of enhancement. Although performing such an action will result in a stable enhancement of the desired source, it is not an optimal solution. This is because the sources that are not spectrally related to $x_\mu(n)$ are also attenuated. In other words, if we aim to enhance a piccolo flute there should be no need to decrease a bass guitar because its spectral content shares little or no relationship with the piccolo. This type of complex frequency-dependent enhancement is familiar to audio engineers and it is what we aim to reproduce.

With this in mind we can design an AM-DAFX source enhancer whose aim is to unmask a source by applying an attenuation to the rest of the sources, relative to their spectral content. Such an enhancer should comply with the following properties:

(1) The enhancer must be able to identify the spectral inter-dependency between channels so that it only attenuates each source in proportion to its spectral relationship to $x_\mu(n)$.

(2) The gain of $x_\mu(n)$ must remain unchanged.

The signal-processing section of such a device is an attenuation multiplier per input channel, and is given by $y_m(n) = cv_m(n) \cdot x_m(n)$. Where the output $y_m(n)$ is the result of multiplying the input signal $x_m(n)$ by the scaling factor $cv_m(n)$. Many other types of enhancements can be achieved by creative modifications of this architecture. For example, the same architecture presented here as a gain enhancer can be used to enhance signals by altering the amount of reverberation added to each channel in proportion to its spectral content. More on such an implementation and detailed references can be found in [PGR08c]. The side-chain processing architecture of such an enhancer will be detailed next.

Feature extraction implementation

The feature extraction algorithm we aim to design takes a digital audio input, $x_m(n)$, and outputs a data signal, $fv_m(n)$, representative of the spectral content of the input source. In order to ensure a clean acquisition we must use a data-validating algorithm. In this particular implementation we make use of an adaptive-gate algorithm. Therefore we will need the aid of an external input, $x_e(n)$, in order to derive the adaptive-gate threshold. This external input is usually taken from a measurement microphone placed in an area that is representative of the ambient noise. Such a feature extraction system is represented by $fv_m(n) = f(x_m(n), x_e(n))$. Given that $fv_m(n)$ must provide us an indication of the spectral content of $x_m(n)$, a system based on spectral decomposition is appropriate, Figure 13.6.

Therefore we can decompose the input $x_m(n)$ after it has been processed by the adaptive gate, $xg_m(n)$ and process it using a filter bank. The filter bank is comprised of K filters with a transfer function $h_k(n)$, where k has a valid range from $0, \ldots, K - 1$. In order to give equal opportunity for input sources to be classified as unique the filter bank can be designed to have $K = M$, where M corresponds to the maximum number of sources involved in the AM-DAFX and has a valid range from $0, \ldots, M - 1$. This also avoids having many sources clustered in the same spectral area. Once $xg_m(n)$ is decomposed into spectral bands we calculate the *root mean square* (RMS) of each k band, $\text{RMS}(h_{k,m})$. Then we identify the RMS element that has the maximum RMS magnitude, $\max(\text{RMS}(h_{0\ldots k,m}))$, and we store it in order to derive the probability mass function. We produce a histogram using the probability mass function $k = \max(\text{RMS}(h_{0\ldots k,m}(n)))$. The x axis of the histogram represents frequency bins, from $0, \ldots, K - 1$, and the y axis corresponds to the probability of the signal $x_m(n)$, to be characterised as having spectral content dominated by a given frequency bin. Given that we are calculating a probability function we must normalise all elements inside the probability mass function so that the overall addition of probabilities per bin is equal to one. This is achieved by continuously dividing the number of occurrences per bin by the total number of elements received. Finally, the maximum peak of the probability mass

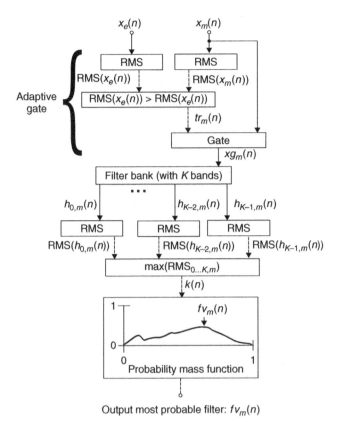

Figure 13.6 Block diagram of a feature extraction algorithm for spectral decomposition of a channel.

function must be found. This peak corresponds to the most probable spectral decomposition band $fv_m(n)$ that characterises the $x_m(n)$ under study. Under the feature extraction schema stated, $fv_m(n)$ corresponds to the most probable filter identification value and has a valid range from $0, \ldots, K - 1$. Such a feature extraction process must be implemented for all M sources.

Cross-adaptive feature processing

Now that we have extracted a feature that represents the spectral content of the input signal $x_m(n)$, a function that maps the inter-relationship between the spectral content of the sources must be found. Given a source to be enhanced, $x_\mu(n)$, we must find a continuous function whose minima are located at $fv_\mu(n) = k$. This function should increase for filter values away from $fv_\mu(n)$. The final implementation should make use of the following parameters:

- User parameters

  - μ: This is the main parameter that states which of the sources is the one to be enhanced.

  - G: Is the maximum attenuation. Any source that shares the same spectral classification as $x_\mu(n)$ will have an attenuation equal to G.

  - Q: Is the amount of interaction the enhancement has with non-spectrally related sources.

- Non-user parameters

  - M: This corresponds to the total number of sources involved in cross-adaptive processing.

  - m: This tells the algorithm which source is being processed, thus getting the proper attenuation level which corresponds to a given source.

An ideal candidate to map the spectral inter-relation between channels is an inverted Gaussian. Such a function is a continuous smooth function and its minima can be made to be located at $fv_\mu(n)$. Therefore we can derive

$$
fg_m(n) = \frac{1}{Q\sqrt{2\pi}} e^{\frac{-(fr_m(n)-\mu(n))^2}{2Q^2}}, \tag{13.1}
$$

where $fg_m(n)$ is a Gaussian function, $fr_m(n)$ is the frequency bin and $\mu(n)$ is the position on the frequency axis where the maximum inflection of the Gaussian function is located. In order achieve maximum attenuation at $fv_\mu(n)$ we normalise and invert Equation 13.1. The user controllable G will also be included as a multiplier, so that it scales the inverted Gaussian mapping function. $a_m(n)$ is the inter-source-dependent mapping function given by

$$
a_m(n) = \left| \left(G\left(\frac{fg_m(n)}{\frac{1}{Q\sqrt{2\pi}}} \right) \right) - 1 \right|. \tag{13.2}
$$

For each source $x_m(n)$ we must find the assigned attenuation value $a_m(n)$. Since $K = M$ we must normalise $fv_m(n)$ with respect to M in order to obtain the correct value for $fr_m(n)$. Such normalisation is given by

$$
fr_m(n) = \left(\frac{2}{M-1} \left(fv_m(n) - 1 \right) \right) - 1. \tag{13.3}
$$

We require that the minima of the mapping function must be centred at $fv_\mu(n) = k$, and the algorithm has K filters with M channels. So we must normalise $fv_\mu(n)$) with respect to M,

$$
\mu(n) = \left(\frac{2}{M-1} \left(fv_\mu(n) - 1 \right) \right) - 1. \tag{13.4}
$$

Recall that our objective is to enhance $x_\mu(n)$ with respect to the rest of sources. So we must maintain the gain of $x_\mu(n)$ unchanged. This is expressed by

$$
cv_m(n) = \begin{cases} 1 & m = \mu \\ a_m(n) & m \neq \mu. \end{cases} \tag{13.5}
$$

The cross-adaptive implementation of such an AM-DAFX is depicted in Figure 13.7. Since our approach only applies gain attenuations, it introduces no phase distortion.

The final mixture is now

$$
mix(n) = \sum_{m=0}^{M-1} cv_m(n) \cdot x_m(n), \tag{13.6}
$$

where $mix(n)$ is the overall mix after applying the cross-adaptive processing. The control attenuation for source m is given by $cv_m(n)$, where $cv_m(n) = 1$ for $m = \mu$. The attenuation control parameter $cv_m(n)$ varies with respect to its spectral content relationship Q, with a maximum attenuation equal to G for all sources in the same spectral category as $x_\mu(n)$.

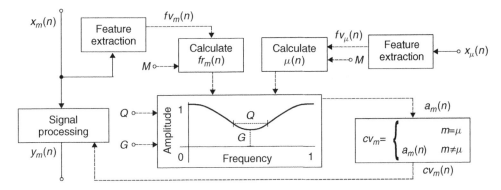

Figure 13.7   Block diagram of an enhancer.

13.4.2   Panner

Stereo panning aims to transform a set of monaural signals into a two-channel signal in a pseudo-stereo field. Many methods and panning laws have been proposed, one of the most common being the sine cosine panning law. In stereo panning the ratio at which the source power has been spread between the left and the right channels determines its position. The AM-DAFX panner aims to create a satisfactory stereo mix from multi-channel audio. The proposed implementation does not take into account knowledge of physical source locations or make use of any type of contextual or visual aids. The implementation down-mixes M input sources and converts them into a two-channel mix, $y_L(n)$ and $y_R(n)$. The algorithm attempts to minimise spectral masking by allocating related source spectra to different panning space positions. The AM-DAFX also makes used of constrained rules, psychoacoustic principles and priority criteria to determine the panning positions. For this panning implementation the source inputs $x_m(n)$ have a valid range from $0, \ldots, M-1$ and the filter bank has a total of K filters $0, \ldots, K-1$. In order to achieve this we can apply the following panning rules:

(1) Psychoacoustic principle: Do not pan a source if its energy is concentrated in a very low-frequency bin. This is because sources with very low-frequency content cannot be perceived as being panned. Not panning these sources will also give the advantage of splitting low-frequency sources evenly between the left and right channels.

(2) Maintain left to right relative balance: Sources with the same spectral categorisation should be spread evenly amongst the available panning space. In order to give all input sources the same opportunity of being classified as having a different spectral content from each other, we will make the amount of filters in the feature extraction block equal to the number of inputs, $K = M$.

(3) Channel priority: This is the subjective importance given by the user to each input source. The higher the priority given by the user the higher the likelihood that the source will remain un-panned.

(4) Constrained rules: It is accepted common practice not to wide pan the sources. For this reason the user should be able to specify the maximum width of the panning space.

Further information can be found in [PGR07, PGR10]. The feature extraction of the proposed AM-DAFX panner is based on accumulative spectral decomposition, in a similar way to the automatic enhancer shown in Figure 13.6. Therefore we can proceed directly to a description of the cross-adaptive feature processing of the AM-DAFX panner.

Cross-adaptive feature processing

Given that we have classified all $x_m(n)$ inputs according to their spectral content, a set of cross-adaptive processing functions may be established in order to determine the relationships between the spectral content of each source and its panning position. Since the algorithm aims to improve intelligibility by separating sources that have similar spectral content, while maintaining stereo balance, we must design an algorithm that makes use of the following parameters:

- User parameters

  - U_m: The user priority ordering of the sources established by the user, that determines which source has more subjective importance.

  - W: The panning width scales the separation between panned sources in order to set the maximum width of the panning space.

- Non-user parameters

  - k: The filter category is used to determine if the spectral content of a source has enough high-frequency content in order for it to be panned

  - R_m: The total repetitions per classification is the number of sources in the same feature category.

In order to assign a panning position per source we must be able to identify the total number of sources in the same feature category as $x_m(n)$, denoted as $R_m(n)$, and the relationship between the user priority, $U_m(n)$, and its spectral classification $fv_m(n)$, denoted as $P_m(n)$. We can then calculate the panning position of a source based on the obtained parameters $R_m(n)$ and $P_m(n)$.

Equation 13.7 is used to obtain the total number of classification repetitions, R_m, due to other signals having the same k classification, given the initial condition $R_0 = 0$.

$$R_m = \sum_{j=1}^{M} R_{j-1} + \begin{cases} 1 & fv_m(n) = fv_{j-1}(n) \\ 0 & fv_m(n) \neq fv_{j-1}(n) \end{cases}.$$ (13.7)

Now we proceed to calculate the relationship between the user-assigned priority of a source $U_m(n)$ and its spectral classification $fv_m(n)$, we will refer to this relationship as P_m. The user-assigned priority U_m has a unique value from $0, \ldots, M-1$, the smaller the magnitude of U_m, the higher the priority. The assigned priority due to being a member of the same spectral classification, P_m, has a valid range from 1 to its corresponding R_m. The lower the value taken by P_m the lower the probability of the source of being widely panned. P_m is calculated by

$$P_m = |\{U_i : fv_i(n) = fv_m(n)\} \cap \{U_i : U_i \leq U_m\}| \quad \text{for} \quad i = \{0...M-1\},$$ (13.8)

where the modulus of the intersection of the two sets, $\{U_i : fv_i(n) = fv_m(n)\}$ and $\{U_i : U_i \leq U_m\}$ gives us the rank position, which corresponds to the value taken by P_m.

Given R_m and P_m, we can relate them in order to obtain the panning control parameter with

$$cv_m(n) = \begin{cases} 1/2 & R_m = 1 \\ W + \left[(1-2W)\frac{R_m - P_m - 1}{2(R_m - 1)}\right] & P_m + R_m \text{ is odd} \\ W + \left[(1-2W)\frac{R_m + P_m - 2}{2(R_m - 1)}\right] & P_m + R_m \text{ is even}, R_m \neq 1, \end{cases}$$ (13.9)

and by evaluating R_m and P_m the assigned panning position can be derived. The panning position $cv_m(n)$ has a valid control range from 0 to 1, where 0 means fully panned left, 0.5 means centred and 1 means panned fully right. The panning width limit, W, can go from wide panning $W = 0$ to mono $W = 0.5$.

Finally, based on the principle that we should not pan a source if its spectral category is too low, we set $cv_m(n)$ to be centred if the spectral category of the input source $fv_m(n)$ is less than a psychoacoustically established threshold tr_{ps}, (set to 200 Hz in [PGR07, PGR10]). This can be implemented by using

$$cv_m(n) = \begin{cases} 1/2 & fv_m(n) \leq tr_{ps} \\ cv_m(n) & fv_m(n) > tr_{ps} \end{cases}. \qquad (13.10)$$

Given that we intend to mix all input sources by combining them in their respective stereo summing buss, the final mixture is given by

$$y_L(n) = \sum_{m=0}^{M-1} \sin(cv_m(n)\pi/2) \cdot x_m(n) \qquad (13.11)$$

$$y_R(n) = \sum_{m=0}^{M-1} \cos(cv_m(n)\pi/2) \cdot x_m(n). \qquad (13.12)$$

Where $y_L(n)$ and $y_R(n)$ correspond to the automatically panned stereo output of the mixing device, $cv_m(n)$ is the panning factor and $x_m(n)$ represents the input signals. Such an AM-DAFX panner implementation has been depicted in Figure 13.8.

13.4.3 Faders

In order to achieve a balanced audio mixture, careful scaling of the input signals must be achieved. The most common interface for achieving such a scaling is sliding potentiometers, commonly known as *faders*. Automatic fader mixers are probably the oldest form of automatic mixing, although most designs are only suitable for speech applications and are not intended for musical use. In [Dug75, Dug89] a dynamic automatic mixing implementation for music is presented. This implementation uses RMS measurements for determining the relationship between levels in order to decide the balance between microphones. One of the problems with automatic mixing implementations that use only low-level features, is that they do not take into account any perceptual attributes of the signal. Therefore a balanced RMS mixture might not be perceptually balanced. In the implementation presented here we aim to obtain a perceptual balance of all input signals. We assume that a mixture in which per-channel loudness tends to the overall average loudness is a well-balanced mixture with optimal inter-channel intelligibility.

We will use accumulative loudness measures in order to determine the perceptual level of the input signals. The main idea behind the proposed implementation is to give each channel the same probability of being heard. That is, every signal must have the same chance of masking each other. The AM-DAFX fader implementation must adapt its gain according to the loudness relationship of the individual input signals and the overall average loudness of the mix. The end result should be to scale all input signals such that they all have equal perceptual loudness. In order to achieve this we apply the following criteria:

(1) Equal loudness probability: By scaling all input signals such that they tend to a common average probability, minimal perceptual masking can be achieved.

(2) Minimum gain changes: The algorithm should minimise gain level changes required in order to avoid the inclusion of excessive gains, this can be achieved by using the overall average loudness of the mix as a reference, given that it is a natural mid starting point.

(3) Fader limit control: There must be a mechanism for limiting the amount of maximum gain applied to the input signals. This avoids unnaturally high gain values from being introduced.

(4) Maintain system stability: The overall contribution of the control gains $cv_m(n)$ should not introduce distortion or acoustic feedback artefacts.

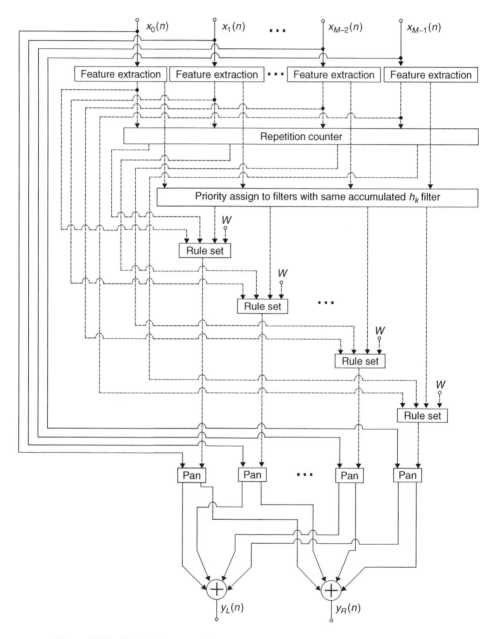

Figure 13.8   Block diagram of an automatic mixing panner [PGR07, PGR10].

The signal-processing section of such a device is an attenuation multiplier per input channel, and is given by $y_m(n) = cv_m(n) \cdot x_m(n)$, where the output $y_m(n)$ is the result of multiplying the input signal $x_m(n)$ by the scaling factor $cv_m(n)$. Further information can be found in [PGR09a]. The side-chain architecture of such perceptually driven automatic faders will be presented next.

Feature extraction implementation

Our feature extraction block will make use of adaptive gating in order to avoid unwanted noise in the measured signals. The feature extraction method requires the input signals $x_m(n)$, together with an external input $x_e(n)$ in order to derive the adaptive gating function. Such a feature extraction method has a function prototype given by $fv_m(n) = f(x_m(n), x_e(n))$.

Loudness is a perceptual attribute of sound. Therefore in order to be able to measure it we require a psychoacoustic model. The model proposed consists of perceptually weighting the input signal $x_n(n)$. Using a set of bi-quadratic filters whose coefficients are calculated so that the transfer function of the filters approximates loudness curves. Given that loudness curves change depending on the sound pressure level, a set of filter coefficients corresponding to different sound pressure levels can be calculated. All calculated coefficients are then stored in a look-up table. A measurement microphone $x_e(n)$, the same used for the adaptive gating, can be used to calculate the sound pressure $SP(n)$ and retrieve the correct set of filter coefficients from the look-up table. With the aim of obtaining a clean measurement, adaptive gating can be implemented. The loudness perceptual weighting of an input signal $xl_m(n)$ is given by

$$xl_m(n) = \frac{1}{S} \sum_{i=1}^{S} (xg_m(n) \star w(SP(n)))_i, \qquad (13.13)$$

where S is an averaging constant that can be used to derive longer-term loudness measurements, as opposed to instantaneous loudness, $SP(n)$ is the sound pressure level derived from the external input and $w(SP(n))$ is the weighting filter loudness curves convolved with the gated input $xg_m(n)$.

Once we have a perceptual representation of the input given by $xl_m(n)$ we can proceed to accumulate it in order to calculate its probability mass function. Given that we are calculating a probability we must normalise the occurrences to sum to unity. Due to the fact that we do not know the perceptual dynamic range limits of the signal we must ensure that in the case where we receive a new $xl_{0...M-1}(n)$ which is greater than a previous sample, we must normalise to that maximum value for all M channels. Then we proceed to find the peak of the probability mass function. This is representative of the most probable loudness value of the input under study, denoted as $fv_m(n)$. The psychoacoustic model proposed here is depicted in Figure 13.9.

Cross-adaptive feature processing

Cross-adaptive feature processing consists of mapping the perceptual loudness of each channel to its amplitude level so that, by manipulating its amplitude, we can achieve the desired loudness level. Given that we are aiming to achieve an average loudness value $l(n)$, we must increase the loudness of the channels below this average and decrease the channels above this average. The average loudness $l(n)$ is obtained as the arithmetic mean of $fv_m(n)$ for all channels.

Since we want a system in which we have a multiplier $cva_m(n)$ such that we scale the input $x_m(n)$ in order to achieve a desired average loudness $l(n)$ its function can be approximated by $Hl_m(n) = l(n)/(cva_m(n)x_m(n))$. Therefore we derive the desired gain parameter as follows:

$$cva_m(n) = \frac{l(n)}{Hl_m(n)x_m(n)}, \qquad (13.14)$$

where $cva_m(n)$ is the control gain variable in order to achieve the target average loudness $l(n)$ and $Hl_m(n)$ is the function of the desired system. Given that our feature extraction block has

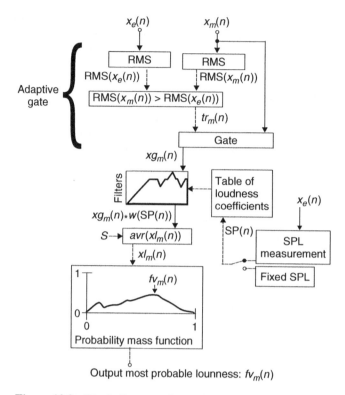

Figure 13.9   Block diagram of an automatic gain fader system.

a function $Hl_m(n) = f v_m(n)/x_m(n)$ we can say that the term $Hl_m(n)x_m(n)$ in Equation 13.14 is equal to $f v_m(n)$. Therefore $cva_m(n) = l(n)/f v_m(n)$. In most cases $cva_m(n)$ will represent a physical fader which has limited maximum gain. In practical applications $cva_m(n)$ has physical limitations. Gain rescaling must be performed in order not to exceed the system limits. This can be achieved by rescaling all channels to have an added gain contribution equal to unity, were unity is the the upper limit of the mixing system. This also ensures that the $cva_m(n)$ values stay below their physical limits and that all the faders perform an attenuation function instead of incrementing gain. This ensures the system does not introduce any undesired distortion or acoustic feedback. The normalisation process can be performed by

$$cv_m(n) = \frac{cva_m(n)}{\sum_{m=0}^{M-1} cva_m(n)},$$

(13.15)

where $cv_m(n)$ is the normalised control gain value that drives the signal-processing section of the AM-DAFX in order to achieve equi-probable average loudness over all channels in the mix. The final mixture is given by Equation 13.6, where $mix(n)$ is the overall mix after applying the cross-adaptive processing. The control attenuation for every source m is given by $cv_m(n)$. The overall system block diagram of the automatic-mixing fader implementation is been shown in Figure 13.10; most cross-adaptive effects that use adaptive gating fit a similar block diagram.

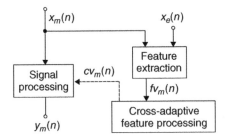

Figure 13.10 Overall block diagram of an automatic gain fader system.

M-file 13.1 (Automatic-Mixing-Framework.m)

```
function Automatic_Mixing_Framework()
% Author: E. Perez-Gonzalez, J. Reiss
% function Automatic_Mixing_Framework()

%---AUDIO INPUT for 8 Mono Files, where x{m} is the input to channel m.
[x{1},Fs]=wavread('x1.wav'); %Read file
% ...
[x{8},Fs]=wavread('x8.wav'); %Read file

%---RECORD FILE BEFORE AUTOMIXING
monoInputSum = 0;
for m=1:length(x) %Mono summing buss
    monoInputSum=monoInputSum + x{1};
end
monoInputSum=monoInputSum *.125; %Mono summing buss scaling
monoInputSumStereo=(repmat(monoInputSum*(1/sqrt(2)),1,2));%Split to Stereo
wavwrite(monoInputSumStereo,Fs,'preAutoMixSum.wav');

%---SIDE CHAIN
tr=0.002;   %%Fixed Threshold
[cv]=LoudnessSideChain_at_Fs44100(x,tr); %Side Chain

%---PROCESSING
[yL,yR]=LoudnessProcessing(x,cv); %Fader Gain

%---RECORD AUDIO OUTPUT
wavwrite([yL yR],Fs,'postAutoMixSum.wav'); %Record file after automixing

%=============================================================
function [cv]=LoudnessSideChain_at_Fs44100(x,tr)
%% LOUDNESS SIDE CHAIN FUNCTION %%%
cv=[0.5 0.5 0.5 0.5 0.5 0.5 0.5 0.5]; %Initial value

%--Noise removal
for m = 1:length(x)
    xg{m}=x{m}(x{m}>tr); %Gate
end

%---Obtain feature
for m=1:length(x)
```

```
    [xg{m}]=Loudness95dB_at_Fs44100(xg{m});
    clear peakA;
end

%---Accumulative feature processing
for m=1:length(x)
    max_vector(m)= max(xg{m});
end
[max_xg,argmax_xg]=max(max_vector);

for m=1:length(x)
    xg{m}=xg{m}/max_xg; %normalize
end

figure(1); %Figure showing accumulated loudness values per channel
for m=1:length(x)
    subplot(2,4,m)
    [maxhist,maxhist_arg]=max(hist(xg{m}));%Calc. max and maxarg of hist
    [num,histout]=hist(xg{m});%Calculate histogram
    bar(histout,num)%Plot histogram
    axis([0 1 0 maxhist+1])
    hold on;
    %Calculate most probable loudness per channel
    fv(m)=(maxhist_arg*(max(xg{m})+min(xg{m})))/length(hist(xg{m}));
    plot (fv(m),maxhist,'ro')%Plot most probable loudness
    hold off;
    clear maxhist maxhist_arg num histout xg{m};
end

%---CROSS ADAPTIVE PROCESSING
l=mean(fv); %obtain average Loudness
for m=1:length(x)
    cva(m)=l/fv(m); %compensate for average loudness
end

%---Unity gain normalisation to maintain system stability
cvasum=sum(cva); %obtain total non-nomalized
for m=1:length(x)
    cv(m)=cva(m)/cvasum; %normalize for cvasum
end

%Print Loudness, control variables and gain
Feature_Loudness=[fv(1) fv(2) fv(3) fv(4) fv(5) fv(6) fv(7) fv(8)]
Control_variables=[cv(1) cv(2) cv(3) cv(4) cv(5) cv(6) cv(7) cv(8)]
Overal_gain=sum(cv) %overal gain equals 1

%==============================================================
function [yL,yR]=LoudnessProcessing(x,cv)
%---AUDIO OUTPUT for 8 Mono Files, where y{m} is the output to channel m.
%---Fader GAIN PROCESSING
for m=1:length(x)
    y{m}=x{m}*cv(m);
    clear x{m}
end;

%---Split mono results to stereo for channels 1 to 8
yL=0; %Left summing bus initialisation
```

```
yR=0; %Right summing bus initialisation

for m=1:length(y)
    yL=yL + y{m}*(1/sqrt(2)); %Scale to split mono to stereo
    yR=yR + y{m}*(1/sqrt(2)); %Scale to split mono to stereo
    clear y{m};
end


%==================================================================
function [out]=Loudness95dB_at_Fs44100(in)%% LOUDNESS FEATURE EXTRACTION
%---Biquad Filter no.1 HPF
B = [1.176506 -2.353012 1.176506]; A = [1 -1.960601 0.961086];
in= filter(B,A,in);

%---Biquad Filter no.2 Peak Filter
B = [0.951539 -1.746297 0.845694]; A = [1 -1.746297 0.797233];
in= filter(B,A,in);

%---Biquad Filter no.3 Peak Filter
B = [1.032534 -1.42493 0.601922]; A = [1 -1.42493 0.634455];
in= filter(B,A,in);

%---Biquad Filter no.4 Peak Filter
B = [0.546949 -0.189981 0.349394]; A = [1 -0.189981 -0.103657];
in= filter(B,A,in);

%---Peak averaging
S=20000; %Frame size for peak averaging
cumin=[zeros(S,1); cumsum(in)];
avin=(cumin((S+1):end)-(cumin(1:(end-S))))/S; % Calculate running average
clear cumin;
Six = (S+1):S:(length(avin));% Times at wich peak amp will be returned
peakA=nan(size(Six));% Create vector holding peaks
for i=1:length(Six)% Calculete peak average
    Si = Six(i);
    peakA(i)=max(abs(avin((Si-S):Si)));%Output peak averaging
end

out=peakA;
```

13.4.4 Equaliser

In order to achieve a spectrally balanced mix, a careful perceptual balancing of the spectral content of each channel is needed. Equalisation per channel is not only done because of the individual properties of the signal, but also because it needs blending with other channels in the mix. In order to achieve a spectrally balanced mix we will employ a cross-adaptive architecture to relate the perceptual loudness of the equalisation bands amongst channels.

Even when we have achieved overall equal loudness in the mixture, as in the previous subsections of this chapter, it is apparent that some frequency ranges appear to have significant spectral masking. For this reason a multi-band implementation of the AM-DAFX gain fader algorithm has been implemented. This algorithm should not only comply with achieving equally balanced loudness per channel, but should simultaneously ensure that there is equal loudness per channel for all equalisation bands. We will apply a signal-processing section per m channel consisting of a graphic equaliser with K bands, using filters described by the transfer function $hq_{k,m}$. By definition, a graphic equaliser has its Q and cut-off frequency points fixed, therefore we will only manipulate the gain parameter for each band. For implementing an AM-DAFX equalisation system we comply with the following design constraints:

(1) Equal loudness probability per band: All the input signals involved should tend to the same average loudness per band.

(2) Minimum gain changes: The algorithm should perform the most optimal gain changes, therefore it should increment or decrement band gain from a natural starting point such as the overall average of the mix.

(3) Overall equal loudness probability: The system must simultaneously achieve equal loudness per band and full bandwidth equal loudness.

The signal-processing section of such a device is

$$y_m(n) = \sum_{k=0}^{K-1} cv_{k,m}(n) \left[hq_{k,m}(n) \star x_m(n) \right], \tag{13.16}$$

where $cv_{k,m}$ is the desired control vector that drives the gain of each k band of the equaliser given a channel m. Further details can be found in [PGR09b]. The side-chain architecture of such perceptually driven automatic equalisers will be detailed next.

Feature extraction implementation

We use an adaptive gating at the input of our feature extraction implementation. The system prototype is described by $fv_{k,m}(n) = f(x_e(n), x_m(n))$, where $x_m(n)$ denotes the side-chain inputs, $x_e(n)$ is the external input used to derive the adaptive threshold and $fv_{k,m}$ is the feature vector describing each k band for every channel m.

We start the feature extraction process by designing a spectral decomposition bank whose filters $h_{k,m}$ match the cut-off frequencies of the filters $hq_{k,m}$ used in the signal-processing equalisation section.

For performing multi-band adaptive gating the system takes each of the spectrally decomposed bands of $x_m(n)$ and $x_e(n)$ and outputs a clean version of each of the bands of $x_m(n)$ denoted as $xg_{k,m}(n)$.

The loudness model per band is the same as presented in the previous subsection, except for the fact that it is performed per decomposition band. This means that there are KM loudness weightings overall. The equation for performing the weighting is given by Equation 13.17,

$$xl_{k,m}(n) = \frac{1}{S} \sum_{i=1}^{S} \left(xg_{k,m}(n) \star w(SP(n)) \right)_i, \tag{13.17}$$

where $w(SP(n))$ is the loudness weighting that changes as a function of the measured sound pressure level $SP(n)$ derived from the external input $x_e(n)$. Given that all the gated and spectrally decomposed bands $xg_{k,m}(n)$ are convolved with the loudness weighting, then $xl_{k,m}(n)$ is a representation of the loudness of the input signal $x_m(n)$. S is the averaging constant used to determine longer-term loudness, as opposed to instantaneous loudness.

The same accumulative process as the one presented in the previous subsection is used per spectral band. In the case of a spectral band having a loudness level greater than the previous loudness value, all bands in all channels, should be renormalised to the new maximum value. The resulting peak value of each probability mass function is an accurate representation of the most

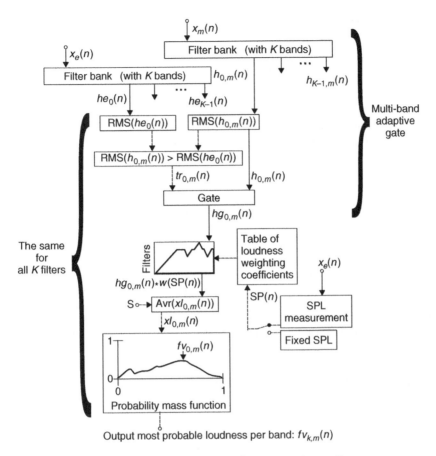

Figure 13.11   Block diagram of an automatic equaliser.

probable loudness per band of a given input and is denoted by $fv_{k,m}(n)$. The block diagram of this multi-band loudness feature extraction method is shown in Figure 13.11.

Cross-adaptive feature processing

Cross-adaptive feature processing consists of mapping the perceptual loudness of each spectral band to its amplitude level so that, by manipulating its gain per band level, we can achieve a desired target loudness level. We aim to achieve an average loudness value $l(n)$, therefore we must decrease the loudness of the equalisation bands for signals above this average and increase the band gain for signals below this average. This results in a system in which we have a multiplier $cva_{k,m}(n)$ per band, such that we scale the input bands $x_{k,m}(n)$ in order to achieve a desired average loudness $l(n)$. The function of the system can be approximated by $Hl_{k,m}(n) = l(n)/(cv_{k,m}(n)x_{k,m}(n))$, where the control vector $cv_{k,m}(n)$ is given by

$$cv_{k,m}(n) = \frac{l(n)}{Hl_{k,m}(n)x_{k,m}(n)}, \tag{13.18}$$

where $cv_{k,m}(n)$ is the control gain variable per band used to achieve the target average loudness $l(n)$ and $Hl_{k,m}(n)$ is the function of the desired system. The feature extraction block has a function

$Hl_{k,m}(n) = f v_{k,m}(n)/x_{k,m}(n)$, so $cv_{k,m}(n) = l(n)/f v_{k,m}(n)$. The target overall average loudness $l(n)$ is

$$l(n) = \sum_{m=0}^{M-1} \left(\sum_{k=0}^{K-1} f v_{k,m}(n)/K \right) /M, \tag{13.19}$$

where $l(n)$ is the average of all $f v_{k,m}$ for all k bands and m channels.

The overall system block diagram is given by Figure 13.10, where the spectral band index k must be added to $f v_m(n)$ and $cv_m(n)$ in order to accommodate the feature vector $f v_{k,m}(n)$ and the control vector $cv_{k,m}(n)$.

The final mixture is

$$mix(n) = \sum_{m=0}^{M-1} \sum_{k=0}^{K-1} cv_{k,m}(n) \left[hq_{k,m}(n) \star x_m(n) \right]. \tag{13.20}$$

Where $mix(n)$ is the overall mix after applying the cross-adaptive processing. The control attenuation for every m source is given by $cv_m(n)$.

The algorithm presented here is a simple equalisation algorithm that only takes into account gain modification per band based on perceptual loudness features. This implementation could benefit from also implementing automatic centre-frequency assignment and automatic filter Q control. One of the areas of automatic mixing which is more underdeveloped is automatic equalisation and there is great scope for further research on this subject within the DAFX community, [Ree00] and [BLS08, BJ09].

13.4.5   Polarity and time offset correction

In music mixing it is a common practice to use more than one signal for a single source. This is the case for using multiple microphones to record a single instrument. A dry signal direct from an electric instrument may be mixed with an acoustic representation of it, such as an electric guitar signal added to the signal of a microphoned guitar amplifier. Paths with different latencies may be summed, such as when adding an unprocessed signal to a processed version. In some cases using multiple representations of a source can improve the quality of the final mix, but if the signals are correlated to each other artefacts in the form of destructive interference can be introduced. The destructive interference can be present in the form of cancelation, due to opposite polarity, and comb filtering, due to offset between the signals. This destructive interference has a direct effect on the frequency content of the mix, introducing undesired frequency cancelations. Given that these artefacts are due to different times of arrival and inverted magnitude sign, we aim fix this by adding delay and polarity compensation. The goal is to achieve a sample accurate compensation in an automatic manner, by implementing an AM-DAFX with the following objectives:

(1) Optimise the delay path of each signal so that there is minimal destructive interference due to time offset errors.

(2) Ensure that the overall delay compensation used for all signal paths is as small as possible.

(3) Optimise polarity of each signal so that it matches the polarity of the signal with more delay offset.

The signal processing of such a device is described by $y_m(n) = cv_{pm}(n) \cdot x_m(n - cv_{\tau m}(n))$, where the polarity signal-processing multiplier is given by $cv_{pm}(n)$ and the signal-processing delay is represented by $x_m(n - cv_{\tau m}(n))$, such that, $cv_{\tau m}(n)$ is the delay in samples added to the signal $x_m(n)$. A detailed implementation of the automatic polarity and time offset correction can be found in [PGR08d]. The side-chain processing architecture of such a device is presented here.

Feature extraction implementation

The transfer function of a system is the Fourier transform of the impulse response of the system. The transfer function can be computed by dividing the Fourier transform of the output of the system by the Fourier transform of the input of the system. The impulse response can then be computed by the inverse Fourier transform. The impulse response of a system determines its dynamic characteristics. If we derive the impulse response of a reference signal with respect to another, given that they are correlated, we can determine the delay between them. The polarity of the maxima of the resultant impulse response can be used to determine the polarity relationship between the two signals with a common source.

In this implementation, $x_\mu(n)$ is denoted as the reference measurement and $x_m(n)$ as the measured signal. We can approximate the transfer function of a system by dividing the FFT of the output of the system by the FFT of its input. Therefore we aim to develop a feature extraction system that calculates the impulse response of a reference signal $x_\mu(n)$ with respect to each and every input given by $x_m(n)$, by deriving their FFTs. The system is given by a function prototype,

$$\mathbf{fv}_m(n) = f(x_\mu(n), x_m(n), tr, reset),\tag{13.21}$$

where $\mathbf{fv_m(n)}$ is the output vector containing the delay and polarity information for every $x_m(n)$ with respect to the reference channel $x_\mu(n)$. This type of transfer function measurement has the advantage of being independent of the input source content. On the other hand, noise added to the system can alter the measurement accuracy in an adverse manner. Therefore great care is taken to ensure that the delay estimation measurements are robust against noise.

The feature processing starts by assigning an arbitrary reference channel $x_\mu(n)$ where μ can take any arbitrary assignment, from $0, \ldots, M - 1$. The inputs and reference signals are weighted by $w_{HN}(n)$, a Hanning window, in order to reduce FFT artefacts. In order to ensure clean valid measurement, the signals $x_\mu(n)$ and $x_m(n)$ must be gated with respect to the RMS amplitude of $x_\mu(n)$, according to a threshold tr. For the sake of simplicity tr is considered to be a constant, but adaptive gating techniques can also be used. The resulting gated outputs will be expressed as $xg_\mu(n)$ and $xg_m(n)$. Once the reference signal $x_\mu(n)$ and its inputs signals, $x_m(n)$, have been gated and windowed, we can proceed to apply an FFT transform to each. Their FFTs are expressed by $X_m(k) = \text{FFT}[w_{HN}(n) \cdot xg_m(n)]$ and $X_\mu(k) = \text{FFT}[w_{HN}(n) \cdot xg_\mu(n)]$, and therefore we can approximate the transfer function of the reference channel against an input signal,

$$Ha_m(k) = \frac{X_m(k)}{X_\mu(k)}.\tag{13.22}$$

In order to make the feature extraction more robust to external system noise we can apply a series of techniques. We start by aiming to obtain an unbiased transfer function [Mey92] by obtaining the auto-spectrum of the measured signal, $X_{mm}(k) = X_m(k)X_m(k)^*$, and the cross-spectrum of the reference signal, $X_{m\mu}(k) = X_m(k)X_\mu(k)^*$, in order to obtain the equivalent cross-transfer function

$$H_m(k) = \frac{X_{mm}(k)}{X_{m\mu}(k)}.\tag{13.23}$$

Thus when the measurement is contaminated by noise, the transfer function may be improved, since the noise is averaged out by the determination of the cross-function of the system.

The transfer-function measurement can also be made more resilient to noise by performing complex averaging. This is achieved by averaging its complex components frames, such that random noise being added to the complex vector is averaged out. The vector averaging is described by

$$Hv_m(k) = \frac{1}{S}\sum_{i=1}^{S}(H_{Rm}(k))_i + j\frac{1}{S}\sum_{i=1}^{S}(H_{Im}(k))_i,$$ (13.24)

where S is a constant representing a number of iterations over which the frequency vectors are to be averaged. The larger the value of S, the longer the system will take to compute.

We use a well-known method for estimating the difference between the arrival times of two signals with a common source [KC76], known as the *the phase transform*, (PHAT). It has been shown that the PHAT presents a prominent peak in correspondence with the actual time delay. Consider two digital signals $x_\mu(n)$ and $x_m(n)$ with a common source, its PHAT is defined by

$$\delta_{PHATm}(n) = \text{IFFT}[Hv_m(k) \cdot |Hv_m(k)|^{-1}].$$ (13.25)

Finally, we use adaptive averaging to obtain reliable and steady delay and polarity measures. When performing adaptive averaging, the number of accumulations needed in order to output a valid datum, adaptively increase or decrease in inverse proportion to the absolute magnitude of the impulse response. This method asumes that the higher the amplitude of the impulse response, the better its signal to noise ratio. This means that if the signal to noise ratio is small, more accumulations are needed before a valid time delay position is output,

$$\delta_m(n) = \frac{1}{B_m}\sum_{i=1}^{B_m}(\delta_{PHATm}(n))_i,$$ (13.26)

where B_m is the averaging value that adapts over time, to the absolute maxima of the impulse response

$$B_m = \text{int}\left(\frac{\alpha}{|\text{max}(\text{abs}(\delta_{PHATm}(n)))|}\right),$$ (13.27)

where α has been chosen to be 2 in order to duplicate the minimum number of operations to validate the calculated delay time. Once we have a stable valid impulse response we can determine its delay with respect to the reference signal by calculating the maximum argument of the impulse response function. This is given by

$$\tau_{\mu m}(n) = \arg\max_{n}(\text{abs}(\delta_m(n))).$$ (13.28)

By evaluating the impulse response by $\tau_{\mu m}(n)$ and extracting the sign we can derive the polarity of the measured signal with respect to the measurement signal,

$$p_{\mu m}(n) = \text{sgn}(\delta_m(\tau_{\mu m}(n))).$$ (13.29)

fv$_m$(n) is the output vector containing the delay and polarity information for every $x_m(n)$ with respect to the reference channel $x_\mu(n)$. The feature extraction method for finding the delay and polarity between the input signals $x_m(n)$ and the references signal, $x_\mu(n)$, is depicted in Figure 13.12.

In Figure 13.12 it can be seen that an extra delay block is applied to the reference signal. This delay allows the feature extraction to see negative delays. This is useful since the initial reference signal may be selected arbitrarily, and some of the measured signals may contain a negative delay. The applied delay is N/4 samples long, where the FFT resolution is equal to N.

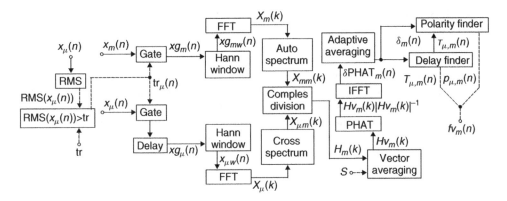

Figure 13.12 Block diagram of a feature extraction algorithm for determining delay between signals.

Cross-adaptive feature processing

If $\mathbf{fv}_{\tau\mu} \neq \max(\mathbf{fv}_{\tau(0...M-1)}(\mathbf{n}))$ we must start by reassigning $x_\mu(n)$ such that the delay added to all $x_m(n)$ is minimum. We then reset the feature extraction process and start a recalculation of the feature vector $\mathbf{fv_m}(\mathbf{n})$ given the new assignation of $x_\mu(n)$.

The components of $\mathbf{cv_m}(\mathbf{n})$ are given by

$$\mathbf{cv}_{\tau m}(\mathbf{n}) = \mathbf{fv}_\mu(\mathbf{n}) - \mathbf{fv_m}(\mathbf{n}), \tag{13.30}$$

and

$$\mathbf{cv_{pm}}(\mathbf{n}) = \begin{cases} 1 & \mathbf{fv}_{p\mu}(\mathbf{n}) = \mathbf{fv_{pm}}(\mathbf{n}) \\ -1 & \mathbf{fv}_{p\mu}(\mathbf{n}) \neq \mathbf{fv_{pm}}(\mathbf{n}) \end{cases}, \tag{13.31}$$

where $\mathbf{cv}_{\tau m}(n)$ corresponds to the delay control data value and $\mathbf{cv_{pm}}(\mathbf{n})$ corresponds to the polarity control data value per signal. Such cross-adaptive processing implementation has been depicted in Figure 13.13.

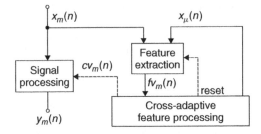

Figure 13.13 Block diagram of a cross-adaptive section of an offset polarity corrector.

The final mixture is then

$$mix(n) = \sum_{m=0}^{M-1} cv_{pm}(n) \cdot x_m(n - cv_{\tau m}(n)), \tag{13.32}$$

where $mix(n)$ is the mixture of all polarity and offset corrected input signals.

13.5   Conclusion

In this chapter we have introduced AM-DAFX; a class of digital audio effects which can do automatic mixing. As well as demonstrating a number of examples, a framework has been presented into which future AM-DAFX can be placed. The system architecture utilises cross-adaptive processing of features extracted from the input signals. Depending on the feature extraction mechanisms, the AM-DAFX have been classed as either dynamic or accumulative. Optimising the accuracy of the feature extraction mechanism can significantly improve the performance of the AM-DAFX.

The intention of AM-DAFX is to aid or replace certain tasks which are normally undertaken by the user. Only time will tell how autonomous a DAFX will become, and to what extent they will be accepted by the user. AM-DAFX is at present a growing field of research and several commercial devices based on such principles have emerged. The use of different configurations and topologies in the implementation remains to be explored. The AM-DAFX proposed here deal mainly with technical mixing constraints, and are meant to be used as a tool which allows the sound engineer to concentrate on more creative aspects of the mix. In the future, more extensive use of perceptual models may not only improve the performance of AM-DAFX, but may also allow more subjective mixing decisions to be explored. Research into these areas is, however, likely to remain controversial.

Video examples of the implementations mentioned in this chapter can be found at: http://www.elec.qmul.ac.uk/digitalmusic/automaticmixing/

References

[ABLAV03]   X. Amatriain, J. Bonada, À Loscos, J. L. Arcos and V. Verfaille Content-based transformations. *Journal of New Music Research*, 32(1): 95–114, 2003.

[BJ09]   J. Bitzer and J. LeBeuf. Automatic detection of salient frequencies. In *Proceedings of the 124th AES Convention*, Preprint 7704, Munich, Germany, May 2009.

[BLS08]   J. Bitzer, LeBoeuf J. and Simmer U. Evaluating perception of salient frequencies: Do mixing engineers hear the same thing? In *Proceedings of the 126th AES Convention*, Preprint 7462, Amsterdam, The Netherlands, May 2008.

[BR09]   D. Barchiesi and J. D. Reiss. Automatic target mixing using least-squares optimization of gains and equalization settings. In *Proceedings of the 12th International Conference on Digital Audio Effects (DAFx-09)*, Como, Italy, Sept 2009.

[Dug75]   D. W. Dugan. Automatic microphone mixing. In *Journal of the Audio Engineering Society*, 23(6): 442–449, 1975.

[Dug89]   D. W. Dugan. Application of automatic mixing techniques to audio consoles. In *Proceedings of the 87th AES Convention*, Preprint 2835, New York, USA, October 1989.

[JT84]   S. Julstrom and T. Tichy. Direction-sensitive gating: A new approach to automatic mixing. In *Journal of the Audio Engineering Society*, 32(7/8): 490–506, 1984.

[KC76]   C. Knapp and G. Carter. The generalized correlation method for estimation of time delay. In *IEEE Transactions on Acoustic, Speech and Signal Processing*, ASSP-24, pp. 320–327, 1976.

[Kol08]   A. B. Kolasinski. A framework for automatic mixing using timbral similarity measures and genetic optimization. In *Proceedings of the 124th AES Convention*, Preprint 7496, Amsterdam, The Netherlands, May 2008.

[Mey92]   J. Meyer. Precision transfer function measurements using program material as the excitation signal. In *Proceedings of the 11th International AES Conference: Test and Measurement*, Portland, Oregon, USA, May 1992.

[Pet78]   R. W. Peters. Priority mixer control. US Patent, 4,149,032, filed 4 May 1978 and issued 10 Apr 1979.

[PGR07]   E. Perez Gonzalez and J. Reiss. Automatic mixing: live downmixing stereo panner. In *Proceedings of the 7th International Conference on Digital Audio Effects (DAFx-07)*, Bordeaux, France, pp. 63–68, September 2007.

[PGR08a]   E. Perez Gonzalez and J. Reiss. An automatic maximum gain normalization technique with appli-
            cations to audio mixing. In *Proceedings of the 124th AES Convention*, Preprint 7830, Amsterdam,
            The Netherlands, May 2008.

[PGR08b]   E. Perez Gonzalez and J. Reiss. Anti-feedback device. UK patent GB0808646.4, filed 13 June 2008
            and published 19 November 2009.

[PGR08c]   E. Perez Gonzalez and J. Reiss. Improved control for selective minimization of masking using
            interchannel dependency effects. In *Proceedings of the 8th International Conference on Digital
            Audio Effects (DAFx-08)*, Espoo, Finland, pp. 75–81, September 2008.

[PGR08d]   E. Perez Gonzalez and J. Reiss. Determination and correction of individual channel time offsets for
            signals involved in an audio mixture. In *Proceedings of the 25th AES Convention*, Preprint 7631,
            San Francisco, USA, October 2008.

[PGR09a]   E. Perez Gonzalez and J. Reiss. Automatic gain and fader control for live mixing. In *Workshop on
            Applications of Signal Processing to Audio and Acoustics (WASPAA)*, New Paltz, New York, October
            2009.

[PGR09b]   E. Perez Gonzalez and J. Reiss. Automatic equalization of multi-channel audio using cross-adaptive
            methods. In *Proceedings of the 127th AES Convention*, Preprint 7830, New York, October 2009.

[PGR10]   E. Perez Gonzalez and J. Reiss. An autonomous audio panning system for live music. In *EURASIP
            Journal Advances in Signal Processing, Special Issue on Digital Audio Effects*, Manuscript submitted
            on Jan, 2010.

[Ree00]   D. Reed. A perceptual assistant to do sound equalization. In *Proceedings of the 5th International
            Conference on Intelligent User Interfaces*, New Orleans, Louisiana, United States, pp. 212–218,
            2000.

[SBI00]   Shure Brothers Inc. Chicago IL, Data sheet models FP410 portable automatic mixer. User Manual
            27B8392(TB), 2000.

[TR09a]   M. Terrell and J. Reiss. Automatic noise gate settings for multitrack drum recordings. In *Proceedings
            of the 12th International Conference on Digital Audio Effects (DAFx-09)*, Como, Italy, Sept 2009.

[TR09b]   M. Terrell and J. Reiss. Automatic monitor mixing for live musical performance. In *Journal of the
            Audio Engineering Society*, 57(11): 927–936, 2009.

[VZA06]   V. Verfaille, U. Zölzer and D. Arfib. Adaptive digital audio effects (a-dafx): A new class of
            sound transformations. In *IEEE Transactions On Audio, Speech, and Language Processing*, 14(5):
            1817–1831, 2006.

[Zöl05]   U. Zölzer. *Digital Audio Signal Processing*, 2nd edition. John Wiley & Sons, Ltd, 2005.

14

Sound source separation

G. Evangelista, S. Marchand, M. D. Plumbley and E. Vincent

14.1 Introduction

When processing a sound recording, sound engineers often face the need to apply specific digital audio effects to certain sounds only. For instance, the remastering of a music recording may require the correction of the tuning of a mistuned instrument or the relocation of that instrument in space without affecting the sound of other instruments. This operation is straightforward when these sounds are available as separate tracks, but becomes quite difficult otherwise. Indeed, the digital audio effects reviewed in this book all apply to the recording as a whole.

Source separation refers to the range of techniques aiming to extract the signals of individual sound *sources* from a given recording. The input recording is called a *mixture* signal. The estimated source signals can then be separately processed and added back together for remastering purposes. In this scenario, the number of mixture channels is typically equal to one or two, or more rarely up to five, while the number of sources ranges from two to ten or more. The need for source separation also arises in many other application scenarios, such as speech enhancement for hearing aids, high-quality upmixing of mono or stereo content to 3D sound formats, and automatic speech and speaker recognition in multi-talker environments.

Source separation is a recent field of research compared to the other audio effects reviewed in this book, so that most techniques are less mature and cannot address the above applications scenarios to date. Yet, some established techniques are gradually finding their way to the industry and will soon be part of professional or general consumer software. This chapter will provide an overview of these established techniques, as well as more recent ones.

DAFX: Digital Audio Effects, Second Edition. Edited by Udo Zölzer.
© 2011 John Wiley & Sons, Ltd. Published 2011 by John Wiley & Sons, Ltd.

14.1.1   General principles

Notion of source

The first step to address when considering source separation is to formalize the notions of source and mixture. The notion of source or track is often ambiguous in the absence of additional assumptions. For instance, a bass drum, a snare drum and a hi-hat may be considered as separate sources or as components of a single "drums" source depending on the targeted degree of separation. In the following, we make the former choice and assume that all sources are point sources emitting sound from a different point in space. We also set additional constraints on the sources in the case of a single-channel mixture.

Modeling of the mixing process

Independently of the application scenario, the notion of mixture can generally be formalized as the result of a multi-channel filtering process. Let I be the number of mixture channels and M the number of sources. The point source assumption implies that each source can be represented as a single-channel signal $s_m(n)$, $m \in \{1, \ldots, M\}$. When the sources are digitally mixed by amplitude panning (see Chapter 5), the ith mixture channel $x_i(n)$, $i \in \{1, \ldots, I\}$, is given by the *instantaneous* mixing model

$$x_i(n) = \sum_{m=1}^{M} a_{im} s_m(n), \tag{14.1}$$

where a_{im} is a scalar panning coefficient. When the mixture is obtained by simultaneous recording of the sources or when additional artificial reverberation is applied, the mixture channels can be expressed by the more general *convolutive* mixing model [SAM07],

$$x_i(n) = \sum_{m=1}^{M} \sum_{\tau} a_{im}(\tau) s_m(n - \tau), \tag{14.2}$$

where $a_{im}(\tau)$ is a finite impulse response (FIR) filter called a *mixing filter* modeling time-varying sound transformations between the mth source and its contribution to the ith channel.[1] In a conventional recording, the mixing filters are room impulse responses reflecting the spatial directivity of the sources and the microphones and acoustic propagation from the sources to the microphones, including sound reflections over the walls or other objects in the room. The length of the filters is then on the order of a few hundred milliseconds in a small room or one second in a concert room. Additional filtering due to the listener's head arises in binaural recordings, so that the mixing filters are equal to the sum of the head-related transfer functions (HRTFs) associated with the direct sound and with all reflections.

Time-frequency domain processing

Despite its accurate reproduction of the mixing process, the time domain signal representation (14.2) is generally considered as inconvenient for sound source separation, since all sources except silent ones contribute to each sample $x_i(n)$ of the mixture signal. Time-frequency representations are preferred, since they decrease the overlap between the sources and simplify the modeling of

---

[1] Models (14.1) and (14.2) both assume that the source positions and the digital audio effects applied upon them are fixed throughout the duration of the recording. Moving source scenarios have received less attention so far. However, such scenarios may be addressed to a certain extent by partitioning the recording into time intervals over which the mixing filters are reasonably time-invariant and applying the techniques reviewed in this chapter to each interval.

their characteristics. Indeed, all sources are typically characterized by distinct pitches or spectra in a given time frame and by distinct dynamics over time, so that one or two predominant sources typically contribute to each time-frequency bin. This property, known as *sparsity*, makes it easier to estimate their contributions and subsequently separate them. This phenomenon is illustrated in Figure 14.1, where the features of a violin source and a piano source are hardly visible in the mixture signal in the time domain, but are easily segregated in the time-frequency domain.

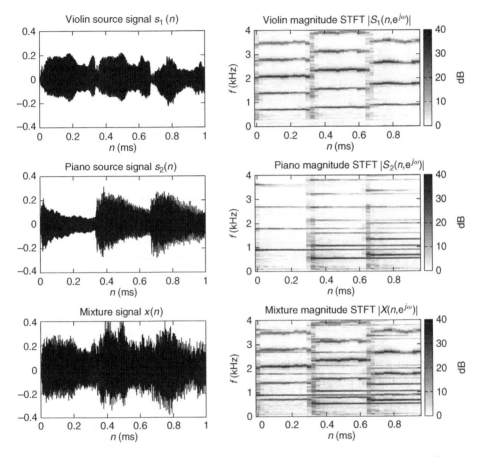

Figure 14.1   Time vs. time-frequency representation of a single-channel mixture of a violin source and a piano source.

Although perceptually motivated representations have been employed [WB06], the most popular time-frequency representation is the Short Time Fourier Transform (STFT), also known as the phase vocoder, which is the subject of Chapter 7. The mixing process can then be modeled directly over the STFT coefficients using the time-frequency filtering algorithm described in that chapter. However, this exact algorithm requires the window length N to be larger than twice the length of the mixing filters, that is typically on the order of several hundred milliseconds, while the optimal window length in terms of sparsity is on the order of 50 ms [YR04]. Also it introduces a dependency between the source STFT coefficients at different frequencies due to zero-padding, which makes them more complex to estimate. Approximate time-frequency filtering based on circular convolution is hence used instead. Denoting by $X_i(n, e^{j\omega})$ and $S_m(n, e^{j\omega})$ the complex-valued STFT coefficients of the ith mixture channel and the mth source in time frame n

and at normalized frequency ω and by $A_{im}(e^{j\omega})$ the frequency domain mixing coefficients corresponding to the mixing filter $a_{im}(\tau)$, the mixing process is approximately modeled as [SAM07]

$$X_i(n, e^{j\omega}) = \sum_{m=1}^{M} A_{im}(e^{j\omega}) S_m(n, e^{j\omega}). \tag{14.3}$$

Denoting by $\mathbf{X}(n, e^{j\omega})$ the $I \times 1$ vector of mixture STFT coefficients and by $\mathbf{S}(n, e^{j\omega})$ the $M \times 1$ vector of source STFT coefficients, the mixing process can be equivalently expressed as

$$\mathbf{X}(n, e^{j\omega}) = \mathbf{A}(e^{j\omega})\mathbf{S}(n, e^{j\omega}). \tag{14.4}$$

where $\mathbf{A}(e^{j\omega})$ is the $I \times J$ matrix of mixing coefficients called *mixing matrix*. Source separation amounts to estimating the STFT coefficients $S_m(n, e^{j\omega})$ of all sources and transforming them back to the time domain using overlap-add STFT resynthesis.

Quality assessment

Before presenting actual source separation techniques, let us briefly introduce the terms that will be used to describe the quality of the estimated sources in the remainder of this chapter. In practice, perfect separation is rarely achieved, e.g., because the assumptions behind source separation algorithms are not exactly met in real-world situations. The level of the target source is then typically increased within each estimated source signal, but distortions remain, compared to the ideal target source signals. One or more types of distortion can arise depending on the algorithm [VGF06]: linear or nonlinear distortion of the target source such as e.g., missing time-frequency regions, remaining sounds from the other sources and additional artifacts taking the form of time- and frequency-localized sound grains akin to those observed in denoising applications (see Chapter 7). These three kinds of distortion will be called *target distortion*, *interference* and *musical noise*, respectively. Minimizing interference alone often results in increasing musical noise, so that a suitable trade-off must be sought, depending on the application. For instance, musical noise is particularly annoying and must be avoided at all costs in hearing-aid applications.

14.1.2 Beamforming and frequency domain independent component analysis

Separation via unmixing filter estimation

One of the earliest paradigms for source separation is obtained by in estimating the sources by applying a set of appropriate multi-channel *unmixing filters* to the mixture. In the time-frequency domain, this amounts to computing the estimated STFT coefficients $\widehat{S}_m(n, e^{j\omega})$ of the sources as [BW01]

$$\widehat{S}_m(n, e^{j\omega}) = \sum_{i=1}^{I} W_{mi}(e^{j\omega}) X_i(n, e^{j\omega}), \tag{14.5}$$

where $W_{mi}(e^{j\omega})$ are complex-valued unmixing coefficients. With similar notations to above, this can be expressed in matrix form as

$$\widehat{\mathbf{S}}(n, e^{j\omega}) = \mathbf{W}(e^{j\omega})\mathbf{X}(n, e^{j\omega}) \tag{14.6}$$

where $\mathbf{W}(e^{j\omega})$ is the $J \times I$ *unmixing matrix*.

These filters act as spatial filters that selectively enhance or attenuate sounds depending on their spatial position. In order to understand how these filters can be designed to achieve source separation, let us consider first the simple case of a two-channel mixture of two sources recorded from omnidirectional microphones. The extension of this approach to more than two channels and two sources is discussed later, in Section 14.1.3. Since each interfering source generates a large number of echoes at distinct positions, sounds coming from all of these positions should be canceled. Under the assumption that these positions are far from the microphones relative to the wavelength, sound from a given position will arrive at the second microphone with little attenuation relative to the first microphone, but with a delay δ that is approximately equal to

$$\delta = \frac{d \, f_S}{c} \cos \theta \text{ samples,} \qquad (14.7)$$

where d is the microphone spacing in m, f_S the sampling frequency in Hz, c the speed of sound i.e., about 344 ms^{-1} and θ the sound *direction of arrival* (DOA) relative to the microphone axis oriented from the second to the first microphone. Since the frequency response associated with delay δ is equal to $e^{-j\omega\delta}$, the *directivity pattern* of the unmixing filters $W_{mi}(e^{j\omega})$ associated with source p, that is their magnitude response to a sound of normalized frequency ω with DOA θ, is given by [BW01]

$$G_m(\theta, \omega) = \left| W_{m1}(e^{j\omega}) + W_{m2}(e^{j\omega})e^{-j\omega\frac{d \, f_S}{c} \cos \theta} \right|. \qquad (14.8)$$

Note that distance or elevation do not enter into account, provided that the distance is large enough, so that all sounds located on the spatial cone corresponding to a given DOA are enhanced or attenuated to the same extent.

Beamforming

Expression (14.8) allows it to design the filters so as to achieve suitable directivity patterns. Let us assume for a moment that the DOAs θ_1 and θ_2 of both sources are known and that we aim to extract the first source. A first simple design is obtained by in setting

$$W_{11}(e^{j\omega}) = \frac{1}{2} \qquad (14.9)$$

$$W_{12}(e^{j\omega}) = \frac{1}{2}e^{j\omega\frac{d \, f_S}{c} \cos \theta_1}. \qquad (14.10)$$

This design, called the *delay-and-sum beamformer* [BW01], adjusts the delay between the two microphone signals before summing them so that they are perfectly in phase for sounds with DOA θ_1, but tend to be out of phase for sounds with other DOAs. The directivity pattern corresponding to this design is depicted in Figure 14.2. Sounds within a beam around the target DOA are enhanced. However, the width of this beam increases with decreasing frequency and it covers the whole space in the range below 400 Hz with the considered microphone spacing of $d = 30$ cm. Sidelobe beams also appear with a regular spacing at each frequency, so that the interfering source is cancelled at certain frequencies only. This results in an average enhancement of 3 dB.

A more efficient design, called the *null beamformer* [BW01], is obtained by in setting

$$W_{11}(e^{j\omega}) = \frac{1}{1 - e^{j\omega\frac{d \, f_S}{c}(\cos \theta_2 - \cos \theta_1)}} \qquad (14.11)$$

$$W_{12}(e^{j\omega}) = -\frac{e^{j\omega\frac{d \, f_S}{c} \cos \theta_2}}{1 - e^{j\omega\frac{d \, f_S}{c}(\cos \theta_2 - \cos \theta_1)}}. \qquad (14.12)$$

The numerator of this expression adjusts the delay between the two microphone signals so that sounds with DOA θ_2 are in antiphase, while the denominator adjusts the gain so as to achieve

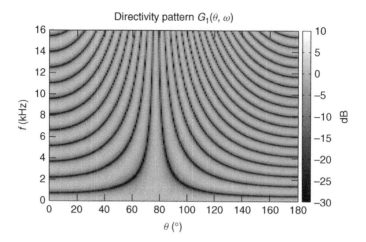

Figure 14.2 Directivity pattern of the two-channel delay-and-sum beamformer pointing to a target source at $\theta_1 = 77°$ with a microphone spacing of $d = 30$ cm.

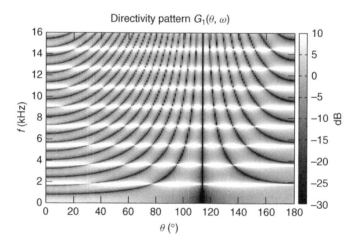

Figure 14.3 Directivity pattern of the two-channel null beamformer for a target source at $\theta_1 = 77°$ and an interfering source at $\theta_2 = 114°$ with a microphone spacing of $d = 30$ cm.

a flat response to sounds with DOA θ_1. The resulting directivity pattern shown in Figure 14.3 confirms that direct sound from the interfering source is now perfectly notched out, while direct sound from the target source is not affected. Note that the notch at θ_2 is extremely narrow so that precise knowledge of θ_2 is crucial. Also, sidelobes still appear so that echoes of the interfering source are not canceled. Worse, sounds from almost all DOAs are strongly enhanced at frequencies that are multiples of 1.8 kHz with the considered microphone spacing and source DOAs. Indeed, both source DOAs result in similar phase differences between microphones at these frequencies, i.e., $\omega d\, f_S/c \cos\theta_1 = \omega d\, f_S/c \cos\theta_2$ (mod 2π), so that the numerator tends to cancel the target source together with the interfering source and a strong gain must be applied via the denominator to compensate for this. Precise knowledge of θ_1 is therefore also crucial, otherwise the target source might become strongly enhanced or attenuated at nearby frequencies.

The delay-and-sum beamformer and the null beamformer are both fixed designs, which do not depend on the data at hand, except from the source DOAs. More robust adaptive designs have been proposed to attenuate echoes of the interfering source together with its direct sound. For example, the *linearly constrained minimum variance (LCMV) beamformer* [BW01] minimizes the power of the source signals estimated via (14.5), which is equal to the power of direct sound from the target plus that of echoes and interference, while guaranteeing a flat response over the target DOA. This beamformer can be interpreted in a statistical framework as achieving maximum likelihood (ML) estimation of the sources under the assumption that the sum of all interfering sounds has a stationary Gaussian distribution. Its implementation via the so-called generalized sidelobe canceller (GSC) [BW01] algorithm does not necessitate knowledge of the interfering source DOA anymore, but still requires precise knowledge of the target DOA. In realistic scenarios, this information is not available and must be estimated from the mixture signal at hand. State-of-the-art source localization algorithms e.g., [NSO09] are able to address this issue in anechoic environments, but their accuracy drops in moderately to highly reverberant environments, so that the separation performance achieved by beamforming drops as well.

Frequency domain independent component analysis

In order to understand how to circumvent this seemingly bottleneck issue, let us come back to the matrix expression of the mixing and unmixing processes in (14.4) and (14.6). By combining these two equations, we get $\widehat{\mathbf{S}}(n, e^{j\omega}) = \mathbf{W}(e^{j\omega})\mathbf{A}(e^{j\omega})\mathbf{S}(n, e^{j\omega})$. Therefore, if the mixing filters were known, choosing the unmixing coefficients as

$$\mathbf{W}(e^{j\omega}) = \mathbf{A}(e^{j\omega})^{-1} \qquad (14.13)$$

would result in perfect separation i.e., $\widehat{\mathbf{S}}(n, e^{j\omega}) = \mathbf{S}(n, e^{j\omega})$ in the limit where time-frequency domain approximation of the mixing process is valid and $\mathbf{A}(e^{j\omega})$ is invertible. In practice, $\mathbf{A}(e^{j\omega})$ can be singular or ill-conditioned at the frequencies for which the sources result in similar phase and intensity differences between microphones. The directivity pattern corresponding to these optimal unmixing coefficients is illustrated in Figure 14.4 in the case of a concert room recording.

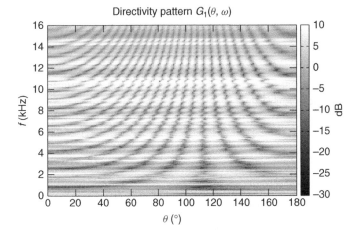

Figure 14.4 Directivity pattern of the optimal unmixing coefficients for a target source at $\theta_1 = 77°$ recorded in a concert room in the presence of an interfering source at $\theta_2 = 114°$ with a microphone spacing of $d = 30$ cm.

Deviations compared to Figure 14.3 are clearly visible and due to summation of direct sound and echoes at the microphones, resulting in apparent DOAs different from the true DOAs.

In practice, the mixing filters are unknown, thus the optimal unmixing coefficients must be adaptively estimated from the mixture signal. This can be achieved in a statistical framework by ML estimation of the unmixing coefficients under the assumption that the STFT coefficients of all sources are independent and follow a certain distribution. It can be shown that the ML objective is equivalent to maximizing the statistical independence of the STFT coefficients of the sources, hence this approach is known as *frequency domain independent component analysis (FDICA)*. A range of prior distributions have been proposed in the literature [SAM07, VJA+10], which typically reflect the aforementioned sparsity property of the sources, i.e., the fact that the source STFT coefficients are significant in a few time frames only, within each frequency bin. Note that this statistical framework is very different from that underlying LCMV beamforming, since the sources are now modeled as separate sparse variables instead of a joint Gaussian "noise."

A popular family of distributions is the *circular generalized Gaussian* family [GZ10]

$$P(|S_m(n, e^{j\omega})|) = \frac{p}{\beta \, \Gamma(1/p)} \exp\left(-\left|\frac{S_m(n, e^{j\omega})}{\beta}\right|^p\right) \tag{14.14}$$

where $\Gamma(.)$ denotes the function known in mathematics as the gamma function. The scale and shape parameters β and p govern, respectively, the average magnitude and the sparsity of the source STFT coefficients. The smaller p, the more coefficients concentrate around zero. Distributions with shape parameter $p < 2$ are generally considered as sparse and those with $p > 2$ as non-sparse with respect to the Gaussian distribution over the magnitude STFT coefficients associated with $p = 2$. In the absence of prior information about the spectral shape of the sources, the scale parameter β is typically fixed so that the coefficients have unit power. Figure 14.5 shows that this distribution with $p = 0.4$ provides a very good fit of the distribution of a speech source after power normalization

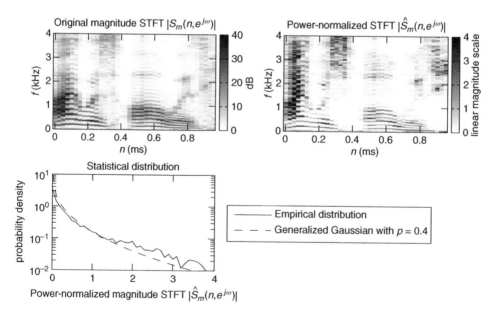

Figure 14.5 Distribution of the power-normalized magnitude STFT coefficients of a speech source compared to the generalized Gaussian distribution with shape parameter $p = 0.4$.

in each frequency bin. The shape parameter value $p = 1$, which results in the slightly less sparse *Laplacian distribution*, is nevertheless a popular choice [SAM07].

The likelihood of the observed mixture signal is obtained by multiplying the probability density (14.14) over all sources, all time frames and all frequency bins. ML estimation of the unmixing coefficients is then equivalent to solving the following optimization problem:

$$\min_{W_{mi}(e^{j\omega})} \sum_{m=1}^{M} \sum_{n,\omega} |\widehat{S}_m(n, e^{j\omega})|^p \tag{14.15}$$

where $\widehat{S}_m(n, e^{j\omega})$ implicitly depends on $W_{mi}(e^{j\omega})$ via (14.5). This problem may be addressed using a range of algorithms, that rely on principles of optimization theory beyond the scope of this chapter. Readers may refer to [SAM07] for details.

Two additional problems remain. Firstly, since the scale parameter β is constant over all frequency bins, the resulting sources have a flat average spectrum. This *scaling indeterminacy* of FDICA may be circumvented by exploiting more advanced models of the source spectra or by multiplying the estimated source STFT coefficients by the mixing coefficients derived from the unmixing coefficients via (14.13) so as to estimate the contribution of each source to one or more mixture channels instead of the original source. Secondly, since the model (14.14) is identical for all sources, the sources can be estimated at best up to a random order. This *permutation indeterminacy* of FDICA can be addressed to a certain extent by exploiting more advanced models of the source spectra or by estimating approximate source DOAs and permuting the unmixing coefficients so that the resulting directivity patterns match the null beamformer pattern in Figure 14.3 as closely as possible. Again, see [SAM07] for details.

14.1.3 Statistically motivated approaches for under-determined mixtures

We have seen that null beamforming or preferably FDICA can be employed to separate a two-channel mixture of two sources. At this stage, most readers will undoubtedly wonder how these methods generalize to more channels and more sources. As it turns out, these algorithms can be extended to any number of sources and channels. However, they are efficient only when the number of sources is equal to or smaller than the number of channels. Indeed, the number of independent spatial notches corresponding to any set of unmixing filters is at most equal to the number of channels. This can be seen in Figure 14.3 where the unmixing coefficients may be chosen so as to form one notch per frequency in the direction of the interfering source in a two-channel mixture, but other notches due to sidelobes cannot be independently adjusted. Mixtures satisfying this constraint are called *determined mixtures*.

In the remainder of this chapter, we shall focus on *under-determined mixtures*, which involve more sources than mixture channels and occur more often in practice. The separation of such mixtures requires a novel paradigm: instead of estimating unmixing filter coefficients, one now wants to estimate the mixing coefficients and the source STFT coefficients directly. Again, this can be addressed in a statistical framework by specifying suitable statistical models for the mixing coefficients and the source STFT coefficients. In practice, for historical reasons, most methods rely on a statistical model of the source STFT coefficients, but adopt a simpler deterministic model for the mixing coefficients based on e.g., perceptual considerations.

Two categories of models have been studied so far, depending on the number of channels. In a multi-channel mixture, spatial information still helps to separate the sources so that weak source models are sufficient. Sparse distributions of the source STFT coefficients have been used in context together with learned mapping functions between the source DOAs and the mixing coefficients. An example algorithm relying on such distributions will be presented in Section 14.2. In a single-channel mixture, spatial information is no more available so that more accurate models of the source STFT coefficients are needed. Example algorithms relying on such models will the described in Section 14.3.

14.1.4 Perceptually motivated approaches

The ability to locate and separate sound sources is well developed among humans and animals who use this feature to orient themselves in the dark or to detect potential sources of danger. The field of *computational auditory scene analysis (CASA)* studies artificial systems able to mimic this localization-separation process. These approaches clearly represent a shift in the paradigm where, rather than modeling the sound production process, focus is in modeling the spatial sound perception processes.

A simple task in source localization is to detect, to a good degree of approximation, the DOA of the source waves from the signals available at the two ears. To a certain extent, humans are able to perform this task even if one of the two ears is obstructed or not functioning, i.e., from monaural hearing. Several models have been conceived to explain binaural perception, which are rooted in the work by Jeffress [JSY98] on the analysis of *interaural time difference* (ITD) by means of a neuronal coincidence structure, where nerve impulses derived from each of the two ears, stimuli travel in opposite directions over delay lines. This model transforms time information into space information since a nerve cell is excited only at the position on the delay lines where the counter-traveling impulses meet.

Back at the beginning of last century, the ITD together with the *interaural level difference* (ILD) were considered as the principal spatial hearing cues by Lord Rayleigh, who developed the so-called *duplex theory of localization*. According to this theory, validated by more recent experimentation, ITDs are more reliable at lower frequencies (roughly below 800 Hz), while ILDs perform better at higher frequencies (roughly above 1.6 kHz). This is due to the fact that the wavelength associated with low audio frequencies is larger than the distance between the ears (typically 12–20 cm). In this case, the perturbation at the two ears is mainly characterized by phase differences with almost equal levels. On the other hand, at higher frequencies, the head is shadowing the perturbation reaching one of the ears, thus introducing relevant ILDs for sound sources that are not placed directly in the frontal direction of the listener. In real measurements, ITDs and ILDs are the result of multiple reflections, diffractions and resonances generated in the head, torso and external ears of the listener. Consequently, the interpretation and use of ITD and ILD as cues for DOA detection is less simple and error prone [Bla01, Gai93, Lin86, ST97].

In perceptually motivated source separation methods, the binaural signals are first input to a cochlear filter bank. The sources are separated by processing linearly or non-linearly the signal in perceptual frequency bands. Typical non-linear processing includes half-wave rectification or squaring followed by low-pass filtering [FM04]. ITD and ILD are also estimated within perceptual bands and used as cues for the separation.

While the accurate modeling of binaural hearing is essential to the understanding of auditory scene analysis as performed by humans or animals, several approaches to sound source localization and separation based on spatial cues were derived for the sole purpose of processing audio signals. In this case, the proposed algorithms are often only crudely inspired by human physiological and perceptual aspects. The ultimate goal is to optimize performance, without necessarily adhering to biological evidence. For example, the frequency resolution at which ITD and ILD cues can be estimated can go well beyond that of the critical frequency bands of the cochlear filter bank.

14.2 Binaural source separation

In binaural separation, the various sources are segregated according to spatial cues extracted from the signals available at both ears. This is the case for signals transduced by the microphones of a two-ear hearing-aid system or of the signals available at the microphones in the artificial ears of a dummy head. The type of apparatus is irrelevant, as long as human-like head shadowing is present in-between the microphones. A common strategy is to first detect and discern sources based on the DOA of waves, which is the object of Section 14.2.1, and then to build suitable time-frequency masks in a two-channel STFT representation of the binaural signal in order to demix them. Each mask, which can be binary or continuous valued with arbitrary values in [0, 1], coarsely represents the time-frequency profile of a given source. Due to energy leakage in finite sliding window time-frequency analysis, the masks are bound to cover broader bands than the ideal time-frequency tracks. The estimation of proper masks is the subject of Section 14.2.2. The masks are multiplicatively applied to both STFT channels and the transforms inverted. The ideal outcome is a set of binaural signals, each representing the sound of a single source spatially placed at the corresponding DOA.

14.2.1 Binaural localization

An important aspect of binaural localization is the estimation of the DOA in terms of azimuth and elevation. Together with the range information (distance from the source), it provides full knowledge of the coordinates of the source. However, we shall confine ourselves to estimates of the azimuth only. Estimates of the range are difficult in closed spaces and if the distance of the source to the listener is not large. Estimates of the elevation are affected by larger error, even in the human hearing system. The so-called cones of confusion [Bre90], show large uncertainty on the elevation of the source, while azimuth uncertainty as sharp as $\pm 5°$ is common in humans. It must be pointed out that the azimuth resolution depends on the angle, with lateral directions providing less sharp results.

In order to estimate the azimuth of the source one can explore spatial cues such as ILD and ITD. For any given source and at any given time, the ILD is the difference in level as received at the ears. Given the STFT of the left and right ear signals, $X_L\left(n, e^{j\omega}\right)$ and $X_R\left(n, e^{j\omega}\right)$, respectively, one can estimate the ILD at any angular frequency ω and time interval indexed by n, where the signal energy is above a certain threshold, as follows:

$$\Delta L_n(\omega) = 20 \log_{10} \left| \frac{X_R\left(n, e^{j\omega}\right)}{X_L\left(n, e^{j\omega}\right)} \right|. \tag{14.16}$$

Basically, the ILD estimate is the difference in dB of the amplitudes in the two channels as a function of frequency and averaged over the STFT analysis interval $[nN, ..., nN + M - 1]$, where the integers N and M respectively denote hop-size and window length of a discrete time STFT.

For any given source and at any given time, the ITD is defined as the time shift of the two signals received at the ears. This time shift could be measured, e.g., by finding a local maximum of the two signals, cross-correlation. However, in the time-frequency paradigm we adopted for the whole localization-separation process, for each angular frequency ω one can estimate the ITD from the STFT of the two ear signals, as follows:

$$\Delta T_{n,p}(\omega) = \frac{1}{\omega} \left(\angle \frac{X_R\left(n, e^{j\omega}\right)}{X_L\left(n, e^{j\omega}\right)} + 2\pi p \right). \tag{14.17}$$

The ITD is estimated from the phase difference of the two ear signals. In fact, through division by ω, it corresponds to a phase delay measurement. Since the phase is defined modulo 2π, there is an ambiguity in the estimate that is a multiple of this quantity, which justifies the term $2\pi p$ in (14.17), where p is any integer.

By the nature of the problem, ITD estimates are sharper at lower frequencies, where the effect of phase ambiguity is minimized, while ILD estimates are sharper at high frequencies, i.e., at wavelengths much shorter than the distance between the ears.

Localization using HRTF data or head models

Azimuth estimation from ITD and ILD can be performed by means of table lookup, using a set of measured HRTFs for a given individual. Given the measurements $HRTF_R^s(\theta, e^{j\omega})$ and $HRTF_L^s(\theta, e^{j\omega})$ of the subjective HRTF for the right and left ears as a function of the azimuth θ and angular frequency ω, one can form the following tables:

$$\Delta L_s(\theta, e^{j\omega}) = 20 \log_{10} \left| \frac{HRTF_R^s(\theta, e^{j\omega})}{HRTF_L^s(\theta, e^{j\omega})} \right| \tag{14.18}$$

and

$$\Delta T_{s,p}(\theta, e^{j\omega}) = \frac{1}{\omega} \left(\angle \frac{HRTF_R^s(\theta, e^{j\omega})}{HRTF_L^s(\theta, e^{j\omega})} + 2\pi p \right) \tag{14.19}$$

for the azimuth lookup, respectively, from ILD and ITD estimates. As shown in Figure 14.6 left column, the measured HRTF tables are quite noisy, depending on the details of multiple head – torso wave reflection. It is practice to smooth these tables along the azimuth axis, as shown in Figure 14.6 right column; we will continue to use the same symbols as in (14.18) and (14.19) to denote the smoothed tables.

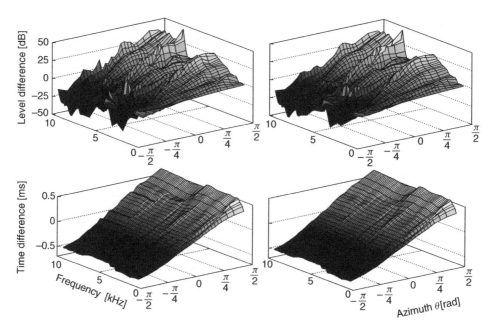

Figure 14.6 Spatial cues from HRTF measurements; Left: Unsmoothed estimates, Right: Estimates smoothed along azimuth axis; Top: Level differences; Bottom: Time differences. Figure reprinted with IEEE permission from [RVE10].

For any frequency, given an STFT-based estimate $\Delta L_n(\omega)$ for the level difference as in (14.16), the azimuth θ can be estimated by finding in (14.18) which value of θ provides the measured ILD. We denote this estimate by $\theta_{L,n}(\omega)$.

Similarly, given an STFT-based estimate $\Delta T_{n,p}(\omega)$ for the time difference as in (14.17), the azimuth can be estimated by finding in (14.19) which value of θ provides the measured ITD.

The time-difference estimate depends on an arbitrary integer multiple p of 2π. Therefore, for any fixed-frame index n and angular frequency ω, each ITD estimate is compatible with a countable infinity of azimuth estimates $\theta_{T,n,p}(\omega)$. However, assuming that the phase difference of the HRTFs does not show large discontinuities across azimuth and that the phase difference at zero azimuth is as small as possible, i.e., zero, it is possible to resolve the phase ambiguity by unwrapping the phase difference of the right and left HRTFs along the azimuth. Even when this ambiguity is resolved, there can still be several values of θ providing the same ILD or ITD values in the HRTF lookup. While smoothing tends to partially reduce ambiguity, majority rules or statistical averages over frequency or other assumptions can be used to increase the reliability of the azimuth estimate.

Usually, the duplex theory is applied here to choose among the estimates as a function of frequency. At low frequencies, the estimate $\Delta T_{s,0}(\theta, e^{j\omega})$ is selected for the azimuth lookup estimates from unwrapped phase difference, while at high frequencies $\Delta L_s(\theta, e^{j\omega})$ is selected. In Section 14.2.1 a procedure for azimuth estimate jointly employing ITD and ILD is described.

Given a head radius of r meters, the cut-off frequency f_c to switch from ITD- to ILD-based azimuth estimates can be estimated as the inverse of the time for the sound waves to travel from ear to ear along the head semicircle, i.e., $f_c = \frac{c}{\pi r}$, where $c \approx 344 \text{ ms}^{-1}$ is the speed of sound in air. Approximately a cut-off frequency of 1.6 kHz is selected to switch from ITD- to ILD-based estimates when the head radius is not known.

The discussed azimuth estimation lookup procedure requires knowledge of the individual HRTFs. When these are not known, it is possible to resort to a slightly less accurate estimation procedure which makes use of average ILD and ITD, respectively obtained from (14.18) and (14.19) by averaging over several individuals in a database of HRTFs. It can be shown [RVE10] that the performance of the averaged model is comparable with that of the method based on individual transfer functions.

At the cost of slightly reduced performance, it is possible to eliminate the need for HRTF-based lookup tables in azimuth estimates. In fact, from simple geometric considerations [WS54], as shown in Figure 14.7 for an idealized face represented by a circular section of radius r, the two ears, path-length difference for a wave reaching from DOA θ is not only due to an "in air" term $r \sin \theta$, but also to the arc length $r\theta$ of a curved path along the face, yielding

$$\Delta T(\theta) = r \frac{\sin \theta + \theta}{c}. \tag{14.20}$$

Due to the fact that the head is not perfectly spherical, the measured ITD is slightly larger than the values in (14.20), especially at low frequencies. A more accurate model, discussed in [RVE10],

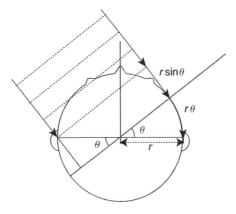

Figure 14.7 Path-length difference model for the ITD based on head geometry.

scales the ITD model (14.20) by a frequency and, possibly, subject-dependent scaling factor $\alpha_s(\omega)$, to obtain

$$\Delta T_s(\theta, \omega) = \alpha_s(\omega) r \frac{\sin\theta + \theta}{c}. \tag{14.21}$$

Given a measure of the ITD $\Delta T_s(\theta, \omega)$, in order to produce an estimate for the azimuth θ one needs to invert (14.21), which can be achieved by polynomial approximation [RVE10].

The ILD is a much more complex function of frequency. However, based on the observation of a large number of HRTFs, the following model [RVE10] can be shown to capture its main features when the sources are at large distances (over 1.5 m) from the listener;

$$\Delta L_s(\theta, \omega) = \beta_s(\omega) \sin\theta, \tag{14.22}$$

where $\beta_s(\omega)$ is again a frequency and, possibly, subject-dependent scaling factor. Inversion of (14.22) in order to produce an estimate for the azimuth does not present any problems.

Localization using ITD, ILD and IC

Since both the ILD and the ITD are related to the azimuth, they can be jointly employed in order to improve the azimuth estimates. The noisy $\Delta L_n(\omega)$ provides a rough estimate of the azimuth for each left/right spectral-coefficient pair. This ILD estimate can be used in order to select the most reasonable value for the parameter p in the ITD estimate, which is the one for which the ILD- and ITD-based estimates provide the closest value for the azimuth. Formally, this is given by

$$\theta_{J,n} = \theta_{T,n,p|p=\mathrm{argmin}_p|\theta_{T,n,p}-\theta_{L,n}|}. \tag{14.23}$$

Comparative experimental results obtained by ILD only, ITD only and the joint method are shown in Figure 14.8 for a single white-noise source located at angles $0°$, $15°$, $30°$, $45°$ and $65°$. Extensive performance evaluation of the joint ILD-ITD azimuth estimates can be found in [RVE10].

In the presence of one source only, the two ear signals x_L and x_R approximately are two delayed and amplitude-scaled versions of the same signal. In that case, the *interaural cross correlation (ICC)*, defined as the normalized cross-correlation

$$\rho_{L,R}(n) = \frac{\displaystyle\sum_m x_L(m)x_R(n+m)}{\sqrt{\displaystyle\sum_p x_L^2(p)\sum_q x_R^2(q)}} \tag{14.24}$$

peaks at a time lag corresponding to the relative delay or global ITD of the two signals. The amplitude of the peak provides a measure of similarity. In the presence of two or more sources with different DOA, the cross-correlation peaks are less distinguishable: since there is more than one characteristic delay, the two ear signals are less similar. The *interaural coherence (IC)* is defined as the maximum of the normalized cross-correlation of the two ears signals, which is a number between 0 and 1. It is useful to evaluate the ICC in time-frequency, i.e., with $x_L(n)$ and $x_R(n)$ in (14.24) replaced by the STFTs $X_L(n, e^{j\omega})$ and $X_R(n, e^{j\omega})$, respectively:

$$\rho_{L,R}(n, e^{j\omega}) = \frac{\left|\displaystyle\sum_m X_L(m, e^{j\omega})X_R^*(n+m, e^{j\omega})\right|}{\sqrt{\displaystyle\sum_p |X_L(p, e^{j\omega})|^2 \sum_q |X_R(q, e^{j\omega})|^2}}, \tag{14.25}$$

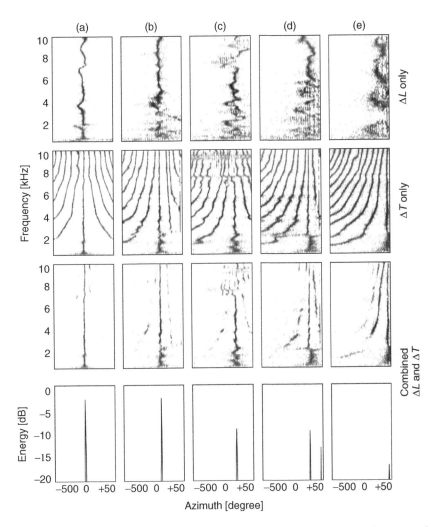

Figure 14.8   2D time histograms of azimuth estimates, in terms of azimuth and frequency, for five different heads and azimuth angles an 0°, 15°, 30°, 45° and 65°, (a)–(e), respectively. First row: based on ILD only. Second row: based on ITD only. Third row: based on combined evaluation of ILD and ITD. Bottom row: marginal histograms obtained by summing the combined ITD-ILD evaluation over all frequencies. Figure reprinted with IEEE permission from [RVE10].

where * denotes complex conjugation. In practice, the ICC is smoothed in time [Men10] in order to mitigate the oscillatory behavior due to the STFT finite window length. The corresponding time-frequency IC cue, defined as the amplitude of the maximum of the time-frequency ICC for any fixed frequency, provides a measure of reliability of the ITD and ILD for each frequency channel [FM04], IC being larger if only one source contributes to a given frequency bin. Furthermore, the time-frequency IC can be effectively employed as a cue to improve separation in the presence of time-frequency overlapping sources, where non-binary demixing masks are optimized by maximizing the IC of the separated sources.

14.2.2 Binaural separation

In Section 14.2.1, methods for the localization of sources in binaural signals are discussed, which are based on DOA discrimination from the STFT of the signals observed at the two ears. The azimuth $\theta(n, \omega)$ estimated for each left/right pair of spectral coefficients pertains to a narrow-band signal component in a short time interval. The ensemble of azimuth estimates can be employed to obtain separate binaural signals where the spatial information is preserved, but where only one source is present in each, which is the object of this section. Starting from the simple method based on binary masks we then explore the construction of continuous-valued masks based on Gaussian mixtures models of the multi-modal distribution of azimuth estimates. We then illustrate the use of structural assumption in the multi-channel separation of overlapping harmonics.

Binary masks

At any given time, each prominent peak of the histogram $h(\theta)$ obtained by cumulating the azimuth estimates $\theta(n, \omega)$ over frequency pertains to a different observed DOA. On the assumption that the sound sources are spatially distributed, so that each has a sufficiently distinct DOA as observed by the listener, the number of peaks equals the number of sources. The position of the peak estimates the DOA $\theta_k(n)$ of the corresponding source, where k represents the source index, which can be tracked over time.

Given the azimuth estimates $\theta(n, \omega)$ and the source azimuths $\theta_k(n)$, a weighting factor $M_k(n, \omega)$ can be given for each spectral coefficient. For each source, the separated binaural signal is obtained by multiplying this weighting factor by the STFT of the left and right ear signals followed by STFT inversion. Respectively, the left and right channel STFTs of the kth reconstructed source signal are given by

$$
\begin{aligned}
Y_{k,L}(n, e^{j\omega}) &= M_k(n, \omega)X_L(n, e^{j\omega}) \\
Y_{k,R}(n, e^{j\omega}) &= M_k(n, \omega)X_R(n, e^{j\omega}).
\end{aligned}
\tag{14.26}
$$

Different approaches can be considered for the definition of the weights. On the assumption that the STFT spectra of the different sources do not overlap significantly, i.e., on the window-disjoint orthogonal (WDO) assumption [YR04]. In this case, only one source contributes significant energy to a given spectral coefficient so that each spectral coefficient can be exclusively assigned to that source. Binary weights can be efficiently employed in this case. A possible strategy is to assign each spectral coefficient to the source whose azimuth estimate is closest. This is formalized by the following choice of weights

$$
M_k(n, \omega) = \begin{cases} 1 & \arg\min_m |\theta(n, \omega) - \theta_m(n)| = k \\ 0 & \text{otherwise.} \end{cases}
\tag{14.27}
$$

This weight system can be considered as a spatial window in which the coefficients are assigned to a given source according to the closeness of direction. However, this choice of weights can lead to artifacts due to the fact that azimuth estimates that are very far from the estimated azimuth of any source are unreliable. Therefore, the corresponding STFT coefficients should not be arbitrarily assigned to a source in this case. It may be better to consider these estimates as outliers and assign to a given source only those STFT coefficients for which the corresponding azimuth estimates lie in a window of width W from the estimated source azimuth. This is formalized by the following choice of weights:

$$
M_k(n, \omega) = \begin{cases} 1 & |\theta(n, \omega) - \theta_k(n)| < \frac{W}{2} \\ 0 & \text{otherwise.} \end{cases}
\tag{14.28}
$$

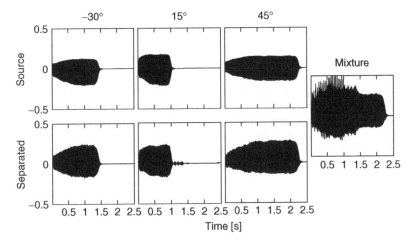

Figure 14.9 Binary mask separation of three trombone sources located at $-30°$, $15°$ and $45°$: time domain.

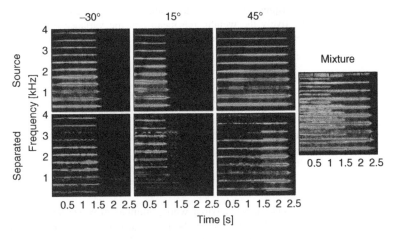

Figure 14.10 Binary mask separation of three trombone sources located at $-30°$, $15°$ and $45°$: spectrograms (gray-scale magnitude).

The result of the separation of three trombone sources, each playing a different note, located at $-30°$, $15°$ and $45°$ are shown in Figure 14.9, together with the spectrogram displayed in Figure 14.10. Artifacts are visible and audible especially in the attack area and during silence. Smoothing in the time direction can effectively reduce artifacts due to mask switching. However, in performed music, more severely than in speech, the overlap of the sources in time-frequency is not a rare event. In fact, musicians are supposed to play with the same tempo notes that are harmonically related, which means that several partials of the various instruments are shared within the same time interval. This results in artifacts of the separation when binary weighting of either of the forms (14.27) and (14.28) is enforced. One way to reduce these artifacts is to enforce non-binary weighting in which the energy of time-frequency bins is distributed among two or more overlapping sources, with different weights. Even in the ideal case where one can guess the exact weights, the separation continues to be affected by error in view of the fact that the phase of the signal components is also important, but not taken into consideration. The relative phase of the source components overlapping in the same bin also affects the total energy by interference.

Gaussian mixture model

In theory, in the case of a single source all frequencies should give the same azimuth, exactly corresponding to the source position θ. However, in practice, the violation of the WDO assumption, the presence of noise and estimation errors make things a little more complicated. As a first approximation, we consider that the energy of the source is spread in the power histogram following a Gaussian distribution centered at the theoretical value θ. The Gaussian nature of the distribution is confirmed by the well-known central limit theorem as well as practical experiments. In this context, the ideal case is a Gaussian of mean θ and variance 0.

In the case of K sources, we then introduce a model of K Gaussians (K-GMM, order-K Gaussian mixture model)

$$P_K(\theta|\Gamma) = \sum_{k=1}^{K} \pi_k \phi_k(\theta|\mu_k, \sigma_k) \quad \text{with} \quad \pi_k \geq 0 \quad \text{and} \quad \sum_{k=1}^{K} \pi_k = 1, \tag{14.29}$$

where Γ is a multi-set of K triples $(\pi_k, \mu_k, \sigma_k^2)$ that denotes all the parameters of the model; π_k, μ_k and σ_k^2 indicate respectively the weight, the mean and the variance of the kth Gaussian component described mathematically by

$$\phi_k(\theta|\mu_k, \sigma_k) = \frac{1}{\sqrt{2\pi\sigma_k^2}} \exp\left(-\frac{(\theta - \mu_k)^2}{2\sigma_k^2}\right). \tag{14.30}$$

We are interested in estimating the architecture of the K-GMM, that is the number of sources K and the set of parameters Γ, to be able to setup the separation filtering.

Unmixing algorithm

In the histogram $h(\theta)$, we observe local maxima whose number provides an estimation of the number of sources in the mixture. The abscissa of the kth local maximum reveals the location θ_k of the kth source. However, in practice, to avoid spurious peaks, we must deal with a smoothed version of the histogram and consider only significant local maxima–above the noise level. Informal experiments show that the estimated source number and location are rather good. This gives the model order K and a first estimation of the means of the Gaussians (μ_k in Γ). This estimation can be refined and completed–with the variances σ_k^2 and the weights π_k–for example by the EM algorithm.

Expectation maximization (EM) is a popular approach to estimate parameters in mixture densities, given a data set x. The idea is to complete the observed data x with an unobserved variable y to form the complete data (x, y), where y indicates the index of the Gaussian component from which x has been drawn. Here, the role of x is played by the azimuth θ, taking values in the set of all discrete azimuths covered by the histogram. We associate θ with its intensity function $h(\theta)$ (the histogram). The role of y is played by $k \in \{1, \cdots, K\}$, the index of the Gaussian component θ should belong to.

The EM algorithm proceeds iteratively, at each iteration the optimal parameters that increase locally the log-likelihood of the mixture are computed. In other words, we increase the difference in log-likelihood between the current with parameters Γ and the next with parameters Γ'. This log-form difference, noted $Q(\Gamma', \Gamma)$, can be expressed as

$$Q(\Gamma', \Gamma) = \sum_\theta h(\theta) \left(\mathcal{L}(\theta|\Gamma') - \mathcal{L}(\theta|\Gamma) \right) \quad \text{with}$$

$$\mathcal{L}(\theta|\Gamma) = \log\left(P_K(\theta|\Gamma) \right). \tag{14.31}$$

We can then reformulate $\mathcal{L}(\theta|\Gamma)$ like this:

$$\mathcal{L}(\theta|\Gamma) = \log\left(\sum_k P_K(\theta, k|\Gamma) \right) \quad \text{with}$$

$$P_K(\theta, k|\Gamma) = \pi_k \phi_k(\theta|\mu_k, \sigma_k). \tag{14.32}$$

The concavity of the log function allows us to lower bound the $Q(\Gamma', \Gamma)$ function using the Jensen's inequality. We can then write

$$Q(\Gamma', \Gamma) \geq \sum_\theta \sum_k h(\theta) P_K(k|\theta, \Gamma) \log\left(\frac{P_K(\theta, k|\Gamma')}{P_K(\theta, k|\Gamma)} \right), \tag{14.33}$$

where $P_K(k|\theta, \Gamma)$ is the posterior probability, the degree to which we trust that the data was generated by the Gaussian component k, given the data; it is estimable with the Bayes rule

$$P_K(k|\theta, \Gamma) = \frac{P_K(\theta, k|\Gamma)}{P_K(\theta|\Gamma)}. \tag{14.34}$$

The new parameters are then estimated by maximizing the lower bound with respect to Γ;

$$\Gamma' = \arg\max_\gamma \sum_\theta \sum_k h(\theta) P_K(k|\theta, \Gamma) \log\left(P_K(\theta, k|\gamma) \right). \tag{14.35}$$

Increasing this lower bound results automatically in an increase of the log-likelihood, and is mathematically easier. Finally, the maximization of Equation (14.35) provides the following update relations (to be applied in sequence, because they modify–update–the current value with side-effects, thus the updated value must be considered in the subsequent relations):

$$\pi_k \leftarrow \frac{\sum_\theta h(\theta) P_K(k|\theta, \Gamma)}{\sum_\theta h(\theta)}, \tag{14.36}$$

$$\mu_k \leftarrow \frac{\sum_\theta h(\theta) \theta P_K(k|\theta, \Gamma)}{\sum_\theta h(\theta) \, P_K(k|\theta, \Gamma)}, \tag{14.37}$$

$$\sigma_k^2 \leftarrow \frac{\sum_\theta h(\theta) \, (\theta - \mu_k)^2 \, P_K(k|\theta, \Gamma)}{\sum_\theta h(\theta) \, P_K(k|\theta, \Gamma)}. \tag{14.38}$$

The performance of the EM depends on the initial parameters. The first estimation parameter should help to get the around the likelihood local maxima trap. Our EM procedure operates as follows:

(1) Initialization step

   ■ initialize K with the order of the first estimation

   ■ initialize the weights equally, the means according to the first estimation, and the variances with the data variance (for the initial Gaussians to cover the whole set of data):

$$\pi_k = 1/K, \qquad \mu_k = \theta_k, \quad \text{and} \quad \sigma_k^2 = \text{var}(\theta)$$

   ■ set a convergence threshold ϵ

(2) Expectation step

  ▪ compute $P_K(k|\theta, \Gamma)$ with Equation (14.34)

(3) Maximization step

  ▪ compute Γ' from Γ with Equations (14.36), (14.37) and (14.38)

  ▪ if $P_K(\theta|\Gamma') - P_K(\theta|\Gamma) > \epsilon$ then $\Gamma \leftarrow \Gamma'$ and go back to the Expectation step else stop (the EM algorithm has converged).

Finally, to separate the sources, a spatial filtering identifies and clusters bins attached to the same source. Many methods, like DUET, separate the signals by assigning each of the time-frequency bins to one of the sources exclusively. We assume that several sources can share the power of a bin, and we attribute the energy according to a membership ratio–a posterior probability. The histogram learning with EM provides a set of parameters for the Gaussian distribution that characterizes each source. These parameters are then used to parameterize automatically a set of spatial Gaussian filters. In order to recover each source k, we select and regroup the time-frequency bins belonging to the same azimuth θ. We use the parameters issued from the EM-component number k, and the energy of the mixture channels is allocated to the (left and right) source channels according to the posterior probability. More precisely, we define the following mask for each source:

$$M_k(t, \omega) = P_K(k|\theta(t, \omega), \Gamma), \qquad (14.39)$$

if $10 \log_{10} |\phi_k(\theta(t, \omega)|\mu_k, \sigma_k)| > L_{dB}$, and 0 otherwise. This mask limits the fact that the tail of a Gaussian distribution stretches out to infinity. Below the threshold L_{dB} (expressed in dB, and set to -20 in our experiments), we assume that a source of interest does not contribute anymore. For each source k, the pair of short-term spectra can be reconstructed according to

$$S_L(t, e^{j\omega}) = M_k(t, \omega) \cdot X_L(t, e^{j\omega}), \qquad (14.40)$$

$$S_R(t, e^{j\omega}) = M_k(t, \omega) \cdot X_R(t, e^{j\omega}). \qquad (14.41)$$

Experimental results

First, we synthesized binaural signals by mixing monophonic source signals filtered through the HRTFs of a given individual corresponding to various azimuths using the HRTF-based technique, then we applied the EM-based unmixing algorithm described in the previous section.

A result of demixing is depicted in Figure 14.11 for a two-instrument mixture: xylophone at $-55°$ and horn at $-20°$; their original spectrograms are shown in Figure 14.12. In the time domain, the xylophone rhythm is respected, its signal looks amplified and its shape is preserved. Perceptively, the demixed xylophone is very similar to the original one. Also, for the horn, we must tolerate some interference effects, and the spectrograms are partly damaged. A portion of energy was absorbed by an unwanted source generated from interferences. We also conducted tests on speech samples. The reconstruction quality was good, much better than for long-distance telephone lines. Figure 14.13 shows the power histogram for the localization of four instruments in a binaural mixture. This histogram, here of size 65, was built using FFTs of $N = 2048$ samples with an overlap of 50%. Figure 14.14 shows the (normalized) Gaussian mixture model associated to this histogram. Of course, the EM algorithm can also be applied on the raw azimuth estimates $\hat{\theta}(t, \omega)$ instead of the data stored in the histogram.

Multi-channel separation of overlapping harmonics

The separation of time-frequency overlapping source components is a very challenging problem. However, in a multi-channel context one can use the sensor signals, together with structural

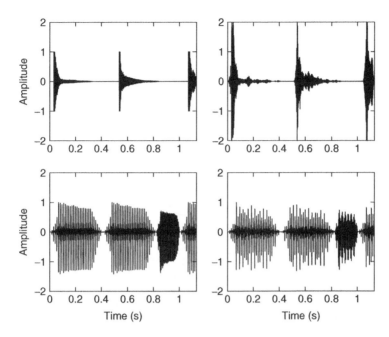

Figure 14.11   Waveforms of the demixtures (on the right, originals being on the left): xylophone (−55°) (top) and horn (30°) (bottom).

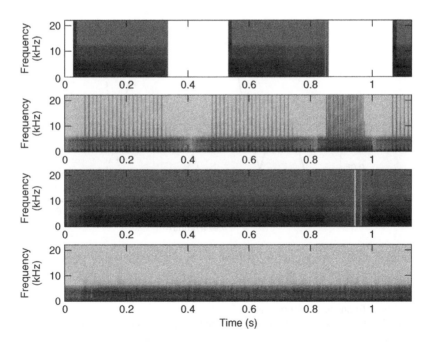

Figure 14.12   Spectrograms of the four sources, from top to bottom: xylophone, horn, kazoo and electric guitar.

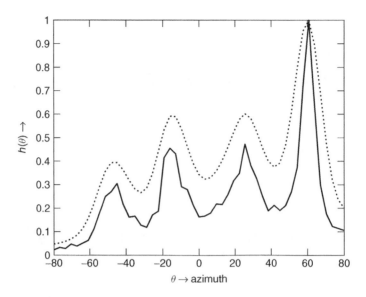

Figure 14.13 Histogram (solid line) and smoother version (dashed line) of the four-source mix: xylophone at $-55°$, horn at $-20°$, kazoo at $30°$ and electric guitar at $65°$.

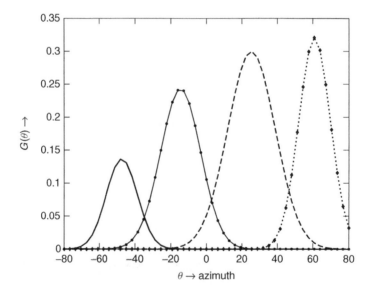

Figure 14.14   GMM (normalized) for the histogram of the four-source mix.

cues, e.g., harmonicity, in order to successfully separate the contributions of the various sources to the shared time-frequency components.

For each bin of the discrete time-frequency spectrum, let us now consider the observed magnitude in this frequency bin as time goes by. If a single stationary sinusoid has amplitude a and frequency exactly equal to the frequency of one of the analysis bin, the observed magnitude STFT at that bin is proportional to the amplitude of the sinusoid.

When two sinusoids are present at the same frequency, then the resulting signal is also a sinusoid of the same frequency (straightforward when considering the spectral domain). More precisely, the complex instantaneous amplitudes of the sinusoids add together as follows:

$$A = a_1 e^{j\phi_1} + a_2 e^{j\phi_2} \tag{14.42}$$

where a_p and ϕ_p are the amplitude and phase of the p-th sinusoid ($p \in \{1, 2\}$). Thus, via the Cartesian representation of complex numbers, the corresponding magnitude is

$$a = |A| = \sqrt{(a_1 \cos(\phi_1) + a_2 \cos(\phi_2))^2 + (a_1 \sin(\phi_1) + a_2 \sin(\phi_2))^2}. \tag{14.43}$$

Physically, the addition of two sinusoidal signals, even of the same amplitude a_0 ($a_1 = a_2 = a_0$), is ruled by a nonlinear addition law which gives a maximum of $2a_0$ (thus ≈ 6 dB above the volume of a_0) when the sinusoids are in phase ($\phi_1 = \phi_2$) and a minimum of 0 when they are opposite phase ($\phi_1 = \phi_2 + \pi$). One might intuitively think that all the cases in the $[0, 2a_0]$ interval are equiprobable. Not at all! For example, in the case where the initial phases of the sinusoids are independent uniformly distributed random variables over $[-\pi, +\pi)$ we have that $a \approx a_1 + a_2$ is the most probable value for the magnitude, as shown in Figure 14.15. The interference of several sinusoids at the same frequency results in one sinusoid. In this situation, it is quite impossible to separate the two sinusoids without additional knowledge. A possible strategy would be to simply ignore time-frequency regions where this interference phenomenon is likely to occur. However, in the case of musical signals, musicians playing in tempo and in harmony often generate frequency overlap at least for some of the partials. Thus, the separated signals would present large time intervals in which all or some of the partials are muted. When properly exploited, structural cues can help disambiguate overlapping partials and provide heuristics for their separation. In fact, under the assumption of quasi-periodicity of the sources, all the signals are nearly harmonic. Although this may seem a particular case of a general inharmonic structure, one can push the methods a little further with simple techniques and minimal side information. In fact, given that at least one of the partials for each source is not completely overlapping in time-frequency with those of the others, one can assume a harmonic structure based on the isolated partials, without additional knowledge of the sources. The overlap of the partials is resolved by assuming that the time envelopes of each partial are similar, with neighboring partials bearing the highest similarity.

A similarity measure was proposed in [HG06], which involved the normalized scalar product of the envelopes;

$$\beta_{p,q} = \frac{\sum_n E_p(n) E_q(n)}{\sqrt{\sum_n |E_p(n)|^2} \sqrt{\sum_n |E_q(n)|^2}}, \tag{14.44}$$

where $E_p(n)$ and $E_q(n)$ are the time envelopes of two components detected in time-frequency, each obtained by detecting and tracking in time contiguous zones of nonzero energy in adjacent frequency bins. When the envelopes are quite similar, like the ones of adjacent harmonics of a single source, the similarity measure $\beta_{p,q}$ is close to one. However, when interference among the sources is present, the similarity measure is much lower than 1.

All the sensor signals can be used in the case of multi-channel signals. The problem of separating the overlapping partials can be stated as that of estimating a mixing matrix from a known number of N sources contributing to M distinct measurements of each partial. For the problem to have a reliable solution there must be at least as many sensors as there are overlapping partials in that region. In view of the narrow-band characteristics of the partials, one can model this mixing process in time-frequency by means of constant complex matrices for each partial [HG06] in

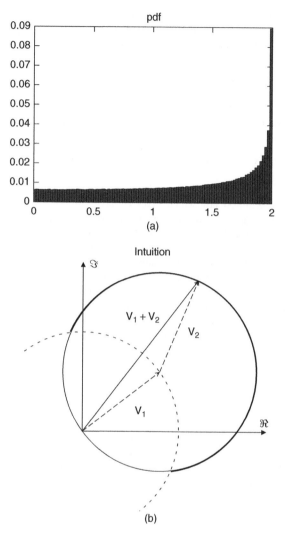

Figure 14.15 Interference of two sinusoids of the same frequency and amplitude 1. The signal resulting from the addition of the these two sinusoids is also a sinusoid with the same frequency, but its amplitude depends on the phases of the initial sinusoids. (a) shows histogram illustrating the probability density function of this amplitude (for uniform distributions of the phases). The sum of the amplitudes (2) is the most probable value. (b) gives an intuitive justification. It shows that, considering the sum of the two vectors corresponding to the complex amplitudes of the sinusoids in the complex plane (see Equation (14.15)), its norm is more likely to be greater than 1 (bold line).

each frequency bin. For a two-sensor two-sources case of overlapping partials at frequency bin ω we have

$$
\begin{bmatrix} P_L(n, e^{j\omega}) \\ P_R(n, e^{j\omega}) \end{bmatrix} = \begin{bmatrix} H_{L,1}(e^{j\omega}) & H_{L,2}(e^{j\omega}) \\ H_{R,1}(e^{j\omega}) & H_{R,2}(e^{j\omega}) \end{bmatrix} \begin{bmatrix} S_1(n, e^{j\omega}) \\ S_2(n, e^{j\omega}) \end{bmatrix}, \tag{14.45}
$$

where $S_i(n, e^{j\omega})$, $i = 1, 2$ represent the STFTs of the original source signals, $H_{L/R,i}(e^{j\omega})$ the frequency responses from source i to left/right sensor channel and $P_{L/R}(n, e^{j\omega})$ the STFTs of mixed overlapping partials at left and right sensors. The matrix composed by the frequency responses $H_{L/R,i}(e^{j\omega})$ is the mixing matrix at frequency bin ω.

In order to proceed with separation, first the envelopes of the other nonoverlapping partials are computed, which are called the model envelopes. Then, for each candidate mixing matrix, its pseudo-inverse is applied to the sensor-mixed partials and the envelopes of the resulting partials are computed. The matrix that gives separated partials with envelopes whose shapes most closely resemble those of the model envelopes is chosen as the estimate of the mixing matrix for that corresponding partial. Thus, the estimate of the mixing matrix is obtained by means of optimization as the one that gives the best match between the separated partials and the model partials according to the criterion (14.44).

Good experimental results are obtained by using the L_1 norm to combine the similarity measures deriving by each partial [Vis04]. An example of separation of overlapping partials from two sources, a violin tone with vibrato and a trombone tone without vibrato, is shown in Figure 14.16, where one can appreciate how closely the envelopes are recovered, together with the fine AM-FM fine structure due to vibrato in the violin tone.

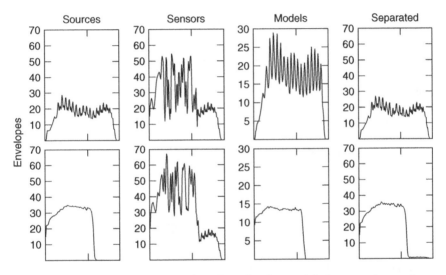

Figure 14.16 Simple example of separation of overlapping partials from two harmonic sources, violin (top row) and trombone (bottom row). Columns from left to right: source envelopes, mixed source envelopes at left and right sensors, model envelopes extracted from nonoverlapping partials at sensor signals, envelopes of separated partials maximizing envelope similarity.

14.3   Source separation from single-channel signals

Separation of sources from single-channel (monophonic) mixtures is particularly challenging. If we have two or more microphones, we have seen earlier in this chapter that we can use information on relative amplitudes or relative time delays to identify the sources and to help us perform the separation. But with only one microphone, this information is not available. Instead, we must use information about the structure of the source signals to identify and separate the different components.

For example, one popular approach to the single-channel source separation problem is to use non-negative matrix factorization (NMF) of the Short Time Fourier Transform (STFT) power spectrogram of the audio signal. This method attempts to identify consistent spectral patterns in the different source signals, allowing these patterns to be associated with the different sources, then allowing separation of the audio signals. As well as NMF, we shall see that methods based on sinusoidal modeling and probabilistic modeling have also been proposed to tackle this difficult problem.

14.3.1   Source separation using non-negative matrix factorization

Suppose that our mixture signal is composed of a weighted mixture of simple source objects, each with a fixed power spectrum a_p, and where the relative energy of the pth object in the nth frame is given by $s_{pn} \geq 0$. Then the activity of each object has a spectrum of $x_{pn} = a_p s_{pn}$ at frame n. If we then assume that the source signal objects have random phase, so that the spectral energy due to each source object approximately adds in each time-frequency spectral bin, then the spectrum of the mixture will be approximately given by

$$x_n \approx \sum_p a_p s_{pn} \tag{14.46}$$

or in matrix notation

$$X \approx AS, \tag{14.47}$$

where X is the mixture spectrogram, $A = [a_p]$ is the matrix of spectra for each source, and $S = [s_{pn}]$ is the matrix of relative source energies in each frame. Since each of the matrices X, A and S represent amounts of energy, they are all non-negative.

In single-channel source separation, we only observe the mixture signal with its corresponding non-negative spectrogram X. But, since A and S are also non-negative, we can use non-negative matrix factorization (NMF) [LS99] to approximately recover A and S from X.

Non-negative matrix factorization (NMF)

In its simplest form, NMF attempts to minimize a cost function $J = D(V; WH)$ between a non-negative matrix V and a product of two non-negative matrices WH. For example, we could use the Euclidean cost function

$$J_E = D_E(V; WH) = \tfrac{1}{2}\|V - WH\|_F^2 = \tfrac{1}{2}\sum_{\omega n}(v_{\omega n} - [WH]_{\omega n})^2 \tag{14.48}$$

or the (generalized) Kullback–Leibler divergence,

$$J_{KL} = D_{KL}(V; WH) = \sum_{\omega n}\left(v_{\omega n} \log \frac{v_{\omega n}}{[WH_{\omega n}]} - v_{\omega n} + [WH_{\omega n}]\right) \tag{14.49}$$

and search for a minimum of J using, e.g., a gradient descent method. In fact we can simplify things a little, since there is a scaling ambiguity between W and H, so we are free to normalize the columns of W to sum to unity, $\sum_\omega w_{\omega p} = 1$. Lee and Seung [LS99] introduced a simple parameter-free "multiplicative update" method to perform this optimization;

$$w_{\omega p} \leftarrow w_{\omega p} \sum_t h_{pn}(v_{\omega n}/[WH_{\omega n}])$$
$$w_{\omega p} \leftarrow \frac{w_{\omega p}}{\sum_\omega w_{\omega p}} \tag{14.50}$$
$$h_{pn} \leftarrow h_{pn} \sum_\omega w_{\omega p}(v_{\omega n}/[WH_{\omega n}]),$$

where this procedure optimizes the KL divergence (14.49).

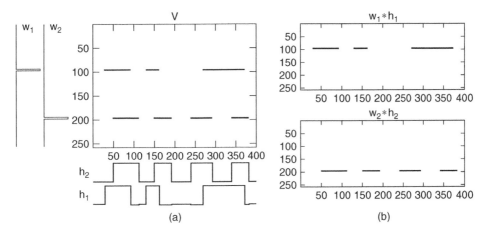

Figure 14.17   Simple example of non-negative matrix factorization.

Figure 14.17(a) shows a simple example where we have two sources w_1 and w_2, each consisting of a single frequency, with their activations over time given by h_1 and h_2. Smaragdis and Brown [SB03] applied this type of NMF to polyphonic music transcription, where they were looking to identify the spectra (w_p) and activities (h_p) of, e.g., individual piano notes.

For simple sources such as individual notes, we could use the separate products $V_p = w_p h_p^T$ as an estimate of the spectrogram of the original source. We could then transform back to the time domain simply by using the phases in the mixture spectrum as estimates of the phases of the original sources. However, in practice this approach can be limited, since it assumes that: (a) the source spectrum is unchanging over time and (b) real sources can often change their pitch, which would produce many separate "sources" from NMF [WP06].

Convolutive NMF

Real sources tend to change their spectrum over time, for example with the high-frequency components decaying faster than the low-frequency components. To account for this, Virtanen [Vir04] and Smaragdis [Sma04, Sma07] introduced a *convolutive* NMF approach, known as *non-negative matrix factor deconvolution* (NMFD). Here, each source is no longer represented by a single spectrum, but instead by a typical spectrogram which reflects how the spectrum of the source changes over time.

For NMFD, our model becomes

$$x_{\omega n} \approx \sum_{p,m} a_\omega p(m) s_{p,n-m},$$ (14.51)

which we can write in a matrix form as (Figure 14.18)

$$X = \sum_{m=0}^{M-1} A(m) \overset{m\rightarrow}{S},$$ (14.52)

where the $\overset{m\rightarrow}{\cdot}$ matrix notation means that the matrix is shifted m places to the right

$$[\overset{m\rightarrow}{S}]_{pn} = [S]_{p,n-m}.$$ (14.53)

Smaragdis [Sma04] applied NMFD to separation of drum sounds, using it to separate bass drum, snare drum and hi-hat from a mixture.

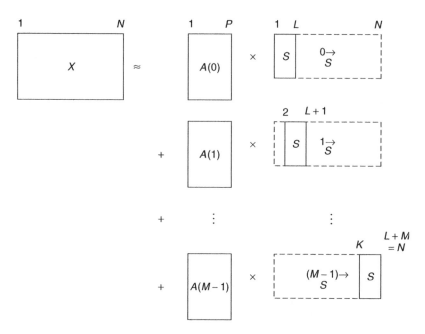

Figure 14.18 Convolutive NMF model for Non-negative Matrix Factor Deconvolution (NMFD).

2D Convolutive NMF

The convolutive approach, NMFD, relies on each drum sound having a characteristic spectrogram that evolves in a very similar way each time that sound plays. However, pitched instruments have a spectrum that is typically composed of spectral lines that change as the pitch of the note changes. To deal with this, Schmidt and Mørup [SM06] extended the (time-) convolutive NMF approach to a 2D convolutive NMF method, NMF2D. NMF2D uses a spectrogram with a log-frequency scale, so that pitch changes become a vertical shift, while time changes are a horizontal shift (as for NMFD).

The model then becomes

$$x_{\omega n} \approx \sum_{p,q,m} a_{\omega-q,p}(m) s_{p,n-m}(q),$$ (14.54)

which we can write in a matrix convolution form as (Figure 14.19)

$$X = \sum_{q=0}^{Q-1} \sum_{m=0}^{M-1} \overset{q\downarrow}{A}(m) \overset{m\rightarrow}{S}(q),$$ (14.55)

where the $\overset{q\downarrow}{\cdot}$ matrix notation indicates that the contents of the matrix are shifted q places down

$$[\overset{q\downarrow}{A}]_{\omega p} = [A]_{\omega-q,p}.$$ (14.56)

Schmidt and Mørup [SM06] used NMF2D to separate trumpet from piano sounds.

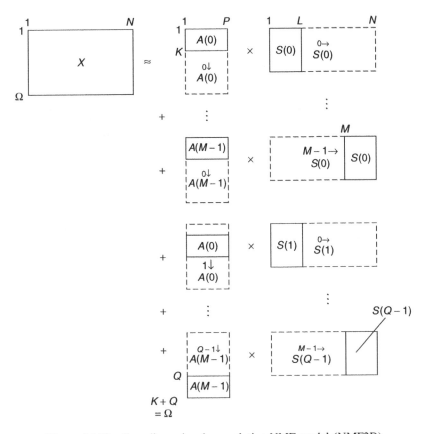

Figure 14.19 Two-dimensional convolutive NMF model (NMF2D).

14.3.2 Structural cues

Sinusoidal modeling

Sinusoidal modeling has solid mathematical, physical and physiological bases. It derives from Helmholtz's research and is rooted in Fourier's theorem, which states that any periodic function can be modeled as a sum of sinusoids at various amplitudes and harmonically related frequencies. Here we will consider the sinusoidal model under its most general expression, which is a sum of sinusoids (the *partials*) with time-varying amplitudes and frequencies not necessarily harmonically related. The associated representation is in general orthogonal (the partials are independent) and sparse (a few amplitude and frequency parameters can be sufficient to describe a sound consisting of many samples), thus very computationally efficient. Each partial is a pure tone, part of the complex sound (see Figure 14.20). The partials are sound structures very important both from the production (acoustics) and perception (psychoacoustics) points of view. In acoustics, they correspond to the modes of musical instruments, the superpositions of vibration modes being the solutions of the equations for vibrating systems (e.g., strings, bars, membranes). In psychoacoustics, the partials correspond to tonal components of high energy, thus very important for masking phenomena. The fact that the auditory system is well adapted to the acoustical environment seems quite natural.

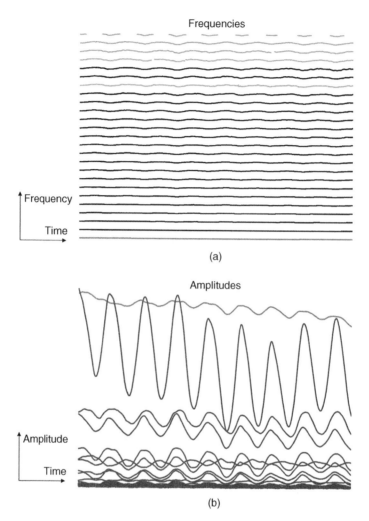

Figure 14.20 The evolutions of the partials of an alto saxophone over ≈ 1.5 second. The frequencies (a) and amplitudes (b) are displayed as functions of time (horizontal axis).

From a perceptual point of view, some partials belong to the same *sound entity* if they are perceived by the human auditory system as a unique sound when played together. There are several criteria that lead to this perceptual fusion. After Bregman [Bre90], we consider:

- The common onsets/offsets of the spectral components.
- The spectral structure of the sound, taking advantage of harmonic relations.
- The correlated variations of the time evolutions of these spectral parameters.
- The spatial location, estimated by a localization algorithm.

All these criteria allow us to classify the spectral components. Since this is done according to the perception, the classes we obtain should be the sound entities of the auditory scene. And the organization of these sound entities in time should give the musical structure. Music transcription is then possible by extracting musical parameters from these sound entities. But an advantage over standard music information retrieval (MIR) approaches is that here the sound entities are still available for transformation and resynthesis of a modified version of the music.

The use of each criterion gives a different way to classify the partials. One major problem is to be able to fuse these heterogeneous criteria, to obtain a unique classification method. Another problem is to incorporate this structuring within the analysis chain, to obtain a partial tracking algorithm with multiple criteria that would track classes of partials (entities) instead of individual partials, and thus should be more robust. Finding solutions to these problems are major research directions.

Common onsets

As noted by Hartmann [Har88], the common onset (birth) of partials plays a preponderant role in our perception of sound entities. From the experiences of Bregman and Pinker [BP78] and Gordon [Gor84], the partials should appear within a short time window of around 30 ms (corresponding to a number of γ consecutive frames, see below), else they are likely to be heard separately. Many onset-detection methods are based on the variation in time of the amplitude or phase of the signal (see [BDA+05] for a survey). Lagrange [Lag04] proposes an algorithm based on the D measure defined as

$$D[n] = \frac{B[n]}{C[n]}, \tag{14.57}$$

with

$$B[n] = \sum_{p=1}^{P} \epsilon_p[n] \bar{a}_p \quad \text{and} \quad C[n] = \frac{1}{2\gamma+1} \sum_{p=1}^{P} \sum_{k=-\gamma}^{+\gamma} a_p[n+k], \tag{14.58}$$

where a_p is the amplitude of the partial p, $\bar{a}_p$ is its mean value, and $\epsilon_p[n]$ is 1 if the partial is born in the $[n-\gamma, n+\gamma]$ interval and 0 otherwise. Thanks to this measure, it seems that we can identify the onsets of notes even if their volume fades in slowly (see Figure 14.21), leading to a better structuring of the sound entities (see Figure 14.22).

Simple- and poly-harmonic structures

The earliest attempts at acoustical entity identification and separation consider harmonicity as the sole cue for group formation. Some rely on a prior detection of the fundamental frequency [Gro96] and others consider only the harmonic relation of the frequencies [Kla03]. A classic approach is to perform a correlation of the short-term spectrum with some template, which should be a periodic function, of period F – the fundamental frequency under investigation. Such a template can be built using the expression of the Hann window

$$g_{1,F}(f) = \frac{1}{2}\left(1 + \cos\left(\frac{2\pi f}{F}\right)\right), \tag{14.59}$$

where f is the frequency and F is the fundamental. However, the problem with these templates is that the width of the template peaks depend on F (see Figure 14.23.a). For a constant peak selectivity, we can propose another function

$$g_{2,F}(f) = g_{1,F}(f)^{-s/\log(g_{1,F}(1))}, \tag{14.60}$$

where $s \in (0, 1]$ allows us to tune this selectivity (see Figure 14.23.b). But this template is still too far from the typical structure of musical sounds, whose spectral envelope (in dB) is often a linear function of the frequency (in Hz), see [Kla03]. Thus, we can consider

$$g_{3,F}(f) = g_{2,F}(f) \cdot 10^{-d(f-F)}, \tag{14.61}$$

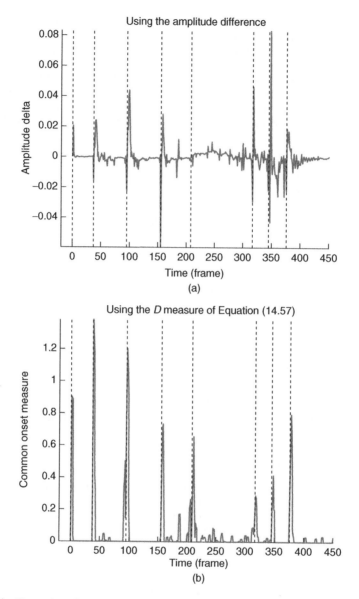

Figure 14.21 Examples of note onset detection using two different measures: (a) the difference in amplitude between consecutive frames and (b) the D measure of Equation (14.57). The true onsets – annotated manually – are displayed as vertical bars. Our method manages to identify correctly the note onsets, even if the volume of the note fades in slowly (see around frame 200).

where d is the slope of the spectral envelope, in dB per Hz (see Figure 14.23.(c)). Multi-pitch estimation is still an active research area, and yet our simple approach gives very good results, especially when the s and d parameters can be learned from a database. However, many musical instruments are not perfectly harmonic, and the template should ideally also depend on the inharmonicity factor in the case of inharmonic sounds.

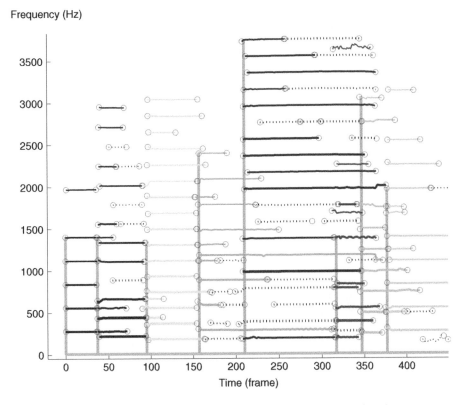

Frequency (Hz)

Figure 14.22   Result of the structuring of the partials in sound entities using the common onset criterion on the example of Figure 14.21.

Similar evolutions

According to the work of McAdams [McA89], a group of partials is perceived as a unique sound entity only if the variations of these partials are correlated, whether the sound is harmonic or not.

An open problem is the quest for a relevant dissimilarity between two elements (the partials), that is a dissimilarity which is low for elements of the same class (sound entity) and high for elements that do not belong to the same class. It turns out that the auto-regressive (AR) modeling of the parameters of the partials is a good candidate for the design of a robust dissimilarity metric.

Let ω_p be the frequency vector of the partial p. According to the AR model, the sample $\omega_p[n]$ can be approximated as a linear combination of past samples

$$\omega_p[n] = \sum_{k=1}^{K} c_p[k]\omega_p[n-k] + e_p[n], \tag{14.62}$$

where $e_p[n]$ is the prediction error. The coefficients $c_p[k]$ model the predictable part of the signal and it can be shown that these coefficients are scale invariant. Conversely the non-predictable part $e_p[n]$ is not scale invariant. For each frequency vector ω_p, we compute a vector $c_p[k]$ of four AR coefficients with the Burg method. Although the direct comparison of the AR coefficients computed from the two vectors ω_p and ω_q is generally not relevant, the spectrum of these coefficients may be compared. The Itakura distortion measure [Ita75], issued from the speech recognition community

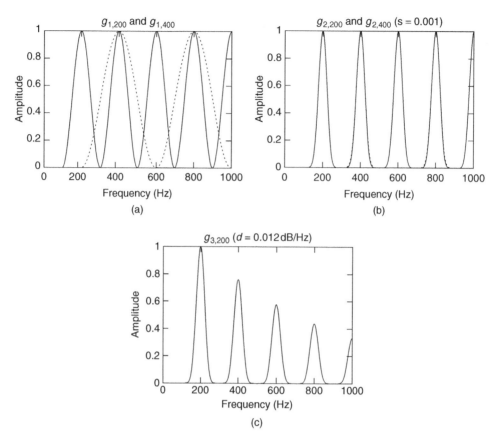

Figure 14.23 Three kinds of templates for the extraction of harmonic structures: (a) simple periodic function, (b) modified version for a constant peak selectivity, and (c) modified version for a more realistic spectral envelope.

can be considered:

$$d_{AR}(\omega_p, \omega_q) = \frac{1}{2\pi} \log \int_{-pi}^{+pi} \left| \frac{C_p(\omega)}{C_q(\omega)} \right| d\omega, \tag{14.63}$$

where

$$C_p(\omega) = 1 + \sum_{k=1}^{K} c_p[k] e^{-jk\omega}. \tag{14.64}$$

Another approach may be considered. Indeed, the amount of error done by modeling the vector ω_p by the coefficients computed from vector ω_q may indicate the dissimilarity of these two vectors. Let us introduce a new notation e_p^q, the cross-prediction error defined as the residual signal of the filtering of the vector ω_p with c_q

$$e_p^q[n] = \omega_p[n] - \sum_{k=1}^{K} c_q[k] \omega_p[n-k]. \tag{14.65}$$

The principle of the dissimilarity d_σ is to combine the two dissimilarities $|e_p^q|$ and $|e_q^p|$ to obtain a symmetrical one:

$$d_\sigma(\omega_p, \omega_q) = \frac{1}{2}\left(|e_p^q| + |e_q^p|\right).$$
(14.66)

Given two vectors ω_p and ω_q to be compared, the coefficients c_p and c_q are computed to minimize the power of the respective prediction errors e_p and e_q. If the two vectors ω_p and ω_q are similar, the power of the cross-prediction errors e_p^q and e_q^p will be as weak as those of e_p and e_q. We can consider another dissimilarity d_σ' defined as the ratio between the sum of the crossed prediction errors and the sum of the direct prediction errors:

$$d_\sigma'(\omega_p, \omega_q) = \frac{|e_p^q| + |e_q^p|}{1 + |e_p| + |e_q|}.$$
(14.67)

Lagrange [Lag05] shows that the metrics based on AR modeling perform quite well.

14.3.3   Probabilistic models

We can also view the source separation problem as a probabilistic inference problem [VJA$^+$10]. In outline, one uses a probabilistic model $p(x|s_1, s_2)$ for the observed mixture x from two sources s_1 and s_2, and then attempt to find the original sources given the mixture. This is typically done using the maximum a posteriori (MAP) criterion

$$(\hat{s}_1, \hat{s}_2) = \arg\max_{s_1, s_2} p(s_1, s_2|x)$$
(14.68)

using the Bayesian formulation $p(s_1, s_2|x) \propto p(x|s_1, s_2)p(s_1)p(s_2)$, where the sources s_1 and s_2 are assumed to be independent, although other criteria, such as the posterior mean (PM) are also possible.

Benaroya et al. [BBG06] use this probabilistic approach, modeling the sources using Gaussian mixture models (GMMs) and Gaussian scaled mixture models (GSMMs). A GSMM is a mixture of Gaussian scaled densities, each of which corresponds to a random variable of the form $g_a = \sqrt{a}g$, where g is a Gaussian with variance σ^2 and a is a non-negative scalar random variable with prior density $p_0(a)$.

They demonstrated their approach on separation of jazz tracks, considering "piano + bass" as one source and drums as another source. The model parameters were trained on a CD containing the separated tracks. This type of CD was originally designed for people to learn how to play jazz, but is also convenient for this type of experiment since it contains separated sources which make a coherent piece of music when mixed together. They found good performance with about 8 or 16 components, although this depended on the particular model used and the estimation method (MAP or PM). For more details about other probabilistic modeling-based approaches, see [VJA$^+$10].

14.4   Applications

In a binaural context, sound source separation has been applied to speech in hearing-aid systems for the reduction of the cocktail party effect. The same is true for mobile telephony, where the reduction of environmental noise plays a critical role in the intelligibility of speech. However, even the listening experience of music, both at home and in concert halls, can be enhanced for the listener, as interfering environmental noise sources can be eliminated or attenuated.

In a broader single-channel or multi-channel context there are other compelling reasons for desiring to separate sound sources. Traditionally, the listener is considered as a receptor who passively listens to the audio signal stored on various medias (CD, DVD audio, etc.) or streamed through the internet. The only modifications that are easy to perform are global to the whole piece, like changing the volume, the tone or adding artificial reverberation. Although new formats such as MPEG Audio Layer 3 (MP3) have changed the way people access music, the interaction with music is still very limited. However, with the availability of higher computing capabilities, people are more eager to interact with the original media, while the sound is playing. This can be seen, for example, with the karaoke, where the listener can replace the voice of the original singer. But more freedom and creativity are also possible.

With the techniques presented in this chapter, new ways are available for the identification, separation and manipulation of the several sound entities (sources) which are perceived by the listener as independent components within the binaural (stereophonic) mix that reaches his/her ears. More precisely, one can find out the sound entities by considering their localization (spatial hearing) and the correlations of their spectral parameters (common onsets, harmonic relations, similar time evolutions). Then, it is possible to apply digital audio effects to each separate sound entity.

This way, listeners are enabled towards an active listening behavior, which entails freedom to interact with the sound in real time during its diffusion. For example, the listener can explore the possibility of changing the spatial locations of the individual sound sources, their relative volumes, pitches and even timbres, as well as their durations, or the rhythm of the music and experiment with these alterations while playing the piece. In other words, by means of sound source separation, the engaging world of mixing and re-editing separate tracks is reopened to the listener without the need to store or stream the separate tracks, which would require much larger storage or higher data rates.

14.5 Conclusions

In this chapter we have reviewed several methods addressing the problem of source separation in various contexts, such as multi-channel, binaural, stereo or mono, with various degrees of a priori information or assumptions on the sources. To date, the results achieved are fairly good considering the complexity and ill-posedness of the problem but near-perfect separation is still beyond reach in most cases. In some applications, such as the addition of audio effects or re-spatialization of the sources, near-perfect separation is not a must as artifacts are less audible in the remixed sound. This field has undergone tremendous development in recent years, of which we could only present a partial view, and a considerable amount of work is still under progress.

Acknowledgements

The authors would like to thank Beiming Wang, Harald Viste and Mathieu Lagrange for assistance with some of the figures in this chapter. MP was supported in part by EPSRC Leadership Fellowship EP/G007144/1 and by the EU Framework 7 FET-Open project FP7-ICT-225913-SMALL: Sparse Models, Algorithms and Learning for Large-Scale data.

References

[BBG06]   L. Benaroya, F. Bimbot and R. Gribonval. Audio source separation with a single sensor. *IEEE Transactions on Audio, Speech, and Language Processing*, 14(1): 191–199, January 2006.

[BDA+05] J. P. Bello, L. Daudet, S. A. Abdallah, C. D. Duxbury, M. E. Davies and M. B. Sandler. A tutorial on onset detection in music signals. *IEEE Transactions on Speech and Audio Processing*, 13(5): 1035–1047, September 2005.

[Bla01]   J. Blauert. *Spatial Hearing*. MIT Press, Cambridge, MA, 2001.

[BP78]   A. S. Bregman and S. Pinker. Auditory streaming and the building of timbre. *Canadian Journal of Psychology*, 32(1): 19–31, 1978.

[Bre90]   A. S. Bregman. *Auditory Scene Analysis: The Perceptual Organization of Sound*. MIT Press, Cambridge, MA, 1990.

[BW01]   M. S. Brandstein and D. B. Ward (eds). *Microphone Arrays: Signal Processing Techniques and Applications*. Springer, New York, NY, 2001.

[FM04]   C. Faller and J. Merimaa. Source localization in complex listening situations: Selection of binaural cues based on interaural coherence. *Journal of the Acoustical Society of America*, 116(5): 3075–3089, November 2004.

[Gai93]   W. Gaik. Combined evaluation of interaural time and intensity differences: Psychoacoustic results and computer modeling. *Journal of the Acoustical Society of America*, 94(1): 98–110, 1993.

[Gor84]   J. W. Gordon. *Perception of Attack Transients in Musical Tones*. PhD thesis, Department of Music, Stanford University, California, USA, 1984.

[Gro96]   S. Grossberg. *Pitch-based streaming in auditory perception*. In N. Griffith and P. Todd (eds.), Musical networks, pp 117–140, MIT Press, Cambridge, MA, 1996.

[GZ10]   R. Gribonval and M. Zibulevsky. Sparse component analysis. In P. Comon and C. Jutten (eds), *Handbook of Blind Source Separation*, pp. 367–420. Academic Press, Oxford, UK, 2010.

[Har88]   W. M. Hartmann. Pitch perception and the segregation and integration of auditory entities. In Gerald M. Edelman, W. Einar Gall and W. Maxwell Cowan (eds.), *Auditory Function: Neurobiological Bases of Hearing*, pp. 623–645. Wiley, New York, USA, 1988.

[HG06]   Viste and G. Evangelista. A method for separation of overlapping partials based on similarity of temporal envelopes in multi-channel mixtures. *IEEE Trans. on Audio, Speech, and Language Processing*, 14(3): 1051–1061, May 2006.

[Ita75]   F. Itakura. Minimum prediction residual principle applied to speech recognition. *IEEE Transactions on Acoustics, Speech, and Signal Processing*, 23(1): 67–72, 1975.

[JSY98]   P. X. Joris, P. H. Smith, and T. C. T. Yin. Coincidence detection in the auditory system: 50 years after Jeffress. *Neuron*, 21: 1235–1238, 1998.

[Kla03]   A. P. Klapuri. Multiple fundamental frequency estimation based on harmonicity and spectral smoothness. *IEEE Transactions on Speech and Audio Processing*, 11(6): 804–816, November 2003.

[Lag04]   M. Lagrange. *Modélisation Sinusoïdale des Sons Polyphoniques*. PhD thesis, LaBRI, University of Bordeaux 1, Talence, France, December 2004. In French.

[Lag05]   M. Lagrange. A new dissimilarity metric for the clustering of partials using the common variation cue. In *Proceedings of the International Computer Music Conference (ICMC)*, Barcelona, Spain, September 2005.

[Lin86]   W. Lindemann. Extension of a binaural cross-correlation model by contralateral inhibition. i.simulation of lateralization for stationary signals. *Journal of the Acoustical Society of America*, 80(6): 1608–1622, 1986.

[LS99]   D. D. Lee and H. S. Seung. Learning the parts of objects by non-negative matrix factorization. *Nature*, 401: 788–791, 21 October 1999.

[McA89]   S. McAdams. Segregation of concurrent sounds: effects of frequency modulation coherence. *Journal of the Acoustical Society of America*, 86(6): 2148–2159, 1989.

[Men10]   F. Menzer. *Binaural Audio Signal Processing Using Interaural Coherence Matching*. PhD thesis, EPFL Lausanne, Switzerland, 2010.

[NSO09]   F. Nesta, P. Svaizer and M. Omologo. Cumulative state coherence transform for a robust two-channel multiple source localization. In *Proceedings of the 8th International Conference on Independent Component Analysis and Signal Separation*, pp. 290–297, 2009.

[RVE10]   M. Raspaud, H. Viste and G. Evangelista. Binaural source localization by joint estimation of ILD and ITD. *IEEE Transactions Audio, Speech and Language Processing*, 18: 68–77, 2010.

[SAM07]   H. Sawada, S. Araki and S. Makino. Frequency domain blind source separation. In S. Makino, T.-W. Lee, and H. Sawada (eds), *Blind Speech Separation*, pp. 47–78. Springer, Dordrecht, The Netherlands, 2007.

[SB03]   P. Smaragdis and J. C. Brown. Non-negative matrix factorization for polyphonic music transcription. In *Proceedings of the 2003 IEEE Workshop on Applications of Signal Processing to Audio and Acoustics*, pp. 177–180, New Paltz, New York, 19-22 October 2003.

[SM06]   M. N. Schmidt and M. Mørup. Nonnegative matrix factor 2-D deconvolution for blind single channel source separation. In *Independent Component Analysis and Signal Separation, International Conference on*, volume 3889 of *Lecture Notes in Computer Science (LNCS)*, pp. 700–707. Springer, New York, NY April 2006.

[Sma04]   P. Smaragdis. Non-negative matrix factor deconvolution: Extraction of multiple sound sources from monophonic inputs. In *Independent Component Analysis and Blind Signal Separation: Proceedings of the Fifth International Conference (ICA 2004)*, pp. 494–499, Granada, Spain, September 22–24 2004.

[Sma07]   P. Smaragdis. Convolutive speech bases and their application to supervised speech separation. *IEEE Transactions on Audio, Speech, and Language Processing*, 15(1): 1–12, Jan. 2007.

[ST97]   R. M. Stern and C. Trahiotis. Models of binaural perception. In R. H. Gilkey and T. R. Anderson (eds.), *Binaural and Spatial Hearing in Real and Virtual Environments*, pp. 499–531. Lawrence Erlbaum Associates, 1997.

[VGF06]   E. Vincent, R. Gribonval, and C. Févotte. Performance measurement in blind audio source separation. *IEEE Transactions on Audio, Speech and Language Processing*, 14(4): 1462–1469, 2006.

[Vir04]   T. Virtanen. Separation of sound sources by convolutive sparse coding. In *Proceedings of the ISCA Tutorial and Research Workshop on Statistical and Perceptual Audio Processing (SAPA 2004)*, Jeju, Korea, 3 October 2004.

[Vis04]   H. Viste. *Binaural Localization and Separation Techniques*. PhD thesis, EPFL, Lausanne, Switzerland, 2004.

[VJA+10]   E. Vincent, M. G. Jafari, S. A. Abdallah, M. D. Plumbley and M. E. Davies. Probabilistic modeling paradigms for audio source separation. In W. Wang (ed), *Machine Audition: Principles, Algorithms and Systems*. IGI Global, Hershey, PA, 2010.

[WB06]   D. L. Wang and G. J. Brown (eds). *Computational Auditory Scene Analysis: Principles, Algorithms and Applications*. Wiley-IEEE Press, Hoboken, NJ, 2006.

[WP06]   B. Wang and M. D. Plumbley. Investigating single-channel audio source separation methods based on non-negative matrix factorization. In A. K. Nandi and X. Zhu (eds), *Proceedings of the ICA Research Network International Workshop, 18-19 Sept 2006*, pp. 17–20, 2006.

[WS54]   R. S. Woodworth and H. Schlosberg. *Experimental Psychology*. Holt, New York, NY 1954.

[YR04]   Ö. Yılmaz and S. T. Rickard. Blind separation of speech mixtures via time-frequency masking. *IEEE Transactions on Signal Processing*, 52(7): 1830–1847, 2004.

Glossary

ADT Automatic double tracking: A time-based signal processor that simulates the effect of playing a part, then overdubbing a second part to give a thicker sound.

Aliasing Frequency components above half the sampling frequency of a sampled signal that are folded back into the audio spectrum (0−20 kHz).

AT constant Time needed for a signal to reach 63% (−4 dB) of its final amplitude. After three time constants it will have reached 95% (−0.4 dB) of its final amplitude.

Attack time AT Time for a signal to rise from 10% to 90% from its final amplitude.

Audio effect A modification of a sound by use of a signal-processing technique. It is sometimes called Audio-FX.

Auto pan To change a signal's spatial position in the stereo field via some modulation source.

Brassage French for time shuffling.

Chorus Detuning effect where the original signal is mixed with a pitch-modulated copy of the original signal. Pitch modulation is achieved by a random variation of the length of a delay line.

Click A slight sharp noise, usually due to a discontinuity of the signal or to some computation error. In some forms of musical production, such as techno or live sampling, the clicks become such an important musical relevance, that they are even emphasized.

Clipping Severe distortion of the signal because the amplitude is larger than the processing system can handle.

Comb filter Filter effect occurring if the original signal is mixed with a delayed version of the original signal. The effect produces notches in the frequency domain at regular frequency intervals.

Compressor A compressor is used for reducing the dynamics of an audio signal. Quiet parts or low levels of a signal are not modified, but high levels or loud parts are reduced according to a static curve.

Controller A device used to modify one or several parameters of an effect.

Convolution Mathematical algorithm which is based on an input signal and another short signal (for example, an impulse response) and leads to an output signal.

Cross-synthesis This effect takes two sound inputs and generates a third one which is a combination of the two input sounds. The general idea is to combine two sounds by spectrally shaping the first sound by the second one and preserving the pitch of the first sound.

Decay rate The time rate at which a signal decreases in amplitude. Usually expressed in decibel per second (dB/s).

Decay time Time for a signal to decrease from 90% to 10% from its initial amplitude.

DAFX: Digital Audio Effects, Second Edition. Edited by Udo Zölzer.
© 2011 John Wiley & Sons, Ltd. Published 2011 by John Wiley & Sons, Ltd.

De-emphasis See **pre-emphasis**.

De-esser A de-esser is a signal processing device for processing speech and vocals and is used to suppress high-frequency sibilance.

Denoising To decrease the noise within a sound.

Dispersion Spreading a sound in time by a frequency-dependent time delay.

Distance rendering The distance of a sound source is largely controllable by insertion of artificial wall reflections or reverberant room responses.

Distortion A modification of the signal that is usually objectionable. When a signal is processed by a nonlinear system, some components appear that were not part of the original signal. They are called distortion products. Some musical instruments such as the electric guitar take advantage of distortions to enlarge and vary their timbre. This modifies the sound color by introducing nonlinear distortion products of the input signal. Related effects are Overdrive, Fuzz, Blender, Screamer.

Dithering Adding a low-level noise to the signal before quantization. It improves the signal quality by decorrelating the quantification error and the signal.

Doppler effect The Doppler effect raises the pitch of a sound source approaching the listener and lowers the pitch of a sound source departing the listener.

Dropout A temporary loss of audio information. This is a typical problem of magnetic-tape-based storage and processing systems.

Dry In general a "dry" sound is a sound that has not been processed by any means. It qualified originally sounds that were recorded in an anechoic room. In our application the phrase "dry signal" denotes the sound before processing. See also **wet**.

Dubbing Adding further material to an existing recording. Also known as overdubbing.

Ducking A system for controlling the level of one audio signal with another. For example, background music can be made to "duck" whenever there is a voiceover [Whi99].

Echo Several delayed versions of the original signal.

Equalizer Filter system to shape the overall sound spectrum. Certain frequency ranges can be either increased or cut. A parametric equalizer allows individual setting of boost or cut, center frequency, bandwidth and filter type.

Exciter Signal processor that emphasizes or de-emphasizes certain frequencies in order to change a signal's timbre.

Expander Expanders operate on low-level signals and increase the dynamics of these low-level signals.

Fade-in Gradually increasing the amplitude of a signal from silence.

Fade-out Gradually decreasing the amplitude of a signal to silence.

Feedback To send some of an effect's output signal back to the input. Also called regeneration.

Flanger Sound effect occurring if the original signal is mixed with a delayed copy (less than 15 msec) of the original signal. The delay time is continuously varied with a low-frequency sinusoid of 1 Hz.

Flatterzunge A sound effect which is produced by rolling the tongue, blowing air through the mouth and performing a rapid fluttering motion of the tongue.

Flutter Variations due to short-term speed variations at relatively rapid rates (above 6 Hz) [Met93]. See **wow**.

Foley Imitation of real sounds for cinema applications. See also **sound effect**.

Formant changing This effect produces a "Donald Duck" voice without any alteration of the fundamental frequency. It can be used for performing an alteration of a sound whenever there is a formant structure.

Freezing (1) Selecting a fragment of sound and playing it as a loop. The time seems to be frozen to the date when the fragment was sampled. (2) Memorizing the spectrum envelope of a sound at a given time in order to apply this envelope onto another sound [Hal95, pp. 59–60].

Frequency shifter A signal processor that translates all the frequency components of the signal by the same amount $f_i \rightarrow f_i + \Delta f$.

Frequency warping A alteration of the linearity of the frequency axis.

FX Shortcut for effects.

Gaussian noise A random noise whose instantaneous amplitudes occur according to the Gaussian distribution.

Glissando Linear transition from one pitch to another. This implies that the frequencies corresponding to the pitches vary according to a logarithmic law. See **portamento**.

Glitch An unwanted short-term corruption of a signal, or the unexplained, short-term malfunction of a piece of equipment. See **click**.

Granulation Extracting short segments from the input signal and rearranging them to synthesize complex new sounds.

Halaphon A four-channel sound projection system that was developed in 1971 by Hans Peter Haller and Peter Lawo. Four amplitude envelope oscillators with different waveforms driving four amplitude modulators allowed complex sound projection patterns at various speeds. An eight-channel version was used in 1973 for the production of "Explosante fixe" by Pierre Boulez and a ten-channel version for the production of "Prometeo" by Luigi Nono. The methods for spatialization proposed by John Chowning could also be implemented [Hal95, pp. 77–90].

Harmonizer A trademark of Eventide for a pitch shifter.

Impulse response The response of a system which is fed by an impulse signal.

Inharmonizer This effect is obtained by frequency warping an original harmonic sound. The resulting sound is enriched by inharmonic partials.

Jitter Degradation of a signal by sampling it at irregular sampling intervals. It can be interpreted as a modulation process where the audio signal equals the carrier and the jitter signal equals the modulation source.

Leslie This effect was initially produced by rotating micro-phones or rotating loudspeakers. It can be approximated by a combination of tremolo and doppler effect.

Leveler A dynamic processor that maintains (or "levels") the amount of one audio signal based upon the level of a second audio signal. Normally, the second signal is from an ambient noise sensing microphone. For example, a restaurant is a typical application where it is desired to maintain paging and background music a specified loudness above the ambient noise. The leveler monitors the background noise, dynamically increasing and decreasing the main audio signal as necessary to maintain a constant loudness differential between the two. Also called SPL controller [Boh00].

LFO Low frequency oscillator. See **modulation**.

Limiter Signal processor that lets the input signal pass through when its level is lower than a defined threshold and limits the output signal to a fixed level when the limiter threshold is exceeded.

Live sampling A musical style that relies on the replay of sounds or fragments of them that are sampled during the performance from other performers or sound sources.

Masking Phenomenon whereby one sound obscures another, usually one weaker and higher in frequency [Alt90].

Modulation Process of altering a parameter, usually through some automatic or programmed means such as an LFO. See **vibrato** and **tremolo**.

Morphing (1) Imposing a feature of one sound onto another. (2) A transition from one sound to another. (3) Generation of an intermediate sound between two others. (4) Generation of one sound out of the characteristics of another sounds. (5) Transforming one sound's spectrum into that of another. See **spectral mutation**.

Morphophone A tape-based multi-delay system with a bandpass filter on the input signal as well as on each of the 10 playback heads. The mixed output can be fed back to the input. This device was designed by J. Poullin [Pou60] and A. Moles [Mol60, p. 73].

Multi-effect A signal processor containing several different effects in a single package.

Mute Cuts off a sound or reduce its level considerably.

Noise gate Signal processor that lets the input signal pass through when its level is higher than a defined threshold.

Normalize To amplify the sound so much that its maximum reaches the maximum level before clipping. This operation optimizes the use of the available dynamic range of the audio format and reduces the risk of corruption of the signal by low-level perturbations that could happen during a further processing or the transmission of the sound.

Octavider Producing a signal one octave below the input signal.

Off-line A process is said to be off-line when it is applied on a recorded signal instead of on a real-time signal. Some processes are inherently off-line such as time contraction. Others are too computationally intensive to be performed in real-time.

Overdubbing See **dubbing**.

Overload To exceed the operating capacity of a representation, transmission or processing system.

Panorama Composing a panorama of acoustic events in the space spanned by loudspeakers.

Patch Another word for program, left over from the days of analog synthesizers. Also, the process of interconnecting various devices.

Peak filter Tunable filter which boosts or cuts certain frequency bands with a bell-like frequency response.

Phasing Effect where phase shifts of a copy of the original signal and mixing with the original signal cause phase cancellations and enhancements that sweep up and down the frequency axis.

Phonogène A special tape recorder playing a loop at various speeds. It "has a circular arrangement of 12 capstan to change the tape speed within the 12 steps of the tempered scale". The pinch roller facing each capstan is activated by a piano-like keyboard. This device was designed by P. Schaeffer. A further development of this device is called the "Phonogène universel". It allows continuous transposition and/or time contraction and expansion. It relies on the rotating drum carrying four heads that was proposed by Springer [Mol60, p. 73], [Sch73, p. 47], [Pou60, Bod84].

Pink noise Noise which has a continuous frequency spectrum and where each frequency band of constant relative bandwidth $\Delta f / f$ contains the same power, e.g., each octave has the same power.

Pitch Subjective perception of frequency.

Pitch scaling See **pitch shifting**.

Pitch shifting Modification of the pitch of a signal. All the frequency components of the signal are multiplied by the same ratio. $f_i \rightarrow r \cdot f_i$. Asynchronous pitch shifting is achieved by varying the output sampling rate [Mas98] (see Section 6.2).

Pitch transposer A signal processor that duplicates the input at a defined pitch interval.

Portamento A gliding effect where the pitch of a sound is changed gradually rather than abruptly when a pitch modification is required.

Post-echo See **print through**.

Precedence effect In a stereo loudspeaker set-up, if we step to one side of the central position and listen to a monophonic music program, we locate the apparent sound source in the same position as our closest loudspeaker, and the apparent position does not move, even if the other channel is significantly louder.

Pre-echo See **print through**.

Pre-emphasis A system to boost high frequencies of a sound before processing it. A de-emphasis should be performed before playing the sound back after processing. This procedure attenuates high-frequency noise contributed by the processing or transmission system.

Print through The undesirable process that causes some magnetic information from a recorded analog tape to become imprinted onto an adjacent layer. This can produce low-level pre- or post-echoes.

Quantize Coding the amplitude of a signal with a given number of bits. Reducing the number of bits used to represent a signal usually degrades the quality of the signal. This effect can be attenuated by the use of dithering. Quantizing and dithering occur usually at the AD and DA stages of an audio processing system.

Random noise A noise whose amplitude cannot be predicted precisely at any given time.

Ratio Quotient of two quantities having the same unit. The transposition ratio is the quotient of the output frequencies to the input frequencies when they are expressed in Hz. The compression or expansion ratio is the quotient of the output amplitudes to the input amplitude when they are expressed in dB.

Real-time A process is said to be real-time when it processes sound in the moment when it appears. A real-time system is fast enough to perform all the necessary computations to process one sample of sound within a sampling period.

Recirculate See **feedback**.

Regeneration See **feedback**.

Release time RT Time for a signal to decrease from 90% to 10% of its final amplitude.

Resonator Narrow bandwidth filter that amplifies frequencies around a center frequency.

Reverberation Natural phenomenon occurring when sound waves propagate in an enclosed space.

Rise time Time for a signal to rise from 10% to 90% of its final amplitude.

Robotization Applying a fixed pitch onto a sound.

RT constant Time needed for a signal to reach 37% (-9 dB) of its initial amplitude. After five time constants it will have reached 1% (-43 dB) of its initial amplitude.

Sampler A digital system for recording and playing back short musical sounds in real-time. It is controlled by a MIDI keyboard or controller.

Scaling As applied to continuous controllers, this determines how far a parameter will vary from the programmed setting in response to a given amount of controller change.

Shelving filter Tunable filter which boosts or cuts the lower/higher end of the audio spectrum.

Shuffling Out of a sequence of time or frequency elements of sound, producing a new sound with a new random order. The time shuffling is called *brassage* in french.

Sibilance High-frequency whistling or lisping sound that affects vocal recordings, due either to poor mic technique, excessive equalization or exaggerated vocal characteristics [Whi99].

Side chain In a signal-processing circuit, such as one employing a VCA, a secondary signal path in parallel with the main signal path in which the condition or parameter of an audio signal that will cause a processor to begin working is sensed or detected. Typical applications use the side-chain information to control the gain of a VCA. The circuit may detect level or frequency or both. Devices utilizing side chains for control generally fall into the classification of dynamic controllers [Boh00].

Side-chain input The side-chain input is necessary for the "ducking" effect, used by disc jockeys to automatically compress the music when they are talking [Whi99].

Side-chain insert This insert can be used to insert an additional equalizer into the side chain, to turn a standard compressor into a de-esser, for example [Whi99].

Slapback Echo effect where only one replica of the original signal is produced.

Sound effect A sound that comes as an audible illustration in an audio-visual or multi-media production.

Speaker emulator A signal processor designed to imitate the effect of running a signal through a guitar amplifier cabinet.

Spectral mutation Timbral interpolation between two sounds, the source sound and the target sound, in order to produce a third sound, the mutant. Operates on the phase and magnitude data pair of each frequency band of the source and target spectra [PE96].

Spectrum inverter An amplitude modulator where the modulating frequency is equal to $f_s/2$. By usual audio sampling frequencies, this effect is usually unpleasant because most of the energy of the signal is located close to the higher limit of the frequency range.

Sweetening Enhancing the sound of a recording with equalization and various other signal-processing techniques, usually during editing and mixing of a production.

Time-constant A time required by a quantity that varies exponentially with time, but less any constant component, to change by the factor $1/e = 0.3679$. The quantity has reached 99% of its final value after five time-constants.

Time warping An alteration of the linearity of the time axis.

Transposition See **pitch shifting**.

Tremolo A slow periodic amplitude variation, at a typical rate of 0.5 to 20 Hz.

Undersampling Sampling a signal at a frequency lower than twice the signal bandwidth. It produces aliasing.

Varispeed Playing back a signal with time-varying speed.

VCA Voltage controlled amplifier.

Vibrato A cyclical pitch variation at a frequency of a few hertz, typically 3 to 8 Hz.

Vocal gender change Changing the gender of a given vocal sound.

Vocoding See **cross-synthesis**.

Wah-wah A foot-controlled signal processor containing a bandpass filter with variable center frequency. Moving the pedal back and forth changes the center frequency of the bandpass.

Wet In practice the sound processed by an audio effect is often mixed with the initial sound. In this case, the processed sound is called the "wet signal" whereas the initial signal is called the "dry signal." The term "wet" was initially used to qualify sounds affected by a lot of reverberation, whether contributed by a room or by an audio processor.

Whisperization Applying a whisper effect onto a sound.

White noise A sound whose power spectral density is essentially independent of frequency (white noise need not be random noise).

Wow Instantaneous variation of speed at moderately slow rates. See **flutter**.

Zigzag During a zigzag process, a sound is played at the nominal speed but alternatively forwards and backwards. The reversal points are set by the performer [Wis94, Mir98].

Zipper noise Audible steps that occur when a parameter is being varied in a digital audio effect [Whi99].

References

[Alt90]   S. R. Alten. *Audio in Media*. Wadsworth, 1990.

[Bod84]   H. Bode. History of electronic sound modification. *Journal of the Audio Engineering Society*, 32(10): 730–739, October 1984.

[Boh00]   D. A. Bohn. http://www.rane.com/digi-dic.htm. *Rane Professional Audio Reference*, 2000.

[Hal95]   H. P. Haller. *Das Experimental Studio der Heinrich-Strobel-Stiftung des Südwestfunks Freiburg 1971–1989, Die Erforschung der Elektronischen Klangumformung und ihre Geschichte*. Nomos, 1995.

[Mas98]   D. C. Massie. Wavetable sampling synthesis. In M. Kahrs and K.-H. Brandenburg (eds), *Applications of Digital Signal Processing to Audio and Acoustics*, pp. 311341. Kluwer, 1998.

[Met93]   B. Metzler. *Audio Measurement Handbook*. Audio Precision Inc., 1993.

[Mir98]   E. R. Miranda. *Computer Sound Synthesis for the Electronic Musician*. Focal Press, 1998.

[Mol60]   A. Moles. *Les Musiques Expérimentales*. Trad. D. Charles. Cercle d'Art Contemporain, 1960.

[PE96]   L. Polansky and T. Erbe. Spectral mutation in soundhack. *Computer Music Journal*, 20(1): 92101, Spring 1996.

[Pou60]   J. Poullin. Les chaines électro-acoustiques. *Flammarion*, pp. 229–239, September-December 1960.

[Sch73]   P. Schaeffer. *La Musique Concrète*. QSJ No 1287, PUF 1973.

[Whi99]   P. White. *Creative Recording, Effects and Processors*. Sanctuary Publishing, 1999.

[Wis94]   T. Wishart. *Audible Design: A Plain and Easy Introduction to Practical Sound Composition*. Orpheus the Pantomime, 1994.

Index

DAFX: Digital Audio Effects, Second Edition. Edited by Udo Zölzer.
© 2011 John Wiley & Sons, Ltd. Published 2011 by John Wiley & Sons, Ltd.

Printed and bound by CPI Group (UK) Ltd, Croydon, CR0 4YY

16/04/2025

14658550-0004